INTERNATIONAL MANAGEMENT

INTERNATIONAL
— MANAGEMENT —
A Cross-Cultural and Functional Perspective

Kamal Fatehi

The Wichita State University

Prentice Hall, Upper Saddle River, New Jersey 07458

Library of Congress Cataloging-in-Publication Data

Fatehi, Kamal.
  International management : a cross-cultural and functional perspective / Kamal Fatehi.
    p. cm.
  ISBN 0-13-099722-6
    1. International business enterprises—Management—Social aspects.
  2. Corporate culture.   3. Intercultural communication.   I. Title.
  HD62.4.F37   1996
  658′.049—dc20   95-24369
                                                      CIP

Acquisitions Editor: David Shafer
Associate Editor: Lisamarie Brassini
Editorial Assistant: Nancy Kaplan
Marketing Manager: Jo-Ann DeLuca
Production Service: Spectrum Publisher Services
Buyer: Vincent Scelta
Cover Art: Hugh Whyte/Stockworks

© 1996 by Kamal Fatehi

 Published by Prentice Hall, Inc.
A Simon & Schuster Company
Upper Saddle River, New Jersey 07458

Printed in the United States of America

10   9   8   7   6   5   4   3   2   1

ISBN 0-13-099722-6

Prentice-Hall International (UK) Limited, *London*
Prentice-Hall of Australia Pty. Limited, *Sydney*
Prentice-Hall Canada Inc., *Toronto*
Prentice-Hall Hispanoamericana, S.A., *Mexico*
Prentice-Hall of India Private Limited, *New Delhi*
Prentice-Hall of Japan, Inc., *Tokyo*
Simon & Schuster Asia Pte. Ltd., *Singapore*
Editora Prentice-Hall do Brasil, Ltda., *Rio de Janeiro*

Contents

Preface

The world economy is moving ever faster toward a highly interrelated, interdependent state, in which no nation will be immune from the forces of the global market. Increased interdependency, however, does not mean market uniformity or universality of management practices. Cultural, political, and to some extent, economic diversity differentiates nations and creates unique market segments. Managing a business, whether domestic or international, in such a milieu requires an understanding of this diversity.

Realizing the impact and the influence of the global market on management of firms, most business schools, following the mandate of American Assembly of Collegiate Schools of Business (AACSB), are offering an international management course, along with other international business courses, to cover the worldwide dimension of the business. This book is for use in such a course. It deals with the fundamental concepts of managing from an international perspective. Although the book is primarily for business students, managers would find it very useful as well. The book offers conceptual frameworks and theoretical explanations useful for the daily challenges of a practicing manager. The insight thus gained could provide managers with added competitive advantages in the global market.

The scope and intensity of operations that expand and exceed the national domestic market vary among firms and industries. This variation determines different levels of commitment by a firm to the global market. Semantically, however, most scholars have not differentiated among these varied levels of commitment. All business activities beyond the domestic market are commonly referred to as *international, multinational, transnational,* or *global*. Strategy differentiation, however, is acknowledged, such as multidomestic versus global. These terms, nonetheless, are beginning to acquire specific meanings, though no consensus has yet been arrived at on their usage.

Among these terms, "international" is more

popular. Many scholars have used the term "international" to connote all business activities that go beyond the domestic market, regardless of the size or scope of the operation. Almost all business schools use the label "International Management" for the title of the course that covers the management concepts of such an operation. For these reasons, in this book, the terms **multinational company** and **international management** are used to describe a firm that operates beyond the domestic market and the management of such a business operation, respectively. Throughout the text, however, to differentiate among firms with various levels of commitment to the world market, whenever necessary, other terminologies have been used.

Cross-cultural Orientation

The book emphasizes the importance of cultural differences and the difficulties of working with people from diverse cultural backgrounds. It provides the readers with the understanding that international management is not just conducting international business transactions abroad, but working with the people who may not share our basic values and assumptions.

Functional Coverage

The book also elaborates on the functional aspects of international management. This particular feature should appeal to instructors who would like the presentation of international management issues to include a flavoring of international business topics. Alternatively, this section could be totally left out or deemphasized in favor of covering the topics through case analyses. For this purpose, there is at least one case per chapter that can be used as an anchor for discussion. These cases are long enough to provide sufficient material for the coverage of the relevant issues, but short enough to be discussed in one class session.

Organization of the Book

The sixteen chapters are divided into four sections. The first section covers strategic aspects in four chapters: introduction, strategic planning, organizational structure, and control. The second part discusses cultural and behavioral dimensions in five chapters: cultural influences, communication and negotiation, motivation, leadership, and human resources. Functional aspects are presented in the third section: international labor relations, manufacturing management, marketing management, financial management, and information systems management. The last part includes two chapters dealing with legal and socio-ethical topics.

Acknowledgment

Of course a book is not a book without a publisher. Mine is Prentice Hall. With apologies ahead of time to anyone whom I may have overlooked I want to thank the people at Prentice Hall who helped me to create the text and the support package: Natalie Anderson, Jo-Ann DeLuca, Nancy Kaplan, Nancy Proyect, David Shafer, Joyce Turner, Pat Wosczyk, and Alana Zdniak.

Many people at various stages of the development of this book have provided me with their support, assistance, and opinions. Their useful recommendations are reflected throughout the book. I am especially indebted to Sandra Hartman of the University of New Orleans who reviewed all chapters and made many constructive recommendations on each. Thank you, Sandra, for your help. My friends, Fariburz Ghadar, Intrados/International Management Group, and V. Baba, Concordia University, Canada, provided me with their intellectual encouragement to make this book a reality. I am grateful for their support. I would like also to express my appreciation to Arvik Naimogieb, Roohsaam Enterprises, who offered interesting anecdotes and thoughtful suggestions.

Several friends and colleagues have contributed their works to this book, as authors or coauthors of different chapters. Their names and affiliations appear on their respective chapters. I appreciate their assistance; they are Mohammad Dadashzadeh, Foad Derakhshn, Deema deSilva, Rauf Khan, Gus Manoochehri, Dwight Murphy, and Alireza Tourani Rad.

I would like to thank the following scholars who reviewed different chapters and offered their helpful comments: Susanata Deb, University of San Francisco, San Francisco, California; Steven Dunphy, Northeastern Illinois University, Chicago, Illinois; Bahman Ebrahimi, University of North Texas, Denton, Texas; Debora Giffiard, Metropolitan College, Denver, Colorado; Caroline Gomez, University of North Carolina at Chapel Hill, North Carolina; Andrea Licari, St. John's University, Jamaica, New York; Karen Middleton, Oklahoma City University, Oklahoma City, Oklahoma; Robert Moore, University of Nevada, Las Vegas, Nevada; Gary Oddou, San Jose State University, San Jose, California; Sam C. Okoroafo, University of Toledo, Toledo, Ohio; James O'Rourke, Notre Dame University, South Bend, Indiana; Keramat Poorsoltan, Frostburg State University, Frostburg, Maryland; Bob Rabboh, Detroit College of Business, Dearborn, Michigan; Martin Roth, Boston College, Boston, Massachusetts; John Stanbury, Indiana University, Kokomo, Indiana; and Phil Van Auken, Baylor University, Waco, Texas.

Finally, I share with my angels Shannon, Shireen, and Linda the joy of accomplishment.

Kamal Fatehi
Western University
Baku, Republic of Azerbaijan

PART ONE

STRATEGIC ASPECTS OF INTERNATIONAL MANAGEMENT

ONE

THE MANAGEMENT OF INTERNATIONAL BUSINESS

This chapter suggests that we are in the midst of a transition period in which economic competition is becoming the new battleground for international rivalry. International business is the instrument with which nations attempt to gain a superior position. To gain competitive advantage, we need to learn how to manage international business operations. To study international management, we need to know what international business is. Therefore, I initially introduce various forms of international business.

The first step in learning how to manage international business is to understand why firms internationalize. This chapter discusses theories of international expansion to illuminate this issue and argues that international management is similar and, at the same time, different from the management of domestic operation. The similarity is due to the fact that both are concerned with achieving organizational objectives through the proper utilization of organizational resources. The dissimilarities are due to variations in managerial mentality, the complexity of business-host government relationship, and cultural and environmental differences. A discussion of these issues concludes the chapter.

Caterpillar, Inc., is an American multinational company (MNC) headquartered in Peoria, Illinois. It designs, manufactures, and sells earth moving, construction, and materials handling equipment and engines as well as electric power generation systems. With a global operation and annual sales of more than $10 billion, the company earns 59 percent of its revenues from foreign markets. Caterpillar employs

approximately 39,000 people in North America, 8,700 in Europe, 4,800 in Latin America, and 2,000 in the Asian/Pacific region.

Caterpillar machines, engines, parts, and components are manufactured in 11 large plants (with more than 500 employees each) and in 12 smaller plants in the United States. Outside the United States, there are 8 large plants and 7 smaller plants. The non-U.S. facilities are operated by wholly owned subsidiaries in Australia, Belgium, Brazil, France, Mexico, and the United Kingdom, and 80 percent-owned subsidiaries in India and Japan. Turbines are manufactured in the United States by Solar Turbines Inc., a wholly owned subsidiary.

Caterpillar products are produced under contract for Caterpillar by independent manufacturers in the United States, Finland, Germany, Norway, South Korea, and the United Kingdom. In addition, products are sold under names other than Caterpillar, produced under license by independent manufacturers in India, Malaysia, New Zealand, People's Republic of China, South Africa, South Korea, and Turkey.

Caterpillar remanufactures diesel engines and related components at two facilities in the United States. Solar Turbines Inc. also operates five turbine overhaul centers, four of which are located outside the United States.

Caterpillar replacement parts are distributed through a network of 22 distribution centers in 10 countries. Caterpillar products are sold and serviced through a worldwide network of 215 independent dealers and one company-owned dealership. Turbines are sold around the world through a sales organization employed by Solar Turbines Inc. Solar replacement parts are distributed through a network of 6 distribution centers in 4 countries.[1]

As a global firm, Caterpillar operates across national borders and has to abide by the laws of the nations in which it does business. In the early 1980s, Caterpillar was caught between conflicting policies of the U.S. and French government. The Soviet Union was building a gas pipeline from Siberia to Western Europe. The pipeline was to deliver natural gas from Siberia to Western Europe, which, in exchange, would provide the Soviet Union with badly needed hard currencies. Caterpillar earth-moving machinery was used in the construction of the pipeline. To punish the Soviets for their expansionist policies in Poland and Afghanistan, the United States decided to halt or delay the construction of the pipeline. President Reagan issued an executive order prohibiting the sale of earth-moving equipment to the Soviets. To the chagrin of the United States, the construction of the pipeline continued undisturbed. Although the shipment of equipment from Peoria, Illinois, had stopped, the French subsidiary, following the French government's strict order, kept shipping the Soviets the same equipment. Caterpillar executives and the U.S. government could do nothing but watch a multimillion dollar business go to Grenoble (near Lyon), France, rather than Peoria, Illinois.

Introduction

From the end of World War II until the 1990s, many countries, particularly the United States, were preoccupied with the threat of communism and the danger of another world war. The United States served as a great security force against communism and provided much needed stability for world trade to flourish. From 1950 to 1972, world trade increased at an average of 5.9 percent per year after adjusting for inflation. Between 1972 and 1990, world trade grew 4.7 percent per year.[2] Of course, new technologies, falling transportation costs, improvements in education, and increased opportunities for international business contributed to economic growth. Without political stability, however, world trade could not have flourished at a steady and healthy rate. During this period the United States acted as the police of the world and was preoccupied with the task of containing communism. To maintain a credible commitment to stability, the United States allocated a relatively large amount of expenditure to defense. The provision of political stability by the United States enabled the world to enjoy economic development at rates that were higher and persisted longer than in any previous period in history.[3]

While the attention of the United States was focused on fighting communism, other nations were able to devote comparatively more time and capital to developing their economies. Under the security umbrella provided by the United States and the concomitant stability, nations began to engage in international trade and export. At a time when other countries, such as Japan, were expanding their markets globally, the United States was busy fighting communism. The commitment of the United States to heavy military expenditure was freeing resources and providing opportunities to other nations, particularly Western Europe and Japan, to challenge directly the U.S. share of the world market.

In military and politics, other countries, except for the Soviet Union, acquiesced to the U.S. leadership. Economically, however, they found much more room and opportunity to contest the U.S. leadership, and they often assumed a prominent position. In the past, military might would often secure economic domination and wealth for the superior nation. In this period, the fruits of U.S. military power, however, accrued to other nations. The relatively safe and secure environment following World War II allowed world trade to expand. Increased world trade produced a higher degree of interdependence among nations. Economic interdependencies and the unacceptable consequences of a nuclear war produced a new mentality. For the first time, nations began rejecting brute force as an acceptable means of conflict resolution. The buildup of the most powerful military force in human history was making military domination less relevant. Economic competition and international business became the arenas for future rivalries.

The world is still going through some fundamental changes. The threat of a major military confrontation among the world superpowers is diminishing. The conditions that forced the United States to seek military supremacy are gradually disappearing. Our former adversaries are seeking our help, and old friends are now posing a serious competitive challenge. In short, political and military rivalries are losing ground to economic competition. Global markets and international business are becoming the new battlegrounds. Some governments, for example, spend heavily to support their industries and to help them achieve global competitive positions. For example, to promote exports, Japan and France expend $5 and $4 per capita, respectively, compared with $0.50 per capita for the United States. According to the U.S. Government Office of Technology Assessment, Japan spends $500 million per year backing 185 technology extension centers.[4]

Faced with the reality of losing markets to these countries, some people are debating the need for a U.S. industrial policy to help secure current market shares and to regain lost market shares. They point out the close relationships between government and industry in Japan that have promoted the expansion of Japanese industries globally. Whatever its relevance or validity, this debate brings the importance of international business into sharp focus. We may not need the type of industrial policy deployed by the Japanese, but we certainly do need to understand the complexity and intricacy of international business and how to manage it. The complexity of international business and the difficulty of managing it was reflected in Caterpillar's predicament presented in the vignette at the beginning of this chapter. The Caterpillar situation highlights the demanding nature of international management and the conflicting pressures that MNCs encounter.

Gaining a competitive advantage in the global market is possible only if we understand the underlying forces and concepts of international management. The application of these concepts in managing the cultural and operational diversity of international business is a challenging task.

Changing Profile of Global Business Environment

As we approach the twenty-first century, there are many factors that increase the impact of international business and, consequently, the role of MNCs in our lives. A corollary factor is that the increase in the volume of international business heightens the importance of international management. Major factors that underline the significance of international business are as follows:

1. It is the tendency of most countries to strive for free world trade and the removal of trade barriers. A good indication of this tendency is the expansion of world trade. As Table

Table 1.1
World Trade Trends: 1970–1992

	Exports (F.O.B.), Millions of U.S. Dollars					
	1970	1975	1980	1985	1990	1992
World	313,792	876,065	1,993,645	1,931,861	3,432,253	3,721,263
Developed countries	223,646	576,272	1,255,548	1,281,230	2,465,055	2,652,276
Developing countries	57,177	221,462	582,945	483,050	794,656	979,530
Other*	30,969	78,332	155,154	167,582	172,453	89,459
United States	43,762	109,317	225,722	218,828	393,592	448,164

	Imports (C.I.F.), Millions of U.S. Dollars					
	1970	1975	1980	1985	1990	1992
World	328,503	902,375	2,047,668	2,006,692	3,562,727	3,849,400
Developed countries	235,319	607,888	1,405,531	1,387,259	2,591,406	2,712,757
Developing countries	61,480	202,415	482,033	453,101	775,446	1,043,197
Other*	31,704	92,074	160,106	166,333	195,802	93,446
United States	42,808	105,880	256,984	361,626	516,987	554,023

* Prior to January 1992, includes Eastern Europe and the former USSR; beginning January 1992, includes Eastern Europe and the European countries of the former USSR.

Source: *1992 International Trade Statistics Yearbook, Volume 1.* (New York: United Nations, 1993), pp. S2–S3, Table A.

1.1 indicates, from 1970 to 1990, world trade expanded more than 10 times. The supporters of free trade believe that free world trade is vital to their economic prosperity. Some, however, would like to take advantage of the open markets of other countries without reciprocating and allowing others free access to their domestic markets. A few countries have been fairly successful in such practices. The imposition of trade and nontrade restrictions has created friction among the European countries, Japan, and the United States. The handling of such friction suggests the willingness of all to solve these problems in a mutually acceptable and amicable manner. Of course, totally free world trade will not arrive overnight, but there is an inexorable movement toward the removal of most trade restrictions and barriers. It may, however, take longer than most people anticipate. Meanwhile, certain transitory arrangements are already developing. For example, Europe is preparing for

full economic integration that would produce a market larger than the United States. The United States, Canada, and Mexico entered into the North American Free Trade Agreement (NAFTA), which removes most of the trade restrictions among these countries and creates a large free trade bloc. Similar events may occur in the Australasian region.

2. The attitudes of many developing countries toward MNCs and foreign direct investment (FDI) have changed. Before the mid-1970s, most developing countries took a dim view of FDI. Expropriation, the forced divestment of foreign assets, was frequently used as a policy choice by many developing countries in their disputes with MNCs. After the mid-1970s, however, the number of expropriations declined dramatically. The large number of pre-1970s expropriations has been attributed to certain problems that developing countries were experiencing. Among these problems were the lack of

administrative capability, the low level of economic development, and an inability to service foreign debts.[5]

As developing countries improved their economic and political capabilities, the need for ownership control through expropriation diminished. Now they can achieve their objectives through taxation and performance requirement rather than by direct control. The changing attitudes of developing countries toward FDI have led some to argue that the attractiveness of foreign investment is growing and its supply is decreasing. Consequently, competition to attract FDI should escalate, and governments may outbid each other with packages of investment incentives and inducements.[6] This may result in increased international trade and may open previously inaccessible markets.

3. Hoping to duplicate the success achieved by Japan, Korea, and other Asian nations, many developing countries are adopting an export-oriented strategy of economic growth. The circumstances, however, under which Japan and, to some extent, Korea employed their export-oriented strategies have changed. During the period in which these countries engaged in an export-oriented strategy, the U.S. market absorbed the bulk of their exports. As a result of a substantial trade deficit, the United States, once the largest creditor nation, was transformed into the largest debtor nation. Since this trend cannot continue unabated and the United States is determined to reverse it, other nations may not fully succeed in emulating Japan. Nonetheless, as more nations engage in export, international business and, along with it, international management will gain prominence.

Export-oriented strategy, in part, involves MNCs' participation. As Lecraw and Morrison have noted, in the mid-1980s, 30 percent of British, 30.3 percent of Japanese, and 40 percent of the U.S. imports were through intrafirm trade by MNCs.[7] As more countries view MNCs as an instrument for achieving this goal, we must understand how these firms operate and how they are managed.

4. Regional trade agreements and pacts are reducing trade restrictions among the members and increasing intraregion trade. Membership in regional trade agreements is on the rise. The most notable trade agreements are the European Community (EC), the Association of South East Asian Nations (ASEAN), and the Andean Pact. The EC members are the 12 Western European countries of Belgium, Denmark, France, Germany, Greece, Luxembourg, Ireland, Italy, Netherlands, Portugal, Spain, and the United Kingdom. The ASEAN countries are Brunei, Indonesia, Malaysia, the Philippines, Singapore, and Thailand. Bolivia, Colombia, Ecuador, Peru, and Venezuela are members of the Andean Pact. NAFTA, when fully implemented, will create another bloc rivaling the EC and ASEAN.

Some speculate that in the future three trading blocks will dominate world trade. The first bloc is EC, with its present 12 members, which may expand to include a few more nations. The second bloc is ASEAN with the expanded membership that could include Australia, India, and Japan. The third bloc is America, with the membership of Argentina, Brazil, Canada, Chile, Mexico, the United States, and Venezuela. There could be relatively free or open trade within these blocs as well as trade restrictions among them.[8] A strategic response to such a scenario would be for the firms to have a foothold within each bloc or to form strategic alliances with those that already operate within the blocs. Either case results in the expansion of the roles and scope of international management.

5. Recent technological developments, particularly in manufacturing, have altered the nature of international business. Robotics, computer-aided design (CAD), computer-aided manufacturing (CAM), and flexible manufacturing have reduced production costs for most products. These technologies have also reduced the labor component of some products. As a result, the traditionally low labor cost countries are losing their competitive position. Therefore,

we expect that these countries will try to tap MNCs for technology transfer.

6. Competition for capital will increase as demand rises. Demand for capital from Eastern European countries, along with those of the Commonwealth of Independent States (CIS) (various republics of the former Soviet Union), will likely intensify competition in capital market. Another factor that has resulted in a rising demand for capital is the sovereign debt crisis of the 1980s. In the 1980s, heavily indebted developing countries experienced great difficulty in paying their debts. This resulted in a serious financial strain on the American and European banks and financial institutions that had lent the money. Ever since, these institutions have become more cautious, and private sources of capital have become scarce and costly. Consequently, more countries are viewing the equity capital from MNCs as a viable alternative. This is another reason for the changing attitudes of developing countries toward MNCs.

7   Slowly but steadily, national borders are losing their effectiveness in dealing with MNCs. Although we are witnessing a rising national fervor among the subjugated people of the former Soviet bloc, simultaneously there is evidence that certain new developments are evolving that defy traditional description. For example, in June 1992, a U.S. citizen, Raffi Ovanesian, became foreign minister of Armenia. One month later, another U.S. citizen, Milan Panic, was elected by the Yugoslavia's parliament as their premier. Furthermore, the top executives of some well-known American firms are foreign citizens. The ranks of recent foreign executives in American corporations included the vice chairman of Pfizer from France, the president and chief executive officer of Esprit de Corp and the president and chief operating officer of Unisys, both from Switzerland, the vice president of worldwide purchasing at General Motors from Spain, the executive vice president of Xerox from Italy,[9] and the head of McKinsey and Company, the prestigious consulting firm, from India.

For many years, Europeans firms have been preparing for a borderless market in which the nationalities of managers have no bearing on their selection and in which cross-national career advancement is a norm. Many well-known European firms regularly promote foreigners to their top executive ranks. Recently, for example, the head of Michelin-Okmoto, a Japanese subsidiary of Michelin of France, was a German, and Electrolux, a Swedish firm, had a French director.[10]

8. The enormous investment required to support new technologies and research and development, and the increasing scale economies needed for an optimum operation, are compelling firms to consider the whole world as a market. In many industries, even the largest and most resourceful firms cannot afford the enormous investments required. For example, the estimated $1 billion needed to develop a new generation of dynamic random-access memory (DRAM) chips has forced International Business Machines to form a joint venture with Toshiba Corporation of Japan and Siemens AG of Germany.[11] The immense operations and marketing costs of new high-technology products, along with other requirements, have been the driving forces behind the recent trend in increased internationalization.

9. International linkages among countries are creating a higher degree of interdependency, characterized by an increasing volume of FDI. Tables 1.2 and 1.3 illustrate the rising FDI during the 1965 to 1990 period. While the U.S. FDI has been increasing, other countries' investments in the United States have been on the rise as well. From 1965 to 1990, the U.S. FDI increased nearly 10 times. In contrast, FDI in the United States expanded more than 40 times. By 1990, FDI in the United States. was almost equal to U.S. investments abroad.

International linkages have been growing since World War II. It began with successive reduction of international trade restrictions, which increased the world trade. The interdependency

Table 1.2

U.S. Direct Investment Position Abroad, 1965–1990*

	Millions of U.S. Dollars					
	1965[†]	1970	1975	1980	1985	1990
Total	49,217	78,178	124,212	215,578	232,667	424,086
Developed countries	29,066	53,145	90,323	158,350	172,750	318,156
Developing countries	18,134	21,448	26,222	53,277	54,474	102,360
International and unallocated	2,017	3,586	7,067	3,951	5,443	3,570

*Because of rounding off, figures may not add up.

[†]For 1965 data, Japan was included in the developing countries category.

Source: U.S. Department of Commerce, Bureau of Economic Analysis. *Survey of Current Business* (1966–1992) Washington, DC.

through trade was followed by financial integration, which was aided by the recycling of the Organization of Petroleum Exporting Countries (OPEC) surplus during the 1970s. Now we are experiencing the third phase of international linkage that often is referred to as **globalization.** Characteristics of this phase include FDIs made by MNCs and the technological alliances among them. A large and growing portion of world trade involves intrafirm trade. For example, in the case of the United States and Japan, more than one-half of the total trade flow is related to intrafirm transactions.[12]

These are signs of changing times and a globalization of business. It is becoming very difficult, if not impossible, to identify the national origin of many products. Today, products are assembled from parts produced around the world. When the U.S. government was questioning whether Honda automobiles had more than 50 percent of U.S. contents, it became clear that General Motors, Ford, and Chrysler were not in a much better position. The issue of national origin is becoming an international trade problem. Consider the following dilemma: Japan insists that products made by American

Table 1.3

Foreign Direct Investment Position in the United States, 1965–1990

	Millions of U.S. Dollars					
	1965	1970	1975	1980	1985	1990
All countries	8,797	13,270	27,662	68,351	184,615	396,702
Canada	2,388	3,117	5,352	10,074	17,131	30,037
Europe	6,076	9,554	18,584	45,731	121,413	250,973
Japan	118	229	591	4,225	19,313	81,775
Australia, New Zealand, and South Africa	—	—	36	253	3,324	6,677
Latin America	—	—	2,774	6,990	16,826	9,616
Middle East			219	753	4,954	4,423
Others	214	370	106	325	1,654	13,201

*Because of rounding off, figures may not add up.

Source: U.S. Department of Commerce, Bureau of Economic Analysis. *Survey of Current Business* (1966–1992) Washington, DC.

corporations that are located in Japan should be counted as American-made, yet Honda of America is claimed to be American. A similar problem arises when cars made in the United States by Japanese companies are exported to Europe. Should these cars be considered Japanese or American?

Imperatives of Globalization of Business

In the following section, I discuss the imperatives of globalization of business. First, I elaborate the need for going international. Then, I present theories of international trade and FDI. Finally, within the framework of product life cycle, I explain the firm's expansion into international markets.

Reasons That Businesses Expand Their Operations Abroad

International competition affects most businesses and results in the globalization of many industries. The unprecedented information explosion unimaginable only a couple of decades ago has greatly contributed to international competition. Technological developments have also reduced transportation costs. Consequently, physical distance between producers and consumers is no longer much of a competitive hindrance. Domestic firms with unique products or services, or with a competitive advantage, can expand beyond their home market easily.

In today's environment, going international is either an inherent extension of successful domestic business operations or a requirement if the company is to remain competitive. Increased worldwide interdependencies, if continued at the present pace, will make internationalization a requisite for survival. Until such a time, many organizations will operate at national and international levels as if they were totally independent. Given this crude assumption, scholars argue about the motives and reasons for the internationalization of firms. Theories of international trade, FDI, and product life cycle have attempted to explain reasons and motives for in-

ternational expansion. These theories provide the following explanations.

Theories of International Trade and Foreign Direct Investment

International trade theorists propose that nations gain from international trade (exports and imports). The gains are the consequences of exploiting relative comparative advantages, which are derived from exporting those goods that a nation holds superior in production cost. This superiority could stem from natural resource endowments such as climate, quality of land, or differences in cost of labor, capital, technology, and entrepreneurship. The opportunity cost plays an important role in comparative advantage. To produce one product a country has to give up production of another product, and this entails an opportunity cost. Nations benefit from international trade when they export products that they specialize in, because they have the greatest comparative advantage, and then import those products in which they have the greatest comparative disadvantage.

Theories of FDI suggest that four factors influence the expansion of MNCs abroad:

1. Change in geographic horizons[13]
2. Possession of an ownership-specific advantage[14]
3. Exploitation of the firm's internal market[15]
4. Effect of locational advantages on host countries

Change in geographic horizons   As firms grow and expand abroad, under the influence of external and internal forces, their geographic horizons widen. The changes in their horizons enable them to perceive the existence of international opportunities and stimulate them to expand internationally.

Possession of an ownership-specific advantage   Compared with local firms, MNCs face certain disadvantages, such as the lack of knowledge about the economic, political, legal, and social situations of foreign countries.

Geographic distance, currency exchange risks, and language barriers create further difficulties. The established relationships among domestic firms and their suppliers, customers, and the regulatory agencies put MNCs at an additional disadvantage. When a firm acquires a global horizon and goes international, it can benefit from investments in foreign countries if it has an ownership-specific advantage, to offset the disadvantage of its foreignness. The ownership-specific advantage, which is also called strategic advantage, could be a patented technology, product differentiation, economies of scale, brand names, managerial skills, or possession of knowledge.

Exploitation of the firm's internal market
A firm's strategic advantage could be licensed, franchised, or traded to local firms. Therefore, ownership-specific advantage alone is not sufficient for a firm to go international. Internal organizational capabilities should allow for a more effective use of strategic advantages rather than contractual agreements with other firms. Scattered throughout the firm, organizational capabilities that could employ the firm's strategic advantages better than outside customers are called the internal market. Specifically, the firm's internal market can best exploit the strategic advantages that are embodied in intermediate products. Some of these strategic advantages, such as knowledge and expertise, which may ultimately result in a patent, could be best capitalized using the firm's internal market. Unless such knowledge and expertise culminate in products, there is no ready market for them in their intermediate states. The creation of an internal market through international expansion ensures full exploitation of these strategic advantages.

Effect of locational advantages on host countries   Building organizational capabilities and the use of strategic advantages through international expansion do not determine the location of foreign investment. MNCs must justify the choice of investment location. In which for-

eign countries should MNCs expand? The answer is very simple. MNCs should locate their operations in countries that offer certain locational advantages, such as sources of raw materials, large markets, or low-cost labor.

Other factors   Once a firm, for whatever reason, expands abroad there is the likelihood that it will develop scanning and learning capability. Its presence in many markets enables the firm to locate alternative low-cost production sources and new technologies, or to learn about market needs that could trigger new product development.[16] In effect, scanning and learning capability enhances the firm's competitive advantage. The worldwide presence could also be used as a competitive weapon and for cross-subsidization of markets. Taking the competition head on by penetrating into their home turf forces foreign competition to allocate resources for defensive purposes. Subsidizing losses in one market with funds from another profitable market could hamper the competitive position of rivals.[17] The penetration of rivals' home markets and cross-subsidization could adversely affect the competition. Competition may suffer from vital cash drain, reduced income, and lost opportunities. This could impair the competitors' abilities to expand into new markets.

International Product Life Cycle

The international product life cycle, first proposed by Raymond Vernon[18] and expanded upon by Adler and Ghadar,[19] suggests a sequential progress for the firm's expansion into an international market that follows the life cycle of products. Vernon proposed a three-stage model of product life cycle that was useful in explaining the expansion of post–World War II manufacturing investment abroad. The three stages proposed by Vernon are as follows: new product stage, mature product stage, and standardized product stage. The model suggests that high-income, economically developed countries are the home for most new products and innovations.

In the first stage, innovative firms in developed countries produce new products for the home market. Foreign markets, which are other high-income countries, are served through exports. At this stage, since products are new, the firms do not face serious competition.

The maturity phase is the second stage, at which products have been perfected and sufficiently standardized. As more firms enter the market, price competition forces firms to establish manufacturing facilities in other high-income countries to serve foreign markets with local production.

Heavy price competition characterizes the standardized product stage. The emphasis on price compels firms to move production to low-cost countries. The home market and other high-income countries are served by exports from these locations.

The three-stage international product life cycle is a useful model that explains internationalization of firms for the 20-year period following World War II. Technological developments, however, have accelerated the life cycle of products, whereby most products become obsolete a few years after introduction. Furthermore, the world has become an integrated market that requires mass customization of products to meet individual needs.

According to Adler and Ghadar, we are now in the fourth stage of the international product life cycle. This stage is characterized by technological diffusion, the high cost of research and development, a global market, mass customization of products, and intense competition among firms from developed and newly developing countries.

In the first three stages, internationalization was in response to specific needs, such as market extension or low-cost production. Adler and Ghadar's argument implies that in the fourth stage, firms internationalize because the demarcation line between domestic and foreign markets, for many manufactured products, is blurring. By the fourth stage, global market is the source of new technology, capital, and other factors of production at low costs. Internationalization is not an extension of the previous stages, but a stage onto itself. The diversity and resources of the global market, the immense consumer base, and the necessity of tapping them instigate FDI and international trade. Due to the unique characteristics of this stage, global operation is the only answer to the pressure of intense competition. As Adler and Ghadar assert, in the fourth stage

> . . . top-quality, least-possible-cost products and services become the minimally acceptable standard. Competitive advantage comes from sophisticated global strategies based on mass customization. Firms draw product ideas, as well as the factors and locations of production, from worldwide sources. Firms tailor final products and their relationship to clients to very discrete market niches . . . the product, market, and price orientations of prior phases almost completely disappear, having been replaced by a strategic orientation combining responsive design and delivery with quick, least-possible-cost production. . . . [At this stage] strategic orientation requires firms to develop global R&D, production, and marketing networks . . . [20]

The preceding discussion highlights various reasons and motivations for the internationalization of the firm. I should add, however, that rarely is the decision to expand abroad based on a solitary reason or motive. The search for enhancing firms' competitive positions entices them to explore global opportunities. The more adaptable and successful firms usually venture into the uncharted waters of the global market. Once there, through first-hand experience, they learn about the expanse of the market and the variety of choices. The vista of the global market thus envisioned creates many more reasons to expand even further.

Types of International Business Operations

The internationalization process covers a variety of transactions and activities. Imports and exports are two of the simplest forms of international business. The most complex form is managing FDI abroad. These activities can be differentiated based on the perspective of the activities or the types of investment commitments.[21]

There are two perspectives to international business—inward-looking and outward-looking. These two perspectives are mirror images of each other. The outward-looking activities have their beginning at home and their ending at a foreign market. Export is the least demanding of the outward-looking transactions, while establishing operational facilities in a foreign country is the most difficult one. The inward-looking perspective covers a range of transactions that start in a foreign location and end at home. It consists of imports at one end and the management of a wholly owned foreign subsidiary at the other end.

As mentioned previously, the firm's internationalization process begins when it starts to buy from, or sell to, foreigners. The most serious aspect of the process, however, does not start until the firm commits resources to international activities. The type of foreign investment commitment that a firm makes to international business could be analyzed across three dimensions. These three dimensions are scale of investment, type of partners, and ownership arrangement. The investment scale could be small or large. An example of small-scale investment is opening a sales office abroad for exporting, while establishing a full-scale production facility abroad is an example of a large-scale investment. The ownership level could vary from minority ownership to wholly owned operations. Partners in an international business could be from the local public, local government, private entities, or other foreign firms. Figure 1.1 illustrates that this typology creates 80 different potential forms of international business.[22] MNCs may choose a combination of these alternatives in their quest to capitalize on global opportunities available to them. In the following chapter, major international business operations are described. The order of presentation follows an evolutionary view of international business that begins with export and ends with FDI.

Export and Import

When a firm explores whether to expand abroad, the first choice is export. Export and its mirror image, import, require careful evaluation of the market and the establishment of cross-cultural relationships. The firm has to decide if it should directly export, use a local importer, or hire an export agent. The decision, of course, reflects the strategic capabilities of the firm. For firms without international experience, direct exporting may not be the best choice. Local middlepersons could be a better option for a first-time exporter. As the firm builds experience and learns about the market, culture, and particulars of the environment, direct exporting becomes a feasible alternative.

Exported products should offer local customer values above competing local products and those sold by other MNCs. An exporter incurs transportation costs and other costs associated with operating in a foreign country. Tariffs, exchange rates, and government supports that prolong the existence of inefficient local firms are among the factors that may increase the final price to customers. Exporters with a competitive advantage that offset these costs could succeed in exporting. Falling transportation costs and new telecommunication technologies that reduce the cost of information acquisition have reduced the costs of exporting. However, costs related to the differences in language, culture, and legal systems are major impediments to exporting.

Countertrade

Countertrade is the exchange of goods for goods. In a countertrade, the exporting firm is required to purchase, from a country, all or a portion of the value of goods sold to it.

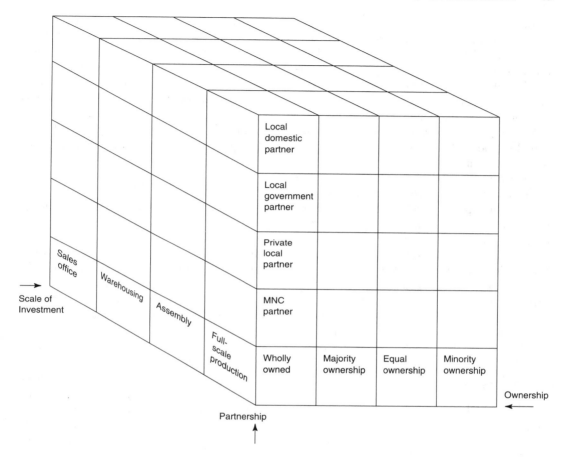

Figure 1.1 Types of International Business Operations
Adopted with permission from P. W. Beamish, J. P. Killing, D. J. Lecrew, and H. Crookell. International Management (Burr Ridge, IL: R. D. Irwin, Inc., 1991), 6.

Countertrade is used to conserve hard currencies, help local businesses, and promote technology transfer. It is estimated that between 25 and 40 percent of the world's exports are through countertrade.[23] Major types of countertrade are barter, counterpurchase, buyback, and switch trading.

Barter Barter is the oldest method of trade. In barter, countries exchange goods without the use of money. The difficulty involved in a barter is to agree on the rate of exchange for the products that are the subject of bartering.

Counterpurchase The obligation by the exporter to purchase a certain amount of goods from the country when exporting to it is called counterpurchase. This obligation could be for all of the export value or a portion of it. Some important conditions to a counterpurchase that are negotiated are the timing, the duration, and the percent of countertrade.

Buyback   The exchange of output of plants or equipment as the payment for goods or services rendered by an exporter is called a buyback. Buyback could be for building a plant, licensing of a trademark or patent, transfer of managerial know-how, or lending of capital. For example, Fiat of Italy built an automobile plant in Russia. The cost of constructing the plant was partially paid with Fiat automobiles manufactured at the plant.

Switchtrading   The barter between three or more countries in a circular fashion is switchtrading. An importer in country X, for example, wants to import machinery from country Y in exchange for grains. Country Y does not need grains and, at the same time, has a trade deficit (debt) with country Z as a result of a pervious import of oil from that country. If country Z accepts grains from country Y to settle the oil account with country X, in part or totally, the switchtrading is complete. A switch specialist usually assists consummation of these transactions.

Turnkey Projects

The design and construction of an operation and the training of personnel to run it could be contracted to an MNC. In return for setting up such a turnkey project, the MNC receives a fee. Turnkey projects usually involve large contracts such as the construction of chemical plants, pipelines, refineries, steel mills, dams, and electric power plants.

Licensing

Licensing is a contract between an MNC and a foreign firm. Under the terms of the licensing agreement, the foreign company is allowed to produce products using the technology, patents, trademarks, manufacturing technologies, trade secrets, and other proprietary advantages of the MNC for a fee. The licensing agreement could be between an MNC and its foreign subsidiary. Quite often, however, the licensing contract is between an MNC and a domestic firm.

Licensing could be an attractive option because of several reasons. It does not require much capital, managerial resources, and understanding of foreign market. Licensing permits the test marketing of products before direct investment. A small market could be exploited that otherwise would have not been economical to enter. In some cases, licensing is the only option because of the government restriction on imports and/or FDI.[24]

International Joint Ventures

A corporate alliance between an MNC and a local company or a foreign government, or between two MNCs, in the ownership of a firm is called an international joint venture. It is beneficial to both partners. The local company benefits from the technology transfer, and the MNC learns about the market through the partnership with a local firm. It has the benefit of dampening nationalistic fervor and antiforeigner sentiment in developing countries. The drawback is the difficulty of blending two different cultures in managing the venture. Cultural misunderstandings and differences in managerial styles sometimes lead to the breakup of the venture. Often, the consequence of such a breakup is the likelihood that the old partner becomes a new competitor.

Direct Investment

The most demanding and complex form of international business operation is direct investment. It involves the ownership and management of physical facilities for producing goods in foreign countries. FDI could be a part of the firm's overall strategy or may be due to trade restrictions imposed by foreign governments. To overcome these restrictions, MNCs find it advantageous to invest directly in a country and establish a subsidiary. When a firm establishes production operation abroad, it creates a long-term commitment and obligation and assumes the associated risks and rewards. Having physical facilities, such as the operation of a mine, manufacturing plants and equipment, and real estate, requires a higher level of financial and human resources commitment. It constrains the firm to the vagaries of sovereign foreign government and local market forces, while also offering many opportunities. The size and scope of FDI and the choice of strategies for expansion abroad create different types of international firms. International management lexicon refers to these firms as international, multidomestic, multinational, transnational, and global. Different scholars have used each term to refer to a specific type of international firm. In this book, we generally use the term *international* for all firms that expand abroad and cross the boundaries of their domestic market. For "industry" identification, however, we distinguish between multidomestic, international, and global industries. We discuss the differences among them in Chapter 2. At this point, it suffices to know that global firms are those enterprises that operate at the global level and treat the whole world as one market.

International Business and International Management

International business deals with business activities and transactions that are carried out across two or more national borders. The management of organizations that are involved in international business is called international management. A couple of decades ago, only large and very resourceful firms could operate successfully at the international level. Although many international businesses still involve large-scale operations, recent improvements in technology, transportation, and communications have made the size less relevant.

Small companies are using new technologies to penetrate markets that previously were the domain of big business. The success of small firms is not limited to any particular industry or market. Semiconductors, medical equipment, laundry equipment, and wastewater treatment systems are among many industries that have al-

lowed small businesses to join their larger counterparts in the global market. For example, Sharper Finish, Inc., of Chicago, a maker of commercial laundry equipment, deals with 300 distributors in 30 countries, using modern communication technologies. In 1991, 60 percent of Sharper Finish's $3 million sales were to overseas markets. Another example is Midwest Tropical, Inc., of Chicago, with annual sales of $5.5 million. Tropical is earning half of its revenues from export.[25] Yet a third example is DSP Group, Inc., of San Jose, California, a producer of specialty semiconductors, with annual sales of $8 million. Nearly half of DSP's sales are to Japan. Albeit from diverse industries, what these firms had in common was an understanding that managing an international business operation is different from managing a domestic firm. They were all effective in adapting to the requirements of their foreign customers and the imperatives of the host country.[26]

Most of U.S. management know-how, as Richman and Copen observed in the early 1970s, if modified properly, is transferable to other environments.[27] The assumption of universality of management concepts and practices, however, could result in utter failure in international business. In other words, there are as many differences as there are similarities between the management of an international enterprise and a domestic business. The differences have less to do with the size of the assets, earnings, the complexity of technology employed, or number of employees, and more to do with environmental factors and cultural variations. International management involves greater environmental diversity, complexity, and uncertainty than managing domestic operations. Social, political, legal, economic, and cultural variations of multiple environments necessitate more careful planning and preparation, as well as greater diligence in implementation and control.

When a firm ventures into international business, it leaves behind the familiar and tested business practices. Everything about forces that govern the market has to be learned anew. The consumers, competition, suppliers, government, labor market, capital market, and above all, culture are all unfamiliar. While a domestic firm has to deal with only one set of rules regarding market forces, an international operation requires understanding of the interaction between all these forces in multiple markets.

Although it may appear that going international is fraught with many problems and difficulties, at the same time it offers many opportunities not available in a purely domestic operation. For example, one of the complexities of international business is doing business in multiple currencies. Exchange rates for foreign currencies fluctuate due to local and global economic forces. Two major forces affect the exchange rate—supply and demand for foreign currency and domestic conditions, such as the inflation rate, balance of payments, economic growth, and political factors. Exchange rate fluctuation can create additional risk, while also offering opportunities. MNCs could use their unique position of operating across national borders to benefit from favorable exchange rates. They could augment the benefits of favorable exchange rates with intrafirm business transactions to boost their profits.

We now examine outstanding features of managing international business operations that distinguish them from domestic businesses.

Major Elements of Managing International Business Operations

The management of international business and domestic operations is similar in that both require the attainment of organizational objectives through coordination of activities and the utilization of resources. They are different because of the differences in their respective environment and cultural settings. The difference is also due to managerial attitudes and mentality. International business has a multi-environmental, multicultural framework. The environmental and cultural diversity add more complexity and uncertainty to international business, which make managing such an operation even more difficult. The difficulty of managing an international business operation is also due to a mismatch between the managerial mentality and the progression of business from a domestic to an international posture. When operational and systemic transition from a domestic position to an international status is not accompanied by a commensurate change in managerial mentality, the firm may not succeed in international competition. For example, a firm that has expanded to many markets and is dealing with people from many cultures can no longer operate with the mentality of a domestic company. Ignoring the expanded role of the firm as a corporate citizen of multiple countries results in a tarnished image and operational restrictions. The consequence may ultimately be failure.

Management View of International Business

In the 1960s, some scholars suggested that the truly international firms could offer the best hope for creating world peace and improving economic conditions of the people. They were asserting that such firms, with supranational frameworks, could conceivably make wars less likely on the assumption that bombing customers, suppliers, and employees is in nobody's interest.[28] We are now witnessing the emergence of such supranational firms that could rightly be called global. The executives of these firms have a global view and mentality. They focus on worldwide and local objectives. They are globally integrated and locally responsive. The relationship between headquarters and subsidiaries is based on mutual understanding and support. Subsidiaries are neither satellites nor are they totally independent. They always ask the question: "Where in the world shall we raise money, build our plant, conduct R&D, and create and launch new ideas to serve our present and future customers?"[29]

Of course, not all firms that are engaged in international business have developed supranational frameworks and mentalities. There appears to be an evolutionary pattern of internationalization that determines the executives' state of mind. This state of mind pertains to the orientation of the executives toward foreign people, ideas, and resources, both at home and abroad. This attitude not only differentiates between the executives of international and domestic firms, but also differentiates among executives of MNCs. Perlmutter proposed that the degree of internationalization of a firm could be estimated by the mentality and orientation of its executives.[30] He identified three states of mind or attitudes toward key decisions on products, functions, and geography. By supplementing the three-stage framework identified by Perlmutter[31] with ideas presented by others,[32] the evolutionary process of multinational firms can be categorized in four stages. The four stages are ethnocentric (or home country mentality), polycentric (or host country mentality), centocentric (or classical global mentality), and geocentric (or supranational mentality). These stages represent managerial mentality and attitudes of MNCs.

Ethnocentric mentality The ethnocentric firm views foreign markets as an extension of the domestic market. It ascribes superiority to everything from the home country and inferiority to everything foreign. Products are produced for the home market and are exported abroad as an additional source of revenue. The firm headquarters and affiliates are identified by the nationality of the home country. Key managerial positions, both at the headquarters and at subsidiaries, are reserved for home country executives. A foreign assignment is not considered a very desirable appointment and does not advance the professional career of a manager. In short, an ethnocentric firm views itself as a domestic firm with foreign extensions.

Polycentric mentality In a polycentric firm, the prevailing attitude is that foreigners are different and difficult to understand. The assumption, therefore, is that the management of foreign affiliates should be left to local people.

Products are produced for local consumption in facilities that are operated by host country personnel. Headquarter's control is exercised through financial reports. The firm could best be characterized as a confederation of loosely connected, semi-autonomous affiliates. Although on the surface it may appear that a polycentric firm, operating in multiple markets and acting as a local company in every market, is a highly internationalized enterprise. That is far from the truth. In a polycentric firm, local managers are not treated as equals to home country managers and are considered somewhat less trustworthy and competent. They cannot aspire to a high-level executive position at the headquarters office. Consequently, local managers who detect the ignorance of the headquarter in managing subsidiaries and resent the treatment they are receiving are pulled into a virulent ethnocentric mentality.

Centocentric mentality The local responsiveness of polycentric firms results in inefficient operations. Attention to local markets and to the demands of local governments creates an infrastructure within each subsidiary that ignores internal market opportunities. Manufacturing facilities are often underutilized and the full benefits of economies of scale are not realized.

Decreasing trade barriers and improvements in telecommunication technologies and transportation allow the use of classical global strategies, viewing the world as one market. We label such an attitude centocentric. Treating the world as one market enables the firm to take advantage of economies of scale in design, manufacturing, and marketing of products, and research and development. Products are designed and manufactured, quite often, at home for the world market. Centocentric firms assume that nations are more similar in tastes and preferences than they are different. The assumption is that the differences could be made inconsequential by providing better quality products at lower prices compared with domestic products. Therefore, uniform products could be produced at centers for distribution to all. Centocentric firms require more central control than others. The headquarters office maintains control by assigning products or business managers with global responsibilities. The firm is still identified with the home country, and business managers are nationals from the home country, as are other key executives. The home country culture and the culture of headquarters permeate the firm and all the subsidiaries. Only local managers who identify with the dominant culture of the headquarters are promoted to key positions. Important strategic decisions are made at the headquarters, and subsidiaries are expected to implement them.

Geocentric mentality   The success of centocentric MNCs and the power they exert on the local market cause resentment and apprehension. Central control over subsidiaries that dictate major decisions from the home office and identification with the home country produce additional concerns. To offset perceived power and control of global firms on the local market, host governments are restricting their operations. They also pressure MNCs for more local investment and technology transfer by enacting local content laws. Some governments demand changes in MNCs' personnel policies to allow for local representation on managerial ranks. Moreover, the global market is proving to be more heterogeneous than centocentric MNCs had assumed. The volatility of the global economic and political environment is an extra impetus for global firms to become locally responsive. Add to all of this the improvements in manufacturing technologies that have enabled more efficient flexible manufacturing and smaller batch production, and the stage is set for localized strategies.

There are two simultaneous demands on global firms. On the one hand, they are expected to be locally responsive; on the other hand, maintaining worldwide competitiveness requires a higher degree of efficiency, which is possible only with a globally integrated operation. This gives rise to emerging geocentric firms. Geocentric firms view themselves as global companies with no geographic center, in which no nationalities dominate the firm. Viewing the world as their home, geocentric firms strive for flexibility and efficiency globally. Successful geocentric firms think globally and act locally. They integrate an interdependent network of decentralized and specialized companies worldwide. Perhaps the best way to describe a geocentric firm is to look at the operation of one. An example of a geocentric firm is Asea Brown Boveri (ABB), a global electrical systems equipment company. ABB started as a Swedish firm that later merged with a Swiss company and made Zurich its headquarters. ABB's annual revenues exceed $25 billion, and it employs 240,000 people around the world. It generates $7 billion in annual revenues from North America with 40,000 employees. It has 10,000 employees in India and 10,000 in South America. Percy Barnevik, president and chief executive officer of ABB, describes his company as follows:

> ABB is a company with no geographic center, no national ax to grind. We are a federation of national companies with a global coordination center. Are we a Swiss company? Our headquarters is in Zurich, but only 100 professionals work at headquarters and we will not increase that number. Are we a Swedish company? I'm the CEO, and I was born in Sweden, and only two of the eight members of our board of directors are Swedes. Perhaps we are an American company. We report our financial results in U.S. dollars, and English is ABB's official language. We conduct all high-level meetings in English.
>
> My point is that ABB is none of those things—and all of those things. We are not homeless. We are a company with many homes.[33]

MNCs and Host Government Relationships

The relationship between business and government has always been an area of considerable concern. Governments, in their quest for economic development and social programs, enact regulations that may restrict business activities or affect earnings. Often, government economic policies and social agendas do not coincide with the goals and objectives of business. In particular, governments are skeptical of the foreign subsidiaries that are controlled by headquarters outside the country. Influencing the strategies of such foreign affiliates is not as easy as influencing those of the domestic firms. They can, nonetheless, affect the local subsidiaries of MNCs through their public policy decisions. In dealing with MNCs, the sovereign power of government renders objections from MNCs mute. This is not to say that governments always have an upper hand in their dealing with MNCs. Usually, the ability of integrated MNCs to acquire capital, material, technology, and labor globally reduces the effectiveness of most government policies.

Host governments would like foreign firms to invest in the country, create jobs, facilitate technology transfer, and help with balance of payment through exports. Foreign firms with limited operations abroad are forced to comply with government policies more readily. Their subsidiaries are also in a better position for compliance because they do not face conflicting demands of multiple governments. But integrated MNCs, due to the nature of their operations, may not be able to respond favorably to host government demands. Demands of one government may differ from the requirements of the other. For example, to earn hard currencies, many developing countries are emphasizing exports. To give in to the pressure by one government to increase exports is to jeopardize the relationship with others. Moreover, the flexibility of globally integrated operation enables these MNCs to withstand the demands of local governments by capitalizing on their internal market. Globally integrated MNCs could supplement operational restrictions imposed on them in one country with increased business in the other countries.

The preceding argument may give an exaggerated impression of the power and flexibility of globally integrated firms. Host government relationships with MNCs are very complex and do not lend themselves to a simple generalization. For instance, it is true that reallocation of resources among subsidiaries, shifting production between various locations, and the use of the firm's internal market are effective tools for foiling the unfavorable policies of a host government. If a host government applies serious pressure on the MNC with the implication of severely hampering its business, the MNC's choices are few. The size of investment and the commitment of MNC to a host country reduces its flexibility. FDI in plants, production equipment, and physical facilities that are not readily mobile reduces the flexibility of integrated strategies, at least in the short run. Accommodating the host government may be the wisest choice in this case.

Host government subsidies to domestic firms or the use of the government's purchasing power to give preference to domestic firms could create unfavorable business conditions for MNCs. Changes in tax laws, labor laws, repatriation of profits, and a host of other regulations and restrictions are sources of additional risk. Political risk increases the cost of doing business abroad and makes FDI a challenging and demanding proposition. Foreign governments have had a history of such practices. The political risk of operating in a foreign country is a reality with which MNCs have to deal. Sudden and dramatic change in government policy toward FDI, though less frequent in recent years, is a distinct possibility that MNCs have to consider when going abroad.

The most troublesome feature of managing across national borders is to deal with the public policies of a home government that are in conflict with host government policies. Complying with the policies of either government could create legal problems for the executives. Consider the quandary of Caterpillar executives during the construction of the Soviet pipeline to Western Europe in the early 1980s. You may recall that the U.S. government, to punish the Soviet Union for its expansionist policies, ordered Caterpillar to stop selling earth-moving equipment to the Soviet Union. Caterpillar executives complied and stopped shipping equipment from its Peoria, Illinois, plant. However, the French subsidiary of Caterpillar, under the order of the French government, continued to deliver equipment to the Soviets. Caterpillar executives, although following the U.S. policies, were not able to satisfy the mandate of the U.S. government.

Host Country Business Environment

Besides the complexity of relationships with host governments, MNCs have to deal with the local work force, domestic and international competition, local suppliers, and customers that are different from those of the home country. The cultural difference is a major source of difficulty for managing a global firm. Faced with multiple cultures, MNCs have to adjust and adapt their managerial practices to accommodate the idiosyncrasies of various cultures. Fluctuations in the exchange rate create an additional burden for the MNCs. These issues are discussed in later chapters.

In short, managing an MNC is not managing a larger domestic firm. It involves a change in management mentality and a greater attention to the requirements of doing business. The requirements of managing global firms stem from the variations of multiple environments of foreign countries and the additional complexity of operating across national borders.

Conclusion

This chapter explains why international business and international management are important to us and why we should learn about them. It is suggested that the prolonged peace after World War II has changed the nature of international rivalry. The diminishing threat of large-scale military conflict among the superpowers has shifted the emphasis from military supremacy to economic competition. The changing attitudes of nations toward global relationships facilitate increased international business.

Therefore, an understanding of the concepts and theories of international business and management has gained added importance.

To learn about international management, we examine the question of why businesses internationalize. Included in our examination are theories of international trade, theories of FDI, and international product life cycle.

International business operations cover a spectrum of activities, from exporting to direct investment. Various types of these operations are explained. It is proposed that the management of these varied business operations is not the same as those of domestic business. The differences between international management and management of domestic business are due to the complexity of the international environment. Internationalization of the firm not only is expansion of the operations abroad but also a change in management mentality. The management view of international business is categorized into four stages: ethnocentric, polycentric, centocentric, and geocentric.

The business-host government relationship is a major source of difficulty for MNCs. The flexibility and resourcefulness of integrated global firms, when paired with the sovereign power of a host government create a challenging and demanding proposition for management. Other factors that make international management different from that of managing domestic operations are cultural differences and currency exchange fluctuations. These issues are covered in other chapters.

Discussion Questions

1. Why is it important to learn about international management?
2. What factors contribute to the increased role of international business in our lives?
3. Explain the reasons for firms' international expansions.
4. Raymond Vernon proposed a three-stage international product life cycle. Describe

these stages. Adler and Ghadar suggested the addition of a fourth stage. What are the characteristics of the fourth stage?

5. What is the difference between the inward-looking and outward-looking perspective of international business?

6. How many different types of international business operations can you identify? Describe, in detail, a major international business operation.

7. Describe international management.

8. In what ways are international management and the management of domestic operations similar? What are their differences?

9. The author of this text asserts that a major differentiating factor among executives of domestic businesses and those of MNCs is managerial mentality (their view of business). This attitude also differentiates among MNC executives. Explain the four stages of managerial mentality.

10. Why do host governments have less influence on integrated global firms?

11. The relationship between the host government and an MNC is more complex than government-domestic business relations. Why?

Endnotes

1. *Caterpillar Annual Report, 1991.*

2. A. H. Meltzer. "U.S. Leadership and Postwar Progress." In *Policy Implications of Trade and Currency Zones* (The Federal Reserve Bank of Kansas City, 1991), 237–57.

3. Ibid., 237–57.

4. C. Farell, M. J. Mandle, K. Pennar, J. Carey, R. Hof, and Z. Schiller. "Industrial Policy." *Business Week* (April 6, 1992), 70–5.

5. M. Minor. "Changes in Developing Country Regimes for Foreign Direct Investment." *Essays in International Business*, No. 8 (September 1990), 30–31.

6. D. Encarnation, and L. T. Wells Jr. "Sovereignty En Garde: Negotiating With Foreign Investors." *International Organization*, 39, (1985), 47–78.

7. D. J. Lecraw, and A. J. Morrison. "Transnational Corporation-Host Country Relations: A Framework for Analysis." *Essays in International Business,* no. 9 (September 1991), 29.

8. A. H. Meltzer. "U.S. Leadership." 249.

9. S. J. Lublin. "Foreign Accents Proliferate In Top Ranks As U.S. Companies Find Talent Abroad." *The Wall Street Journal* (May 21, 1991), Sec. B, p. 1.

10. M. Maruyama. "Changing Dimensions In International Business." *Academy of Management Executive, 6,* No.3, (1992), 88–96.

11. L. Hoper and M. W. Miller, "IBM, Toshiba, Siemens Form Venture To Develop DRAMs For Next Century," *The Wall Street Journal* (July 13, 1992), sec. B, p. 7.

12. S. Ostry. "The Domestic Domain: The New International Policy Arena." *Transnational Corporation, 1,* No. 1 (1992), 9.

13. Y. Aharoni. *The Foreign Investment Decision Process* (Boston: Harvard Business School, 1966).

14. S. H. Hymer. *The International Operations of National Firms: A Study of Direct Investment* (Cambridge, MA: MIT Press, 1976).

15. P. J. Buckely, and M. Casson. *The Future of Multinational Enterprise* (New York: Holmes and Meier, 1976).

16. R. Vernon. "Gone Are the Cash Cows of Yesteryear." *Harvard Business Review* (November/December 1980), 150–5.

17. C. M. Watson. "Counter Competition Abroad to Protect Home Markets." *Harvard Business Review* (January/February, 1982), 40.

18. R. Vernon. "International Investment and International Trade In the Product Cycle." *Quarterly Journal of Economics*, 80, no. 2 (1966), 190–207.

19. N. J. Adler, and F. Ghadar. "International Strategy From the Perspective of People and Culture: The North American Context." In A. M. Rugaman, ed. *International Business Research For the Twenty-First Century* (Greenwich, CO: JAI Press), 179–205.

20. Ibid., 189.

21. P. W. Beamish, et al. *International Management,* (Burr Ridge, IL: R. D. Irwin, Inc., 1991), 3–6.

22. Ibid., 6.

23. A. V. Phatak. *International Dimensions of Management* (Boston, MA: PWS-Kent, 1989), 9.

24. P. W. Beamish, et al. *International Management,* 61.

25. W. J. Holstein, and K. Kelly. "Little Companies, Big Exports." *Business Week* (April 13, 1992), 70–2.

26. C. J. Chipello. "Small U.S. Companies Take the Plunge Into Japan's Market." *The Wall Street Journal,* (July 7, 1992), sec. B, p. 1.

27. B. M. Richman, and M. Copen. *International Management and Economic Development* (New York: McGraw-Hill, 1972), 5.

28. H. V. Perlmutter. "The Tortuous Evolution Of the Multinational Corporation." *Columbia Journal of World Business* (January/February 1969), 9–18.

29. Ibid., 13.

30. Ibid., 9–18.

31. Ibid., 9–18.

32. D. A. Heenan, and H. V. Perlmutter. *Multinational Organizational Development* (Reading, MA: Addison-Wesley, 1979), 71–86. C. A. Bartlett, and S. Ghoshal.

Transnational Management (Homewood, IL: Richard D. Irwin, 1992), 11–14.

33. W. Taylor. "The Logic Of Global Business: An Interview With ABB's Percy Barnevik." *Harvard Business Review* (March/April, 1992), 92

R A Y T H E O N
C A N A D A   (A)

J. ALEX MURRAY AND
DAVID L. BLENKHORN

As Bob Carpenter, contracts administrator for Raytheon Canada Limited (RCL), waited for clearance from Korea on the proposal to use Koshin as a supplier for advanced electronic components, he questioned the countertrade system of offsets. Even if Koshin were selected to fulfill the offset agreement, they were an unknown company in the United States. He had no idea whether their components would sell or whether they could be used internally by RCL. He had no doubt about the desirability of making the sale, but he wondered if the demands were becoming too stringent.

To put the decision regarding the countertrade system of offsets in perspective, this case will first provide the history of Raytheon Canada and its involvement with the Radar Modernization Project (RAMP). Following that will be a discussion of how it came to be involved with Ground Controlled Approach Systems in Korea.

This case was prepared by Professors J. Alex Murray and David L. Blenkhorn with special assistance from executives of Raytheon, Hyundai and External Affairs Canada, for the sole purpose of providing material for class discussion. Alterations of the facts were used to disguise events. Copyright © 1986 by Wilfrid Laurier University. Distributed through the Laurier Institute, School of Business and Economics, Wilfrid Laurier University, Waterloo, Ontario, Canada, N2L 3CS. Please address enquiries to the Coordinator of Management Case Sales.

Canadian Operations

RCL was incorporated in January 1956 as a wholly owned subsidiary of its American parent—Raytheon Company. Operations covered the fields of electronics, aircraft products, energy services and major appliances, in addition to several other lines. The company was among the nation's 100 largest industrial companies ranked by *Fortune* magazine each year. In 1984, sales were $6 billion with just under 50 percent of the total from the U.S. government. Raytheon Company's sales to customers outside the United States comprised 19 percent revenues. Exhibit 1 gives a summary of the continuing operations for 1982 to 1984.

The head office of Raytheon Company was in Lexington, Massachusetts, and the firm had 12 major operating subsidiaries and more than 80 plants and laboratories in 26 states. The major overseas subsidiaries and affiliates were located in six countries with a principal one being RCL, which received a world product mandate from its parent to design, manufacture, and market air traffic control (ATC) systems worldwide. The RAMP project explained below was an integral part of this world product mandate and was to be completed in 1992. A second major commitment for RCL was their international radar program for air defense surveillance radars and ground control approach radars

Exhibit 1

Business Segment Reporting—Continuing Operations (dollars in millions)

		Operations by Business Segments				
Years Ended December 31	Electronics	Aircraft Products	Energy Services	Major Appliances	Other Lines	Total
Sales to unaffiliated customers						
1984	$3,399	$723	$ 680	$797	$397	$5,996
1983	2,995	642	926	710	358	5,631
1982	2,656	568	1,124	565	304	5,217
Income from continuing operations before taxes						
1984	431	6	14	61	33	545
1983	385	14	17	53	28	497
1982	319	61	65	22	23	490
Capital expenditures						
1984	136	188	35	37	18	414
1983	103	83	34	21	13	254
1982	101	34	57	16	16	224
Depreciation and amortization:						
1984	81	27	36	18	12	174
1983	70	17	33	16	12	148
1982	63	10	32	16	10	131
Identifiable assets at						
December 31, 1984	1,697	959	306	455	183	3,600
December 31, 1983	2,071	741	354	391	172	3,729
December 31, 1982	1,934	654	412	359	151	3,510

Operations by Geographic Areas

	United States	Outside United States (principally Europe)	Consolidated
Sales to unaffiliated customers			
1984	$5,450	$546	$5,996
1983	4,903	728	5,631
1982	4,419	798	5,217
Income from continuing operations			
1984	327	13	340
1983	294	15	309
1982	273	30	303
Identifiable assets at			
December 31, 1984	3,326	274	3,600
December 31, 1983	3,430	299	3,729
December 31, 1982	3,187	323	3,510

(GCAs). Typically, GCA systems were composed of three basic units: an airport surveillance radar (ASR), a precision approach radar (PAR) to assure accurate approach on landings, and a secondary surveillance radar (SSR) for systems operations. An international radar marketing team had been organized with the president of RCL as team coordinator to sell GCA systems worldwide. Exhibit 2 gives an organizational chart for the Marketing Group.

The Radar Modernization Project (RAMP)

In 1978, the Canadian government developed a formal plan to update the present antiquated radar system in Canada. This plan was based on a conclusion of the specially appointed Dubin Commission of Inquiry on Aviation Safety that "radar equipment presently in use at Canadian airports was obsolete." The plan, known as

CASP (Canadian Air Space Programs) was massive in scope with an expected cost totaling $3.5 billion by 1992.[1] Two years later, the federal government set specifications for the first of the new systems that made up CASP and made a Request for Proposals (REP). Six firms responded with proposals for the project; RCL was one of these companies. In order to position itself competitively, RCL had increased its research and development on radar technology and by 1980 was well along on the development of the world's most advanced civil airport surveillance radar. Among other advances it fea-

---

[1] Called RAMP/RSE (Radar Modernization Project/Radar Site Equipment), this first project covered the radar equipment (sometimes called sensors) at 41 sites and would be followed by an RFP for the RAMP DSE/RDPS (RAMP Display Site Equipment/Radar Data Processing System) about one year later.

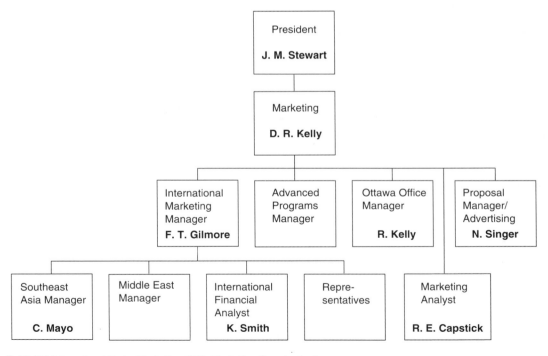

Exhibit 2 International Radar Marketing (RCL Marketing Organization)

tured solid state technology in the transmitter rather than the more conventional high voltage glass output tubes and this was a factor in winning the contract valued at $390 million. It was the involvement with the huge RAMP project and being at the forefront in airport radar technology that put RCL in good contention for contracts in the international marketplace.

The Canadian government, through the Minister of Transportation, the Department of Supply and Services and the Department of Regional Industrial Expansion were all actively involved with the RAMP negotiations. Canadian air traffic engineers had complained quite vehemently about the outdated system which had been in place for over 22 years. In order to upgrade the system, and at the same time spread the benefits across Canada, three important requirements were included in the RFP:

1. The radar system should provide maximum safety for civil air traffic.
2. Many Canadian jobs should be created by the project.
3. Control of the technology should reside in Canada so that Canada could export the radar system to other countries.

Initially, the government had compiled a list of 27 national and international firms to which REPs would be sent, early enough for international firms to find Canadian partners and quality for the bidding process. The government established several criteria in order to evaluate different proposals:

1. Demonstrated experience in the field of radar systems.
2. Canadian entity; however, the government would accept a joint venture between a Canadian firm and an international firm contingent on there being an active Canadian component.
3. The financial stability of the company.
4. Evidence of good management.
5. Acceptable performance in past government contracts.

6. Present facilities or access to facilities capable of completing a project as large as RAMP.

The Raytheon Proposal

RCL assembled a team in order to present an integrated package for the proposal. In addition to an advanced engineering and technology system which would cover all the specifications listed by the RFP, RCL planned the following strategy:

1. RCL would own the radar technology.
2. RCL would export this and other technologies to other countries worldwide through world product mandates from their U.S. headquarters, Raytheon Company.
3. Jobs would be distributed throughout Canada so that all areas would benefit, not just southern Ontario. RCL estimated that employment would be created as follows:

    242 person years in the Atlantic region.
   1,310 person years in Quebec.
   2,310 person years in Ontario.
    790 person years in western Canada.
4. The U.S. and U.K. content would be 100 percent offset by Raytheon Company purchases in Canada.
5. The price would be competitive.
6. The building of a working model would cost approximately $1 million and would demonstrate the radar's effectiveness.

The RAMP contract was critical to the future direction of RCL; however, Westinghouse was a strong competitor. Both RCL and Westinghouse had existing products that were similar to what was needed for RAMP. Their respective proposals, while meeting the rigid specifications of the Canadian government, were considerably different technically in the management approach and in the countertrade programs (socioeconomic benefits or SEBs). The role of SEBs in awarding the contract to a specified firm was given added weight as a factor in the award. The Canadian government had developed a unique set of offset procedures in which items not produced in Canada had to be balanced with exports of "like" products. It also developed that the Westinghouse bid had an appreciably higher price than the RCL submission.

International Radar Marketing

RCL was awarded the RAMP project on May 9, 1984. This was the world's largest and most comprehensive civil airport radar system yet implemented. Establishing a bid for this initial phase had required over $5 million of input funding over approximately three years. The major phase of the contract required the construction of 24 terminal surveillance radar (TSR) installations, providing primary and secondary surveillance radars at airports across the country. In 1985, RCL expanded its Waterloo, Ontario plant to a 126,000-square-foot office and manufacturing facility on a 25-acre site. However, even before the RAMP award, RCL increased its export efforts to demonstrate its commitment to the Canadian government by undertaking the sale of its world mandate products to a number of foreign countries. Marketing strategies were initiated in the Pacific Rim, Middle East, Africa, and South America in order to implement a new ATC marketing plan. Of particular interest were Indonesia, Australia, Korea, Thailand, and Greece, in which the military was very interested in talking to RCL about its ground approach systems.

Ground Controlled Approach Systems

In mid-1983, RCL received a world product mandate from its U.S. parent for ground control approach radar systems (GCAs). Such GCA systems consisted of three separate units. The first was the Airport Surveillance Radar (ASR) which provided for primary surveillance up to a range of 60 nautical miles. This unit displayed "blips" corresponding to approaching objects.

The second was the precision approach radar (PAR) which displayed all approaching aircraft

and tracked as many as six aircraft on final approach. It displayed precise locations and other critical information needed to guide an aircraft into a landing. The third was the secondary surveillance radar (SSR) which addressed a transponder on the aircraft triggering a response that included an identification code, speed, and azimuth bearing. An integrated system of the above three units was first produced by the parent company as both a guidance for approaching aircraft and a surveillance radar system.

RCL identified three immediate overseas markets for the system—Korea, Thailand, and Taiwan—because of their need to provide both military surveillance of the skies and landing guidance for their own aircraft. Frank Gilmore, RCL's international marketing manager, pinpointed, in particular, the Korean need in 1983 for GCAs. The Korean Air Force had inherited a number of radars from the United States at the end of the Korean war in 1954, and had continued to periodically purchase new or updated equipment. They naturally went to the United States for their radar requirements when it became a priority. The only possible suppliers were those in the U.S. Armed Forces Inventory, that is, Westinghouse, ITT, RCL, and Texas Instruments. The Korean market appeared to be the most promising in 1983 since a general budget allocation had been designated for such general systems.

Raytheon's GCA systems were already used in South Korea by the U.S. Air Force because of their advanced technology. The Korean Air Force was familiar with the system and this made it preferable as a military defense purchase.

The Korean Government had committed 25 percent of its budget (6 percent of GNP, compared to 1 percent for Japan) to defense, and the military agencies were anxious to obtain the most sophisticated equipment available. Strained diplomatic relations with North Korea, China, and the USSR had placed a serious obligation on the government to assure a military alertness possible only with the most advanced systems.

The Republic of Korea

Korea existed as a part of various personal kingdoms and dynasties until 1910, when it was taken over by Japan. At the end of the Second World War, the struggle for its control escalated into the Korean "Conflict" when the country was divided, with the Communists ruling North Korea and an elected government in South Korea (the Republic of Korea). In 1961, Colonel Park Chung Hee seized military power and preached that the key to South Korea's economic success lay in exports. This commenced the move toward manufacturing for export, taking advantage of an inexpensive labor force.

Since 1980, Chun Doo Hwan, the current president, had taken a vigorous stand attacking inflation and improving living standards. He succeeded in reducing inflation from 25 percent to 4 percent, while the per capita GNP rose from $100 U.S. to $2,500 U.S. This was accomplished through rigorous fiscal control and zero-based budgeting for all departments of the government.

Korea enjoyed five years of steady growth and social stability since the turmoil of 1980, when troops crushed an uprising in Kwangju. Unfortunately, this newfound wealth had not been broadly distributed with the resulting inequality lending support to the opposition efforts of Kim Dae-Jung, who returned from exile a short while later to make significant gains in recently held elections.

Contract Negotiations

Preliminary to successfully winning an order from the Republic of Korea for GCA system, lengthy and involved negotiations were necessary. RCL's negotiation team consisted of two executives—Cy Mayo, project manager and Bob Carpenter, contracts administrator, both from the Waterloo company.

Mayo had an extensive technical background and could keep all interested parties up-to-date with the capabilities of the equipment. He also could help explain the feasibility and expense of "peripheral" features in a system demanded by the Korean government. Carpenter was an expert negotiator and handled the commercial end of the negotiations.

The Korean negotiating team consisted of Lieutenant-Commander Choi from the Korean Navy as the senior negotiator, General Lee from the Defense Procurement Agency (DPA), and Major Chang of the Republic of Korea Air Force (ROKAF). DPA was RCL's immediate contact. The three were experienced and patient negotiators. Like negotiators in many Pacific Rim countries, they were not above using the tactic of threatening to cancel the negotiations and award the contract to a competitor if certain progress and objectives were not met.

The bargaining began when the field was narrowed to RCL and one of its traditional competitors. The other contenders did not have equipment which specifically met the Korean requirements, while RCL had produced such equipment, and ITT had similar equipment in the developmental stage. RCL had a competitive advantage in that the U.S. Air Force used their system at its Korean bases.

From October 20 to November 17, 1983, representatives from each potential supplier met with the Korean bargaining team for all-day sessions. By mid-November, offers and counteroffers had been proposed, discussed, and revised. Three major items of contention had been resolved.

First, there was an agreement on price. RCL's price was significantly higher, which was a major problem at the beginning since the Koreans were under a very strict budget and had many other items to procure with a fixed sum. Eventually it was agreed that RCL's price was acceptable. Since its competitors had never actually built the required system, cost overruns could be a problem or quality might suffer in order to meet the cost objectives.

Second, the terms of payment were another major hurdle which was overcome. The original plan called for payments in the first year which would exceed budget and was unacceptable to the Koreans. At the same time, RCL needed to ensure that working capital was coming in as fast as project expenses were going out. Finally an agreement was reached to pay more money up front in return for add-on peripheral components being included in the package.

Third, performance bonds had presented a severe problem in the negotiations but that issue too was eventually resolved. A compromise was struck, whereby complaints would be arbitrated by a panel of three—one independent and one appointed by each side of the contract.

Offset Agreements

In the world of international trade where goods are frequently bartered and countertrade among nations is commonplace, offset agreements are often used. An offset is broadly defined as a commitment by an international seller to do something that favorably impacts the economy of the buying country and describes a wider range of transactions than is usually referred to by the term "countertrade." Offsets may be contrasted to countertrade in that in the case of offsets, the purchaser is a foreign government, the bilateral trade agreement covers a long period of time, and the transactions often include a technology transfer to the buying country as the items involved have a high value. Benefit packages, besides technology transfer, may include industrial spin-offs and guaranteed purchase commitments.

By the time the contract reached discussions of offsets in the spring of 1984, the Koreans were only beginning to develop an operational policy on the items and delivery to be included in any offset package.

The Raytheon Offset Proposal

When confronted with the offset requirement, John Stewart, president of RCL, decided to ap-

proach Korean companies presently doing business in Canada. His aim was to initiate importation to Canada of Korean Products in order to satisfy the offset requirement. The government provided a list of candidates, three of whom were in Toronto. The international marketing manager was assigned the task of reviewing the candidates, the first on the list being Hyundai Canada Inc. of Markham, Ontario. Their parent proved to be an $11 billion conglomerate with vast interests that included shipbuilding, construction, manufacturing, electronics, automobiles, and engineering.

Hyundai Canada's parent in Korea, Hyundai Engineering and Construction Company Ltd., was founded in 1947 and grew from a small trucking firm. The company was also a major factor in the Korean financial and service industry including banking, insurance, marketing stocks and bonds, and hotels. The Hyundai motor division was one of the larger components of Hyundai Industries.

First discussions with Mr. Hyo-Won O, general manager and director, found that Hyundai was indeed interested, and had plans to import the Hyundai Pony. They were presently negotiating with FIRA (Foreign Investment Review Agency) for permission to import the automobiles, but needed something like the RCL proposal to make it happen. An agreement was signed, and for a fee, Mr. O agreed to make imports of Korean-made products that would satisfy RCL's 100 percent offset requirement. In turn, Hyundai would use the GCA contract to persuade FIRA to approve the import of Ponys. It was clear in the agreement that if insufficient Ponys were in fact imported, Hyundai would import one of its many other products. No difficulty was foreseen in the amount of imports required.

Counter Offers

By 1984, an offset program had been established by the Korean government, as detailed in the Appendix. The guidelines called for support of high-priority industries and attempted to offset with "like" products. The Koreans were seeking electronic product offsets to match the purchase of electronic equipment as an entry into the North American market. There was also a general feeling on the part of the Koreans, that the Hyundai Pony would have succeeded without the help of RCL. Since the approval of FIRA had been expected, and sales were actually projected to be higher than the levels proposed by Raytheon, the Koreans felt that this was not a very advantageous offset and sought additional ones.

The ministry watchdog for promoting Korean high technology, the Defense Industry Bureau (DIB), wanted to negotiate the best offset contract to assist in technology transfers and employment to selected companies, particularly those firms the DIB felt had the most promise. RCL located and contacted Koshin,[2] a supplier to a large U.S. retailer of branded television sets. They agreed to be part of the offset arrangement. This left only two items on the agenda—the dollar amount needed to satisfy the additional offset requirement and the timetable for the offset purchase in order to satisfy the agreement.

By the fall of 1984, Bob Carpenter was ready to go back to the Korean government with these questions. He was prepared to purchase 5 percent of the contract's value (about $1 million U.S.) and take delivery over the next five years. The Koreans demanded 50 percent of the contract price in additional offset purchases (about $10 million U.S.) and delivery within the two-year span of the ASR agreement.

The Koreans said they would consider Koshin as a supplier for the offset, but to Carpenter's surprise television sets could not be the product of the offset. He was told these were not considered "like" products under the guidelines. RCL would have to take electronic components (e.g., integrated circuits) from a specified supplier in order to satisfy the terms of the offset agreement. This was the only line manufactured in Korea which was considered "favored" by the government.

Appendix: Summary Guide for Korean Offset Program

Defense Industry Bureau
Ministry of National Defense
Republic of Korea

1. PURPOSE

   The purpose of this "Guide" is to outline definitions, objectives, basic guidelines and procedures in support of Offset Programs, directed by the Defense Industry Bureau (DIB), Ministry of National Defense (MND), Republic of Korea.

2. SCOPE OF APPLICATION

   This "Guide" applies to all agencies under the Ministry of National Defense and Korean industries as well as all foreign contractors incurring obligations under the Republic of Korea Offset Program.

3. DEFINITIONS

   A. Offset Program: The Offset Program is work, or the provision of work, or other compensatory opportunities, directed to the Republic of Korea by foreign contractors as a result of receiving, or in anticipation of receiving, a major order for equipment, material (including spare parts), or services in which the Government of the Republic of Korea is involved. There are two offset categories— direct and indirect. The determination of category, as well as project qualification, will be made by DIB, MND.

      i. Direct Offset: Activities in the direct offset category are those which are directly related to the original purchase by the Republic of Korea, or foreign equipment, material, or services. Direct Offset includes the following:

         a. Transfer of technology to achieve the capability to manufacture and

---

[2] Koshin, as the parent holding company, is in several industries such as pharmaceuticals and banking, and through one of its groups has become a major exporter of electronic products and components.

manage the production of parts and components to meet follow-on logistic support.

b. Provision of opportunities to manufacture and export parts and components related to the original purchase.

c. Transfer of technology to obtain a maintenance capability for equipment purchased within the Republic of Korea.

d. Assistance in obtaining maintenance opportunities in overseas markets for which the Republic of Korea has the technological capability.

ii. Indirect Offset: Activities in the Indirect Offset Category are those activities which are not directly related to the production of equipment originally purchased. Indirect Offset activities include the following:

a. Korean Industry Participation (KIP)

1. Activities in paragraphs 3A. (1) (a) through (d) which are not directly related to the original purchase.

2. Opportunities to participate in major research and development projects.

3. Assistance in establishing industrial facilities and developing technological capabilities.

4. Assistance in creating new employment opportunities.

5. Any approved activity that will further Korean national, political, economic, military, and industrial interests.

b. Counterpurchase: Counterpurchase activities include those which are related to the purchase of general commodities and financial assistance. It should be noted that general commodity purchases will not be indiscriminate and credit will only be allowed when a commodity purchase has been given approval from DIB, MND. Counterpurchase activities include the following:

1. Direct purchase by the contractor of Korean products or services.

2. Assistance in selling, or the direct purchase of, self-defense articles from original Korean sources.

3. Assistance in arranging sales to third parties from the original Korean manufacturer.

4. Efforts to obtain financial assistance for Korean products.

B. Memorandum of Agreement (MOA) for Offset Programs: An addition to the basic contract setting forth the obligations and understandings of foreign contractors and the Government of the Republic of Korea with respect to the Offset Program.

4. OFFSET PROGRAM OBJECTIVES

The primary objective of the offset Program is to assist the Republic of Korea in developing and expanding its manufacturing and industrial capability. The goal of the program is to obtain new technology, provide design and development work, assist underutilized sectors of industry, selectively stimulate sectors of the economy, and create new employment opportunities. The program is intended to increase technological and industrial capability with an emphasis on the area of National Defense.

5. BASIC GUIDELINES

A. The Offset Program will apply, on a case-by-case basis, to all major equipment, material, and services purchased by the Government of the Republic of Korea for more than $1 million U.S.

B. The national goal for an individual Offset Program will be at least 50 percent of the basic contract value. At least 20 percent of the basic contract value will be in the Direct Offset Category.

C. The basic offset proposals will be considered on a competitive basis and foreign contractors will submit Offset Program Proposals to DIB, MND within a specified period of time. Offset Program Agreements will be an important factor in awarding the final contract.

D. The Memorandum of Agreement for the Offset Program will be part of, and attached to, the basic contract.

E. In executing the Offset Program, all values that exceed program goals will be credited to the foreign contractor for follow-on contract.

6. EVALUATION CRITERIA

A. The technological sophistication, the total dollar value and the length of time to complete the Offset Program will be major factors in the evaluation process.

B. It is expected that Korean equipment, material, and services will be used to the maximum extent possible. Priority will be given to those Offset Program Proposals containing a greater amount of Korean material and services.

C. Some projects will not be approved by MND because they do not meet selection criteria.

D. The following categories are listed in order of importance; Activities of National high priority which promote political, economic, military and industrial development objectives:

a. Participation in advanced technological development projects.

b. Transfer of advanced technology and know-how.

c. Creation, or improvement of, self-reliance in equipment purchased by providing for:
   i. Ability to produce equipment independently.
   ii. Ability to produce equipment jointly.
   iii. Ability to produce spare parts independently.
   iv. Ability to maintain equipment independently.

d. Creation or improvement of self-reliance in related equipment/industry by providing for:
   i. Ability to produce related equipment independently.
   ii. Ability to produce related equipment jointly.
   iii. Ability to produce spare parts independently.
   iv. Ability to maintain related equipment independently.

SUJI-INS K.K.

WILLIAM H. DAVIDSON

Mike Flynn, president of the International Division of Information Network Services Corporation, was undecided as to how he could best approach several delicate issues with his

Source: This case was written by Professor William H. Davidson on the basis of original research by Professor Michael Yoshiuo at the Harvard Business School. Copyright © 1988 by the University of Southern California. Reprinted by permission.

Japanese joint venture partner. He needed to develop an agenda for his trip to Japan, scheduled for the following day. In many ways, he considered this trip of vital importance. For one thing, the problems to be discussed were likely to affect the long-term relationship between his company and the Japanese partner in the management of their joint venture. Moreover, this was his first trip to Japan in the capacity of president of the International Division, and he was anxious to make a good impression and to begin to build a personal relationship with senior executives of the Japanese firm.

Flynn had assumed the position of president several months previously in May of 1988. He was 40 years old and was considered to be one of the most promising executives in the company. After 2 years of military service followed by business school, he had joined a consulting company for several years prior to accepting a position with Information Network Services Corporation (INS). Prior to his promotion to the presidency of the International Division, he had served as managing director of INS's wholly owned subsidiary in Canada.

INS was a major provider of value added network (VAN) services in the United States. Its principal products included high-speed data communications (packet switching), data base management, transaction processing services, and a variety of industry-specific information services. The company's total sales for 1988 were roughly $250 million, and it had recently established successful presences in the United Kingdom and other European countries. International operations accounted for roughly 25 percent of the company's total sales, and the company's top management felt that international markets represented a major field for future growth.

The company's management recognized that in order to capitalize on the rapidly growing Japanese market, a direct presence was needed. By the mid-1980s, the company began to receive a number of inquiries from major Japanese corporations concerning licensing possibilities. INS was particularly interested in the possibility of establishing a joint venture to provide VAN services.

The company, after 2 years of demanding negotiations, was successful in establishing a joint venture in Japan with Suji Company, a leading Japanese telecommunications equipment manufacturer. The arrangement was formalized in the summer of 1987.

Suji was one of the companies that approached INS initially to arrange a licensing agreement involving VAN technology and expertise. It appeared to be an attractive potential partner. Suji was a medium-sized telecommunication equipment vendor that was directly tied to one of the major Japanese industrial groups. The company had only limited sales to Nippon Telegraph and Telephone (NTT), the national telephone company. About half of its sales were exported, and the remainder went largely to other Japanese firms within the same industrial group. Suji had established a reputation for high quality, and its brands were well established.

In the mid-1980s, as the Japanese telecommunications market was deregulated, Suji began to explore opportunities in the telecommunication services market, particularly in paging and mobile phone services. Prior to deregulation, telephone and related services were monopoly markets served only by NTT. Under the terms of the 1984 New Telecommunications Law, other Japanese firms were permitted to offer these services to the general public. VAN services in particular could be initiated simply by notifying the Ministry of Posts and Telecommunications. The Ministry of International Trade and Industry had established several programs to provide incentives for new VAN services, including tax breaks and low-cost loans. Suji's management felt that VAN services, would be a major growth area. Suji's management, after some investigation, concluded that the quickest and most efficient way to achieve entry into these markets was through either licensing or a joint venture with a leading U.S. company. Suji's management felt that timing was of particular importance, since its major competitors were also considering expansion into these markets. Suji's expression of interest to INS was timely, as INS had become increasingly interested in Japan. Suji was at first interested in a licensing arrangement, but INS, anxious to establish a permanent presence in Japan, wished to establish a joint venture.

The negotiations concerning this joint venture were difficult in part because it was the first experience of the kind for both companies. INS had virtually no prior experience in Japan, and for Suji this was the fist joint venture with a foreign company, although it had engaged in licensing agreements with several U.S. and European firms.

The ownership of the joint venture was divided between the two companies, such that Suji owned two-thirds and INS one-third of its equity. Japanese law limited foreign ownership in telecom services vendors to one-third equity participation. In addition to a predetermined cash contribution, the agreement stipulated that INS was to provide network technology and the Japanese partner was to contribute facilities and network equipment. The joint venture was first to market data communication services and later was to introduce transaction processing services. The services were to be marketed under the joint brands of INS and Suji. The agreement also stipulated that both companies would have equal representation on the board of directors, with four people each, and that Suji would provide the entire personnel for the joint venture from top management down to production workers. Such a practice was quite common among foreign joint ventures in Japan, since given limited mobility among personnel in large corporations, recruiting would represent a major problem for foreign companies. The companies also agreed that the Japanese partner would nominate the president of the joint venture, subject to approval of the board, and the U.S. company would nominate a person for the position of executive vice president. INS also agreed to supply, for the time being, a technical director on a full-time basis.

INS had four members on the board: Flynn, Jack Rose (INS's nominee for executive vice president of the joint venture), and the chair and the president of INS. Representing the Japanese company were the president and executive vice president of Suji, and two senior executives of the joint venture, the president and vice president for finance.

By the fall of 1988, the venture had initiated tests of its data communication services, and a small sales organization had been built. Although the venture was progressing reasonably well, Flynn had become quite concerned over several issues that had come to his attention during the previous 2 months. The first and perhaps the most urgent of these was the selection of a new president for the joint venture.

The first president had died suddenly about 3 months before at the age of 68. He had been a managing director of the parent company and had been the chief representative in Suji's negotiations with INS. When the joint venture was established, it appeared only natural for him to assume the presidency; INS management had no objection.

About a month after his death, Suji, in accordance with the agreement, nominated Kenzo Satoh as the new president. Flynn, when he heard Satoh's qualifications, concluded that he was not suitable for the presidency of the joint venture. He became even more disturbed when he received further information about how he was selected from Jack Rose, the executive vice president of the joint venture.

Satoh had joined Suji 40 years previously upon graduating from Tokyo University. He had held a variety of positions in the Suji company, but during the previous 15 years, he had served almost exclusively in staff functions. He had been manager of Administrative Services at the company's major plant, manager of the General Affairs Department at the corporate headquarters, and personnel director. When he was promoted to that position, he was admitted to the company's board of directors. His responsibility was then expanded to include overseeing several service-oriented staff departments, including personnel, industrial relations, administrative services, and the legal department.

Flynn was concerned that Satoh had virtually no line experience and could not understand why Suji would propose such a person for the presidency of the joint venture, particularly when it was at a critical stage of development.

Even more disturbing to Mr. Flynn was the manner in which Satoh was selected. This first came to Mr. Flynn's attention, when he received a letter from Rose, which included the following description:

> By now you have undoubtedly examined the background information forwarded to you regarding Mr. Satoh, nominated by our Japanese partner for the presidency of the joint venture.
>
> I have subsequently learned the manner in which Mr. Satoh was chosen for the position, which I am sure would be of great interest to you. I must point out at the outset that what I am going to describe, though shocking by our standards, is quite commonplace among Japanese corporations: in fact, it is well-accepted.
>
> Before describing the specific practice, I must give you a brief background of the Japanese personnel system. As you know, the major companies follow the so-called lifetime employment where all managerial personnel are recruited directly from universities, and they remain with the company until they reach their compulsory retirement age, which is typically around 57. Career advancement in the Japanese system comes slowly, primarily by seniority. Advancement to middle management is well-paced, highly predictable, and virtually assured for every college graduate. Competence and performance become important as they reach upper middle management and top management. Obviously, not everyone will be promoted automatically beyond middle management, but whatever the degree to which competence and qualifications are considered in career advancement, chronological age is the single most important factor.
>
> A select few within the ranks of upper-middle management will be promoted to top management positions, that is, they will be given memberships in the board of directors. In large Japanese companies, the board typically consists exclusively of full-time operating executives. Suji's board is no exception.

Moreover, there is a clear-cut hierarchy among the members. The Suji board consists of the chair of the board, president executive vice president, three managing directors, five ordinary directors, and two statutory auditors.

Typically, ordinary directors have specific operating responsibilities such as head of a staff department, a plant, or a division. Managing directors are comparable to our group vice presidents. Each will have two or three functional or staff groups or product divisions reporting to them. Japanese commercial law stipulates that the members are to be elected by stockholders for a 2-year term. Obviously, under the system described, the members are designated by the chair of the board or the president and serve at their pleasure. Stockholders have very little voice in the actual selection of the board members. Thus, in some cases, it is quite conceivable that board membership is considered as a reward for many years of faithful and loyal service.

As you are well aware, a Japanese corporation is well known for its paternalistic practices in return for lifetime service, and they do assume obligations, particularly for those in middle management or above, even after they reach their compulsory retirement age, not just during their working careers. Appropriate positions are generally found for them in the company's subsidiaries, related firms, or major suppliers where they can occupy positions commensurate to their last position in the parent corporation for several more years.

A similar practice applies to the board members. Though there is no compulsory retirement age for board members, the average tenure for board membership is usually around 6 years. This is particularly true for those who are ordinary or managing directors. Directorships being highly coveted positions, there must be regular turnover to allow others to be promoted to board membership. As a result, all but a fortunate few who are earmarked as heir apparent to the chair, presidency, or executive vice presidency must be "retired." Since most of these executives are in their late fifties or early sixties, they do not yet wish to retire. Moreover, even among major Japanese corporations, the compensation for top management positions is quite low compared with the U.S. standard, and pension plans being still quite inadequate, they will need respectable positions with a reasonable income upon leaving the company. Thus, it is common practice among Japanese corporations to transfer senior executives of the parent company to the chair or presidency of the company's subsidiaries or affiliated companies. Typically, these people will serve in these positions for several years before they retire. Suji had a dozen subsidiaries, and you might be interested in knowing that every top management position is held by those who have retired from the parent corporation. Such a system is well routinized.

Our friend, Mr. Satoh is clearly not the caliber that would qualify for further advancement in the parent company, and his position must be vacated for another person. Suji's top management must have decided that the presidency of the joint venture was the appropriate position for him to "retire" into. These are the circumstances under which Mr. Satoh has been nominated for our consideration.

When he read this letter, Flynn instructed Rose to indicate to the Suji management that Satoh was not acceptable. Not only did Flynn feel that Satoh lacked the qualifications and experience for the presidency, but he resented the fact that Suji was using the joint venture as a home to accommodate a retired executive. It would be justifiable for Suji to use one of its wholly owned subsidiaries for that purpose, but there was no reason why the joint venture should take him on. On the contrary, the joint venture needed dynamic leadership to establish a viable market position.

In his response to Rose, Flynn suggested as president another person, Takao Toray, marketing manager of the joint venture. Toray was 50 years old and had been transferred to the joint venture from Suji, where he had held a number of key marketing positions, including regional sales manager and assistant marketing director. Shortly after he was appointed to the latter position, Toray was sent to INS headquarters to be-

come acquainted with the company's marketing operations. He spent roughly 3 months in the United States, during which time Flynn met him. Though he had not gone beyond a casual acquaintance, Flynn was much impressed by Toray. He appeared to be dynamic, highly motivated, and pragmatic. Moreover, Toray had a reasonable command of English. While communication was not easy, at least it was possible to have conversations on substantive matters. From what Flynn was able to gather, Toray impressed everyone he saw favorably and gained the confidence of not only the International Division staff but those in the corporate marketing group as well as sales executives in the field.

Flynn was aware that Toray was a little too young to be acceptable to Suji, but he felt that it was critical to press for his appointment for two reasons. First, he was far from convinced of the wisdom of adopting Japanese managerial practices blindly in the joint venture. Some of the Japanese executives he met in New York had told him of the pitfalls and weaknesses of Japanese management practices. He was disturbed over the fact that, as he was becoming familiar with the joint venture, he was finding that in every critical aspect such as organization structure, personnel practices, and decision making, the company was managed as though it were a Japanese company. Rose had had little success in introducing U.S. practices. Flynn had noticed in the past that the joint venture had been consistently slow in making decisions because it engaged in a typical Japanese group-oriented and consensus-based process. He also learned that control and reporting systems were virtually nonexistent. Flynn felt that INS's sophisticated planning and control system should be introduced. It had proved successful in the company's wholly owned European subsidiaries, and there seemed to be no reason why such a system could not improve the operating efficiency of the joint venture. He recalled from his Canadian experience that U.S. management practices, if judiciously applied, could give U.S.

subsidiaries abroad a significant competitive advantage over local firms.

Second, Flynn felt that the rejection of Satoh and appointment of Toray might be important as a demonstration to the Japanese partner that Suji-INS was indeed a joint venture and not a subsidiary of the Japanese parent company. He was also concerned that INS had lost the initiative in the management of the joint venture. This move would help INS gain stronger influence over the management of the joint venture.

Rose conveyed an informal proposal along these lines to Suji management. Suji's reaction to Flynn's proposal was swift; they rejected it totally. Suji management was polite, but made it clear that they considered Flynn unfair in judging Mr. Satoh's suitability for the presidency without even having met him. They requested Rose to assure Flynn that their company, as majority owner, indeed had an important stake in the joint venture and certainly would not have recommended Satoh unless it had been convinced of his qualifications. Suji management also told Flynn, through Rose, that the selection of Toray was totally unacceptable because in the Japanese corporate system such a promotion was unheard of and would be detrimental not only to the joint venture but to Toray himself, who was believed to have a promising future in the company.

Flynn was surprised at the tone of Suji's response. He wondered whether it would be possible to establish an effective relationship with the Japanese company. Suji seemed determined to run the venture on their own terms.

Another related issue which concerned Flynn was the effectiveness of Rose as executive vice president. Flynn appreciated the difficulties he faced but began to question Rose's qualifications for his position and his ability to work with Japanese top management. During the last visit, for example, Rose had complained of his inability to integrate himself with the Japanese top management team. He indicated that he felt he was still very much an outsider to the company,

not only because he was a foreigner but also because the Japanese executives, having come from the parent company, had known each other and in many cases had worked together for at least 20 years. He also indicated that none of the executives spoke English well enough to achieve effective communication beyond the most rudimentary level and that his Japanese was too limited to be of practical use. In fact, his secretary, hired specifically for him, was the only one with whom he could communicate easily. He also expressed frustration over the fact that his functions were very ill-defined and his experience and competence were not really being well utilized by the Japanese.

Flynn discovered after he assumed the presidency that Mr. Rose had been chosen for this assignment for his knowledge of Japan. Rose graduated from a midwestern university in 1973, and after enlisting in the Army was posted to Japan for 4 years. Upon returning home, he joined INS as a management trainee. In 1984, he became assistant district sales manager in California, Oregon, and Washington. When the company began to search for a candidate for executive vice president for the new joint venture, Rose's name came up as someone who was qualified and available for posting to Japan. Rose, although somewhat ambivalent about the new opportunity at first, soon became persuaded that this would represent a major challenge and opportunity.

Flynn was determined to get a first-hand view of the joint venture during his visit. He had many questions, and he wondered whether he had inherited a problem. He was scheduled to meet with Mr. Ohtomo, executive vice president of Suji Corporation, on the day following his arrival. Ohtomo, who had been with Suji for over 40 years, was the senior executive responsible for overseeing the joint venture. Flynn had not met Ohtomo, but he knew that Ohtomo had visited the United States and spoke English reasonably well. He wondered how best to approach and organize his meetings and discussions with

Mr. Ohtomo. He also wondered if his planned stay of 1 week would be adequate to achieve his objectives. While practicing with chopsticks, he returned to reading *Theory Z,* a popular book on Japanese management, in the hope of gaining insight for the days ahead.

T W O

INTERNATIONAL STRATEGIC PLANNING

International strategic planning as a response to environmental changes and challenges, in pursuit of organizational goals, is the subject of Chapter 2. In general, domestic and international strategic processes are very similar, differing only in the specifics. The differences are due to forces governing the international business environment. These forces include host governments; political and legal issues; the currency exchange rates; competition from local business, government-supported firms, and other MNCs; and cultural variations among nations. Cultural differences result in variations in the strategic planning process among MNCs. For example, Japanese MNCs prepare strategies to respond to changing environmental forces. They have, however, a different concept of strategy. As a major force in the process of planning a strategy, the relationships between host governments and MNCs are analyzed. Host governments' methods of dealing with MNCs and the MNCs' management of host government relations are examined.

Notwithstanding the similarities between domestic and international strategic processes, the differences necessitate the application of specific strategies. Three different strategic choices—global integration, host country focus, and a hybrid international strategy—are described.

In 1987, looking across the Atlantic Ocean and assessing the European market for consumer paper products, James River Corporation saw a growth rate twice that of the United States. James River realized the advantage of developing a pan-European manufacturing and marketing strategy, and noted that the European consumer paper product market was highly fragmented. To create a pan-European firm, in partnership with Italian and Finnish corporations, it acquired 13 companies in 10 countries. In 1990, these acquisitions were combined into "Jamont" as a joint venture.

Jamont started a program of capital investment, the overhaul of manufacturing, and the development of consistent quality. By investing in new tissue machines, by consolidating plants, and through other cost-cutting measures, revenues increased significantly and net profit doubled. Now, Jamont is the second largest paper producer in Europe, behind Scott Paper Company of the United States, which has been operating in Europe for 30 years.

In the process of integrating across national borders, Jamont learned a lot about selling toilet tissue to the people of different cultures. The assumption always has been that German-speaking countries bought strength, the French wanted soft, and Americans craved very soft. It turned out that consumers everywhere wanted both softness and strength. All these years, the manufacturers were dictating tastes instead of the consumers.

Jamont set out to offer consumers quality products at a low price, but getting 10 cultures to cooperate was not an easy task. To produce napkins efficiently, for example, Jamont needed to make them the same size throughout its operations. But in some countries napkins were produced in sizes of 30 centimeters by 30 centimeters (12 inches by 12 inches), and in others they were 35 centimeters by 35 centimeters. They were other problems that increased the costs. The French, for example, were using 20 outside suppliers. They were asked to use only 2 suppliers owned by Jamont. That reduced costs and helped quality tremendously. Each company used to make its own deep-colored napkins, a very time-consuming process. Now they are all produced at one plant in Finland.

Creating uniformity in measuring efficiency proved to be challenging. Some companies were counting a year with 330 days, allowing for holidays and maintenance time, others counted it as 350 days. Comparing the up-time (the time a plant was in operation) of one factory to another was not a straightforward task. A 95 percent up-time for one was not necessarily better than the 89 percent up-time of another.

Jamont executives believe that they have solved many of the major problems of integration and consolidation. Most of the operational and strategic issues are resolved with the help of committees. Where issues cannot be resolved by the committees, Singer, the chief executive officer, and his staff take over. The staff consists of four Frenchmen, two Americans, two British, two Italians, a Finn, a Spaniard, and a Dutchman. Mr. Singer is an American with a master's degree in economics from Cambridge University.

Source: Janet Guyon. "A Joint-Venture Papermaker Casts Net Across Europe," *The Wall Street Journal,* Monday, December 7, 1992, p. B6. Reprinted by permission of *The Wall Street Journal,* © 1992 Dow Jones & Company, Inc. All rights reserved worldwide.

Introduction

Planning is the process of establishing organizational goals and the determination of methods to attain those goals. Strategic planning is the alignment of organizational capabilities with the present and anticipated future environmental changes, in the pursuit of goal attainment. Because organizations are formed to satisfy societal needs, and because their survival depends on securing the resources needed to achieve these goals, understanding and awareness of environmental forces are essential to the strategic planning process. Environmental forces are not constant; they change over time. In the past, organizations faced fewer environmental changes at a slower pace. Today, more changes are taking place at faster rates, and this trend is accelerating. The environmental simplicity and relative stability of the past has been replaced by the dynamic complexity of today. Moreover, strategic planning itself is relatively new and can be traced back to the 1970s.

The predecessor of strategic planning was long-range planning.[1] Long-range planning is based on two premises. First, environmental changes are assumed to be continuous. Second, these changes are assumed to be predictable through extrapolation of the historical growth. Both of these premises, however, pose potential problems for today's planners. When environmental conditions were simple and relatively stable, firms could expect that the future would be an extension of the past. Under those assumptions, planning was an optimistic projection of past organizational performance, with the expectation of future growth. In other words, the future was presumed to be better than the past. Environmental factors were expected to change in magnitude and not in character. Long-range planning, therefore, was pursuing organizational goals by matching its capabilities with the economic considerations of the market.

The events of the 1970s, such as the energy crisis, proved the fallacy of those assumptions.

It became evident that the past may not be a reliable predictor of the future and that many environmental changes are discontinuous. With its questionable premises, long-range planning was displaced by strategic planning.

The premises of strategic planning are different: The future may not necessarily be an improvement over the past, nor may it extrapolated.[2] The patterns of the past events may not continue in the future. Most of the environmental changes are discontinuous. To succeed in such an unpredictable milieu, firms need to strategically plan and manage the present and future operations. As Figure 2.1 illustrates, the strategic planning process begins with a determination of organizational mission and goals. After establishment of the mission and goals, the process proceeds with two interdependent and simultaneous analyses: internal assessment and environmental scanning. Internal assess-

ment provides information regarding internal capabilities and limitations of the firms. Environmental scanning enables the firm, domestic or international, to identify the existence of opportunities and threats in the environment. These interdependent, simultaneous analyses should permit the firm to assess the appropriateness of its goals and, if necessary, modify them. Changes in the premises on which the organizational mission and goals are based may require a modification or a total revision of those goals.

Once the appropriateness of the organizational mission and goals is resolved, two sequential phases of strategy formulation and implementation begin. The formulation phase creates the plan for future activities, and the implementation phase is the execution of that plan. In its simplest form the process of strategy formulation and implementation entails four major steps. The first two steps are environmental

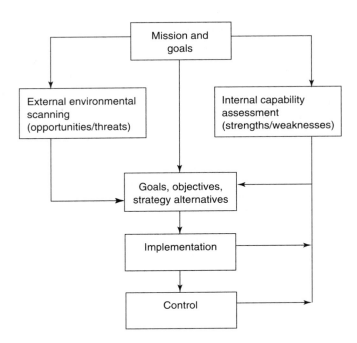

Figure 2.1   Strategy Formulation Process

scanning and internal capability analysis. Based on these two simultaneous analyses, the firm develops a plan to accomplish organizational goals and to exploit environmental opportunities through the deployment of its strengths. In so doing, the firm should be careful not to expose its weaknesses, and should be prepared to face threatening conditions or avoid them all together. The process is concluded when a control mechanism assures the proper execution of the strategy process.

There are no substantive differences between this strategic planning process for a domestic company or a multinational company (MNC). The strategic process, domestic or otherwise, entails the matching of organizational capabilities and the imperatives of the environment and the achievement of organizational goals in the face of changing environmental conditions. Irrespective of the nature of the operation, the strategic management process remains basically the same, for the domestic enterprise and the MNC. Just because a firm expands abroad it does not mean that there will be a different strategy formulation and implementation process. By expanding to foreign markets, however, the firm will encounter additional complexity from operating across national borders.

Internationalization of the firm brings about many new problems that require careful resolution. These new problems increase the burden of managing an MNC. The multiplicity of cultural, sociopolitical, legal, and economic environments creates quantitative and qualitative difficulties. Quantitatively, there are many national markets, each with its own requirements and problems that demand special attention. Qualitatively, because of historical, cultural, political and economic variations, each national market is unique. Each changes differently and at a different pace. Confounding the problems are the interdependencies among national markets in a network of customers, suppliers, creditors, competitors, etc., that culminate in a complex global market. Successful MNCs learn how to deal effectively with the multiplicity of environmental conditions.

In the following, we examine environmental forces that influence international management. Each of these forces alone, or in combination with other forces, makes the job of an international manager a challenging task. Although these forces are often the sources of difficulty, they have the potential to open up many opportunities for MNCs. They can hinder or help MNC operations and can improve the overall profitability or cause substantial loss.

International Environmental Forces

The difference between strategy formulation and the implementation processes of a domestic or an international operation is in the degree of environmental and organizational complexities and uncertainties. MNC operations are more complex, and they face many more environmental uncertainties and complexities. In addition to all of the forces that influence the strategy of a domestic business, the MNCs have to deal with many more forces. The major international environmental forces include (1) cultural differences; (2) host governments and political and legal issues; (3) competition from local businesses, government agencies, and other MNCs; and (4) international finance and currency exchange rates. We will discuss the cultural differences in Chapter 5. The following delineates the host governments, political and legal issues, and the competition. Financial aspects of international operations, including currency exchange rates, are presented in Chapter 13.

Host Governments and Political and Legal Issues

The most influential of all international environmental forces are political, legal, and governmental. Chapter 15 is devoted to the discussion of legal and political difficulties facing the MNCs. Political uncertainty and risk associated with the instability of host governments are discussed in Chapter 13 that covers international financial issues. But here it suffices to remind ourselves that legal and political issues could hinder the MNCs' overseas operations. The lack of understanding of local laws could cost the MNCs dearly. Political turmoil that simmers under the surface may be very difficult for outsiders to detect. Yet an inappropriate response could result in substantial earning and property loss.

Host governments use their sovereign power by restricting or assisting MNCs. When host countries believe that the operation of MNCs is compatible with their national goals, they may provide various incentives to attract and maintain MNC operations. If, however, MNCs' activities do not meet the host governments' expectations, many restrictions and obstacles are routinely placed in their paths. At the heart of this difficulty lies the difference between host countries' objectives and those of the MNCs. The major strategic goals of the MNCs and host governments are summarized in Table 2.1. The challenge is to find common areas where there are mutual benefits.

Host governments have a love–hate relationship with the MNCs. It is safe to say that the feeling is mutual. In general, this feeling is more intense in the case of developing nations. The power of MNCs and the fact that they operate across national borders make their operations less susceptible to influence and control by the host governments. When the strategic requirements of the MNCs are not compatible with the host government's economic plans, the relationship may not be very beneficial to the host country. The power, resources, and flexibility of the MNCs could overwhelm most host governments' plans, and render them less effective. However, MNCs are the source of new technology, capital, and tax revenues. The MNCs' global network of distribution channels could assist host countries to reach world markets. For many developing countries that are burdened with heavy national debts, MNCs are the only source of needed capital. While the host government relationship is a major concern for the MNCs, the relationship with the governments of developing countries poses unique problems for them.

Table 2.1
Host Government and MNC Strategic Goals*

Host Governments	Multinational Corporations
Increase of national income	Return on investment and increase of corporate assets
Economic modernization	Competitive position
More and better employment	
Broadly based development and dissemination of industrial skills	Efficient, low-cost production
Diversification of economic activity	Selective hiring and training of employees
	Specialization of production for efficiency
Avoidance of foreign takeovers of domestic firms	Acquisition of indigenous capacity
Development of domestic research capability	Location of research and development facilities in countries with best universities and other scientific institutions
Stimulation of investment in backward regions and rural areas	Location in large cities where infrastructure and labor supply are most developed
Balance of payments equilibrium	Free convertibility of currencies
Control over pattern of economic development	Freedom of trade and investment
Maximization of public revenues	Minimization of tax burden

*Adapted from Endel-Jacob Kolde. *Environment of International Business* (Boston, MA: Kent Publishing Company, 1985), 405. Used with permission.

Developing countries and the MNCs Although most countries welcome the MNCs, and find the relationship with them mutually beneficial, some developing nations have expressed disappointment with the relationship. Some have argued that the needs of developing countries and the objectives of MNCs are not compatible. They view the main objectives of MNCs as exploitation of foreign markets and maximization of profit. MNCs do business with developing countries based solely on economic reasons, such as cheap raw materials and untapped markets. They are not seriously concerned with the impact of their operations on developing countries. Developing countries, however, want to maximize the MNCs' contribution to national goals with a minimum effect on national sovereignty.[3]

Historically, the developing countries' relationships with the MNCs have been marred by misunderstandings and unfulfilled expectations. Although both parties believe they can benefit from the relationship, the outcomes have been less than satisfactory to some developing countries. The disappointment with the MNCs, according to Peter Wright, stems from dissimilar views in three aspects of the relationship: expectation of wealth, incongruency in values, and technology transfer.[4]

Wealth expectation. Developing countries expected MNCs to assist them in their pursuit of economic development. They assumed that major economic gains and technology transfer would take place through the operation of MNCs. The reality was different from the assumptions. Developing countries maintain that the benefits of the relationships accrued to the MNCs only. While the MNCs enjoyed higher sales and revenues, developing countries' quest to join the ranks of rich nations through cooperation with the MNCs was not realized. Developing countries assert that the MNCs exploited their natural resource and low labor costs without providing them with a corresponding wealth gain. MNCs and developed na-

tions argue that the plight of developing countries may be traced to sociocultural values that are not congruent to economic growth.

Value incongruency. There are certain inherent values that support and sustain industrialization and modernization. The most salient values of industrial societies are the utility of mass production and the economic benefits of efficiency. To operate efficiently, a mass production system necessitates adherence to certain organizational requirements. These requirements include certain man-machine ratios, and specific interfaces between the person and the machine. At the micro level, for example, the efficiency of an assembly line operation is fatally damaged if it is interrupted for the daily prayers that are expected of the devout in certain religions. At the macro level, business decisions that are dictated by market force are not always congruent with the political and economic priorities of host countries.

Technology transfer. Developing nations were hoping that the operation of MNCs would result in technology transfer, and would assist them in joining the rank of industrialized nations. They were disappointed to discover that whatever transfer of technology took place, particularly in the extractive industries, was industry specific, and not applicable elsewhere. Such technology was also useless once the natural resources were depleted. Also, the viability of technology transferred in the manufacturing sector was heavily dependent on the MNCs. Without the provision of parts and components, for example, car manufacturing or appliance facilities in developing countries would be rendered idle.

While past relationships between developing countries and MNCs were marred by misunderstanding and dashed hopes, not many would dispute the benefits that MNCs could provide. Host governments, in general, however, have a few concerns in their dealings with the MNCs.

Host government concerns The relationship with MNCs, particularly globally integrated MNCs, raises concerns of host governments over several specific issues.[5] These issues are (1) the flexibility of MNCs, (2) interdependency and control, (3) efficiency, (4) the effect on the domestic strategic industry, (5) taxation, and (6) the MNCs' headquarters as decision centers.

MNC flexibility. Host governments fear that the MNC network of integrated facilities around the world could be used to the disadvantage of domestic firms. Their fear is based on MNC characteristics. First, MNCs have an information advantage over locally oriented domestic firms. Significant changes in market conditions could be detected by the global scanning capabilities of the MNCs. They are able to switch out of unattractive business activities much faster than domestic firms. Second, MNCs have multiple locations around the world that enable them to respond immediately to changing circumstances. They can quickly respond to changes in the global market and shift production and manufacturing facilities to countries with a relative cost advantage. Also, because they are not particularly committed to any country, except possibly their home base, the MNCs can easily relocate on short notice.[6]

Interdependency and control. With increased trade comes interdependence among trading partners. A decision made by one of the partners influences the other, and vice versa. It compels governments to consider the ramification of decisions made outside their national borders on their economies. Increased globalization of industry creates international interdependency among nations and exposes national economies to forces beyond the control of governments. In other words, governments lose some control over their economies, and even some of their sovereign power, to global market forces, including the MNC. Free trade brings about free movement of capital and investment. Free trade also influences labor-management relationships and restricts labor union strategies. Globalization of industry and free trade pressure national economies to adjust to changes that take place globally. A change in the competitive position of an industry due to changes in the price of raw material or labor, for example, may require changing national priorities and economic programs. During the oil crisis of early 1970s, for example, Japan realized that its high energy-consuming aluminum industry could not compete with the American aluminum industry. The American aluminum could rely on domestic oil as a buffer against the high price of imported oil, whereas the Japanese had to satisfy all of their needs through imports. Therefore, Ministry of International Trade and Industry (MITI) decided not to provide the aluminum industry with any additional source of cheap financing, causing it to wither away. In effect, the forces of the global market left the Japanese government no choice but to watch the demise of its aluminum industry.

The competitive pressure resulting from the globalization of the industry as well as advancement in telecommunication and transportation has exposed the vulnerability of many domestic firms. MNCs, with a presence in many markets, have information and resource advantages over domestic firms. These advantages include capital, distribution channels, and technical and managerial expertise. MNCs can detect changes in consumer needs and purchasing patterns, and learn about new technologies, much before their domestic counterparts. The technological explosion of recent years has also shortened industry life cycles and has increased the cost of data gathering and analysis. Government concerns are heightened by the realization that this information advantage, when coupled with their resource advantage, provides MNCs with a decisive edge over their locally based domestic firms. Those concerns are more pronounced for mature industries. Mature industries, characterized by price competition, operate in the most fiercely contested markets. Since barriers to entry are low in these industries, competition is intense and comes from many countries. Therefore, governments would like to see domestic firms branch out into emerging industries, where competitive pressures are low and the opportunities for profits are high.

Faced with the pressure of global market forces and motivated by the desire to regain control, some governments have established a much closer relationship with the industry. The cooperative relationship between MITI and Japanese industry is a good example. It has enabled Japan to reduce the cost and uncertainty for private firms in committing resources to emerging industries. Characteristically, emerging industries require heavy investments for extended periods of time. Although, the eventual returns could be high, the high cost of capital and economic and technological uncertainties discourage private long-term investment in emerging industries. As Japan has demonstrated, governments can reduce the cost and uncertainties of investment and can increase the participation of private firms in emerging industries.

Efficiency.   On the one hand, if allowed unrestricted access to the domestic market, the MNCs' competitive advantage may force less resourceful domestic businesses out of the market. On the other hand, if MNC participation in the domestic market is restricted or prevented, consumers may pay higher prices, and inefficient domestic industry may unnecessarily be preserved. Even if government follows a policy of free trade, without actively encouraging the development of new and emerging industries, the country may find itself saddled with aging MNC subsidiaries. When faced with heavy competition from low-cost producers in other countries, the large-scale departure of these subsidiaries will have a harmful effect on the economy. A couple of decades ago, for example, the United Kingdom found itself in such a position. When a number of traditional plants, such as Singer's sewing machine and Caterpillar's tractor plants, lost their competitive position vis-à-vis the Asian counterparts, the impact on the United Kingdom was painful. In contrast, the

government of Singapore has enjoyed the positive effects of encouraging quick adjustments to international competition and the development of emerging industries.[7]

Domestic strategic industry.   Globalization of business leads to specialization. If globalization is allowed to take its own course, some domestic firms may be forced out of business, while others may flourish. It is possible that the MNCs' participation in the domestic market may hinder the development of domestic industry. The MNCs, with their information and resource advantage, may crowd the market and leave no room for domestic competition to evolve. Therefore, host governments believe industries that are vital for national security should be protected from the pressure of global market forces. Without support and protection from the government, these industries may not have a chance of developing and, if they exist, may disintegrate. Even those countries that are active participants in the global market and, therefore, have accepted interdependency, are very fearful of depending on outsiders in strategically important areas. To be able to control telecommunication and defense industries, for example, governments would like domestic firms to develop them exclusively. But the small size of many domestic markets for these industries raises concerns over efficiency and costs. For that reason, to make it possible to produce in large volumes and reduce costs, global arms sales is an attractive option for many industrialized countries to bolster their defense industry. It is, especially, for this reason that efforts to curb the arms race among developing countries have not been successful. Without having modern manufacturing capabilities of their own, historically, developing countries have been eager customers of modern weaponry.

Taxation.   In industries where direct costs are small and allocated costs (R&D, patents, administrative costs) are large, MNCs can manipulate subsidiaries' earnings. Through transfer pricing, where subsidiaries are charged for their intrafirm purchases, and by allocating research and development expenditures, a subsidiary could show fewer profits to reduce its tax obligations. It is very difficult for the governments to prove the actual violations and prevent them from happening. For many years, to no avail, developing countries complained about such abuses by the MNCs. The inability of host countries to thwart these abuses became amply clear when in the late 1980s and early 1990s, without much success, the U.S. government took legal actions against a few MNCs, accusing them of such practices.

MNC headquarters as the decision center. An aggravating issue for the host country is that a subsidiary of an MNC may not have real decision-making authority. Subsidiary managers, in a global firm, very seldom can make an important decision all by themselves. Often, the strategic ramifications of a subsidiary's decisions for the total MNC operation compel the headquarters to intervene. Subsidiary managers regularly have to consult with headquarters on any agreement made with the host government. In many cases subsidiary managers are not even allowed to involve themselves in negotiations with host governments. Although host government officials deal with these managers regularly, they cannot count on them to make decisions affecting the domestic market. The real decision makers are thousands of miles away in a foreign country.

Characteristics of MNC–host country relationships Until recently, many countries regarded MNCs as evil institutions that could provide some benefits. The question was whether or not their presence should be tolerated. The very same countries now assume a more practical stance and search for the best way to use the MNCs to further their national goals.[8] In the mid-1970s, for example, the government of Venezuela took over the oil industry from foreign MNCs. In the 1990s, the same government envisions a major new role for foreign MNCs, especially oil companies such as Exxon Cor-

poration and Royal Dutch/Shell Group. There are plans for these firms to participate in a \$40 billion project to speed development of Venezuela's vast energy base. Similarly, the British Petroleum Company that was nationalized in the mid-1970s by the Nigerian government has been called back to resume the search for oil.[9] Many host governments see the MNCs' operations as beneficial to the national economy in the development of an industrial base, creation of jobs, and generation of tax revenues.

Although there is no formal market for foreign investment, in practice market conditions prevail. Similar to the competition among producers for the market share of consumer expenditures, countries compete for market share of new foreign investment.[10] Firms that are looking for plant sites for international expansion are "buyers," and host governments that are offering plant locations are "sellers." In this market, the bargaining power of "buyers" and "sellers" determines the characteristics of the transactions.

The host governments and MNCs have a very complex and interdependent relationship. Many factors determine the amount of influence that each can exert on the other. Among the factors that could dictate the nature of the relationship are their relative bargaining power, the type of strategy MNCs employ, and the structure of the industry.

MNCs' bargaining power. An MNC's relative bargaining power increases under five conditions: First, if it has a monopolistic position. Second, if it utilizes a technology that requires a large investment in R&D, without many viable substitutes. Third, if it exports a large part of its outputs, and has control over the market downstream (e.g., distribution channels). Fourth, if it employs factors of production, such as unskilled labor, that are easily substitutable across countries. Fifth, if its operations require a small investment that could very easily be liquidated or moved, meaning the operations are relatively immune from excessive pressures on the part of the host government.[11]

Bargaining power of host countries. Just as there are certain conditions that increase the relative power of MNCs, there are also conditions that influence the relative bargaining power of the host countries (see Table 2.2). A country in the early stages of economic development that is heavily dependent on technology importation may be in a weak bargaining position vis-à-vis the MNCs. For these countries, the MNCs are the only vehicle of technology transfer, and they cannot afford to alienate them. A government in dire need of hard currencies can ill afford to restrict MNC operations. In general, the relative power of the host government is a function of control over three factors: access to product markets, access to the domestic capital market, and access to production technology.[12]

Host governments have the power to control access to domestic markets, and usually exercise this power. The importance of access to a domestic market is a function of one or a combination of three factors. First, the MNC may desire access to the market because of its size. Brazil, Mexico, and India have large domestic markets. Their huge size and the fact that these markets cannot be supplied by locating plants in other countries make them attractive to MNCs. The low purchasing power in these countries, however, tempers their attractiveness. Control over a large domestic market gives the government a monopoly power, similar to that enjoyed by countries with desirable raw materials that

are limited in supply. Second, a market may be attractive to MNCs because of its export potential. As a part of its global strategy, an MNC may be interested in the low labor costs of a country for setting up export-oriented manufacturing facilities. Third, a country's domestic market could be attractive due to its membership in a regional trade pact. It could be used for entry into a market that otherwise would be difficult to access. Each of the members of the European Common Market, for example, could be an attractive alternative for reaching the European market.

The domestic capital market is typically controlled by the governments. Host governments can generate alternative sources of capital, both internal and external, such as domestic savings and foreign commercial loans. This willingness and ability to provide or assist in securing investment finances increases the bargaining power of host governments, and the attractiveness of their domestic markets. Likewise, the availability of indigenous technology or of licensing agreements could improve the host government's bargaining position.

Methods of dealing with MNCs   In their quest to exploit the MNCs to advance their own national policies, host governments involve themselves in specific corporate decisions. Attempts by host governments to wrest more benefits from the MNCs may not be very successful. Such attempts may fail not because the

Table 2.2
Factors Influencing Host Government's Bargaining Power

Increasing Bargaining Power	Decreasing Bargaining Power

1. Control access to product market: Domestic market is attractive because of
  a. Size
  b. Potential for export (low labor costs)
  c. A regional pact member
2. Control access to domestic capital market
3. Control access to production technology
	1. Dependence on the MNCs for technology
	2. The need for hard currencies

MNCs might resist them due to their adverse effects on the revenues (although that could be the case). The MNCs may not be able to respond favorably to host government demands for other reasons. An integrated global firm that operates across the national borders may not be able to give in to the demands of one host government without alienating others. An increase in production, exports, employment, technology transfer, or capital in one place may require a corresponding decrease in other places. Also the effectiveness of a firm's global strategies could be undermined if it heeds requests that are inconsistent with those strategies. Often MNCs utilize their worldwide operations and effectively nullify host government policy decisions that they consider to have an adverse impact on the business. The difficulties that host governments experience in forcing MNCs into a particular action was highlighted in the case of the Soviet gas pipeline embargo.[13]

The preceding discussion may imply that host countries are at the mercy of the MNCs for the benefits they provide. Although MNCs have a considerable amount of power and flexibility, they face many difficulties in exercising their power. To induce the MNCs into a desired action, certain policy instruments are employed by the host countries.

To encourage or discourage certain action in targeted industries, direct or indirect measures are commonly used by host governments. Direct measures are subsidies and taxes that are designed as incentives for inducing MNCs into a particular action. Indirect measures are various regulations and restrictions that increase the cost of doing business and induce the MNCs to curtail or halt certain operations. On the other hand, as a positive inducement, a host country may reduce or exempt the MNCs from paying taxes. Investment in production facilities, increased exports, or technology transfers, which increase employment and benefit the local population, may be granted government subsidies. For example, in exchange for agreeing to locate

an automobile assembly operations in the United States, Volkswagen received subsidies from federal, state, and local governments worth $50 million. It was also granted more than $40 million in wage concessions by the United Auto Workers. The province of Quebec offers a 10 percent credit on salaries paid to research workers. If the corporation fails to have taxable income in a given year, this credit can be converted into cash.[14]

While incentives are used to encourage and persuade, regulations, restrictions, and increased taxes may be used to dissuade MNCs from undertaking certain actions. For instance, imports of luxury products or items that compete directly with local products may face higher taxes. Local content laws could prevent MNCs from completely relying on imports for their production operations.

Although host governments have certain concerns regarding MNC operations in their countries, they still make attempts to court them. Many have actively sought the MNC participation in the local market by encouraging foreign direct investment. In their dealings with MNCs, host countries have commonly employed two methods for promoting FDI. The first method is a policy approach, and the second is negotiation. The two methods are described next.[15]

Policy approach. Countries using the policy approach do not negotiate with individual investors over important issues. These countries determine in advance the general policies that specify the industries in which foreign investors would be accepted and the terms of foreign investment. Such policies can range from very lenient to very restrictive toward foreign investment. Hong Kong and Burma are respective examples. Hong Kong follows an open policy, and imposes minimum restrictions on foreign investment, whereas Burma is relatively closed to the outside world and is very cautious in its dealings with foreigners.

Negotiation approach. Governments using the negotiation approach fall along a continuum at one end of which is a decentralized method, and at the other a centralized one. In a centralized approach, all negotiations with investors are centralized in one organization. This organization has the full authority to accept or reject an applicant and to conclude agreements with foreign investors. Singapore and Ireland have used the centralized policy approach in dealing with potential foreign investors. In a decentralized method, negotiations with foreign investors are dispersed across several agencies and ministries, such as the ministries of trade and finance and central banks. Almost all countries, at one point in their history, have relied on this approach. India, Mexico, and many developing countries are still using this approach.

Managing host government relations MNCs handle government relations, and respond to government demands and policy actions in many different ways. The response to government actions and demands may be centralized at headquarters, be placed with the regional managers, or be delegated to the country managers.[16] The latter method, however, is not very popular with MNCs. Usually, country managers have limited authority and autonomy in their dealings with host governments. Mahini and Wells have identified four factors that largely determine the location of decision re-

sponse in the organizational hierarchy, and the method of handling host government relations. The four factors that determine the location of decision response are (1) the firm's bargaining power in dealing with host governments, (2) the significance of the international operations to the enterprise, (3) the degree of interdependence of the subsidiaries, and (4) the political salience of the industry, where the industry accounts for the major part of the host country's foreign exchange earnings and the host government revenues. By considering these factors, we elaborate on four different approaches to government relations: (1) policy, (2) centralized, (3) diffuse, and (4) coordinated approaches (see Figure 2.2).

In the policy approach the major areas of possible conflict with host governments are identified in advance, and policies are devised for handling them. The centralized approach directs and supervises government negotiations from headquarters. Foreign subsidiaries are responsible for host government relations in the diffuse approach. A middle ground approach, between the extreme positions of the centralized and diffuse approaches, is followed by firms using the coordinated approach. The following paragraphs provide details for these four approaches.[17]

Policy approach. In the policy approach, the firm decides in advance its position regarding the issues of major importance for negotia-

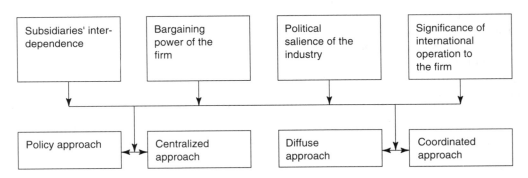

Figure 2.2   Managing Host Government Relationships

tion with host governments. The location of decisions regarding government relations is at headquarters, and managers have little or no discretion to depart from the policy on these matters. The policy approach might be employed where the firm is in a very strong bargaining position, and the host government is dependent on the resources of the firm. Although the policies are made centrally at headquarters, the host government deals with the local MNCs' managers who implement them.

Except for IBM, no firm has used the policy approach recently. In dealing with host governments, IBM had established policies regarding matters of strategic importance, such as the ownership of foreign subsidiaries, location of R&D facilities, and trade among its affiliates. These matters were subject to strict company policies and not open for negotiation with host governments. In the mid-1970s, for example, the Indian government demanded that IBM reduce its equity ownership from 100 percent to 40 percent. IBM had already established that it would not assume less than 100 percent ownership position. Rather than setting a precedent by giving in to the government demand, IBM withdrew from India.[18] Soon after that incident, it withdrew from Nigeria on the same policy position too.[19] In both cases, IBM felt that the host governments could not obtain its sophisticated know-how and technology from other firms. Also, it considered the issue of full ownership of its manufacturing and R&D facilities of strategic importance.

The policy approach, although rigid, is a proactive position. As illustrated by the IBM case, the areas of possible conflicts with host governments are identified in advance, and steps are taken to implement the predetermined solutions before a possible confrontation with the host government. IBM, for example, had decided that the ownership of manufacturing facilities, trade between subsidiaries, and the location of R&D facilities would remain internal policy decisions. It would, however, provide widespread R&D facilities for activities that were not crucial to its core operation. It would also follow a balanced policy of trade between its subsidiaries, making sure that none would become a net importer in relation to others.

Centralized approach. In the centralized approach, similar to the policy approach, the decision location is at a high level in the organization. A specialized unit at headquarters is given the responsibility for dealing with host governments. The subsidiary manager may be present at the negotiation with the host government, but would take a subordinate position to that of the specialized negotiating unit. The major difference between the policy approach and the centralized approach is in their dealing with the most important government relations matters. In the former, these issues are decided in advance by top management and are not negotiable. In the latter, headquarters is willing to negotiate on them.

This approach is common among international oil companies. These firms have a specialized staff for handling government relations. The most important personnel are assigned to the exploration and production division. This division is usually in charge of the negotiation with host governments and takes the lead role for new exploration and production contracts. Firms using this approach take a proactive position too, and government relations are an integral part of overall international strategy. Therefore, top management closely supervises the government relations unit, and even sometimes participates directly in the negotiations. For example, when Arco was negotiating new exploration and production rights with the government of Dubai, the head of the Exploration and Production Division was Arco's chief negotiator. Besides legal and tax specialists from headquarters, the negotiating team included the division's technical specialists, engineers, and economists. The bargaining limits were, however, defined by senior management. For renegotiations, regional management from the geographic division usually took the lead. Nonetheless, even in renegotiations, senior management would often get involved. As an example, when in 1974 Arco was renegotiating with the government of Indonesia, the president of the Eastern Operating Group headed the team of specialists from the division and the headquarters.[20]

Interdependency among foreign subsidiaries of oil companies also makes the choice of a centralized approach a necessity. Oil companies have a large network of foreign subsidiaries that are linked through vertically integrated operations. In the vertical chain, each subsidiary may be involved in any of the activities of exploration, production, transportation, refining, and distribution. They are connected with others in the chain with a supply line that starts with the exploration and ends with distribution. In a vertically integrated firm, the actions of one subsidiary would affect the rest of the operation in the vertical chain. It would also impact other foreign subsidiaries at the same level. Therefore, the activities of subsidiaries are important, both to globally integrated operations and to overall earnings and profits of the oil companies. This internal interdependency coupled with the political saliency, makes host government relations a very critical and complex undertaking that could not be left to foreign subsidiaries.

The operations of oil companies are politically salient to host countries. Most oil-producing countries rely on the oil industry for a major part of their foreign exchange earnings and government revenues. They are very much interested in, and keep informed about, contracts and agreements that oil companies negotiate with other countries. The terms of a new agreement that is favorable to a host country will quickly become a model for other countries to follow. Often host countries demand renegotiation of their contract if they learn about a more favorable term granted to other countries. Before the 1960s, for example, contracts between oil-producing countries and multinational oil companies, allowed for less than 30% royalties. In the early 1960s, the government of Libya signed a contract with Occidental Oil Company with a 75% royalty. Very soon, all other oil-producing countries demanded renegotiation of their contracts. All new contracts followed the pattern established by Libya.

Because oil companies do not have the strong bargaining power of IBM in negotiation with host countries, the use of the policy approach would be impractical. Because the operations of oil companies would dramatically impact the host countries' economy, direct involvement of top management and a centralized approach to government relations would be a logical choice.

The diffuse approach. In firms that follow the diffuse approach, the responsibility of the host government relations rests with different managers. Depending on the issues at hand, the foreign subsidiaries, the regional manager, or a functional department such as marketing might be responsible for host government relations.

The diffuse approach seems to be more appropriate for firms in which the degree of interdependency between their foreign subsidiaries is minimal or nonexistent. If the actions, or activities, of one subsidiary do not greatly impact the other subsidiaries, the ad hoc nature of this approach allows local managers to take the initiative, and develop a close working relationship with host governments. Therefore, firms with strategies that emphasize local (national) responsiveness are ones that can afford limited or no coordination of their government relations. Also, when foreign operations do not account for a major portion of the firm's earnings and profits, decisions made by a subsidiary do not dramatically impact overall corporate profitability. Hence, the headquarters' arms-length involvement, which typifies a diffuse approach, would provide a closer relationship between the subsidiary and the host government. Ultimately, the benefits of such a relationship may be less friction between the host government and the subsidiary. Having built a close relationship with the host governments, the subsidiary executives may be spared the arbitrary operational restrictions that often beset firms with arms-length government relations.

International Harvester, the earth-moving and heavy equipment manufacturer, and Cummins, the diesel engine manufacturer, have used this approach. Before the reorganization of 1977 at International Harvester, local government relations were among the responsibilities of country managers. When three worldwide product divisions were formed in 1977, although the decision-making power was moved to the divisional level, government relations were handled on an ad hoc basis. In negotiation with the government of Mexico, for example, subsidiary management was completely bypassed by division management. However, similar negotiations with Canada, which took place around the same time period, were handled by subsidiary managers.[21]

In 1976, Cummins was interested in establishing facilities in the Andean Pact countries of Latin America. It started negotiating with Brazil and Mexico on exporting and the expansion of their production lines. These negotiations were handled by the corporate manufacturing staff. When Cummins learned that Mexico had begun negotiating with General Motors, the threat to Latin American expansion became evident. Therefore, the responsibilities for these two sets of negotiations were assigned to the head of the international marketing division.[22]

Coordinated approach. Compared with the extreme positions of the policy, centralized, and diffuse approaches, the coordinated approach is a middle ground position. Firms using the coordinated approach usually clarify who is responsible for host government relations, and assign most of the authority to subsidiary or other front-line managers. At the same time, the responsible manager is directed and/or encouraged to coordinate the major decisions with the other subsidiaries. The coordinated approach involves front-line managers, while the headquarters maintains some degree of centralization. With this approach, the firm intends to minimize the reactive nature of the diffuse approach and to install some degree of initiative or forecasting to government relations. Xerox, ITT, Ford, and Eli Lilly are among the firms that have used the coordinated approach.

In the mid-1980s, for example, Xerox, at one of its regions, had each country manager prepare a quarterly report on government issues. These reports were discussed with regional managers to produce a list of proposed objectives for government relations. Subsequently, these objectives were integrated into the company's system of management-by-objectives (MBO). In this way, the annual performance review explicitly included the country manager's handling of government relations. In addition, every quarter, the neighboring country managers discussed with regional managers, the possible impacts of each subsidiary's undertakings on all other subsidiaries. At the end of the sessions, country managers were supposed to have objectives that were acceptable to them and the regional management. These sessions helped in developing a convergence of views among country managers, and between country managers and the regional functional staff. In this way, MBO serves as a coordination mechanism.

The Competition

A major difference between the management of MNCs and that of the domestic firm is the nature of the competition each faces. MNCs operate in a more competitive environment. In some or all aspects of their operations, many MNCs have to deal with competition from local and state-owned firms. Besides the competition from local firms, rivalry among MNCs creates a very intense competitive pressure. As previously discussed, government involvement in business creates an environment of constraints and control. Through direct or indirect support and subsidies of local businesses, governments force MNCs to evaluate their strategies carefully.

Competition from domestic and state-controlled firms In the following pages we learn that industries may be classified along a continuum by extent of internationalization. Multidomestic industries are at the low end of this continuum and at the high end are "global" industries. International industries are in the middle. In multidomestic industries, where product characteristics and consumer choices are heavily influenced by local tastes and cultural norms, domestic firms can effectively challenge the MNCs. In effect, in multidomestic industries, most of the advantages of being an MNC are nullified by market characteristics. Unless MNCs behave like domestic firms, they will not be able to capture much of a market share. Domestic firms, due to their insider position and familiarity with the cultural, legal, and logistical requirements of doing business, have an edge over the MNCs. In some countries the stigma of being a foreign company is by itself a drawback. The older generation of Japanese managers, for example, is still reluctant to deal with foreign companies. They tend to consider it unpatriotic to buy from the foreigners. Some U.S. firms have capitalized on the consumers' patriotic feelings as well. Wal-Mart, for example, has used its support of American suppliers, whenever these suppliers are competitive on quality and price, as an effective marketing tool.

Certain industries are considered by host governments to be strategically important for national security. These industries receive government support in competing with MNCs. Host government policies regarding domestic strategic industries vary. In some countries, these industries are government owned. In other countries, they are the exclusive domain of domestic firms with the government effectively controlling them. Still in others, MNCs are allowed limited participation in some aspects, but are barred from others. Most host governments, however, effectively tilt the competitive position of strategic domestic firms against their MNC competitors. Industries that are commonly controlled by governments include airlines, coal, electricity, gas, oil, automobile, the post office, railroads, shipbuilding, steel, and telecommunication. In addition, in all countries that have modern manufacturing capabilities, defense industries are the exclusive domain of governments and domestic firms. Where private firms are allowed to participate in arms production, their sales to foreign countries are under strict government control. In addition to the benefits mentioned earlier, weapons sales to foreign governments is an important instrument of foreign policy implementation. Global weapon sales generate huge sums annually. In 1993, for example, the U.S. arms sales to foreign governments were more than $34 billion. In 1994, the British companies were expecting to sell more than $9 billion worth of weapons abroad. Russia claims that complying with international arms embargos against Libya and Iraq and others has cost the country more than $7.5 billion in sales.[23]

Host governments can control an industry without an ownership share. A host government may be the only customer of the industry's products, and through its purchasing power it can effectively bar MNC participation in that industry. By buying only from domestic firms, governments can create artificial entry barriers. Exclusive domestic purchasing may not be a formal government policy, but a *de facto* practice. Nor does it have to be practiced only by the government to have an impact on MNC participation in the industry. The government of Japan, for example, only recently, and with the extensive pressure from the United States, allowed American firms to participate in contract biddings for large public construction projects. In the supercomputer industry, Cray Research's bid was rejected in favor of a Japanese firm even though performance specifications and the Cray price were much better. Often Japanese manufacturers restrict their purchases to domestic suppliers that are members of their *Keiretsu* (a Japanese-type conglomerate that is made up of a family of firms in supplier–buyer relationship, including banks and insurance companies). Such a practice makes it almost impossible for non-Japanese firms to compete in the Japanese market.

In many cases, when an MNC is successful in securing an initial contract, it can confidently expect a long-term relationship with the host government. Suppliers are abandoned only if government becomes extremely disgruntled with their performance or technologies.[24] For this reason, it is very difficult for a new manufacturer to break into established national markets that are controlled by governments. Only new markets of developing countries, although small in size, offer significant opportunities for newcomers. These countries, however, rely on the advice of independent consultants, and use only very reputable suppliers with proven performance in developed countries. The choice of LM Ericsson, a Swedish manufacturer, by the Australian government is an example. In 1977, the Australian government, through detailed comparative tests among telecommunication equipment from a few manufacturers, chose LM Ericsson's AXE electronic digital switching system. Ericsson then used this contract as a reference in successful deals with Kuwait, Saudi Arabia, and Panama.[25]

In obtaining a new business contract in the government-controlled industries of developing countries, MNCs that can offer new technologies have a competitive advantage over those who cannot or are not willing to do so. As noted, developing countries are very much interested in technology transfer. Therefore, by providing technological assistance, for example, CIT-Alcatel, the French supplier of switching equipment, was able to win a sizable contract from the Indian government. CIT-Alcatel agreed to set up an Indian digital telecommunication equipment industry, backed by a guarantee and agreements between the French and Indian governments.[26]

To assure that these industries remain responsive to national interests, some governments have demanded joint ventures with MNCs. In response to government demands, the MNCs have acted in two different ways. Some have established subsidiaries in each country with no interaction among them. The resulting firms are joint ventures that operate as domestic firms. ITT has used this strategy. The other strategy is to negotiate with host countries to establish a partly integrated manufacturing network and to share the ownership of each with respective host countries. Ericsson, for example, set up such an arrangement with France in the 1960s, and another deal with Italy in the 1980s. To both countries, Ericsson offered entrance into its partly integrated manufacturing network. The French were given the production of crossbar relays, and the Italian received manufacturing of AXE processors.[27]

Competition from other MNCs Competition to MNC operation comes from other MNCs, as well as domestic firms. The nature of competition, of course, varies with industry characteristics. For the automobile and consumer electronics industries, for example, which employ mature technologies and have products and market characteristics that are less influenced by cultural norms, competition is not limited to developed countries' MNCs. Similarities in consumer tastes and preferences provide opportunities for standardization in manufacturing and economies of scale and make them very attractive. Since these products do not require cutting-edge technologies, MNCs from newly industrialized countries, such as those of the South Korea, Taiwan, and Malaysia, are joining the melee too. In contrast, the leading-edge industries, such as medical technology, biomedicine, or computer chip design, are the exclusive domain of the MNCs from a few advanced industrialized countries.

Even in government-controlled industries, MNCs are not totally immune from competition. As mentioned earlier, if host governments become dissatisfied with MNCs' operations, they may choose new suppliers. In the 1970s, for example, to demonstrate its dissatisfaction with ITT, Spain invited LM Ericsson to compete with ITT.[28] The availability of new technology could also undermine the exclusive contracts the MNCs have with host governments. In the early 1970s, when all domestic new product development programs and deliveries were behind by at least one year, the British Post Office chose LM Ericsson to supply new switching equipment.

To encourage exports, many governments provide subsidies to domestic firms. With the financial and sometimes technological assistance from governments, international markets are becoming the scene of very intense competition. For instance, Airbus Industries, a consortium of aviation firms from Europe, which is backed by the French and British governments, has been able to make successful inroads into markets that previously were exclusively served by Boeing. A U.S. Department of Commerce study puts the total subsidies received by Airbus at $26 billion.[29] Airbus has been able to use these subsidies to develop a technologically advanced passenger airplane and undercut Boeing prices. Consequently, in recent years, even some American airlines have chosen Airbus over Boeing.

Another very well publicized example of government involvement in international competition is the practice of the Japanese government. Japanese industries have effectively captured market shares from their competition by using cheap financing and support from the Ministry of International Trade and Industry (MITI). Other countries, noticing Japan's success, have begun emulating them. Even in the United States the government's involvement in business has increased. Traditionally the U.S. government has maintained a hands-off policy toward business and industry. Recently, however, serious consideration has been given to establishing closer ties with business. After years of insisting in vain that Japan behave more like America, the United States may aim to compete with Japan by borrowing a page from Tokyo's playbook. The U.S. administration has indicated that it prefers an industrial policy that, in addition to trade pressures, will use more public funds for civilian research and provide incentives to nurture high-tech industries.[30] As a sign of the changing times, in 1988, when it was faced with the prospects of losing the lead in computer chip manufacturing to Japanese firms, the U.S. government followed a traditional Japanese practice. It aided in the establishment of Sematech, a consortium of leading semiconductor firms. Sematech was designed to help U.S. manufacturers build a technologically advanced and less expensive chip than those of the Japanese. After five years, and more than $1 billion financing from both the government and the member firms, Sematech was successful in improving on the industry standard by 100 percent.[31]

In the preceding pages we have argued that the international strategy process is the same for both domestic and MNC operations; however, the management of an international operation is more demanding and difficult. The difficulty of international management is due to the higher level of complexity and uncertainty involved in the international environment. Equipped with knowledge about the major environmental forces of international management, we now turn to the strategic choices available to MNCs.

Generic MNC Strategies

In dealing with environmental complexities and uncertainties, MNCs have a range of alternative strategic choices. Because there are some similarities, as well as differences, among national markets, the choice of strategy is determined by considering these similarities and differences. An emphasis on similarities calls for producing products that can be sold globally, without many modifications. To take advantage of differences among national markets would necessitate strategies that treat each market based on its own merits. Therefore, each market is considered as a unique business opportunity, which requires responding to its special characteristics and demands. In terms of strategy, therefore, the choice is between global integration and national responsiveness. The old decision quandary of efficiency versus effectiveness prevails in the international marketplace too. An attempt to serve many countries with the same range of products is efficiency oriented. To serve the unique needs of each market by catering to their requirements is effectiveness oriented. Of course, the choice does not have to be between integration-efficiency and responsiveness-effectiveness. Depending on circumstances, firms can establish a middle ground position and lean toward either one or the other. Alternatively, a firm could combine some features of both strategies, as circumstances demand. These choices are presented under three generic strategies: global integration, host country focus, and hybrid international.

Global Integration Strategy

To capitalize on the economies of scale and to take advantage of the diverse opportunities for cost reduction that the global market provides, the choice of strategy is global integration. Following a global integration strategy, MNC production and distribution facilities expand over national borders in a network of specialized operations. Firms using a global integration strategy capitalize on the similarities among the national markets, and sidestep the differences. Global integration can be based on product or process specialization.

MNCs using product specialization produce only part of a common global product range in each country. Each foreign subsidiary, however, offers a complete range of products in its national market. Through intrafirm trade, each subsidiary imports from other subsidiaries what it is not producing, and exports to them its specialized outputs. The process specialization involves a multistage manufacturing process, where each subsidiary produces certain parts and components for a common product or product range. American semiconductors have used this strategy by farming out to border plants in Mexico and the Far East. The U.S. automobile industry has employed this strategy by building various cars and components in different countries.[32]

Global integration benefits are realized through cost reduction by, for example, locating manufacturing facilities where costs of doing business are low. The emphasis on cost may come at the expense of flexibility and responsiveness to national markets. By using a global integration strategy the MNC is compelled to find a mix of products for all of its foreign markets. Standardization of products among its subsidiaries does not allow for customizing products to national criteria and tastes.

To take advantage of the large-scale operations that provide for economies of scale, manufacturing operations are centralized. The manufacturing concentration increases intercompany product shipment. If the pattern of intercompany shipments (trade) causes a country to be the net importer, it could raise the risk of host government intervention. Similar efforts to improve efficiency through centralization of R&D activities may raise the same risk. Also, large-scale centralized operations expose the MNC to foreign currency exchange risk.[33] Although MNCs face certain risks by concentrating manufacturing and R&D activities, in general, the benefits outweigh the associated risks. Caterpillar, Ford Motor Company, IBM, and Brown Boveri have relied on global integration strategies.

Host Country Focus Strategy

If global integration strategy could be regarded as the "efficiency" choice, the host country focus strategy is the "effectiveness" option. In a host country focus strategy, subsidiaries are treated as if they are autonomous national firms. They are allowed to respond to local demands as they see fit. The MNC's headquarters office maintains overall coordination among various subsidiaries (using some of the techniques discussed previously) in a way that maximizes the MNC's global performance. A relatively complete range of products is manufactured by each subsidiary. Since each subsidiary is responsible for its own domestic market needs, a minimum amount of trade occurs between subsidiaries. Consequently, subsidiaries are not directly responsible for the total MNC efficiency. Indirectly, however, they all are involved with the MNC's total performance.

The MNC that pursues a host country focus strategy has a different way of using its worldwide presence and resources for a competitive advantage. While the MNCs with a global integration strategy compete with other MNCs, firms using host country focus vie for market share with domestic firms and the subsidiaries of other MNCs that employ the same strategy. Whereas the competitive advantage of global integration strategy is based on corporatewide standardization and similarities among national markets, host country focus strategy employs the MNC's worldwide resources for a competitive edge.

In competition with their domestic counterparts, the MNC subsidiaries use headquarters resources in several ways.[34] First, even when national subsidiaries are managed as fully autonomous profit centers, the financial umbrella of the headquarters allows more risk taking by the subsidiaries. Second, because of the headquarters support, lower cost financing is available to national subsidiaries. Third, centralized R&D activities reduce costs and can increase the benefit to the subsidiaries. Fourth, the subsidiaries have access to a global distribution network and logistics that are beyond the reach of their domestic counterparts. Fifth, national subsidiaries may supply their customers the same product from several sources within the MNC's global operations. Through their sister subsidiaries, they can take advantage of bilateral trade agreements among many developing countries. Such arrangements potentially make them more competitive than their domestic or globally integrated counterparts. Finally, with central control in pricing and marketing policies by the headquarters, each subsidiary can become a more resilient competitor. Instead of competing as individual firms in national markets, they can coordinate their competitive response for a better result. As an example, Goodyear's reaction to the Michelin's entry into the U.S. market was a very aggressive response in Europe. If Goodyear had to respond to Michelin in the U.S. market only, it would probably have hurt itself more. In this vein, the inability to respond in the home market of their competition puts domestic firms at a competitive disadvantage versus MNC subsidiaries. Of course this is true only if MNC subsidiaries are centrally controlled and coordinated from the headquarters. However, the drawback is a reduction in flexibility.[35]

Operating as semi-autonomous firms, the entrepreneurial flexibility and innovation of national subsidiaries enable them to identify market needs and requirements and respond to them quickly. Since national subsidiaries operate autonomously, and most of their activities are carried out on a local basis, unlike the global firms, they are not affected by the extreme fluctuation of currency exchange rates. Among the firms that have followed this strategy are European firms such as Unilever, Philips Electronics, and Nestle.

Hybrid International Strategy

An attempt by MNCs to combine the benefits of global integration and host country focus strategies brings about a hybrid international strategy. In choosing a hybrid international strategy, the MNC intends not to be committed to the extreme positions of global integration and host country focus. Both extreme strategies have certain shortcomings. As noted, the global integration forgoes the flexibility of the host country focus, whereas the host country focus does not enjoy the economies of scale and efficiency of global integration. A hybrid international strategy aims to combine both features and, therefore, to enable the MNCs to decide each major situation based on its own merits and plan accordingly. For example, faced with a saturated market for soup in the United States, Campbell Soup is expanding abroad with locally responsive strategies. In Argentina, it offers split pea with ham, for the Chinese it has a watercress and duck-gizzard soup, and in Mexico it is selling Creama de Chile Poblano.[36] These locally developed products are supported by the vast marketing and financial resources of the headquarters office.

Compared with the clarity of the other two strategies, however, the hybrid strategy is ambiguous. It is an option when there is no clear-cut preference for either global integration or host country focus strategies. It attempts to trade off the costs and benefits of the other two strategies on a case-by-case basis, in order to maximize the overall results.[37] Some situations may call for a host country focus strategy, with limited opportunity for global integration. Other situations may allow global integration, with moderate responsiveness to host government demands. Maintaining some manufacturing and R&D facilities, and forming joint ventures with domestic firms in each country, for example, could satisfy host government demands, yet allow for corporatewide integration.

Hybrid international strategy requires the ability to respond quickly to changing situations and to shift different aspects of the operation among countries when circumstances change. If interventions by host governments create unacceptable conditions, the MNC should have the alternative of shifting its priorities between national subsidiaries. It also calls for a close working relationship between the managers of national subsidiaries and host government officials. The headquarters, therefore, has to rely on the managers of national subsidiaries and permit their involvement in major decisions. Because of their working relationships with the local community and host government officials, these managers are in the best position to assess the need for local responses.

To benefit from the global resources of the MNC, the worldwide operations should be integrated. Integration, however, requires a global perspective and specialized resources.[38] Local managers very seldom concern themselves with a global perspective. Similarly, specialized resources, such as a global marketing staff and manufacturing specialists, are more readily available at the headquarters. Therefore, a close and supportive relationship between the subsidiaries and the headquarters will improve overall corporate performance. At first, this may sound like an easy and acceptable choice. Closer scrutiny, however, reveals that it can cause problems. National subsidiaries may not be aware or willing to consider the ramifications of their recommendations on the rest of the MNC operation. Or they may reject out of hand alternatives that would enhance the overall corporate performance, but would require a sacrifice on their part. The case of ITT in the 1970s and 1980s is a classic example of the difficulties of merging the varied positions and views of dispersed subsidiaries.[39]

ITT is one of the largest suppliers of telecommunications equipment in the world. Its foreign subsidiaries traditionally operated much like independent local firms, developing and implementing their own strategies. Over the years, these subsidiaries became powerful and independent entrepreneurial firms. Most of ITT's major innovations came from these subsidiaries. These national firms insisted on tailoring products to local needs. For example, when the French subsidiary developed a highly successful telecommunications switch, the British,

Belgium, German, and Italian subsidiaries opted for a different version with many modifications. Because of the subsidiaries' insistence on producing the switches to their own specifications, integration attempts were not successful. For the same reason, the effort to standardize other products to a global design failed as well.

The emergence of digital switching technology and the deregulation of many national markets in the late 1970s challenged the strategic posture of ITT with its many autonomous national subsidiaries. The new technology required hundreds of millions of dollars for development and manufacturing. Economically, it was not feasible for national subsidiaries to develop their own local products. Global integration for designing, developing, and manufacturing the new switching equipment became a strategic imperative. While ITT's British and French subsidiaries held many original patents in digital signal processing, ITT was not successful in integrating its technological advantages. Various subsidiaries independently started to develop their own digital switches under the broad title of "System 12." The expenses of these dispersed development programs exceeded $1 billion. In the early 1980s, in response to deregulation, ITT attempted to use System 12 in the United States. The managers of the U.S. operations, however, opted to develop their own product. These scattered efforts cost ITT several hundred million dollars in R&D expenditure, and no standardized product resulted. Because of the inability to apply its leading-edge technology to the U.S. market, ITT was forced to withdraw from its home market, and eventually from direct involvement in the global market. ITT's withdrawal from direct involvement in the global telecommunications industry could be attributed to its choice of host country focus strategy, and its inability to form consensus among it national subsidiaries.

Industry Characteristics and MNC Strategy

From our discussion of generic MNC strategies one could surmise that the world market is made up of three industries: global, international, and multidomestic. Such a categorization is shown in Figure 2.3, which depicts the world market on two dimensions: product and market requirements, and operational requirements of the firm. Product requirements consist of product characteristics, such as product specifications, size, colors, shapes, tastes, functions, and features. Market characteristics are the attributes that differentiate among markets, such as distribution channels and service needs and expectations. Product and market requirements may be determined by market forces or dictated by the government. For example, most host governments would like to develop a national telecommunications industry and impose product specifications that effectively leave the industry in the hands of domestic firms and/or the autonomous subsidiaries of MNCs. Operational requirements are the factors that enable a firm to situate itself in a favorable competitive position vis-à-vis other firms. These factors include, but are not restricted to, economies of scale, investment requirements in research and development, and manufacturing facilities. The interaction between these two dimensions creates three industries: multidomestic, international, and global. Multidomestic industry has local product and market requirements and national operational requirements. Global industry is just the opposite of multidomestic industry. Global industry is characterized by worldwide product and market requirements and global operational requirements. International industry shares the worldwide product and market requirements with the global industry, and national operational requirements with multidomestic industry.

The MNCs operating in each industry need to adopt the strategy suitable for that industry. To succeed in a global industry, a global integration strategy is needed. A host country focus strategy is appropriate for multidomestic industry. Competitive advantage can be gained in international industry by using a hybrid international strategy. These three types of industries are discussed next.

Figure 2.3 Industry Characteristics

Global Industries

The theoretical concept of international expansion, as it was discussed in Chapter 1, explains the success of MNC expansion in the global market. We reiterate the major points here. We can attribute the MNCs' successes to their ability to exploit the economies of scale and experience, location, product differentiation, process technology, and the control of distribution channels. The exploitation of some of these advantages is possible only with a global integration strategy.[40] Certain technologies and products require a huge investment in R&D and manufacturing facilities. In such situations, organizational efficiency demands a large production run, and a market share on a global scale. The efficiency imperative, therefore, creates global industries. Global industries are characterized by highly centralized large-scale manufacturing and R&D operations and standardized products. The automobile, chemical, consumer electronics, heavy equipment, commercial aircraft, supercomputer, and shipbuilding industries are considered to be global.

The global operational requirement necessitates an enormous investment capital for establishing the global manufacturing and distribution network. R&D investment needs are large too. Economic imperatives have forced global industries toward globalization of their operation. Over the years, for example, successive technological innovations in consumer electronics have increased the minimum economic production run from 50,000 units per year to 3 million per year.[41] There are no national markets with an annual absorption capacity of this size. This huge increase in the size of an economic production run has made globalization a necessity. Falling transportation and communication costs, along with relatively low restrictions on imports, has also made globalization in these industries a possibility.

In these industries, because product and market requirements are worldwide, products are produced, sold, and serviced worldwide, without many variations. In other words, consumer product needs are homogeneous across markets. For these products, national and local tastes do not vary, and there is no need to customize products to national standards. Government intervention and regulation are relatively low in global industries. Therefore, firms can locate manufacturing facilities wherever in the world that provides the most economical advantages. Manufacturing facilities for automobiles and consumer electronics, for example, are established almost everywhere—in the United States, in Europe, in Latin America, and in Asia.

Theodore Levitt has argued that technology is driving all national markets toward a converging commonality.[42] A complete and total commonality of tastes and preferences may never arrive. In the global industries, however, this commonality has already taken place. The convergence of consumers' preferences and technical standards allows the production of a narrow range of standardized products for all markets from these factories. Because rationalization and integration of these manufacturing facilities that are scattered worldwide requires a strong internal control, there is no premium for partnership with local firms.[43] Local partners whose knowledge of local culture is the source of the competitive advantage in multidomestic industries have limited attraction to global firms. Therefore, global industries are dominated by MNCs that compete with each other on a global scale.

Multidomestic Industries

Multidomestic industries are characterized by local product and market requirements. National, cultural, social, and political differences lead to diverse product standards and different consumer tastes. These differences create a strong need for customized products to meet the local tastes and preferences. The operational requirements of multidomestic industries are on a national scale. Therefore, separate manufacturing facilities, to serve each national market independently, are economical. There are no economies of scale in functional areas, such as R&D and marketing, beyond the national market. This means that channels of distribution, for

example, are unique to each country, and R&D carried out in one market could not be duplicated in other markets. What a firm learns about the requirements of the construction industry in one country, for example, has little relevance for others. It also means that national subsidiaries are less dependent on the headquarters for R&D.

Since the benefits directly derived from the headquarters office are limited, the national subsidiaries behave more like domestic firms. The benefits of localization and the loose control by the headquarters over foreign subsidiaries provide opportunities for joint ventures with local firms. In fact, some have argued that partnership with local investors is frequently a preferred option in multidomestic industries.[44] Laundry detergents, cosmetics, construction, prepared food products, and furniture are examples of multidomestic industries.

The host country focus is an appropriate strategic choice for a multidomestic industry. The need to respond quickly to local standards and changes necessitates the responsiveness of a host country focus strategy. If a firm correctly identifies local preference for a particular product or products with certain features or functions, it can effectively apply the host country focus strategy to that market segment. In effect, by doing so it carves out a market segment representing domestic preferences. The example of an upstart British electronic firm is a case in point.[45] The company correctly identified the unhappiness of the English consumers with modern hi-fi equipment referred to as "music centers." The equipment had been designed to global standards, and was made to be simpler and more functional. Gone were the teak exterior and complex control panel that gave the user a feeling of technical mastery and wizardry. To the British consumers, the metal casing of the new global design, in silver or black, was no match for the old, warm, teak furniture look. Amstrad responded by bringing back the old exterior features, and combined them with modern technology high-fidelity sound delivery. It then chose the largest discount retailer for its sales outlets. The results were that Amstrad captured the market leadership from its global competitors in England.

International Industries

The dominance of technological forces and the need to develop and distribute innovations in multiple markets are characteristics of international industries. Success in this industry depends on the ability to exploit technological forces, to produce new products, and to duplicate the process in different national markets. Typically, new products are developed in the home market. Then sequentially these products and their related technologies are applied to other national markets. Since competitive advantage hinges on expensive technological development, the ability to duplicate the technology in multiple markets is an economic necessity. The imperative of the new-technology application in multiple national markets gives impetus to the emergence of international industries.

When host governments restrict the operation of a global industry and force it to produce to national standards, international industries could emerge. As Figure 2.4 illustrates, an overlap between the multidomestic and global industries characterizes international industries. When there are demands on the firm for both localization and globalization, success could come from the ability to exploit both imperatives. In the telecommunications industry, for example, both forces for globalizing and localizing are present. However, it is the ability to innovate and to adopt the innovation in national markets that differentiates the winners from the losers.[46] General Electric, Kraft, Pfizer, and Procter and Gamble are among the U.S. firms that use this strategy.

Cultural Aspects of Strategy

The central issue in strategy formulation is identification of environmental forces that may have an influence on the organization and preparation of a plan of action to deal with them. Environmental scanning should enable the firm to identify these forces. Doing this not only calls for information gathering, but also for deciding what to look for, where to look, and what to select from the multitude of information available. The process is not an objective and mechanistic activity that is free of human biases. The scanning and information gathering is a culturally based perceptual process. The external environmental assessment aspect of strategy formulation has been described by Susan Schneider as a five-step process of scanning behavior, information selection, interpretation, validation, and prioritizing. Because these steps are based on culturally programmed perception processes, country differences can be expected in each step.[47]

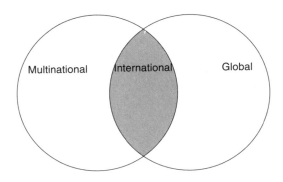

Figure 2.4 International Industries

Strategy formulation and implementation also deal with internal organizational issues that center around relationships among people, such as the place of individual and group, the hierarchy, power, and authority. In this section, we examine strategy implications of cultural differences relating to the environment and existing in relationships among people.

Relationship with the Environment

American and many other Western societies consider exploitation of nature as a desirable action. People are considered to be masters of the world. This belief leads to an engineering orientation toward nature. It means that the physical environment should conform to the design made by people. If there is any mismatch, it is the physical environment that should be changed to fit plans, and obstacles in the path are destroyed. In contrast to this proactive and engineering view, some cultures believe in a symbiotic relationship with nature. Native Americans, for example, instead of attempting to change the environment, believe in living in harmony with the surroundings, and trying to be a part of it, not apart from it. The mental framework used by an engineering-oriented person is very different from a symbiotic mentality. Each mentality leads to a different scanning behavior. An engineering-oriented person looks for data in support of change and intervention in the environment. In contrast, preference to live in harmony with the environment leads a symbiotic-oriented person to search for nondestructive alternatives.

Scanning behavior is also influenced by the belief that people are able to control the environment. The fatalist beliefs of Buddhists and the Muslims' conviction that events are predetermined limit their scanning behavior. If environmental forces are beyond the control of individuals, and if events are preordained, what is the usefulness of a strategy? This is not to say that Moslem or Buddhist businesses function with no plans or strategies. It involves the ac-

knowledgment in these cultures of the limits of human control. This is in sharp contrast to the American "can do" mentality and belief in self-determination.

Strategy formulation above all is a mental exercise and a thought process. Thinking patterns among people vary. This variation is due to cultural programming that influences perception and shapes the individual psyche. In the simpler life of preindustrial societies, people were accustomed to direct contact with objects and persons. In their thinking, they relied on *visual associations* between events and the environment. Industrial societies have grown complex and have substituted *abstract concepts* for the visual association, concrete objects, and relationships.[48] Daily life in civilized societies therefore relies more on conceptualization and abstraction. Cultures, however, vary in their methods of conceptualization and abstraction. There are cultural differences in the use of cognitive models of environment for interpretation of nature and the world. An important cognitive model that very much influences organizational life is a causation model, which is used to explain events.

Research findings suggest, for example, that there is a difference between the way Americans and Japanese perceive causation.[49] In short, the type of information that we select from our scanning process is a function of cultural upbringing. Cultural differences result in various perceptual models that are the product of our abstraction process. Synthesizing these findings, Robert Doktor suggests that the managerial practices of Japanese and Americans are due to different views of causation. A different use of brain structure and differences in cognitive models lead to two different causation maps. American thinking is shaped by Aristotelian logic that assumes an action-reaction process, the position that events occur in "response" to one or more prior events. Most Japanese use an "environmental" model of causation. They rely on the concrete data received from primary senses. They emphasize the more concrete environmental relationships such as group consensus, nation, and security.

The American cognitive model is logical, sequential, and it is based on an abstract concept of universal reality. Japanese cognition is based on concrete perception, which relies on sense data, emphasizes the particular rather than universal reality, is not abstract and has a high sensitivity to environmental context and relationships. The abstract concepts used by Americans to explain organizational behavior, such as leadership, morale, and decision making, are not well defined in the Japanese language.[50]

Western cultures, and particularly the American culture, place a high value and priority on rational, objective, and factual information in support of business decisions. Aristotelian logic used by Europeans, North Americans, and other nations assumes the existence of an "objective" truth. Errors are considered to be the source of differences. Quite often, people attempt to reach an understanding by discarding areas of disagreements and building on the areas on which they agree. Japanese, however, try to include multiple views and build on variations. This is similar to the variation between the two different images of the same object. A three-dimensional view is due to the differences between the two images. Discarding the variations between the two images results in a two-dimensional, flat object. For the Japanese the objective truth of Aristotelian logic is a foreign concept, which does not have an exact equivalence in Japanese and therefore does not make sense. The translation of the term *objectivity* into Japanese does not quite match the meaning implied by it in the English language. The Japanese translation for the foreign word *objectivity* is *kyakkanteki,* which means the guest's point of view, and subjectivity is *shukanteki,* meaning the host's point of view.[51]

We can surmise from the preceding argument that scanning behavior is a function of assumptions regarding the nature of "truth and reality."[52] It also brings to our attention that other aspects of the scanning behavior, namely, selection, interpretation, validation, and prioritization, are influenced by mental frameworks and the interpretation of our observation of environmental phenomenon. Observations of the managerial practices of other nations, for example, are interpreted using our cultural cognitive maps. Application of our cultural cognitive maps for understanding and evaluating the people of other cultures is also called a *self-reference criterion* (SRC). SRC is the unconscious reference to one's own cultural values.[53] SRC may lead us to wrong conclusions. For instance, in the past couple of decades, the success of Japanese business has lead to the study of Japanese managerial practices, in a search to find the "secret" to their achievements. Using SRC, we have erroneously interpreted the Japanese decision-making process as consensus. Because Japanese include input from different levels of the hierarchy and involve many employees in the process, their collective decision making has been labeled as reaching consensus. If consensus means reaching the same decision, then interpreting the Japanese approach as consensus decision making is incorrect. The Japanese collective decision making can best be described as the process of informing all involved about future adjustments and paybacks. The outcome of any decision will cause inconvenience for some and benefit for others. To the Japanese, the main focus of the decision-making process is for all to make a mental note of each individual's benefits and inconveniences for future adjustment. This, therefore, would call for a collective participation in the process.[54]

In the same vein, the use of SRC in the interpretation of Japanese practices has resulted in another misunderstanding. According to American cultural models, conformity implies losing uniqueness, accepting uniformity, and submission to the rule of the majority. Therefore, it is not a complement to call someone a conformist. Conformity, however, is translated into Japanese "as sharp perception of the situation, unique sense of adaptation with reality, quick orientation and reaction to cope with various situations, responding to the needs of the overall situation." "Conformity" to the Japanese, using their own standards of desirability in judging behaviors, implies something desirable because it involves understanding others and the ability to comprehend situations from their viewpoints. It seems that the Japanese sense of conformity more closely corresponds to the "flexibility" of the Americans. In contrast, the American sense of conformity implies rigidity and inability to change.[55] Along the same line, the most important function of job rotation, for the Japanese, is to make each worker think "in one another's head" and become mentally connected with others,[56] while the purpose of job rotation in America is to reduce monotony and boredom. As a side benefit, of course, job rotation is utilized to build different skills among the workers, so that they can be employed interchangeably.

Relationships Among People

Managerial functions, including strategy formulation, are based on the premise involving patterns of interpersonal relationships. It is accepted that in a business enterprise people will relate to each other in a predictable fashion. This predictability of behavior involves cultural programming such that a superior's order, and a subordinate's response, follow an expected pattern, and agreed on modes of behavior. The same is true for other relationships in the organization. Organizational hierarchies are established to deal with these relationships. The American work relationship is based on contractual arrangements, based on earnings and career opportunities.[57] An American, for example, in fulfilling his or her job responsibilities expects to receive corresponding rewards. No one is expected to make an individual sacrifice, unless other employees do the same. On that ba-

sis, strategies are formulated, and environmental opportunities are considered worthwhile to pursue, if they fit this framework.

In contrast, the Japanese firms have a larger assortment of alternatives for strategic choices. It is understood that each individual may be called on to make personal sacrifices for the benefit of the company. Such sacrifices, however, are interpreted differently. A Japanese employee's sacrifice for the sake of his company is ultimately for his or her own benefit rather than self-sacrifice. If his or her sacrifice makes the company prosper, it will be his or her gain.[58]

At the heart of the American strategic planning process is the concept of a fully functional market. The governing force of this market is pure, albeit theoretical, competition. The fairness in contractual agreements provides continuity of business transactions between the managers as employers, and employees. In effect, in this market the employee sells his or her labor for a price.[59] The strategy process and the associated scanning behaviors are bound by these rules. In contrast, the governing principle for the French organization is the honor of each class, in a society that has always been, and still is, extremely stratified. In France, "superiors behave as superior beings and subordinates accept and expect this, conscious of their own lower level in the national hierarchy but also of the honor of their own class."[60] Unlike the Americans, French consider management a "state of mind." Successful French managers share a distinctive sense of belonging to the French managerial class called *cadre*.

Most French managers come from engineering schools and see managerial work as requiring an analytical mind, independence, intellectual rigor, and the ability to synthesize information. French managers are excellent at quantitative thoughts and expression, and the numeric aspects of strategy formulation. They believe that their achievement and high position is due to their intellectual ability. Consequently, senior French managers think that their intellectual superiority entitles them to make the most critical and important decisions. Large French organizations are characterized by a centralized decision-making, hierarchical, and compartmentalized structure. Senior managers make all the important decisions, and expect to know all that happens in the firm, so they can check everyone's decisions. This hierarchical arrangement is reflected in the physical structure of the typical large French firms. Often, the chief executive's office is on the top floor, and the typing pool in the basement. Large public and private institutions hire the best students from top engineering schools, and assign them to fast-track positions. These proteges develop an informal network that exists throughout the French managerial class. The French educational system is set up such that a high proportion of the best brains from each generation is channeled into business, the civil service, and government. Such a system brings close cooperation between the French government and business. The special relationship between the French education system and business and also French cultural attributes create a unique managerial mentality. A simple way of explaining this uniqueness is to use the often-cited statement by a GM president. The French equivalent of "What is good for General Motors is good for the United States," is "What is good for France is good for Peugeot."[61]

Management literature has begun to recognize that American management theories are not universal. The strategic management process as it was described at the beginning of this chapter is the product of management theories and practices that are rooted in the American culture. Although the general framework, namely, the objective of winning in a competitive global marketplace, is universal; the methods, approaches, and orientation to it are not universal. Recognition of cultural differences in the strategy process enables MNCs to understand not only the competition, but also the orientation and attitudes of local managers of its foreign

subsidiaries. Acknowledging the influence of culture in the strategy process results in relevant and appropriate managerial practices.

Conclusion

The strategy formulation and implementation process, as suggested in this chapter, is a plan of aligning organizational goals with the environmental situations and requirements, and the attempts to achieve those goals. The difference between the strategic planning process in a domestic firm and that of an MNC is the complexity and uncertainty of the international environment. The more demanding, complex, and uncertain the situations, the more challenging the strategy process.

The additional complexity, uncertainty, and challenge of international management are due to several factors, including political and legal differences, currency exchange rate fluctuations, competition from local businesses, host government agencies and other MNCs, and the involvement of host government in business. Each of these environmental forces is the subject of a separate chapter. In this chapter we discuss the role of host governments and elaborate on the relationship between the host governments and MNCs. This relationship is portrayed as mutually beneficial and interdependent. We learned that host governments are concerned that their relationships with MNCs may lead to dependency and the loss of the sovereign power. Therefore, host governments attempt to influence the operation and strategies of MNCs so as to serve their own national priorities. Consequently, MNCs employ various methods in their government relationships. Variations among these methods are a function of industry characteristics and of the bargaining powers of the MNCs and the host governments.

The MNC strategic choices were presented in the form of three generic strategies: global, host country focus, and hybrid international. We learned that industry characteristics and host government domestic policies may determine the appropriateness of each generic strategy. For instance, a global strategy may be effective in an industry when consumer preferences and tastes do not vary across national borders, and standardized products could be sold in all markets. Also a global strategy could be effective when host government involvement in the industry is at a minimum.

Besides the differences due to environmental situations, the cultural differences among countries create additional difficulties for international managers. Although strategy is a response to environmental changes and challenges, the formulation process depends on cultural values and assumptions. Since the essence of strategy formulation is perceptual and intellectual, international managers with different cultural backgrounds approach their jobs from different mental frameworks. In this vein, there are differences between the Eastern and the Western strategy formulation process. A simple way of explaining this difference is the use of analogies. Cooking practices among Americans and Japanese reflect their differences in thinking and relating to environment. There is a tendency for Americans to adhere as precisely as possible to the recipe. People of other cultures, including the Japanese, cook more by playing with the ingredients and cooking techniques as the situations demand. The Japanese tendency for situational conformity is reflected in all aspects of life, including the work life. When a Japanese manager needs to get out of the office for a while, all he or she has to say to the staff is *"yoroshiku tanomu,"* meaning "do as you think fit." The staff would keep on working without needing any other instruction. An American counterpart usually provides specific instruction for the staff before leaving the office.[62]

process in a domestic or a multinational corporation.

2. Describe qualitative and quantitative difficulties that a firm faces as it goes international.

3. Why is there a love–hate relationship between host governments and MNCs?

4. Why have some developing countries expressed disappointment with MNCs?

5. What are a host country's major concerns when dealing with MNCs?

6. Elaborate on the argument that the relationship between a host country and an MNC is shaped by their relative bargaining powers.

7. Host countries use direct and indirect measures to influence MNC strategic and operational decisions. Give an example of each.

8. MNCs could handle host government relations in four different ways: the policy approach, the centralized approach, the diffuse approach, and the coordinated approach. Briefly describe each approach.

9. In their competition with domestic firms, MNCs may enjoy a superior position. What are the sources of their superiority?

10. Under what conditions could a global integration strategy be effective?

11. What are the differences between a hybrid international strategy and a host country focus strategy?

12. Describe the strategy implications of cultural differences.

13. How could the use of our cultural cognitive maps mislead us in judging other peoples' actions and decisions?

14. The American concept of the strategy formulation process is anchored around the concept of a fully functioning "market" that governs employee–employer relationship. Is this the same in other countries?

Discussion Questions

1. Explain why there are no substantive differences between the strategic planning

Endnotes

1. H. I. Ansoff and E. McDonnell. *Implanting Strategic Management* (New York: Prentice Hall, 1990), 13.

2. Ibid., 14.

3. K. Fatehi and F. Derakhshan. "Appropriate Technology, Appropriate Management and International Trade: An Integrative Proposal." *Approtech*, 5 (1982), 19–22.

4. P. Wright. "MNC-Third World Business Unit Performance: Application of Strategic Elements." *Strategic Management Journal*, 5 (1984), pp. 231–40.

5. Y. L. Doz. "Government Policies and Global Industries." In M. E. Porter, ed. *Competition in Global Industries* (Boston, MA: Harvard Business School Press, 1986), 237.

6. Ibid., 232.

7. Ibid., 232.

8. A. Mahini. *Making Decisions in Multinational Corporations* (New York: John Wiley and Sons, 1988), 4.

9. J. Tanner, "Venezuela Now Woos Oil Firms It Booted in '70s Nationalization." *The Wall Street Journal* (October 2, 1991), p. 1.

10. D. J. Encarnation and L. T. Wells, Jr. "Competitive Strategies in Global Industries: A View from Host Governments." In M. E. Porter, ed. *Competition in Global Industries*, 267–90.

11. Ibid., 269–70.

12. Ibid., 270.

13. D. F. Vagts, "The Host Country Faces the Multinational Enterprise," *Boston University Law Review*, 53, no. 2 (1973), 261–77.

14. C. Y. Bladwin, "The Capital Factor: Competing for Capital in a Global Environment." In M. E. Porter, ed. *Competition in Global Industries*. 185–223.

15. Encarnation and Wells, "Competitive Strategies," pp. 277–8.

16. A. Mahini and L. T. Wells, Jr., "Government Relations in the Global Firm." In M. E. Porter, ed. *Competition in Global Industries*. 291–312.

17. Ibid., 291–312.

18. J. M. Grieco, "Between Dependence and Autonomy: India's Experience with the International Computer Industry." *International Organization* (Summer 1982), 36.

19. Mahini and Wells. "Government Relations," 303.

20. Ibid., 298.

21. Ibid., 299.

22. Ibid., 299.

23. J. Cole and S. Lubman. "Bombs Away." *The Wall Street Journal* (January 28, 1994), A1, A4–A5.

24. Y. Doz. *Strategic Management in Multinational Companies* (Oxford, UK: Pergamon Press, 1987), 93.

25. Ibid., 94.

26. Ibid., 103.

27. Ibid., 105–6.

28. Ibid., 95.

29. K. Labrich. "Airbus Takes Off." *Fortune* (June 1992), 102–8.

30. A. Borrus, J. Carey, and K. L. Miller. "How Clinton Will Deal with Japan." *Business Week* (January 18, 1993), 42–43.

31. K. Pope, "Sematech Claims Major Advance by Halving Size of Chip Circuits." *The Wall Street Journal* (January 22, 1993), Sec. B, p. 6.

32. Doz, *Strategic Management*, 12–13.

33. C. A. Bartlett and S. Ghoshal, *Transnational Management* (Homewood, IL: Richard D. Irwin, 1992), 286.

34. Doz. *Strategic Management*, 16–17.

35. Ibid., 16–17.

36. P. Engardio and J. Weber. "Campbell: How It's M-M-Global." *Business Week* (March 15, 1993), 52–54.

37. Doz. *Strategic Management*. 214.

38. Ibid., 214.

39. C. A. Bartlett and S. Ghoshal. *Managing Across Borders*. (Boston, MA: Harvard University Press, 1991), 10–12.

40. Doz. *Strategic Management*. 19.

41. Bartlett and Ghoshal. *Transnational Management*. 116.

42. T. Levitt. "The Globalization of Markets." *Harvard Business Review* (May/June 1983), 92–102.

43. F. J. Contractor. "Contractual and Cooperative Forms of International Business: Towards a Unified Theory of Modal Choice." *Management International Review*, 30, no. 1 (1990), 31–54.

44. Ibid., 31–54.

45. Bartlett and Ghoshal. *Transnational Management*. 113.

46. Ibid., 117.

47. S. C. Schneider, "Strategy Formulation: The Impact of National Culture," *Organizational Studies*, 10, no. 2 (1989), 149–68.

48. E. J. Kolde. *Environment of International Business* (Boston, MA: PWS-Kent Publishing Company, 1985), 423.

49. H. Nakamura. *Ways of Thinking of Eastern People* (Honolulu, HI: East-West Center Press, 1964). T. Tusunoda. "The Differences of Recognition Mechanism Toward Natural Sounds Between Japanese and Westerners." *Medicine and Biology*, 88, (1975), 309–14.

50. R. Doktor. "Some Tentative Comments on Japanese and American Decision Making." *Decision Sciences*, 14, no. 4 (1983), 607–15.

51. M. Maruyama. "Alternative Concepts of Management: Insights from Asia and Africa." *Asia Pacific Journal of Management* (January 1984), 102.

52. Schneider. "Strategy Formulation." 156.

53. J. A. Lee. "Cultural Analysis in Overseas Operations." *Harvard Business Review* (March/April 1966), 106–14.

54. Maruyama. "Alternative Concepts." 100–11.

55. Ibid., 109.

56. Ibid., 103.

57. G. Hofstede. "Cultural Constraints in Management." *Academy of Management Executive,* 7, no. 1 (1993), 81–94.

58. Maruyama. "Alternative Concepts." 104.

59. Hofstede. "Cultural Constraints." 81–94.

60. Ibid., p. 84.

61. J. Bardoux and P. Lawrence, "The Making of a French Manager." *Harvard Business Review* (July/August 1991), 58–67.

62. R. Iwata. *Japanese-Style Management: Its Foundations and Prospects* (Tokyo: Asian Productivity Organization, 1982), 23–24.

MINSEARCH (A)

BRIAN LEGGETT AND ALAN WATSON

In his office on the outskirts of Charn, Narnia (a country in the Middle-East), Keith Ellerman, MinSearch's general manager, put down the letter that the Deputy Ministry messenger had delivered a few minutes earlier and looked out of the window. His sources at the Deputy Ministry of Mineral Resources had warned him that the Finance Ministry people were taking a lot of interest in the contract arrangements that the Deputy Ministry had with MinSearch. However, he hadn't really expected THIS!.

The letter was signed by the Deputy Minister and read as follows:

Dear Keith,

The Minister of Finance has recently informed me that, with effect from the beginning of next year, they want to change the basis for awarding the contract which the Deputy Ministry of Mineral Resources has with your company from the present discretionary award system to one in which the contracts will be awarded to the lowest cost bidder in an open

Case of the Research Department at Institute de Estudios Superiors de la Empiesa. This case was prepared by Professor Brian Leggett and Alan Watson, MBA 1988, June 1988. It is intended to be used as a basis for class discussion rather than to illustrate either effective or ineffective handling of an administrative situation. Copyright © 1988, by IESE. No part of this publication may be reproduced without the written permission of IESE.

tender. I am not entirely in favour of the new idea but I can see the Ministry of Finance's point of view. There will be a prequalifying stage to the bidding process and, of course, I will invite MinSearch to take part in it.

We will need your assistance to draw up the specifications for the coming contract and my Technical Adviser will be visiting you shortly to begin outlining the work program that will need to be carried out by the successful tenderer.

I am sure you will give this matter your most urgent attention.

Osman Sudairy

"Open tendering with the contract going to the lowest bidder—what a crazy idea for a mineral exploration program!" Keith was sure that this would set back the mineral resource assessment of Narnia by years. If contracts were awarded on the lowest price basis, then the quality of the mineral resource assessment being carried out in the country was sure to plummet. Some fly-by-night company would hire a bunch of second-rate geologists, put in a really low bid and win the contract! They would then achieve exactly nothing during the five-year span of the contract.

He had to convince the Deputy Minister that the Finance Ministry move should be rebuffed. He had to act quickly—there was a meeting of the Council of Ministers in two days' time in

Charn. He would write a letter to the Deputy Minister stating as clearly and persuasively as possible the case AGAINST the open tender idea and FOR the retention of the present system of discretionary awarding of contracts.

Keith Ellerman phoned the Deputy-Minister on receiving this letter and on being informed that Mr Sudairy was engaged elsewhere decided to write to him.

MINSEARCH

Date

Address

Your Excellency,

Thank you for your recent letter in which you informed me of the Ministry of Finance's plans to change the basis on which MinSearch's contract is awarded.

As always, MinSearch's resources are at your disposal to help you and your staff resolve this difficult matter satisfactorily.

Your Excellency will of course be aware that I regard the Ministry of Finance's proposal to use a "lowest price" system with extreme misgivings.

I have no doubt that the Ministry of Finance have done a superficial cost-benefit analysis when examining the situation and have concluded that since MinSearch has not found any major mineral deposits in 10 years we have somehow been deficient in carrying out our contract. The Ministry of Finance are very wrong to think that mineral resource asssessment contracts can be treated in a similar fashion to those used for infrastructure projects such as roads and airports. MinSearch's work is complicated and long-term in nature. Success in mineral resource assessment cannot be measured by the same criteria used for the majority of the contracts with which the Ministry of Finance is familiar.

The nature of mineral resource assessment is such that nobody who truly understands the situation would entrust the task to any company with less than a top class reputation in the field. Your Excellency will recall that a first-class record in its dealings with developing countries was the reason why MinWorld, our parent company, was invited 10 years ago by the Minister of Petroleum and Mineral Resources to form MinSearch and begin the mineral resource assessment of Narnia.

As your Excellency knows, MinSearch has taken a very vigorous approach to its work. Our teams of geoscientists have accumulated sufficient knowledge to be able to identify the areas of the country which have the greatest potential for yielding minerals in economic quantities. We are confident that we have done a good job in the past and we feel that if we are allowed to continue we will maintain our high standards.

I realise that you will have great difficulty persuading the Ministry of Finance not to go to lowest price bidding for MinSearch's contract. May I suggest that the Narnian Government request a reputable outside organization such as the World Bank to assign a team of consultants to assess the quality of MinSearch's work in the past and to provide independent recommendations for how the mineral resource assessment contract should be awarded.

Assuring you of my continued loyalty.

signed-Keith Ellerman
MinSearch General Manager

The letter was delivered by hand that afternoon. However, when no reply was received within the next five or six days, Keith Ellerman phoned the Deputy-Minister's office. He was informed by a secretary that the letter had been received, but that Mr Sudairy was heavily engaged at the time-being. The following morning, a letter was delivered to the MinSearch office.

Ministry of Mineral Resource

Date

Address

Dear Mr Ellerman,

Your recent letter regarding the mineral contract has been received. Your comments seem most practical and are receiving our attention.

Yours sincerely,

Osman Sudairy.

Time passed and as Keith Ellerman had received just the two-line reply to his letter, his anxiety began to mount. It was at this point that he decided to fly to London to seek the advice of his colleagues at MinWorld. "Perhaps", he thought, "some other channel of communicating with the ministry could be found through the Consular service or other such channel in London".

It was quite by accident that on the plane to London he fell into conversation with an American who was also living in Charn. The conversation soon turned to business, and Ellerman in his frustration told the American about the high possibility of losing the contract with the DMMR.

The American, an engineer with a multinational corporation, understood Ellerman's plight exactly, and referred him to various articles which explained the cultural differences between Islamic and western mentalities. He showed him one such article from the HBR, that had been written on the subject of doing business in Islamic countries. Ellerman glanced through it and his attention was caught by the following piece:

The American neophyte dealing with an Islamic government and business community soon learns that formal enquires, letters, office memos, contracts, and other business are given life only after understanding has been reached and goodwill achieved—and agreement sealed with a handshake. Whatever precise formal arrangements have been worked out, the relationship between the parties determines the success or the failure of any undertaking.

A fundamental goal in these relationships is to develop friendly alliances inside and outside the business organisation. Particularly important to business undertakings is the establishment of ties with government officials, the business community, and the company's bankers.[1]

The American pointed out that these were differences and that one way of life was not necessarily superior to the other; people have to tackle their problems the best way they can within the environment in which they find themselves. "We all have to adapt ourselves to the situation in which we find ourselves," he said. Ellerman did not reply as he basically believed the Anglo-Saxon way of life to be superior to all others. The material progress of the West was sufficient evidence for him.

During this period in Narnia, government officials were by and large educated in the West. Many of these had attained a high academic distinction, but now lacked individual practical experience, especially in the technological areas. In order to overcome this situation, many technical advisers depended on the assistance of technical experts from the established multinational corporations. This help was mainly in drawing up specifications and ensuring that the resultant work met these requirements. Specifications were drawn up normally to meet very high standards, which had the great advantage of eliminating the fly-by-night companies.

The American explained to Ellerman that he knew of situations where the government technical adviser worked closely with the corporation expert in drawing up the specifications, advertising, and adjudicating the tenders. Usually in these cases the contact remained with the corporation whose technical expert worked with the government technical adviser. For the government, this ensured that the high specifications were met at a reasonable cost. For the company, it ensured the continuation of the contract.

Ellerman reported this conversation to his colleagues in London, who thought that he

---

[1] Peter Wright. "Doing Business in Islamic Markets," *Harvard Business Review* (Jan.–Feb. 1981), 34.

should take whatever steps necessary to maintain the contract. Ellerman himself thought the whole idea wrong. His company's future would depend more on the friendship between himself and the technical adviser, than on its professionalism. This was like saying that his ability to behave in a manner socially acceptable to the Narnians was more important than his talents and capabilities.

On returning to Charn, Ellerman received a call from the technical adviser, and a meeting was arranged. The technical advisor indicated during his call that the Ministry had taken a poor view of Ellerman's letter but had decided to call the meeting in which Ellerman would be given an opportunity to forward his proposal formally. The Junior Minister, a senior civil servant from the Department of Finance, two technical experts from the DMMR, and the technical advisor would attend this meeting.

Exercise: Draft a persuasive presentation based on the information given, with special attention to Ellerman's previous attitude.

Exhibit 1
Minsearch (A)

The Country

This episode took place in Charn, Narnia, in 1985. Narnia was nearing the end of an unprecedented 10 year economic boom fuelled by oil revenues.

During the previous decade, Narnia had reaped vast rewards as a result of OPEC's crude oil price increases. This wealth had been controlled by the Narnian royal family. Since oil revenues made up most of the Gross National Product of Narnia at that time, the royal family, through the government ministries, effectively controlled the national economy. Members of the royal family and their ministers accumulated vast wealth at this time. The stability of their regime was due to their ability to:

1. Satisfy the material needs of the average Narnian (through adoption of Western living styles, industrialisation, and an excellent social security system);
2. Pacify the moderate religious leaders by ensuring that much of the country's income was spent on Islamic works. Narnia's leaders went to great lengths to show that theirs was an Islamic country "par excellence". They frequently acknowledged their duty to protect the Holy Cities of Islam—Mecca and Medina—and spent much money to improve the conditions of the pilgrims who come from all over the Moslem world to perform the Hajj.
3. Ruthlessly control any attempted insurrections by opposition groups. The army was well equipped, well paid, and was controlled by members of the inner royal family.

At the time the case takes place, Narnia was being buffeted on two main fronts:

1. The dramatic drop in the price of crude oil had reached such proportions that the country, long considered one of the most wealthy in the world, was in serious danger of running a budget deficit for the first time in its history;
2. The Iran-Iraq war was having an unsettling influence on certain Moslem sects within Narnia.

Mineral Exploration in Narnia

As part of a policy of diversifying the country's industrial base away from dependence on oil, the Narnian government had established the Deputy Ministry of Mineral Resources (DMMR). DMMR's brief was to make an inventory of the country's mineral resources.

Such a task is a daunting one in any country. In a large and sparsely populated country like Narnia with little history of organized mineral exploration, this is a monumental job.

DMMR had resorted to a response typical of any developing country when faced with a similar problem. In the early 1960s DMMR had entered into long term agreements with specialist organizations affiliated to foreign governments.

The United States Geological Survey (USGS) and the French Bureau de Recherches Geologiques et Minières (BRGM) had been given the task of unravelling the geological history of the country. Both these organizations had been mapping the country for 20 years. Scientific understanding of the geology was on a firm base. By the mid-1970s, mineral provinces (areas where economic mineral deposits were likely to be found) were more or less defined. However, neither USGS not BRGM was greatly skilled in the demanding work of actually locating and assessing mineral deposits. Faced with this situation, and knowing that no Western private mining company was willing to use its own money to explore for minerals in Narnia due to the high cost of working in the country, the (still) poorly developed infrastructure, generally difficult working conditions, and doubts over political stability, the DMMR decided to invite MinWorld to take up a contract to assess the mineral resource potential of the country.

MinWorld was one of the world's largest mining companies and had an unparalleled record in developing countires for assessing mineral deposits. MinWorld was able to call on a formidable array of technical experts with experience of many types of mineral deposit in virtually all parts of the world. After a period of negotiations, MinWorld and DMMR came to agreement over the terms of a contract whereby MinSearch, a company created by MinWorld, would carry out mineral resource evaluation work within Narnia. In common with many contracts of this type in Narnia, the MinSearch contract ran for renewable five year periods in phase with the five year development plans which were used by the Narnian government. The contract terms were flexible with regard to work program content.

The DMMR Technical Adviser and his team of expatriate experts kept a close watch on the progress of MinSearch's work. MinWorld earned a handsome management fee from DMMR from the contract.

Minsearch

From the beginning of their first contract, MinSearch's managers had taken their work very seriously. Top class staff had been hired and extensive use was made of MinWorld's experience in geologically and climatically similar terrain in other parts of the world. The latest technology in mineral exploration and the best available consultants were used.

MinSearch's offices, workshops and residential quarters were in a walled compound on the outskirts of Charn. Fieldwork was carried out by well-equipped teams of geologists and technical support staff from mobile camps spread throughout the country. MinSearch staff had an uncompromising attitude towards their work. Senior managers were consistent in devoting the maximum amount of available funds to the task of searching for economic mineral deposits. Unlike the other organizations contracted by DMMR, MinSearch had avoided being tainted with rumours of mis-direction of funds.

At the peak of its activities in 1980, MinSearch employed about 400 people. Virtually all the senior managerial and scientific staff were either British or Australian. Narnians occupied several administrative posts, some of which, like the liaison function with the Deputy Ministry, were very important. The scarcity of Narnians in the higher echelons of MinSearch was mainly due to the fact that there were very few Narnian geologists with adequate training and experience. MinSearch had initiated an ambitious training programme for young Narnian geologists. This included further academic training periods at universities in U.K. and on-the-job training on field projects in Narnia. Unfortunately, several of the trainees did not feel comfortable with the hard-driving, professional attitudes of the expatriate geologists and they left the programme. However, a core of live young Narnian geologists was developing very satistactorily and they were looked upon as being capable, in a few years time, of taking charge of mineral exploration projects.

Despite MinSearch's very professional and aggressive attitude towards mineral resource assessment, it had been unsuccessful in discovering any large mineral deposits. Several mineral deposits of a promising nature had been discovered, but to prove or disprove the economic viability of such deposits would take at least two more years. Such time spans were not unusual for mineral deposit assessment and it was actually quicker than might be expected in a developing country such as Narnia.

MinSearch had coped with an earlier crisis, when the Narnians, worried about the seemingly slow progress that MinSearch was making, employed a firm of consultants to assess MinSearch's work. The consultants' final report had highly commended MinSearch for their exemplary work and recommended that the Narnians maintain their contract.

The Crunch!

The Deputy Ministry had recently informed MinSearch's management that funds for the coming year would be cut and that their mineral exploration contract arrangement was being examined by the Ministry of Finance.

MinSearch had been expecting budget cuts. The Narnian state budget expenditure was directly linked to the oil price and this had dropped in recent years from over $30 per barrel to less than $20 per barrel. The price showed no sign of stabilizing.

Re-definition of the contract terms was a different and potentially more serious matter. The present system of a gentlemen's agreement between DMMR and MinSearch brought benefits for both Narnia and MinWorld. In return for handsome management fees for MinWorld, MinSearch carried out top class mineral deposit investigation.

If MinSearch's mineral exploration contract were put out to open tender next year, both sides would lose. MinWorld would lose a very useful foothold in the Middle East as well as the hefty management fees which it earned from the contract. If DMMR signed a contract with the lowest bidder in an open tender process, the mineral exploration effort in the country would be very seriously delayed since it was very likely that the contract winner would be technically deficient.

MinSearch's Communication Practice

Over the previous ten years Keith Ellerman had submitted quarterly reports on the company's activities to the Ministry. In these formal reports he explained operation procedures and some technical matters concerning mining. Otherwise, reporting was restricted to the DMMR's technical advisor, who reported directly to the deputy-minister. Ellerman's communication policy could be summed up as follows:

(i) Organizing periodic visits to operation sites for Ministry officials;
(ii) Restricting reporting to explanation of current plans and technical matters; and
(iii) Creating an image of seriousness in order to create trust and confidence in the company.

LARSON INCORPORATED

ISAIAH A. LITVAK

David Larson, vice-president of international operations for Larson Inc., was mulling over the decisions he was required to make regarding the company's Nigerian operation. He was disturbed by the negative tone of the report sent to him on January 4, 1979 by the chief executive officer of the Nigerian affiliate, George Ridley (see Exhibit 1). Larson believed the future prospects for Nigeria were excellent and was concerned about the action he should take.

Company Background

Larson Inc. was a Montreal-based multinational corporation in the wire and cable business. Wholly owned subsidiaries were located in the United States and United Kingdom, while Mexico, Venezuela, Australia, and Nigeria were the sites of joint ventures. Other countries around the world were serviced through exports from the parent or one of its subsidiaries.

The parent company was established in 1925 by David Larson's grandfather. Ownership and management of the company remained in the hands of the Larson family and was highly centralized. The annual sales volume for the corporation worldwide approximated $575 million in 1978. Revenue was primarily generated from the sale of power, communication, construction, and control cables. Technical service was an important part of Larson Inc.'s product package, so the company maintained a large force of engineers to consult with customers and occasionally supervise installation.

The Nigerian Operation

Larson Inc. established a joint venture in Nigeria in 1974 with a local partner who held 25

Reprinted with permission of Isaiah A. Litvak, York University.

percent of the joint venture's equity. In 1978 Larson Inc. promised Nigerian authorities that the share of local ownership would be increased to 51 percent within five to seven years.

Sales revenue for the Nigerian firm totalled $28 million in Canadian funds in 1978. Of this revenue, $24.5 million was realized in Nigeria, while $3.5 million was from exports. About 40 percent of the firm's Nigerian sales ($10 million) were made to various enterprises and departments of the government of Nigeria. The company was making a reasonable profit of 10 percent of revenue, but with a little bit of luck and increased efficiency, it was believed it could make a profit of 20 percent.

The Nigerian operation had become less attractive for Larson Inc. in recent months. Although it was believed that Nigeria should become one of the key economic players in Africa in the 1980s and that the demand for Larson's products would remain very strong there, doing business in Nigeria was growing more costly. Furthermore, Larson Inc. was becoming increasingly unhappy with its local partner in Nigeria, a lawyer who was solely concerned with quick "pay-backs" at the expense of reinvestment and long-term growth prospects.

David Larson recognized that having the right partner in a joint venture was of paramount importance. The company expected the partner or partners to be actively engaged in the business, "not businessmen interested in investing money alone." The partner was expected to hold a substantial equity in the venture. In the early years of a joint venture, additional funding was often required, and thus it was necessary for the foreign partner to be in a strong financial position.

The disillusionment of George Ridley, the Nigerian firm's CEO, had been increasing since his early days in that position. He was an expatriate from the United Kingdom who, due to his background as a military officer, placed a high value upon order and control. The chaotic situation in Nigeria proved very trying for him. His problems were further complicated by his inability to attract good local employees in Nigeria, while his best expatriate staff requested transfers to Montreal or Larson Inc.'s other foreign operations soon after their arrival in Nigeria. On a number of occasions Ridley was prompted to suggest to head office that it reconsider its Nigerian commitment.

David Larson reflected on the situation. He remained convinced that Larson Inc. should maintain its operations in Nigeria; however, he had to design a plan to increase local Nigerian equity in the venture to 51 percent. Larson wondered what should be done about Ridley. On the one hand, Ridley had been with the company for many years and knew the business intimately; on the other hand, Larson felt that Ridley's attitude was contributing to the poor morale in the Nigerian firm. Larson knew Ridley had to be replaced, but he was unsure about the timing and the method to use, since Ridley was only two years away from retirement.

Larson had to come to some conclusions fairly quickly. He had been requested to prepare a plan of action for the Nigerian operation for consideration by the board of directors of Larson Inc. in one month's time. He thought he should start by identifying the key questions, whom he should contact, and how he should handle Ridley in the meantime.

Exhibit 1
The Ridley Report

In response to the request from head office for a detailed overview of the Nigerian situation and its implications for Larson Inc., the following report was prepared. This report will attempt to itemize the factors in the Nigerian environment that have contributed to the problems experienced by Larson Inc.'s joint venture in Nigeria.

The Nigerian Enterprises Promotion Decrees

1. There can be no doubt that the Nigerian Enterprises Promotion Decree of 1977 represents very severe and far-reaching indigenization legislation. The cumulative damaging effects of the decree have been exacerbated by some aspects of its implementation. In particular the valuation of companies by the Nigerian Securities and Exchange Committee has in many cases been unrealistically low. This has represented substantial real-capital asset losses to the overseas companies concerned, which have had no opportunity of appeal to an independent authority. This unsatisfactory aspect has been made worse by the difficulties and delays experienced by many companies in obtaining foreign currency for the remittance of proceeds from the sale of shares. A disquieting feature has been the enforced imposition, in certain cases, of a requirement to issue new equity in Nigeria instead of selling existing shares with the consequent ineligibility to remit even part of the proceeds from Nigeria and a dilution of value to both Nigerian and foreign shareholders. Another aspect causing great concern is related to the time constraint for compliance, particularly as the Nigerian authorities concerned appear to be literally snowed under with applications. There is also doubt as to the continuing ability of the market to absorb the very large amount of equity that must inevitably be offered for sale within a period of a few months.

Remittances

2. In addition to the problems of remittances of the proceeds from the sale of shares under the 1977 decree, there has been a steadily increasing delay in the granting of foreign exchange for remittances from Nigeria, such as payment for supplies and services from overseas. Whereas early this year delays of about three months

were being reported, delays of up to eight months or even more are now not unusual. Larson Nigeria cannot continue to operate effectively if it is unable to remit proceeds and pay bills in a reasonable time frame. It is in the position of importing $5.5 million (Can.) in products and services annually. These delays in remittances, coupled with delays in payments (see paragraph 4(a) below), also raise problems related to export guarantees, which normally are of limited duration only.

3. A problem regarding remittances has arisen as a result of the Nigerian Insurance Decree No. 59, under which cargoes due for import to Nigeria have to be insured with a Nigerian-registered insurance company. Though claims related to cargo loss and damage are paid in Nigeria, foreign exchange for remittance to pay the overseas supplier is not being granted on the grounds that the goods have not arrived.

Problems Affecting Liquidity and Cash Flow

4. A number of problems have arisen during the last two years or so that are having a serious effect upon liquidity and cash flow, with the result that local expenses can only be met by increasing bank borrowing, which is not only additional cost but also becoming more difficult to obtain. These problems include:

(a) Serious delays in obtaining payment from federal and state government departments for supplies and services provided, even in instances where payment terms are clearly written into the contract concerned. This is particularly true for state governments where payment of many accounts is twelve months or more in arrears. Even when paid, further delays are experienced in obtaining foreign currency for the part that is remittable abroad. This deterioration in cash flow from government clients has in turn permeated through to the private clients.

(b) The 1978 federal budget measures, whereby companies are required to pay tax in ad-

vance of auditied accounts, with the result that over a period of about twelve months Larson Nigeria is faced with paying virtually two years' tax.

(c) The requirement for 100 percent deposit on application for some Letters of Credit.

(d) The fairly recent requirement by the Nigerian Port Authorities for the payment of 50 percent of customs duty before a ship is even permitted to berth.

Incomes and Prices Policy Guidelines

5. Many of the guidelines issued by the Productivity. Prices and Incomes Board are a direct discouragement, as they make operations in Nigeria increasingly less attractive in comparison with other areas in the world. Among these guidelines are:

(a) Continued restrictions on wage and salary increases, fees for professional services, audit fees, etc.

(b) Unrealistic restrictions on price mark-up for many imported goods. The permitted mark-up of 25 percent is totally inadequate to meet the very high operating costs in Nigeria and to provide good sales and after-sales service.

Dividends

6. While Larson Inc. welcomed the raising of the level of dividend restriction from 30 percent gross ($16^1/2$ percent net) to 40 percent gross (20 percent net) of issued capital, the exclusion of scrip/bonus issues post October 1, 1976 is still a matter of concern where profits that would otherwise have been available for remittance have been reinvested. It seems inequitable that investors, both indigenous and foreign, should not receive a return on this reinvestment. Furthermore, it results in an artificial dilution of share value for both indigenous and overseas shareholders.

7. The regulations regarding interim dividends are also a matter of concern. The require-

ment to pay advance income tax on such dividends prior to the due date for payment of tax on the full year's income is unreasonable, and the rule under which remittance to overseas shareholders have to await final account is discriminatory.

Offshore Technical and Management Services

8. Restrictions on the reimbursement of expenses to the parent company for offshore management and technical services are a cause of great concern, since such services are costly to provide.

Professional Fees

9. The whole position regarding fees for professional services provided from overseas is most unsatisfactory. Not only are the federal government scales substantially lower than in most other countries, but the basis of the project cost applied in Nigeria is out of keeping with normally accepted international practice. The arbitrary restriction on the percentage of fees that may be remitted is a further disincentive to attracting professional services. Moreover, payment of professional fees in themselves produce cash flow problems exacerbated by long delays in payments and remittance approvals (referred to above).

Royalties and Trade Marks

10. The Nigerian government's apparent unpreparedness to permit payment of royalties for the use of trade marks for a period of more than ten years is out of keeping with the generally accepted international practice.

Expatriate Quotas, Work Permits, and Entry Visas

11. It must be recognized that expatriate expertise is a very important element for this business, but expatriate staff is very costly.

Unfortunately, at the present time there are a number of difficulties and frustrations, such as the arbitrary cuts in expatriate quotas at very short notice and the delays in obtaining, and in some cases the refusal of, entry visas and work permits for individuals required for work in Nigeria.

Expatriate Staff

12. In general the conditions of employment and life in Nigeria are regarded as unattractive as compared with many other countries competing for the same expertise. This is due partly to the general deterioration in law and order, to the restrictions on salary increases, to the restrictions placed on home remittances, to the unsatisfactory state of public utilities such as electricity, water and telecommunications, and to general frustrations related to visas and work permits, mentioned above. The situation has now reached a stage where not only is recruitment of suitably qualified skilled experts becoming increasingly difficult, but we are also faced with resignations and refusals to renew contracts even by individuals who have worked and lived here for some years. Furthermore, the uncertainty over the length of time for which employment in Nigeria will be available due to doubts whether the necessary expatriate quotas will continue to be available to the employer is most unsettling to existing staff. This and the restriction of contracts to as little time as two years are important factors in deterring the more highly qualified applicants from considering posts in Nigeria. This is resulting in a decline in the quality of expatriate staff it is possible to recruit.

Public Utilities

13. The constant interruption in public utility services not only affects the morale of all employees, it has a very serious impact upon the operation of the business itself. Unless reason-

able and continuing supplies of electricity, water, and telecommunications can be assured, the costs related to setting up and operating escalate.

Continuity of Operating Conditions

14. The general and growing feeling of uncertainty about the continuity of operating conditions is a matter of considerable concern. It would seem that this uncertainty is engendered by a whole range of matters related to short-notice changes (sometimes even retrospective) in legislation and regulations: imprecise definition of legislation and regulations, which lead to long periods of negotiation and uncertainty; delays between public announcement of measures and promulgation of how they are to be implemented; and sometimes, inconsistent interpretation of legislation and regulations by Nigerian officials.

Bribery

15. Surrounding many of the problems previously listed is the pervasive practice of bribery, known locally as the "dash." Without such a payment, it is very difficult to complete business or government transactions with native Nigerians.

T H R E E

ORGANIZATION OF MULTINATIONAL OPERATIONS

In Chapter 3 we present the various organizational structures of MNCs and we will learn that many factors influence an MNC's selection of the proper organizational structure. Some of these factors are external forces and demands. Among the external forces that could determine an MNC's choice of structure are economic conditions at home and abroad, host government policies, product-market characteristics, and information technology. Factors that are related to the firm itself are the history of the company, top management philosophy, nationality, corporate strategy, and the degree of internationalization. We first discuss the development of an organizational structure designed to deal with the export of products to foreign markets. The subsequent major structural designs for MNCs including the autonomous foreign subsidiary, the international division, geographic and product divisions, and the matrix structure are explained in this chapter.

Asea-Brown Boveri (ABB) is a global electronic equipment giant that is bigger than Westinghouse and could challenge General Electric in a head-to-head competition. It is a world leader in high-speed trains, robotics, and environmental control. ABB was created by merging Asea, a Swedish engineering group, to Brown Boveri, a Swiss competitor, and adding on more than 70 other companies in Europe and the United States, with joint ventures in South Korea and Taiwan. The architect of this global organization is Percy Barnevik, a Swede who has created the most successful cross-border merger since Royal Dutch Petroleum was linked to England's Shell in 1907. IBM sought

his help in reducing its own overstaffed bureaucracy, and Du Pont put him on its board of directors.

ABB became very efficient by getting rid of excess capacity and eliminating duplication and reducing waste. It cut more than one in five jobs, closed dozens of factories, and decimated headquarters staffs throughout Europe and the United States. There are only 13 executives at the headquarters in Zurich, making up the executive committee. The committee consists of Americans, Germans, Swedes, and Swiss managers. Since there is no common first language, they speak only English. The executive committee is responsible for ABB's global strategy and performance. More than fifty business area managers report to the executive committee.

To leverage its core technologies and global economies of scale without sacrificing local responsiveness, ABB is using a loose, decentralized version of the matrix organizational structure. ABB is organized along a matrix system of 50 or so business areas (BAs) which are grouped into eight business segments. A member of the executive committee is responsible for each business segment. An example of a business segment is a group of five BAs that sells components, systems, and software to firms for automating their industrial processes. This business segment includes metallurgy, drives, and process engineering, and is headed by a German board member whose office is in Stamford, Connecticut.

BA managers devise strategies to optimize the business areas globally. They are responsible for cost and quality standards, allocation of export markets to factories that are located around the world, and the sharing of expertise by rotating people across borders. National managers, who are responsible for local firms within national borders, report to BA managers. Most of the national managers are host country citizens. The local companies act as national firms, and have their own boards including eminent outsiders, presidents, financial reporting, and career ladders for employee advancement. They are very much like any other national corporation. In other words they are local companies that are responsive to local demands and needs. The managers of local firms have a global boss, the BA manager, who sets the overall framework for the operation of the BA. They also report to the country manager, who coordinates the activities of national firms.

ABB has 1,100 of these local firms around the world. This allows ABB to run each operation locally with intense global coordination. Simply put, ABB is running a successful model of "multidomestic" structure. The power transformer BA, for example, has 25 factories in 16 countries, and its leader is a Swede who is stationed in Mannheim, Germany. Each BA leader is responsible for the global performance of a business, and supervises the operations and manufacturing facilities spread all over the world.

Sources: "Asea-Brown Boveri: Generating New Hope for Europe." *Multinational Business* (1987), no. 4, 35–37; C. Rappoport. "A Tough Swede Invades the U.S." *Fortune,* (June 1992), 77–79; W. Taylor. "The Logic of Global Business: An Interview With ABB's Percy Barnevik." *Harvard Business Review* (March/April 1991), 91–105; "Asea-Brown Boveri." *The Economist* (May 28, 1988), 19–22; "Asea-Brown Boveri Union Underscores Industry's Move Toward Consolidation." *The Wall Street Journal* (August 12, 1987), p. B13; and "Swedish-Swiss Merger Braces European Electronic." *Electronic Business* (December 10, 1988), 32.

Introduction

Collective endeavors, such as businesses, require a certain amount of order and organization, without which failure ensues. Organizational goal achievement is dependent on the effective combination of the contributions and work output of the individual members. Because organizational activities are interdependent, complementary, and varied in types and timing, they require a certain degree of coordination and integration. The coordination and integration of these activities is facilitated through their operational proximity. Operational proximity means making allowances for the synchronization of activities in time and space. Simply put, physical proximity allows the members of the organization to perform their tasks together and in a timely fashion. Organizational activities need to be grouped in such a fashion that it is easy for people to work together and so that progress toward goals is expedited. In arranging the operational proximity of organizational activities and tasks, different methods and frameworks are available for organizing. The methods of organizing are based on work specialization, division of labor, and economies of scale that were first articulated by Adam Smith. The frameworks that are used should allow for appropriate job designs, reporting and communication arrangements, authority and responsibility distribution, and the physical layout of the organization. In short, an organization needs form and structure.

Definition and Functions of Organizing

The organizing function involves designing the skeleton and the structure that delineate the nature and extent of formal relationships among various internal components, including tasks, jobs, positions, and units of the organization. It is the physical and nonphysical form that the organization assumes in response to its internal requirements and external environment. It allows for the distribution of power and authority among the members, and the establishment of communication lines between them. The internal requirements of a firm are the type of technology used, the nature of tasks performed, and type of strategy employed. The external environment is the combination of outside constituencies and forces that are influential in determining the fate of the organization. Because firms have different internal requirements and external environments, they employ various structural configurations. Simply put, the structure of the firm is a tool for goal attainment and a means to an end.

The structure of the organization defines the boundaries of organizational components (units); the relationships among various parts; the extent, limits, and location of authority and power; and the formal communication patterns. The architects of organizational structure need to answer four basic questions about the firm: (1) What should the units of organization be? (2) Which components should be joined and which kept apart? (3) What size and shape pertain to different components? (4) What is the appropriate placement and relationship of different units?[1]

To respond to these questions, the basic principle for organizing is to group activities that have similar characteristics and functions from the lowest levels of the firm and proceed upward. In doing so, tasks are clustered into jobs, jobs are combined to form departments, and departments are put together to create business units. Larger firms that serve multiple markets and have many products lines consequently have a number of different business units. These business units are organized into a corporate structure. The clustering of activities just described is commonly referred to as *departmentalization*.

There are six common bases for departmentalization or grouping of the organizational activities: knowledge and skill, work process and function, time (shifts in a factory), output (products), client, and place (geographic).[2] Figure 3.1 represents organizational structures resulting from two of the most commonly used types of departmentalization: functional and geographic.

The Organization of Multinationals

The fundamental structural considerations of MNCs are similar to those of domestic firms. Internal requirements and the external environment of MNCs, however, pose additional design challenges. The MNC structure should accommodate for physical distance, legal and governmental considerations, headquarter–subsidiary relationships, and many other factors. Because of the environmental diversity, the coordination and integration needs of the MNCs are different from those of the domestic firms. Therefore, requirements of operating across national borders create additional concerns for organizing. In addition to those issues pertinent to organizing domestic firms, three major concerns surround the design of an MNC organizational structure:

- How to encourage a predominantly domestic organization to take full advantage of growth opportunities abroad.
- How to blend product knowledge and geographic area knowledge most efficiently in coordinating worldwide business.
- How to coordinate the activities of foreign units in many countries while permitting each to retain its own identity.[3]

As consumers' tastes converge globally, the firms that respond to this convergence in product preferences could gain competitive advantage. The MNCs respond to these changes by adopting various strategies. These strategies were discussed in the previous chapter. Therefore, we could add another item to this list:

Figure 3.1   Two Types of Departmentalization

• How to exhibit local responsiveness while maintaining a global orientation.

An MNC's response to these concerns is influenced by many factors including the size and history of the company, top management orientation, product-market characteristics, and corporate strategy. As MNCs expand abroad, under the influence of these factors, their structures evolve to facilitate the accomplishment of corporate objectives. Consequently, there are many variations among MNC structures.

The organizing variations among firms are usually discussed at a level directly below the chief executive officer. We differentiate among various forms of MNC designs by focusing our presentations on this level. We also confine our discussion to the managerial organization, as opposed to the statutory or legal organization. To satisfy the host countries' legal and statutory requirements, MNCs create legal entities that exist on paper only. The statutory entities are designed to fulfill legal obligations while promoting the MNCs' objectives of ease of operation

and increased earnings. It is through these entities that the legal and ownership relationships between the headquarters and its various subsidiaries are specified. Many different statutory and legal forms link the parent company to its foreign operations, including branch offices, subsidiaries, and holding companies. The legal requirements of the host country and tax implications determine the MNC's statutory organization.[4]

Factors Influencing MNC Structure

Many factors influence an MNC's choice of organizational structure. These are either external environmental forces, or factors related to the firm itself, or a combination of both.

External Forces

Major external environmental forces that influence an MNC's structure are economic conditions, host governments, technological developments, product-market characteristics, and information technology.[5]

Economic conditions Changes in economic conditions at home and abroad create opportunities and threats to the operation of MNCs. Unemployment and reduced purchasing power resulting from recessions and slower economic growth force adjustments in MNCs' business operations. Reduced market share and earnings in mature markets may prompt firms to diversify. Internationalization may partly be the consequence of home market saturation and maturity.

Technological developments In some industries, the high level of risk and huge investment required for developing new products are straining the financial capabilities of many MNCs. This is prompting international joint ventures between competitors. Also, globalization of some markets has created conditions in which MNCs face the same competitors in many markets. Consequently, local advantages are quickly eroded by the immediate responses of international rivals. The reality of competition between partners of international joint ventures and the need for fast response require a flexibility in structure and a closer integration of the worldwide operations.

Technological developments are considered to be the most important factor influencing structural changes in MNCs. New product development, and new manufacturing methods offer opportunities for expansion into new markets. In turn, expanded foreign operations resulting from the technological advances necessitate the provision of organizational support systems and structural changes. Technological advances have increased international competition and have caused the global integration of the MNCs. Telecommunications and information processing technology have improved the ability of the headquarters office to monitor subsidiary performance in a timely fashion. Improved communication between the subsidiaries and headquarters allows the adoption of either a centralized or decentralized mode of control. In either case, the management of information provides an opportunity for devising a proper structure.

Product-market characteristics Recent shifts in regional economic growth have resulted in the emergence of new international competitors from newly industrialized countries such as South Korea and Taiwan. The emergence of new competition has increased market uncertainty and instability. Simultaneously, advances in manufacturing technologies, new product development, and marketing, along with convergence of consumer tastes and preferences for certain products, have created a global market. To compete in this market, MNCs need global economies of scale and quick response. Consequently, firms require a greater degree of internal integration and coordination among their dispersed worldwide operations, while allowing local responsiveness to their national subsidiaries. Therefore, in designing a new structure, the MNCs are concerned with the reconciliation of these two conflicting needs. An MNC's organizational structure should facilitate global integration and local responsiveness. Other product-market characteristics such as diversity of product line and the nature of competition affect the organizing efforts of MNCs. A product division structure and centralized decision-making process, for example, would serve well those firms that have a diverse product line and are competing with other MNCs in national markets. If competition in national markets is limited to local firms, granting more autonomy to the subsidiary would be appropriate. With competition limited to local firms, intimate knowledge of local conditions and a closer relationship with domestic businesses would be necessary.

Host government policies Host government policies are influential factors shaping the strategies and, in turn, the structure of the MNCs. Investment incentives offered by host governments stimulate FDI and the expansion of MNC operations. Many forms of trade and business requirements and restrictions influence the management of MNCs. Taxes and tariffs, the need for local content, local ownership, technology transfer, local employment, and minimum exports exert pressure on foreign subsidiaries. Of course, an MNC's responses to host government policies influence headquarters–subsidiaries relationships, and subsequently result in structural changes.

Company Factors

Major company factors include its history, top management philosophy, nationality, corporate strategy, and degree of internationalization.[6]

Company history   Firms at the early stages of internationalization have a few managers with experience and expertise in coping with a complex worldwide operation. As the firms continue operating abroad and learn how to manage their worldwide businesses, the decisions regarding the organizational structure will be affected by the years of experience in foreign markets. Therefore, when there is a small pool of managers with international experience, the most feasible structure is an international division. The use of other types of structure has to wait for more advanced stages of internationalization.

Top management philosophy   Top management philosophy regarding the autonomy granted to subsidiaries is reflected in various control mechanisms that the headquarters employs. The organizational structure is a means for exercising headquarters control over subsidiaries. A loose federation of national subsidiaries under the general direction of headquarters, for example, is a sign of management belief that local executives are better qualified to run their own operations.

Nationality   There are differences among the organizational design of American, Japanese, and European MNCs. European subsidiaries, for example, tend to have more autonomy than the Americans. The type of control used also varies among the MNCs from different countries. A higher level of output control tends to be exercised by the U.S. MNCs over their subsidiaries, while the Europeans tend to exert a higher level of behavioral control.[7] Foreign subsidiaries of Japanese MNCs appear to have more local decision-making power. Executive selection, socialization, and acculturation of Japanese managers assure the subsidiaries' strict compliance with the headquarters' norms, and renders other control mechanisms less necessary. Consequently, there is no need for Japanese MNCs to receive extensive and frequent performance data from their foreign subsidiaries of the sort that the American subsidiaries are required to send to their headquarters. Another unique feature of Japanese MNCs is the structure of the *keiretsu* system. Many Japanese manufacturing firms have been using keiretsu systems. A keiretsu is a very close collective of many firms in manufacturer–supplier relationships. The Japanese have effectively used keiretsu systems to gain international competitiveness and successfully penetrate world markets.

Corporate strategy   Corporate strategy greatly influences the structure of the firm. From the pioneering work of Chandler,[8] and subsequent research by others, we have learned that, among other factors, the strategy of the firm sets the stage for structuring the organization. The popular phrase "structure follows strategy" suggests the link between the two. An internationalization strategy that moves the firm away from the familiar domestic market also results in structural variations. Some organizational structures employed by the MNCs appear to work better with certain strategies.[9] International division structure tends to fit a strategy that calls for a low level of foreign sales with a few products. Strategies that involve product diversity tend to be associated with product division structures.

Degree of internationalization   The degree of internationalization affects organizational structure through headquarter–subsidiary relationships. Foreign subsidiary autonomy and internationalization of the firm are related. Internationalization could be thought of as the number of foreign countries in which a firm has subsidiaries. As the number of foreign subsidiaries increases, so does the complexity of

Keiretsu Structure

Many large manufacturers in Japan have formed *keiretsu,* or company coalitions, by grouping the subcontractors who supply them with parts. The result is a production system, distributed among many firms, that has helped Japanese manufacturers strengthen their global competitiveness.

Japan's traditional keiretsu-type "distributed production" system appears to have two major characteristics. First, a key manufacturer takes care of only a small portion of a multistage production process, with the remaining processes subdivided among a chain of subcontractors (more than 50% of small- and medium-sized companies in Japan operate as subcontractors for manufacturer). Second, the key manufacturer assures subcontractors of long-term and continuous relationships. In turn, the subcontractors offer advice on quality control and impose stability to the flow of parts. They offer technical assistance and promote joint development projects.

Recently, however, the subcontracting system has started changing to reflect the structural sophistication in Japanese industries. This trend is expected to accelerate as Japan's economic conditions change.

Large Japanese manufacturing firms, which have experienced sagging demand and decreasing earnings, are increasingly pressuring subcontractors to cut production costs. If they do not comply, they will be excluded from the keiretsu. An increasing number of subcontractors are now seeking ways to gain independence from keiretsu, although most simultaneously seek to improve their technology and production to satisfy key manufacturers.

Excerpted from I. Umebayashi. "New Trends in the Keiretsu System." *The Wall Street Journal* (November 16, 1992), p. A10. Reprinted by permission of *The Wall Street Journal,* © 1992 Dow Jones & Company, Inc. All rights reserved worldwide.

managing them. It is expected that the MNCs with a high degree of internationalization may be forced to allow more autonomy to their subsidiaries for certain decisions such as marketing. For other decisions such as finance, however, they may exert more control. The intimate knowledge of local situations is more critical in marketing than in finance.

Development of International Corporate Structure

As a mechanism that facilitates progress toward goals, organizational structure evolves to accommodate the implementation of strategies. Since firms follow different paths to international expansion, they assume many different forms. The organizational structure of most international operations evolves to serve the growing needs of their diverse markets. Consequently, their choice of structure depends on the type of strategy employed. An organization's structure not only signifies distribution of power and authority, and a formal relationship between organizational members, but it also tells of the importance the company places on certain aspects of the business. A company organized along the customer groups, for example, signals the importance it attaches to meeting the needs of its customers.

As the firm grows, so does the importance of its structure. A small business requires a simple formal organization. But as it expands, increased specialization of tasks and duties creates additional demand for coordination and integration. A more sophisticated structure is needed to handle the complexity of the operation, and the coordination and integration requirements of a large firm. Such a structure would also facilitate the efficient distribution of the firm's resources and the execution of its strategies. The structure that served the business of a domestic firm may well be ill equipped to handle the diversity of the international marketplace. International expansion brings about structural changes. A three-phase evolutionary process characterizes the changes in organizational structure of MNCs. The progression through these phases parallels the three stages of introduction, growth, and maturity of a product's life cycle.[10] These changes transform the firm from domestic orientation through three phases of international, multinational, and global perspectives.

In the first phase, competition is limited to a small number of companies located in developed countries. These firms manufacture products with functions, features, and characteristics that are designed for the domestic market. International operation to these firms is nothing but exports. Although exports may be an important source of revenues, they constitute a small portion of total corporate earnings. Therefore, international operations are carried out as an appendage to domestic business. At this stage, the firms continue using the existing domestic structures with some minor additions to accommodate business activities across national borders.

In the growth stage, technology diffusion and price competition, particularly from domestic firms, force firms to establish manufacturing facilities in low-cost locations abroad. As the increased foreign sales make up a larger share of corporate revenues, firms enter phase two by a change in the organizational structure. In this phase, MNCs use the international division structure. All international business activities are organized into a division comparable to other divisions in the domestic side of the business. No attempt is made to integrate foreign subsidiaries. Operations within each foreign country remain separate from one another. Some firms go through a transition phase before entering phase three. Firms in the transition phase attempt to learn the intricacies of the international environment through their autonomous foreign subsidiaries. A major portion of the MNC earnings come from these autonomous foreign subsidiaries, which are given substantial decision-making freedom.

In phase three, most of the corporate revenues are generated from abroad. At this stage the MNCs organize their operations on a global basis. Domestic operation becomes one aspect of their business and receives corresponding attention along with foreign operations. Various forms of organizational structure that involve the transition from a domestic form to an international structure are discussed next.

The Extension of the Domestic Structure

The first attempts at doing business across national borders result in some organizational changes. The firm begins to learn about other markets beyond its own familiar domestic surroundings. It carries business transactions in other currencies, and learns about foreign business protocols. Foreign correspondence appears among the firm's official communications. To accommodate all these events and activities, some structural changes have to take place. None of these changes, however, require major structural modifications. Since the firm's business activities only marginally expand into the international domain, the corresponding formal changes are handled under the existing domestic structure.

At the early stage of international expansion, the firm's interest and expertise are centered around the domestic operations, and its international involvement is incidental. Often, international sales are triggered by foreigners' inquiries and are insignificant compared with domestic sales. The lack of competition and the firm's superior technology lead it to export the existing products or product line without many modifications. All export jobs are contracted to an independent agent. With the increased sales to foreigners, the firm may set up an in-house export desk or export unit. An export manager, who reports to the marketing executive, is given the responsibility of handling all export activities. The position and reporting arrangement for the export manager depends on the breadth of product line. In a firm with a narrow product line, the export manager reports to the chief marketing officer. The export manager reports directly to the chief executive officer in a firm that has a broad product line.[11] Figure 3.2 depicts the international organizational structure of the firm at this early stage of expansion abroad.

As the volume of export increases, the firm may establish an office abroad to handle sales and service of its products. Except for the addition of an export manager, the basic organizational structure of the firms at this stage remains virtually intact. Most American firms' early internationalization experiences fit this description. Japanese firms, however, have adopted a different approach. For expanding into foreign markets, the Japanese have relied on trading companies called *sogo shosha*. These trading companies perform all the necessary business functions for Japanese firms.[12] Although sogo shoshas play a vital role in Japanese international business, Japanese companies in the automobile and consumer electronic industries have followed a pattern of international expansion similar to that of American and European firms.[13]

As the firm gains experience, it may get involved in other facets of international business

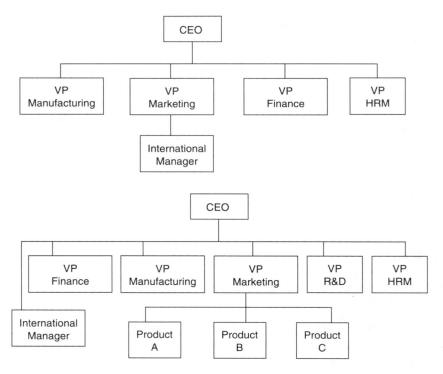

Figure 3.2   Position of International Manager

such as licensing and manufacturing abroad. With the passage of time the market matures, and local and foreign competitors enter the market. With increased competition and market maturity local demands could not effectively be addressed with exports only. A change in the firm's foreign involvement is also hastened due to host government demands. Increased volume of exports into a host country may prompt the host government's demand for local participation in the business. Export restrictions are imposed, and local content laws are passed to assure the MNC's operations provide benefits to the country in additional jobs, improved skills, and technology transfer. A combination of market pressure and government demands forces the firm to establish local manufacturing facilities.

When the firm establishes manufacturing facilities abroad, the diversity and scope of international operations brings about a change in the organizational structure. At this stage, the firm leaves behind the simplicity of the international organizational structure of an exporter, and instead enters the world of managing foreign subsidiaries. It needs a control and coordination mechanism to integrate its geographically dispersed international operations.

The Transition: Autonomous Foreign Subsidiary

Initially, local subsidiaries are allowed a considerable amount of autonomy. The headquarters' lack of experience in managing a distant operation in a foreign land leaves it no choice but to grant the subsidiary managers most of the decision-making power usually reserved for top executives. To control dispersed foreign subsidiaries, MNCs commonly use financial reporting. As long as the operations remain profitable, the headquarters follows a hands-off policy. The need to learn exceeds the desire to control.[14]

A direct reporting relationship links the foreign subsidiary managers to the president at the corporate headquarters. These managers are fully responsible for all aspects of the subsidiaries' operations. For most American firms this type of structure has a short life. The longevity of autonomous foreign subsidiary structure depends on two factors: its growth rate and the rate of international experience accumulated by the headquarters. When a subsidiary's contributions to corporate earnings become large enough to warrant closer scrutiny, headquarters begins a search for ways to exercise more control. Also, as the corporate executives' familiarity with foreign operations increases, they begin to feel more confident in establishing more coordination and control among foreign operations through organizational design modifications.

Sometimes, the foreign subsidiary has its own local board of directors, with the headquarters representative as a member.[15] This arrangement is practiced more by European firms. Two factors were influential in the creation of autonomous foreign subsidiaries by the European MNCs. First, some European firms expanded into international markets before the advent of modern communication technologies. It was not possible to closely control and integrate their foreign subsidiaries. Without the aid of modern communication technologies, European MNCs had no choice but to allow their subsidiaries a considerable degree of self-rule. Second, starting with small domestic operations, European MNCs then found their foreign subsidiaries to be a significant part of the corporation, and therefore treated them accordingly.[16]

The unique relationship between the European subsidiaries and their parent corporation is labeled a "mother–daughter" relationship. Among the many reasons given for such a relationship three stand out. First, European MNCs created a strong organizational identification among their managers through a long period of acculturation and indoctrination to the norms and ways of the corporation. Second, they avoided joint ventures with foreign partners and assigned expatriate managers to be in charge of foreign subsidiaries. These managers could be relied on to abide by corporate norms without close supervision by the headquarters. Third, barriers to trade kept national markets separate from one another and limited the need for cross-boarder communication in most European MNCs. Even without a formal system of reporting, some of these MNCs were able to achieve total worldwide standardization of policies for product mix and diversity, product quality, product design and formulas, brand names, internal or external financing, and human resource management procedures for promotions and rewards.[17]

For years, Procter and Gamble operated strong national subsidiaries in Europe. Differences in market conditions, consumer habits, and competition resulted in the creation of these subsidiaries, each of which resembled a miniature Procter and Gamble. They had their own manufacturing facilities, product development capabilities, marketing and advertising agencies, and responded to local conditions as they saw fit. Honeywell is another MNC that allowed its European subsidiaries much autonomy. Autonomous country managers were responsible for all operations in their countries. Each subsidiary sold the full line of Honeywell products. Some also had manufacturing and service facilities. The headquarters at Minneapolis provided administrative and marketing support. As one executive put it, "Honeywell has always distinguished between centralized 'what-to-do' decisions and decentralized 'how-to-do-it' decisions in international areas. The philosophy is to have a tight 'what' and loose 'how' because Danes will know the business in Denmark better than the Minnesotans do."[18]

The structure of an autonomous foreign subsidiary is better suited to satisfy the career aspiration of local nationals. It also is more amiable to host government demands for local ownership. Having host nationals in visible high-level managerial positions and sharing ownership with local investors can subdue nationalist feelings against the MNCs and reduce tension between the MNCs and host governments.[19]

Advantages Autonomous foreign subsidiaries have the freedom to operate as independent, responsible enterprises within the host country environment. MNCs use a host country focus strategy for managing these subsidiaries. The host country focus strategy was presented in the previous chapter. Relatively free from close supervision by the parent firm, autonomous foreign subsidiaries can integrate into the economic context of the host country and develop their own competitive posture. They gain competitive advantage by setting up local manufacturing, marketing, and purchasing. By operating as a local firm, they can tap the domestic source of cheap labor, and are faced with fewer restrictions. Their independence from the headquarters enables them to consider local consumers' needs in making major decisions and to be sensitive to local markets and governments. The direct relationship between the foreign subsidiary and the headquarters makes it possible to present the subsidiary problems at the highest corporate level without additional levels of bureaucracy. It also elevates the prestige of subsidiary managers in the eyes of host government officials and immensely improves their negotiation status.[20]

Disadvantages An autonomous foreign subsidiary structure has certain drawbacks. Allowing each subsidiary local decision-making power may cause subsidiaries to ignore the benefit of the corporation as a whole. As discussed in the previous chapter, certain benefits are associated with the operation of an integrated multinational. The benefits are realized by managing the firm as a whole and maximizing worldwide performance. The subsidiary manager has a local horizon, whereas the maximization of worldwide performance requires a total corporate perspective. One way to overcome this weakness is to tie some part of the subsidiary manager's rewards to overall corporate performance.[21]

The International Division

With increased sales and revenues from dispersed foreign subsidiaries, MNCs are compelled to impose more coordination and control. The organizational structure of an export office or the creation of independent foreign subsidiaries is inadequate to deal with the diversity of expanded foreign business. At this stage, MNCs adopt an international perspective and use international division structures (Figure 3.3).

Four factors prompt the establishment of an international division structure that enjoys sufficient organizational status on par with the other divisions.[22] First, increased international involvement, both operationally and strategically, requires the attention and involvement of a senior executive, and the structure of a separate organizational unit. Second, at this early stage of internationalization, concentration of all international activities in a single organizational unit is the best way to deal with the complexity of the global market and to exploit the worldwide business opportunities. Third, there is the realization that internal specialists are needed to deal with the special features of international market opportunities. Last, there is a desire to develop proactive global scanning capabilities to assess global opportunities and threats rather than passively respond to conditions that are presented to the firm.

In an international division structure, the management of foreign operations is coordinated by a department usually located at the headquarters. Each subsidiary manager reports directly to the head of the international division. The executive in charge of the division is a member of the corporation's executive board. All activities of foreign operations are centralized at the international division, and the head of the international division is given line authority over foreign subsidiaries. Through the international division, the MNC headquarters exercises control and coordination over foreign operations without much change in the corporation's existing structure. With the creation of an international division, the foreign subsidiaries' loss of autonomy is matched by a corresponding measure of guidance and support from the corporate staff.[23] In effect, the international division allows the firm to maintain separate domestic and foreign businesses and to use its limited international expertise efficiently. Since the firm basically has a domestic orientation, not many executives have international experience. Concentration of international staff in the international division allows for integration, coordination, and control of foreign subsidiaries without placing undue demands on other executives.

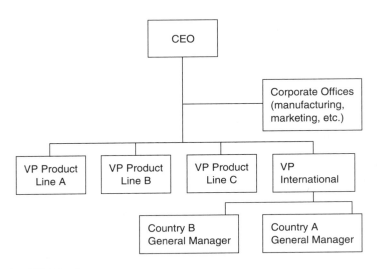

Figure 3.3   International Division Structure

International division corporate structure is likely to be adopted by firms with a dominant domestic business, a narrow product line, a limited geographic diversity, and few managers with international business expertise and experience. With the dominance of domestic business over the international operations, upward mobility of the executives in the corporate hierarchy is not tied to international expertise and experience. Therefore, not too many executives see the knowledge, experience, and expertise of international business as necessary for their career progress. Often, a foreign assignment may be an organizational hinderance that could limit their managerial advancement. By spending a few years abroad on foreign assignments, they could become foreigners to domestic corporate network. They could be bypassed for promotion in favor of those who are active in the domestic operations and a part of internal power network.

An international division structure is a manifestation of the firm's international orientation and geographic interests that are translated into design arrangements fitting the multinational nature of their foreign operations. The firm at this stage considers each geographic area to be a separate market that requires differentiated business practices that are handled by foreign subsidiaries. These subsidiaries, although separate operationally, could benefit from the overall guidance and integration efforts of the headquarters. There is a need to balance the self-interest of foreign subsidiaries with overall corporate performance. This is accomplished by the standardization of information control mechanisms of foreign subsidiaries. The structure of international division and the associated standardization allow for the application of international corporate practices that improve corporate performance, such as transfer pricing, resource acquisition and allocation, and product distribution.[24]

Polaroid is an example of a firm that has used the international division structure. During the 1980s, nearly 40 percent of Polaroid's revenues came from international operations. Its international division controls all manufacturing and marketing functions outside the United States. It has three facilities in Scotland, Ireland, and the Netherlands that handle many aspects of manufacturing Polaroid products. It essentially sells abroad the same products as those sold in the domestic market, with some modifications to accommodate special market conditions, local regulations, and the metric measures. The international division markets the full line of Polaroid products through wholly owned subsidiaries in 20 countries. The international division is treated as a profit center and seems to enjoy a degree of independence within the corporation that is envied by other divisions.[25] With the recent reorganization that has carved the firm into three major business units—consumer, industrial, and magnetic—it seems that Polaroid is experimenting with the goal of creating a matrix organization design.[26]

Coleman Corporation based in Wichita, Kansas, is another firm that has employed the international division structure for many years.[27] Coleman is the largest manufacturer of outdoor products in the world. Its outdoor product line, especially gasoline-powered lanterns and insulated coolers, has gained worldwide recognition. Coleman started its international operations in 1919, and has had an international division structure since the 1940s. The division is headed by an executive-level vice president and is located a few miles from the corporate headquarters.

The international division structure works well for Coleman, which has a rather centralized manufacturing operation and a narrow, homogenous line of products. Coleman has principal manufacturing sites in Wichita and Inheiden, Germany. Other smaller manufacturing sites are in Texas, South Carolina, Utah, and Washington. Outdoor products are manufactured in Wichita, Inheiden, and Texas sites. Utah and South Carolina facilities make textile products, such as sleeping bags, and tents. It produces portable generators in Nebraska and water skiing equipment in Washington.

Coleman outdoor products generally need little modification for sales in foreign markets. The changes that are made are generally cosmetic, such as labeling and packaging changes. In the United States and developed countries, Coleman products are used for recreational purposes. In these countries, advertising and marketing is relatively undifferentiated. Adjustments are made for variations in the infrastructure of the markets and for differences in cultures and languages. An example is Japan, where there are many small retailers and long channels of distribution. Products are used recreationally, however, so advertising and marketing tactics are similar to those of Europe and the United States.

In developing countries, Coleman products often serve basic utility functions. Lanterns are a primary source of light, and insulated coolers are a principal source of refrigeration. Therefore, in these countries the marketing mix is differentiated, and the distribution is through dealers with an emphasis on product promotion. Coleman does not coordinate advertising, but instead provides free products for demonstration based on the distributor's promotion efforts.

Except for Inheiden, the international division is centralized at the headquarters. At Inheiden, Germany, Coleman manufactures products for sale to European markets. Inheiden also coordinates European sales operations, and regional sales and distribution offices in Bristol, England, and Alphen aan den Rijn, Netherlands. The international division coordinates all other regional sales and distribution offices, including Tokyo, Singapore (which covers the rest of Asia), Sydney, New Zealand, and San Juan, Puerto Rico (which includes Latin America and the Caribbean).

The international division structure at Coleman reflects characteristics of various foreign markets and the strategic approach of Coleman in serving those markets. Europe has long held business opportunities in outdoor products. The Europeans' interests in outdoor recreation and their higher level of income make Europe a large market for Coleman products. Consequently, the European operations are significantly larger than operations in other countries and are afforded more local decision-making power. In a sense, market characteristics determine either centralization or autonomy of the operating units.

While Europe has been Coleman's largest foreign market, Japan is its fastest growing market. During the 1980s, Coleman became the largest vendor of outdoor products in Japan. The increasing popularity of outdoor activities among Japanese, combined with the fast rate of market growth, may make the Japanese market equal to that of the United States for Coleman's products. It is also expected that market for outdoor equipments will increase in the rest of the Asian and Latin American countries. These changes in the external environment will have a structural impact on Coleman, as foreign sales surpass domestic sales. Until then, an international division structure seems to be appropriate for Coleman, based on its narrow product line and a dominant domestic business.

The MNCs typically continue to use the international division structure as long as it remains smaller than most domestic divisions. It is abandoned in favor of other structures when it rivals the largest domestic divisions. The international division structure, however, may last longer if the rest of the MNC is organized along the geographic structure. There is a better fit between a geographic structure and an international division. Increased volume of business results in increased size, which in turn strains the capacity of the division to handle the product diversity and geographic dispersion of the MNC. At this point the worldwide activities are in need of corporate direction. A very strong international division, however, hampers headquarters' direction of worldwide operations. The increased size of the international division, which is accompanied by more independence, tends to insulate the headquarters from international operations. As Clee and Sachtjen observed, "the more independent an international division becomes, the more it tends to insulate corporate management from overseas problems and opportunities."[28] Also the international division needs the product expertise possessed by domestic divisions. Domestic division staff, however, are reluctant to share their expertise with foreign operations. Consequently, the need to reorganize leads to one of the two forms, an international product division or international geographic division.

Advantages   The choice of any organizational design represents the trade-offs between the benefits gained and the limitations imposed on the management of the firm. International division design provides a few benefits, which we briefly discuss.[29] Among the benefits are adequate top management attention to foreign business, concentration of international management expertise at headquarters, and the acquisition of capital and resources worldwide. With the head of the international division as a member of the senior executive team, the firm is constantly reminded of the international implication of strategic decisions. The existence of international expertise at headquarters expedites coordination between functional units, such as marketing, finance, and production, and foreign operations. The presence of international managers at the top corporate hierarchy and their participation at strategy making committees allow for evaluation of investment decisions on a worldwide basis.

Disadvantages   The international division structure has drawbacks.[30] There is an inherent conflict between the goals of the domestic and international division. Almost always, products that are sold abroad are those produced for the domestic market. The international division does not have its own R&D and engineering staff. Therefore, it cannot cater to the special needs of its foreign customers. Domestic functional specialists are reluctant to give priority to foreign customers because the evaluation of

their performance is based on domestic criteria. The international division, therefore, relies heavily on the cooperation of domestic functional departments, and such cooperation may not be forthcoming. There is also another source of conflict. Some activities, such as financing and resource acquisition, need to be coordinated internationally at the divisional level. Attempts at the division level to exercise central control on financing clashes with country-level activities such as local marketing. Domestically the firm gives a high priority to product coordination as compared with area coordination (a divisional activity). The international division, however, needs both product and area (geography) coordination.

The Geographic Division Structure

The geographic or regional structure divides the worldwide operations into regional divisions. The responsibility of managing each geographic area is given to a senior-level executive (see Figure 3.4). These executives have operational and human resource management responsibilities for their regions, while the headquarters maintains strategic planning and control for worldwide corporate operations. Some regional divisions may operate as self-contained units, producing and selling all needed products locally. Other geographic divisions may rely on other divisions for some of their needs. For the MNCs with geographic division structure, the domestic market is but one of many markets worldwide. Nestle is an example of a firm using an international division form, based on geographical grouping of its foreign subsidiaries and operations. It has 75 country managers who report to five regional managers. The five regions under the supervision of these managers are Europe; South and Central America; Africa and the Middle East; Asia, Australia, and New Zealand; and North America, United Kingdom, and Ireland.[31]

Advantages   The geographic division structure is suitable for certain products and market characteristics. Advantages of the geographic

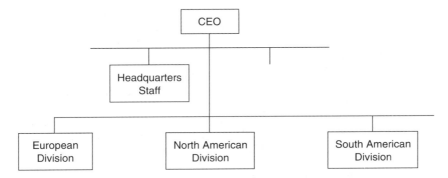

Figure 3.4 Geographic Division Structure

division form are the possibility of regional economies of scale and the treatment of country subsidiaries as profit centers. Geographic division works well when regional similarities in customers' preferences allow for standardization and create the opportunity for economies of scale. It is also suited to situations where, with modest marketing modifications for individual countries, whole regions can be treated as a market. Firms using regional structures tend to have mature businesses and narrow product lines. They have a greater growth prospect abroad where their products are at earlier stages of the life cycle. Since these firms generate large earnings from foreign markets, they need an intimate knowledge of the local environment. They generally emphasize low-cost manufacturing by establishing large plants and using stable technologies. They try to create competitive advantages through marketing techniques and price and product differentiation. Automotive, beverages, containers, cosmetics, food, farm equipment, and pharmaceutical industries have characteristics favoring the regional structure.[32]

Disadvantages Although a regional structure simplifies the task of top management by creating regional specialists, it may cause problems.[33] A firm with a diverse product range may find a regional structure inadequate in handling coordination among product lines and between the country subsidiaries. Regional structure tends to emphasize coordination and integration within an area at the expense of overall corporate integration. It may focus too much attention on regional performance, which may not necessarily optimize overall corporate interests. Rivalry among the regions may sacrifice cooperation needed for global competition. It may also create too much duplication of functional and product specialists among the regions. Strong regional managers may block or delay implementation of strategies aimed at taking advantage of global economies of scale and worldwide opportunities. MNCs using a geographic division structure may experience difficulties with the transfer of new production techniques and new product ideas from one country to another, and the optimum flow of products and material from diverse sources to world markets. Firms facing this problem may respond by establishing a worldwide product manager at corporate headquarters. This manager is assigned the responsibility for particular products or product lines worldwide. Product managers promote the development, progress, and dissemination of product ideas and production worldwide. They recommend global product strategies and act as a clearing house for the transfer of successful developments from an area to the rest of the MNC. It is likely, however, that they encounter an ambiguous operating relationship with geographic division managers, who have line responsibilities.[34]

The Product Division Structure

Firms using a product division structure arrange their business into product groups, and assign a senior line executive the total responsibility for each product division (Figure 3.5). Similar to the regional structure, strategic decisions within each product division that affect the total MNC operations are made by headquarters. Products using similar technologies and having similar customers are grouped within a division. The total responsibility of serving the world market rests with each product division. Within the guidelines established by headquarters, each product division prepares plans to serve the world market. These plans are subject to approval by the headquarters before they are implemented. Financial, legal, technical, and other functional services and guidance are provided by corporate staff to all product divisions.

Firms with diverse product lines and growth opportunities tend to use the product division structure. Their products typically have a relatively high level of technological content and different end users. Because marketing requirements for these products are varied, there is a need for product and market integration among them. The product division structure makes it easier to market such products. It also provides product and market integration.

Hewlett Packard is a firm that has been using the product division structure to serve the world market. In 1970, Hewlett Packard established its first product groups with four divisions. Later, in 1975, the product groups were expanded to six: Electronic Test and Measurement Instruments, Computer and Computer-based Systems, Calculators, Solid-State Components, Medical Electronic Products, and Electronic Instrumentation for Chemical Analysis. Each division was responsible for all aspects of business within their product group including manufacturing, sales, and services. Product groups also prepared sales forecasts and recommended prices. The general managers of product divisions reported to two executive vice presidents who were jointly responsible for operations. Product divisions were supported by the corporate staff reporting to the vice president for administration.[35]

Advantages   The benefits of product division are realized when high transportation costs, tariffs, and other considerations favor local manufacturing of the product. By emphasizing the product market and taking advantage of advanced technology and product expertise, multinational operations are better served by this type of structure. The flexibility of division by product allows the MNCs with growth strategies to add new product divisions without disturbing the rest of the organization.[36] It also permits fast response to the global competitive pressures against specific product lines. Global competitive maneuvers of international rivals are more

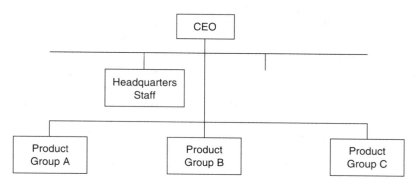

Figure 3.5   Product Division Structure

readily noticed by the product division executives. Therefore, the MNC can concentrate and apply its resources at the location of the competitive attack effectively.

Disadvantages A product division structure may result in wasteful duplication of management, sales representation, and plant capacity utilization within regions.[37] A customer, for example, may be visited by representatives from different product divisions. To eliminate duplication and waste, coordination among divisions would be necessary. Within a given geographic area, however, coordination of different product division activities may represent a difficult task. The addition of country managers, who do not have profit responsibility, may be used to overcome this shortcoming. The country managers report to appropriate product divisions for their share of local activity, and perhaps to a regional staff specialist for their role in maintaining local presence.[38] In this manner, the country managers function as if they are operating in a matrix organization. A review of the matrix structure is given later.

The Functional Structure

In a functional structure the responsibilities of managing the MNC's operations are organized by functions. Each business function such as manufacturing, marketing, finance, research and development, human resource management, etc. is assigned to a top-level executive. Each executive has worldwide responsibility in his or her functional area, and reports to the chief executive officer of the MNC (Figure 3.6). The manufacturing executive, for example, has line authority over, and is responsible for, all manufacturing activities, domestic and foreign, within the MNC organization. This form of structure works well in a situation where the firm has a narrow, standardized product line,[39] and its global coverage and demand have reached a plateau, with no serious changes in the competitive challenge.[40] A functional organization allows tight centralized control with a small cadre of functional managers.

Except for raw material extractive industries, the functional form is less popular among MNCs. In a survey of 92 American MNCs, only 10 had functional structure, and all were in the raw material extractive industry.[41]

Advantages A functional structure seems to work well in this industry because raw materials are very homogeneous and processes do not differ substantially from one country to another. Coordination among the functions such as exploration, production, and sales is of strategic importance, not the introduction of new products or marketing. All major oil companies, for example, have exploration, crude oil production, transportation (tankers and pipelines), refining, and marketing worldwide. Functional design permits functional line managers to control directly all activities at each step globally through the process of product flow.

Disadvantages For a firm with a multiple product line, the use of a functional structure could create problems. It puts undue demands on functional managers that are not easily met. These managers would need expertise in multiple product lines and regions. Another problem is the inherent divergence of objectives among

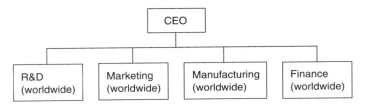

Figure 3.6 International Functional Structure

functional managers, such as production and marketing. The conflicts resulting from differences in objectives between functional managers, such as marketing and production, which cannot be resolved at the country level need to be referred to headquarters. A headquarters overburdened with reconciling and resolving conflicts among the functional divisions has less time for strategic decisions.

Mixed Structure

Some firms may find geographic and product division structures inadequate for their expanding operations. These forms are too restrictive for the ever-changing pattern of international business activities. These organizations have opted either for a mixed design or a matrix form. The mixed or overlapping design is a combination of other structures (Figure 3.7). One option is to combine functional and product divisions. Another choice is to mix geographic and product lines. A third version is functional and geographic divisions.

A major reason for the adoption of a mixed structure is that the other designs do not allow for optimum integration of inputs from regional, functional, and product areas. An optimum level of interaction and cross-fertilization among the three areas is necessary for gaining a competitive position in the ever-changing global markets. MNCs are constantly in search of the structure that combines area knowledge with product and functional skills.[42]

Matrix Structure

Ever since its introduction, the matrix structure has been praised and criticized both by business scholars and managers. Matrix management is an organizational form in which a normal hierarchy is overlaid by some form of lateral authority, communication, and influence. A matrix organization does not follow the traditional principle of unity of command that prescribes each subordinate to have only one superior. It usually combines two chains of command, one along functional lines and the other along project lines (Figure 3.8). There are dual channels of authority, performance responsibility, evaluation, and control in a matrix organization.

Dow Chemical pioneered the matrix management structure in the 1960s and is still using a more flexible version of it. Dow's operations are arranged into three overlapping components: functional, business, and geographic. The functional components include manufacturing, R&D, marketing, and the like. The business segment consists of product lines. The geographic part encompasses the countries where Dow has business operations.[43] Citicorp, Digital Equipment, General Electric, Shell Oil, and Texas Instruments are among the well-known firms that have used matrix design.[44] However, some large companies such as Xerox have recently abandoned the matrix structure, claiming it had created a stranglehold on product development.[45] Peters and Waterman even asserted that the tendency toward hopelessly compli-

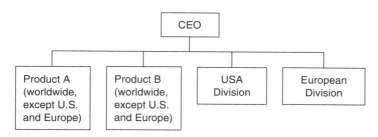

Figure 3.7 International Mixed Structure

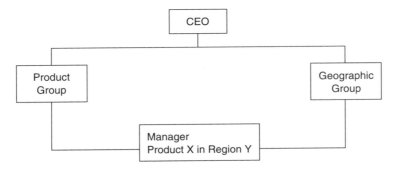

Figure 3.8   International Matrix Structure

cated and ultimately unworkable structures "reaches its ultimate expression in the formal matrix organization structure."[46] Of course, Peters and Waterman were referring to the U.S. domestic operations, which combine functional and product structures. An international matrix often combines product and regional forms.

Matrix structure could be viewed as the end product in a sequence of lateral coordinating arrangements. These coordinating arrangements encompass liaison roles, task forces, teams, integrating managers, integrating departments, and finally matrix.[47] The matrix structure is a delicate system to manage. Experience indicates that firms that succeeded in building multidimensional organizations, such as the matrix, are those that begin by building an organization instead of installing a new structure. In other words, these firms first altered organizational psychology and built a strong organizational culture. Then they reinforced organizational psychology with improvements in organizational physiology by building the proper structure.[48]

Advantages   A matrix structure offers many advantages. It allows the efficient use of organizational resources. Specialists as well as equipment can be shared across multiple projects or countries. It also provides a clear and workable mechanism for coordination work across functional lines, facilitating project integration.

Vertical information flow should improve in a matrix form since one role of the country manager or the project manager is to be a central communication link with top management. In addition, lateral communication is normally very strong due to the necessity of such communication. The result is improved interaction both vertically and laterally. Frequent contacts between members from different areas expedite decision making and enhance management flexibility.

Disadvantages   The matrix structure has several disadvantages. Proponents praise the matrix efficiency and flexibility, while critics say the matrix is costly, cumbersome, and overburdening to manage. It has a built-in tension between country managers and product managers who are in competition for control over the same set of resources. Such conflict is viewed as a necessary mechanism for achieving an appropriate balance between product issues and unique country requirements. The effect on morale, however, can be very damaging. Often work conflicts resulting from differences in objectives and accountability, disputes about credits or blames, and infringements on professional domains spill over to a more personal level. Any situation in which equipment and personnel are shared across projects lends itself to conflict and competition for scarce resources. The time-consuming nature of shared decision making, while enhancing the flexibility, increases costs. Additional administrative overhead is associated with the addition of managers. The very nature of matrix structures creates situations in which "when everyone is responsible, no one is responsible." In effect, "passing the buck" is easy in a matrix organization.

Firms using the matrix structure are aware of the problems and some have moved to minimize their impact on the organization. Dow Chemical, for example, found that instead of promoting communication, a matrix design created a labyrinth of bureaucracy, many committees, and miles of red tape. In the 1970s, to establish a more direct line of communication and to clarify authority and accountability, the firm gave the ultimate authority to geographic managers. In so doing, however, it discovered that a new rivalry began among the different area (geographic) managers. As each tried to grow faster and bigger than the others, a series of poor investment decisions resulted. To overcome the problem of rivalry and still reduce ambiguity and confusion in authority, in 1978 the company again revamped its matrix structure. It established a small team of senior executives at the headquarters to set priorities, such as return on investment, market share, expansion into a new market, or new product development, for each type of business. After establishing the priorities, one of three components of the matrix— function, product, or geography—is chosen to carry more responsibility in the decision-making process. Of course, the component that takes the lead varies depending on the type of decision, the market, and locational considerations.[49]

Other Organizational Structures

MNCs and domestic firms alike are in constant search for the best possible organization design. Although functions, products, and geographic areas remain the three basic models of organizational structure, each has shortcomings that limit its application. The efforts to combine the benefits of all three models while keeping the drawbacks at a minimum produced the matrix structure. Although the matrix design offers the flexibility and quick response needed in a dynamic global business environment, it is not the final answer to the organizing needs of the MNCs. Many firms that were enthusiastically promoting the matrix earlier now are not quite sure of its benefits. Some have found it too cumbersome and confusing and have abandoned it in favor of market-based designs.

A market-based design takes into account market difference in structuring the firm. A market could be a group of countries that have similar pattern of needs, purchasing behaviors, and product use. Based on these criteria the world could be divided into a few markets that could be served with similar products and services. The physical proximity that is the basis for the geographic division structure is abandoned in favor of more meaningful market characteristics. Instead of dividing the world into geographic regions such as South America, Europe, and East Asia, for example, countries could be categorized by their level of economic development. On that basis, for example, Brazil, Mexico, South Korea, Taiwan, Turkey, and the OPEC countries could form one market.[50]

Following this line of reasoning, General Electric established its planning around *strategic business units* (SBUs). These SBUs are families of businesses that encompass product and geographic dimensions. The older structure serves as a supportive skeleton on which the newer structure of strategic business units could be overlaid. Xerox Corporation has done similarly by discarding its matrix structure in favor of SBUs.[51] While the limitations of travel and communication over long distances coupled with advantages of physical proximity for managing were the basis for adopting the geographic division structure, advances in telecommunications and information processing have reduced both those limitations and the benefits. Such developments have, in turn, enabled firms to use market-based structures.

Conclusion

Organizational structure is a means and a tool with which the firm can accomplish its goals and implement its plans. The same basic organization design concepts used by domestic firms can be useful to MNCs. To operate a worldwide operation, however, MNCs need a more careful examination of their organizational structures. Spread across the globe, it is through an effective structure that they can maintain a productive relationship between the various foreign operations and the headquarters.

External environmental conditions and circumstances along with the firm's characteristics determine an MNC's proper organization structure. The MNC's history, top management philosophy, nationality, corporate strategy, and degree of internationalization are attributes that affect the proper choice of organization structure. Also, economic conditions, host government policies, product-market characteristics, and information technology are major external forces that influence the MNC attempts to choose an organizational structure.

Five types of organizational structure are commonly used by the MNCs. At the early stage of expansion into foreign markets, the firms use the international division. When the revenues from foreign sales become a substantial part of corporate earnings, and when the firm has gained sufficient international experience, other forms are employed. When an international division no longer is adequate for dispersed MNC operations, product division or geographic division structures are employed. Some firms go through a transition stage before establishing product or geographic divisions. In the transition stage independent foreign subsidiaries handle almost all business transactions of the MNCs. A functional organizational structure is used by firms with limited product diversity such as the raw material extractive industry. Finally, the need for flexibility, coordination, and integration among their worldwide businesses prompts some MNCs to establish matrix structures.

Discussion Questions

1. What are the similarities and differences of the organizing needs of MNCs compared to those of domestic firms?
2. Use product life-cycle theory in explaining the development of the organizational structure of MNCs.
3. When do MNCs abandon the use of existing domestic organization structure and reorganize to support their international expansion?
4. In modifying a domestic organization to handle international operations what is the most common structure employed by MNCs?
5. Describe the structure of an autonomous foreign subsidiary. What are its strengths?
6. Explain the differences between the structure of an autonomous foreign subsidiary and an international division.
7. Elaborate on conditions that prompt a firm to use the international division structure.
8. Why might a firm with diverse products find a geographic organizational structure inadequate for its need? What type of organization do you recommend for such a firm?
9. While the functional organizational structure has not been very popular among MNCs some have used it effectively. Do you think more firms may use it in the future? Elaborate on your answer.
10. What are the advantages of using a matrix structure. Which MNCs benefit from it? How can we minimize the problems of using a matrix structure?
11. Discuss in detail two internal and external factors that influence an MNC's choice of organization structure.

12. What are the differences between a *keiretsu* and a *sogo shosha*?

Endnotes

1. P. Drucker. *Management* (New York: Harper and Row, 1974), 529.

2. H. Mintzberg. "The Structuring Of Organizations." In J. B. Quinn, H. Mintzberg, and R. M. James, eds. *The Strategy Process,* (Englewood Cliffs, NJ: Prentice Hall, 1988), 283.

3. M. G. Duerr and J. M. Roach. *Organization and Control of International Corporations* (New York: The Conference Board, 1973), 5.

4. S. H. Robock and K. Simmonds. *International Business and Multinational Enterprises* (Homewood, IL: Richard D. Irwin, Inc., 1989), 253.

5. *Structure and Organization of Multinational Enterprises* (Paris, France: Organisation for Economic Co-Operation and Development, 1987), Chap. III; S. B. Prasad and Y. K. Shetty. *An Introduction to Multinational Management* (Englewood Cliffs, NJ: Prentice-Hall, 1976) 97–99.

6. Ibid.

7. W. G. Egelhoff. "Patterns of Control in United States, United Kingdom and European Multinational Corporations." *Journal of Business Studies,* 15 (1984), 73–84.

8. A. D. Chandler, Jr., *Strategy and Structure* (Cambridge, MA: The MIT Press, 1962).

9. J. M. Stopford and L. T. Wells, Jr. *Managing the Multinational Enterprise* (New York: Basic Books, 1972); W. G. Egelhoff. "Strategy and Structure in Multinational Corporations: A Revision of the Stopford and Wells Model." *Strategic Management Journal,* 9 (1988), 1–14.

10. S. M. Davis, "Organization Design." In I. Walter and T. Murray, eds. *Handbook of International Management.* (New York: John Wiley and Sons, 1988), 13.4.

11. A. V. Phatak. *International Dimensions of Management* (Boston: PWS Kent Publishing Company, 1989), 82.

12. D. deSilva. "Global Business Acumen and Strategy of Sogoshosha." *Proceedings of Pan-Pacific Conference,* Kuala Lumpur, Malaysia, June 6–8, 1991, pp. 326–31; D. deSilva. "Management Forte of Japan's Sogoshosha." *Proceedings of International Conference on Comparative Management,* Taipei, Taiwan, June 4–7, 1989, pp.

13. Robock and Simmonds. *International Business.* 254.

14. Stopford and Wells. *Managing the Multinational Enterprise.* 20.

15. J. Picard. "Organizational Structure and Integrative Devices in European Multinational Corporations." *Columbia Journal of World Business* (Spring 1980), 31.

16. Robock and Simmonds. *International Business.* 256.

17. L. G. Franko, *The European Multinationals* (Stamford, CT: Greylock Publishers, 1976), 192–93.

18. F. V. Cespedes and J. King, "Honeywell, Inc.: International Organization for Commercial Avionics." In R. D. Buzzel, J. A. Quelch, and C. Bartelett, eds. *Global Marketing Management.* (Reading, Massachusetts: Addison-Wesley Publishing Co. 1992), p. 535.

19. Robock and Simmonds. *International Business.* 257.

20. Robock and Simmonds. *International Business.* 257.

21. Robock and Simmonds. *International Business.* 258.

22. G. H. Clee and W. M. Sachtjen, "Organizing a Worldwide Business." In J. C. Baker, J. K. Ryan Jr., and D. G. Howard, eds. *International Business Classics,* (Lexington, MA: D.C. Heath and Company, 1988), 265–66.

23. Davis. "Organization Design." 13.5; Phatak. *International Dimensions.* 85.

24. Davis. *Organization Design.* 13.5.

25. H. Mintzberg and J. B. Quinn. *Strategy Process: Concepts, Contexts, Cases* (Englewood Cliffs, NJ: Prentice-Hall, Inc., 1991), 513.

26. S. Adams and A. Griffin, *Polaroid Corporation.* In T. L. Wheelen and J. D. Hunger, eds. *Cases in Strategic Management* (Readings, MA: Addison-Wesley, 1990), 102.

27. Based on a presentation of Coleman's international strategy at the October 24, 1991, meeting of the World Trade Council of Wichita, and from discussions with executives of the Coleman Corporation, with the assistance of graduate students, N. Al-Agha, B. Baumgart, and G. Becker.

28. Clee and Sachtjen. "Organizing a Worldwide Business." 257.

29. Phatak. *International Dimensions.* 85–86; Robock and Simmonds. *International Business.* 259–60.

30. Clee and Sachtjen. "Organizing Worldwide Business." 256–57. Phatak. *International Dimensions.* 85–86; Robock and Simmonds. *International Business.* 259–60.

31. J. A. Quelch and E. J. Hoff "Nestle S.A.: International Marketing." In Buzzel, Quelch and Bartelett, eds. *Global Marketing Management.* 407–08.

32. Clee and Sachtjen. "Organizing Worldwide Business." 13.7.

33. Davis, "Organization Design." 13.9; Robock and Simmonds. *International Business.* 264.

34. Clee and Sachtjen. *Organizing a Worldwide Business.* 261.

35. H. Mintzberg and J. B. Quinn, "The Hewlett Packard Company." In H. Mintzberg and J. B. Quinn, eds. *The Strategy Process: Concepts, Contexts, Cases* (Englewood Cliffs, NJ: Prentice-Hall, Inc., 1991), 462–63.

36. Prasad and Shetty. *An Introduction to Multinational Management.* 97–99.

37. D. B. Zenoff. *International Business Management* (New York.: Macmillan, 1971), 262.

38. Davis. "Organization Design." 13.11; Robock and Simmonds. *International Business.* 266.

39. Prasad and Shetty. *An Introduction to Multinational Management.* 94.

40. Robock and Simmonds. *International Business.* 259–60.

41. J. D. Daniels, R. A. Pitts, and M. J. Tretter. "Strategy and Structure of U.S. Multinationals: An Exploratory Study." *Academy of Management Journal,* 27, no. 2, (1984), 292–307.

42. Prasad and Shetty. *An Introduction to Multinational Management.* 95.

43. "Dow Draws Its Matrix Again—And Again, And Again. . . ." *The Economist* (August 5, 1989), 55.

44. J. A. Pearce II and R. B. Robinson. *Strategic Management* (Homewood, IL: Richard D. Irwin, 1991), 333.

45. "How Xerox Speeds Up the Birth of New Products." *Business Week* (March 19, 1984), 58–9.

46. T. Peters and R. Waterman. *In Search Of Excellence* (New York: Harper and Row, 1982), 49.

47. J. Galbraith. "Matrix Organization Design: An Information-Processing View." In J. W. Lorsch and P .R. Lawerence, eds. *Organization Planning: Cases and Concepts,* (Homewood, IL: Richard D. Irwin, 1972), 49–74.

48. C. A. Bartlett and S. Ghoshal. "Matrix Management: Not a Structure, a Frame of Mind." *Harvard Business Review* (July–August 1990), 140.

49. "Dow Draws Its Matrix." *The Economist,* 55–6.

50. Davis. "Organization Design." 13.14.

51. "How Xerox Speeds Up," 58.

BANCIL CORPORATION

LAWRENCE D. CHRZANOWSKI

Struggling to clear his mind, Remy Gentile, marketing manager in France for the toiletry division of Bancil, stumbled to answer the ringing telephone.

"Allo?"

"Remy, Tom Wilson here. Sorry to bother you at this hour. Can you hear me?"

"Sacrebleu! Do you know what time it is?"

"About 5:20 in Sunnyvale. I've been looking over the past quarter's results for our Peau Doux . . ."

"Tom, it's after 2:00 A.M. in Paris; hold the phone for a moment."

Remy was vexed with Tom Wilson, marketing vice president for the toiletry division and acting division marketing director for Europe, since they had discussed the Peau Doux situa-

tion via telex no more than a month ago. When he returned to the phone, Remy spoke in a more controlled manner.

"You mentioned the Peau Doux line, Tom."

"Yes, Remy, the last quarter's results were very disappointing. Though we've increased advertising by 30 percent, sales were less than 1 percent higher. What is even more distressing, Remy, is that our competitors' sales have been growing at nearly 20 percent per year. Furthermore, our percent cost of goods sold has not decreased. Has Pierre Chevalier bought the new equipment to stream-line the factory's operation?"

"No, Pierre has not yet authorized the purchase of the machines, and there is little that can be done to rationalize operations in the antiquated Peau Doux plant. Also, we have not yet succeeded in securing another distributor for the line."

"What! But that was part of the strategy with our increased advertising. I thought we agreed to . . ."

Tom Wilson hesitated for a moment. His mind was racing as he attempted to recall the specifics of the proposed toiletry division strat-

This case was prepared by Lawrence D. Chrzanowski under the supervision of Ram Charan, Associate Professor of Policy and Environment, as a basis for class discussion rather than to illustrate effective or ineffective handling of an administrative situation. The case was made possible by a corporation which prefers to remain anonymous. All names, figures, and locations have been disguised. Copyright © 1975 by Northwestern University. Reprinted with permission.

egy for France. That strategy had guided his earlier recommendations to Gentile and Pierre Chevalier, the Bancil general manager in France, to increase advertising and to obtain a new distributor. Tom wanted to be forceful but tactful to ensure Gentile's commitment to the strategy.

"Remy, let's think about what we discussed on my last trip to Paris. Do you recall we agreed to propose to Chevalier a plan to revitalize Peau Doux's growth? If my memory serves me well, it was to increase advertising by 25 percent, groom a new national distributor, reduce manufacturing costs with new equipment, increase prices, and purchase the 'L'aube' product line to spread our marketing overhead."

"Oui, oui. We explored some ideas and I thought they needed more study."

"Remy, as you recall, Peau Doux has a low margin. Cutting costs is imperative. We expected to decrease costs by 5 percent by investing $45,000 in new equipment. Our test for the new strategy next year was to increase advertising this quarter and next quarter while contracting for a new distributor. The advertising was for naught. What happened?"

"I really don't know. I guess Pierre has some second thoughts."

Tom spoke faster as he grew more impatient. Gentile's asking Tom to repeat what he had said made him angrier. Tom realized that he must visit Paris to salvage what he could from the current test program on Peau Doux. He knew that the recent results would not support the proposed toiletry division strategy.

"Remy, I need to see what's going on and then decide how I can best assist you Chevalier. I should visit Paris soon. How about early next week, say Monday and Tuesday?"

"Oui, that is fine."

"I'll fly in on Sunday morning. Do you think you can join me for dinner that evening at the Vietnamese restaurant we dined at last time?"

"Oui."

"Please make reservations only for two. I'm coming alone. Good night, Remy."

"Oui. Bon soir."

Company Background

Bancil Corporation of Sunnyvale, California, was founded in 1908 by pharmacist Dominic Bancil. During its first half century, its products consisted primarily of analgesics (branded pain relievers like aspirin), an antiseptic mouthwash, and a first-aid cream. By 1974, some of the top-management positions were still held by members of the Bancil family, who typically had backgrounds as pharmacists or physicians. This tradition notwithstanding, John Stoopes, the present chief executive officer, was committed to developing a broad-based professional management team.

Bancil sales, amounting to $61 million in 1955, had grown to $380 million in 1970 and to $600 million in 1974. This sales growth had been aided by diversification and acquisition of allied businesses as well as by international expansion. Bancil's product line by 1970 included four major groups:

	Sales ($ millions)	
	1970	1974
Agricultural and animal health products (weedkillers, fertilizers, feed additives)	52	141
Consumer products (Bancil original line plus hand creams, shampoos, and baby accessories)	205	276
Pharmaceutical products (tranquilizers, oral contraceptives, hormonal drugs)	62	107
Professional products (diagnostic reagents, automated chemical analyzers, and surgical gloves and instruments)	60	76

In 1974, Bancil's corporate organization was structured around these four product groups which, in turn, were divided into two or three divisions. Thus, in 1973 the consumer products group had been divided into the Dominic division, which handled Bancil's original product line, and the toiletry division, which was in charge of the newer product acquisitions. The objective of this separation was to direct greater attention to the toiletry products.

International Operations

International expansion had begun in the mid-1950s when Bancil exported through agents and distributors. Subsequently, marketing subsidiaries, called National Units (NUs), were created in Europe, Africa, Latin America, and Japan. All manufacturing took place in the United States. Virtually the entire export activity consisted of Bancil's analgesic Domicil. An innovative packaging concept, large amounts of creative advertising, and considerable sales push made Domicil a common word in most of the free world, reaching even the most remote areas of Africa, Asia, and South America. A vice president of international operations exercised control at this time through letters and occasional overseas trips. By the mid-1960s, overseas marketing of pharmaceutical and professional products began, frequently through a joint venture with a local company. Increasing sales led to the construction of production facilities for many of Bancil's products in England, Kenya, Mexico, Brazil, and Japan.

Bancil's international expansion received a strong commitment from top management. John Stoopes was not only a successful business executive but also a widely read intellectual with an avid interest in South American and African cultures. This interest generated an extraordinary sense of responsibility to the developing nations and a conviction that the mature industrial societies had an obligation to help in their development. He did not want Bancil to be viewed as a firm that drained resources and

money from the developing world; rather, he desired to apply Bancil's resources to worldwide health and malnutrition problems. His personal commitment as an ardent humanist was a guideline for Bancil's international operations.

While Bancil had been successful during the 1960s in terms of both domestic diversification and international expansion, its efforts to achieve worldwide diversification had given rise to frustration. Even though the international division's specific purpose was to promote all Bancil products most advantageously throughout the world, the NUs had concentrated mainly on analgesics. As a result, the growth of the remaining products had been generally confined to the United States and thus these products were not realizing their fullest worldwide potential.

According to Bancil executives, these problems had their roots in the fact that the various product lines, though generically related, required different management strategies. For consumer products, advertising consumed 28 percent to 35 percent of sales; since production facilities did not require a large capital investment, considerable spare capacity was available to absorb impulses in demand created by advertising campaigns. For agricultural and animal health products, promotion was less than 1 percent of sales, but the capital-intensive production (a facility of minimum economic scale cost $18 million) required a marketing effort to stimulate demand consistently near full production capacity. Furthermore, the nature of the marketing activity for the professional and pharmaceutical products placed the burden on personal selling rather than on a mass-promotion effort.

In response to this situation, a reorganization in 1969 gave each product division worldwide responsibility for marketing its products. Regional marketing managers, reporting to the division's vice president of marketing, were given direct authority for most marketing decisions (e.g., advertising, pricing, distribution channels) of their division's products in their area. The manufacturing division, with head-quarters in Sunnyvale, had worldwide responsibility for production and quality control (See Exhibit 1 for the 1969 organization chart.)

Corporate management also identified a need in key countries for a single local executive to represent Bancil Corporation's interests in local banking and political circles. There was no single criterion for selecting, from the divisions' representatives in each country, the Bancil delegate, the title given to this position. A corporate officer remarked: "We chose whom we thought was the best business executive in each country. There was no emphasis on functional specialty or on selecting an individual from the division with the greatest volume. In one country, the major candidates were opinionated and strong-willed, and we therefore chose the individual who was the least controversial. The Bancil delegate generally had a marketing background if marketing was the primary Bancil activity in the country or a production background if Bancil had several manufacturing facilities in the country."

While international sales had grown from $99 million in 1970 to $147 million in 1972, profit performance from 1971 to 1972 had been disappointing. A consultant's report stated:

> There are excessive communications between the NUs and Sunnyvale. The marketing managers and all the agents are calling for product-line information from the divisional headquarters. Five individuals are calling three times per week on an average, and many more are calling only slightly less often.

It appeared that a great deal of management time was spent on telex, long-distance communications, and travel. In response to these concerns, the divisions' staffs increased in each country. Overhead nearly tripled, affecting the growth rate of profits from international operations.

With the exception of financial decisions which were dictated by corporate headquarters, most decisions on inventories, pricing, new product offerings, and facility development were made by corporate headquarters in conjunction with the local people. Local people, however, felt that the key decisions were being postponed. Conflicting demands were a problem as every division drew on the local resources for manpower inventories, receivables, and capital investment. These demands had been manageable, however, because even though profits were below target no cash shortages had developed.

Current Organization of International Operations

To improve the performance of its international operations, Bancil instituted a reorganization in mid-1973. The new organization was a matrix of NU general managers and area vice presidents, who were responsible for total resource allocation in their geographic area, and division presidents, who were responsible for their product lines worldwide. (See Exhibit 2 for a description of the matrix in 1975.)

The general manager was the chief executive in his country in charge of all Bancil products. He was also Bancil's representative on the board and executive committee of local joint ventures. The Bancil delegate usualy had been chosen as the general manager. He was responsible for making the best use of financial, material, and personnel resources; pursuing approved strategies; searching for and identifying new business opportunities for Bancil in his NU; and developing Bancil's reputation as a responsible corporate citizen. The general manager was assisted by a financial manager, one or more plant managers, product-line marketing managers, and other functional managers as required.

The divisions were responsible for operations in the United States and Canada and for worldwide expertise on their product lines.

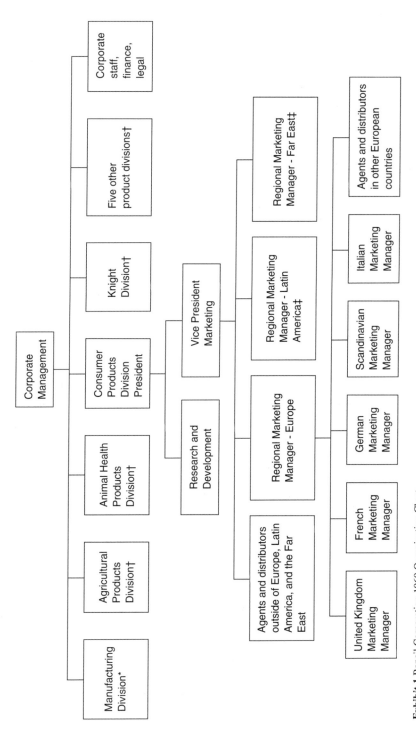

Exhibit 1 Bancil Corporation 1969 Organization Chart

Source: Company records.

*The manufacturing division manufactured products for all the product divisions. Overseas manufacturing (not shown) reported to the manufacturing division in Sunnyvale.

†Organization similar to that of the consumer products division.

‡Organization similar to that for Europe.

| Product group vice presidents | Division presidents | Vice president international operations Clark B. Tucker — Europe Andre Dufour | | | Latin America Juan Vilas | | | Far East | Area vice presidents |
		France P. Chevalier	Germany D. Rogge	Four other national units	Argentina and Uruguay S. Portillo	Brazil E. Covelli	Two other national units	Four national units	General managers
Agricultural and animal health (3 divisions)	Rodgers division								
	Division B								
	Division C								
Consumer products (2 divisions)	Dominic division								
	Toiletry division (Robert Vincent)								
Pharmaceuticals (2 divisions)	Division A								
	Division B								
Professional (3 divisions)	Knight division								
	Division B								
	Division C								

Exhibit 2 Bancil Corporation Shared Responsibility Matrix
Source: Company records.

Divisions discharged the latter responsibility through local product-line marketing managers who reported on a line basis to the NU general manager and on a functional basis to a division area marketing director. The latter, in turn, reported to the divisional marketing vice president. Where divisions were involved in other functional activities, the organizational structure was similar to that for marketing. The flow of product-line expertise from the divisions to the NUs consisted of (1) operational inputs such as hiring/termination policies and the structure of merit programs, and (2) technical/professional inputs to the NU marketing, production, and other staff functions on the conduct of the division's business within the NU.

Only the Dominic division was represented in every NU. Some divisions lacked representation in several NUs, and in some cases a division did not have a marketing director in an area. For example, the Rodgers division had area marketing directors in Europe, the Far East, and Latin America, all reporting to the divisional vice president of marketing to whom the division's U.S. marketing personnel also reported. However, the Knight division, which had a structure similar to that of the Rodgers division, could justify area marketing directors only in Europe and Latin America.

The new matrix organization established for each country a National Unit Review Committee (NURC) with its membership consisting of the general manager (chairman), a financial manager, and a representative from each division with activities in the NU. Corporate executives viewed the NURC as the major mechanism for exercising shared profit responsibility. NURC met quarterly, or more frequently at the general manager's direction, to (1) review and approve divisional profit commitments generated by the general manager's staff; (2) ensure that these profit commitments, viewed as a whole, were compatible with and representative of the best use of the NU's resources; (3) monitor the NU's progress against the agreed plans; and (4) review and approve salary ranges for key NU personnel. When the division's representatives acted as members of the NURC, they were expected to view themselves as responsible executives of the NU.

Strategic Planning and Control

NURC was also the framework within which general managers and division representatives established the NU's annual strategic plan and profit commitment. Strategy meetings commenced in May, at which time the general manager presented a forecast of Bancil's business in his NU for the next five years and the strategies he would pursue to exploit environmental opportunities. The general manager and the divisional representatives worked together between May and September to develop a mutually acceptable strategy and profit commitment. If genuine disagreement on principle arose during these deliberations, the issue could be resolved at the next level of responsibility. The profit commitment was reviewed at higher levels, both within the area and within the product divisions, with the final approval coming from the Corporate Executive Committee (CEC), which required compatible figures from the vice president of international operations and the product group executives. CEC, the major policy-making forum at Bancil, consisting of the chief executive officer, the group vice presidents, the vice president of international operations, and the corporate secretary, met monthly to resolve policy issues and to review operating performance.

For each country, results were reported separately for the various divisions represented, which, in turn, were consolidated into a combined NU statement. The NU as well as the divisions were held accountable, though at different levels, according to their responsibilities. The division profit flow (DPF) and NU net income are shown in the following example for the Argentine National Unit in 1974:

	Rodgers Division	Dominic Division	Toiletry Division	National Unit
Division sales	$250,000	$800,000	$1,250,000	$2,300,000
Division expenses	160,000	650,000	970,000	1,780,000
Division profit flow (DPF)	$ 90,000	$150,000	$ 280,000	$ 520,000
NU other expenses (general administrative interest on loans, etc.)				350,000
NU income before taxes				170,000
Less: Taxes				80,000
NU net income				$ 90,000
Working capital	$100,000	$300,000	$ 700,000	

The product divisions were responsible for worldwide division profit flow (DPF), defined as net sales less all direct expenses related to divisional activity, including marketing managers' salaries, sales force, and sales office expenses. The NU was responsible for net income after charging all local divisional expenses and all NU operating expenses such as general administration, taxes, and interest on borrowed funds. Because both the general managers and the divisions shared responsibility for profit in the international operations, the new structure was called a shared responsiblity matrix (SRM). The vice president of international operations and the division presidents continually monitored various performance ratios and figures (see Exhibit 3). In 1975 international operations emphasized return on resources, cash generation, and cash remittance, while the division presidents emphasized product-line return on resources, competitive market share, share of advertising, and dates of new product introductions.

The impact of the 1973 organizational shift to the SRM had been greatest for the general managers. Previously, as Bancil delegates, they had not been measured on the basis of the NU's total performance for which they were now held responsible. Also, they now determined salary adjustments, hiring, dismissals, and appointments after consultations with the divisions. In addition, general managers continued to keep abreast of important political developments in their areas, such as the appointment of a new finance minister, a general work strike, imposition of punitive taxes, and the outbreak of political strife, a not-infrequent occurrence in some countries.

Under the new organizational structure, the area marketing directors felt that their influence was waning. While they were responsible for DPF, they were not sure that they had "enough muscle" to effect appropriate allocation of resources for their products in each of the countries they served. This view was shared by Nicholas Rosati, Knight division marketing manager in Italy, who commented on his job:

The European marketing director for the Knight division keeps telling me to make more calls on hospitals and laboratories. But it is useless to make calls to solicit more orders. The general manager for Italy came from the consumer products division. He will neither allocate additional manpower to service new accounts for the Knight division nor will he purchase sufficient inventory of our products so I

Exhibit 3
Bancil Corporation Control Figures and Ratios

Vice President of International Operations for National Unit		Division President for Product Line
X*	Sales	X
X	Operating income: percent sales	X
X	General manager expense: percent sales	
X	Selling expense: percent sales	X
X	Nonproduction expense: percent operating income	
X	Operating income per staff employee	
X	Percent staff turnover	
X	Accounts receivable (days)	X
X	Inventories (days)	X
X	Fixed assets	X
X	Resources employed	X
X	Return on resources	X
X	Cash generation	X
X	Cash remittances	
X	Share of market and share of advertising	X
X	Rate of new product introduction	X

* X indicates figure or ratio on organization's (national unit or division) performance of interest to the vice president of international operations and the division presidents.

Source: Company records.

can promise reasonable delivery times for new accounts.

Divisions, nevertheless, were anxious to increase their market penetration outside the United States and Canada, seeing such a strategy as their best avenue of growth. The recent increase in international sales and profits, which had by far exceeded that of domestic operations (see Exhibit 4), seemed to confirm the soundness of this view. Not all NU general managers shared this approach, as exemplified by a statement from Edmundo Covelli, the general manager of Brazil:

The divisions are continually seeking to boost their sales and increase their DPF. They are not concerned with the working capital requirements to support the sales. With the inflation rate in Brazil, my interest rate of 40 percent on short-term loans has a significant effect on my profits.

The Peau Doux Issue

The telephone conversation described at the begining of the case involved a disagreement between Tom Wilson, who was both marketing vice president for the toiletry division and acting division marketing director for Europe, and Pierre Chevalier, Bancil's general manager for France. It also involved Remy Gentile, who reported on a line basis to Chevalier and on a functional basis to Wilson.

Pierre Chevalier had been a general manager of France for 18 months after having been hired from a competitor in the consumer products business. Upon assuming the position, he iden-

Exhibit 4
Sales and Profits for Bancil Corporation, Domestic and International ($ millions)

	Domestic		International		Total	
Year	Sales	Profit	Sales	Profit	Sales	Profit
1955	61	5.5	—	—	61	5.5
1960	83	8.3	6	0.2	89	8.5
1965	121	13.5	23	1.3	144	14.8
1969	269	26.7	76	9.2	345	35.9
1970	280	27.1	99	12.3	379	39.4
1971	288	28.7	110	14.2	398	42.9
1972	313	32.5	147	15.8	460	48.3
1973	333	35.3	188	21.4	521	56.7
1974	358	36.7	242	30.9	600	67.6

Source: Company records.

tified several organizational and operational problems in France:

> When I took this job, I had five marketing managers, a financial manager, a production manager, and a medical specialist reporting to me. After the consumer products division split, the new toiletry division wanted its own marketing manager. Nine people reporting to me was too many. I hired Remy for his administrative talents and had him assume responsibility for the toiletry division in addition to having the other marketing managers report to him. That gave me more time to work with our production people to get the cost of goods down.

In less than two years as general manager, Chevalier had reduced the cost of goods sold by more than 3 percent by investing in new equipment and had improved the net income for the French NU by discontinuing products which had little profit potential.

Remy Gentile had been the marketing manager for the toiletry division in France for the past year. In addition, five other marketing managers (one for each Bancil Corporation division operating in France) reported to him. During the previous six years Gentile had progressed from salesman to sales supervisor to marketing manager within the Knight division in France.

Although he had received mixed reviews from the toiletry division, particularly on his lack of mass-marketing experience, Chevalier had hired him because of his track record, his ability to learn fast, and his outstanding judgment.

The disagreement involved the Peau Doux line of hand creams which Bancil Corporation had purchased five years earlier to spread the general manager's overhead, especially in terms of marketing, over a broader product offering. Wilson's frustration resulted from Chevalier's ambivalence toward the division's strategy of increasing the marketing effort and cutting manufacturing costs on the Peau Doux line.

The total market in France for the Peau Doux product line was growing at an annual rate of 15–20 percent, according to both Wilson and Gentile. However, Peau Doux, an old, highly regarded hand cream, had been traditionally distributed through pharmacies, whereas recently introduced hand creams had been successfully sold through supermarkets. The original Peau Doux sales force was not equipped to distribute the product through other outlets. To support a second sales force for supermarket distribution, the toiletry division sought to acquire the L'aube shampoo and face cream line. When Gentile had informed Chevalier of this strategy, the latter had questioned the wisdom of the move. The current volume of the Peau Doux line was $800,000. Though less than 10 percent of Chevalier's total volume, it comprised the entire toiletry division volume in France.

Tom Wilson viewed the Peau Doux problems primarily in terms of an inadequate marketing effort. On three occasions within the past year, he or his media experts from Sunnyvale had gone to Paris to trouble-shoot the Peau Doux problems. On the last trip, Robert Vincent, the toiletry division president, had joined them. On the return flight to Sunnyvale, Wilson remarked to Vincent:

> I have the suspicion that Chevalier, in disregarding our expertise, is challenging our authority. It is apparent from his indifference to our concerns and his neglect in allocating capital for new machinery that he doesn't care about the Peau Doux line. Maybe he should be told what to do directly.

Vincent responded:

> Those are very strong words, Tom. I suggest we hold tight and do a very thorough job of preparing for the budget session on our strategy in France. If Chevalier does not accept or fundamentally revises our budget, we may take appropriate measures to make corporate management aware of the existing insensitivity to the toiletry division in France. This seems to be a critical issue. If we lose now, we may never get back in the French market in the future.

After Wilson and Vincent had departed for Sunnyvale, Chevalier commented to Dufour, his area vice president:

> I have the feeling that nothing we say will alter the thinking of Wilson and Vincent. They seem to be impervious to our arguments that mass advertising and merchandising in France do not fit the Peau Doux product concept.

Andre Dufour had been a practicing pharmacist for six years prior to joining Bancil Corporation as a sales supervisor in Paris in 1962. He had progressed to sales manager and marketing manager of the consumer products division in France. After the untimely death of the existing Bancil delegate for France in 1970, he had been selected to fill that position. With the advent of SRM he had become the general manager and had been promoted to vice president for Europe a year later. Dufour had a talent for identifying market needs and for thoroughly planning and deliberately executing strategies. He was also admired for his perseverance and dedication to established objectives. Clark B. Tucker, vice president of international operations and Dufour's immediate supervisor, commented:

> When he was a pharmacist he developed an avocational interest in chess and desired to become proficient at the game. Within five years he successfully competed in several international tournaments and achieved the rank of International Grand Master.

In the fall of 1974, Dufour had become the acting vice president of international operations while his superior, Clark Tucker, was attending the 13-week Advanced Management Program at the Harvard Business School. Though Dufour had considerable difficulty with the English language, he favorably impressed the corporate management at Sunnyvale with his ability of getting to the heart of business problems.

The toiletry division had only limited international activities. In addition to the Peau Doux line in France, it marketed Cascada shampoos and Tempestad fragrances in Argentina. The Cascada and Tempestad lines had been acquired in 1971.

Tom Wilson and Manual Ramirez, toiletry division marketing director for Latin America, were ecstatic over the consumer acceptance and division performance of Cascada and Tempestad in Argentina. Revenue and DPF had quintupled since the acquisition. In his dealings with Gentile, Wilson frequently referred to the toiletry division's clearly stated responsibility for worldwide marketing of toiletry products.

Wilson felt that his position in proposing the new strategy for France was strong.

On the other hand, Sergio Portillo, general manager of Argentina and Uruguay, and Juan Vilas, vice president for Latin American operations, had become alarmed by the cash drain from marketing the toiletry division products in Argentina. The high interest charges on funds for inventories and receivables seemed to negate the margins touted by the division executives. In describing the Cascada and Tempestad operation to Vilas, Portillo commented:

> I have roughly calculated our inventory turnover for the toiletry division products marketed in Argentina. Though my calculations are crude, the ratio based on gross sales is about four, which is less than one half the inventory turnover of the remainder of our products.

Neither Portillor nor Vilas shared the toiletry division's enthusiasm and they suspected that Cascada and Tempestad were only slightly above breakeven profitability. Chevalier and Dufour were aware of this concern with the toiletry products in Argentina.

As Chevalier contemplated the toiletry division strategy, he became convinced that more substantive arguments rather than just economic ones would support his position. In discussing his concerns with Dufour, Chevalier asked:

> Are the toiletry division product lines really part of what John Stoopes and we want to be

Bancil's business? Hand creams, shampoos, and fragrances belong to firms like Colgate-Palmolive, Procter & Gamble, and Revlon. What is Bancil contributing to the local people's welfare by producing and marketing toiletries? We have several potentially lucrative alternatives for our resources. The Rodgers division's revenues have been increasing at 18 percent. We recently completed construction of a processing plant for Rodgers and we must get sales up to our new capacity. The Knight division is introducing an electronic blood analyzer that represents a technological breakthrough. We must expand and educate our sales force to take advantage of this opportunity.

Chevalier sensed that Gentile was becoming increasingly uneasy on this issue, and the feeling was contagious. They had never faced such a situation before. Under the previous organization, NUs had been required to comply, although sometimes reluctantly, with the decisions from Sunnyvale. However, SRM was not supposed to work this way. Chevalier and Gentile stood firmly behind their position, though they recognized the pressure on Tom Wilson and to a lesser degree on Vincent. They wondered what should be the next step and who should take it. Due to the strained relationship with Wilson, they did not rule out the possibility of Wilson and Vincent's taking the Peau Doux issue to the consumer products group vice president and having it resolved within the corporate executive committee.

FOUR

CONTROL OF INTERNATIONAL OPERATIONS

No organization can accomplish its goals without proper control. The imperative of organizational control is heightened when firms cross national borders and expand into unfamiliar foreign markets. Chapter 4 presents control of international operations and foreign subsidiaries. First, various control mechanisms are described. Next, three approaches to control are discussed. Then, cultural aspects of NMC control are elaborated. Afterward, within the context of the historical evolution of the international environment, the corresponding MNC coordination and control mechanisms are summarized. There are differences between the control of an MNC and that of a domestic firm. These differences are due to the complexity of and uncertainties surrounding the MNC environment, with a resulting potential for difficulty. The host government relationship creates additional problems. Following a discussion of control problems of the MNCs, the influence of host government actions on MNC control is analyzed.

During the 1980s, many developing countries experienced financial crises. Most were forced to block the transfer of hard currencies abroad. Multinational companies (MNCs) operating in these countries were unable to repatriate earnings or assets. In effect, the MNCs' control of these funds and, indirectly, a partial control of their businesses, was subject to host government policies. Some firms used unique methods to move the blocked funds abroad. Columbia Pictures, for example, filmed a movie in Kenya to use up blocked funds generated by its parent company Coca-Cola. Another firm, for a while, booked all of its airline tickets for all destinations in or out of Dar es Salaam, Tanzania, to spend money blocked in that country.[1]

Host country interference into the normal business operation of MNCs is not limited to blocking funds. Often, MNCs lose some control over their foreign subsidiaries due to host government demands. Renegotiation of contracts to terms more favorable to host countries is a common practice. Sometimes, the original agreement is so much in favor of the MNC that a renegotiation is an expected eventuality. A famous example is the case of the General Motors (GM) wholly owned subsidiary in Australia in the mid-1950s. In 1954–55, the GM subsidiary's profit after taxes amounted to 560 percent of the original investment, and the dividend paid to GM represented 8 percent of the Australian balance of payments.[2]

The loss of control over foreign subsidiaries is not always the result of one-sided contracts, nor do they necessarily happen because of renegotiations. Cases of outright takeover of foreign subsidiaries for political reasons have occurred. Whenever, and for whatever reasons, host governments initiate a renegotiation process, MNCs are usually reluctant participants. Consider the Papua, New Guinea, government and the three mining companies that own most of the big Porgera gold mine in that country.

The government of Papua, New Guinea, shared the ownership of Porgera mine with subsidiaries of Placer Dome of Vancouver, Canada; Hanson plc of Britain; and M.I.M. Holdings Ltd. of Australia. The three companies each owned 30 percent, and the government *owned 10 percent of the mine, until the government decided to increase its share to 25 percent. This reduced each firm's stake in the mine to 25 percent. To finance the purchase of the additional 15 percent worth of shares, Papua's government proposed that $136 million needed for the purchase would be generated by the cash flow from the same amount. In effect, according to a financial analyst, Papua is paying the firms with their own money, at a price 20 percent below its market value. When it declared the intention to raise its stake, however, the government of Papua suggested that production and profit from the mine had exceeded initial expectations. It claimed that the companies had withheld information and understated the mines potential in their first negotiation.[3]*

Introduction

The effective management of an organization, among other factors, depends on securing continuous and sufficient progress toward goals. Management must determine if the organization is following the right strategies and if these strategies are being implemented correctly. Sound management also involves asking whether the organization is moving in the proper direction, and if the results obtained are those intended. Organizational control could provide answers to these questions. Control is needed not only for detecting problems and deviations from plans, but for anticipating problems before they occur. Simply put, control and strategic planning functions are very closely related and interdependent. A good plan has a built-in control system that monitors the implementation of the plan and provides information on goal attainment. It often involves highlighting problem areas and identifying the deficiencies in carrying out the plan. The validity and appropriateness of a strategy is also assessed with the information supplied by various control mechanisms.

In the following pages we introduce the major elements of the traditional control system. Using this introduction as a background, control tactics for MNCs are then discussed.

Purpose and Functions of the Control Process

Organizational control refers to the process of monitoring and evaluating the effectiveness and efficiency of organizational performance, and taking corrective action when performance falls short of expectations. Based on this definition, there are four major components to a control system. First, spell out the intended results, and establish standards against which organizational activities and accomplishments could be measured. Second, monitor and collect information on organizational activities that are aimed at goal accomplishment. Third, evaluate organizational performance and results for effectiveness. Fourth, make necessary adjustments to correct deficiencies during and after the implementation of the strategy. Deficiencies could be due to shortcomings in implementation or flaws in the strategy. The failure of a strategy could also be related to changes in environmental factors that were the basic premises of the strategic plan. In any case, a properly constructed control mechanism should provide information regarding the shortcomings. Therefore, control could be viewed as the last step in the strategic management process, coming after planning and implementation but with the potential to feed information back into those systems as it is learned.

Problems may arise at any point along the four stages of the control system. Inadequate information, for example, could result in inaccurate standards being established. In turn, the use of deficient standards in measuring progress toward goals could falsely indicate performance failure on the part of organizational members.

Based on the differences in time horizons and scope of coverage, planning may be either strategic or operational. Strategic planning involves the total organization, deals with long-term survival of the organization, and requires nonroutine solutions. Operational planning takes into account shorter term performance requirements, and deals with recurring problems that are often the domain of individual organizational units. The two types of planning have their corresponding controls, strategic control and operational control.

Control Mechanisms

Several control mechanisms can be used individually or in combination in an organization. Some are very formal, such as various reports from lower levels to higher levels of the organizational hierarchy. Others are informal, such as socialization and acculturation that instill organizational values in members and create uniformity in decisions and actions. In the following section, we review major control mechanisms.

Input and Output Controls

Organizational activities and performance may be regarded either as inputs or as outputs. In using various control mechanisms, a firm has the choice of controlling the inputs, the outputs, or a combination of both. Input control is regarded as behavioral control, where expectations are communicated to employees in advance. Then, through personal supervision and surveillance they are guided and directed to achieve goals. Of course, rewards and punishment are the instruments used to induce goal-oriented behavior modification. Input control relies on feedforward information. It works best in small organizations, and where the low level of complexity allows managers to identify the desired behavior in advance. Also, input controls could be more useful at the lower levels of the organization where activities and their outcomes are more predictable.

Output control is result oriented and utilizes impersonal measures such as the difference be-

tween the expected and final outcome. It relies on feedback information to correct the deviations. Output control works well for large organizations where the complexity and heterogeneity of activities require standard objective measures for comparison. Organizations tend to use more output controls at the higher levels of the hierarchy, where there is a high level of complexity and interdependence among tasks. Output control systems are reactive, whereas input controls are proactive. Of course, the two control systems are complementary.

Locus of Decision Making

Usually, all major strategic and critical decisions are made by top-level executives. Some organizations may allow dispersion of decision-making power for other important matters among lower level managers. *Centralization* of decision making is characteristic of a firm in which most decisions are made by top-level managers. In a centralized MNC, foreign subsidiaries have limited decision-making authority, and most important matters are decided by the headquarters. The opposite is *decentralization,* where decision-making power is dispersed among more managers. Decentralized MNCs give more autonomy to their foreign subsidiaries. Centralized firms exert much tighter control over various parts of the organization than decentralized firms.

Many factors determine the degree of autonomy granted to the subsidiary. Major factors include the nature of decisions that need to be made and the impact on the rest of the MNC, the type of technology employed, and the product and industry characteristics. In situations where the decision outcomes affect only the subsidiary and the host country market, managers are often given more autonomy. In large, globally integrated firms, decision making is more centralized so that the activities of various subsidiaries can be closely coordinated. Also, for the most important matters, such as negotiating new agreements with host governments, subsidiaries are required to clear their decisions with headquarters.

Technology and market characteristics may dictate the need for closer coordination among various subsidiaries. When products are mature, price competition is the norm. Also, when product components are produced by a number of subsidiaries, there is a high degree of interdependency among subsidiaries. Price competition and interdependency require uniformity of activities and coordination among subsidiaries. Consequently, the headquarters is more apt to exercise central control.

Decision-making autonomy also varies within the functional areas. A study by Hedlund of 77 subsidiaries of 39 MNCs in the United States, United Kingdom, Germany, Japan, and Sweden indicated that subsidiary autonomy was highest for personnel decisions and lowest for finance decisions. For production and marketing decisions, subsidiary autonomy was at an intermediate level.[4] A similar pattern of decision making was reported by the Conference Board for 109 U.S., Canadian, and European MNCs. The overall result of the Conference Board findings are summarized in Table 4.1. These firms exercised stricter financial control, and allowed greater local freedom for labor, political, and business decisions. Also, the home office of these MNCs made the decisions to introduce new products and to establish R & D facilities.

Communication and Information Flow

Information collection on organizational performance is the linchpin in any control system. To assess the firm's viability and the relevance of its strategy, a variety of data must be collected from inside and outside the firm. To monitor performance, a variety of information is communicated among different parts of the organization. Strategies, goals, and expectations are communicated from the headquarters to subsidiaries. Data on implementation of strategies, fulfillment of goals, and market information are sent to the headquarters.

Communication and information flow range from periodic financial and operations reports to occasional face-to-face meetings. Telecom-

munications technology has expanded the information processing capability of MNCs and has resulted in movements toward both centralization and decentralization. Through telephone, facsimile, and electronic mail, the headquarters is able to receive timely information from dispersed foreign operations. Timely information allows more centralization of the decision-making process. However, decentralization efforts have also been aided by the speed and accuracy of surveillance and better control. Consequently, the headquarters feels better informed and that it has more potential control and as a result is less reluctant to grant decision-making authority to subsidiary managers. On the other hand, when circumstances call for centralization, headquarters will have more confidence in making decisions that are going to be applied in far away operations.

Formal reports Formal reporting on financial and operations aspects along with local market data are essential means of subsidiary control by the MNC. Most MNCs rely heavily on financial reports for control of foreign subsidiaries. Financial data such as return on investment and inventory turnover allow comparison with industry norms and provide information on strategy implementation progress. Intrafirm business transactions and corporate tax variations among host countries make the use of financial data by MNCs more complex. This aspect of MNCs' control is the subject of conflict between host countries and the MNCs. Often, host countries claim MNCs abuse intrafirm transactions to reduce taxable earnings and consequently corporate taxes.[5]

The use of financial data for control of foreign operations has several limitations. For example, currency exchange rate fluctuations distort financial data, and strategic decisions by headquarters may limit a subsidiary manager's choice of the best possible business options. MNCs are aware of these limitations, and temper the use of financial data with personal judgment.

Informal communication Informal communication is used along with formal communi-

Table 4.1
Decision-Making Authority in Local Units

Decision Area	Number of Operations Where Local or Regional Unit Has		
	Full Authority	Authority to Take Action, But Must Consult with Higher Level	Authority to Recommend; Parent Must Approve Any Major Action
Capital expenditures			
Acquire local business	3	19	299
(Local interests control)	5	14	59
Enter joint venture	4	30	288
(Local interests control)	5	17	56
Build new plant	8	24	285
(Local interests control)	4	21	52
Miscellaneous			
Build research facility	16	63	255
(Local interests control)	9	24	46
Top personnel issues			
Choose new director	9	74	241
(Local interests control)	6	30	46
Select new head	15	78	226
(Local interests control)	7	34	37
Territorial and jurisdicational issues			
Enter new territory	7	60	241
(Local interests control)	6	20	48
Business decisions			
Product introduction	62	98	150
(Local interests control)	17	25	32
Labor and external relations			
Discuss political issues	60	186	68
(Local interests control)	22	38	14
Negotiate labor contract	175	124	15
(Local interests control)	57	19	5

Note: Sample of 109 companies. For each decision area, level of authority in local or regional unit is given for two situations, where local interests (particularly eight host governments) do not have a controlling interest and (in parentheses) where they do exert a controlling interest.

Source: R. E. Berenbeim. "Operating Foreign Subsidiary." Conference Board Report No. 836 (1983). Used by permission.

cation to convey to members of the organization what the performance expectations are, and to cajole them to comply with norms. Informal communication is more subtle and indirect in enforcing organizational standards. Some firms, for example, communicate dress codes to members without making a formal statement about it. Note, however, that physical distance and limited opportunities for regular, face-to-face contacts with subsidiary managers compel the MNCs to a greater reliance on the formal system of control.

Organizational Structure

In Chapter 3, we discussed MNC organizational structure within the framework of the organizing function. As a tool in implementing strategy, and as a skeletal framework that regulates and channels activities in prescribed directions, organization structure is an effective control mechanism. It is within this structure that formal communication channels and superior–subordinate relationships are established.

Increased competition and changing market conditions require timely, concerted, and uniform response from various organizational units. To increase organizational capabilities for proper response to competition and other market forces, firms may need to institute more central control. For example, MNCs that find themselves faced with intense competition may require tighter control, and could centralize their operations by restructuring. In response to increased competition in the United States, for example, Sony consolidated its electronic and entertainment operations under one corporate umbrella headed by an American executive. When Sony bought its entertainment companies, it was hoping to capitalize on the synergies between the electronic and entertainment businesses. The expected synergies did not fully materialize because of the strained relationship between the two divisions. The electronics executives were often critical of the huge amounts that Sony spent on its Hollywood operations. Also, there was a cultural gap between the more prosaic hardware operations and the glamorous entertainment division. With the restructuring, Sony intended to bring the two sides closer together and eliminate each division's preoccupation with its own priorities.[6]

Integrative Mechanisms

To control and manage interdependencies among various organizational units, various integrative mechanisms are used. The more common integrative mechanisms are liaison positions, cross-unit committees, integrators, and the matrix structure.[7] These mechanisms form a continuum from simple to complex, moving from liaison to matrix in terms of complexity. Obviously, the effective control is gained by matching the level of interdependency among organizational units with the complexity of integrative mechanisms. A low level of interdependency calls for the use of a simple integrative mechanism such as a liaison role. A more complex integrative mechanism such as a matrix is appropriate for the management and control of a high level of interdependency. Therefore, it is of no surprise that some global firms, such as Asea-Brown Boveri, with a high degree of interdependency among their worldwide operations have chosen a matrix form.

To improve coordination among interdependent divisions and to facilitate communication between them, a liaison role could be used. A liaison bypasses long lines of communication, if the two units have to refer to a higher level on the corporate hierarchy for solving their differences and working out their interdependence. Liaison roles are used more at the lower and middle levels of organizations and, therefore, are more appropriate for operational control.

To solve problems of control and interdependence, integrative roles or departments are created whose responsibility is to enable the two units to work together smoothly. Typical titles and positions are product managers, program managers, and project managers. A product manager, for example, may integrate the marketing and production activities of a product between two separate divisions. Committees are frequently used at various levels of organizations for control problems that other mechanisms cannot handle. Committees could be used on an ad hoc or permanent basis. Many firms have permanent executive committees that handle corporatewide strategic problems of control and integration.

Resource Allocation

The primary relationships among various units of a business organization center on economics. One way of exerting control is through resource allocation. The pattern of resource distribution (anything that people value, e.g., money, material, promotion, knowledge, technology, vacation, a large office, etc.) indicates to the members the performances and outcomes desired by the organization. By changing the allocation of resources among subsidiaries, MNCs effectively exercise control over them. In many MNCs, the direction of resource flow is from the headquarters to the subsidiaries; in integrated MNCs, however, the flow of resources is multidirectional. A subsidiary's influence and its autonomy within the MNC is a function of the amount of resources it provides to the rest of the MNC. Ultimately, however, it is the headquarters that determines the pattern of resource allocation and control, and it generally uses the budgeting system as the associated control system.

Budgeting system   Budgeting is the allocation of resources among various organizational units on the basis of present needs, past performance, and the projection of future needs. Budgets are standards against which actual performance can be measured. Firms use different budgets for monitoring important activities and functions, such as the capital expenditure budget, the marketing and promotion budget, and the research and development budget.

With a budgeting system MNCs not only monitor subsidiaries' activities, but establish priorities that are reflective of corporate strategies. Increasing or decreasing the budget is an effective way of dictating the direction of a subsidiary's development and progress. Earlier in this chapter, it was mentioned that because of physical separation and the unique relationship between foreign subsidiaries and the home office, MNCs are very much concerned with the performance of their dispersed global operation. One way of reducing the level of concern is to centralize the most critical decisions at the headquarters. The most obvious and easily centralized decisions are those dealing with finance. Through a budgeting system, most of the subsidiaries activities are translated into financial reports and are available for closer scrutiny.

Control Approaches

The three approaches to control are the market approach, rules approach, and cultural approach. Based on the ideas of Ouchi and Maguire,[8] Lebas and Weigenstein[9] proposed that the three approaches form a triangular continuum along which organizations use a combination of two methods of control: input control and output control (see Figure 4.1). The three approaches do not exist in pure form. Each, however, may be a dominant form in a given organization. Among the three approaches, as we will argue, cultural control may be needed to respond to the uncertainty and complexity of the international environment.

The Market Approach

Control mechanisms employed in a market approach are external market forces. Competition, supply and demand, and contractual agreements govern the relationships among organizational units. An MNC using the market approach resembles a federation of autonomous units that are free to deal with internal (other units and subsidiaries) or external suppliers. Output control is the dominant method in a market approach, which includes transfer pricing, bargaining, and management compensation. The market approach is efficient when performance

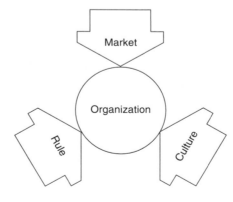

Figure 4.1   Three Approaches to Control

ambiguity is low and goal incongruence is high.[10]

Rules Approach

In most organizations, the rules approach seems to be more visible than other controls. A rules-oriented organization utilizes both input and output controls. It relies extensively on established rules and procedure such as planning, budgeting, formal reports, performance evaluation, and hierarchical structure. Rules work best when both goal incongruence and performance ambiguity are moderately high, and when the environment is relatively stable. When there is less congruence among various goals pursued by the members, a rules-oriented control system provides a common ground for action and coordination. In a relatively stable environment, rules provide the specifics needed to clarify goals and performance requirements. A rules-oriented system will only be viable when the environment allows sufficient time to respond to feedback information when corrections are needed. Of course, environmental conditions, and particularly those of the international environment, are not stable. Often the time needed to make corrections and adjustments is short. Therefore, very seldom does the feedback process of error–information–correction work well for MNCs.

Cultural Approach

In a cultural approach, external rules and procedures are internalized. Instead of the supervisory surveillance that is common in a rules-oriented organization, individuals exercise self-control and abide by cultural norms and expectations. The time required to respond to feedback information is shorter, and the cost of control is lower than is the case in the other two approaches. The shortcomings of other control systems make the cultural approach more attractive for MNC operations. Due to their personalized nature, the effectiveness of behavioral controls (input), is limited to a single unit of the organization. Because of their specificity and narrow scope, and the required response time, rules-oriented controls have a narrow application and are tied to an organizational unit. There are always exceptions to rules with which the upper level managers have to deal. Since MNCs operate in a dynamic environment, the market and rules approaches will have limited applicability and MNCs will need to make increasing use of cultural controls.

When through cultural controls, the norms, values, and goals of the organization are internalized, there is no need for personal supervision or formal rules. Since they are not narrow and specific, when applied to input and output controls, cultural norms are applicable on an organization-wide basis. The internalized values provide guidelines that are broad enough to cover most situations. These guidelines allow individuals to follow cultural norms where ambiguity of the situation renders rules and established standards, for example, in budgeting and performance criteria, inappropriate. People's knowledge of these broad informal rules enables them to extrapolate those rules into new situations and to act quickly.[11] Therefore, compared with market and rules approaches, the cultural approach to control provides a better ability to handle the performance ambiguity that is a characteristic of MNC operations. To summarize the contrasting ideas in the approaches, Ouchi explains the limitations of the market and rules approaches and describes the advantages of a cultural approach.[12] He builds his argument on the informational prerequisites of each approach. The informational prerequisites of the market and rules approaches are prices and rules, respectively. Prices charged for intrafirm business transactions are the basis for control in a market system. Rules and procedures form a foundation for control in a rules-oriented system.

> Prices are a highly sophisticated form of information for decision making. However, correct prices are difficult to arrive at, particularly when technological interdependence, novelty,

or other forms of ambiguity obscure the boundary between tasks or individuals. Rules, by comparison, are relatively crude informational devices. A rule is specific to a problem, and therefore it takes a large number of rules to control organizational responses. A decision maker must know the structure of the rules in order to apply the correct one in any given situation. Moreover, an organization can never specify a set of rules that will cover all possible contingencies. Instead, it specifies a smaller set of rules which cover routine decisions, and refers exceptions up the hierarchy where policy makers can invent rules as needed.[13]

Compared to the market and rules approaches, the cultural approach has minimal informational prerequisites. As information prerequisites, cultural norms and expectations are implicit rather than explicit rules that govern behavior. They prescribe performance and evaluation requirements in a general way, which must be interpreted in a particular situation. These norms, however, "in a formal organization may produce a unified, although implicit philosophy or point of view, functionally equivalent to a theory about how that organization should work. A member who grasps such an essential theory can deduce from it an appropriate rule to govern any possible decision, thus producing a very elegant and complete form of control."[14] Characteristics of the three approaches are summarized in Table 4.2.

Cultural control has the potential to be very effective in dealing with the diversity, complexity, and uncertainty of the MNC environment. MNCs, however, cannot totally abandon market and rules approaches. Creating culturally based controls takes a long time—cultures are not built overnight. Also, cultures change very slowly, whereas most environmental conditions are subject to sudden changes. Additionally, MNCs are comprised of diverse people. Diversity always makes it difficult to create uniform cultural norms. Therefore, it is impractical for the MNC not to apply other means of control, and wait for the development of a corporate culture and the concomitant cultural controls. Moreover, it is important to acknowledge the influence of cultural diversity on the effectiveness of market and rules approaches to control. In the following, we elaborate on this aspect of cultural control.

The effectiveness of various control systems is influenced by cultural differences among nations. Because of cultural differences, for example, the usefulness of different control mechanisms could vary in the U.S., the European, and Asian countries. In a country such as France, for example, where the hierarchical authority is more readily accepted, "a vertical organizational structure, minimal lateral relationships, dependence on chain of command, and rules and procedures set by superiors are natural control system components."[15] A market-oriented or cultural control system may be more appropriate in a country such as Sweden, where inequalities among the members are minimized,

Table 4.2
Characteristics of the Three Control Approaches

Control Approach	Dominant Method of Control	Information Prerequisite	Scope
Market	Output	Prices	Wide
Rule	Input/output	Rules	Narrow
Cultural	Input/output	Norms and expectations	Wide

and participative decision making is favored. In traditional societies that avoid radical departures from established norms, and where resistance to change is strong, people prefer specificity of rules and regulations. Therefore, organizational hierarchy and formal authority could be an effective control system. Cultures also vary in their emphasis on the role of individuals in the society. Where individualism is dominant a market-oriented control may function better. In contrast, where the individual's concerns are subordinate to the collective interests and benefits of groups or institutions, a culture-oriented control system may be more applicable.

Cultural Aspects of MNC Control

Culture is the most effective control mechanism. Societies effectively manage and control their people by devising cultural controls. Through the socialization process members internalize the values and norms of the society, which become the criteria for judging behavior. They are also strong motivating forces that induce people to behave according to the values and norms. Organizations employ culture and socialization for control purposes too. Because the MNCs operate in culturally diverse environments, the challenge, however, is to build a control system that capitalizes on the synergy of cultural diversity.

Corporate Socialization

Corporate socialization could be described as the process by which the members learn what behaviors and perspectives are customary and desirable in the work environment.[16] Through the corporate socialization process, the new members "learn the ropes," and are indoctrinated about the basic goals of the organization, the preferred means of goal achievement, the responsibilities of the members, the behavior pattern required for effective performance, and the rules for the maintenance of corporate identity and integrity.[17]

Corporate socialization takes place through a combination of obvious and subtle means. The obvious means of corporate socialization include job rotation, management development programs, and informal company-sponsored events. Of course, the corporate reward and compensation system is an obvious and powerful tool for shaping employee behavior and promoting the socialization process. A subtle socialization process encompasses the interaction and interpersonal relationship of top management with colleagues and the rest of the employees. The socialization process is closely related to the values inherent in the corporate culture. In this vein, corporate culture is both a reinforcing mechanism and an ever-present instrument of corporate socialization.

For a domestic firm, socialization of employees is a relatively routine process. Almost all organizations establish "the way we do things around here." Every management veteran has stories to tell about the process of breaking-in new employees, a process that makes future control less troublesome. One manager's strategy of dealing with what he was considering unwarranted arrogance on the part of new engineers, for example, was to demonstrate to them their lack of practical knowledge and their dependence on experienced managers.

> He would ask the new engineer "to examine and diagnose a particular complex circuit, which happened to violate a number of textbook principles but actually worked very well. The new [engineer] would usually announce with confidence, even after an invitation to double-check, that the circuit could not possibly work. At this point the manager would demonstrate the circuit, tell the new [engineer] that they had been selling it for several years without customer complaint." Then he would direct the engineer to explain why it did work. None he had tested were able to do it, but were convinced of the need for supplementing their textbook knowledge with practical know-how. From then on, establishing a good give-and-take relationship with the new engineer would be easy.[18]

The dispersed operations of an MNC make the socialization process more difficult and challenging. Aware of the challenge, many MNCs use job rotation to introduce employees early in their careers to the firm, the culture, and "the ropes" around their global operations. For example, to demonstrate that, contrary to employees' perceptions, international experience was not a roadblock to career advancement, General Electric revamped its job rotation program. It started sending its brightest stars to foreign assignments rather than the run-of-the-mill managers it once picked for posts abroad.[19] Motorola is another U.S. MNC with a similar program. Motorola has included in its job rotation program foreign engineering recruits. The program, called "Cadres 2000," is designed to permit its operation in the People's Republic of China to put up to 20 top recruits into leadership training and rotate them through its worldwide operations.[20]

Evolution of MNC Coordination and Control

Because of the additional coordination and control difficulties that MNCs face, they need more sophisticated control mechanisms than are used by domestic firms. The need to respond simultaneously to different strategic requirements of foreign countries necessitates much flexibility. MNCs have to be flexible in order to take advantage of global opportunities while remaining responsive to local differences. This calls for developing a much more sophisticated control mechanism. Consequently, in addition to formal means of control and coordination, MNCs need to rely on a wide range of informal mechanisms[21] including informal networks of communication, corporate culture and socialization, and career path management.

As the international competitive environment changes, so does the MNC's strategies and operations. The implementation of new strategies and the management of new operations require different methods of coordination and control from those used in day-to-day management. As a result, the MNC's coordination and control tactics are an evolutionary response to their environmental circumstances. The historical evolution of the international environment, and the corresponding pattern of coordination and control mechanisms used by MNCs, are summarized in Table 4.3. As Table 4.3 shows, over the years, emphasis has shifted from simpler to more complex coordination and control mechanisms.

The evolutionary changes in the international business environment can be divided into three periods.[22] Period I (1920–1950) brought about political changes that discouraged international competition and were conducive to competition on a country-by-country basis. Forces that restricted international business activities included nationalist sentiments, protectionist barriers, and communication and transportation difficulties. The strategic response to environmental imperatives was the establishment of semi-autonomous businesses within each country. The European firms, in particular, adopted country-centered strategies. They organized a decentralized, loosely connected federation of independent national subsidiaries. Each subsidiary served its domestic market. No integration onto a total corporate operation was sought, and local subsidiaries were nationally responsive firms. The management of a federation of semi-autonomous firms needed little coordination and control. MNCs managed their foreign subsidiaries as a "portfolio" of investments. As long as the subsidiaries were generating earnings, they were left to the discretion of expatriate managers. These managers were the equivalent of "Roman proconsuls that were given responsibilities only after years spent absorbing the values and practices of the parent company."[23] Headquarters control was assured through loyal, expatriate managers who provided an informal link with subsidiaries and preserved the corporate management style even in faraway countries. Direct reporting of subsidiary managers to the head of

Table 4.3

Historical Evolution of the International Competitive Environment and Corresponding Coordination and Control

Pattern of International Competition	Strategic Response of MNCs	Coordination and Control
PERIOD I: 1920–1950		
Multidomestic (or country-by-country basis)	*Country-Centered*	*Limited Control and Coordination*
Competition in each country is essentially independent of competition in other countries	Direct investment in many countries Self-contained and autonomous branches Differentiated and nationally responsive strategy Competitive advantage in downstream value activities	MNCs manage their activities as portfolios of subsidiaries (especially Europeans) No integration Decentralized federation of national subsidiaries Periodic financial reports
PERIOD II: 1950–1980		
International	*International*	*Formal*

International MNC's competitive position in one country is strongly influenced by its competitive position in other countries.	Concentration of production in few plants to achieve scale economies
	Serve the world from these few manufacturing locations through exporting
	Centralized control of worldwide marketing activities
	Standardization of product design
		Budgeting, standardized programs (e.g., marketing, manufacturing)
		Centralized R&D
		Structural mechanisms:
		  Product divisions, regional divisions
		  Centralized "hub"
		Output control

PERIOD III: 1980–		
Global (or worldwide basis)	*Global with Increasing Foreign Investment*	*Formal and Informal*
MNC's competitive position in one country is strongly influenced by its competitive position in other countries.	Decentralization of production in many plants in the world, each specialized in processes and/or products, with a strong interdependence among them Interorganizational transfer of technology and ideas Simultaneous response to national interests and local needs, and to economic forces toward globalization	Period I & II mechanisms, plus: Task forces, committees, integrators Informal communication networks Socialization of home-country and foreign managers Corporate culture

Source: Adopted from Tables 4a and 4b of Jon I. Martinez and J. Carlos Jarillo. "The Evolution of Research on Coordination Mechanisms in Multinational Corporations." *Journal of International Business Studies,* 20, no. 3 (1989), 504–506. Used by permission.

the MNC was a formal means of control exercised by headquarters. Subsidiaries supplied the headquarters with periodic financial reports, assuring compliance with the profit objectives of the MNC.

The international environment during Period II (1950–1980) represented a reverse of the conditions in the previous period. Economic and political forces favored international competition. Advancements in production technologies increased economies of scale. Decreased transportation and communication costs, along with economies of scale, allowed concentration of production in low-cost countries. These developments combined with the easing of protectionist barriers to increase international competition. MNCs responded by adopting an international strategy in which decision making was highly centralized and foreign subsidiaries were tightly controlled from headquarters. In terms of control, the MNCs relied on formal mechanisms, centered on budgeting, and on standardized programs in manufacturing and marketing. In addition to frequent financial reports, subsidiaries provided the headquarters with reports on all major functional areas. Formalization and standardization of policies, rules, and procedures strengthened the headquarters' tight output control over subsidiaries' operations.

Currently, MNCs are experiencing the environmental changes comprising Period III (1980–present), which are challenging their coordination and control capabilities. In the early 1980s, dichotomous and conflicting demands began to create a new set of pressures on the MNCs. On the one hand, technological developments have resulted in the globalization of business and competition in many industries. On the other hand, many governments demand that MNCs invest locally to create jobs, transfer technology, and contribute to the balance of payments. These factors plus a rise in nontariff barriers and protectionism have called for local responsiveness. In turn, the contradictory demands of global strategies and local responsiveness have required a higher level of coordination and control. MNCs discovered that the hands-off approach that relied on formal control and coordination mechanisms of the first two periods was inadequate for period III. Recognizing the need for flexibility and responsiveness, they have instituted both formal and informal control mechanisms. In addition to the formal controls of pervious periods, MNCs are using informal and subtle means that overlap the existing organizational structure and formal reporting procedures. Included among the new control mechanisms are teams, task forces, committees, and integrators. Additionally, the free flow of informal communication among all managers—from the headquarters to subsidiaries and vice versa, and among the foreign subsidiaries—supplements formal communication channels. Philosophical changes at the headquarters allow the MNCs to offer career paths that enable all managers, regardless of their country of origin, to advance to positions previously reserved for home country executives. In doing so, the MNCs create a corporate culture that effectively controls managerial actions without the reliance on formal rules and procedures. Acculturation of these managers, through continuous assignments to key positions throughout the global operation of the MNCs, works to develop a strong corporate culture and induce internalization of organizational objectives, values and beliefs, and corresponding policies and procedures.

Of course, this chronological progression in the application of control mechanisms is not uniform among all MNCs. Technological developments and competitive forces of the industry, among other factors, may propel a firm to use specific control mechanisms. The trend toward globalization, however, has been compelling MNCs to abandon the less appropriate control mechanisms of earlier periods. Also, MNCs may not change their structural and formal tools of coordination and control, but may also establish more informal mechanisms that are hidden under the surface. Procter and Gamble and Unilever, for example, have not changed their formal coordination and control mechanisms significantly in more than two decades. Instead, the internal management processes have changed. "Subsidiaries have assumed new and specific roles to respond to changing local conditions, and the headquarters' control mechanisms have evolved from ubiquitous 'company ways' to multidimensional gestalts that are applied differently to different parts of the organization. . ."[24]

Additional Control Problems of MNCs

In addition to the control problems associated with global operations, MNCs also encounter several other specific control problems. The additional control problems of the MNCs are a result of: (1) geographic distance between the headquarters and subsidiaries, (2) language and cultural differences, (3) legal differences, (4) intrafirm business transactions (transfer pricing), and (5) currency exchange rate fluctuations. Currency exchange rate fluctuations and other international financial issues are presented in Chapter 13. In the following, we discuss the other control problems of MNCs.

Language and Cultural Differences

Diversity in language and culture among various foreign operations is the source of many of the difficulties encountered by the MNCs' headquarters. The assignment of expatriates who are "acculturated" at headquarters to key managerial positions in the subsidiaries, and identification of local managers who are proficient in the language of the headquarters can reduce some of the problem. Typically, however, most staff at headquarters have limited or no foreign language skill, and the language problem remains real. The result is that communication between much of the headquarters staff and foreign subsidiaries is limited to contacts with those sub-

sidiary personnel who can speak the headquarters' language. This reality reduces the amount of information headquarters staff receives and processes. Without the ability to directly reach the sources of most information, they are at the mercy of subsidiary staff who have the language skills or interpreters.

This problem is magnified if several languages are spoken by the local workforce. Such is the case in Africa and India. Even in European countries, which employ a large number of guest workers, control problems arise from linguistic variety. In Germany, for example, many plants employ guest workers from Spain and Turkey, as well as the local German workers. The codetermination laws (covered in Chapter 10) require periodic meetings with workers. These meetings are held in Spanish, in Turkish, and, of course, in German. Additionally, the German subsidiaries of American firms that have American general managers hold top management meetings in English.[25]

Language diversity often creates fewer strategic and more operational control problems. In part, it is typical for upper level managers to be involved in strategic control, and there is a higher level of foreign language proficiency among this group of managers. In contrast, there are two reasons why language diversity creates problems with operational control, particularly in developing countries. First, and as noted, operational control affects more lower level foreign subsidiary personnel, and these are less likely to be proficient in the MNC's home country language. Second, since language and culture reflect the level of technological development, the language of many developing countries does not have equivalents for technical, industrial, and commercial terms used in modern business enterprises. Often it is impossible to translate these terms into the local language. The use of a common language, which in most cases is English, is very difficult for a workforce with minimal education, and may require the MNC to institute language training programs.

To overcome the language problem for servicing of its equipment, for example, Caterpillar has devised a unique method. They have developed an 800-word vocabulary called Caterpillar Fundamental English. With this tool it is possible for local suppliers, dealers, and service personnel to work with Caterpillar equipment without the need for a translation.[26]

Even without language difficulties, cultural differences have the potential to create control problems. Cultural norms and role expectations may result in inaccurate information and misunderstanding. Criticisms in public, for example, are avoided in most Oriental cultures; therefore, on-the-spot suggestions for improvements may not produce the intended results. Group harmony and cohesion is very much valued in many Asian countries. Consequently, people from these cultures may not report problems to higher levels immediately, hoping instead to find a solution without unduly disturbing the group.

Geographical Distance

Telecommunications technologies and improvements in transportation facilities have greatly aided the expansion of MNC operations. Vast geographical distances between the MNCs' subsidiaries, however, pose control problems that even today's modern telecommunications and travel facilities have not been able to fully overcome. Nothing can substitute for face-to-face communication and personal visits. Written communication, telephone calls, and voice and computer messages are not the same as personal visits. Often to travel from the headquarters and visit a foreign subsidiary takes at least a couple of days and much advance preparation. In some cases, this added travel time permits host country staff to rig personal visits by headquarters to show a different and rosier picture of the operations. Consider the following incident:

> A foreign importer in an Asian country was given the exclusive regional distribution rights of an American paint manufacturer. The importer was supposed to act as a middleman between the retailers and the paint company. Therefore, by contract, he was not permitted to be a retailer as well. In violation of the contract, the importer had established a full retailing operation, and in effect had become a monopoly. He had set up a bogus wholesale office separate from his main business that was temporarily staffed only when he was expecting a visit by the headquarters. Language barriers and long physical distance allowed this masquerade to go undetected for a few years.

Legal Differences

Although a whole chapter is devoted to the legal aspects of international management, here we briefly examine some major legal problems with MNC control. Laws and legal procedures are central to the concept of organizational control. The control of a business firm relies on the legal institutions and practices of the host country. The practices that legally are accepted or rejected in one country are not necessarily honored by the other. The MNCs' control of foreign subsidiaries can take place only within the confines of the legally accepted business norms of host countries. In effect, the host country's legal system may place limitations on the control that can be exercised by headquarters. In Germany, for example, most firms including the MNCs are bound by codetermination laws that require the membership of labor representatives on the board of directors. Because the law dictates power sharing and sharing of organizational control between management and labor, managers cannot unilaterally make certain decisions, such as the closing of a plant.

Host country legal requirements in virtually all aspects of business operations including labor relations, finance, marketing, and manufacturing limit MNCs' control over subsidiaries. Some countries limit the equity ownership of domestic firms by the MNCs. The equity ownership limits are more common among developing countries. In these countries, instead of direct control over the subsidiary operations, the

MNCs may assume the minority position and have to rely on advice and persuasion. The major problems of sharing equity ownership with host countries are discussed in a subsequent section.

Intrafirm Business Transactions

As discussed in Chapter 2, firms can use various strategies for entering into foreign markets, including export, contractual agreements, and direct investment. An export-oriented firm is dominated by product flows from the home country to foreign markets. The flow of capital from home country to host countries characterizes the firms using investment as an entry strategy. Knowledge flows from MNCs to host countries through licensing and contractual agreements. Within this context, therefore, an MNC could be viewed as a network of products, capital, and knowledge flow across national borders among business units controlled by the headquarters. In this network, knowledge, capital, and products primarily flow from the MNC's headquarters located in the home country to subsidiaries in foreign countries. Additionally, there are intersubsidiary business transactions that are controlled by the headquarters.

Because the flow of resources among various units of a domestic corporation takes place within national boundaries (i.e., where the firm manufactures in one area of the country but sells its products in others), it creates no special problem. The same is not true for MNCs. In some countries, MNCs cannot exercise their property rights fully. Various host government restrictions imposed on the MNCs limit the free flow of resources among subsidiaries. When repatriation of profits is restricted by host governments, for example, control and exercise of property rights on corporate earnings are limited. Some countries even go further and establish production requirements for the MNCs, which effectively curtail operational control over the subsidiary.

Furthermore, resource flow patterns between headquarters and the subsidiaries, on the one hand, and between the subsidiaries, on the other hand, raise special control issues. Although the pattern of resource flow is mostly from the MNC headquarters to subsidiaries, increasing globalization of business and diffusion of technology is beginning to alter this arrangement. An MNC may find it necessary to concentrate certain aspects of their business in a country. In the microcomputer industry, for example, it would be beneficial to locate R&D facilities in Silicon Valley (San Jose, California). Proximity to, and interaction with, a large number of firms at the cutting edge of a new technology provides easy access to a highly qualified workforce and immediate knowledge of the latest developments. A foreign subsidiary located in Silicon Valley could become responsible for the supply of advanced technology to the rest of the company. The dependence of various units of the MNC on this subsidiary for technology increases the subsidiary's importance to the MNC, and along with it the amount of attention and scrutiny it receives from the headquarters. In fact, internal resource interdependence is felt by many researchers to have an very important influence on decision-making patterns within the various units of an MNC.[27] Some even consider the headquarters' resource dependence on its subsidiary the most important determinant of subsidiary autonomy.[28] Empirical evidence suggests that the higher the importance of a subsidiary to the parent MNC and the rest of the firm, the lower its decision-making authority. The more the parent company delivers to, and receives resources from a subsidiary, the more critical decisions, such as investment and finances, are concentrated at the headquarters. Thus, there is an inverse relationship between the importance of a subsidiary to the MNC and its decision-making authority.[29]

The pattern of intrafirm resource flow could be used to chart the decision-making autonomy of MNC units. Figure 4.2 illustrates the pattern

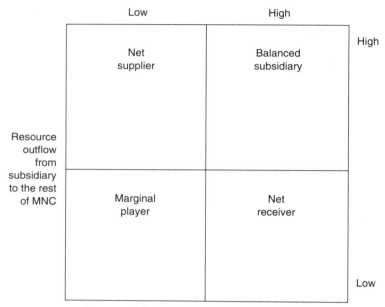

Figure 4.2   MNC Intrafirm Resource Flow

of intrafirm business transactions along a two-dimensional model.[30] One dimension of this model is the flow of resources from a subsidiary to the rest of the MNC, and the other dimension is the flow of resources from the rest of the MNC to the subsidiary. Four types of subsidiaries are represented in this model: net supplier, net receiver, balanced subsidiary, and marginal player. A net supplier sends more resources to the rest of the MNC than it receives. A net receiver is just the opposite of a net supplier, it receives more resources from the rest of the MNC than it sends to them. There is a roughly equal inflow and outflow of resources between the balanced subsidiary and the rest of the MNC. A minimum number of business transactions with the rest of the MNC characterizes a marginal player.

Based on Figure 4.2, there could be variations in subsidiaries' importance and autonomy within the MNC. The most important subsidiary is the balanced subsidiary, and the least important is a marginal player. A net supplier is more important than a net receiver, which in turn is more important than a marginal player. Both the net supplier and the net receiver are less important than a balanced subsidiary. Everything else being equal, the importance of a subsidiary to MNC operation is directly related to the amount of resource inflow and outflow that occurs between the subsidiary and the rest of the MNC. On this basis, a balanced subsidiary will be more closely controlled than the other subsidiaries, and marginal players may be afforded considerable freedom from controls. Table 4.4 depicts these relationships.

Other Factors

The pattern of resource allocations and the amount of control exerted by the headquarters is determined by many factors, among them are the importance of a subsidiary to the MNC and

Table 4.4
Resource Flow, Subsidiary Importance, and Headquarters Control

	Resource Flow to Subsidiary	Resource Flow from Subsidiary	Importance of Subsidiary to Headquarters	Control Exercised by MNC
Marginal player	Low	Low	Very little	Very little
Net receiver	High	Low	Some	Some
Net supplier	Low	High	Moderate	Moderate
Balanced subsidiary	High	High	Very much	Considerable

the required relationship between the subsidiary and the host government. A subsidiary, for example, may be given more decision-making authority if it has to establish certain links with the local community and to do so it requires more autonomy. Also, the headquarters confidence in the managers of subsidiaries determines the amount of central control exercised over them. MNC confidence is a function of a managers' skills, experience, and nationality. More experienced and competent managers are given more decision-making authority. Also expatriates have more autonomy than host national managers.

The pattern of resource allocation among foreign subsidiaries is an important means of control. This is particularly important when dealing with some developing countries. Sociopolitical instability and capricious government policies are often the source of political risk in these countries.[31] To reduce political risk, control of resource flow is an effective strategy. MNCs can exert substantial control even from a minority ownership position through the flow of technology, management know-how, and control of export marketing channels.[32] Centralization of R&D activities at the headquarters is a common and effective means of control that assures the dependency of foreign subsidiaries on the headquarters. For this reason, MNCs are very reluctant to establish R&D facilities outside their headquarters. Prior to the 1970s, oil-producing countries that had nationalized MNC operations were forced to invite the MNCs back because

the local governments lacked the technological and managerial capabilities to run the nationalized industries. Similarly, domination of export marketing channels by global oil companies was effectively used against the risk of nationalization.

Ownership and Host Government Involvement

In discussing control concerns of multinational corporations, two separate, but interrelated issues stand out. The first one is the control of organizational performance as just discussed. It deals with the activities and operation of the enterprise, and provides information and assurances that the corporate plans are accomplished. Typically, it is the control of organizational performance that comes to mind when discussing the subject of control. The second issue is the legal and ownership control that deals with business-government relationships, and participation of the host country in the ownership of a foreign subsidiary. The legal and ownership issues of control are even more challenging and complex than those involving corporate strategies.

Host Government Involvement

Host governments regularly interfere in the normal business operations of MNCs and infringe on their decision-making power and control. Typically, host governments get involved in the operation of MNCs' subsidiaries, rather than at the headquarters level. Consequently, the amount and type of control exercised by the headquarters over foreign subsidiaries are altered as host government involvement increases. Host government interference falls into three major categories: financial and investment decisions, business decisions, and human resource management.[33]

Financial and investment decisions   The most prevalent demand by host governments is for financial participation in foreign subsidiaries. Particularly, in Asia and South America, host governments pressure MNCs to share equity ownership of their subsidiaries with domestic investors or host government agencies. Under pressure some MNCs succumb to these demands and share equity ownership with locals. Most MNCs do not strongly object to a minority equity ownership by locals. In fact, an effective protection against the host government policy decisions that could adversely affect the MNC operations is sharing of ownership with host country investors. Some MNCs, however, have refused to do business with countries where they are not permitted to assume a majority equity ownership. From the MNCs' point of view, the effective control of a business is much easier with a majority equity position.

Interference in repatriation of assets is another financial restriction imposed on the MNCs. Some host governments limit repatriation of MNC assets. This limitation is considered most troublesome by the MNCs because it severely curtails their investment strategies and forces them to reinvest in the host country. Reinvestment in the host country may not necessarily be the best alternative. Asset repatriation restrictions are more common among developing countries with growing markets.

Another financial decision that is the source of contention with host governments is the allocation of R&D expenses to foreign subsidiaries. Some host governments have policies limiting the amount of fees the MNCs charge their foreign subsidiaries for R&D work carried out by their central laboratories. Another R&D issue is the location of research facilities. All countries, particularly developing nations, are very much interested in technology transfer. They are demanding that MNCs establish research laboratories within the host countries. Research and development facilities are not only the source of new technology, but they do contribute to the improvement of skills and knowledge of the local workforce.

Sharing equity ownership with host countries affects utilization, and sometimes control, of MNC resources. Without full control over a subsidiary, MNCs may not be willing to use the best available technology. State-of-the-art technology transfer that could not effectively be safeguarded against pilferage and piracy is not a wise choice. It may not, however, be wise to limit technology transfer. One MNC executive expressed this dilemma in the following terms. "Local participation can interfere with the free flow of the best technology available for each market. When you slow the development of the local units this can sometimes result in the loss of management control over the decision-making process."[34] The requirement for a large local equity ownership may reduce an MNC's control over how to maintain and expand a business. Extractive industry is an example where the full development of a business requires a large investment. In some countries sufficient local capital may not be available to meet a 50 percent, or more, local ownership requirement. In such a case, MNCs may be forced to operate the foreign subsidiary at a less than optimum size.

Business decisions   Host governments interfere with business decisions by establishing certain performance criteria for foreign subsidiaries. These criteria include local component requirements, market share limits, and tie-in products. Local component requirements involve the demand by many host governments that products sold by the MNCs in the host markets incorporate local components or raw materials purchased locally. The aim is to increase the MNCs' contribution to the local economy and employment, and to reduce hard currency spending. Host governments are also very much interested in regulating domestic competition and preventing total domination and control of local markets by MNCs. Setting a limit on the local market share that foreign subsidiaries can gain assures the viability of fledgling domestic businesses. Also, tie-in products are used to increase the MNCs' contribution to the domestic economy. As a condition for allowing access to the domestic market, a host country may "tie-in" by requiring that the MNC produce or sell certain products. These requirements and demands transfer partial control of the business operation from the MNC to the host country and reduce the decision-making authority of MNC managers.

Human resource management decisions
The desire on the part of host governments to increase the employment, skills, and knowledge of their people becomes manifest in several ways. The host government may demand that host nationals be appointed to top managerial positions within local subsidiary operations. Compliance with this demand makes the control of local operations more difficult especially where trust and competence become issues.

MNCs become more cautious and increase headquarters control when they are forced to appoint a host national as the head of a foreign subsidiary. Most MNCs grant more decision-making authority to expatriate managers than to host nationals, and having home country nationals at the head of foreign subsidiaries is perceived to reduce the need for other means of control. An alternative effective control technique utilized by most MNCs is to identify expatriate managers who have internalized corporate values.

Appointments at lower organizational levels are considered less important. These and other human resource management issues, such as hiring, promotion, and negotiation with locals,

are made by the subsidiary. Usually, only important and critical decisions are centralized at the headquarters. Other matters are left very much at the discretion of the subsidiary. Those decisions that might directly affect the headquarters or other subsidiaries, or might influence the profitability of the affiliates or the parent company, are closely controlled. Often, these decisions are exclusively made by the parent MNC. Sometimes subsidiaries are permitted to participate in making these decisions, but the final choice is still made by the headquarters.

Ownership and Control of Foreign Affiliates

Beside the nature of the decisions, other factors influence the centralization of decision making at the headquarters and reduce the autonomy of affiliates. We have already referred to a few of these factors, including the skills and experience of managers and their nationality. Other factors are the size and degree of internationalization of the MNC, the type of product produced by the subsidiary, the markets that the affiliate serves, and the size of equity owned by others. From a survey of U.S. affiliates in Mexico and France, Garnier[35] concluded that a subsidiary's autonomy is less when (1) it belongs to a large MNC that operates in many countries, (2) its products are fairly standardized, (3) the MNC is fairly integrated with important intrafirm flow of resources, (4) beside its own home market, it serves other markets as well, and (5) a large portion of its equity is owned by the parent MNC.

At the outset of expansion abroad, due to unfamiliarity with the host country environment, a firm may prefer joint ownership with locals. At that time, the MNC may not have a majority equity ownership, and therefore not have full control over the foreign operations. The MNC, however, can exercise significant control through other means. As it gains experience and self-confidence, it will probably favor creating an integrated global operation, which requires majority or full ownership of foreign subsidiaries.[36] Of course, even with a majority or full equity ownership by the MNC, host governments control a wide range of the subsidiaries' operating decisions, such as profit repatriation and expatriate employment.

The ownership pattern of U.S. MNCs indicates that they prefer to retain total ownership of foreign subsidiaries.[37] The management of a jointly owned foreign operation is a very difficult undertaking. Cultural differences and limited commonality among partners exacerbate the operational and strategic problems of a joint venture. Except for the learning period at the beginning of expansion into a host market, a jointly owned firm is less attractive to the MNCs than a wholly owned subsidiary. Sometimes, however, as mentioned before, in a politically unstable environment a joint venture with host country partners reduces the risk of adverse host country policy decisions. Joint ventures are inherently unstable and subject to frequent "renegotiation" imposed by the majority partner. Usually, through these renegotiations the joint venture is converted into a wholly owned subsidiary.[38]

It is much easier to manage a firm without having to share decision-making authority with other parties. The preference for full ownership of foreign subsidiaries is therefore almost a direct result of control problems. In a marketing oriented MNC such as Coca-Cola, for example, where commitment to certain marketing strategies for the global operation is very important, and where the firm possesses special marketing skills, a wholly owned subsidiary is preferred. To implement the overall marketing strategy at the subsidiary level, control by the headquarters is needed. In this case, strategy implementation could be compromised if conflicts arise with the partner over centralized control.

Where control could be exercised by other means than the equity ownership, MNCs have shown a considerable amount of practical flexibility. The MNC, for example, may agree to share equity ownership in a joint venture manufacturing project with a host government, if it can maintain control by the full ownership of the sales operations. Consequently, the host government's demand is met, and the headquarters' control over subsidiary operations is maintained.

Conclusion

To manage an organization successfully, an effective control system is needed. In MNCs, control is a much more complex and demanding issue than it is in a domestic business. Unlike a domestic operation, a foreign subsidiary cannot, for long, subordinate its business requirements, which are often dictated by the host country, to those of the parent MNC. An effective MNC control system should allow for local adaptability, and responsiveness to the host country environment. A challenging task for MNC top management is to build a control system that, while promoting the overall corporate competitive position, is beneficial to individual subsidiaries as well. In other words, if subsidiaries consider the strategy process and associated control system fair, they more readily accept it. The inclusion of subsidiaries' interests directly into corporate strategy increases the attractiveness of the strategy to subsidiaries' managers. Moreover, when subsidiaries' interests are not totally abandoned in favor of promoting corporate objectives, the strategy process will be considered more fair. This, in turn, provides more incentive for compliance by the subsidiary and makes corporate control much easier.

Compliance with headquarters decisions will be higher when an MNC's strategy-making process is judged to be fair by the top managers of its subsidiaries.[39] Five conditions determine the fairness of the strategy-making process: (1) Headquarters is knowledgeable about the local conditions of subsidiaries, (2) two-way communication exists in the multinational's strategy-making process, (3) the headquarters' decisions are fairly consistent across subsidiaries, (4) subsidiaries can legitimately challenge the headquarters strategic views, and (5) the MNC's final strategic decisions are fully explained to subsidiaries.[40] Of course, a fair strategy-making process has a built-in control mechanism that is also fair. This means, for example, if return on investment is used to evaluate the performance of a subsidiary manager, allowances should be made to compensate for the shortcomings of this evaluation technique. Thus, return on investment evaluations do not reflect the impact of decisions that are made by the headquarters for the benefit of the whole MNC operations. Those decisions may have a negative impact on the subsidiary's earnings.

Various control mechanisms and approaches used by domestic firms are applicable to MNCs. The diversity of the international environment, however, makes it more difficult to apply these controls. Effective MNC control employs a combination of formal, informal, direct, and indirect mechanisms to account for the uniqueness of each subsidiary, while addressing the total MNC strategic and operational requirements.

Discussion Questions

1. What are the differences between the control processes of MNCs and domestic firms?
2. Describe various control mechanisms that the MNCs could use.
3. What control mechanisms work well for an integrated MNC?
4. Why is the MNC control more difficult than the control of a domestic business?
5. Does geographical distance create any difficulty for the control of the MNC?
6. What is the impact of an increase in intrafirm business transactions on control of a foreign subsidiary?
7. What attributes of the managers influence the amount of autonomy granted to a foreign subsidiary?
8. Why do host governments interfere with MNC operations?
9. Which one of the three approaches to control is more appropriate for the MNCs? Why?

Endnotes

1. M. R. Sesit. "Funds Blocked Abroad by Exchange Controls Plague Big Companies." *The Wall Street Journal* (December 3, 1984), 1.

2. E. T. Penrsoe. "Foreign Investment and the Growth of the Firm." *The Economic Journal,* 66 (June 1956), 220–35.

3. L. M. Greenberg. "Mining Firms Cede Portion of Porgera." *The Wall Street Journal* (March 18, 1993), A2.

4. G. Hedlund. "Autonomy of Subsidiaries and Formalisation of Headquarter-Subsidiary Relationships in Swedish Multinational Enterprises." In L. Otterbeck, ed. *The Management of Headquarters Subsidiary Relationships in Multinational Corporations* (Stockholm: Gover, 1981), 51–64.

5. R. Wartzman. "Clinton Plan Opens Debate Over Degree Foreign Concerns Cheat on U.S. Taxes." *The Wall Street Journal* (June 26, 1993), A12.

6. P. M. Reilly, "Sony Combines U.S. Operations Under Schulhof." *The Wall Street Journal* (May 25, 1993), B1.

7. J. R. Galbraith. "Organization Design: An Information Processing View." *Interface,* 4 (1977), 28–36; D. A. Nadler and M. L. Tushman. *Strategic Organization Design* (Glenview, IL: Scott, Foresman Co., 1988).

8. W. G. Ouchi and M. A. Maguire. "Organizational Control: Two Functions." *Administrative Science Quarterly,* 20 (1975), 559–69.

9. M. Lebas and J. Weigenstein, "Management Control: The Roles of Rules, Markets and Culture," *Journal of Management Studies,* 23 (1986), 259–72.

10. W. G. Ouchi. "Markets, Bureaucracies, and Clan." *Administrative Science Quarterly* (March 1980), 129.

11. Lebas and Weigenstein. "Management Control." 264.

12. The terms "clan" and "tradition" as used by Ouchi are very much the same as cultural traits. Since the framework of his writings was adopted by Lebas and Weigenstein to elaborate on cultural control, we too use Ouchi's argument on "clans" and "tradition" in our discussion of cultural control.

13. Ouchi. "Markets, Bureaucracies, and Clan." 138–39.

14. Ouchi. "Markets, Bureaucracies, and Clan." 139.

15. Lebas and Weigenstein. "Management Control." 266.

16. I. Van Maanen and E. H. Schein. "Toward a Theory of Organizational Socialization." In B. M. Staw, ed. *Research in Organizational Behavior* (Greenwich, CT: JAI Press 1979), Vol. 1, 209–64.

17. E. H. Schein. "Organizational Socialization and the Profession of Management." In B. M. Staw, ed. *Psychological Foundations of Organizational Behavior,* (Santa Monica, CA: Goodyear Publishing Co., 1977), 210–24.

18. Schein. "Organizational Socialization." 214.

19. A. Bennett, "GE Redesigns Rungs of Career Ladder." *The Wall Street Journal* (March 15, 1993), p. B1.

20. P. Engardio. "Motorola in China: A Great Leap Forward." *Business Week* (May 17, 1993), 59.

21. J. I. Martinez and J. C. Jarillo. "The Evolution of Research on Coordination Mechanisms in Multinational Corporations." *Journal of International Business Studies* (Fall 1989), 500.

22. Martinez and Jarillo, "The Evolution of Research on Coordination Mechanisms." 500–08.

23. L. G. Franko, "Organizational Structure and Multinational Strategies of Continental European Enterprises." In M. Ghertman and J. Leontiades, ed. *European Research in International Business,* (Amsterdam: North-Holland, 1978), 118.

24. S. Ghoshal and C. A. Bartlett. "The Multinational Corporation as an Interorganizational Network." *Academy of Management Review,* 15 (1990), 620.

25. V. Terpstra and K. David. *The Cultural Environment of International Business* (Cincinnati, OH: South-Western Publishing Co., 1991), 36.

26. Caterpillar business manual. *Business International* (April 6, 1973), 107.

27. *Structure and Organisation of Multinational Enterprises* (Paris, France: Organisation for Economic Co-Operation and Development, 1987), 32.

28. G. H. Garnier. "Context and Decision-Making Autonomy in the Foreign Affiliates of United States Multinational Corporations." *Academy of Management Journal,* 25 (1982), 893–908.

29. Organisation for Economic Co-Operation and Development. 33.

30. Patterned after A. K. Gupta and V. Govindarajan.

"Knowledge Flows and the Structure of Control Within Multinational Corporations," *Academy of Management Review,* 16 (1991), 768–92.

31. K. Fatehi, "Capital Flight from Latin America as a Barometer of Political Instability." *Journal of Business Research,* 30, no. 2 (June 1994), 187–95.

32. J. Fayerweather, "Four Winning Strategies for the International Corporation." *Journal of Business Strategy,* (Fall 1981), 25–36.

33. R. E. Berenbeim, *Operating Foreign Subsidiaries: How Independent Can They Be?* The Conference Board, Report No. 836, 13–14.

34. Berenbeim. *Operating Foreign Subsidiaries.* 18.

35. Garnier. "Context and Decision-Making. 906.

36. A. R. Negandhi and M. Welge. *Advances in International Comparative Management* (Greenwich, CT: JAI Press, 1984), 32.

37. Negandhi and Welge. *Advances in International Comparative Management.* 32–34.

38. L. L. Blodgett. "Factors in the Instability of International Joint Ventures: An Event History Analysis." *Strategic Management Journal,* 13 (1992), 475–81.

39. W. C. Kim and R. A. Mauborgne. "Procedural Justice, Attitudes, and Subsidiary Top Management Compliance with Multinationals' Corporate Strategic Decisions." *Academy of Management Journal,* 36 (1993), 502–26.

40. W. C. Kim and R. A. Mauboregne. "Implementing Global Strategies: The Role of Procedural Justice." *Strategic Management Journal,* 12 (1991), 17–31.

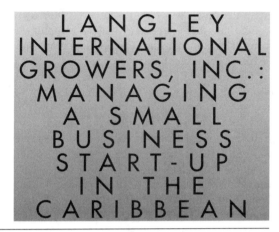

LANGLEY INTERNATIONAL GROWERS, INC.: MANAGING A SMALL BUSINESS START-UP IN THE CARIBBEAN

RAE ANDRE

David Langley was the 58-year-old president of Langley International Growers, Inc., a New York-based firm with annual sales close to $4 million. Like his father and grandfather before him, Langley grew flowers for distribution to wholesale markets along the Eastern coast of the United States. Domestically, he ran about 12 acres of greenhouses, putting the company among the top ten greenhouse operations in the United States. To compete with flower growers from Latin America, Langley started a subsidiary in Santa Nueva, an island republic in the Caribbean. The following text is based on discussions with him two years after he successfully started the new operation.

Managing the International Start-up

We first became interested in going abroad when we heard about it from one of our competitors. We had decided it might be a good idea to hedge our bets and move to a climate where there is no fuel requirement. So we went down

This case is based on an actual company. Facts have been altered to protect the identity of those involved. Santa Neuva is a fictional country. Reprinted with permission of Rae Andre, Northeastern University, Boston, MA 02115.

to Santa Neuva to see the competitor's operation and we thought he was doing a good job. Sixty percent of the flowers used in the United States today are imported. Those flowers are grown with labor at $2 a day, versus what we have to pay at minimum wage, around $3.35 per hour. We thought there was money in it.

But establishing yourself in a foreign country is not easy. There are pitfalls. The laws of these governments look like they welcome business coming in. It's all on the books: the laws are there to help you. The government itself wants you there in a lot of these countries. What they spend nationally on oil alone exceeds the money they get from exports, which constantly puts them in the doghouse internationally. They can't buy anything outside, so they're constantly in a state of devaluation relative to everybody else. In addition to that, they have an enormous birthrate which constantly keeps their poverty in place. (You go down there with the idea you're going to help them out from that standpoint, forget it, because they're not going to let you do it.) There's a lot of money to be made if you know how. You go down there and start spending your money and then you find out that the laws have to be administered by people, and the people are where the hangups come because they don't obey the law. They circumvent it to their own benefit. In other words, they make it difficult for you for various reasons. The political aims start to disappear in the bureaucracy.

For example, we have to import a lot of things into the country because they don't have them. Well, they can let that stuff sit down at that dock until some guy clears it. They let our crates of greenhouses sit there for two to three *months*. It threw us way back, cost us thousands of dollars. We had importers down there who knew their business. All the paperwork was right, but all the government guy says is "I don't think this is right," and it gets kicked back and forth. One problem is that a lot of the government income is taxes on imports, so that they're very strict, particularly if it's an American company that's shipping. This holdup means that everybody's benefiting except the poor guy who has to cut the flowers, because they've made work for the phone operator and everybody else. You're constantly checking, checking, checking. It's a make-work scheme, in any sense of the word, whether it's in Detroit or the Caribbean, and they're masters at it. A lot of these foreign countries, they don't operate, they make work.

For example, down where we are, the bureaucracy has increased 50% in four years— 50% more government employees. Going through the airports, there's a guy who puts the tag on your thing and there's a guy who takes it off, five feet away. You can tell them your problem, but they don't understand the problem of business having to get that money moving that's sitting there. They don't realize that they have to collect their taxes and build their country from business. Even answering the phone: the conversations are long, the conversations are flowered. They don't get to the point, and this, of course, is frustrating if you're not used to it. And especially if you're paying for a long-distance phone call. It takes them a half hour to say good morning!

Back about six months ago, we needed this particular type of spreader for an insecticide and I wanted to make sure it was there. We wanted it the following morning and I wanted it delivered that day. And my secretary is on the phone talking to this guy twenty-five miles away. He kept saying, "Manana" (tomorrow), and I kept saying, "Ayer" (yesterday). The secretary kept saying, "Manana" and I kept saying, "Ayer." Finally, with negotiations back and forth, I got it.

So you have to tighten things. They don't respect you if they know they're getting away with it, because everybody is watching everybody else. We made that mistake. We were too easy. Of course, these people are very hungry. Their unemployment rate is tremendous. The established rate is 40%, but they don't count everybody. If they counted everybody, it's around 80%. You learn as you go, and you learn from talking to people. They don't respect softness and, yet, they don't respect anybody who's going around shouting and yelling either. You've got to have them understand who's boss. We had a guy who was coming in late all the time, so we gave him a written notice. After you hire him for three months, the government says you own him: it costs you money to let him go. If he's there three months, you might have to give him another three months pay. After a year, you might have to give him another six months pay. The guy was late. We gave him the notice. He still was late, so we had to let him go. It didn't cost us anything. See, if he breaks the company rules and they're allowable rules according to the law, then you can get rid of him without any pay. But we had to get tougher and tougher and tougher. It's so easy to be easy because the labor's cheap. But you have to realize that any time you're not making money, it's coming out of capital, so labor's not cheap then.

We weren't knowledgeable about the culture. We assumed that they're like us—sort of like us—if you have the language. That's the mistake you make. You can hire a Neuvan to run the place if you've got the language yourself, but you have to know the language so well that you get the innuendoes and that's something none of us have. Very few Americans have that. You could hire a Cuban, Mexican, or a Puerto Rican, but even they do not think like we do. They're more apt to identify with the person instead of identifying with the problem. They identify with their emotions and they think, "Well, poor guy."

We hadn't taken one dime out of there yet, and we were asked for a raise. They'll say, "Look at these poor people here. Don't you think they ought to be given hope?" When we went into the village there the only means of transportation was the truck that we had bought. Now, almost everybody rides up in a new Honda motorcycle. The standard of living has gone up. We hired them and they had 60% unemployment in the town, and yet I didn't give them hope? They're big on expectations and poor on execution down there.

You have to have an American boss, period. All those guys underneath can be Neuvans, but you got to have an American boss because you have to teach those Neuvans how you want it. If you go down there and take their way of doing it, you've lost everything you've ever had.

There was a lot of petty thievery when we built the place. A bar down the end of the street was built in the last year since we built. The owner didn't have a thing before. He's the guy that plowed our property and worked the field before we put our greenhouses up. Right after we built, he was able to build himself a bar and a dance hall from similar materials that were used to construct Langley Greenhouses. I call it Langley's bar. It's right at the end of our road. I often stop in for a cerveza.

All the foreigners do better than we Americans do. Number one, they can bribe the governments. We put strings on our businessmen that are absolutely abominable and then holler that we can't export anything. Another

thing is the gringo approach. The Japanese are a new face in there and they operate a little differently than we do. They always say, "Yes." We say, "No," but they say "Yes" and don't mean it, so it doesn't hurt as much. It's a different approach and they've sold one hell of a lot of cars. In fact, I have never driven an American car down there. If you want to go buy an American truck, just forget it. We have a little two-cylinder Japanese truck that's running up and down those hills for fifty kilometers per gallon.

Local Operations

Our manager there came originally from Puerto Rico. I hired him when he was fifteen or sixteen years old. He has worked for me for seventeen years. We usually have about 75% Puerto Ricans working for us up North. I am like a father to him. He had a child and named it after me.

I sent him down and he's been as happy as a lark, but that's Jorge. That's not everybody. You can't generalize on Jorge.

He's doing a good job. Of course, he lost his first wife because she thought the girls were a little too loose in Santa Neuva. She wasn't wrong. She walked out on him. I don't know whether he got divorced, but he got married again. To give you just a brief insight into it, we won't allow him to hire any woman under forty. We don't want him to be passing his favors out. There's another reason for that. They'll come and work for you, but if they get pregnant, you have to give them at least a month off with pay. Sure enough, they'll come when they're already pregnant. First thing you know, you have five young ladies pregnant, nobody to do the work and you're paying for it.

We hired the first secretary, thought she could speak English, took me nine months to get rid of her. I fired her. She couldn't speak a word of English. "Yes" or "No." She had the books all fouled up. Pregnant, too. She lied to us about it. She came back and had the kid here. Now he's an American citizen.

It's a very loose society. It's amazing, underneath. On top, if you walk into a bar or a dance hall, you can't dance with those girls in that bar, unless you know somebody who knows them. But down underneath. . . it's a different story. Jorge's getting worse, being down there. He's forgetting his English, too. He has to think twice.

We have three managers and twenty employees. That's what we call the office help—managers. We have an office manager, a pack and ship manager, and an overall manager. These people can all speak Spanish. Then we have about twelve men and eight women. The women do the bunching. The men do the cutting, are night watchmen and all kinds of things. You look in that packing shed down there and it's probably identical to this one up here, only there are no conveyers.

God forbid I ever put a conveyer down there because it'll only work about three hours. And that's when I'm working. The more we check up on them, the more controls we put on them in equipment, the more apt they are to say, "This doesn't work now." It's so simple to break a computer. You spit at it or push the wrong damn buttons and it's done. We sent down one of the finest little power mowers you can buy. We started it up before it went down. It worked perfectly. It was eight or nine months later and three mechanical overhauls before we got that thing working.

Last year I arrived and found ten or fifteen men cutting the fields with machetes. I'm still not sure that isn't the cheapest. If you hire them for $2 a day, they're telling you something. They really are telling you something. You can hire their people, on certain jobs anyway, cheaper than you can use the damned equipment. You won't see a lot of bookkeeping machines in Santa Neuva. They use people and they'll get it right. They'll have a calculator, but that's about the extent of it. You might in a very big American company, but not generally.

We have parameters for the manager: checklists for his rounds, a checklist for his maintenance, a checklist for his nightman. You must be specific. You don't just walk out and say "clean." You've got to say, "Clean this table, clean that table, clean this." Write it down and give to him. If you don't do that some of it will be forgotten, some of it just won't be done. And then you can't come in and holler, because the guy will say he didn't hear you. They're really sharp this way. You have to be specific. You have to draw it step by step or they just won't do it. If they have a package of cigarettes, the empty packs will go onto the floor, until you tell them, "The next time you do that . . . out. We are not going to have that. This is not the way we're going to be." You go to the company next door to ours where he never enforced these things and it's a dump. Not that he doesn't make money, but it's a dump, a literal dump. It's terrible.

We have the manager take videotape pictures around the plant every week so we see what the plants look like, see what the surroundings look like, see what the housekeeping looks like. We also have him send all the bills, the bank balances, and the payroll up each week.

We have a problem with visitors, too. We have to keep them out. They'll just drop in and say, "Can I see the place?" and they'll take up the manager's time and they'll take up the office time. When they get to talking, they'll talk about their grandfather, their father, their brothers, their sisters, and it's on your time. So we had to discourage that. We had to fence the place to keep the horses out, the cows out, and the people out. Just so you can keep control of the flowers. I don't know if we stopped it. If you have a fence, you have to say, "Don't crawl over the fence."

A lot of growers don't do things the way we do them, even up North. I like it written down. I hate verbal orders, unless it's just a day order. If it's a long-term deal it should be written down and put in the policy. "This is what we do in this way at this particular time." We're known to have the best place in Santa Neuva and there are a lot of flower growers. In the town, we're known as operating a very tight ship.

The President's Personal Involvement

I've spent a lot of hard times down there. When I go down there, I'm alone most of the time. There are many, many nights you're all alone. There's no one in the hotel. That's why I like to take somebody with me to play gin or to go out to eat. You're just there in the mountains and you're all alone. It's not a bad hotel as hotels go. Jorge has a list he puts in my room for me. I have a toaster, coffee, water, coke, beer, vodka, insecticides, and other stuff. Of course, they haven't changed the linen in the three years we've been going there. They say you don't go in the kitchen or you'll never eat there again. I spray the room for cockroaches and watch them wiggling. In the middle of the night you hear them. I spray all over the room every time I go out.

The hotels are owned by the government and they're rented from the government. It's amazing. These beautiful hotels rent for two or three hundred dollars a month. Any you should see the way they keep it. Terrible. You can't swim in the swimming pool. It's green. It's a beautiful swimming pool and I know how to tell them to keep it, but they won't. If I were going to be down there a lot, I'd take my own chlorine and fix it. It would only cost $100 to use the pool the whole time I was there. Probably, they'd give me free drinks out of it, they'd make it up. They just don't know how to do things. They fool around.

When I was robbed at the hotel, I went to the police station and gave them a list just because I wanted it for the insurance company. Nothing happened. Nobody found anything. I didn't eat in that hotel for the next two months, the next two times I was there. I wouldn't go in their dining room, because I knew those guys knew who did it. I was there alone. Somebody had to be

watching and the town is too small not to know the thief and I knew the police knew. I found out the hotel was responsible, but you can't get blood out of a stone, so I said "All right, I want a 10% discount rate until this is paid off on my hotel room," which they went along with. After that, they put a guard on me. Every night I have a guard—a private guard. They give him a peso. He's sitting right outside my door. I've never felt physically afraid, just alone, that's all.

I went down to town one night trying to negotiate for this land. Downtown at night looks like a country road. The house lights are on, but there are no street lights. I went down there negotiating with this family right in their house. (The guy who said that he owned the land just pissed me off. I had it all negotiated and later found out we couldn't get a clear title.) Anyway, I'm sitting there in this house with this family. Nobody can speak English, and I can't speak Spanish, but we're negotiating. It was this guy and his son, who could speak English a little, and the whole family—his wife, and relatives. They all come in to look at me. Everybody was just staring. All of a sudden, I started to wiggle my ears, and I'll tell you, they had a hilarious time. My wife was up in the hotel. She was worried I'd disappeared in the middle of the night down in a strange country. I didn't get home 'til one or two o'clock in the morning.

It's just a new ball game and you should detail it right from the beginning. We should have had notebooks which was my fault. We should have had everything detailed—the duties, the laws of the country, the work rules. If I were to do it now, I would have all this stuff researched and if we ever expand again, we'll know what the hell we're doing. And there'll be no problem. I spent quite a bit of time down there last June when we were planting, but I should have spent two months down there. I did spend practically that much time down there off and on, but I should have been right there and taken over the job of doing it. It's not the Neuvan's fault at all. I might lose it if I don't get down there more.

If I were going to do it over again, I wouldn't invest down there, but if I had to do it, I'd still pick that country. I didn't make a mistake in the country. We did not do that. It's probably the best of the lot. They're more democratic than most. The problem is that poverty does strange things. Poverty will turn those people into almost anything if they don't get it straightened out. That birth rate should be zero right now, but the population is going to double by the year 2000. That's why their university is a hotbed of Communism. They've got all this intelligence and they see the country like it is, and they don't know what to do.

Our government ensures us if we're taken over down there because of riot or insurrection or government acquisition. Otherwise, you couldn't get any loans. You'll see people with jobs there and you wouldn't believe it. Take the waiters in the hotels. You'll go down there today and five years from now and they're practically working for nothing. There's nobody in the hotels from one day to the next. Yet, they'll be there. They have no place to go. There's no place to go except the United States and there are 500,000 Neuvans working in the United States. You literally can't get a plane reservation back to the States during the first two weeks of January.

But it's gorgeous. It's a paradise. You couldn't believe it until you see it. Everything grows. You can have a terrific amount of flowers; I love to go there. I'm getting homesick for it. I would say they've treated us very well. After all, it's their country. It's not up to them to change . . . we're trying to take a profit out of it.

PART TWO

CULTURAL AND BEHAVIORAL ASPECTS OF INTERNATIONAL MANAGEMENT

F I V E

INTERNATIONAL MANAGEMENT AND THE CULTURAL CONTEXT

To manage a business organization effectively, an understanding of people and their values and assumptions is necessary. The values and assumptions of people are shaped by their cultures. Although there are certain similarities among cultures, these cultural norms and values are not universal. Among the similarities of cultural norms and values we find a preference to be helpful, respect for authority and power, and the desire for comfort. But even those concepts and values that at first glance appear to be universal show vast differences upon closer scrutiny.

In this chapter we learn how cultural differences influence the management of business organizations. The definitions of national culture and corporate culture allow an explanation of the relationship between the two. A discussion of the typology of an organization illustrates how cultural diversity of the MNCs could improve organizational capabilities. The differences between the most prominent American cultural values and those of other nations are used as a framework for the discussion of managerial implications of cultural differences.

A few decades ago, when MNCs started sending their employees abroad, they learned about a phenomenon called cultural shock. Manifested as feelings of bewilderment, loss, and anxiety, cultural shock besets people who in a foreign land do not find the familiar clues that make everyday life a comfortable exercise. Now many MNCs are being introduced to another cultural shock. This time, strategic alliances between large MNCs, which create multicultural teams and result in many unforeseen problems between these teams, are sending cultural shocks through the corporate spines. Take the case of

International Business Machines (IBM), which started a cooperative project with Siemens AG of Germany and Toshiba Corporation of Japan, to develop a revolutionary computer memory chip. At the East Fishkill, New York, facilities, in mostly windowless offices, more than 100 scientists from culturally diverse backgrounds were brought together.[1]

Cooperative projects combining culturally diverse people are supposed to produce synergy. Americans, for example, look at the objects and relate them in a linear fashion. Japanese look at the harmony between the objects and the spatial relationships. To Americans the harmony is a symmetrical balance when every object is balanced by an equal object on the opposite side. To Japanese the harmony is a fit, a match, an asymmetrical balance that creates a coherent pattern without forcing parallels and matching opposites. Combining the two divergent styles could produce new solutions.

In this case, however, from the onset and before the full realization of potential synergies, problems began to slow down the project.[2] Siemens' scientists were shocked to find that Japanese seemingly fall sleep during meetings. (It is a common practice for overworked Japanese managers to close their eyes and rest when talk does not concern them.) The Japanese found it painful to sit in small, individual offices and speak English. The Americans complained that the Germans planned too much and the Japanese were not making clear decisions.

Before getting together for the project, all the scientists were sent to training programs in their home countries.

Toshiba, for example, provided language training. Siemens briefed its scientists about "hamburger" managerial styles. They were told that when criticizing a subordinate the Americans start with small talk: "How is the family?" This is the top of the hamburger. Then, they slip in the meat, the criticisms, which is followed by more bun, the encouraging words, such as "I know you can do better." With Germans all you get is the meat. Japanese offer only the soft bun, you have to smell the meat.

The toughest adjustment problem for Toshiba scientists was in the area of corporate culture. They were accustomed to working in large rooms with a lot of people, constantly overhearing all the conversations, like living in a sea of information. IBM's small offices could not accommodate this important information exchange. Germans were horrified to see windowless offices. They also did not like to step outside the offices for smoking. For a few months they were all on their best behavior. With the passage of time, however, the three groups grew more isolated. Even after-hours socializing and softball games were marred by cultural differences. Americans and Japanese knew the game but Germans did not. In short, participation in the project was a frustrating experience for all.

Introduction

The survival of an organization depends on its ability to respond to environmental changes and societal demands. The successful adaptation of the organization to these changes and demands creates among its members widely shared assumptions and values that are referred to as the corporate culture. The organization is dependent on the effective interaction with its environment for existence and survival. This dependency includes the relationship between the corporate culture and the cultural environment. Various aspects of national culture are reflected in the culture of the firm. Although the transfer from national culture to the firm is never complete, it is irresistible. Very seldom could irreconcilable contradictions exist between the two. Any difference is either temporary or a normal variance of the national norms.[3] Incongruity between the corporate culture and societal values results in organizational demise. Only those organizations survive that adopt cultures reflective of the society and its dominant cultural characteristics.

Cultural Framework

Although the domain of a culture is not limited by national borders, for simplicity and practicality, we will often use national boundaries as the basis for discussing cultural phenomena. National boundaries delineate the social, legal, and political environments of host countries. It is within these boundaries that multinational corporations (MNCs) have to operate, and may encounter difficulties due to cultural misunderstandings.

While a domestic firm embodies the basic attributes of its national culture, an MNC is influenced by the multicultural nature of their global market. Each firm, however, develops its own unique corporate culture that exhibits the basic values of the society, the requirements of its industry, and the shared philosophy and beliefs of its members, and particularly the values and philosophy of its top management. Therefore, there are many cultural similarities and also some difference among firms. Since domestic firms share the same national culture, cultural variations among firms are attributed not only to the philosophy of their founders, but to the differences in industry characteristics[4] and the composition of their members. MNCs, however, are not limited to the influence from one national culture. Through their affiliates around the world, they are exposed to diverse cultures. Similar to the diversity among domestic firms, MNCs develop corporate characters that are the representations of the cultural diversity of their affiliates. Successful MNCs develop an understanding of cultural differences and learn how to take advantage of the opportunities that cultural diversity may provide. Otherwise, problems similar to those that beset the participants in the IBM project at East Fishkill may plague the operation of MNCs and detract from the benefits of internationalization.

Cultural Values and Organizational Behavior

Culture could be viewed as the way people live and relate to each other and their environment. Culture has physical and nonphysical manifestations. The physical manifestation of culture can be seen in functional objects and artistic products, crafts, music, literature, and poetry. The nonphysical aspects of culture are manifested through the mental frameworks that people use in dealing with their surroundings. Even the most mundane daily activities such as our view and visualization of the surrounding objects are influenced by these cultural assumptions and frameworks. The following[5] is an example of variations in mental frameworks between two different cultures.

When Nissan chose a car design developed by the American designers for the new Infinity J30 over the Japanese design, the Americans were naturally elated. They were, however, surprised by the proposed modifications. Nissan's Japanese executives liked the low, gently sloping back end, but they hated the front. The rejection highlighted cultural differences in visual perception. When Westerners conjure up an image of a car, it is a side view. With the Japanese, however, it is the front. The Japanese read personality and expression into the "face" of the car. All discussions for modifications were centered on whether the "eyes" were sleepy or

awake, and whether the "mouth" gesture was appropriate, a reference to the shape and size of headlights and the grill. In the end, the headlights and the grill were redesigned to make for bigger, more expressive "eyes" and a smaller "mouth."

Likewise, a review of advice columns in Japanese newspapers reveals some of the cultural characteristics that distinguish Japanese from others. The Japanese version of Ann Landers may sound very parochial or even "antifemale" to Americans, but it fits well with the Japanese. Most of the advice given dwells on the maintenance of social harmony, the avoidance of confrontation, and the importance of hard work. The most common piece of advice offered to suffering questioners is *Gaman,* the stoic virtue of endurance, tolerance, and bearing pain without complaint. The following are two samples:

Sample 1: Mrs. T. of Yamagochi complained to the Jinsei Annai (Guide to Life) column of the Yomiuri Shimbun newspaper that her husband has no time at all for the children. She wrote: He leaves home early and comes home late, therefore, he never sees them. Even on his days off, he leaves early and does not return home till late at night, when the children are already in bed. When the children ask him to play with them, he says he will, but goes out anyway. My heart aches to see my children play alone on Sundays, while watching with envy the neighborhood kids who are playing with their fathers.

The Advice: Be patient with your husband, please. You did not mention what kind of job your husband has. He could be involved in scientific research. People involved in scientific works often ignore their families. So, please treat him warmly, and spend more time with the children yourself. We hope that your husband is successful in his work.

Sample 2: Mrs. C. of Ibaragi had a different problem. She was married three years ago and now lives in her husband's home. She wrote that the house is always very dirty. Nobody ever cares to clean the house except her. It drives her crazy to see her baby to crawl in all that filth. Her request to her husband to move to another house was answered so rudely that she was considering divorcing him.

The Advice: You have to learn to get along with others. If your in-laws are not concerned about cleanliness, you have to be patient. If you respond by smiling brightly and clean the house as well as you can, this may have an impact on them.[6]

A typical American newspaper would offer quite different advice. Hypothetical answers to these troubled women would proceed to deal with the issues more directly. For example:

Answer 1: Evidently, he is unable to realize his obligations and fulfill his role as a father/husband, and is attempting to find satisfaction in his work. He may not feel comfortable at home, so he, therefore, avoids spending time at the house. Whatever the reason, you and your husband should seek professional help while the children are young and the marriage is still intact.

Answer 2: I do suggest that you find an affordable home of your very own. Help your husband see the benefits of living separately from his family. Explain to him how his family will enjoy the additional space and freedom that this will provide them. Keep trying, and don't give up. He may come to his senses. After all, nobody dislikes more privacy, more space, and a clean home.

To continue our discussion of the influence of culture on international management, we should define culture and corporate culture.

Culture Defined

There are many definitions of culture. Culture could be defined as a system of knowledge and standards for perceiving, believing, evaluating, and acting. It is a system of socially transmitted patterns of behavior that serves to relate people

to the environment.[7] It develops over time, and is constantly and slowly evolving. A simpler definition is offered by Hofstede who described culture as "the collective programming of the mind which distinguishes the members of one category of people from those of the other."[8]

Language, ethnicity, and religion are the major components of culture. With some exceptions, ethnicity is a geographically based attribute, as are language and religion.

To understand a culture fully, knowledge of its religious foundation is necessary. There are several major religions and many minor ones. The major religions include Buddhism, Christianity, Confucianism, Hinduism, Islam, Judaism, and Shinto. Even a cursory examination of their fundamentals would require voluminous discussion. People who are seriously pursuing international careers would benefit greatly by studying these religions. To whet the appetite of the curious, a few comments suffice here. With a high level of simplicity, we can say that the three religions originating from the Middle East—Judaism, Christianity, and Islam—have much in common and share the same basic framework. These three religions, for example, believe in one god who is omnipotent, omnipresent, and omniscient. They also believe in life after death and the day of judgment. The Oriental religions such as Hinduism and Buddhism, however, have a different structure. Many abstract religious concepts that have shaped Western thoughts and beliefs are alien to followers of these two religions. A characterization of these differences by H. L. Telshaw, Jr., is illuminating. Mr. Telshaw, an executive of General Motors, has many years of international experience, especially with Asians. He asserts:

"the adherents of Confucius, Buddha and Lao Tsu's Tao have been molded by the thoughts, ideals and teachings of these Oriental philosophers which incidentally tend to concentrate on developing strong personal and family values unencumbered by such intellectual hurdles as "immaculate Conceptions", "Resurrections", miracles, etc. . . . .

We in the Occident, having been reared on a battleground contested by the forces of good and evil, have developed an unusual capacity for guilt, not found in the same extremes in the Orient. Captivated by the promises of heaven and the threats of hell, we tend to be idealistically and fearfully motivated. Moreover, because of the widely held belief that we are individually accountable at the judgement seat for our deeds, we tend toward self centeredness and egotism. Orientals, on the other hand, see themselves as merely another manifestation of the creation, and strive to be "in harmony" with its other elements and therefore tend to be more realistic—more fatalistic, humble, even innocent."[9]

Cultural differences can be analyzed along many dimensions. Two dimensions that are relevant to international business are complexity and heterogeneity.

Cultural complexity The amount of inherent background and contextual information that provide meaning to and explain a given situation or condition is referred to as *cultural complexity.* Unspoken, unformulated, and unexplicit rules are used by all cultures in interpersonal relationships and communication. Subtle information supplied by these clues is vital for the interpretation of situations and interpersonal behavior. Cultures vary in their use of contextual information. The more contextual information required for understanding social situations, the more the cultural complexity. The higher the cultural complexity, the more difficult it is for outsiders to correctly assess and interpret the social circumstance. Countries can be categorized as having a high level of cultural complexity to a low level, according to the amount of contextual information needed for understanding daily life situations. Low-context cultures are more explicit and overt in their communication and social interaction, while high-context cultures are covert and implicit.[10] Examples of low-context cultures are the United States, Germany, and Switzerland. China, Japan, Latin America, and the Middle Eastern countries are high context, while France is moderate context.

In low-context cultures communication is explicit and direct; the opposite is true for high-context cultures. In high-context cultures, much information is transmitted by physical context or internalized in people. Without familiarity with this hidden information, interpretation of a message would be incomplete and misunderstood. For example, in a business deal, when an American responds affirmatively to a proposal it means that the proposal is being accepted. A Japanese "yes," however, may not mean acceptance. Depending on circumstances surrounding the message it may mean yes, maybe, or no. Japanese are very reluctant to say "no," fearing the damage they may cause to interpersonal relationships. They are particularly sensitive not to embarrass others by saying no in public.

There are many more implicit rules and requirements governing the daily life of people in countries with a high level of cultural complexity. These rules and understandings determine the appropriateness of behavior. Violations of these rules are not taken lightly. For example, in Japan, the place of people around a negotiation table is strictly based on their seniority. The same is true in the Middle East. In the Middle East, no business transaction should begin unless participants have exchanged pleasantries, had time to learn about each other, and feel comfortable carrying out the business transactions. The desire for efficiency and fast action that prompts Americans to get to the business at hand immediately will be regarded as rude and impolite. In such situations, in effect, the Americans are missing the contextual ingredient by which they should interact with others.

In countries with a low level of cultural complexity, interpersonal relationships tend to be temporary and shallow. Friendships are very easily formed and dissolved. The ease and speed with which Americans get to know people often leads visitors to the United States to comment on how "unbelievably friendly" Americans are. There is a worldwide complaint, however, that Americans are capable of only informal, superficial friendships that do not involve an exchange of deep confidences.[11] In contrast, in countries with high-context cultures, interpersonal relationships are often more difficult to form, but are longer lasting and much stronger and deeper. Their cultural norms tend to have a long life and resist change. People from high-context cultures are inclined to get more involved in each others lives.

Considering these cultural differences, without proper training and preparation, managers of low-context cultures would face difficulties when dealing with people of high-context cultures, and vice versa. Taking words at their face values, ignoring unspoken signals, and lacking background information embedded in the cultural tradition could result in gross misunderstandings. The tendency of low-context cultures for direct communication and specificity could be interpreted as rude and impolite. The preference to not meddle in other people's lives could be regarded as cold and indicative of the absence of feelings. Of course, people of high-context cultures experience difficulties of their own in low-context cultures.

Cultural heterogeneity   Language, ethnicity, and religion are the major components of culture. A relatively large degree of dissimilarity and diversity among the many constituencies of a culture is regarded as *cultural heterogeneity*. A country with diversity in language, ethnic make-up, and religion is culturally heterogeneous. Examples are Canada, the United States, and India. These countries are made up of many subcultures. Other countries have a relatively low diversity in language, ethnicity, and religion and include Japan and Saudi Arabia, which are culturally homogeneous.

It is more demanding and challenging for expatriate managers to function in cultures with a high level of cultural heterogeneity and complexity. All managerial functions demand a more careful assessment of the situations and understanding of circumstances in which they are going to be performed. It is more difficult, for example, to manage a firm in India than in the United States. While both the U.S. and India are culturally heterogenous, India has a higher level of cultural heterogeneity and complexity. Conducting business transactions in a country with a relatively homogeneous culture is much simpler. Understanding the cultural complexity and heterogeneity of host countries should be a top priority of MNCs. To succeed in the multi-cultural environment of the world market, MNCs should show sensitivity to their host countries' cultures, and attempt to understand the cultural differences. Also, in a heterogenous culture, many opportunities are lost by not recognizing the needs of members of subcultures as a result of focusing on the dominant culture. To wit, only recently have American businesses begun to cater to the Mexican-American subculture.

Corporate Culture

Corporate culture indicates organizationally shared values, beliefs, assumptions, and understandings that are the basis for relevant corporate norms and behavior patterns. A very simplified definition of corporate culture is "the way things work around here."[12] Cultural phenomena are detectable in organizations at three levels[13]: Overt behavior and other physical manifestations, such as artifacts and literature, are at the first level. The second level consists of values, a sense of what "ought" to be. The third level contains the basic assumptions and the "correct" ways of coping with the environment. Formal communication style and dress code are first-level examples; promoting from within the organization and lifetime employment are examples of the second level; and strategic choices and the method of facing competition are third-level examples.

Corporate culture, according to Davis,[14] is based on internally oriented beliefs of how to manage, and externally oriented beliefs of how to compete. Since corporate culture is influenced by societal culture, successful firms reflect the basic attributes of their cultural environments. Because of differences in national cultures, accepted managerial practices vary around the world, as do the norms of relating to other businesses and the way of competing. For example, management-by-objectives (MBO), which was successfully applied by many U.S. firms, failed to work in Europe. MBO was designed based on American cultural values. In the hierarchial organizations of France, superiors and subordinates were uncomfortable negotiating the future goals as required by MBO. In Sweden and Holland, MBO procedures were considered too autocratic.[15] What is considered a business gift in other countries might be regarded as a bribe in the United States. In contrast, lobbying, which is regarded by Americans as a normal political practice, is considered to be influence peddling and corruption by other countries.

Corporate culture is a product of the firm's environment and the interpersonal relationships among its members. Initially, the firm's culture is influenced by the national culture of its origin, the country where it initially was established. Once the firm expands its operations outside the borders of its own nation-state and outside the dominance of its own home culture, the influence of the host countries' national cultures becomes a reality.

The performance of business organizations depends on their ability to maintain external compatibility and internal consistency. External compatibility is the congruity of the firm with its host environment. Internal consistency is the equilibrium and balance between the various internal components of the firm. By creating external compatibility, an organization should be careful not to create too much internal inconsistency. In an effort to create external compatibility and to represent the cultural diversity of the global market in their corporate cultures, the MNCs may create a morass of cultural mismatch. Reflecting the diversity of their markets and building a patchwork of too many cultures can cause internal inconsistency for the MNCs. The challenge is to bring about external compatibility and at the same time manage a cultur-ally diverse work-force without creating an internal conflict. Many believe that cultural diversity enhances organizational competitiveness. Failure to manage cultural diveristy properly, however, could lead to increased conflict and communication breakdowns. Consequently, depending on their approach to cultural diversity, MNCs could either enhance their worldwide competitiveness or fall victim to cultural quagmires.

Because of unfamiliarity with the culture in each environment, MNCs face potential problems associated with the peculiarities of that culture. Of course, not all functional areas of the firms are affected similarly. The extent of difficulties arising from the lack of cultural understanding is a function of the amount of interaction between various functional areas of the firm and the host culture. The higher the interaction between a functional area and the host culture, the higher its potential for experiencing problems. For example, marketing and sales functions interact with the host culture much more than the R&D function. Consequently, marketing and sales have the potential to encounter many more occasions for cultural misunderstanding.

The success of an MNC's global expansion, therefore, depends on its ability to adopt the practical aspects of host countries' cultural norms, while maintaining core aspects of the corporate culture that are the basis of its competitiveness. Although cultural adaption to national cultures is axiomatic, no direct, one-to-one correlations between the MNC's corporate culture and host country cultures is conceivable. Instead of seeking intimate identification with the host cultures, it is practical to aim for the avoidance of cultural incompatibility. Therefore, a more realistic expectation is to achieve a certain degree of compatibility, or constructive neutrality, with the host country cultures.[16] Kolde defines constructive neutrality as a positive system of principles and norms to guide the decision-making processes of all of an MNC's

The Mismatch of Corporate Cultures

Global media mergers often do not succeed. When products are information, ideas, words, and images, crossing national boundaries will rarely be as easy as initially envisioned by the parties involved. The acquisition of Diamandis Communication Inc. by the French magazine empire, Hachette S. A., illustrates this point well. The executives' dining tastes were indicative of many of their cultural differences. Diamandis' managers ate at Gallagher's, a Manhattan smoky, he-man steakhouse. Hachette's executives dined at Le Bernardin, an expensive French seafood restaurant, which served black bass with zucchini, tomato, and basil as a part of an ornate $42 lunch. Therefore, by swallowing Diamandis, Hachette experienced a serious case of corporate indigestion.

Two years after the merger, Mr. Diamandis, who was considered a great asset to the company, and his two top lieutenants severed their relationships with the company. This move followed months of disagreement between Hachette's Vice Chairman, Daniel Filipacchi, and Diamandis.

Cultural differences were the root cause of their problems, which were manifested in the managerial styles of the American and French executives. Hachette's executives, like most Europeans, used instinct to guide them, they made most of their decisions on gut-level feelings, without the benefit of meetings or marketing studies. By involving themselves in the tiniest details, suggesting covers and new page designs for magazines, even deciding what pictures should be used, and where they should be used, French executives clashed with U.S. editors who used a more systematic, planned approach.

Adapted from P. M. Reily. "Egos, Cultures Clash When French Firm Buys U.S. Magazines." *The Wall Street Journal* (February 15, 1991), A1.

entities and affiliates to avoid or minimize clashes with its various national environments, and to facilitate optimal involvement and participation of the company in the productive systems of its host countries.[17]

Achieving constructive neutrality is easier if MNCs adopt a multicultural composition and orientation. A unicultural organization that is not exposed to cultural diversity, and an ethnocentric firm that believes in the superiority of its own culture, may have difficulty relating to the idiosyncracies of other cultures. In the multicultural environment of the world business, it is, therefore, advisable for organizations to become multicultural and develop a geocentric mentality. This is done by adopting the best attributes of both local and corporate cultures, to function effectively in different cultural environments. What are the characteristics of a muticultural firm? In the following we examine those attributes.

Cultural Typology of the Organization

On the basis of cultural diversity, business organizations could be categorized into monolithic, plural, and multicultural. We examine these organizations using six factors: acculturation, structural integration, informal integration, cultural bias, organizational identification, and intergroup conflict.[18] These factors influence the cultural diversity of the organizations and are depicted in Figure 5.1. The following is a brief description of these factors:

1. The method of resolving the difference between the dominant culture and any minority culture is called *acculturation*. Acculturation could be by assimilation, the unilateral adop-

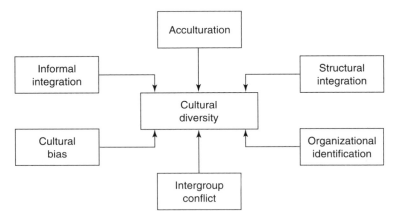

Figure 5.1   Factors Influencing Cultural Diversity of the Organization

tion of the norms and values of the dominant culture by other cultural groups; by pluralism, combining some elements of the dominant and any minority cultures; or by separation, where there is little adoption from either culture.

2. Structural integration is the presence of members of different cultural groups in various organizational levels.
3. Informal integration is the inclusion of the members of minority cultures in informal networks and activities taking place outside the ordinary work activities.
4. Cultural bias is the existence and the practice of prejudice and discrimination in the organization.
5. The extent of personal identification with the firm by its workforce is organizational identification.
6. Intergroup conflict refers to friction, tension, and power struggles between various cultural groups within the firm.

Having described different factors with which cultural diversity is examined, we now elaborate on the organizational types.

Monolithic organization Monolithic organizations are highly homogeneous with a minimum amount of structural integration. They

consist of one dominant cultural group. If the members of other cultural groups join the firm, to survive they must adopt the existing cultural norms. Because of the lack of structural and informal integration, prejudice and discrimination against the members of the cultural minority are prevalent. Consequently, organizational identification among the host country personnel is very low. The homogeneity of the workforce, however, leaves little room for intergroup conflict.

Firms at their early stages of involvement with international business are mostly of the monolithic type. When they expand abroad, they represent the culture of their home country. Their parochial attitudes and ignorance of the host cultures prevents them from taking full advantage of opportunities that host cultures could present to them. If the firms expand beyond simple import and export activities, the forces of competition for local talent, and the pressure from local governments for the inclusion of locals in the MNCs operations, alter their cultural composition. Therefore, eventually, the homogeneity of the monolith firm gives way to the heterogeneity of a plural organization.

Plural organization The attempt by the MNCs to include the host country citizens in their workforce creates opportunities for the representation of norms and values from other cultures in the MNC cultures. The necessity of tapping indigenous knowledge to learn about the host markets and the host government demands for participation of local personnel in MNC operations compel the firms to change their human resource management practices. As a result, the MNCs gain a higher level of structural integration than monolithic firms, leading to a plural organization that is culturally heterogeneous. The home country personnel, however, are still dominant in number and occupy key decision-making positions at all organizational levels. The top managers of plural organizations have an ethnocentric attitude, believing that "our way is the best way."

Although structural integration is incomplete in plural organizations, partial structural integration results in the inclusion of some host country citizens into the MNCs' informal networks. The consequences of informal integration are moderation of prejudice and reduced discrimination. The partial structural and informal integration brings about greater identification with the firm among host country personnel. With the increased number of host country personnel, plural organizations experience more intergroup conflict than would be present in monolithic firms. Similar to monolithic organizations, plural firms rely on assimilation for acculturation. Personnel who are not from the dominant culture of the firm and do not strongly ascribe to the prevailing cultural norms of the firm will have difficulty progressing in the organizational hierarchy. Examples of plural organizations include many subsidiaries of U.S. MNCs operating abroad, such as Exxon, Ford, and Apple Computer.

Multicultural organization Both plural and multicultural firms are culturally heterogeneous. Plural organizations, however, do not value their cultural diversity, while multicultural firms do. Multicultural organizations have overcome the shortcomings of plural firms. They recognize the value of cultural heterogeneity and understand the potential contributions of cultural diversity to organizational performance. Multicultural organizations adopt a synergistic approach to management.

Multicultural organizations are characterized by full structural and informal integration, an absence of prejudice and discrimination, and minimum intergroup conflict. Members of minority cultures identify with the organization, and acculturation takes place by the integration of all participating cultures into a synergistic whole. It is doubtful that many MNCs have reached the goal of multiculturalism. But it seems reasonable to expect that the competitive environment of the global market will conceivably necessitate the adoption of a multicultural posture. The ability of MNCs to attract and maintain qualified personnel from host countries will depend on an orientation that values cultural diversity. To be competitive in the global job market, MNCs need to provide not only good wages, fringe benefits, and a good quality of work life, but they should offer cross-national career advancement, the promotion of foreign employees across national borders.[19] Effective cross-cultural career advancement in firms that do not value cultural diversity is extremely difficult. Therefore, the future growth and fortune of global firms, one can argue, is facilitated by their success in forming multicultural organizations. Multiculturalism bestows upon firms certain benefits, and improves the firm's organizational capabilities. Asea-Brown Boveri (ABB), a global firm that was originally established as a Swedish company, and Jamont, a subsidiary of James River Corporation operating in Europe, are examples of multicultural organizations. Jamont was the subject of the vignette in Chapter 2, and ABB was detailed in Chapter 3.

The Benefits of Multiculturalism

Until recently, most organizations were primarily concerned with the problems and costs created by the ethnic and gender diversity of their workforce. They ignored the potential benefits of cultural diversity. Diversity of the workforce could be a source of competitive advantage. The following are major potential advantages of multiculturalism[20]:

1. *Reduced costs:* There is evidence that as the cultural diversity of firms increases, so does the cost of poor integration. The experiences of minorities and women at work indicate that when cultural minorities are not fully integrated into the workforce, they tend to have lower job satisfaction and higher absenteeism and turnover. Firms that properly manage cultural diversity could have cost advantage over those that do not due to lower absenteeism and turnover rates.

2. *Resource acquisition:* With the increasing globalization of business, competition for qualified personnel has become more intense. Firms with a good reputation for handling cultural diversity attract more and better qualified personnel. This benefit of cultural diversity is especially critical to an MNC's international expansion. A well-qualified pool of managers adds expertise and knowledge to the firm. In addition, these managers, with their diverse background, understand the value of cultural diversity, and are better suited to nurture cultural diversity. Consequently, they could set the stage for a mutually reinforcing process.

3. *Marketing advantage:* The insight and cultural sensitivity of the multicultural workforce with roots in other countries improves marketing efforts. Multicultural personnel enable MNCs to understand and adopt the cultural perspectives of their multiple markets.

4. *Creativity:* Creativity is encouraged when there is less emphasis on conformity. Creativity flourishes when there is a diversity in perspective. Multicultural organizations are potentially more hospitable to creativity.

5. *Problem solving:* A broader and richer base of experience is available to a multicultural firm. Heterogeneity allows the examination of a wider range of perspectives and a more thorough critical analysis of issues. Therefore, heterogeneous groups have the potential for making better decisions.

6. *Organizational flexibility:* Research has demonstrated that bilinguals have a higher level of divergent thinking and cognitive flexibility.[21] MNCs that value cultural heterogeneity actively recruit and employ host country personnel. Many of these employees are bilingual. The inclusion of bilinguals who also have different cultural perspectives enhances the cognitive flexibility of the MNCs. Moreover, to accommodate the inclusion of culturally diverse people, organizational policies and procedures are broadened. A combination of less standardization of the norms and a tolerance for culturally different viewpoints should create more flexibility and a feeling of oneness.

These benefits could be realized only in multicultural firms, since by definition, they are fully integrated organizations. Communication problems and conflict could beset a firm that does not fully integrate and take advantage of cultural diversity.

The advantages outlined above could enhance the competitiveness of multicultural firms in the global market. To create a multicultural organization, MNCs should strive to create heterogeneity in their workforce through effective human resource management practices. Proper human resource management is also a function of the organizational culture. This subject will be discussed in Chapter 9.

Cultural Aspects of Management

Managerial concepts such as motivation, superior–subordinate relationships, authority, leadership, and control are rooted in cultural values and norms. The meaning attached to, and the application of these concepts, varies from one culture to another. The roles and expectations of managers and subordinates are different across cultures. Consider the accompanying conversation between an American manager (A) and a Greek worker (G).[22] Based on his cultural norms, the American manager, who favors employee participation, expects certain initiatives and self-direction from the worker. The Greek worker, however, expects a superior to exercise managerial authority and be direct in giving orders. Each attributes certain meaning to the dialogue, using their cultural assumptions and frame of reference, and each has certain culturally determined expectations regarding superior–subordinate relationships. Conversation between them, and their interpretation of it, are depicted in the dialogue at the bottom of the page.* Because of cultural differences, the American and the Greek were unable to understand each other. The consequence of such ineffective interaction is a disappointment for the individuals and results in a performance loss for the firm.

The interaction between the Greek and the American is probably typical of the encounters that occur when two persons from two different cultures, who are not familiar with the idiosyncrasies of the other culture, interact. Though cultures differ from one to another, cultural differences between traditional and modern societies are more noticeable in international business. Many norms of modern societies either do not have equivalents in traditional cultures or they are totally in variance with them. The concept of time, for example, as a tangible commodity that could be saved,

Behavior	Attribution
A: How long will it take you to finish this report?	A: I asked him to participate.
	G: His behavior does not make sense. He is the boss. Why doesn't he tell me?
G: I do not know. How long should it take?	A: He refuses to take responsibility.
	G: I asked him for an order.
A: You are in the best position to analyze time requirements.	A: I press him to take responsibility for own actions.
	G: What nonsense! I better give him an answer.
G: 10 days.	A: He lacks the ability to estimate time; this time estimate is totally inadequate.
A: Take 15. Is it agreed you will do it in 15 days?	A: I offered a contract.
	G: These are my orders: 15 days.

In fact, the report needed 30 days of regular work. So the Greek worked day and night, but at the end of fifteenth day, he still needed one more day's work.

A: Where is the report?	A: I am making sure he fulfills his contract.
	G: He is asking for the report.
G: It will be ready tomorrow.	(Both attribute that it is not ready.)
A: But we had agreed it would be ready today.	A: I must teach him to fulfill a contract.
	G: The stupid, incompetent boss! Not only he did give me the wrong orders, but he does not even appreciate that I did a 30-day job in 16 days.
The Greek hands in his resignation.	The American is surprised.
	G: I can't work for such a man.

* From H. C. Traindis. "Cultural Training, Cognitive Complexity and Interpersonal Attitudes." In R. W. Brislin, S. Bochner, and W. J. Lonner, eds. *Cross Cultural Respectives on Learning* New York: John Wiley & Sons, 1975). Copyright © 1975. Reprinted by permission of John Wiley & Sons.

wasted, used, and given away is alien to many traditional cultures. Modern societies have much more differentiation and compartmentalization of various facets of daily interaction. In traditional societies, however, most aspects of daily life blend together. Business transactions, for example, are combined with interpersonal relationships such that differentiating them may not be possible. For instance, to babysit for a neighbor, an American is expected to get paid, while in most Asian countries, since neighborhood children are all part of a big family, an expression of appreciation suffices. An attempt to pay for a favor that requires just a compliment could cause much embarrassment.

The most notable compartmentalization and differentiation are the separation of the individuals' work roles in the organization and the roles outside the organization. Americans leave behind much of the trappings and circumstances of their roles as superiors when they finish their daily work. In a traditional culture, a superior's organizational distinction and status extend far beyond the firm and the work relationship. In the Middle East, for example, superiors are considered as role models even outside the organization. A good boss is someone who is concerned about the family problems of the subordinates, and lends a helping hand in their resolution. The same is true in Latin America.

Because the influence of culture in the daily lives of people is pervasive, the underlying cultural values and assumptions form a foundation for accepted and expected managerial practices and corporate culture. These assumptions and values prescribe the way individuals perceive, think about, and evaluate the world, themselves, and others.

Our Way and Cultural Values

To appreciate the influence of cultural values and assumptions on management, let us examine some fundamental values that are relevant to the business. In particular, we will start with a discussion of some basic values of American culture. These values and assumptions serve as anchors in our perception of the environment and guide our decisions. We will compare and contrast them with those of other cultures. The resultant understanding could safeguard us against cross-cultural mistakes and mishaps.

People of most cultures have a tendency for ethnocentrism. The inclination to display an attitude of superiority is symptomatic of ethnocentrism. When doing business abroad, such a tendency could undermine the competitive position of an MNC. Unlike the 1950s and 1960s, today, American managers have a much more enlightened understanding of the people of other cultures. Previously, American MNCs dispatched their managers to other countries not to learn and understand more about the host culture, but to improve and change it for the better. As it was usually put, they wanted to "help introduce modern managerial values."[23] This was more pronounced in dealing with the developing countries. As Kolde asserts, because of their material "backwardness," developing countries were assumed to be formless matter waiting to be shaped and developed to American concepts of good management. To the surprise of many, the subsequent interaction with these cultures brought the sobering realization that the social fabric of any society, whether or not it is industrially advanced, can be as tenacious as that of our own.[24]

Most of us do not want to be considered as insensitive and ignorant. Learning about other cultures certainly allows us to be sensitive to other people and their perspectives. This is not only helpful at a personal level, it additionally has the potential to produce organizational performance through successful business deals and reduced failures in business transactions. We will not be able to become proficient in the knowledge of all cultures, but understanding our own basic cultural values could go a long way toward increasing our sensitivity to cultural differences. It could certainly reduce the "ugly American" charge. As a Lebanese cab driver once told a visiting American, "There is nothing more ugly than an American trying to be an Arab. America is a good country. You must be proud."[25] Let us now examine these basic American cultural values.

The individual   An organization is made up of a group of people and is the result of their purposeful collective efforts. People are the essence of organizations. All organizational activities are based on assumptions regarding the individuals, their interpersonal relationship, and how they relate to the society. These assumptions are culturally determined and differ among nations. There is a big difference, for example, between the Western, particularly the American, concept of the "person" and the place of a person within the society, and the corresponding understanding of the Japanese. Westerners have an isolationist concept of the "person." To them, an individual is a person standing alone and clearly separate from his or her environment. Such a concept of an individual is alien to Japanese. In the Japanese language, there is no equivalent for the English word "I," denoting a person isolated from the surroundings. For Japanese, individuals exist only in relation to others. "The individual is a node of interrelations with others around him/her. Each has a special way and meaning in relating with others, which becomes his/her individuality. Without such relations, there is no individuality."[26] The "I" of teacher–student, or a superior–subordinate situation (Watakushi, for male or female), for example, is different from the "I" of parent–child or sibling relationships (Watashi or Ore, a female or male about 14 years or older; Atashi or Boku, a girl or a boy under 14 years).

The differing views of an individual predicate divergent concepts of organizational relationships. In countries with an isolationist view of the individual, such as the United States, an individual is expected to perform certain functions with clearly defined responsibilities. Fundamental to the individual's participation in business organizations is a clear demarcation of

each person's performance from others and the importance attached to the individual's contribution to the organization. Job descriptions clearly specify the domain of each person's responsibilities, and the management expectations of a person occupying a position. This situation is totally different in Japan.[27] Japanese business organizations do not necessarily define the scope of the job assigned to each individual. The basic unit of work is not the individual's job but the job of a work unit, a section, or a department. The responsibility of performance, therefore, rests with the work unit not the individuals. This is consistent with the "Japanese vagueness of individual responsibility, the idea of joint group responsibility, and the strong sense of responsibility toward the small, close group."[28]

Because of different cultural heritages, the differences between the Americans and the Japanese are not surprising. However, there are also differences in perspectives between the Americans and other Western cultures. For example, the difference between the Germans and the Americans could be illustrated using the concept of social distance proposed by Kurt Lewin.[29]

An individual could be depicted as having a multilayered personality with two major regions: the peripheral region and central region as illustrated in Figure 5.2. The Americans have a much larger peripheral region and smaller cen-

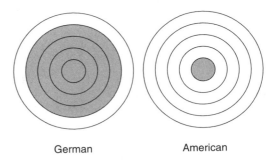

German   American

Figure 5.2   Social Distance

tral region than the Germans. The peripheral region is the "public self" and the central region is the "private self." The Americans have more layers of the peripheral, and these layers are easier to penetrate. Their deeper layers of the central region, however, are relatively inaccessible. In comparison, the Germans, have low accessibility at the peripheral region, but share a larger area of the central region with intimate people.

The accessibility of a larger peripheral region means that the Americans are more willing to open to others than the Germans. In the United States, it is quite common for strangers to greet each other with a smile. Such behavior is unusual in Germany. The Americans seem more friendly and ready to help strangers. A visitor to the United States is more apt to receive an invitation to dine with people in their homes than someone visiting Germany. It seems that the Americans need less privacy in certain aspects of their lives. Many executives of the American corporations or government agencies leave the door of their offices open, and everyone can see their daily activities. For German managers, even those at lower managerial positions, it is unthinkable to leave their doors open. To the Germans, such accessibility is an indication of low prestige.

The openness of the peripheral region does not extend to the more private, intimate region of the American personality. Friendship in the United States progresses much faster through the layers of the peripheral region, and up to a certain point where the central core of personality is reached. It is as difficult to reach the central region of the American personality as that of the Germans. It seems that the boundary leading to intimate relationships is more clearly marked for Americans than for the Germans. In Germany, the transition from the peripheral region to the very intimate region is more gradual and more involved.

Interpersonal relationships involve less of the central core of the Americans and more of the central region of the Germans. For the Americans it is possible to form relatively close relations with others without a deep personal and emotional involvement. This makes it possible to have less personal friction and fewer disappointments. It also makes it as easy to say goodbye to the friends of many years as the acquaintances of a few weeks.

The size and the number of layers in each region may explain certain behavioral differences among the Germans and the Americans. This also may explain the American and German communication patterns. When faced with small difficulties and misfortunes in daily life, for example, the Americans tend to express less open anger. Their reaction is more from the point of view of an action taking place, and the remedies needed to prevent a similar occurrence. The Germans react to these accidents more from the moral point of view of whose fault it is. These differences in reaction to the events reflect the differences in the layering of the peripheral and central regions for the Germans and the Americans. It is less likely that these events will touch the central regions of an American, and more possible that they may touch the Germans' central region. Therefore, the German reaction is more one of anger and moral judgment because it involves more of the private, central core of the person.

The peripheral layers of the personality, according to Lewin,[30] include the "executive" region of a person. These layers are closer to the environment and correspond to the appearance and the action of a person. It seems that compared to the Germans, the Americans emphasize achievement more than ideology and status, and in science the emphasis is more on practice than theory. The Americans are pragmatic and Germans are idealistic.

Ecological relations   Besides the isolationist view of the individual, the Americans also have a different ecological concept of the individual, the relationship between the person, the environment, and other people. Americans believe that people are the masters of their own destiny. They are very optimistic about their ability to shape the future through hard work. They believe that individuals have a considerable choice in what happens to them and around them. Americans take pride in doing everything by themselves without help from others, and have a very strong sense of independence. The concept of self-determination has a counterpart of individual responsibility. Individuals are held responsible for their deeds. The limits of each person's responsibilities are clearly defined. Business organizations assign work to individuals and hold them accountable for the outcome. Personal accomplishment has a high value in the American culture, and failures are considered stepping stones to eventual success. Of course, the American self-determination concept is tempered with pragmatic realism. Cost and benefit analyses serve as a decision guide. The idealism of pursuing a dream for the sake of the pursuit has less appeal to Americans. An endeavor should have a realistic chance of producing a tangible outcome; otherwise it is not worth the effort.

The American concept of the individual as an independent, self-sufficient, self-reliant, and hard-working person who should be held responsible for the outcomes has been an anchor around which other social values were constructed. Various cultures have different views of the individual and the ecological relations. In some cultures, the concept of the individual as a lone entity all by itself and separate from the surrounding milieu does not have much appeal. The individual responsibility that is practiced in American firms is not recognized and practiced by the Japanese, and has a different scope in the Middle East and Southeast Asian cultures.

In Japan, there is little awareness of "individual responsibility." The scope of individual responsibility is very small and obscure. Instead, the responsibility is with the group. As a corollary, there is an exceptionally strong presence of "solidarity of responsibility" among members of a family, a work group, and other social organizations. The solidarity of responsibility is a given. Willingly or not, membership in a group puts a person in the position of assuming a joint responsibility.[31] This sense of joint responsibility is more toward lower level groups, which are closer at hand in face-to-face contact, such as work groups, than to larger groups. The joint responsibility creates "responsibility of the stronger." "When the weaker element in the group is in trouble or placed in an awkward situation, it is considered natural in Japan that he or she seek succour, and that the 'stronger' will be considered as being 'irresponsible' should he not respond to and take appropriate measures."[32]

The self-determinism of the American culture makes little sense to a devout Moslem who believes in preordained faith based on God's will. It is not uncommon to hear a Moslem responding to a business request with a reply of "Insha Allah," which means "if God is willing." Since the destiny of the people and all events are dependent on the will of Allah, it is irreligious for a devout Moslem to think he or she can influence the future. Consequently, planning for the future, and striving to succeed in the American sense, take on a different meaning for the Moslems. In this vein, business strategy and planning are carried out within the context of God's will. Successes are regarded as the blessings of God, and failures are viewed as what God did not mean to be. This does not mean lack of effort or a disbelief in struggle. It means submission without fuss to what has happened. This fatalist view of life (from the American perspective) is also shared by the Buddhists of Southeast Asia, where people believe that the selfish desire for possession and enjoyment is the source of all suffering. Hard work seems futile, and self-determination has no meaning where forces beyond human control influence events. The same is true in Latin America, where the culture promotes a strong belief that fate has more to do with success than effort.

The status of individuals in American society is based on many factors. Besides family and wealth, the status of an American is largely dependent on the level of education, the amount of expertise, and his or her accomplishments. In other societies, such as the Arabs, the familial links overshadow everything else. Although education level, knowledge, and expertise confer prestige and status on the individuals, the status of an Arab in the society is largely determined by his or her family position and social contacts.[33] Likewise, in the Indian society, the caste system will likely determine the profession a person is permitted to pursue.

Work and material gain   Hard work is considered a requisite for goal achievement. It is not only a requirement for success, but a virtue. The frontier heritage of America has made hard work the gospel. The prolonged siesta of other lands, the leisurely luncheon, and the hour-long teas are frowned upon.[34] Without hard work goal accomplishment should not be expected, and in all likelihood it would not happen, and if by luck it happened the recipient does not deserve it. Americans take pride in hard work and believe that it will eventually pay off. Work permeates all aspects of American life. Social occasions, religious gatherings, and leisure activities are quite often used as opportunities to facilitate or conduct business. Many Americans spend their weekends doing what others consider manual labor, such as painting the house, washing the car, mowing the lawn, or tinkering in the garage. It seems to others that the Americans live to work, while others work to live. To the people of many cultures, work is a necessary burden, which if possible should be avoided. Australians, for example, admire the "bludger," a person who appears to work hard while actually doing little work.[35] Most Middle Easterners look down on manual work with contempt, and consider it undignified to engage in manual labor. The undignified status of manual work may be one reason why some oil-rich nations of the Persian Gulf region traditionally import virtually all their labor force from other countries, notably Pakistan. Manual work is particularly demeaning for the educated and the wealthy. Some Europeans do not share the American attitudes toward work. The following story describes the Italian view of a person who is too much consumed by the work ethic. Italians consider such a person as one dimensional.[36]

> An Italian air force officer gave me his impressions of Germans. He likes Germany, but found the Germans very *lineare,* meaning direct, purposeful and efficient. "Lineare" is not a compliment. It characterizes a one-dimensional person, while Italians feel it is important to develop the whole person, not just the work side. I said I thought the Americans were probably just as bad as the Germans, but he shook his head and grinned. "Worse," he said, "much worse."

While Americans work hard because they consider hard work as a virtue and enjoy it as an activity, Japanese work hard for a different reason. Japanese people work hard because of their loyalty and obligation to the group, and because of a sense of responsibility to the group. To perform well is considered fulfilling a duty. When the group succeeds, so do the individual members, and when the group fails, its members have failed. The failure of an individual member to do his or her part in a group situation usually results in a deep sense of agony and shame, the loss of face. So people work hard, stay overtime, or come to work sick to assure the group's success.

Japanese work more hours than their American or European counterparts. Japanese workers in the manufacturing sector, for example, worked 2,124 hours a year on average in 1990, compared to 1,948 hours for Americans, 1,598 hours for Germans, and 1,683 hours for the French.[37] White collar workers work even longer. The Ministry of International Trade and Industry (MITI) figures for 1988 indicated that Japanese workers put in 2,246.8 hours of work.

When Peter Kuper, an American journalist, was discussing MITI's report with a Japanese editor, the Japanese responded "That is too low. They must be leaving out overtime. If I could work 2,500 hours a year, I'd feel as if I was on vacation."[38] (The reader should note that this is more than 8 hours a day, six days a week with no annual vacation.) Very seldom does anyone refuse to work overtime. Since everybody seems to works hard, most individuals feel obligated to do the same. Doing otherwise could cause collective failure, and result in loss of face. It would plunge the individual into a deep pool of personal agony and shame. Japanese feel, if you lose face once, you lose face forever.[39]

The pressure to work hard, and the feeling of obligation and duty to do so, critics say, has resulted in a phenomenon called *karoshi,* meaning sudden death from hard work. It is estimated that karoshi claims 10,000 victims each year. Jun Ishii was a typical karoshi victim. As one of the factory automation specialists working for Mitsui, and the only Russian-speaking specialist, he was shouldering the bulk of the growing Russian business for Mitsui. The 47-year-old specialist, during the previous year, had made 10 Russian trips totaling 115 days. When he returned home from his last trip, Mitsui immediately sent him out to guide a group of Russian clients on a factory tour near Nagoya. Later, while taking a shower in his hotel room, he died of a heart attack. His widow filed a complaint with Tokyo labor regulators and won $240,000 from MITI. She was also granted an annual worker's compensation. Kazuhiro Nakanishi, the family's lawyer, asserted "Finally, the government recognizes that white-collar workers can die of karoshi."[40]

While wealth has universal appeal, the significance of wealth and wealth acquisition varies among nations. Wealth has two basic dimensions. First, wealth is an instrument for the provision of sustenance and physical comfort for self and others. Second, wealth is a measure of success and accomplishment. The Americans' penchant for wealth is not only aimed at providing material comfort but is also an indication of accomplishments. Often, the Americans focus more on the second dimension. As Billington and Ridge have asserted, the American emphasis on wealth acquisition is a frontier heritage. From the early days of the frontier experience, the abundance of natural resources had resulted in a state of mind in which material progress was the only measure of the worth of people. Wealth was the talisman that would create social status, influence, and political power. Money was the primary objective in the life of many frontier settlers. The root of the materialistic attitudes of contemporary Americans is the affluence of the frontiers.[41]

Other nations have different perspectives on wealth, money, and status. In contrast to the Americans, the Germans, for example, consider the intrinsic value of the material things. Consider the purchase of books. Americans feel remiss if they buy books but do not read them. The Germans feel owning books, even if not reading them immediately, is important. For that reason, hardcover books sell more in Germany, and paperback sales are higher in the United States.[42]

Americans have the tendency to display their wealth conspicuously and flaunt their material possessions. They enjoy displaying to others their accomplishments. Some cultures are more subtle about the display of wealth. The Americans view wealth more from the consumption aspect. They view wealth as something to be used. Usefulness is a criterion to measure the worth of the material things. If something is not useful, it should be thrown away. The American penchant for wastefulness is probably also an indirect result of the frontier mentality. To those settling in the frontiers, it must have seemed that the plentiful resources of America were inexhaustible. Therefore, there was no reason for conservation. The resulting wastefulness is evident in the activities of everyday life. To feel warm and comfortable at home, for example, a typical American, who is wearing only light clothes, may increase the heat and warm up the whole house. A European would put on an additional sweater for warmth and comfort.

The worth of a position or an occupation is determined by several primary factors, including honor, power, prestige, and the monetary earnings associated with the position, as well as the impact it may have on the family. In some cultures, the nonmonetary aspects of a job are more important. In other cultures, the monetary gains are emphasized more. It is not unusual for an American to set a goal of becoming a millionaire by a certain age, and to take on more than one job in pursuit of that goal. This narrow pursuit of material gain is frowned on by many traditional cultures with a close family relationship. Faced with an opportunity to earn more money or help a family member, for example, a Hindu may choose the latter.

> When in 1981 a United Nations observer was assigned to Kashmir, as it was customary there, he hired a local boy as a servant to perform household services and help with the housework of his family. The family was so much pleased with his performance that after a short time he was given a good raise. To the surprise of the Swedish family, the servant did not show up the next week and sent his younger brother instead. With his new salary the boy could employ his younger brother, providing him with an income and maintaining the same life style without working.[43]

The method and manner of wealth acquisition are of concern to all cultures. However, the Americans' high regard for business, and wealth acquisition through business, is not universal. In cultures where there is not a high regard for business, outsiders often fill the gap in business and commercial activities. The Indians in East Africa and the Chinese in Southeast Asia, for example, have been successful in business and commerce due to the tendency of locals to hold low regard for business and commerce.[44]

Informality   Informality is a salient characteristic of the Americans. The American informality has its roots in the frontier experience.[45] When in search of a better life Americans moved to the West, they left behind much of the complexity of the Old World cultures. There were no rules or protocol, and no opportunity to practice the old customs. Very soon a much more informal way of speaking and dressing and engaging in social relationships and etiquette was developed.[46] The Old World formal social rules, ceremonies, and traditions never took roots in frontier America. As Robert Cruden explains, frontier people under the pressure of hard work and isolation had to shuck off the grace and amenities of the Eastern cities. They cultivated only those values necessary for survival: sheer physical strength and courage, pragmatic thinking, assertive egalitarianism, and obsession with purely material things. They simply evolved their way of life.[47]

This informality has persisted over the years, and the Americans have never shown much interest in rules and practices that are impractical, restrict behavior, or limit interaction with others. Too much formality is considered by Americans as unfriendly, and they are ill at ease with it. A striking example of this fondness for informality can be found on the pages of the annual reports of American firms. American corporate annual reports are full of pictures of smiling executives. In contrast, in other countries, very seldom is a picture of a smiling executive seen on a corporate annual report. To other nations, the smiling face of an executive is not a dignified pose.

This informality has become such a strong American trait that many Americans assume it is universal. In reality, however, many cultures rigidly adhere to customs and ceremonies. Germans, for example, are very much aware of official and formal titles when addressing each other. In Germany, students never call college professors by their first names. The protocol is to refer to a professor as *herr* (Mr.) *doktor professor*. In work and office situations, Germans always call each other formally and may spend 20 minutes each morning in shaking hands and formal greetings. German executives call their secretaries by an honorific and last name such as *Frau Schmidt*. The use of the first names is regarded as too familiar and condescending by Germans.[48]

Latin Americans are very much interested in pomp and circumstance. Personal etiquette and hospitality rules are strictly observed. Any failure to observe ceremonial practices is construed, at best, as a lack of culture and savoir faire and, at worst, as impolite and rude. The practice of keeping family names going back several generations is a means by which Latin Americans can show a relationship to prominent families or to the Iberian peninsula.

The Japanese are very much concerned with the strict observance of the rules of interpersonal relationships, proper manners, and discipline. In the days of samurai rule, a serious disregard for manners and the failure to show proper respect to a samurai could be punishable by death. A very precisely prescribed way of eating, greeting, gesturing with hands, wearing clothes, walking, and sleeping was practiced. Even today, the daily life of a Japanese is governed by a very strict code of conduct.[49] James Mortellaro, an American executive, who worked for 10 years for Japanese firms, made the following observations on Japanese formality[50]:

> Employees at a typical Hitachi factory in Tokyo remove their shoes before entering their work areas. They wear slippers, color-coded for different jobs, functions, and departments. There are stripes of many colors painted side-by-side on the floor at the main entrance. Employees follow these stripes into the depths of the plant, each color leading off in a different direction. They must follow the color corresponding to their slippers. This practice constantly reminds them of their place and their position in the company.

A naive foreigner, uninformed about the Japanese code of conduct, for example, may lose a business deal just because of an inappropriate manner of exchanging business cards. When Japanese are handed a business card, they acknowledge each individual and his card, they carefully study them, and then respectfully stow them away. In so doing they are trying to understand the person's relationship to the organization and his or her position within it. In a way, they create a context for the future interaction.

Certain American characteristics are closely and directly related to their affinity for informality. In particular, Americans are very exuberant, they like simplicity and brevity of expression, and joking and kidding is a common practice in most formal and informal occasions.[51]

Americans work hard, and with the same vigor, wholeheartedly participate in fun and games. The open enjoyment of life and the hearty expression of pleasure displayed by the Americans is in contrast with the attitudes of Latin Americans. Latin Americans are much more formal and reserved. They never remove their jackets in public, and are very careful to preserve a dignified composure. Relaxed manners, unabashed drinking, and hearty laughter are reserved for family and a circle of close friends. Latin Americans, or for that matter the people from many other cultures, would be truly at a loss at a Shriner's convention, a college class reunion, and would certainly be surprised at a typical college fraternity hazing.

Simplicity and brevity of expression and frank, open, and direct actions are favored by the Americans. The "bottom line" and "getting to the point" are the common currencies of daily language. Tact and diplomacy are not the favorite American styles of interpersonal relationships. The no-nonsense attitude of directly discussing the substance and the main point of business at hand is not favored by other cultures. Where social acceptance, preserving harmony, and saving face are considered important, people avoid candor and frankness. To avoid embarrassment and hurt feelings, the Japanese and many Asians are very reluctant to criticize others publicly, give direct answers, and put oth-

The Failure of an International Joint Venture

After two and a half years of alliance, Corning company and a Mexican glass manufacturer, Virto, had to call off their marriage. Virto, Sociedad Anonima, is a well-known glass manufacturer based in Monterrey, Mexico. It has a large, well-educated and highly trained workforce. Through its subsidiaries and joint ventures with Ford, Samsonite, and Whirlpool, Virto manufactures everything from glass bottles to plastic containers to washing machines and suitcases. Corning is the glass and ceramic giant with a long history of successful joint ventures. Besides alliances with a number of American firms, Corning has joint ventures with Japanese, Korean, German, and French companies. More than half of Corning's operating income comes from joint ventures. Corning's success in alliance with other companies is mostly due to its ability to cope with the constant give-and-take that joint ventures require.

Not all of Corning's alliances, however, are successful. The joint venture with Virto is an example. While some past failures were due to economic and political factors, this one was attributed to cultural differences. At the beginning, the alliance seemed to be a perfect match. Both had the same corporate philosophy that emphasized service to the customers. On the surface the companies appeared very similar. Deep down, however, they had some basic cultural differences. Corning managers, for example, were sometimes left waiting for important decisions about marketing and sales. In Mexican culture only top managers could make those decisions, and at Virto those people were busy with other matters. Conversely, Mexicans sometimes saw the Corning managers as too direct, while Virto managers, in their effort to be very polite, sometimes seemed unwilling to acknowledge problems. Often, the Virto managers thought Corning people moved too fast, while Corning managers thought Virto people were too slow. Mexican managers were taking very long lunch breaks, while Americans had no trouble eating lunch at their desks. While Americans were willing to discuss what went wrong and learn from it, Mexicans were reluctant to criticize anyone, especially a partner. Therefore, many mistake were left unattended.

Sources: C. Mitchell. "Partnerships Are Way of Life for Corning." *The Wall Street Journal* (July 2, 1988), 6; N. A. Nichols. "From Complacency to Competitiveness." *Harvard Business Review* (September–October, 1993), 163–171; A. DePalma. "Still Under Construction." *The Wichita Eagle* (July 10, 1994), 1E–2E.

ers on the spot. Americans, on the other hand, are very much interested in quick and timely feedback of the sort that would require a direct and frank response.

Americans enjoy joking and kidding very much. They use it to break the ice and feel comfortable around people. It also seems to be an equalizer that removes artificial social barriers and brings everyone to the same level. In the rest of the world, the American kidding and joking can be offensive. Outside a close circle of friends, formality and courtesy govern all inter-

personal relationships. The practice of roasting, a ceremony in which colleagues affectionately elaborate on the behavioral or physical shortcomings of a designated person, would be unthinkable in other cultures and extremely offensive.

In the United States, many formal presentations are opened with a joke. Americans like to lace their speeches and presentations with jokes. In other cultures, jokes are not suitable for formal occasions and should be told only among friends and in informal settings. It is considered abnormal to tell a joke in a formal presentation.

An American businessman was preparing for a business trip to Japan. His cultural consultant told him not to use a joke for the opening of his presentation. American jokes, he was told, lose much of their funny meaning in translation into Japanese. Besides, Japanese do not use jokes and funny remarks in business presentations. When in Japan, he followed the advice and started his presentation very formally. It seemed to him that the interpreter was translating his presentation very effectively. That gave the American confidence, and in the middle of his presentation when he remembered a very appropriate joke, he could not help telling it. To his surprise the audience of Japanese managers broke into hearty laughter. When the speech was finished he asked the Japanese interpreter how he translated the joke. To that question the interpreter answered "I did not. I told them that your American guest just told you a joke, you are supposed to laugh."

Attitude toward time   The phrase "time is money" explains the American attitude toward time. Time is a very valuable and scarce commodity that should be employed in useful purposes. Americans are very conscious of time and try very hard to make the most efficient use of their time. In the eyes of many foreigners, Americans are always in a hurry. Foreigners who spend some time in the United States have a common complaint: "There is a deadline for everything" or "From the beginning of everything, Americans look forward to the finish, they do not take time to enjoy life and whatever they do. Everything is instant. Instant coffee, instant pictures, instant life." The high value that Americans place on time could explain their penchant for action and their disdain for inactivity. Moreover, Americans typically have a low tolerance for silence in meetings. By contrast, most Asians can remain silent for long periods where nobody utters a word. To them, the silent period is an opportunity for contemplation and for organizing and evaluating one's thoughts.[52]

The American dislike for long periods of silence many have gotten many American negotiators into serious trouble. An international vice president of a large U.S. company illustrates.[53]

In one of my company's deals overseas, our buyer was sitting across the table from the Japanese manufacturer's representative for the purpose of bidding on an item in which we were interested. Following the usual niceties, our man offered $150,000 per batch. On hearing the bid, the Japanese sat back and relaxed in his chair to mediate. Our buyer, interpreting this silence to be disapproval, instantly pushed his offer higher. It was only after the session was over that he realized he had paid too much.

Time perspective   Individuals, organizations, and cultures vary in their attitudes and orientation toward time. The time perspective could be considered a continuum, at one end of which is monochronic time and the other end polychronic.[54] To engage in one activity at a time and finish each activity before beginning the next is monochronic. To do two or more activities concurrently or intermittently during a time period is polychronic. Americans and many Northern Europeans have a monochronic time perspective, while many traditional societies are polychronic.[55]

Polychronic time.   Industrialization seems to be a major factor influencing time perspectives. We develop time perspectives in relation to the environment. Before the industrial revolution and the emergence of factory work, people in agrarian societies observed natural changes in the environment, and used those changes as anchors in the organization of their lives. Life progressed through days, nights, seasons, and years. Time was measured by the occurrence of natural phenomena, which were real and not artificial. In a circular fashion, day would lead to night, and night to day; spring to summer, summer to fall, fall to winter, and winter to spring. Important events would reoccur and were interrelated. Work and activities did not have precise deadlines. While there were certain times for planting and harvesting, delaying either one by a few days was not disastrous. Interrupting one activity to engage in another did not seriously hamper normal daily life. Unlike today's industrial societies, agrarian life went on without a rigidly imposed structure. In relating to the environment, people developed a time concept very much in tune with the requirements of their daily lives.

Similar to natural events that occur concurrently, polychronic people spend their time according to the dictates of the events. As events evolve around them, polychronic people tend to those events according to their importance, without hesitating to postpone less important ones. They may do many things concurrently, moving from one to another, without predetermined deadlines. The progression of events and activities are more consequences of the urgency of the moment and the requirements of interpersonal relationships than are governed by the modern concept of time. The life of a polychronic person centers around people and interpersonal relations, while for a monochronic person, time is the essence.

The industrial revolution and the requirement of working with machines and following a work schedule made polychronic time problematic. The natural measures of time were no longer appropriate for factory work and machine operations. A new abstract concept of time based on the movement of a mechanical object, the clock, replaced natural time measurement.

Monochronic time. Monochronic cultures perceive time in a linear way, like a road that extends from the past into the future. Linear time is divided into segments, compartmentalized, and scheduled. Monochronic people devote their attention to scheduled activities, one at a time. They assign property values to time. Time could be owned, spent, saved, or given away. Since time is viewed in a linear fashion and activities are scheduled with a clear expectation of starting and finishing times, a request for an un-

scheduled task or meeting could bring the familiar response "I don't have time for it." Similarly monochronic people "spend" their time at work or home, "save" or "set aside" time for family gatherings, and "waste" time waiting. If their expectations are met, monochronic people "enjoy" their time, and have a "good time," otherwise they are having a "hard time" or "lousy time."

Monochronic cultures emphasize punctuality and promptness. To be late for a meeting or to not finish a task on time cause considerable annoyance. Therefore, unscheduled interruptions are avoided as much as possible. In contrast, polychronic people consider unscheduled meetings and events as a normal part of social interactions where business and nonbusiness activities intermingle. The difference in time perspective for punctuality and strict adherence to timetables and schedules could create problems for international managers. In traditional societies, for example, a combination of polychronic attitudes and concern for interpersonal relationships results in business practices that from a monochronic perspective are unacceptable. In the Middle East, for example, changing work schedules and appointments to fit the regular visits by clients, friends, and relatives is very common. A Northern European or an American manager unfamiliar with the cultural values of Middle Easterns could interpret such practices as the lack concern for business at hand. Similarly, a Latin American may be late for a business appointment due to a preference for finishing a conversation with a friend rather than due to a lack of interest or commitment.

Age and gender   Attitudes toward age and gender vary among cultures. Americans have a special admiration for youths, and females are gaining more equality with their male counterparts. Although in many aspects a complete parity between sexes does not exist, the equalization attempts are paying dividends. The laws have made it clear that there should be no discrimination between sexes in business practices.

The American cultural values still favor males. Usually, however, both sexes are treated similarly. Unlike the traditional societies where females play a subservient role, American females consider themselves equal to males, and societal values are changing in that direction.

Other societies have a different attitude toward females. Except for a few Western societies, in the rest of the world females are not granted the same opportunities as males, and do not enjoy the same privileges. The Japanese society, by all accounts, is still a strictly male society. Females are not given prominent roles in business and government. Females who hold a job before they are married are expected to quit after the marriage. The same is true for other countries in Asia, Africa, and even Australia. In some countries, females are denied the most basic rights, such as holding a job outside the home, voting in the political process, or even driving a car. In Saudi Arabia or Kuwait, for example, females do not have the right to drive a car, they can only be passengers. In many orthodox Moslem countries, females are supposed to adhere to a very rigid code of conduct and personal appearance. They should not be seen in public in any fashion that may draw attention to them. Males and females have different status and, consequently, different rights.

Most American executives seem to be aware of the low social status of women in other countries, and the difficulties American female managers could face working abroad. For that reason, they are reluctant to send female managers on such assignments. In a survey of 13,338 North American MNC executives, it was found that only 3% were women.[56] A survey of North American personnel managers found that nearly three-quarters believed that foreign countries' cultural patterns were a major barrier to female expatriate managers.[57] Some firms saw certain disadvantages associated with sending women abroad. They feared that the possibilities of sexual harassment, physical hardship, isolation, and loneliness would adversely affect their perfor-

mance. Some had strong reservations about female expatriate managers, because they believed the failure of a good female manager would have a more negative impact on their firm than that of a male counterpart. These firms were more apt to send a female manager to a staff but not a line position, or to internal but not client-contact positions. They reasoned that the limited opportunity to interact directly with locals, in these positions, would leave less room for concern. There are indications, however, that American female executives abroad are first recognized for their *American* status. Gender has a secondary or nominal role for them.

While Americans are aware that many countries have different attitudes toward females, they will be surprised to learn that the admiration for the youths and youthfulness is not universal either. The United States is a very young country. The vigor and strength of its youth made this country expand and prosper. Unlike the Old World, there were no restrictions and limitations on how far a person could advance. Particularly, the rugged frontier life favored the physical stamina and strength of youth.[58] Since then, Americans have come to admire youthfulness and consider young age as a favorable characteristic. The elderly people do not have as high a place in society as in other nations. In other nations, old age is a sign of experience and wisdom, and youth is synonymous with naivety and lack of sophistication. In many Asian countries, senior citizens are highly respected, and there is a clear ascending order of status according to age. Older people are expected to be in positions of authority and power, in business and the government, and they are. It is highly unusual to see younger people occupying high offices. American MNCs that ignore these cultural values and send the most qualified younger or female managers abroad may not receive a favorable reception. The assignment of a young person or a female is interpreted as an indication of lack of interest and commitment or the low value of the business to the MNC. Traditional societies will place a higher value on seniority than performance in choosing to fill a position.

Conclusion

A firm's global business environment is made up of a multitude of value systems, cultural practices, and nationalistic viewpoints. To operate successfully in this diverse and dynamic environment, the multinational firm must change its frame of reference. The provincial local/national perspective that serves the domestic firm well cannot be effective in a global setting, and should be abandoned in favor of a global perspective. The firm needs to develop an understanding of cultural forces that could impact its operations globally. As the firm learns how to deal with varying cultural forces and sentiments existing in various national markets, it learns to adopt appropriate strategies. These strategies aim to combine the diversity of national markets in an overall corporate plan, yet allow it to be responsive to the unique characteristics and demands of each host country. A successful international enterprise is a firm that could be viewed by the host country as an "insider," a firm that understands and responds to the uniqueness of the host country. To gain the status of an "insider," the MNC is required to understand the host country's national culture and learn how to avoid cultural pitfalls. Also, the cultural diversity of a global firm should provide it with additional competitive advantage.

Discussion Questions

1. Define culture.
2. Describe cultural complexity. How does cultural complexity affect the management of international business?
3. Why do MNC managers have more difficulty in a culturally heterogeneous country?
4. What is corporate culture? Elaborate on the relationship between corporate culture and national culture.

5. What is the basis for the cultural typology of an organization? Describe the differences between multicultural and monolithic firms.
6. Explain the benefits of cultural diversity. How could MNCs gain a competitive advantage through cultural diversity?
7. There are differences between the American and Japanese concepts of "individual." How could such a difference affect the management of a business firm in either country?
8. According to Kurt Lewin, Americans form friendship much quicker and easier than Germans. Why?
9. Why are Americans more informal than other nations? How could this informality cause difficulties for American managers abroad?
10. Both the Americans and Japanese value hard work, but for different reasons. Explain.
11. How could the Americans' penchant for informality create problems when doing business abroad?
12. Explain why a monochronic manager would have difficulty with polychronic workers.
13. What are the problems that an American female manager would face in foreign assignments?

Endnotes

1. E. S. Browning. "Computer Chip Project Brings Rivals Together, But the Cultures Clash." *The Wall Street Journal* (May 3, 1994), A1, A8.

2. Ibid.

3. E. J. Kolde. *The Multinational Company* (Lexington, MA: Lexington Books, 1974), 80.

4. G. G. Gordon. "Industry Determinants of Organizational Culture." *Academy of Management Journal*, 16, no. 2 (1992), 396–415.

5. L. Armstrong. "It Started with an Egg." *Business Week* (December 2, 1991), 142.

6. These examples are based on a news story that appeared in *The Wichita Eagle*, November 26, 1992. The original column was written for *Los Angles Times/Washington Post*, by T. R. Reid.

7. Y. Allaire and M. E. Firsirotu. "Theories of

Organizational Culture." *Organizational Studies*, 5 (1984), 193–226.

8. G. Hofstede. "Cultural Relativity of Quality of Life Concept." *Academy of Management Review*, 9, no. 3 (1984), 389–398.

9. H. L. Telshaw, Jr. "ABCD—Asian Business and Cultural Disparities." *American Institute for Decision Sciences Conference Proceedings* (1985), 250–51.

10. E. T. Hall. *Beyond Culture* (Garden City, NY: Anchor Books, 1977), 16.

11. E. T. Hall and M. R. Hall. *Understanding Cultural Differences* (Yarmouth, ME: Intercultural Press, 1987), 5.

12. V. Terpstra and K. David. *The Cultural Environment of International Business* (Cincinnati, OH: South-Western Publishing Co., 1991), 13.

13. E. H. Schien. *Organizational Culture and Leadership* (San Francisco: Jossey-Bass, 1986).

14. S. M. Davis. *Managing Corporate Culture* (Cambridge, MA: Billinger, 1984).

15. G. Hofstede. "Do American Theories Apply Abroad?" *Organizational Dynamics*, 10, no. 1 (1981), 63–80.

16. Kolde. *The Multinational Company*. 82.

17. Ibid., 83.

18. T. Cox, Jr. "The Multicultural Organization." *Academy of Management Executive*, 5, no. 2 (1992), 34–47.

19. M. Maruyama. "Changing Dimensions in International Business." *Academy of Management Executive*, 6, no. 3 (1992), 88–96.

20. T. H. Cox and S. Blake. "Managing Cultural Diversity: Implications for Organizational Competitiveness." *Academy of Management Executive*, 5, no. 3 (1991), 45–56.

21. W. Lambert. "The Effects of Bilingualism on the Individual: Cognitive and Sociocultural Consequences." In P. A. Hurnbey, ed. *Bilingualism: Psychological, Social, and Educational Implications* (New York: Academic Press, 1977), 15–27.

22. H. C. Traindis. "Cultural Training, Cognitive Complexity and Interpersonal Attitudes." In *Cross Cultural Perspectives on Learning* (New York: John Wiley and Sons, 1975), 42–43.

23. Kolde. *The Multinational Company*. 84.

24. Kolde. *The Multinational Company*. 85.

25. L. Copeland and L. Riggs. *Going International: How To Make Friends and Deal Effectively In the Global Marketplace* (New York: Random House, 1985), 3.

26. M. Maruyama. "Epistomological Source of New Business Problems in the International Environment." *Human Systems Management*, 8 (1989), 71–80.

27. R. Iwata. *Japanese-Style Management: Its Foundations and Prospects* (Tokyo: Asian Productivity Organization, 1982), 5.

28. Ibid., 5.

29. Kurt Lewin, *Resolving Social Conflict* (New York: Harper and Row, 1948), 18–25.

30. Ibid., 25.

31. Iwata. *Japanese-Style Management*. 2.

32. Ibid., 2.

33. C. Pezeshkpur. "Challenges to Management in the Arab Work." *Business Horizons* (August 1978), 47–55.

34. R. A. Billington and M. Ridge. *Westward Expansion* (New York: Macmillan Publishing Co., 1982), 688.

35. Copeland and Griggs. *Going International*. 13.

36. Ibid.

37. U. C. Lehner. "Is It Any Surprise That Japanese Make Excellent Loafers?" *The Wall Street Journal* (February 28, 1992), 1.

38. Pert Kuper. "Death of a Salaryman." *Esquire* (September 1991), 83–85.

39. Ibid., 84.

40. K. L. Miller. "Now, Japan Is Admitting It: Work Kills Executives." *Business Week* (August 3, 1992), 35.

41. Billington and Ridge. *Westward Expansion*. 688.

42. Hall and Hall. *Understanding Cultural Differences*. 46.

43. N. J. Adler. *International Dimensions of Organizational Behavior* (Boston, MA: Kent Publishing Co., 1986), 21.

44. Terpstra and David. *The Cultural Environment of International Business*. 119.

45. T. O. Wallin. "The International Executive's Baggage: Cultural Values of the American Frontier." *MSU Business Topics* (Spring 1976), 49–58.

46. F. S. Philbrick. *The Rise of the West, 1754–1830* (New York: Harper and Row, 1965), 347–50.

47. R. Cruden. *Many and One: A Social History of the United States* (Englewood Cliffs, NJ: Prentice-Hall, 1980), 40.

48. Hall and Hall. *Understanding Cultural Differences*. 64–65.

49. Copeland and Griggs. *Going International*. 11.

50. J. S. Mortellaro. "Japanese Management Imperialism." *Business Marketing* (February 1989), 66.

51. Wallin. "The International Executive's Baggage." 49–58.

52. A. M. Whitehill. "American Executives Through Foreign Eyes." *Business Horizons* (May/June 1989), 42–44.

53. Ibid., 44.

54. A. C. Bluedorn, C. F. Kaufman and P. M. Lane. "How Many Things Do You Like To Do At Once? An Introduction to Monochronic and Polychronic Time." *Academy of Management Executive*, 6, no. 4 (1992), 17–26.

55. Hall and Hall. *Understanding Cultural Differences*. 13–22.

56. N. J. Adler. "Women in International Management: Where Are They?" *California Management Review*, 16, no. 4 (1987), 78–9.

57. N. J. Adler. "Expecting International Success: Female Managers Overseas," *Columbia Journal of World Business* (Fall 1984), 79–85.

58. W. Nugent. *Structures of American Social History* (Bloomington: Indiana University Press, 1981), 68–9.

JOHN HIGGINS: AN AMERICAN GOES NATIVE IN JAPAN

MICHAEL YOSHINO

In the fall of 1962, Mr. Leonard Prescott, vice-president and general manager of the Weaver-Yamazaki Pharmaceutical Company Ltd. of Japan, was considering what action, if any, to take regarding his executive assistant, Mr. John Higgins. In Mr. Prescott's opinion, Mr. Higgins had been losing his effectiveness as one who was to represent the U.S. parent company because of his extraordinary identification with the Japanese culture.

The Weaver Pharmaceutical Company was one of the outstanding concerns in the drug field in the United States. As a result of extensive research it had developed many important drugs and its product lines were constantly improved, giving the company a strong competitive advantage. It also had extensive international operations throughout many parts of the world. Operations in Japan started in the early 1930's, though they were limited to sales activities. The Yamazaki Pharmaceutical House, a major producer of drugs and chemicals in Japan, was the franchise distributor for Weaver's products in Japan.

Export sales to Japan were resumed in 1948. Due to its product superiority and the inability of major Japanese pharmaceutical houses to compete effectively because of lack of recovery from war damage, the Weaver company was able to capture a substantial share of the market for its product categories. In order to prepare itself for increasingly keen competition from Japanese producers in the foreseeable future, the company decided to undertake local production of some of the product lines.

From its many years of international experience, the company had learned that it could not hope to establish itself firmly in a foreign country until it began manufacturing locally. Consequently, in 1953 the company began its preliminary negotiations with the Yamazaki Company Ltd., which culminated in the establishment of a jointly owned and operated manufacturing subsidiary. The company, known as the Weaver-Yamazaki Pharmaceutical Co. Ltd. of Japan, was officially organized in the summer of 1954.

Initially, the new company only manufactured a limited line of products. However, through the combined effort of both parent companies, the subsidiary soon began to manufacture sufficiently broad lines of products to fill the general demands of the Japanese market. For the last several years, importation from the United States had been limited to highly specialized items.

The company did a substantial amount of research and development work on its own, though it was coordinated through a committee set up by the representatives of both parent companies to avoid unnecessary duplication of research effort. The R&D group at the subsidiary had turned out a substantial number of new products, some of which were marketed successfully in the United States and elsewhere.

This case was prepared by Dr. Michael Yoshino under the direction of Professor J. S. Ewing, in Tokyo, as a basis for class discussion rather than to illustrate either effective or ineffective handling of an administrative situation. Reprinted with permission of Stanford University Graduate School of Business. Copyright © 1963 by the Board of Trustees of the Leland Stanford Junior University.

The management of the Weaver company looked upon the Japanese operations as one of the most successful international ventures it had undertaken. It felt that the future prospect looked quite promising with steady improvement in the standard of living in Japan.

The subsidiary was headed by Mr. Shozo Suzuki, as president, and Mr. Leonard Prescott as executive vice-president. Since Mr. Suzuki was executive vice-president of the parent company and also was president of several other subsidiaries, his participation in the company was limited to determination of basic policies. Day-to-day operations were managed by Mr. Prescott as executive vice-president and general manager. He had an American executive assistant, Mr. Higgins, and several Japanese directors who assisted him in various phases of the operations. Though several other Americans were assigned to the Japanese ventures, they were primarily concerned with research and development and held no overall management responsibilities.

The Weaver company had a policy of moving American personnel around from one foreign post to another with occasional tours of duty in the international division of the home office. The period they spent in a country generally ranged from three to five years. Since there were only a limited number of Americans working in the international operations of the company, the personnel policy was rather flexible. For example, it frequently allowed a man to stay in the country for an indefinite period of time, if he desired to. As a result of this policy, there were, though few in number, those Americans who had stayed in one foreign post over 10 years.

The working relationship with the Japanese executives had been generally satisfactory, though there had been a number of minor irritations, which the companies believed were to be expected from any joint venture. The representatives of both parent companies were well aware of these pitfalls and tried to work out solutions to these problems amicably.

Mr. Leonard Prescott arrived in Japan in 1960 to replace Mr. Richard Densely who had been in Japan since 1954. Mr. Prescott had been described as an "old hand" at international work, having spent most of his 25-year career with the company in its international work. He had served in India, the Philippines and Mexico prior to coming to Japan. He had also spent several years in the international division of the company in New York. He was delighted with the challenge to expand further the Japanese operations. After two years of experience in Japan, he was pleased with the progress the company had made and felt a certain sense of accomplishment in developing a smooth functioning organization.

He became concerned, however with the notable changes in Mr. Higgins' attitude and thinking. Mr. Higgins, in the opinion of Mr. Prescott, had absorbed and internalized the Japanese culture to such a point where he had lost the United States point of view and orientation. He had "gone native," so to speak, in Japan which resulted in a substantial loss of his administrative effectiveness as a bi-cultural and -lingual executive assistant.

Mr. Higgins was born in a small Midwestern town. After completing his high school education there in 1950, he went on to attend a large state university nearby, where he planned to major in accounting. During his junior year at college, he was drafted into the Army. After his basic training, he was given an opportunity to attend the Army Language School for an intensive training in a foreign language, providing that he would extend his period of enlistment for another year. Since he had taken much interest in foreign languages, primarily German and Spanish during his high school and college days, he decided to volunteer for this assignment, knowing that the Army would decide the language for him to study. He was enrolled in a Japanese language section with several others. After fifteen months of intensive training in the language, he was assigned as an interpreter and translator to the Intelligence Detachment in Tokyo.

Shortly after he arrived in Tokyo, he was selected to do more intensive work with Japanese and he attended an advanced course emphasizing reading and writing. By the time he completed the program, he was able to read newspapers and political and economic journals of a fairly sophisticated level. His assignment at the Intelligence unit consisted primarily of going over Japanese newspapers and periodicals and translating those parts which were of interest to the United States Army. While he was in Japan, he took evening courses in the Japanese language, literature and history at a well-known Japanese university in Tokyo. At the same time, he acquired many Japanese friends whom he visited quite frequently in his off-duty time. He thoroughly fell in love with the Japanese culture and determined to return to live in Japan for some time.

Immediately upon his release from the Armed Forces in 1957, he returned to college to resume his education. Though he had thought seriously about majoring in Japanese, upon close examination, he decided against it for several reasons. First of all, he felt that majoring in the language would limit his career to teaching or to specialized forms of government service, neither of which he wanted. Secondly, this would mean many more years of intensive graduate study leading to a terminal degree. Finally, he was desirous of using the language as a means rather than as an end in itself. For these reasons, he decided to finish his college work in business management.

In 1958 he graduated from the university with honor and took a position as a management trainee with the International Division of the Weaver Pharmaceutical Company. The company had a policy of assigning new international trainees to domestic operations for a period of six months to get him acquainted with the overall company operations. They then were given six months to a year training at the International

Division of the company in New York prior to an assignment overseas. In the fall of 1959, Mr. Higgins, having successfully completed both of the training programs, was assigned to the Japanese operations as executive assistant to the general manager. Mr. Richard Densely.

He was pleased with his first overseas assignment. He was anxious to return to Japan not only because of his interest in the Japanese language and culture, but also for the opportunity to do something about improving the "Ugly American" image many Americans had created in Japan.

Because of his ability of the language and his intense interest in Japan he was able to assess the attitude toward the United States of far broader segments of the Japanese population than was possible for many. He noted that Americans had a tendency of imposing their value systems, ideals and thinking patterns upon the Japanese, because many of them were under the illusion that anything American was universally right and applicable. They did not, in his opinion, show much desire to understand and appreciate the finer points of the Japanese culture. Generally their adaptations to the Japanese culture did not go beyond developing a taste for a few typical Japanese dishes or learning a few simple Japanese sentences. He had felt indignant on numerous occasions over the inconsiderate attitudes of many Americans he had observed in Japan and was determined to do something about it.

His responsibilities as executive assistant under Mr. Densely covered a wide scope of activities ranging from trouble shooting with major Japanese customers, attending trade meetings, negotiating with the government officials, conducting marketing research projects and helping out Mr. Densely in day-to-day administration of the firm. Mr. Densely was well pleased with Mr. Higgins' performance and relied heavily upon his judgment because of his keen insight into Japan.

When Mr. Prescott took over the Japanese operations in 1960, he found Mr. Higgins' assistance indispensable in many aspects of the operations. For the next two years, he depended much upon Mr. Higgins' advice on many difficult and complex administrative and organizational problems. Mr. Prescott found him to be a capable administrative assistant and staff member.

However, Mr. Prescott began to note a gradual change in Mr. Higgins' basic values and attitude. Mr. Higgins, in Mr. Prescott's opinion, had become critical of the company's policy in managing the Japanese operations and Prescott became increasingly apprehensive of his effectiveness as an executive assistant. He attributed this change to his complete emotional involvement with the Japanese culture, with a consequent loss of objectivity and identification with the U.S. point of view. Mr. Prescott mentally listed a few examples to describe what he meant by Higgins' "complete emotional involvement" with the culture.

In the summer of 1961, Mr. Higgins married a Japanese girl whom he had met shortly after he returned to Japan. His wife was an extremely attractive and intelligent woman by any standard. She had been graduated from the most prominent women's college in Japan and had studied at a well-known Eastern university in the United States for a brief period of time. Shortly after their marriage, Mr. Higgins filed a request through Mr. Prescott with the personnel director of International Division in New York, asking to extend his stay in Japan for an indefinite period of time. The personnel director approved the request upon consultation with both Mr. Densely and Mr. Prescott. Mr. Prescott noted that marriage was a big turning point for Mr. Higgins. Until that time, he was merely interested in the Japanese culture in an intellectual sense, but since his marriage he was observed to have developed a real emotional development with it.

He and his wife rented an apartment in a strictly Japanese neighborhood and he was often seen relaxed in his Japanese kimono at home. He was also observed to use the public bath, a well-known Japanese institution. His fluent Japanese combined with a likeable personality and interest in the Japanese culture won him many friends in the neighborhood. Everyone, including small children, greeted him with a big smile and friendly gestures addressing him as "Higgins-san" whenever they saw him.

His mode of living was almost entirely that of a typical Japanese. He seemed to have completely integrated himself with Japanese life. He was invited to weddings, neighborhood parties and even to Buddhist funerals. On these occasions, he participated actively and fulfilled whatever part was required by the customs and traditions.

The Weaver Pharmaceutical Company had a policy of granting two months home leave every two years with transportation paid for the employee and his family. When Mr. Higgins' turn came, he declined to go home even on vacation on the ground that his parents were already dead and his brothers and sisters were widely scattered throughout the United States. Consequently, he did not feel he had many home ties in the United States. He and his wife took his two months leave and visited many of the remote historical sites throughout Japan.

None of these points by itself disturbed Mr. Prescott greatly. However, he was afraid that accumulations of these seemingly insignificant factors would tend to distort Higgins' cultural orientation and identification, thereby losing his effectiveness as a bi-lingual and cultural representative of the American parent company. In administrative relationships, there have recently been a number of incidents which tended to support Mr. Prescott's anxiety over his attitude. A few of the specific examples were these.

In performing his responsibilities as executive assistant Higgins had taken on many of the characteristics of a typical Japanese executive.

For example, Mr. Higgins was reported to spend a great deal of time in listening to the personal problems of his subordinates. He maintained close social relationships with many of the men in the organization and he and his wife took an active interest in the personal lives of the employees. They even had gone as far as arranging marriages for some of the young employees.

Consequently, many of the employees sought Mr. Higgins' attention to register their complaints and demands with the management. For example, recently a group of middle management personnel approached Mr. Higgins concerning the desirability of more liberal fringe benefits. These were particularly in the areas of company-sponsored recreational activities such as occasional out-of-town trips and the acquisition of rest houses at resort areas.

On another occasion, the middle management personnel registered their objections concerning a recent company policy of promoting personnel based upon merit rather than length of service and education, the two most important criteria in traditional Japanese approach. Shortly after Mr. Prescott took over the Japanese operations, he was appalled with Japanese promotion practices and decided to change these to a merit system. In the process, he consulted with Mr. Higgins as to its applicability in Japan.

The latter objected to the idea, saying that the Japanese were not quite ready to accept what he considered a radical approach. Since Mr. Prescott did not see it as a radical concept, he went ahead and announced the policy. At the same time, he installed an annual review system, whereby every one of the management personnel would be evaluated by his immediate superior and this would constitute an important basis for promotion.

The Japanese objections were primarily based upon the ground that their traditional personnel practices were so different from those of the United States, that a mechanical imposition of the U.S. method would not work in Japan. The system had, as Higgins expected, created many undesirable problems. The Japanese group contended that Mr. Prescott, not understanding the language, was not aware of the magnitude of the anxiety and insecurity the policy had caused. Because of the traditional superior–subordinate relationship characterized by distance, fear, and obedience, they were not willing to take these problems directly to Mr. Prescott. Therefore they asked Mr. Higgins to intercede on their behalf by reporting their feelings to Mr. Prescott.

Mr. Prescott felt that though it was helpful to have Mr. Higgins report back to him the feelings and opinions of the middle management personnel, which otherwise might never come to his attention, he did not appreciate the latter's attitude in so doing. In these cases, Mr. Higgins' sympathy was with the Japanese group and he usually insisted that these demands were reasonable and well justified, according to the Japanese standard and traditions. Mr. Prescott found it necessary to deal with Mr. Higgins on these demands instead of being able to work with him as it had been in the past. His perception had been so colored that Mr. Prescott became hesitant to ask Mr. Higgins' opinions on these matters. Lately, whenever Mr. Prescott proposed a change in administrative procedures which might be contrary to Japanese traditions or culture, Mr. Higgins invariably raised objections. In Mr. Prescott's thinking, there were dynamic changes taking place in traditional Japanese customs and culture and he was confident that many of the points Mr. Higgins objected to were not tied to the cultural patterns as rigidly as he thought they might have been. Besides, Mr. Prescott thought that there was no point for a progressive American company to copy the local customs and felt that its real contribution to the Japanese society was in bring in new ideas and innovations.

To substantiate this point, he learned that some of his Japanese subordinates were much more susceptible to new ideas and were willing to try them out than Mr. Higgins. This fact had convinced Mr. Prescott that Mr. Higgins was too closely and overly identified with the traditional pattern of the Japanese culture, not sensing the new and radically different development taking place in Japan.

Moreover, two recent incidents raised some doubts in Mr. Prescott's mind as to the soundness of Mr. Higgins' judgment, which he, heretofore, had never questioned. The first incident was in connection with the dismissal of Mr. Nonogaki, chief of subsection in the Purchasing Department. In the opinion of Mr. Prescott, Mr. Nonogaki lacked initiative, leadership and general competency. After two years of continued prodding by his superiors, including Mr. Prescott himself, he has shown little interest, if any, in self-improvement. As a result, Prescott had decided to dismiss him from the organization. Both Higgins and Takahinshi, personnel manager of the subsidiary objected vigorously on the ground that this had never been done in the company. Besides, in Japan the management was required to live with a certain amount of incompetent executives as long as their honesty and loyalty were not questioned. They further claimed that the company was partially responsible for recruiting him initially and had kept him on for the last ten years without spotting his incompetency, thus it was not completely fair to require Mr. Nonogaki alone to take the full burden. Mr. Prescott, unimpressed by their arguments dismissed him after serving proper notice.

A few weeks later, Mr. Prescott learned quite accidentally that Mr. Nonogaki was re-employed by one of the other subsidiaries of the Japanese parent company, the Yamazaki Pharmaceutical Co., Ltd. Upon investigating, he found, to his surprise that Messrs. Higgins and Takahinshi had interceded and arranged for him to be taken back without informing Mr. Prescott. For understandable reasons, Mr. Prescott did not appreciate their action and confronted Mr. Higgins with this, who in turn told Mr. Prescott that he had done that which was expected of a superior in any Japanese company.

Another incident was in connection with his relationship with the government. In Japan, the government plays a substantially greater part in business and economic activities than it does in the United States. It is important for companies to maintain a good working relationship with government officials of those agencies which have control over their activities. This is particularly true of foreign subsidiaries. Because of many complicated intricacies, government relations had been entrusted to Mr. Higgins and his two Japanese assistants.

Mr. Prescott had observed a basic difference in the view with which he and Higgins looked upon practices of this sort. Prescott, knowing the differences in business ethics in various countries, accepted some of these activities as a necessary evil but felt that they had to be kept to the minimum in order to preserve the overall integrity of the company. Whereas Mr. Prescott felt Mr. Higgins had become a willing participant in the system without much reservation or restraint.

Mr. Prescott believed these problems to be quite serious. Mr. Higgins had been an effective as well as efficient executive assistant and his knowledge of the language and the people had proved invaluable. On numerous occasions, his American friends envied Prescott for having a man of his qualifications as an assistant. He also knew that Mr. Higgins had received several outstanding offers to go with other American companies in Japan.

Prescott felt that Higgins would be far more effective could he take a more emotionally detached attitude toward the Japanese people and culture. In Mr. Prescott's view, the best international executive was the one who retained a belief in the fundamentals of the U.S. point of view while also understanding foreign attitudes. This understanding, of course, should be thorough or even instinctive, but it also should be objective, characterized neither by disdain nor by strong emotional attachment.

He was wondering how he could best assist Mr. Higgins to see his point of view, so that they could collaborate more effectively in fulfilling their administrative responsibilities.

Questions

1. What are the significant characteristics of Mr. Higgins' attitude? Of Mr. Prescott's attitude?
2. What do you think are the underlying causes for changes in Mr. Higgins' attitude?
3. Do you agree with Mr. Prescott's definition of an "effective" international executive? How would you go about developing a man of these qualities?
4. What objectives should Mr. Prescott have in working with Mr. Higgins?
5. What actions should Mr. Prescott take?

SIX

INTERNATIONAL COMMUNICATION AND NEGOTIATION

Kamal Fatehi and Deema deSilva,
Wichita State University

No business transaction can be carried out without communication. International management involves communicating over national borders and dealing with cultural differences. To communicate we use language, signs, and symbols, which are all culturally determined. In this chapter we learn that effective international communication requires an understanding of cultural influences. We learn about cultural differences in verbal as well as nonverbal communication. Finally, we conclude the chapter with a discussion of cultural differences in international negotiation.

It was his second month of a stay in New York City when Moda Esphenaaj asked Bob Balladur "Why do people sell their garages? Are parking spaces for cars at a premium in New York?"

Moda was an Asian student on a training assignment with a large bank in New York. The bank had extensive business in Moda's home country. Bob had volunteered to become Moda's mentor and was assisting him during his stay in New York.

Of course, Bob's answer to the second question was affirmative. On many occasions, Bob and Moda had searched in frustration for a spot to park his black Saab. Surely, Moda by now should have noticed New York's parking problem. However, he could not understand what Moda was getting at with the first question. When he asked, Moda's response sent him into a roaring, hearty laughter. Moda had seen many signs for "garage sales" and thought that people

were selling their garages separately. When Bob explained the meaning of those signs, Moda's face turned red with embarrassment. Being a sensitive man, Bob offered to tell his experience of many years ago that was not only embarrassing, but very costly.

The story went like this: Bob was working in an American bank in Paris as a senior manager in charge of les cambistes, as the fast-and-furious foreign exchange traders are called. One day, a currency exchange trader from the Bourse (the word for stock and currency market in French) called to say that the U.S. dollar was sinking fast. Bob yelled a profanity and slammed down the phone so hard that it broke into two pieces. A few seconds later the trader called him on another phone and dutifully reported the purchase of a large block of U.S. dollars. "You did what?" Bob angrily inquired. To which the protesting trader answered "but you said Achet"—the French word meaning "buy." That afternoon, Bob walked into his boss's office and told him "I've got a funny story to tell you, but it will cost you a quarter of a million dollars to hear it."

Moda could not wait for Bob to finish his story. By the last sentence, he was already laughing loudly, and Bob joined him in utter fun and relief.[1]

Introduction

During the course of a day we are judged by the effectiveness of our communication. We are judged by the way we speak, the accent of our speech, body language, the way we write and listen, and even the manner in which we read.

Communication is a skill that has to be learned and sharpened. In this changing world, we are expected to continue to improve our communication skills. Do you spend most of your time listening, speaking, or writing? Do you think you will have to continue to do so? The answers to these questions provide you with clues as to the importance of the communication process, which encompasses almost all daily activities.

When people get together, communication is inevitable. In other words, it is impossible not to communicate in the presence of other people. It is not, however, guaranteed that the communication taking place is accurate or reflects the intention of the participants. This is because even silence or inadvertent movements and actions are perceived and interpreted. Sometimes we send erroneous messages by the manner of our dress or tone of our voice, or simply by being where we are physically. We may, for example, mistake someone as a successful financial consultant if he or she dresses in a conservative style, carries a leather briefcase, and reads a financial newspaper. However, if the person responds to a finance quiz with a far-fetched answer, it is obvious that we have made a mistake and the person just fits the stereotypic image of a financial consultant.

The successful management of an enterprise is directly related to the ability of its management to communicate to organizational members the mission and objectives of the enterprise. Communication among organizational members is essential for task accomplishment. Members have to communicate in order to receive and send information. To work in a team, to send a message, to give an order, to assist a coworker, to report a task accomplishment, to negotiate a business transaction, or to do any of the myriad of other business activities in a typical day, we need to communicate.

As organizational complexity increases so does the need for a more effective communication system. Because all business activities involve communication, and because international management is more complex than the management of domestic businesses, effective communication is crucial to the success of an international operation. To deal with customers, suppliers, government agencies, and a host of other organizations, it is necessary to communicate across national borders. In other words, to manage internationally, effective communication is imperative.

Macro and Micro International Communication

International communication can be viewed from two different perspectives, the macro and micro levels. At the macro level it entails understanding the problems and opportunities that arise from the flow of information and communication between countries. At this level, international communication encompasses information exchange and communication through mass media, telecommunications and high technology transfer that could have far reaching political, economic, social, and cultural consequences on nations. The micro level involves communication and information flow between the firm, its employees, and its external constituencies. At the micro level, intrafirm, interpersonal, and intercultural communication are intertwined. Of course, MNCs are more concerned with the communication issues at the micro level. The macro level issues of international communication and information dissemination, however, may potentially be the source of future difficulties. Therefore, before addressing the micro level international communication, we will present the major points of macro level international communication. The macro level of international communication, according to Mowlana, can be viewed from four different perspectives[2]:

1. The idealistic-humanistic approach views international communication (IC) as a means by which nations and people can be brought together. IC is considered a source of power that

international organizations (e.g., the United Nations) can employ to serve the world community. As such, it could increase understanding among nations and peoples and improve conditions that are conducive to world peace.

2. The political proselytization approach considers IC as a medium of propaganda, advertising, and creating myths. Viewed in this light, IC is used by industrialized countries to manipulate people of the Third World.

3. The economic power approach is an increasingly visible view that postulates IC to be the source of economic power. Through international business activities that result in technology transfer and "modernization," weaker nations are dominated by industrialized countries. By adopting the ways and views of industrialized countries, developing countries are more amenable to control by Western powers. Conversion to Western ways may also result in the loss of cultural identity and paralysis of indigenous creative power.

4. International communication may also be viewed as the source of political power. Countries communicate through mass media, literature, films, and data transmission. Increased communication among countries can potentially increase understanding among nations and peoples and improve conditions that are conducive to world peace. International communication through media, films, etc., conveys the cultural content associated with the source too. This, however, may not always be in the best interests of the recipient country. It may lead to cultural domination.

All four approaches have been criticized. The first approach is idealistic and assumes the objective transfer of information and values—an impossible feat. It also assumes a universally accepted view of international order and peace. Of course, there is no consensus on an ideal world. The political proselytization view of IC has created distrust of international media, and has fueled intolerance and hatred among people and nations. The economic and political views

have equated IC with other commodities to be traded and used for manipulation and domination.

An integrative view of international communication is more realistic. International communication encompasses elements of the four approaches and can offer a more practical venue for addressing major cross-cultural and international concerns. Seen from this perspective, a major concern is the widening gap between developed and developing countries' capacity to deal with international communication and information management. While many people of developing countries are waiting for their first telephone, for example, the residents of the developed world are moving to "smart" houses, ones with sophisticated electronic equipment already built-in. These houses are wired to receive a significant number of broadcasting and information services. They could also be programmed, on-site or remotely, to perform many functions, such as turning the lights on, cooling and heating the house, making coffee at a designated time, and filling the bath tub with the right temperature water.[3]

The accelerating rate of technological development coupled with major political changes, including the fall of Communism in the former Soviet Union, is shrinking distances among nations, and creating increased interdependencies among them through more communication and interaction. With the aid of the new communication technologies the world increasingly resembles a "global village." In this global village, communication technologies are instruments that can be used or misused.[4] "Since information is a resource convertible to all kinds of power, there is, and in all probability will be, intensive competition and conflict over its production and utilization."[5]

Developing countries contend that the international flow of information and communication heavily favors the developed countries. They assert that the existing pattern of international communication is creating a dependency relationship that is similar to business and trade dependency. This means that developed countries are the source and supplier of information, and developing countries are the naive consumers. The values, traditions, and cultures of developing countries are slowly, but inexorably losing ground to those propagated by developed countries. As Mowlana puts it ". . . the nature, pattern, and direction of the world economy more or less parallel and depict the directionality of the world information flow."[6] McPhail has argued that the pattern of information flow between developed and developing countries fosters "electronic colonialism":

> The dependency relationship established by the importation of communication hardware, foreign-produced software, along with engineers, technicians, and related information protocols, that vicariously establish a set of foreign norms, values and expectations which, in varying degrees, may alter the domestic cultures and socialization processes.[7]

Even if we consider the concerns of developing countries as exaggerated and paranoid, we cannot ignore the fact that the gap in information and communication technology may increase the vulnerability of these countries. Often, there is more information available, for example, about a developing nation in the research centers of developing countries than in the developing country itself. "When others know more about you than you know yourself, their power to dominate is enhanced significantly."[8]

For an international manager, an appreciation of these views and a familiarity with the concerns of host nationals could provide for better understanding and more productive relationships. In terms of these issues, sensitivity and empathy with the people of host countries could create a more friendly atmosphere conducive for conducting international business transactions.

We next consider the various aspects of cross-cultural communication. Our discussion begins with the presentation of the classic communication model.

Classic Communication Model

Communication comes from the Latin word *communis* meaning "common." When we attempt to communicate with another person, we seek to establish "commonness" by sharing information, knowledge, ideas, or attitudes. Communication is a two-way process and takes place when a person transmits ideas, knowledge, meanings, and feelings to others.

A typical process of communication involves a sender or source of communication, the receiver or the target of communication, and the feedback loop. For sending a message to the target a medium is used, such as a telephone, a computer, a letter, or a face-to-face position. Communication can take place only if the sender's message falls within the receiver's realm of understanding and knowledge. The commonality in language, experience, knowledge, and culture provides a framework for communication between people. Cultural differences, language diversity, and differences in experience and knowledge create barriers to communication. If the receiver of a message, due to any of these differences, is unable to decode the message and comprehend it, the message will not reach its destination. In the following, we examine the three components of the communication process.

Origination

As Figure 6.1 depicts, any communication process has three major segments, the origination, the destination, and the feedback loop. The origination segment consists of the sender and his or her field of experience, which includes attitudes, experience, knowledge, environment, sociocultural background,[9] and values that differentiate him or her from others. Also, the origination segment includes the meaning and the information that the sender intends to share with other(s). To share the meaning that a sender has

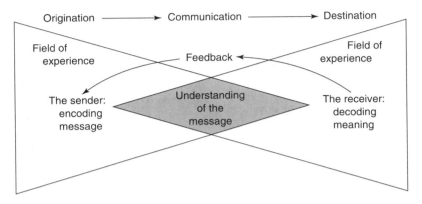

Figure 6.1   A Communication Model

in mind with the target, "encoding" of the meaning into codes (signs, symbols, and words) that the receivers can understand is necessary. The sender has to ensure the accuracy of the information that is to be transmitted by composing the message in his or her mind and organizing it into a logical sequence. In doing so and in "encoding" the meaning into an understandable form, a message is created. After encoding the message, the sender channels the message to the receiver.

Destination

The destination segment consists of the receiver, decoding, and the meaning of the message. After receiving the message, the receiver attempts to decipher the meanings of the words, symbols, and nonverbal signals, such as the hand gestures and tone of voice. Listening to the composition of the words, the manner of presentation, and other signs and signals used in the communication, the receiver uses his or her field of experience for interpreting the message. He or she may encounter some "noise" in the form of confusion and misunderstanding of the message. All of the elements that could cause distortion in the communication process and result in misunderstanding are called "noise." Many potential sources of noise exist when communicating across cultures. We consider several of them next.

There may be a limited commonality of the fields of experience between the receiver and the sender of the communication. The field of experience is used as a frame of reference for the interpretation of what people encounter in their daily activities. When the sender and the receiver have similar fields of experience they have much the same frames of reference. Therefore, interpretation of the information that is exchanged between them encounters limited distortion. As Wilbur Schramm described it:

> . . . . the greater the overlap of the source and the receiver's fields of experience, the greater the probability of successful communication. In other words, they have things in common that facilitate better communication. An individual engaging in communication with another person of a significantly different background should be aware that greater effort may be needed to ensure successful communication.[10]

The commonality of fields of experience between the origination segment and the destination segment reduces the noise and increases the fidelity of the communication. Even in a domestic situation, for example, the sender of the message may be a manager who uses technical computer jargon. If the receiver is a new salesperson in the company, he or she may not have much experience with the technical language, and may have limited information about the manager. Consequently, the lack of enough commonality between the sender and the receiver results in some "noise," which in turn causes the receiver to not understand the message. There might be other reasons for communication "noise." The receiver of the message may not pay close attention to the message. He or she might be a new recruit, nervous, and anxious to impress the supervisor. In this case too, the message is distorted and is not the same as the original.

Cultural differences are major sources of communication distortion. Communication difficulties arising from cultural differences are due to the lack of commonality of values, beliefs, and norms between the people of two cultures. Sometimes, in cross-cultural communication, these differences could lead to misunderstandings and cause serious problems. An example of a serious cross-cultural communication misunderstanding happened years ago at Ain Shams University in Cairo, Egypt.

In the midst of a discussion of a poem in the sophomore class of the English Department, the professor, who was British, took up the argument, started to explain the subtleties of the poem, and was carried away by the situation. He leaned back in his chair, put his feet up on the desk, and went on with the explanation. The class was furious. Before the end of the day, a demonstration by the university's full student body had taken place. Petitions were submitted to the deans of the various faculties. The next day, the situation even made the newspaper headlines. The consequences of the act, that was innocently done, might seem ridiculous, funny, baffling, incomprehensible, or even incredible to a stranger. Yet, to the natives, the students' behavior was logical and in context. The students and their supporters were outraged because of the implications of the breach of the native behavioral pattern. In the Middle East, it is extremely insulting to have to sit facing the soles of the shoes of somebody.*

Feedback

An important component of the communication process is feedback. Feedback is a loop connecting the destination segment to the origination segment. It provides information regarding the message to both the sender and the receiver. Through feedback, the receiver sends information back to the sender indicating the results of communication. Without feedback, the sender would not know whether the message has been received or understood. In short, feedback is a response and a control mechanism in the communication process. For feedback to serve as an effective control, however, it must be given by the receiver and it must be understood by the sender. The differences in giving and understanding of feedback can further complicate communication in cross-cultural settings. For example, in the communication between a Japanese and an American, when the Japanese, who desire harmony and want to save face, politely avoid publicly contradicting the American, the American may take this feedback at its face value. In such a case, the feedback has not served its purpose.

International Verbal Communication

Like their domestic counterparts, international managers use verbal communication more than other media. What makes verbal communication different for international managers is the use of foreign languages. Often, when discussing the communication process, as described earlier,

* Reproduced by permission of the Society for Applied Anthropology from Fathi S. Yousef. "Cross-Cultural Communication: Aspects of Contractive Social Values Between North Americans and Middle Easterners." *Human Organization,* 33, no. 4 (1974), 383–7.

the assumption is that the sender and the receiver are using a common language that both understand. In MNC operations this may not necessarily be the case. The most visible and important factor that international managers deal with is language diversity. Because of the variety of languages spoken in an MNC, without the foreign language skill, international managers have to rely on interpreters. No matter how competent the interpreter, and how accurate the translation, some meaning is always lost in the process of translation. There are always meanings and shades of meanings that cannot be conveyed by translation. Some words cannot be translated at all. The difficulty of translation is but one of the many problems associated with the use of interpreters. Good interpreters are in short supply. A good interpreter is more than a translator of words. There are many factors that make up a good interpreter, including sensitivity to cultural and social differences, understanding what makes people laugh in other cultures, and political sensitivity.[11] Sometimes, when using an interpreter, people may let their guards down and use less tact. In such occasions, a socially and culturally sensitive interpreter would not faithfully translate verbatim. The following is an example:

> Before addressing a Chinese audience, a Western scientist noticed a number of children were playing and chattering in the aisles. To his dismay, no one was attempting to quiet them down. After impatiently waiting for a while, he exploded angrily at the interpreter, "Will you tell those little brats to shut up!" The interpreter quietly spoke into the microphone in Chinese what roughly translates, "Little friends, would you please be just a bit more quiet, if you don't mind."[12]

Humor is very difficult to translate. An important attribute of a good interpreter is the knowledge of what is humorous in other cultures. Recall the story in Chapter 5 about an American executive in Japan telling his audience a joke. The interpreter probably knew the

translation would not do justice to the joke, and therefore told the audience that "the American guest just told a joke, you are supposed to laugh," and the audience responded with hearty laughter.

In translation, the awareness that certain issues are politically off limits, permits the avoidance of potential mine fields. For example, the Middle East is made up of a number of countries and cultures. A frequent mistake is the assumption that all are Arabs. This is politically and culturally a sensitive matter to Persians and Turks. A good interpreter would make an appropriate distinction and would refer to each culture accordingly.

The reliance on interpreters reduces the amount of information an international manager may collect. It shrinks the circle of sources that could be contacted and increases the time involved in communication. The ability to communicate in the local language allows managers to convey the meaning more accurately than with the use of an interpreter. Choosing your own words and picking your own sentence patterns in a foreign language are superior to relying on the precise—or sometimes imprecise—reproduction of your ideas, phrases, and nuances by someone else. Besides its obvious benefits, foreign language skills also contribute to the international managers' adjustment to the local culture and society. According to Mendenhall and Oddou, language skills can be viewed as a means to create and foster interpersonal relationships or as a means to understand the dynamics of a new culture. On that basis, language skill is a useful help toward international managers' adjustment to a host country environment.[13] Language skills not only allow international managers to communicate with the locals more easily and accurately, it permits them to be treated more like "insiders," which by itself is a competitive advantage.

We have discussed language differences in communication, and have noted that language differences make international communication

Danish and Swedish Communication

In the Danish culture the main purpose of interpersonal communication is maintenance of familiar atmosphere and relation of affection. . . . It is impolite to explain things, because such an act assumes that someone is ignorant. It is also impolite to ask questions on anything beyond immediate personal concern, because the respondent may not know the answer. It is often considered aggressive or offensive to introduce new ideas. One prefers to repeat the same old jokes. Discussion of politics or economics is taboo except in marginal enclaves. . . . Safe topics of intellectual conversation are art, literature, and music, on which people are expected to disagree without embarrassment.

In contrast, in Sweden, the purpose of daily interpersonal communication is transmission of new information or frank feelings. One prefers to be silent unless one has an important message, while in Denmark one must keep talking.

Source: Mogoroh Maruyama. *Mindscape in Management* (Aldershot, England: Dartmouth Publishing Co. Ltd., 1993), 49.

---

very difficult. Additional difficulties arise from cross-cultural differences in nonverbal communication. Managers who are assigned to international operations may gain foreign language proficiency. They may, however, experience difficulty comprehending the full meaning of verbal communication unless they can read and understand nonverbal communication cues. We now consider issues in nonverbal communication.

Cultural Differences in Nonverbal Communication

Communication consists of verbal and nonverbal components. Nonverbal communication clues impart meanings that are usually not presented in verbal communication. Just as there are cultural differences among various national groups, so are there differences in communication patterns, especially in nonverbal cues. Differences in nonverbal communication cues can be the source of misunderstanding. International managers could greatly improve their understanding of the people from other cultures by learning the subtleties of meanings that these nonverbal cues convey.

To elaborate on differences in nonverbal communication cues among cultures we could discuss country-by-country differences. This would be a tedious process. Signs and motions using the hands, fingers, eyes, and head, for example, convey different meanings in different cultures. Several examples of these motions are depicted in Table 6.1. Some of these signs convey just the opposite meanings in two different cultures. Although learning these signs is very beneficial, and can prevent potentially embarrassing experiences, it is very time consuming. While those contemplating an international assignment are well advised to make a specific study of nonverbal signs in the interested host country, a better alternative is to compare these differences on some common dimensions. We choose the six most commonly discussed dimensions of culture.[14] The six dimensions are expressiveness, individualism, gender role rigidity, power distance, uncertainty, and contextual variations. In the following pages we discuss cultural differences in nonverbal communication along these dimensions.[15]

Expressiveness

If we consider the expressiveness dimension as a continuum, at one end of this continuum are actions that communicate closeness, accessibil-

Table 6.1

Implications of Various Nonverbal Behavior in Different Cultures

Nonverbal Behavior	Country	Meaning
Thumbs up	United States	An approval gesture/OK/good job!
	Middle East	A gesture of insult
	Japan	A sign indicating "male"
	Germany	A sign for count of "one"
A finger circulating next to the ear	Argentina	A telephone
	United States	That is crazy!
A raised arm and waggling hand	United States	Goodbye
	India, South America	Beckoning
	Some Africans	Beckoning
	Much of Europe	A signal for "no"
Showing the back of the hand in a V-sign	England	A rude sign
	Greece, Middle East	A sign for count of "two"
Showing a circle formed with index finger and thumb	United States	Very good!
	Turkey	Insult gesture/accusation of homosexuality
Crossing first two fingers	United States	Good luck!
	Taiwan	No smoking!
Touching a person's head	United States	Affection
	Thailand	A major social transgression
Eye contact, gazing	United States	A sign of attentiveness
	Japan	A rude behavior/invasion of privacy
	Most Asian countries	Sign of disrespect to senior people
Widening eye	United States	An indication of surprise
	Chinese	An indication of anger
	Hispanic	Request for help
	French	Issuance of challenge
Shaking the head side to side	Western countries	A sign for disagreement/no
	Bulgaria	A sign for agreement/yes
Nodding the head up and down	Western countries	A sign for agreement/yes
	Greece, Bulgaria	A sign for disagreement/no
A hand-shake	Western countries	A greeting action
Bowing	Japanese	A greeting action
Hands placed together in front of the face	India	A greeting action

ity, and approach. At the other end are behaviors that express avoidance and distance. In the United States, for example, smiling, touching, eye contact, nearness, open body positions, and more vocal animations are highly expressive behaviors. In a positive relationship, individuals tend to reciprocate expressive behaviors. Cultures in which people exhibit much expressiveness, such as standing closer to one another and touching more, have been labeled as "high-contact" cultures.[16] People of low-contact cultures tend to stand apart and touch less. South

Americans, Southern and Eastern Europeans, Middle Easterners, and Indonesians are considered high-contact cultures. Asians, North Americans, and Northern Europeans are classified as low-contact cultures. Australians are moderate in their cultural contact level.

Face-to-face communication and interaction between people of high-contact and low-contact cultures could create moments of uneasiness and anxiety. The Americans' preference in keeping their distance during interpersonal communication may be interpreted by South Americans or Middle Easterners as cold, suspicious, and unfriendly. Conversely, Americans may feel anxious and imposed on by the Middle Easterners' habit of staying very close and frequent touching during a conversation. Taiwanese, for example, tend to prefer seating arrangements that allow side-by-side contacts with the persons of the same sex. Americans, on the other hand, prefer seating people of the opposite sex side by side.

Individualism

Individualism is the culture's emphasis on personal identity. It encourages self-serving behaviors. This cultural dimension is one of four identified by Hofstede as being important in showing how a given culture operates. In individualistic cultures, it is expected that individuals primarily look after their own interest and those of their immediate family. Therefore, individualistic cultures are loosely integrated. The opposite of individualism is collectivism. Collectivist cultures emphasize groups (e.g., family, neighborhood, organizations, and the country), not the individuals. In a collectivist society, the interests and goals of the individuals are subordinate to those of the group.[17] Individuals seek fulfillment and happiness in the harmony of the group. Groups provide security to the members, and protect their interests in exchange for their complete loyalty. Compared with individualistic societies, collectivists are tightly integrated societies.[18]

Individualism is directly related to the use of space and accessibility.[19] Individualistic societies heavily emphasize owning space. The heavy emphasis on individual ownership in turn tends to distance people from one another, limit sensory stimulation, regulate accessibility, and promote privacy. Most Western cultures are individualistic, whereas Eastern and most South American cultures are collectivists. People of individualistic cultures rely on personal judgment, while collectivists value collective judgment and emphasize harmony between people.

Collectivist cultures are more interested in living in harmony with nature, while an individualistic culture attempts to dominate nature.

The nonverbal behaviors of individualistic cultures are different from those of collectivist cultures. The greater interdependence of people of collectivist cultures is manifested in their day-to-day activities. They play, work, sleep, and live in close proximity to each other. They also tend to synchronize these activities more, while individualistic people tend to do "their own thing" separately.[20] Because compliance with norms is central to collectivists, they may suppress emotional displays that are contrary to the group mood. Therefore, people of collectivist cultures seem to be more reserved and formal in their demeanor. It is possible that this tendency explains a frequently expressed stereotype that "Orientals are inscrutable." Conversely, since individual freedom is of paramount value in individualistic cultures, they encourage the expression of emotion.

In collectivist cultures most of the norms governing interpersonal relationships are socially prescribed, while individuals bear this responsibility in individualistic cultures. Therefore, in individualistic cultures, individual initiatives are used for building many interpersonal relationships, including establishing opportunities for intimacy. In the United States, for example, flirting, small talk, initial acquaintance, and dating are more important than in collectivist cultures.[21] Similarly, it is not unusual in collectivist societies for families to arrange opportunities for meeting the members of the opposite sex and eventual marriage among young people. Consequently, in individualistic cultures like the United States, it is easier to meet people, and communication is more open. The usually transient and casual nature of these relationships, however, may make it appear to collectivists that the Americans are noncaring people.

Interdependence and socially prescribed interpersonal relationships are reflected in the way collectivist people use time. They tend to schedule more tasks simultaneously, and interrupt meetings to tend to the requests of friends, family members, and business associates. In a way they are more people oriented than the people of individualistic cultures.

Gender Role Rigidity

This dimension refers to the rigidity of socially prescribed gender roles. In some cultures gender roles are narrowly defined. In such cultures people are expected to behave within the socially prescribed gender roles. Masculinity is identified with traits and behaviors such as strength, speed, assertiveness, competitiveness, dominance, anger, ambition, and the pursuit of wealth. Feminine characteristics and behaviors are associated with emotionality, affection, compassion, warmth, and nurturing of the weak and needy. The emphasis on one or the other set of attributes characterizes the masculinity or femininity of a culture. In societies where gender roles are more clearly specified, masculine manners are expected from men, and females are expected to behave in feminine ways. In masculine cultures, men avoid crying in public, while most women do not feel any compelling need to suppress their emotion, and do not hold back their tears in public.

Although there are considerable cultural variations in gender-related behaviors, certain behaviors are generally associated with males or with females almost regardless of culture. Similarly, in most cultures, smooth gestures, graceful movements, and nonverbal inviting behaviors are predominantly used by females, and are avoided by males. Females are conditioned to avoid raising their voices, while loud-speaking manners by men are not frowned upon. Masculine cultures tend to be less tolerant of feminine behavior from males, and vice versa, while a feminine culture tends to tolerate more deviations in norms and behavior.

Hofstede has developed an index rank ordering countries with respect to four cultural dimensions, one of which is gender role rigidity.[22]

The 10 countries with the highest masculinity index are Japan, Australia, Venezuela, Italy, Switzerland, Mexico, Ireland, Great Britain, Germany, and the Philippines. The highest feminine value countries on this index are Sweden, Norway, the Netherlands, Denmark, Finland, Chile, Portugal, Thailand, Peru, and Spain. Although not among the 10 highest on masculinity index, the United States tends to be a masculine society. Compared with the people of most countries, American people of both sexes seem to be loud, aggressive, and competitive. In the United States feminine people are more expressive, nurturing, relational, and provide more personal information. Masculine people are more dominant, argumentative, assertive, and goal oriented. Emotional expressions, such as crying, are associated more with femininity.

Power Distance

Variation in the distribution of power among the members of the society is called *power distance* (PD). It is the difference in the amount of power possessed by the least powerful and the most powerful members of the society. Power distance is the third of four basic cultural dimensions identified by Hofstede. Various degrees of power inequality exist in all cultures. According to Mulder's power distance reduction theory, superiors will try to maintain and increase the power distance between themselves and subordinates, and subordinates will try to reduce this distance.[23] Hofstede, however, proposed that there is a culturally based equilibrium level at which both the most powerful and the least powerful person will find inequality acceptable. Cultures with a high power distance tend to concentrate influence and control in the hands of a few. Distribution of power and influence tends to be more equal among the people of low PD cultures.

Power distance could be measured using Hofstede's power distance index (PDI). The 10 highest in PDI are the Philippines, Mexico,

Venezuela, India, Singapore, Brazil, Hong Kong, France, Colombia, and Turkey. Western Europeans, Israel, New Zealand, the United States, and Canada are the lowest PD cultures. There is less emphasis on power among the people of low PD countries. As one Swedish university official has said "in order to exercise power, he tries not to look powerful."[24] Interpersonal relationships between the people of high PD countries tend to be more along the hierarchical line. In general, Asian and African cultures maintain hierarchical role relationships.[25]

Power distance creates communication barriers among people and affects nonverbal behaviors. When there is a high level of power distance, subordinates show more respect and appear to be more polite in the presence of superiors. It has been suggested that the continuous smiles of many Orientals who are reared in high power distance countries are attempts to produce social harmony or appease superiors.[26] Also, compared to low PD countries, people of high PD cultures appear to speak in a lower voice, apparently not wanting to disturb others. Conversely, those in low PD cultures are generally less aware that their loud voices may be offensive to others.

Uncertainty

Cultures view risk and uncertainty differently. Some cultures have more aversion to risk and uncertainty, and avoid situations that are ambiguous and risky. Other cultures can tolerate such situations with less discomfort and anxiety. "Cultures with a strong uncertainty avoidance are active, aggressive, emotional, security-seeking, and intolerant. Cultures with a weak uncertainty avoidance are contemplative, less aggressive, unemotional, accepting of personal risk, and relatively tolerant."[27]

Uncertainty avoidance is the fourth of Hofstede's basic cultural dimensions. He found that the top 10 countries that are high on the uncertainty avoidance dimension in descending order, are Greece, Portugal, Belgium, Japan,

Peru, France, Chile, Spain, Argentina, and Turkey. The 10 lowest uncertainty avoidance cultures are Singapore, Denmark, Sweden, Hong Kong, Ireland, Great Britain, India, the Philippines, the United States, and Canada.[28] Countries that are lower on uncertainty avoidance tend to be Catholic cultures, while Protestant, Hindu, or Buddhist cultures tend to be more tolerant of ambiguity and risk.[29]

Uncertainty and ambiguity could create stress and anxiety especially in cultures with less tolerance for uncertainty and ambiguity. Since freedom can lead to more uncertainty, to avoid uncertainty some cultures increase rules governing behavior. Other cultures are able to tolerate freedom without excess stress or anxiety.[30] On that basis one could speculate that there are more communication formalities and more codification of nonverbal behavior among high uncertainty avoidance cultures. Conversely, among the people of low uncertainty avoidance cultures there might be fewer communication formalities and less codification of nonverbal behavior. Americans, for example, are less worried about the specifics of eating rituals in informal dinners than the people of most other cultures.

Contextual Variations

Cultures vary in their use of context in the communication process.[31] In high-context (HC) cultures, attention is paid to the surrounding circumstances or context of an event for interpretation of the message.[32] The physical surroundings, the manner of delivery, the situation, and the nature of the issue at hand are all an integral part of the communication process and serve to impregnate it with information. Though not explicit, this information is understood within the culture since people are accustomed to practicing implicit communication. Therefore, in such cultures, words cannot be taken at their face value, and not knowing the hidden meaning behind the words may lead to embarrassment and misunderstanding.

People of HC cultures are more self-reflective, group oriented, and sensitive to group harmony. They are more deferring to others, and have respect for hierarchy of status and authority. Family honor and obligations are important to them, including the respect for ancestors. Asians, most Africans, South Americans, and the Southern and Eastern Mediterranean and Middle Eastern peoples are considered HC cultures.

In contrast to HC cultures, people of low-context (LC) cultures convey most information explicitly by the message itself. Unambiguity and specificity are characteristics of LC communication in which messages are spelled out clearly. People of LC cultures are interested in straightforward answers of "yes" or "no" to most inquiries, and feel uncomfortable in situations where they have to decipher the meaning out of the context of communication. To people of LC cultures, a good communication is one that is direct and does not leave much to personal judgment and interpretation. Low-context cultures attempt to remove all ambiguity and try to anticipate all contingencies in their contractual relationships. Consequently, most business contracts and agreements are lengthy documents. Conversely, in high-context cultures business contracts are viewed as documents formalizing business relationships that are already built on trust. A few pages would be sufficient as a legal basis for such relationships.

People of low-context cultures are direct and outward in their communication patterns and problem-solving style. They do things in sequence, one thing at a time, and tend to be more individualistic. In contrast to the people of high-context cultures, low-context people progress better in a planned manner, are technology oriented, and display and reward initiative. Low-context cultures have a frontier spirit, possess a strong drive toward accumulating knowledge, material products, and capital wealth; need to control the environment to suit their individual needs; and rely on written rules and regulations for social interaction, cohesion, and control.

Because of these tendencies, low-context cultures are stereotyped by others as selfish, individualistic, work-driven, inflexible in dealing with human situations, use more external control, and are results oriented. The major attributes that low-context cultures are identified with are "things," "efficiency" over "people," abstract and linear, and tend to use one-dimensional thinking in planning and problem solving. Most Westerners including Australians, Britons, Germans, New Zealanders, North Americans, Swiss, and Scandinavians are considered low context cultures. People of these countries are concerned with specifics, details, and precise timetables for most of their activities.

Low-context cultures put much emphasis on verbal communication and downplay the value of nonverbal communication. The people of LC cultures are usually perceived by others as excessively talkative, redundant, and belaboring the obvious. Conversely, HC people are described as sneaky, mysterious, and nondisclosing.[33] Nonverbal communication is more important to people of HC cultures. LC cultures do not perceive many of the contextual communication cues that are common to HC cultures. Much meaning is communicated among the people of HC cultures with contextual cues, such as facial expression, tension, speed and location of interaction, pause and silent moments, and other subtleties of the occasion. People of HC cultures are more active participants in the communication, and expect the same from the other party in a communication. They will try to interpret and understand the unspoken signs, unarticulated moods, and environmental clues present during a conversation. These clues are often overlooked by most people of LC cultures.

High- and low-context cultures have contrasting communication styles. The differences in communication are often the source of misunderstanding and mistrust between people of HC and LC countries. Understanding these differences can pave the way for better relationships and improved business activities among nations.

Emotions

Emotional expressions have an important place in communication. For many years scientists assumed that nonverbal communication cues expressing emotions were culture-specific and were learned differently across cultures. Evidence gathered recently, however, suggests that there are at least six universal emotional cues. The six universal emotional cues are facial expressions for anger, disgust, fear, happiness, sadness, and surprise. It seems that these emotional cues are understood by the people of many cultures.[34] There are, however, some cultural differences in experience and evaluation of emotions. The results of cross-cultural research indicate that antecedents of emotions vary between cultures. Matsumoto, Wallbott, and Scherer reviewed research findings regarding these differences.[35] The highlights of their review that are pertinent to our discussion are presented next.

Physical pleasures, cultural pleasures, birth of a new family member, and achievement-related situations were more frequently reported by Americans and Europeans as the antecedents of joy. World news, permanent and temporary separations, and death were reported more frequently by Europeans and Americans as the elicitors of sadness. For the Japanese, relationships were more frequent elicitors of sadness, anger, and fear. For American and Europeans fear of strangers and risky situations were more frequent elicitors of fear (Table 6.2).

The intensity and duration of these emotions vary among the three cultures, too. Americans report feeling their emotions more intensely and for longer periods of time than Europeans and Japanese. Also, there are cultural differences in the effect of emotion-causing events on self-esteem, attributions, and responsibility. Americans have reported greater positive self-esteem and self-confidence for the emotion-eliciting events than the Japanese. Probably, this is a reflection of the individualistic tendency that emphasizes self more than others. Finally, it seems that the Japanese are more reluctant than Americans to make any attribution of responsibility for their sadness-producing experiences. Consequently, they also believe no action is needed even when they report strong negative emotions.

The review of cross-cultural research by Matsumoto, Wallbott, and Scherer also revealed a difference in the physiological responses to emotional experience among the three cultures. In contrast to Europeans and Americans, Japanese respondents reported fewer stomach troubles and muscle symptoms for the four emotions; less blood pressure change for joy, fear, and anger; and less feeling of cold for fear. These differences may be related to the differences in intensity and duration of the emotions reported by the people of the three cultures.

Observing nonverbal communication differences along cultural dimensions provides expatriates an insight to cross-cultural communication. In some situations, the real meaning is not conveyed by the verbal language. Verbal communication might be a convenient way out of a potentially embarrassing situation. In a public discussion, for example, Japanese may agree verbally in order to avoid the appearance of insulting others by disagreement. Verbal communication may be just the opposite of the real message, which is hidden beneath the words. In those situations, the real meaning and the true message are conveyed through nonverbal silent language, nonverbal behavior, by the context of communication, and the manner of delivery. Learning these signs, signals, and silent codes of communication could improve cross-cultural relations and consequently it can influence the managers' performance. Condon and Yousef's description (see "Poor Richard" article) of an American manager's experiences with three situations vividly illustrates problems of cross-

Table 6.2
Antecedents and Elicitors of Emotion

Emotions	More Frequently Reported by Americans and Europeans Antecedents	More Frequently Reported by Japanese Elicitors
Joy	Physical pleasures	
	Cultural pleasures	
	Birth of a new family member	
	Achievement-related situations	
Sadness	World news	
	Temporary or permanent separation	Relationships
	Death	
Fear	Fear of strangers	Relationships
	Risky situations	
Anger	Relationships	Relationships
	Situation of injustice	(strangers)

cultural communication. Sensitivity to cultural differences could minimize the adverse impact of these problems on business transactions.

Communication Competence

The importance of communication competence for international managers cannot be overemphasized. Expatriates are heavily dependent on their communication skills to bridge the cultural gaps with locals and to overcome the experience of culture shocks on foreign assignments.

Spitzberg and Cupach[36] have defined communication competence as the social judgment made by the parties involved in the communication process (interactants) regarding the "goodness" of self and others' communication performance. Communication skills are the basis of communication competence. Verbal and nonverbal behaviors are communication skills, while communication competence is social judgment made by interactants regarding the possession of these skills.

There are two approaches to the study of communication competence: culture specific and culture general. The culture-specific approach views intercultural communication competence as the degree of adjustment to and adoption of the communication patterns and practices of the host country. The culture-general approach assumes that there is a certain communication competence useful to all cultures. It focuses on those aspects of communication competence that can generalize to intercultural communication for all cultures.[37]

In international communication an integrative view is more practical, in which features of both approaches are combined. While universal communication skills may exist (the claim of the culture-general approach), there might be cultural differences for the behaviors that reflect those skills (the culture-specific view). Communication skills such as empathy and respect, for example, might be universal. The expressions and interpretations of them, however, might vary across cultures.[38]

The effectiveness of expatriate managers depends on their ability to adapt to cultural and environmental differences. Among the most

Poor Richard

Meet Richard, a model American: friendly, easy-going, unpretentious, well-intentioned, practical. But poor Richard inevitably seems to run into problems when he is in other countries. The problems are especially annoying because they so often seem to arise when everything is going well and communication appears to be at its best.

While visiting Egypt, Richard was invited to a spectacular dinner at the home of an Egyptian friend. And what a dinner it was! Clearly the host and hostess had gone out of their way to entertain him. Yet, as he was leaving their home he made a special effort to thank them for their spectacular dinner and sensed that something he said was wrong. Something about his sincere compliment was misunderstood.

In Japan he had an even less pleasant experience, but he thought he had handled it well. A number of serious mistakes had occurred in a project he was supervising. While the fault did not lie with any one person, he was a supervisor and at least partly to blame. At a special meeting called to discuss the problem, poor Richard made an effort to explain in detail why he had done what he had done. He wanted to show that anybody in the same situation could have made the same mistake and to tacitly suggest that he should not be blamed unduly. He even went to the trouble of distributing materials which explained the situation rather clearly. And yet, even during his explanation, he sensed that something he was saying or doing was wrong.

Even in England where he felt more at home, where he had no problems with language, this kind of misunderstanding occurred. He had been invited to take tea with one of his colleagues, a purely social, relaxed occasion. Tea was served along with sugar and cream. As he helped himself to some sugar and cream, he again sensed he had done something wrong.

Let us see what went wrong with cross-cultural communication in these three situations?

Dinner. In Egypt as in many cultures, the human relationship is valued so highly that it is not expressed in an objective but impersonal way. While Americans certainly value human relationships, they are more likely to speak of them in less personal, more objective terms. In this case, Richard's mistake might be that he chose to praise the food itself rather than the total evening, for which the food was simply the setting or excuse. For his host and hostess it was as if he had attended an art exhibit and complimented the artist by saying, "What beautiful frames your pictures are in."

The conference. In Japan the situation may be more complicated (or at least the typical Western image of Japan invites mysterious interpretations). For this example we can simply say that Japanese people value order and harmony among persons in a group, and that the organization itself—be it a family or a vast corporation—is more valued than the characteristics or idiosyncrasies of any member. While this feeling is not alien to Americans—or to any society—Americans stress individuality as a value and are apt to assert individual differences when they seem justifiably in conflict with the goals or values of the group. In this case, Richard's mistake was in making great efforts to defend himself. Let the others assume that the errors were not intentional, but it is not right to defend yourself, even when your unstated intent is to assist the group by warning others of similar mistakes. A simple apology and acceptance of the blame would have been appropriate. (In contrast, for poor Richard to have merely apologized would have seemed to him to be subservient, unmanly. Nothing in his experience had prepared him for the Japanese reaction—in fact he had been taught to despise such behavior.)

(continued)

Taking tea. As for England, we might be tempted to look for some nonverbal indiscretion. While there are some very significant differences in language and language style, we expect fewer problems between Americans and Englishmen than between Americans and almost any other group. In this case we might look beyond the gesture of taking sugar or cream to the values expressed in this gesture: For Americans, "help yourself"; for the English counterpart, "Be my guest." American and English people equally enjoy entertaining and being entertained, but they differ somewhat in the value of the distinction. Typically, the ideal guest at an American party is one who "makes himself at home," even to the point of answering the door or fixing his own drink. For persons in many other societies, including at least this hypothetical English host, such guest behavior is presumptuous or rude. Poor Richard may object to this explanation, saying, "In other words, English people like to stand on ceremony." If so, he still does not understand. Another analogy may help Richard to appreciate the host's point of view: An American guest at an American party who would rearrange the furniture without being asked, suggest the dinner menu, and in other ways "make himself at home" also would seem to be presumptuous.

Source: Reprinted with the permission of Macmillan College Publishing Company from J. C. Condon and F. S. Yousef. *An Introduction to Intercultural Communication* (New York: Macmillan Publishing Co., 1975). Copyright 1975 by Macmillan College Publishing Company, Inc.

important skills needed for cross-cultural adaptation are cross-cultural communication skills, ability to deal with stress, and ability to establish interpersonal relationships.[39] Cross-cultural research has identified seven communication skills that influence success in foreign countries.[40] These skills are (1) the ability to express respect for the other persons and their cultures, (2) the ability to respond to others nonjudgmentally, (3) the recognition of the individual basis of our knowledge, (4) empathy, the ability to see the world through other people's eyes, (5) the ability to function both in people-oriented and task-oriented roles, (6) the ability to take turns and not dominate the interaction and relationship, and (7) the ability to tolerate ambiguity and adjust to a new situation with little discomfort.[41] Mastering these skills prepares expatriate managers for building interpersonal relationships in most cross-cultural situations.

Intercultural communication competence is enhanced by learning the value systems of other cultures and by developing verbal and nonverbal communication skills. Knowing the foreign language alone is not sufficient for communication competence. In Japan, for example, a person speaking Japanese and politely interacting with people may not create a favorable impression if in response to a polite bow of the Japanese he or she naively extends a hand for greeting.

Sensitivity to cultural differences in communication styles improves intercultural communication competence. To be effective in cross-cultural communication, for example, one should be aware that the type and pattern of interaction and response is influenced by cultural upbringing. Most Americans' visualization of a classroom is a place in which students are informally dressed, and where frequent interaction among the teacher and the students takes place. Asians, on the other hand, think of a classroom as a place with formally dressed students who listen silently to their teacher's lecture. Interpersonal interactions and responses to the same questions vary even within a country. In the United States, for example, children of middle-class parents are generally taught more elaborate ways of communication at home. Therefore, these children's classroom answers tend to be long and involved. Children of lower class parents learn more restrictive communication codes at home, and are more likely to respond in the classroom with one-word answers. Much backchanneling is involved in Afro-American communication and interaction. The speaker is encouraged by the listeners' backchanneling of vocal utterances like "yeah," "right on," "ahuh," "tell it," "amen," and "go on." A white, middle-class teacher, who is uninformed about cultural differences, may misinterpret the short answers of these students as an indication of less knowledge. Similarly, such teachers are often offended by backchanneling, and consider the constant interruption annoying rather than reinforcing.[42]

Do's and Don'ts of Communication with Foreigners

Communication between the people of different cultures is more difficult not only due to cultural differences but also due to differences in language. Many people who speak a foreign language may not fully comprehend its subtleties and nuances. To improve communication with someone who is not fully proficient in a language, there are certain caveats. Adler has recommended ways of improving understanding when dealing with people whose native language is not English. Her recommendations were addressed to English-speaking North Americans.[43] These recommendations, however, could work both ways, when speaking in English to foreigners, as well as when using a foreign language:

> Do not confuse foreigners by the use of colloquial expressions. Make it easier for them to understand you by enunciating each word clearly. Use simple vocabulary, and avoid long, compound sentences that require language proficiency. Repeat important ideas as often as you can, and pause frequently to allow

time for mental translation and comprehension. Highlight important issues by providing summaries at important junctures in your discussion. Spontaneous translation takes time and energy. Allow listeners enough time to think. Do not rush to fill the silent periods that are normal in bilingual conversations. It is a mistake to equate poor grammar and mispronunciation with the lack of intelligence. Provide verbal and nonverbal encouragement, and do not embarrass novice speakers.

International Negotiations

One of the most difficult and important tasks facing international managers is negotiation. To conclude successfully a business deal, a labor agreement, or a government contract with foreigners who are in most respects quite different from us requires a considerable amount of communication skill. International negotiation is very complex and difficult, because it involves different laws, regulations, standards, business practices, and above all cultural differences. Most of the difficulties in international negotiations, however, are due to cultural differences. The saying "When in Rome, do as the Romans do" is an indication of our awareness that to succeed in international negotiation we need to suppress our ethnocentric tendencies. This awareness, however, has not translated into substantial knowledge and understanding. Today, much of the literature on negotiation deals with intracultural settings. Only recently has intercultural negotiation received the attention of management scholars.

Acuff has defined negotiation as "the process of communicating back and forth for the purpose of reaching a joint agreement about differing needs or ideas."[44] In any negotiation we can identify three components: the process, the parties in the negotiation, and the agreement or the outcome of the negotiation. Negotiating entities could be from the same culture or from different cultures. On that basis, there are two types of negotiation: intracultural and intercultural. In the following we summarize the elements of negotiation from an intracultural perspective. Next, we study the role of cultural differences in intercultural negotiation.

Intracultural Negotiation

Intracultural negotiation assumes similarity in culture and fields of experience among negotiating parties. Based on this assumption, negotiation strategies are devised to influence the other party's position. Goldman, for example, suggested that much of negotiation skills involves accomplishing three tasks: "(a) bringing your own perceptions in line with reality, (b) ascertaining the other side's perceptions of the proposed transaction and the available alternatives, and (c) finding ways to favorably alter the other side's perceptions."[45] He asserts that in negotiation what counts is not the reality, but the parties' perception of reality. Implicitly, he assumes negotiating parties are from the same culture and have similar views and perception of the reality.

There are two extreme negotiating positions of "hard" and "soft." Those taking a hard position see every negotiation as a contest of wills. They believe that by taking extreme positions and holding out longer they will fare better. Taking a hard position may lead to conformation, however. Often the other party responds by taking an equally hard position. This exhausts both parties and damages their long-term relationship. If a hard position is confrontational and adversely affects long-term relationships, a soft position may create a one-sided deal and ill feelings. Avoiding confrontation and taking a more accommodating soft position may result in undue advantage for the other party. By making concessions, a soft negotiator often ends up with less than a desirable deal and may feel bitter about it.[46]

Both hard and soft approaches to negotiation are not constructive. Fisher and Ury[47] suggest that *principled negotiation* (PN) or negotiating on merits is a better alternative. Although PN was proposed for intracultural situations, with some modifications, it is applicable to intercultural negotiations as well. Cultural differences, however, render some of its aspects less useful for negotiations that cross-cultural boundaries. The PN method involves four basic factors of people, interests, options, and criteria. It is applicable to all stages of negotiation. We could divide any negotiation into three stages. The three stages are analysis, planning, and discussion. In each stage, according to Fisher and Ury, you could consider the four factors of people, interests, options, and criteria. In the following section we discuss the four factors of PN that could produce a constructive negotiation process and also examine the three stages of negotiation.

Four factors of PN

People.   Separate the people from the problem. Often negotiating parties confuse people with the problem. They get emotional and instead of attacking the problem, they attack each other. This produces defensive behavior, which is not conducive to constructive negotiation. Reducing the emotional overtone and building a good working relationship improves the chance of success. Allow room for the expression of emotions without taking them personally. In general, promote good communication. Without communication there is no negotiation. It is difficult for strangers to reach an agreement. Try to build a relationship with the other party. Finally, allow the other party a "face-saving" position.

Interests.   Focus on interests, not positions. Sharing information creates understanding. Try to uncover the "interests" of the participants which are behind their positions. Positions are "what" the parties say they want, and interests are "why" they want them. Beware of the situation where each party tries to learn the other party's interests without revealing its own.

Options.   Invent options for mutual gain. Considering multiple options, instead of one option at a time, may provide for more commonality of interests. Look for areas of mutual gain, and search for alternatives that give both sides something to gain. Before deciding how to cut the pie, increase its size.

Criteria. Insist on objective criteria. Use objective criteria that can be used in selecting the final option. Do not give in to the pressure, and do not permit the negotiation to become a contest of wills. Agreement on objective criteria, such as market value, expert opinion, custom, precedence, law, and industry practices, eliminates one-sided outcomes. Following the four preceding factors in the three stages of negotiation should lead parties to an agreement that both parties can accept. Now, let us consider the three stages of PN.

The three stages of principled negotiation

Analysis. Before getting to the negotiation table, make certain preparations. The analysis stage deals with gathering and organizing information for diagnosing the situation. You should review the issues pertinent to the four basic factors of people, interests, options, and criteria. Consider the people problems that may arise during the negotiation, such as perception, emotion, and communication. Define your interests and those of the other party to the negotiation. Review the options already on the table, and identify the criteria and the framework suggested for the negotiation.

Planning. In the planning stage, again you are dealing with the same four factors of people, interests, options, and criteria. Here you want to generate ideas and decide how to use them. You want to determine how to deal with the people problems. Prioritize your interests, and set realistic objectives. Generate more options, and devise criteria for selecting the best option.

Discussion. Similar to the previous stages, here, the four factors of PN are the best subjects for discussion. Parties communicate back and forth looking for ways to agree on various issues. On the people factor, perceptions, feelings, and difficulties in communication could be addressed. The interests of both parties are acknowledged. Options that are mutually benefi-cial are identified, and agreements are sought on objective standards that could resolve opposing interests.

PN provides participants to the negotiation with a method of focusing on the basic interests and mutually advantageous solutions. Unlike inefficient bargaining within a political framework, PN enables parties to reach agreement without all the haggling and posturing. By separating the people from the problem, PN makes it possible to agree amicably and efficiently. Cultural differences, however, make some aspects of PN less viable for intercultural negotiations.

Unfortunately PN does make culturally based assumptions regarding the fields of experience and values of negotiators, and views negotiations from an American perspective. While these assumptions may be true for intracultural negotiations, they might not be as effective in intercultural situations. In the following we examine the American negotiation style and its shortcomings. We discuss how these shortcomings could lead to ineffective intercultural negotiation.

The American Negotiation Style

Quite often, Americans enter international negotiations assuming that their knowledge and experiences at home in dealing with suppliers, buyers, bankers, labor, and U.S. government agencies will be sufficient in securing a good agreement. They take a self-centered, objective, problem-solving approach. Although they are very well aware that it takes two to make a deal, they concentrate on their side and attempt to maximize their gains. In the same vein, Kuhn advises negotiators:

> Don't worry what others get. Don't worry what others think. Just know what you want to accomplish. Keep your eye on the ball and don't allow extraneous pressures to distract you. A good deal maker is constantly enhancing his or her perceived power. The trick is track record. Everyone wants to associate with a winner.[48]

Confident of their own skills and believing that most negotiations can be dealt with in a logical and systematic order, Americans venture into negotiations with others by making several assumptions that can lead to problems. Most of these assumptions are the same ones made by the PN, and which can lead to ineffective international negotiation. Let us look at some of these assumptions.[49]

Doing it alone Individualistic tendencies of Americans lead them to believe that they can handle any situation alone. Americans often enter negotiations very self-confident that they can handle whatever difficulties they encounter. They stress individuality and the importance of asserting the self, and they value autonomy and independence.[50] They take the "Lone Ranger" approach to negotiations.[51] From the other party's vantage point, this may look as if Americans are not taking the negotiation seriously and are not prepared for it. In practice, by going alone Americans may find themselves in strange situations, unfamiliar settings, and outnumbered.

Informality and open communication To Americans, informality is not only a desirable attribute, it is efficient. It allows one to get down to business quickly without wasting time. The assumption is that getting to the point and discussing the "bottom line" saves time and energy. Time spent on formalities and protocol is the time taken away from doing business. Americans prefer direct and open communication. They like to get to the heart of the matter quickly. Americans believe that honest information exchange should facilitate negotiation. They like to put all their cards on the table. The desire for efficiency and getting things done in less time make them appear hasty and impatient. Many foreigners see open and direct communication as crude. In some cultures, it is offensive and rude to jump into the final issue without following proper preparation and protocol.

Foreign language skills Most American managers are not proficient in foreign languages. By contrast, their foreign counterparts are often well versed in at least several foreign languages. The inability to communicate in any language but English is a handicap for Americans. Often, American negotiators watch in frustration while foreigners argue among themselves in their mother tongues, aware that Americans cannot comprehend the content of their arguments.

Silence Unlike the Orientals, who use silent periods to reflect and organize their thoughts, Americans do not like silence. Because of their concern for time, silent periods appear to Americans as inactivity and a waste of time. They get frustrated in what appears to be a slow-moving negotiation process because of their inability to read the nonverbal, silent language of the Oriental. The following complaint is a typical example:

> I spent a week in Japan negotiating a deal that seemed to be good for both parties. For the life of me, I could not make any sense, one way or another, if they were interested or not. They just sat there listening to me, with no expressions on their faces. Yes! They apologized a lot for nothing. I am forced to make another trip just to find out if they like my proposal!

Persistence and competitiveness Americans prize persistence and will not give up easily. They do not take no for an answer. Their competitive nature and their desire to win makes persistence a very valued attribute. "If at first you don't succeed, try and try again" is a hallmark of the American mentality. Americans view negotiations as a win–lose situation. Moreover, they assume that others have the same view of the negotiation. Unfortunately, projecting such unwarranted similarities can lead to disappointment when negotiations bog down due to cultural differences.

Legalistic and linear approach A linear approach to problem solving is used by most American negotiators. Complex problems are broken down into simpler issues, and each issue is tackled separately. On a linear fashion, one issue at a time is solved until the total problem is settled. Americans prefer precise, written contracts that cover every detail of the business transaction in a legal, formal framework.

Now that we have learned about the American style of negotiation, we examine intercultural negotiations.

Intercultural Negotiations

Effective communication is the foundation of a successful negotiation. Intercultural negotiation has all the pitfalls of intracultural communication—in addition to other difficulties. Based on the proposition suggested by Bangert,[52] in the following we examine the influence of culture on various components of negotiation.

Cultural influences on negotiation In general, the complexity of the issues in a negotiation may determine the size of the negotiating parties. Negotiations on complex issues such as oil exploration and marketing rights with a foreign country require the use of many specialists. Most negotiations between the MNCs and their foreign partners are complex. In these negotiations, MNCs employ many staff specialists. Not all the staff need to attend the negotiation session. Negotiating teams may simply benefit from the behind-the-scene services of the specialist staff. Cultural differences influence the size of the team directly involved in the negotiation. Negotiating teams from collectivist societies tend to be large, while, for an individualistic culture, a single person represents an acceptable negotiating team. The Japanese, for example, prefer to use a large negotiating team, while Americans do not hesitate to send only a couple of persons to the negotiation table. Negotiators from individualistic societies that send only a couple of persons to the negotiation table may be overwhelmed by the team of negotiators from a collectivist society.

Collectivist societies consider people very important. Long-term relationships, consensus, and harmony among organizational members are important to them. We already have dis-

cussed the blurring of boundaries between the people and the environmental situations in collectivist cultures. Contrary to the suggestion of PN, it is difficult for collectivists to separate the issues from the people. For the same reason, collectivists are very much reluctant to express disagreement openly. They fear this may cause hurt feelings. Consequently, nonverbal and indirect communication cues play an important role in negotiation with collectivists. To succeed in business in Korea, for example, a person needs an extraordinary skill to read *nunch'i* (noonchee). "*Nunch'i* means the look in a person's eyes, the nonverbal reaction of a person to a question, an order, or any interaction with another person. Koreans are very skilled at this subtle art, and take it for granted that others are also."[53] In a classic case of cross-cultural communication failure, a foreign manager learned the role of *nunch'i* the hard way. Paul Dredge, a senior associate of Korean Strategy Associations, recounted the incident as follows[54]:

> The office of a joint venture company in Seoul, Korea was located in a prestigious but inconvenient area of the city. To make it more convenient for both the visitors and the employees, the foreign manager decided to move the office to a nice down-town location. In his discussion of the issue with his Korean colleagues he did not encounter any objections. All along he assumed they agreed with his choice of the location. He was baffled, however, when at the last moment the Korean president, without any explanation, refused to allow the move. It created an impasse, and a great deal of ill will on both sides.
>
> From the beginning, the Korean president and personnel had opposed the move. They had not directly expressed their opposition, however. They did not want to confront him openly in a contest that they knew the foreign manager could not win. To be polite, in a face saving attempt, they were not specific about their objection to the move. It was up to the foreign manager to ask the right questions and understand the right answers. They had relied

on his ability to read *nunch'i*. His failure had caused the loss of face on both sides.

Negotiations between people of masculine and feminine cultures may also run into difficulties. For the negotiators from masculine societies, ego preservation is important. For them to compromise may give the appearance of giving in, which could be considered a sign of weakness. Consequently, they may be in greater danger of taking a rigid position that may lead to breakdowns in the negotiations. Negotiators from a feminine culture may not be aware of the importance of ego to people of masculine cultures. Building the ego of their counterparts and focusing on the task at hand may help advance negotiations faster.

We know that differences in the fields of experience create barriers to communication. Similarly, negotiation is more difficult between the people of different cultures who have different value systems. Negotiators from a high power distance culture, for example, may need more information to convince their superiors of the value of the agreement. They may also take a longer time, because they have to clear most decisions with those in the position of power.

Views of the expected outcomes of negotiation may also be culturally based. Specifically, the expected outcomes of any negotiation may be either integrative or distributive. Integrative outcomes, or win–win situations, produce mutual benefits to both parties. To produce integrative outcomes, both parties must locate and adopt options that reconcile their needs. Integrative negotiations result in great benefits for both parties and stable relationships. By cooperation, the parties increase the size of the pie that they will eventually divide among themselves.[55] Distributive outcomes are the result of competition among the negotiators, each trying to get a larger share of the same pie without attempting to increase its size. Distributive negotiation is a win–lose scenario in which negotiators believe that they have opposing interests and incompatible alternative choices.[56]

Americans tend to have a short-term, distributive view of negotiation. Since Americans are concerned with their own interests, and view negotiations competitively, they often arrive at distributive outcomes. In contrast, most Asians view negotiation as a long-term relationship, and a cooperative task. Based on laboratory experiments, we can make certain propositions for intercultural negotiations. Viewing negotiations as a win–win proposition tends to produce an integrative outcome. Negotiations between those with distributive views (e.g., Americans) and those with integrative views (e.g., Japanese) tend to produce distributive outcomes.[57]

Given the differences in the negotiation perspective that can occur between Americans and the people of other nations, it is not surprising that international negotiations are marred by many difficulties, misunderstandings, and mistakes. Learning about the cultural perspectives of negotiation can reduce some of the problems of intercultural negotiations. The first step in improving international negotiations is to understand the influence of cultural differences on negotiation styles. Armed with knowledge about various cultural perspectives on negotiation, steps could be taken to reduce difficulties and increase the chance of success in dealing with the people of other cultures. The following examples illustrate style differences in international negotiation and point out the pitfalls to avoid.

We know, for example, that there are differences in time orientation and other cultural values between Americans and other people. These cultural differences influence the objectives, content, and direction of discussion in negotiations. Americans, for example, value youth and rely more on expertise and knowledge than age and seniority in selecting the members of negotiating teams. Younger negotiators are not uncommon among American teams. In other cultures, such as the Middle East, South America, and Asia, team members are often selected on the basis of age, seniority, social standings, and family connections. Some foreigners may not look favorably on a negotiation when they sit across the table from much younger managers representing American companies.

Oriental, and particularly Japanese, decision-making styles are different from that of the Americans. The Japanese include more levels of the hierarchy and many more people in most decision processes. Involving more people in the decision-making process when the intention is to arrive at a consensus becomes more time consuming. The implementation of consensus decisions takes less time, however. The American style of proposal–counterproposal negotiation does not fit well with the Japanese consensus-building, group-based decision-making process. Persuasive arguments are not as effective with the Japanese as is detailed information. They would prefer first reaching an agreement informally, then formalizing it with a short, written contract.[58]

Bargaining and negotiation are a part of daily life in the Middle East. It is unusual to walk into a shop and purchase merchandize at a specific price. No one expects to complete a deal quickly without bargaining. Patience and protocol are prized. They enjoy flowery prose and poetry, and often sprinkle their talks with the recitation of poetry. They are more concerned with personal integrity and building a relationship than with the formality of concluding an agreement. Similar to the Oriental, saving face and preserving their honor and reputation is very important to Middle Easterners. Middle Easterners take pride in their hospitality, are very generous, and appreciate generous people. They have little respect for those who are tight fisted with their wealth. Foreigners who want to establish business relationships in the Middle East should be ready to combine personal relationships with business transactions. In the following, a foreign negotiator's recounting of his experience gives us a glimpse of the Middle Eastern personal approach to business transactions. It is a typical example of the personal nature of doing business in the Middle East.

> The Labour Minister for the United Arab Emirates was in my office to help negotiate an end to a work stoppage by the local Dubai construction workers. The meeting went well until we finished our discussions. While walking with His Highness to the door of my office, I mentioned that he had a beautiful briefcase (mine was in a general state of disrepair). As I reached the door I noticed that he was no longer walking with me. I turned around to see His Highness emptying the contents of his briefcase on my desk.
>
> "Did you lose something?" I tried to ask helpfully.
>
> "No, no," he replied. "I want you to have," he added, as he presented his briefcase to me. "This is for you. You are my friend."
>
> After profusely apologizing, I convinced him that I really couldn't accept the briefcase.
>
> The lesson learned? In that part of the world, don't go around complimenting people on their possessions. You just might end up with them.[59]

Besides learning about other cultures and understanding variations of negotiation styles among different countries, there are certain overall approaches that, if followed, will improve the chances of successfully conducting a negotiation abroad. Frank Acuff suggests the following ten negotiation strategies that will work anywhere[60]:

1. Plan the negotiation.
2. Adopt a win–win approach.
3. Maintain high aspirations.
4. Use language that is simple and accessible.
5. Ask lots of questions, then listen with your eyes and ears.
6. Build solid relationships.
7. Maintain personal integrity.
8. Conserve concessions.
9. Be patient.
10. Be culturally literate and adapt to the negotiating strategies of the host country environment.

Conclusion

Without communication no organization can function. By communicating we share information, knowledge, beliefs, and values; we also share our ideas, opinions, and feelings with others. It is through communication that we negotiate a deal, buy and sell products, and exchange information. Communication is complete when the meaning we intended to send with our message reaches its destination, and is understood by the receiver. This requires commonality of the fields of experience between the sender and the receiver. Cultural differences that create different fields of experience make communication across cultures very difficult. International managers need to understand the influence of cultural differences on communication. They can improve intercultural communication by recognizing cross-cultural variations in communication patterns.

Although verbal and written communication is the predominant form of communication, nonverbal cues are used to supplement or replace oral and written forms. Similar to differences in languages, there are cultural variations in the nonverbal cues, signs, and signals used in communication. Because language differences are apparent, we learn foreign languages to communicate with other people in their mother tongue. Nonverbal cues, signs, and signals used in communication are less evident, therefore, less attempt is made to understand them. International managers who do not familiarize themselves with the idiosyncracies of nonverbal communication will face more communication problems. Not learning about nonverbal, cross-cultural communication can have serious consequences. Often unfamiliarity in reading the meaning behind the verbal messages could lead to misunderstanding, confusion, and business failure.

To negotiate a business deal, international managers need to recognize the cultural differences in communication. They also need to understand cultural differences in negotiation styles. Skills developed in intracultural negotia-

tions are not sufficient for conducting intercultural negotiations. "Projective similarity," assuming others negotiate the same way as we do, could lead to disappointing results. The American view that negotiation is a competitive game is not necessarily shared by other people. Some other cultures view negotiation as a relationship building exercise. Such a view of negotiation calls for a different type of negotiation and different skills. Attempts at maximizing our gains with such groups may produce a short-term result but may damage the long-term relationships. International managers who succeed remember the saying "When in Rome, do as the Romans do."

Discussion Questions

1. What are the differences between macro and micro international communications?
2. Explain developing countries' concerns regarding international communication.
3. Much of the difficulties in international communication are due to cultural differences among nations. In what way could cultural differences cause communication problems?
4. Why is understanding of nonverbal communication more important to international managers?
5. Give an example of American nonverbal communication that may have a different meaning in another culture.
6. Based on the material in this chapter, how would you advise a person from a culture that is high on the femininity index in negotiations with an individual from a culture that is high on the masculinity index?
7. Why do negotiators from high power distance societies need more information to take home?
8. Use at least two cultural dimensions discussed in this chapter for explaining the assertion that Americans are very legalistic and short-term oriented in negotiations.

9. Based on material presented in this chapter, what advice do you have for "Poor Richard"?
10. What is the principled negotiation (PN) method? How different is PN from other negotiation methods?
11. Compare the American style of negotiation with that of the Japanese.

Endnotes

1. Bob's story is adopted from R. Brown. "The Maverick Who Yelled Foul At Citibank." *Fortune* (January 10, 1983), 46.

2. H. Mowlana. *Global Information and World Communication* (New York: Longman, 1986), 180–2.

3. A. Dunkin. "Smart Houses: Getting Switched On." *Business Week* (June 28, 1993), 128–30.

4. K. Nordenstreng and W. Kleinwachter. "The New International Information and Communication Order." In M. K. Asante and W. B. Gudykunst, eds. *Handbook of International and Intercultural Communication* (Newbury Park, CA: Sage Publications, 1989), 87.

5. H. Mowlana. *Global Information and World Communication*. 207.

6. H. Mowlana. *Global Information and World Communication*. 198.

7. T. L. McPhail. *Electronic Colonialism: The Future of International Broadcasting and Communication,* 2nd. rev. ed. (Newbury, CA: Sage Publication, 1987), 18.

8. Ibid., p. 56.

9. W. Schramm. "How Communication Works." In W. Schramm, ed. *The Process and Effects of Mass Communication* (Urbana, IL: University of Illinois Press, 1963), 6.

10. Schramm. "How Communication Works." 6.

11. J. C. Berris. "The Art of Interpreting." In L. A. Samovar and R. E. Porter, eds. *Intercultural Communication* (Belmont, CA: Wadsworth Publishing Co., 1991), 265–9.

12. Ibid., 265.

13. M. Mendenhall and G. Oddou. "The Dimensions of Expatriate Acculturation: A Review." *Academy of Management Review,* 10, no. 1 (1985), 39–47.

14. P. Anderson. "Explaining Intercultural Differences in Nonverbal Communication." in L. A. Samovar and R. E. Porter, eds. *Intercultural Communication* (Belmont, CA: Wadsworth Publishing Co., 1991), 286–96.

15. M. L. Hecht, P. A. Anderson, and S. A. Ribeau, "The Cultural Dimensions of Nonverbal Communication." In M. K. Asante and W. B. Gudykunst, eds. *Handbook of International and Intercultural Communication,* (Newbury Park, CA: Sage Publications, 1989), 163–85.

16. E. T. Hall. *The Hidden Dimension* (Garden City, NY: Doubleday, 1966).

17. H. C. Triandis, R. Comtempo, and M. J. Villareal. "Individualism-Collectivism: Cross-Cultural Perspectives on Self-Grouping Relationships." *Journal of Personality and Social Psychology,* 54 (1988), 323–38.

18. G. Hofstede. "Cultural Relativity of Quality of Life Concept." *Academy of Management Review,* 9, no. 3 (1984), 390.

19. I. Altman. *The Environment and Social Behavior* (Monterey, CA: Brooks/Cole, 1975).

20. Anderson. "Explaining Intercultural Differences." 287–96.

21. Anderson, "Explaining Intercultural Differences." 291.

22. G. Hofstede, *Culture's Consequences* (Beverly Hills, CA: Sage Publications, 1984).

23. M. Mulder. *The Daily Power Game* (Leiden, Netherlands: Marinus Nijhoff Social Sciences Division, 1977), 3–5.

24. Hofstede, *Culture's Consequences*. 94.

25. W. B. Gudykunst and Y. Y. Kim, *An Approach to Intercultural Communication* (New York: Random House, 1984).

26. P. Anderson and L. Bowman. "Positions of Power: Nonverbal Cues of Status and Dominance in Organizational Communication." Paper presented at the 1985 Annual Convention of the Interpersonal Communication Association, Honolulu, cited in Anderson, "Explaining Intercultural Differences." 293.

27. Hofstede, "Cultural Relativity." 390.

28. Hofstede. *Culture's Consequences*. 122.

29. Hofstede. *Culture's Consequences*. 135.

30. Hecht *et al.* "The Cultural Dimensions of Nonverbal Communication." 175.

31. E. T. Hall. *The Silent Language* (New York: Doubleday, 1959); E. T. Hall. *The Hidden Dimension* (New York: Doubleday, 1966).

32. C. E. Halverson. "Managing Differences on Multicultural Teams." *Cultural Diversity at Work* (May 1992), 10–5.

33. Anderson. "Explaining Intercultural Differences." 294.

34. D. Matsumoto, H. G. Wallbott, and K. R. Scherer. "Emotions in Intercultural Communication." In M. K. Asante and W. B. Gudykunst, eds. *Handbook of International and Intercultural Communication* (Newbury Park, CA: Sage Publications, 1989), 225–46.

35. Ibid.

36. B. H. Spitzberg and W. R. Cupach. *Interpersonal Communication Competence* (Beverly Hills, CA: Sage Publishing Co., 1984).

37. M. R. Hammer, "Intercultural Communication Competence." In M. K. Asante and W. B. Gudykunst, eds. Handbook of International and Intercultural Communication (Newbury Park, CA: Sage Publications, 1989), 247–60.

38. B. Ruben. "Assessing Communication Competency for Intercultural Adaptation." *Group and Organizational Studies,* 1 (1976), 334–54.

39. Mendenhall and Oddou. "The Dimensions of Expatriate Acculturation." 39–47.

40. Ruben. "Assessing Communication Competency." 334–54.

41. Ruben. "Assessing Communication Competency." 334–54.

42. J. E. Andersen, "Educational Assumptions Highlighted from a Cross-Cultural Comparison." in L. A. Samovar and R. E. Porter, eds. *Intercultural Communication: A Reader* (Belmont, CA: Wadsworth Publishing Co., 1985), 160–4.

43. N. J. Adler. *International Dimensions of Organizational Behavior* (Boston, MA: Kent Publishing Co., 1991), 84–5.

44. F. L. Acuff. *How to Negotiate Anything with Anyone Anywhere Around the World* (New York: American Management Association, 1993), 21.

45. A. L. Goldman. *Settling for More* (Washington, DC: The Bureau of National Affairs, 1991), 6.

46. R. Fisher and W. Ury. *Getting to Yes: Negotiating Agreements Without Giving In* (Boston, MA: Houghton Mifflin Co., 1981).

47. Ibid.

48. R. L. Kuhn. *Dealmaker: All the Negotiating Skills and Secrets You Need* (New York: John Wiley and Sons, 1988), 27.

49. J. L. Graham and R. J. Herberger. "Negotiators Abroad Don't Shoot from the Hip." *Harvard Business Review,* 61 (1983), 160–8; Acuff, *How to Negotiate.* 41–66.

50. H. R. Markus and S. Kitayama, "Culture and the Self: Implications for Cognition, Emotion, and Motivation." *Psychological Review,* 98, no. 2 (1991), 224–253.

51. Acuff, *How to Negotiate.* 45.

52. D. C. Bangert. "Culture's Influence on Negotiations." Paper presented at the Academy of International Business, Maui, Hawaii, October 21–24, 1993.

53. B. De Mente. *Korean Etiquette and Ethics in Business* (Lincolnwood, IL: NTC Publishing Group, 1991), 83.

54. De Mente, *Korean Etiquette.* 83–4.

55. M. H. Bazerman and M. A. Neal. "Improving Negotiation Effectiveness Under Final Offer Arbitration: The Role of Selection and Training. *Journal of Applied Psychology,* 67 (1982), 543–54.

56. D. G. Pruitt. *Negotiation Behavior* (New York: Academic Press, 1981).

57. R. Lituchy. "Negotiating with the Japanese: Can We Reach Win–Win Agreements?" Paper presented at the Academy of International Business Conference, October 21–25, 1993.

58. S. A. Hellweg, L. A. Samovar, and L. Shaw. "Cultural Variations in Negotiation Styles," in L. Samovar and R. E. Porter, eds. *Intercultural communication: A Reader* (Belmont, CA: Wadsworth Publishing Co., 1991), 185–92.

59. Acuff, *How to Negotiate.* 57.

60. Acuff. *How to Negotiate.* 97.

BUCKEYE GLASS COMPANY IN CHINA

JAMES A. BRUNNER

In November 1988, Buckeye Glass sent a highly skilled team to Qinhuangdao, People's Republic of China, to negotiate a joint venture for the manufacture of glassware. The team consisted of John Brickley, Vice-President of Marketing; Bob Caines, Production Manager; and Steve Miller, Chief Engineer. Brickley had carefully selected an interpreter, Ling Sida, who knew Mandarin Chinese, the dialect spoken in Northern China, as he was concerned that a language barrier might arise.

Company Background

Buckeye Glass headquartered in Columbus, Ohio, produced glassware, including wide and narrow mouth containers, and glass prescription ware. It had over 25,000 customers worldwide in diverse industries such as food processing, liquor, beer, wine, cosmetics, soft drinks, and proprietary and prescription drugs. Its 10 month worldwide sales in 1988 were $3.0 billion, and it had plants in Europe, Asia, North and South America, employing 44,000 people. Its earnings have been flat for the past 5 years and management was exploring new avenues for growth of sales and earnings. The plant being considered for construction in China would produce all types of glassware under the name of Buckeye, its brand name worldwide. It is known as a high quality producer and a leader in its field.

Year	Sales (billion)	Profits (million)
1988*	$3.0	$120
1987	$3.4	$138
1986	$3.0	$140
1985	$3.0	$136
1984	$2.8	$135

* 10 months.

Qinhuangdao

Qinhuangdao is a Chinese international port city in Northern China. Located on the Bohai Sea, it is only 277 kilometers (166 miles) southeast of Beijing and serves as the gateway to the capital as it has a large, modern harbor, which is ice and salt free. The weather is milder than inland, and its beaches at Beidaihe attract thousands annually, including leading government officials from Beijing.

By 1988 Qinhuangdao had developed into an important economic center and was the glass capital of the People's Republic of China. It is one of 14 coastal cities opened to the outside world in 1984; and has a new economic and technical development site which had attracted foreign investors from the United States,

Australia, and several other countries. This site had a 12,000-unit Swedish program controlled telephone system. One of the companies located there manufactured silicon solar batteries, and another, special tubing for refrigerators and buses. There were 25 glass factories in the area producing laminated glass, thermal glass, medical glassware, fiberglass, and heat-absorbing glass. These companies engage in lateral economic cooperation and pool both technologies and skilled personnel, thereby enhancing the quality and efficiency of production. The area is rich in quartz, a major ingredient in the manufacturing of glass.

Trip to Qinhuangdao

The Buckeye Glass team had flown for 26 hours and stayed overnight in Beijing at the Great Wall Hotel. The next morning they traveled by train for 6 hours to Qinhuangdao. Enroute they discussed their plans and were anxious to meet the Chinese and begin negotiating as soon as possible.

When they arrived there, they were greeted warmly by their Chinese hosts and escorted to the Jinshan Hotel, expressly reserved for foreigners. They found to their surprise that their accommodations were comparable to those of first-class hotels in the United States. The rooms were complete with comfortable beds, baths, TV, and telephones. Wake-up service and a dining room were available for meals, which were served in both Chinese and Western styles.

Pleased by their surroundings and encouraged by the congeniality of their hosts at dinner that night they retired; confident that the meeting scheduled for the next day would establish a beneficial working relationship with the Chinese. At 10 PM strains of Brahm's lullaby flowed from the intercom system, and the negotiators slept peacefully after their arduous journey as they began to adjust to their jet lag.

The Chinese arrived promptly at 9 A.M. The Chinese delegation was led by Tien Chao, the Deputy Director of the Foreign Affairs Office.

Through his interpreter, he introduced the others in his party. Pi Zhao, Director of the Xia Xian Glass Factory, the leading glass manufacturer in China, and Mah Ai-qi, his personal secretary and interpreter. Tien Chao was tall, thin, erect, and very dignified in bearing. After formal introductions and an exchange of pleasantries, the group left for a tour of Xia Xian Glass Factory's manufacturing facilities.

Arriving at the factory, the group was greeted by Poh Jiwei, the Managing Director, who escorted them on a tour of the facilities. The Americans were surprised by what awaited them. The floor of the factory was dirty, and there was a large number of glass container crates located haphazardly on the floor. Groups of employees were loitering, playing cards, conversing, and laughing, while others were engaged in various work activities. Surprised at the minimal level of activity in the plant, Caines asked through their interpreter, Ling Sida, "Why aren't all these people working or are some of them on break?"

Poh Jiwei smiled and replied proudly, "Our plant has met its production quota for the year; but these men report in each day to be with their friends and do whatever work is planned for that day. You know, in China we provide jobs for all our people and unemployment is nonexistent. When we receive our new quota from the government, production will begin again at a higher level."

Caines, still perplexed, replied, "Wouldn't it be more profitable to close down some of the production facilities and lay off at least some of the workers until the new quotas are announced and thereby increase the profits of the company?"

Poh Jiwei replied politely as he smiled, "In China, we do what is best for the workers in order to give them steady incomes. Our concern is more about the workers, than the income of the factory."

Caines, noting that some workers were arriving late, asked, "I've known that Chinese facto-

ries practice this *iron rice bowl* concept whereby all workers are assured they will have jobs. But some of them are late in arriving for work. Aren't they expected to be on time?" Poh Jiwei smiled and replied, "Well, in the past we have not enforced your Western-style work ethic of being punctual, but we are beginning to change. But please understand that the middle-aged and elderly workers are hard to change and they resist this new approach. The younger workers, however, agree that punctuality should lead to increased productivity, and are willing to accept these changes. In fact we now give bonuses to those who exceed their quotas and stay on their jobs until closing time. You may be interested to know that our workers retire when they reach the age of 55, and we have only a few older workers in the factory."

As the tour progressed, Caines continued to be amazed by the antiquated machinery in operation, but was startled when they came to an installation which had the latest container glass manufacturing technology. When he openly praised the equipment, Poh Jiwei smiled broadly and replied humbly to the surprise of the Americans, "Oh, our factory is very ill-equipped, with few modern machines unlike those you have in your country." Brickley, confused by Poh Jiwei's statement since they had just viewed a great deal of modern machinery, quickly assured Poh that the plant was indeed impressive and very well equipped.

After the tour of the plant, the Buckeye executives were escorted to a conference room which was plainly decorated, had 24 chairs arranged around the walls of the room, and a conference table with 10 chairs. They were invited to be seated at the table, and were served tea by their hosts. Pi Zhao thanked the Buckeye team for visiting the plant and commented for 5 minutes upon their proposed relationship with Buckeye Glass. He elaborated upon the economic development plans of the People's Republic of China and noted that even though the government had not given top priority to glass container production, he assured them it looked favorably upon the possibility of building a plant in Qinhuangdao for that purpose. He stressed the need for the development of a long-term relationship and hoped those present could become "old friends." After elaborating further for 20 minutes, he sat down.

John Brickley immediately stood up and responded by expressing his sincere appreciation for the plant tour, and also his hope that a close relationship could be developed with the Chinese in this endeavor. He stressed how a glass manufacturing plant would be beneficial to the economic progress of the country as well as the living standards of the Chinese. He profusely thanked Poh Jiwei for the tour of the factory and continued to elaborate for about 10 minutes on this relationship and its mutual benefits.

After he finished, Tien Chao proposed that after lunch they should tour Qinhuangdao and visit the eastern section of the Great Wall of China. He proudly stated that the sea end of the wall was in Qinhuangdao and at one time had been over 23,000 meters long, but that only 2300 meters of it still existed. He stated it had been originally constructed by Emperor Qin Shi Huang of the Qin dynasty, commencing in 221 B.C. He also announced, "We should visit other features of interest, such as the "Old Dragon's Head" at the sea end of the wall, the park and, of course, the beach in Beidaihe."

The rest of the afternoon was, therefore, spent touring the area. A photographer went with the party to photograph the Americans at the various points of interest, which were proudly described in detail by Tien Chao through an interpreter. (Appendix 1 provides a brief review of Chinese culture and negotiating styles.) Brickley was frustrated as he wanted to discuss the proposed joint venture. He attempted not to show his impatience, and expressed interest in the special features of the region. At 6 PM they returned to the hotel. The Chinese joined them for dinner and left promptly at 8 PM.

Initial Meeting

The next morning, the Chinese delegation arrived promptly and escorted the Buckeye team to the hotel's meeting room. The Chinese delegation now consisted of 12 members including Pi Zhao, the Director of Xin Xian Glass Factory, its plant manager, two assistant plant managers, several engineers, and the interpreter. The Chinese arranged themselves on one side of the table and the Buckeye Glass team was seated opposite them. After they were served tea, Brickley rose, thanked the Chinese for inviting them, and described the services of his company.

Brickley then introduced Caines who elaborated for approximately 20 minutes upon the history of Buckeye Glass, its premier position in the worldwide market in the production of containers for a wide range of industries such as food, soft drinks, beer, cosmetics, and pharmaceuticals, and how profitable they had been internationally. He then turned to Steve Miller who introduced the engineers. As a team, they presented a slide presentation of the company's production and sales facilities, and a statistical review of sales and profits for the previous decade. They continued by elaborating on the technological capabilities of Buckeye Glass. Brickley then rose and commented at length about the strong managerial team which the company had. He elaborated upon the integration of the marketing, finance and production activities at Buckeye Glass, which he explained had been highly effective in thrusting the company into a leading position in the international glass container industry.

He commented briefly upon his opinions concerning observations made the previous day in the factory, and noted that his company could assist the Chinese by introducing its production workers and managers to Western concepts of production and marketing. He emphasized the need for management to introduce Western management know-how and methods in the Xia

Xian Glass Factory in order that it could effectively serve the needs of the Chinese people.

During his presentation, the Chinese seemed somewhat passive, but occasionally asked questions and probed for information. Brickley and the other members of the Buckeye Glass team carefully and patiently answered the questions raised. They also endeavored to sense the priorities of the Chinese concerning the various types of problems that they had and what they wanted the American team to do. In their discussions, it became evident that breakage was a major problem as the Chinese workers were not well trained in the use of the equipment. Further, they learned the Xia Xian's customers wanted different types of glass containers than were being produced in this plant, but the company was still manufacturing ware no longer in heavy demand. They had a sizable overaged inventory of these outmoded containers.

Further, the Chinese noted that their products were not meeting the quality specifications demanded by foreign buyers. Thus, it was evident that a quality control training program was essential. Poh Jiwei observed further that the corregated shipping containers for the glass products were inferior and oftentimes broke in shipment, which then led to damaged merchandise.

While Brickley was aware of these problems, he had no idea of the order in which the Chinese would prioritize them, and specifically, which of Buckeye's services were considered to be the most important to the Chinese.

After the discussion had continued for 3 hours, Pi Zhao suggested that they break for lunch; and that after lunch they should go on a sightseeing tour of Yanshan University, a new educational institution founded in the 1980s to train engineering and technical students in the latest scientific developments and technology. Pi Zhao assured the Buckeye team that he would like to meet the next day to discuss the possibility of signing a letter of intent. The meeting then adjourned.

The next morning promptly at 9 AM Tien Chao, Pi Zhao, and Poh Jiwei arrived with their interpreter and 3 engineers. They escorted the Buckeye Glass executives to the conference room and they arranged themselves on one side of the table while the Americans occupied the other. Through his interpreter, Tien Chao expressed his appreciation to the Americans for their informative presentation and announced that they were interested in signing a letter of intent. Tien Chao observed that the Xia Xian Glass Factory had inadequate equipment, and elaborated on a low level of skill possessed by the production workers as well as the managers. Brickley silently concurred with Tien Chao's observations concerning the workers, but he was surprised to hear this comment concerning the managers as some of them were present at the meeting. Further, Tien Chao expressed his admiration of the Buckeye Glass executives, acknowledging that the company was one of the leading glass manufacturers in the world, and that his company was humbly appreciative of the opportunity to join them in a joint venture. Brickley was amazed at this sense of humbleness by the Chinese as he didn't feel that they were as inferior as Tien Chao was suggesting.

Tien continued, "We feel that the time has arrived for us to sign a letter of intent and to express the general principles under which our venture will operate. Our objective is the modernization of the Xia Xian plant in Qinhuangdao and propose that it be located in the new economic and technical development zone. Further, Buckeye Glass will provide for managerial training of the Chinese managers and also for the factory workers and service staff of the joint venture." He paused and then announced, "Further, Buckeye Glass will provide for the transfer of technology to improve the product's quality and performance, reduce production costs and conserve energy and materials. This technology should also enable the company to expand the exportation of glass containers and thereby increase the foreign exchange revenues of the Xia Xian Glass Factory. Finally Buckeye will be the marketing agent for the joint venture, not only in China but on a worldwide basis."

Brickley was silently pleased. On second thought, he was somewhat perplexed as the objectives proposed were very broad and outlined the general principles of the accord without spelling out the specific details. Nevertheless, he thanked Tien Chao and added, "I think it's important that we also include the specific details of our mutual obligations in order to avoid any misunderstandings in the future."

Tien Chao smiled and replied, "We appreciate your concern, but it is not necessary to specify the particulars of the joint venture at this point. But we need to reach a general agreement on the principles in your letter of interest."

As the executives of Buckeye Glass were surprised at the Chinese proposed letter of intent, they began to fire questions concerning the specific details. Tien Chao again smiled and asserted, "The details can be worked out later but first we must come to an agreement on general principles. We propose that we break for a period of time in order that you may have an opportunity to review our broad objectives, I propose that we meet again after lunch."

The meeting adjourned and the 2 groups went to separate meeting rooms. The Buckeye team met in Brickley's room and after pouring each a cup of tea, Brickley, exasperated, stated, "Well this certainly isn't what I expected. I thought we could reach some general agreement on the specific details. Evidently the Chinese are only interested in general principles. Frankly, I'm concerned they didn't specify the time period for the joint venture and the financial details. How much each of us is going to have to put up front is also up in the air. What products are to be produced? This is certainly different than any joint venture I've ever written in the United States. I propose that we come up with recommendations so that we can get this show on the road." Brickley noted further, "After listening to their monologue, I'm sure glad that I

took notes, but I'm not certain what their priorities are. There is a lot we can bring to the table, but it would be helpful if we knew their priorities. I will press that issue after lunch."

At noon, Tien Chao and his team met Brickley and his associates and they went to the dining room. While the Chinese remained reserved and occasionally talked among themselves, the atmosphere was still friendly. After lunch they adjourned again to the conference room and Brickley stated their concern about the missing details and made some specific suggestions. Tien Chao commented, "I know we are old friends, but you are insisting upon being very specific about the details, and are not willing to agree only on the general principles. We regret this and don't understand why." Brickley's interpreter told him the Chinese felt he was behaving dishonorably and acted as though he did not trust the Chinese. Brickley feeling intimidated quickly responded, "I'm disappointed we can't agree. However, if it is not customary in China to be specific in a letter of agreement but only to reach agreement only on the general principles, we will go along to demonstrate our sincerity. After we have signed it, I would like to give it to the press in order that my company may publicize it in the United States as it will be good publicity and will demonstrate Buckeye's interest in economic development in the People's Republic of China."

Tien Chao agreed, but asked that no dates be stated concerning when it was to commence, and that no mention be made of the investment that would be involved, nor the city in China in which it was to be located.

Brickley knew that the Chinese had mixed feelings about publicity and preferred to maintain secrecy in the negotiating process as they had a mistrust of publicity and perceived it as a form of pressure. Moreover, he sensed that they were concerned that their superiors might feel they were endeavoring to promote themselves. On the other hand, he thought that if he didn't publicize the agreement, the Chinese might be offended. He was aware that they might sense a violation of confidentiality if he revealed too much. It was a minor dilemma for him. Brickley paused, and then agreed to all of these stipulations with the exception that the city should be specified as it was known in the United States that his company had representatives in Qinhuangdao. Tien Chao agreed reluctantly.

The next day they met again and signed a joint agreement, which Brickley recognized was not binding on either parties, but at least served as a basis for commencing the substantive negotiations. He personally felt quite gratified with the progress made, as the Chinese indicated that they were now willing to work out the specific details.

Formal Banquet

That evening the Chinese team escorted the Buckeye Glass representatives to a Chinese banquet to celebrate the signing of the letter of intent. Brickley was surprised to observe that place cards had been arranged on the tables in order to facilitate the seating arrangements. He was seated next to Tien Chao's left and the Chinese were interspersed among the Americans around 2 tables. When the first course consisting of braised prawns were served, the Chinese to the right of a Buckeye executive served him a portion of the prawns. While they were awaiting the second course, Tien Chao gave a speech lauding Sino-American relations and the signing completed that afternoon. As he closed he offered a toast of Mao Tai wine to the Buckeye Glass team. Brickley, aware of the effect of Mao Tai which has a 40% alcoholic content, toasted cautiously.

Following this, in sequence, scallops fried in tomato sauce, sautéed conch, fillet of fish stir-fried, pork steak fried, crabmeat stir-fried, heart of rape with mushroom, and sea slugs were served. During each of these 7 courses, the Chinese served the Americans saying, "Quing, Quing" ("please, please").

During the course of the 2 hour banquet, innumerable toasts were made by the Chinese and the Buckeye team reciprocated, oftentimes going from table to table to present toasts. Both teams used the white wine on the table for their toasts on these occasions, rather than the Mao Tai. However, when Tien Chao offered his toasts, Brickley followed protocol, and drank the complete glass of wine, on the urging by Tien Chao, who proposed, "Ganbei" ("bottoms-up").

During the dinner, the conversation naturally turned to the different cuisines of the various regions of the People's Republic of China. Miller asked facetiously if it was true that the Chinese in Southern China ate dog, snake and monkey brains. Tien Chao smiled broadly and replied affirmatively. Encouraged by Tien Chao's smile, Miller began joking about some of the other delicacies that appeared on the menu; such as heart of rape on mushrooms and the sea slugs. The Chinese apparently enjoyed this humorous approach as they were grinning and nodding their heads in response. Encouraged, the Americans began to tell Western jokes. Apparently, the atmosphere was friendly and relaxed.

Brickley, encouraged by this feeling of cordiality, sensed that the time was appropriate to again address the subject of the joint venture. Turning to Tien Chao, he said, "With our technology and investment, Buckeye Glass can pull China from its backwardness and make it a world power." Tien Chao replied, "Yes, yes, Buckeye Glass is a world leader, and a very powerful company from the United States. Xia Xian certainly must make use of a liaison with it."

Encouraged by Tien Chao's reply, Brickley continued, expounding upon the mutual benefit which this joint venture would provide both parties. He observed that Buckeye Glass could train the management of Xia Xian in modern managerial techniques and assist them in training their workers to use Western technology. He noted further that their close contacts would enable Buckeye to establish a foothold in the Chinese market and become a major power in the glass industry in the Pacific Basin countries.

While the guests were eating the stir-fried crabmeat course, Tien Chao rose and commented on the close ties being established with Buckeye Glass. He then presented Brickley a gift of 2 Chinese exercise balls, which he stated had been in use in China since the fourteenth century and were used to stimulate important acupressure points below the wrist. He then demonstrated that they emitted soft chiming sounds in two different pitches to calm the nerves and soothe the soul. Tien Chao then gave Brickley a 4 × 6 foot tapestry of the Great Wall. Brickley thanked him profusely, but was embarrassed as he had no gifts to reciprocate this show of friendship and cordial relations.

After the pastry had been served, the next course consisted of soup, rice and fruit. The Americans found the soup to be delicious and each took two servings of the rice as they especially enjoyed it. Tien Chao listened politely as Brickley sipped his tea. After a third cup, Tien Chao rose and thanked the Buckeye executives for attending the dinner. The hosts escorted them back to their room and quickly departed.

Political and Economic Environment

That night, Brickley reflected on the economic and political environment of China in order to gain a broader perspective. He was aware that the PRC had a population of over a billion, and that its economic system was being developed aggressively by the government. He noted that labor was inexpensive, and quite abundant without any problem of labor strikes. Further, he was aware that although raw materials and other supplies were less costly than in some countries, there were some difficulties in their procurement. He had heard that in the PRC the availability of materials and supplies was oftentimes dependent upon connections which one had with others. These relationships in China were referred to as *guanxi* and Brickley was aware that if one formed such ties, they signified close bonding. This permitted either party to call upon the other for any favors if they were within the power of a *guanxi* member to grant and he would be obligated to do so. Further, he knew that *guanxi* ties were also important for getting things done when working with the governmental bureaucracy as the PRC does not have an institutionalized legal system. Therefore, getting favorable interpretations by bureaucrats was dependent largely upon whom one knew and who had *guanxi* with whom.

Moreover, he noted that the PRC had a culture which traditionally shunned legal considerations and stressed rather the ethical and moral principles of everyday living; and that formal agreements were based more upon moral obligations than the law. He also recognized that although the People's Republic was a socialist country, it suffered from political instability, and the recent *open door* policy was primarily the endeavor of their senior leader Deng Xiaoping. Brickley knew that in November, 1983, Deng had launched a movement to put his mark on China's new emerging economic development. He had devised a 5 year plan to purge the Communist party's 40 million members of 1 million leftists, most of whom were ill educated. This had been accomplished through a reedification program of self criticism and prescribed study. Deng endeavored to clear the way for his protégés to rise to positions of power in order to ensure continuation of his economic, political and open-door policies.

In October, 1987, Zhao Ziyang became the party general's secretary succeeding Deng and a sixth 5 year plan was announced. Deng, however, remained a paramount figure in the decision making process and was encouraging some capitalistic practices to be adopted in China, such as, using quotas and holding managers accountable for the profitability of their factories.

In general, China's semiclosed economy was modified to an open economy with international exchanges encouraged. In moving toward a market mechanism for setting prices, however, inflation surged in 1988 to an unofficial but acknowledged annual rate of nearly 50% in cities.

There was evidence that government officials were capitalizing on entrepreneurism by accepting bribes and engaging in other unsavory activities. The economy was clearly overheated and industrial output had risen 7% in the first half, and investment in capital construction had increased 14%. China's inefficient factories were unable to keep up with the demand for goods and thereby added to the inflationary pressures. Demand for consumer goods was far outstripping supply and black market activities were thriving with inflationary price rises as a consequence.

The government attempted to slow the economy by controlling the money supply, but this had proven to be ineffective as the money supply rose 30% in the first 5 months of 1988. Finally, in order to get better control on the economy and slow down the inflationary pressures, the state council in October 1988, announced that as of December 1, it would reduce investment in a variety of nonessential industries, ranging from textile processing to consumer electronics and plastics. However, this would not apply to projects involving foreigners or those in priority areas such as energy and transportation. It was anticipated that the roll back would be huge, and that Beijing would cutback capital investment in 1989 by 50 billion Chinese yuan (13.5 billion dollars). Fortunately for Buckeye Glass, this would not pertain to glass containers but rather involved such products as cotton textiles, rubber goods, tractors, television sets, and those which consumed too much energy such as irons, vacuum cleaners and rice cookers. The crux of the problem was that the Chinese enterprises were state owned and the managers were not inclined to think in terms of economic efficiency.

Substantive Negotiations

Negotiations commenced promptly the next day and continued for 2 days. Both teams had copies of the Law of the People's Republic of China on Joint Ventures. (See Exhibit 1.) On occasion, the Chinese would engage in detailed questioning about topics which apparently were not too significant. Brickley sensed that this stalling tactic was used to gain time to enable the Chinese to elicit the comments of their superiors concerning various parts of the contract. He observed that when points requiring clarification arose, the Chinese during informal breaks would gather around the Buckeye Glass interpreter in order to attempt to persuade her to get concessions for the Chinese or to clarify Buckeye's proposals. Further, when the Americans expressed their views on a point under negotiation, Tien Chao would say, "We'll take note of your position," but then go on to the next issue under discussion. Brickley sensed that this indicated that the Chinese did not agree, but wished to avoid confrontations.

He also noted that the Chinese were extremely sensitive when pricing was being discussed and were apparently concerned that they might be given unfavorable treatment or were being cheated. From his interpreter, Brickley learned that this was true and that the Chinese were apprehensive that their superior would deal with them harshly if favorable terms were not obtained. Brickley also noted that in order to gain concessions from the Chinese, it was necessary to give one in return, thereby engaging in a face-saving action.

American Hosted Dinner

That evening, the Buckeye Glass executive hosted a dinner for the Chinese. The menu was simpler than the Chinese banquet as the Buckeye executives felt that the Chinese meal was too exotic for their tastes and digestion. Speeches were again given by Tien Chao and Brickley and frequent toasts were offered. Miller again told some Western jokes accompanied by friendly backslapping. The Buckeye executives attempted to lighten the ongoing formal conversation by steering it to familiar topics, such as, the families of the Chinese, personal tastes and ideas, and sexual patterns in China. The Chinese responded with much smiling and laughter even though their replies to the questioning were vague.

Exhibit 1

The Law of the People's Republic of China on Joint Ventures Using Chinese and Foreign Investment (adopted in 1979 at the second session of the Fifth National People's Congress)

1. Foreign companies and individuals within the territory of the People's Republic of China may incorporate themselves into joint ventures with Chinese companies or other Chinese entities with the objective of expanding international economic cooperation and technological exchange.
2. The Foreign Investment Commission must authorize joint ventures, and if approved, ventures are required to register with the General Administration for Industry and Commerce of the PRC, which will then issue a license within 3 months.
3. Joint ventures shall have limited liability and the foreign parties will contribute not less than 25% of the registered capital.
4. The participants will share profits, risks, and losses of the joint venture in proportion to their capital contributions.
5. The equity of each party may be capital goods, industrial property rights, cash, etc., in the ventures.
6. The contributors of technology or equipment contributed run the risk of forfeiture or damages if the technology or equipment contributed is not truly advanced and appropriate for Chinese needs. If losses are casued by deception through the intentional provision of outdated equipment or technology, compensation must be paid for the losses.
7. Investments by the Chinese participants may include the right of use of a site but it shall not constitute a part of the investment as the joint venture shall pay the Chinese government for its use.
8. A joint venture will have a Board of Directors and the Chairman of the board is to be appointed by the Chinese participants. The foreign parties may appoint 2 Vice-Presidents. These do not necessarily have to be Chinese but must be approved by the partners to the joint venture.
9. A jont venture agreement must stipulate procedures for the employment and discharge of the workers and staff members and comply with Chinese laws.
10. The net profit of a joint venture shall be distributed in proportion to the parties' respective investment shares after deductions for reserve funds. Bonuses and welfare funds for the workers and the expansion funds of the venture and the profit or losses shall be in accordance with the capital investment of the parties involved and be subject to the tax laws of the People's Republic of China and expatriation.
11. Joint ventures must maintain open accounts in a bank approved by the Bank of China.
12. All foreign exchange transactions shall be in accordance with the foreign exchange regulations of the People's Republic of China.
13. Joint ventures may borrow funds directly from foreign banks. Appropriate insurance will be provided by Chinese insurance companies. A joint venture equipped with up-to-date technology by world standards may apply for a reduction of or an exemption from income tax for the first 2 or 3 profit-making years.
14. A joint venture is encouraged to market its products outside China through direct channels, its associated agencies, or Chinese foreign trade establishments. Its products may also be distributed on the Chinese market.
15. The contract period of a joint venture must be agreed upon by both parties and may be extended subject to authorization by the Foreign Investment Commission.
16. Disputes which cannot be settled through consultation may be settled through consultation or arbitration by an arbitral body of Chinese or arbitral body agreed upon by the parties.

Proposed Joint Venture Contract

After a long weekend, during which the Americans and Chinese separately developed proposals for the joint venture, the Buckeye team were the first to present their terms for negotiations. Brickley submitted the financial requirements as he and his team perceived them (see Exhibit 2) and their terms for the joint venture (see Exhibit 3).

Negotiations Concluded

As Brickley was willing to negotiate and make concessions, he was puzzled that the Chinese did not present their terms. He commented on the key issues of the joint venture agreement and the Chinese listened intently. As they were passive and remained silent, Brickley couldn't tell whether they agreed or not with his proposal, and the team was perplexed about how to

Exhibit 2
Proposed Joint Venture, Dragon Glass Company: Financial Requirements (U.S. $000)

First year capital			Loan from Bank of China	$ 200
Working capital		$ 898	Long-term debt	400
Installations and equipment		790	Total liabilities	600
New	$450			
Old	40			
Factory		800	Net worth	
Land			First 2 year loss	200
Technology		550	Initial capital	2338
Total		$2738	Total	$3038
Partners' Investments				
Xia Xian Glass Company		55%	Buckeye Glass	25%
Factory		$ 400	Factory	$ 400
Installations and equipment		490	Technology	550
New	$750		Cash equivalent	102
Old	40			
Cash/equivalent		396		
Total		$1286	Total	$1052

cope with these periods of silence. Tien Chao thanked him and proposed they continue their discussions at 2 PM that afternoon. He was most concerned about the confidentiality of the transfer of technology in China as he knew there were no comprehensive commercial laws to protect his company, and China did not have trade secret laws. He had been told that the Chinese, on occasion, take technology and copy it. Moreover, he was aware margins initially would be nonexistent for goods sold on the world markets, and the joint venture would undoubtedly incur losses until the company could become more efficient.

In the afternoon session, the Chinese were cordial but remained passive. Tien Chao observed, "We have reviewed your proposal and can agree on most of its provisions. However, the value placed on the technology is far greater than we believe can be justified. As you have already paid for its development, we insist that in the spirit of friendship, a much lower figure be used. Further, we believe that Buckeye Glass should contribute all of the money for the investment in installations and equipment as we

are providing labor at a considerably lower level than can be obtained elsewhere. We will cover the cost of the factory in our investment. We believe that 80% of the goods should be sold in the export market. Before proceeding, we wish to resolve these issues."

Brickley then endeavored to explain that although his company had already invested in the glass technology, that on world markets it would be valued at this level. Further, he was quite puzzled by the large percentage of output which was to be destined for the export market as he had assumed the Chinese were interested in raising the standards of living of the people in the PRC. Obviously the need for foreign hard currency was more paramount. Discussion continued for another hour, at which time Tien Chao then proposed they adjourn and meet the next morning. At the meeting Tien Chao presented Xias Xian's proposal. Buckeye Glass was to invest 35% of the capital in the form of cash, installations, and technology. He specified that the technology must be advanced, lead to improved product quality and performance, and contribute to export expansion.

Exhibit 3
Proposed Joint Venture

Name: Dragon Glass Company.

Capital Contributions: 55% of the capital for the venture should be provided by the Xia Xian Glass Factory and 25% by the Buckeye Glass Company. In meeting this requirement, the Chinese were to obtain the right to use a site in the Qinhuangdao Economic Development Zone. It was agreed that the joint venture should rent the property from the Chinese government. Buckeye Glass was to invest $400,000 in the building and installations.

Training: Buckeye Glass was also to provide for training of the joint venture's managers and engineers in the United States for a period of 3 months.

Marketing: Buckeye Glass shall be the sole sales agent in the world market and provide for the maximum market penetration by its products internally in China and in the Pacific Basin countries, with the objective of 40% being sold domestically and the remaining 60% in the export market.

Pricing: The prices established in the world market would provide a 20% after tax return on the total investment of each party to the contract.

Technology: Technology provided by Buckeye Glass shall comply with the technology transfer regulations of the People's Republic of China and provide for the improvement of product quality and performance, reduce production costs, and increase foreign revenues. The value of the technology in the first year shall be $550,000.

Imported Materials: All silica and related production materials imported will not be subject to the standard 12% import duty if used for exported products, but a duty will be applied to those used for glassware produced for domestic sales. An 18% tax of value-added nature on domestic sales shall be levied. Sales in the world market shall provide a 20% after-tax return on the total investment of each party to the contract.

Work Force: The work force shall consist of the normal staff of production workers and include staff employees including engineers, office workers and managers. The joint venture shall not hire additional workers for the factory or office workers with the approval of the Board of Directors.

   The initial work force for the plant shall be limited to 200 factory workers and 50 service employees in the offices, including the managers.

Wage Compensation: The direct salary and benefits for the workers shall be determined by the Chinese government. The range for factory workers in the first year will be for 1200 Yuan and in the second year 1800 Yuan and will be for 2000 hours annually.

   The annual wage rate for the production workers will include direct and fringe benefits. The wage rate will be modified after the first year in conformity with those paid in other Chinese corporations for production workers by the Board of Directors.

Technology Confidentiality: The joint venture partners will be obliged to maintain confidentiality of the technology and shall be required during the life of the joint venture and beyond. Damages for the breach of contract will be pursuant to the Foreign Economic Contract Law and recoverable against a contract transferee who discloses the confidential information.

Expansion: The joint venture should secure from the Chinese government an additional 10 acres for expansion of this manufacturing facility.

Board of Directors: The management of the joint venture shall consist of 7 members on a Board of Directors, 4 of whom will be appointed by the Chinese and 3 by the Buckeye Glass Company. The board will follow modern management principles and establish a 5 year marketing and production plan. A planning budget shall be developed for the same period of time. It will be the responsibility of the joint venture board to specify the types and numbers of workers and managers for the venture.

Taxation: With approval of the tax authorities, the joint venture may be exempt from taxation for the first 2 profit-making years and granted a 50% tax reduction for the following 5 years. A profit-making year shall be defined as the year in which a joint venture realizes profits after the accumulated operating losses from prior years have been deducted. Further, as this joint venture is in a Special Investment Zone, the tax rate applicable to the enterprise shall be 15%, and no withholding tax on repatriated profits shall be levied.

Currency: This joint venture will use Reminbi (RMB) to calculate its income and tax liabilities. It may maintain its accounting records and books in dollars.

Brickley thereupon assured him that the technology proposed would do all these things, but insisted that the most advanced technology would not be appropriate at this time in China. He agreed that the value of the property in the buildings should be fixed by the People's government of Qinhuangdao according to a relative industry index. When Brickley inquired concerning the availability of silica and other raw materials for this project the Chinese were evasive, but assured him their "connections" would be able to find the necessary materials at reasonable prices.

To relieve some of the tension, Mr. Brickley and his team avoided the topics about which the 2 groups were in most disagreement; and again emphasized the great mutual benefits which would result from this venture. The afternoon meeting ended well. There were still some disagreements remaining, however, much ground had been covered. The remaining differences were considered by the Buckeye Glass negotiators to be minor, and they agreed to go back over them for the discussion on the next day, but Brickley was becoming impatient as he thought about the considerable investment his company had made in order to conduct these negotiations in Qinhuangdao. Buckeye had already committed over $25,000 for lodging, food, transportation and other expenses, and at least another million could be required for the equity capital.

The next morning the negotiators met again and to Brickley's dismay, the Chinese were adamant and refused to modify their terms. However, Tien Chao proposed that production be expanded to include containers for the wine and soft drink industries rather than only for food. This astounded Brickley as these industries were expanding rapidly and naturally he wanted to be involved in the early phase of development of these markets. He knew that the Chinese had strong loyalty to their initial suppliers and it was essential to establish these relationships before other foreign competitors entered the Chinese market. "What do we do now

to break this impasse?" he agonized to his team. "What concessions can we make to enable the Chinese to save face and alter this position?"

Brickley was aware that any joint agreement proposal would be subject to review by not only the Chinese government but also his legal department. At least another year would be required to formalize the agreement. His team had been in China for 2 weeks and the potential for profit in the long run was in the millions after the shakedown period in the first 2 years. He perceived several options at this point. They could drop the idea and move on to more promising ventures in the short run, make some concessions, and bring in an agent who resided on a permanent basis in Beijing who had strong Chinese ties, as he was a successful Chinese negotiator; they could offer to invite the Chinese to come to America as Buckeye's guests in order to visit the corporate plant and observe the technology and training facilities, or they could set a date for departure with the objective of forcing the Chinese to move off dead center and reach an agreement on the terms. He murmured to himself, "Patience, John, getting a joint venture signed in the PRC is like building Rome—it takes longer than a day! Freight trains move faster than negotiations in the PRC!"

Appendix 1: Chinese Culture and Negotiating Styles

Face

Paramount to an understanding of Chinese behavior in relationships is an understanding of face behavior. In China, face has two forms: lien and mien-tzu. Lien refers to one's moral character and is a person's most precious possession. Without it, one cannot function in society. It is earned by fulfilling one's duties and other obligations. Mien-tzu refers to a person's reputation or prestige and is based on personal accomplishments, political status or bureaucratic power. It also refers to one's ability to deal smoothly with people face-to-face. Face enhancement can be attained by acts of generosity in terms of time or gifts, or praise of others.

Face is the cooperative manner in which people behave toward one another in order to avoid loss of self-respect or prestige by either party. While the concept of face is often a fiction in practice, it retains its importance in actual dealings. For example, given a situation where 2 people are bargaining with each other, 1 must win and the other must lose. Each side expects that the other will consider face in the transaction. In reality, both sides know at the end who has won and who has lost, but the winner makes token concessions to save the loser's face. This is important in that it allows the loser to win in that he or she has been respected by the other, the winning party. Without the saving of face, the loser will be justly offended and avoid dealing with the winner in the future. This avoidance reaction carries with it obvious consequences and hinders any potential ongoing business relationship.

Another aspect of face is similar to the Western concept of being a good sport, or being a good winner. Modesty over one's own achievement and appreciation of the loser's skill and effort are central to saving face.

Face most often requires little effort but merely an attention to courtesy in relationships with others, yet will have a great positive effect upon the recipient. If lost, face will have a negative effect; which, if shown by the loser, results in still further loss of face. With the exception of a show of controlled anger by a person in authority, such as by a policeman, loss of self-control, sulking, and displays of anger or frustration create further loss of face rather than drawing respect or conciliation.

Once face has been lost, the loser will prefer to avoid the winner and ignore the face-losing incident as though it never occurred. In circumstances where the 2 parties must continue a relationship, the loser will return to formal and polite etiquette, pretending that the incident had not occurred. The other party should accommo-date the loser's preference and not refer again to the incident. Face involves a high degree of self-control, social consciousness, and concern for others.

Smiling and Laughter

Laughter and smiling in Chinese culture represent the universal reaction to pleasure and humor. In addition, they are also a common response to negative occurrences, such as death and other misfortunes. When embarrassed or in the wrong, the Chinese frequently respond with laughter or smiling which will persist if another person continues to speak of an embarrassing topic or does not ignore the wrong. Westerners are often confused and shocked by this behavior, which is alien to them. It is important to remember that smiling and laughter in the above situations are not exhibitions of glee, but are rather a part of the concept of face when used in response to a negative or unpleasant situation.

Guanxi (The Value of an Ongoing Relationship)

Guanxi is the word that describes the intricate, pervasive network of personal relations which every Chinese cultivates with energy, subtlety and imagination. Guanxi is the currency of getting things done and getting ahead in Chinese society. Guanxi is a relationship between 2 people containing implicit mutual obligation, assurances and intimacy, and is the perceived value of an ongoing relationship and its future possibilities that typically govern Chinese attitudes toward long-term business. If a relationship of trust and mutual benefit is developed, an excellent foundation will be built to future business with the Chinese. Guanxi ties are also helpful in dealing with the Chinese bureaucracy as personal interpretations are used in lieu of legal interpretations.

Due to cultural differences and language barriers, the visitors to China are not in a position to cultivate guanxi with the depth possible between 2 Chinese. Regardless, guanxi is an important aspect of interrelations in China and deserves attention so that good friendly relations may be developed. These connections are essential to get things accomplished.

Formal and Informal Relations

At present it is likely that the majority of social contacts foreigners have with the Chinese are on a more formal than informal level. Informality in China relates not to social pretension or artifice, but to the concept of face. Great attention is paid to observance of formal, or social behavior and corresponding norms. The social level is the level of form and proper etiquette where face is far more important than fact. It is considered both gauche and rude to allow one's personal feelings and opinions to surface here to the detriment of the social ambience. It is much more important to compliment a person or to avoid an embarrassing or sensitive subject than it is to express an honest opinion if honesty is at the expense of another's feelings. Directness, honesty, and individualism that run counter to social conventions and basic considerations of politeness have no place on the social level; emotions and private relationships tend to be kept private in Chinese society.

Chinese Etiquette for Social Functions

Ceremonies and rules of ceremony have traditionally held a place of great importance in Chinese culture. Confucianism perpetuated and strengthened these traditions by providing the public with an identity, mask, or persona with which a person is best equipped to deal with the world with a minimum of friction. Confucianism consists of broad rules of conduct evolved to aid and guide interpersonal relations. Confucius assembled all the details of etiquette practiced at the courts of the feudal lords during the period c. 551–479 B.C. These rules of etiquette are called the li and have long since become a complete way of life for the Chinese.

The li may appear overly formalistic to Westerners at first glance. Upon closer inspection it is apparent that the rules of etiquette play a very important role in regulating interpersonal relations. Some basic rules of behavior are as follows:

- A host should always escort a guest out to his car or other mode of transportation and watch until the guest is out of sight.
- Physical expression is minimal by Western standards. A handshake is polite, but back-slapping and other enthusiastic grasping is a source of embarrassment.
- At cultural functions and other performances, audience approval of performers is often subdued by American standards. Although the accepted manner of expressing approval varies between functions and age groups, applause is often polite, rather than roaring and bravo-like cheers.
- A person should keep control over his temper at all times.
- One should avoid blunt, direct, or abrupt discussion, particularly when the subject is awkward; delicate hints are often used to broach such a topic.
- It is a sign of respect to allow another to take the seat of honor (left of host), or to be asked to proceed through a door first.
- The serving of tea often signals the end of an interview or meeting. However, it is also served during extended meetings to quench the thirst of the negotiators.

S E V E N

CROSS-CULTURAL MOTIVATION

Foad Derakhshan, California State University
San Bernardino

Kamal Fatehi, Wichita State University

Chapter 7 examines motivation from a cross-cultural perspective. Like domestic companies, global companies rely on motivation as a source of energy to carry out their goals. Companies engaged in international business need to develop extra sensitivity to cultural variations in order to satisfy and motivate their employees. Major motivation theories and their validity from a cross-cultural standpoint are examined in this chapter. Furthermore, the success of the Japanese economy in recent years has been attributed to its unique management style. Whether what motivates Japanese workers will work in other cultures, including America, is a question worthy of investigation. According to some scholars, the removal of the Iron Curtain and major developments in communication technology have fostered a trend toward a global culture. These developments along with the influence of culture on motivation and their implications for international management are examined in this chapter.

Looking at the approaching lights from the commuter train window, Masayoshi Ito pondered about how he would break the news about his promotion to his wife Yoshiko and their five-year-old son. This morning Mr. Ogawa, his supervisor, called Masayoshi to his office and informed him of his promotion to the position of Associate Sales Director for the U.S. region. Masayoshi worked for the Tokyo Sun Coast, a member of a new chain of hotels, which catered primarily to business people and tourists from Asian countries. The persistent occupancy problem that plagued the industry had forced the management to consider extending its market to

American customers. Masayoshi felt very proud of his long-awaited promotion. After graduating from college, he started working in his present job, almost since their hotel had opened. Masayoshi's boss told him that his promotion included an increase in salary, allowances, and other fringe benefits.

Passing next to a Coca-Cola sign, he pondered about his last trip to Los Angeles. In recent years, Masayoshi had traveled to the United States several times and was fairly familiar with the American lifestyle. He remembered the relaxed atmosphere and the colorful scenery in California. He knew that in America people left work at five in the afternoon. This could never happen in his hotel. There were always things to finish and someone who needed help after the closing hour. In Tokyo everything looked gray and everyone was in a hurry. Masayoshi had heard that his pay was comparable, if not higher, to his American counterparts and his fringe benefits, including job security, were more impressive. But the cost of everything seemed to be higher in Tokyo. His family lived in a small two-bedroom apartment one and a half hours away from his work. The image of large houses in California with gardens flashed in his memory. With his promotion came additional responsibility, which meant spending even more time at work.

Masayoshi also remembered what he had heard from his American friend, Jack, about the drawbacks of living in Los Angeles. The crime rate was so high that some children carried guns to school, and some even used drugs. These could never happen in Japan. Living in

America could be very difficult for families with children, he thought. Masayoshi was very proud of their son. He was also proud of his new position and how important his work was in the company.

The train had come to a stop. Rushing out, he looked at his watch, and noticed it was 10 o'clock. Perhaps it was too late for his son to hear the news. Yoshiko would feel happy and proud of him after he told her the news.

Introduction

Masayoshi's case illustrates the complexity and diversity of employees' motivations. Factors surrounding Masayoshi's dilemma remind us of the effect that motivation has on job satisfaction as well as on overall life satisfaction. Masayoshi, though happy about his promotion, is very much concerned with the effect it will have on his family. For most Japanese, motivation, job satisfaction, and job performance are heavily influenced by group affiliation. In contrast, in the United States, a person's motivation and satisfaction are more independently and individually determined. An American bears the main responsibility for her or his job performance. Americans emphasize individualism, nonconformity, and competition, while Japanese promote cooperation and conformity. Japanese employees are under more pressure to conform and work long hours. Long hours and job stress create health-related problems. Recent increases in the rates of heart attacks and suicides among Japanese employees are attributed to increased job stress. There is even a word for the death from hard work and stress, *karoshi,* which means sudden death by a heart attack or stroke triggered by overwork. By some estimates, more than 10,000 Japanese fall victim annually to karoshi.[1] The international expansion of Japanese industries has created additional demands on some employees' time and energy. Job-related overseas travels have strained family relationships. Mass communication technology and especially, television, has also expanded the reference base a person uses to determine his or her satisfaction. For Masayoshi, the exposure to the American lifestyle has increased his expectations. This problem is not unique to Japan. Today, companies in England, France, Argentina, China, and many other parts of the world have to find new ways of motivating a new class of employees who would like to earn an American salary, live in an Italian villa, drive an expensive German car, and wear the latest European fashion.

Employees' Motivation

Motivation has long been a major concern for management due to its linkage to productivity, creativity, job turnover, absenteeism, etc. The word *motivation* comes from the Latin word *movere* meaning "to move."[2] Motivation is defined as the process through which behavior is mobilized to reach certain goals, which in turn satisfy individual and/or organizational needs. Motivation is the total of all forces within individuals that accounts for the effort he or she applies to the job at hand. Figure 7.1 shows the three main phases a person undergoes during the need-satisfaction process.

Although, in their daily activities, managers primarily focus on accomplishing business objectives and satisfying organizational needs, to accomplish this, they must also attend to their employees' need satisfaction. An effective motivation program utilizes the individual's needs to generate internal energy and to direct energized behavior toward achieving organizational and individual goals. The individual's satisfaction with the job, and ultimately with his or her life, plays an important role in sustaining the desired behavior and achieving the much needed

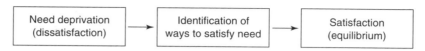

Figure 7.1   Need Satisfaction Process

predictability necessary for planning organizational activities.

Employee dissatisfaction can lead to absenteeism, poor quality products, accidents, family problems, and deterioration of mental health. Job satisfaction is a part of the overall satisfaction with life, and in turn is affected by it. Effective managers show concern for and closely monitor both employee job satisfaction and work performance. They are aware that job satisfaction can lead to a better working relationship with superiors, peers, and subordinates. A satisfied employee working in a less disruptive work environment should be a more productive worker. For most people of many cultures, work attributes are among the most important motivating factors. In a survey of more than 8,000 randomly selected employees from Belgium, Great Britain, West Germany, Israel, Japan, the Netherlands, and the United States, Harpaz found workers place much emphasis on interesting work. He found that the paramount work goal by a wide margin was "interesting work." For these workers "good pay" and "good interpersonal relations" were second and third in degree of importance.[3]

The Universality Assumption and Ethnocentrism

One major obstacle for effective motivation of employees in multinational companies is the "universality" assumption of the available motivation theories. These theories erroneously assume that human needs are universal. Therefore, people will respond similarly to a motivation program. Of course, the assumption that "one size fits all" is a faulty assumption. There are culturally based differences in people's needs and the ways to satisfy them. Unfortunately, because of the difficulties in understanding other cultures, and due perhaps to ethnocentric tendencies, many studies on motivation, either explicitly or implicitly, have ignored cultural differences. In fact, until recently most management literature paid little attention to the effect of culture on motivation.

Roots of the universality assumption can also be traced to stereotyping, oversimplified conceptions or beliefs about others, and ethnocentrism, the belief in the superiority of one's own ethnic group. When faced with an unfamiliar situation, we rely on stereotypes to simplify our perception of the environment. Stereotypes may be correct or incorrect. When confronted with an unfamiliar culture, people assume similarity with their own culture unless other stereotypes are present. Ethnocentrism leads to the belief that "our way is the best way of doing things." Ethnocentrism is an attitude found in almost any culture. Studies have found that people usually think of their country as disproportionately important in the world. In most countries, maps used in the classrooms usually illustrate that country as the center of the world. In Chinese writings, the character for China means the "center of the earth."[4]

Ethnocentrism often leads to prejudiced behavior. Many people of industrialized countries equate lack of industrialization with the lack of culture. Equally erroneous is the tendency to equate the materialism of industrial societies with spiritual corruption. As Kolde puts it:

A widely propounded fallacy in the advanced industrial countries holds that all nations evolve in a series of evolutionary steps in a unilinear path. The Americans, British, and French are likely to place their own respective countries at the pinnacle of this path, and look upon all other peoples' cultures as backward and inferior to theirs. Cultural maturity, thus, is rationalized to be a correlate of economic progress. The claim for cultural superiority by members of subindustrial societies, who regard the relatively greater reliance on materialistic considerations in industrial societies as evidence of moral and spiritual degeneration, is similarly irrational.[5]

Incorrect stereotypes and ethnocentric attitudes are often harmful. They can be changed, however, by training and exposure to other cultures. To be effective in motivating an international workforce, managers need to understand the influence of stereotyping and ethnocentrism, and multinational company (MNC) management development and educational programs should attempt to reduce ethnocentrism and harmful stereotyping.

Motivation and Culture

Human motivation is the product of the interaction between people and the physical and social environment. It is important to recognize, however, that most management literature on motivation is psychologically oriented and is based on psychological models developed and tested almost exclusively in the United States. While psychological models of motivation are very useful for the management of U.S. businesses, they are inadequate for international management. We all accept in principle that there are differences among people of different cultures. In studying human motivation, however, U.S.-based researchers have taken a simplistic view by ignoring cultural influences on people's behavior. To understand human motivation we need to understand not only the people themselves but their environment and their culture. More specifically, as D'Andrade puts it, "to understand why people do what they do, we have to understand the cultural constructs by which they interpret the world."[6]

Culture plays an important role in the formation of many of our needs, their relative importance, and the way we attempt to satisfy them. Except for the basic needs that have a biological basis, many human needs such as security, love, and esteem are learned through cultural influences. Through socialization with others, people learn acceptable ways of satisfying their needs. In other words, there are cultural norms for satisfying our needs, and we follow these norms in pursuit of need satisfaction.

The importance and priorities that people assign to their needs are also determined by their cultures. Americans place a particular importance on individual needs, such as personal comfort and self-actualization. In contrast, Japanese may sacrifice individual comfort to achieve social acceptance. Middle Easterners often sacrifice personal comfort, and even encounter financial hardship, to offer hospitality to their guests. Cultural values are the foundation of socially acquired needs, and define the acceptable methods of need satisfaction. Americans, for example, value individualism very much. Individualism is the foundation for many other American values. It is even expressed in the Declaration of Independence[7] that speaks of "life, liberty, and the pursuit of happiness." To the Americans, freedom of choice and expression are the basis for many individual needs and need satisfaction. Very few Americans, for example, would tolerate interference by others in their choice of a mate. By contrast, in many traditional families in India, China, and the Middle East, those decisions are made by parents, often with little or no consideration for an individual's opinion. Often, the respect for older parents inhibits the children from even expressing their opposition.

In Chapter 5 we learned that culture influences people's perceptions of time and space, as well as attitudes toward work and authority. In turn, the perception of time, space, and the attitudes toward work and authority influence people's motivation. Even among subcultures—various groups of the same culture—these differences are noticeable. Nord, for example, identified age, rural versus urban background, ethnicity and sex as important factors that influence individual behavior in work organizations.[8] Research in the United Sates has found that younger employees are more motivated by money, while for older employees job security and fringe benefits are more important. In a comparative study of attitudes toward work in China and Taiwan, Derakhshan and Khan found a generation gap, in both cultures, between younger and older workers that influenced their work attitudes. There was also a difference between the attitudes of the two samples, with the Taiwanese sample reflecting attitudes closer to Western values.[9]

In a case study, Whyte and Braun identified a group of patterns in socialization and education that appear in less developed economies. Autocratic teachers, glorification of military heroes, and disrespect for businesspersons were among the factors that led to the lack of independence training and, therefore, the lack of motivation.[10] However, in a study of similarities among 14 countries, Haire, Ghiselli, and Porter discovered that countries cluster along ethnic rather than industrial lines.[11] Black and Porter studied managerial behaviors and job performance of U.S., Hong Kong Chinese, and American expatriates in Hong Kong. They found that those managerial behaviors that were significantly related to job performance in the United States did not seem to be relevant to job performance in Hong Kong.[12] The effect of culture on behavior is complex and cannot be discounted.

Cultural Influences on Motivation

Organizational performance is a function of employees' work contributions to organizational goals. The efforts exerted by employees at work are influenced by their motivation. A motivated worker is a more productive worker. If we consider motivation a psychological state that compels a person to expend a certain amount of effort in accomplishing a job, we are dealing with two main concepts. The two concepts that are central to the understanding of motivation are

"work" and the person, or "self." In studying cross-cultural motivation, care should be exercised not to assume that these concepts have universal meanings. There is a growing body of research that indicates people of different cultures have different views about these two concepts. The perception of "self" is a product of cultural upbringing, so is the meaning of work.

Cultural Definition of Work

Throughout the history of Western civilization, work has been regarded variously as drudgery, a necessary evil, an obligation, a duty, and a way to salvation. To engage in physical work has been considered undignified and demeaning in one extreme, and honorable, glorified, and exemplifying piety on the other extreme. According to Max Weber, a contributing factor to the emergence of modern capitalism, characterized by large organizations, was the value and importance that the Protestant religion accorded to work and the accumulation of wealth. "Perhaps because of our Puritan work ethic and the basic belief in cause and effect, we take pride in our work; we conduct business at social functions and we take work home with us. . . . Work gives us identity; we often define ourselves and others by what we do; elsewhere identity often stems from religion, family and village."[13] Thus, personal introductions vary among Americans and the Japanese. In the United States individuals will typically talk about *what* they do, the content of their work: i.e., "I'm a doctor" or "I'm a machinist." In contrast, in Japan, people identify themselves by a reference to their employer such as "Morio of Mitsubishi" or "Tanaka of Toyota."

Regardless of the kind of work in which a person is engaged, Americans expect the person to be willing to do whatever it takes to do the job. A common expression indicating such an attitude is that "we must be willing to get our hands dirty." Of course, the positive attitudes that many Americans have toward work is not universal. To some cultures, a negative meaning of work is more pervasive. In some South American cultures, involvement in physical work is regarded as demeaning and beneath a well-respected person. Various kinds of work are considered low or high status. In extreme cases, college-educated people will not concern themselves with the problems on the shop floor. They consider that type of work degrading. Their college degree should raise them above such low status jobs.[14] The same is true in some Middle Eastern countries. Even in Australia, as we learned in Chapter 5, people admire "bludgers," those who appear to work hard but actually do very little.[15]

People work for many reasons. The first reason that immediately comes to mind is the instrumentality of work, a term which means that to live a comfortable and dignified life, most of us need to work. Therefore, work is an important vehicle for obtaining what we need for our living. To have a comfortable life, we are motivated to work. Taking only this meaning of work into account, organizations devise a variety of techniques, such as pay and fringe benefits, for motivating their employees.

However, work has other meanings. In addition to being a necessity, work can be an attractive activity in and of itself. It may also provide people with an opportunity to socialize and interact with others, and to satisfy their gregariousness. Many people will continue to work even if they are financially secure. It is the interesting activity itself that draws them to work. For others, work is a very important aspect of their life. Without work they feel something is missing in their lives. It assumes a very central position in their lives. We have learned that the centrality of work (its importance) in people's lives varies from culture to culture. In a seven-country study of the meaning of work, for example, researchers found a wide range of work centrality among the countries studied. They

Americans' Faith in Hard Work

William H. Newman has suggested that anyone contemplating a transfer of U.S. management practices to other cultures should understand the premises of these practices. The American faith in rewards for persistent hard work and the value of hard work, for example, is not a universal belief.

Both our lore and our experience underscore the necessity for hard work if objectives are to be achieved. Even among those who do not accept the Puritan ethic that hard work is a virtue in itself, there is a strong belief that persistent, purposeful effort is necessary to achieve high goals. Hard work is not considered to be the only requisite for success; wisdom and luck are also needed. Nevertheless, the feeling is that without hard work a person is neither likely to achieve, nor justified in expecting to achieve, his objectives.

This belief in the efficacy of hard work is by no means worldwide. Sometimes a fatalistic viewpoint makes hard work seem futile. In other instances, it is more important to curry the favor of the right man; and in still other situations, hard work is considered unmanly.

Source: William H. Newman. "Cultural Assumption Underlying U.S. Management Concepts." In J. L. Massie, J. Luytjes, and N. W. Hazen, eds. *Management in an International Context* (New York: Harper and Row, 1972), 347.

found work centrality to be highest for Japan and lowest for the United Kingdom. The sequence of rank ordering was Japan, Yugoslavia, Israel, United States, Belgium, Netherlands, Germany, and the United Kingdom.[16] Jyuji Misumi's research has confirmed that the Japanese consider work highly important in their lives. Among the four countries, Misumi found that work importance was highest among the Japanese, followed by Americans, Germans, and Belgians.[17]

The cultural differences in the meaning of work have practical implications for international managers. Variations in the meaning that the people of different cultures attach to work requires the application of differentiated motivational programs. To motivate those who consider physical work undignified, for example, we may have to rely more on the monetary outcomes of the work. For others, making the work more interesting or socially rewarding may be a better choice.

Although there are cultural differences in the meaning of work, cross-cultural research also suggests that there is substantial commonality among cultures about certain facts of work. Among the major features of work that people of many cultures agree about are "good pay" and "interesting work."[18] The implication for international management is that if pay is good and if the jobs are interesting, managers will have an easier time motivating people of diverse cultural backgrounds.

Cultural Definition of Self

Many consider individualism as the most salient feature of the American culture. Individualism is a value to which other American ideals, such as equality and objectivity in treating people based on their own merits, and not on their social standing or political connections, are anchored. Describing Americans as individualistic does not fully explain cultural differences between the Americans and people of the other nations. Individualism only tells us about the so-

cietal and external view of an "individual," the view that the society holds in regard to a person and his or her relationship with the other members of the society. To fully comprehend the difference between Americans and the people of other cultures, we need to explore the concept of "individualism" from the personal aspect of "self."

The concept of "self" has many facets. Westerners view the individual as a self-contained, autonomous, and independent entity. Based on this understanding, the individual comprises a unique configuration of attributes such as traits, abilities, motives, and values. These attributes are the basis for the individual's behavior.[19] Three major facets of self are *physiological-ecological*,[20] *inner-private*, and *public-relational*.[21] We assume that people everywhere are likely to develop an understanding of themselves as physically distinct and separate from others. This is the ecological self; the self that is referred to as "I." The inner-private self is the sense of awareness that each person has about internal aspects such as dreams, feelings, and the continuous flow of thoughts, which are private and cannot be directly known by others. Some aspects of the inner-private self are probably universal, but many other aspects of the self may be culturally determined. As we relate to others, we develop an understanding of the public-relational self that is defined by social relationships.

People of different cultures see the public-relational self as either *separate and independent* from others, or as *connected and interdependent* with others. Many Westerners, including Americans, believe in inherent separateness of distinct persons. It is the norm, and people are expected to become independent from others, and discover and express their unique attributes. Markus and Kitayama describe the attempt at developing such a self as follows:

> Achieving the cultural goal of independence requires constructing oneself as an individual

whose behavior is organized and made meaningful primarily by reference to one's own internal repertoire of thoughts, feeling, and action, rather than by reference to the thoughts, feelings, and actions of others. . . . This view of the self derives from a belief in the wholeness and uniqueness of each person's configuration of internal attributes.[22]

The independent view of the self gives rise to concepts such as "self-actualization," "self-esteem," "realizing one's potentials," "being true to the self," and many other expressions describing and canonizing self and self-centered activities and concepts.

In contrast to the Western view, many Eastern cultures have maintained an interdependent view of self. These cultures believe in the fundamental connectedness of humans to each other. While the American common expressions of independent self could be "stand up and be counted" and "do your own thing," the Japanese saying that "the nail that stands up gets hammered down" represents the concept of interdependent self. To experience "interdependent self" requires "seeing oneself as part of an encompassing social relationship and recognizing that one's behavior is determined, contingent on, and, to a large extent organized by what the actor perceives to be the thoughts, feelings, and actions of *others* in the relationship."[23] An interdependent self is not separate from the social context. It is more connected to and less differentiated from others. Such a connectedness motivates people to fit and to become a part of the social context and to fulfill the obligation of belongingness with relevant others.

The internal attributes of an interdependent self are less fixed and concrete and more situation specific, and are sometimes elusive and unreliable. In such a case, the attitudes will not directly regulate overt behavior, especially if the behavior implicates significant others. In many social contexts, the interdependent self must constantly control and regulate his or her opinion, abilities, and characteristics to come to terms with the primary task of interdependence. In an interdependent, collectivist culture, an independent behavior, such as expressing an opinion, is likely to be influenced and somewhat determined by the forces of interdependence. Such behavior has a different significance than the one exhibited by an independent self in an independent culture.[24] The contrast between the external source of what Westerners consider inner attributes, such as conscience, and an external source of such attributes for the Japanese is described by Dore[25]:

> The Christian who believes that his conscience is the voice of God within him feels that it is a duty to God to obey its dictates and that he has sinned in the sight of the Lord if he fails to do so. The Japanese who conceives of the voice of his conscience as the voice of his parents and teachers feels it to be a duty towards them to obey it, and if he fails to do so it is they whom he has let down. Even after their death his feelings of guilt may take the form of imagining how displeased these honored parents and teachers would be. . . .

Parsons, Shils, and Olds have suggested that self-orientation (independent self) versus collectivity orientation is an important variable that determines human action. Giving priority to one's own "private interests, independently of their bearings on the interests or values of a given collectivity" is self-orientation. Taking into account the values and interests of collectivity before any action is collectivity orientation.[26]

Interdependent cultures assume that a person is mostly defined by situations and by the presence of others. Therefore, a person is inseparable from the situations of others. This interconnectedness, for example, is the basis for the Chinese culture's emphasis on synthesizing the constituent parts of any situation or problem into a harmonious whole. The Japanese *jibun*, for self, more accurately describes "one's share of the shared life space."[27] For the Japanese, according to Hamaguchi,[28] "a sense of identification with others (sometimes including conflict) pre-exists and selfness is confirmed only through interpersonal relationships. . . . Selfness is not constant like the ego but denotes a fluid concept which changes through time and situation according to interpersonal relationships."

In contrast to independent cultures, in interdependent cultures the relationships are often valued for and by themselves, not as a means of achieving personal objectives. People are constantly aware of the others and will try to account for the others' goals and desires in the pursuit of their personal goals. A reciprocity arrangement exists within which people passively monitor their contributions to others' goals and vice versa. The importance of others to one's life and the resultant relationships and social obligations are limited to persons of "in-groups," such as family members or members of social or work groups. The following excerpt from Dore illuminates the issue:

. . . . the individual surrenders a part of himself not to a group of which he is a member,

but to particular individuals whose leadership he accepts, with whose fortunes he identifies himself, on whose help he depends for securing his own advancement or happiness, on whose goodwill he depends for his emotional security, and whose approval he depends for his self-respect.[29]

A summary of the key differences between the independent and interdependent selfs is presented in Table 7.1. The two different concepts of "self" have various implications for motivation. An independent self takes pride in his or her own attributes and accomplishments. In contrast an interdependent self may be motivated to avoid such a selfish expression. Instead, the overt expression of pride may often be directed at a collective of which the self is a part.[30] The following is an example of how Japanese feel proud of the accomplishments of their superiors, and how every member of the group experiences a shared pride in those accomplishments:

In a Tokyo office, (a company employee) let me witness a gesture of devotion to his office

Table 7.1
Summary of Key Differences Between an Independent and an Interdependent Concept of Self

Feature Compared	Independent	Interdependent
Definition	Separate from social context	Connected with social context
Structure	Bounded, unitary, stable	Flexible, variable
Important features	Internal, private (abilities, thoughts, feelings)	External, public (statuses, roles, relationships)
Tasks	Be unique	Belong, fit-in
	Express self	Occupy one's proper place
	Realize internal attributes	Engage in appropriate action
	Promote own goals	Promote others' goals
	Be direct; "say what's on your mind"	Be indirect; "read other's mind"
Role of others	*Self-evaluation:* others important for social comparison, reflected appraisal	*Self-definition:* relationships with others in specific contexts define the self
Basis of self-esteem*	Ability to express self, validate internal attributes	Ability to adjust, restrain self, maintain harmony with social context

*Esteeming the self may be primarily a Western phenomenon, and the concept of self-esteem should perhaps be replaced by self-satisfaction, or by a term that reflects the realization that one is fulfilling the culturally mandated task.

Source: H. R. Markus and S. Kitayama. "Culture and Self: Implications for Cognition, Emotion, and Motivation." *Psychological Review,* 98 (1991), 230. Copyright 1991 by the American Psychological Association. Reprinted by permission.

superior which I had never experienced in the Western world. We were at the end of an interview in his office which, being that of a lower-middle ranking officer, was small and sparsely furnished. But the size and nature of his office were never part of our conversation. As I was preparing to take my leave, he said, "Let me show you the office of my Section Chief." He took me to an office three times as big as his, very well furnished, pointed to the empty chair behind the big desk ornamented with lots of bric-a-brac and proudly said: "This is the desk of my Section Chief."[31]

According to most Western theories, motivation is more a personal phenomenon and others indirectly influence the process as a means of contributing to individual goal accomplishments. The concept of an interdependent self implies a more fundamental and vital role for significant others in shaping and directing the behavior of a person. In the preceding discussion we have implied that in interdependent cultures most of the individual motives are shaped by the group. Therefore, there are a number of motives that have more relevance to an interdependent self than to an independent self. Murray[32] presented a list of such motives including affiliation; avoidance of blame; similance, the need to imitate others; deference, the need to willingly follow superiors and those we admire; nurturance, the need to nurture, protect, and aid another; abasement, acceptance of self-deprecation; and succorance, the need to seek aid, sympathy, and dependence. Since, for an interdependent self, it is imperative to socially integrate, seek harmony with others, and immerse the "self" in the collectivist whole, then all of these needs would be more relevant and even desirable to the interdependent self.[33] For interdependent Chinese, for example, the achievement need has a different meaning that is more socially oriented. For them, achievement is to meet the expectations of others who are important and close to the individual.[34]

Cognitive consistency has also been considered as a motivating force. Individuals seek to establish consistency in their cognitions. Cognitive inconsistency creates dissonance,[35] an unpleasant anxiety producing a psychological state that motivates the individual to take action. An example of cognitive inconsistency is the case of a person who smokes cigarettes and believes that smoking is detrimental to his or her health. In this example, the individual can pursue a number of alternatives to eliminate the dissonance. An interdependent self whose internal attributes are more flexible is less likely to quit smoking as long as his or her reference group smokes. For this individual, the confirmation for self-harm comes from the group. When the private feelings of interdependent persons are regulated in accordance with the situational requirements, there is less room for experiencing inconsistency and dissonance.

Major Motivation Theories

Motivation theories are classified into two groups: content theories and process theories. Content theories explore what motivates people; i.e., arouses and energizes the behavior. The most famous content theories are Maslow's need hierarchy, Herzberg's two-factor theory, and McClelland's three-factor theory. Process theories research the specifics of the motivation process. Vroom's expectancy theory and Adam's equity theory are well-known process theories.

Content Theories of Motivation

All of the well-known motivation theories just mentioned have been developed by American theorists, and historically research on the theories has involved only U.S. subjects. More recently, some international research on content theories has been conducted. However, cross-cultural studies on the process theories remain rare due to the complex nature of this type of research. In the following we briefly discuss major content theories and elaborate on their relevance to international management.

Hierarchy of needs The cornerstone of most content theories is Abraham Maslow's concept of hierarchy of needs.[36] Maslow identified five categories of human needs, which follow a hierarchical order of importance and satisfaction. In this hierarchy, the lowest needs have to be reasonably satisfied before the next level of needs is activated. Ranging from the lowest to the highest, these need categories are physiological, security, social (affection), esteem (self-esteem and esteem of others), and self-actualization. Two principles form the foundation of this theory. The *deficit principle* states that a deprived need is a motivating force. People attempt to satisfy the lower and unfulfilled need on the hierarchy. According to the *progression principle*, people seek the satisfaction of their needs in a progression from the lower levels to the higher levels. Each level of need is activated only after the preceding lower level need has sufficiently been satisfied. Figure 7.2 depicts this hierarchical relationship among groups of needs.

The suggestion that these needs might have an instinctive origin led to a universality assumption in later interpretations of Maslow's theory. Maslow himself cautioned against overgeneralization due to a number of exceptions he had noted to hierarchical satisfaction. As we see in the next part, Herzberg and many management scholars believe that in the American cul-

ture, the true motivator is the need for achievement and its satisfaction is relatively independent of the lower level needs. Hofstede has suggested that although achievement may be a strong motivator in some cultures, in countries with a low tolerance for uncertainty, security is more important than self-actualization. He argued that the word *achievement* does not even translate into many other languages. In his presentation of four dimensions of culture—power distance, uncertainty avoidance, individualism, and masculinity/femininity—he elaborated on the relevance of Maslow's motivation theory to various cultures. He mapped the management attributes of 40 countries on the two dimensions of uncertainty avoidance and masculinity/femininity. Figure 7.3 shows the resulting four quadrants and country clusters. Using country clusters along these dimensions, Hofstede questioned the applicability of North American motivation theories, including McClelland's (discussed later) and Maslow's. Hofstede asserted[37]:

> The consequence of country differences along these two dimensions is that management conceptions about the motivation of employees, common in North America, do not necessarily apply abroad. . . . [For example] the countries in which McClelland's nAch [Achievement need] is strong are characterized by weak uncertainty avoidance [personal risk-taking] and strong masculinity. McClelland's nAch may represent one particular combination of cultural choices.
>   . . . the ordering of needs in Maslow's hierarchy represents a value choice—Maslow's value choice. This choice was based on his mid-twentieth-century U.S. middle-class values. First Maslow's hierarchy reflects individualistic values, putting self-actualization and autonomy on top. Values prevalent in collectivist cultures, such as "harmony" or "family support," do not even appear in the hierarchy. Second, the cultural map suggests even if just the needs Maslow used in his hierarchy are considered—the needs will have to be ordered differently in different cultural areas.

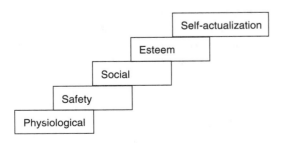

Figure 7.2   Maslow's Hierarchy of Needs

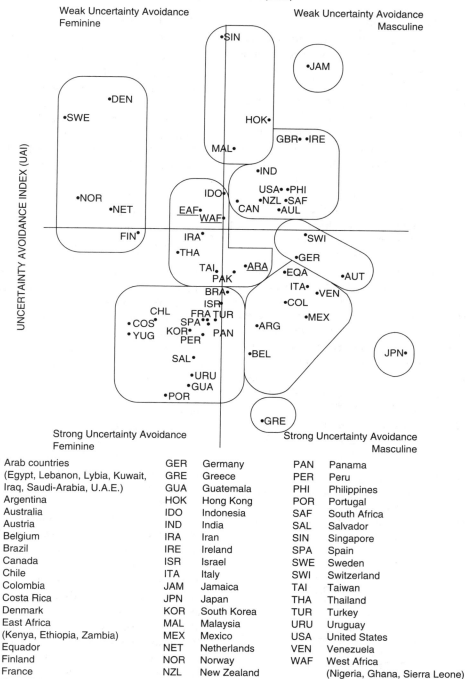

Figure 7.3 Country Clusters

ARA	Arab countries (Egypt, Lebanon, Lybia, Kuwait, Iraq, Saudi-Arabia, U.A.E.)	GER	Germany	PAN	Panama
		GRE	Greece	PER	Peru
		GUA	Guatemala	PHI	Philippines
ARG	Argentina	HOK	Hong Kong	POR	Portugal
AUL	Australia	IDO	Indonesia	SAF	South Africa
AUT	Austria	IND	India	SAL	Salvador
BEL	Belgium	IRA	Iran	SIN	Singapore
BRA	Brazil	IRE	Ireland	SPA	Spain
CAN	Canada	ISR	Israel	SWE	Sweden
CHL	Chile	ITA	Italy	SWI	Switzerland
COL	Colombia	JAM	Jamaica	TAI	Taiwan
COS	Costa Rica	JPN	Japan	THA	Thailand
DEN	Denmark	KOR	South Korea	TUR	Turkey
EAF	East Africa (Kenya, Ethiopia, Zambia)	MAL	Malaysia	URU	Uruguay
		MEX	Mexico	USA	United States
EQA	Equador	NET	Netherlands	VEN	Venezuela
FIN	Finland	NOR	Norway	WAF	West Africa (Nigeria, Ghana, Sierra Leone)
FRA	France	NZL	New Zealand		
GBR	Great Britain	PAK	Pakistan	YUG	Yugoslavia

Source: G. Hofstede. *"The Cultural Relativity of Quality of Life Concept." Academy of Management Review, 9, no. 4 (1984).* *Reprinted with permission.*

Most of the interpretations of the need hierarchy theory are made within the individualistic framework of Western cultures, which overemphasize needs such as self-esteem and self-actualization. Redding suggested that it is questionable to apply Western "ego-centered paradigms" that focus on individual needs to other cultures that emphasize relationships.[38] Similarly, Nevis,[39] in a comparison of Chinese and American cultures, suggested that the society, rather than the individual, determines the four-level hierarchy of needs for Chinese. Ranging from the lowest to the highest, these needs are belonging, physiological, safety, and self-actualization in the service of society. As depicted in Figure 7.4, there are three major differences between Maslow's hierarchy and the Chinese need hierarchy as suggested by Nevis. First, belonging (social) need has replaced physiological need as the most basic need. Second, self-esteem is not included in the hierarchy. Self-esteem, Nevis proposed, as a driving force makes sense for cultures that emphasize individualism. It is not a necessary, universal requirement that could be found in all cultures. In particular, as F. L. K. Hsu[40] has pointed out, in the collectivist Chinese culture, the concept of "self" is quite different from that of the Western concept:

> . . . the Chinese use a concept of "jen" (man), which is defined as the person plus the salient, intimate societal and cultural environment that makes her or his life meaningful. This implies much less differentiation in the self-concept of individuals and stresses identity as a *social* phenomenon.[41]

Third, although self-esteem is considered unimportant, self-actualization is still present. In China, self-actualization is defined as moral imperative and social confluence: "My country needs me to be the best. . . ."[42] Therefore, it becomes a duty for the individual Chinese to fully develop the "self." Failure at self-development could bring severe shame and loss of face. For Chinese, achieving the goal of the extended family is more motivating than trying for individualized self-fulfillment.[43]

In many cultures social needs are much more prominent. It is not uncommon to mix business dealings with a heavy dose of socializing. The vignette on "Yugoslavian Lunch" provides a glimpse of the importance of social needs among Yugoslavians.

Within a given culture, ethnic and individual differences also complicate the applicability of Maslow's theory. To remedy this problem, Hofstede has suggested using work-related culture, and job levels and categories, to map need satisfaction hierarchies. Based on his study, he recommends using physical rewards for lower level employees, while using challenge, autonomy, and cooperation as motivators for middle and upper managers.[44] Cross-cultural studies have found managers and professionals are more responsive to higher order needs in Maslow's hierarchy.[45]

Although there is some support for the universality of a need hierarchy, support is inconclusive. In an early study of 14 countries, mainly industrial and European, Haire, Ghiselli, and Porter found some support for Maslow's theory.[46] Later, in a study of eight countries selected from different parts of the world, Reitz also found some support for the order of satisfaction as suggested by Maslow.[47] The failure to support a universal hierarchy of needs in other research has led critics to argue that the theory may only be good for European, and more specifically Anglo, cultures. They argue that in

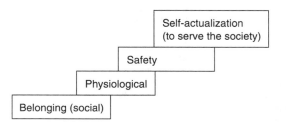

Figure 7.4 Chinese Need Hierarchy

Yugoslavian Lunch

When Mark arrived to pick up his company client for lunch, he was surprised to find out that the Yugoslavian manager had invited four other people to accompany them. Mark was on a hastily arranged visit to work out the final details on a sales agreement with a client in Zagreb. While driving to the restaurant in a crowded car, he discovered that none of these four had anything to do with the negotiations. They had dropped by the manager's office right before Mark got there, and his Yugoslavian partner had invited them to come along.

When they finally arrived at the small cafe in the outskirts of the city, Mark quickly ordered his food and took out his papers to start working on the contract. He was soon frustrated by the slow progress due to the little attention his partner paid to the work at hand. Instead he was making jokes and telling stories. Mark could not understand how the manager could be so relaxed when they were negotiating such an important deal. He decided to postpone discussing business to after lunch. After lunch, Mark and his counterpart went over the list and completed the details. Then, the manager ordered a bottle of wine to toast. There were more stories and more wine was ordered. The lunch meeting took four hours. Going back to his hotel, Mark felt tired and in need of a nap. Next time, he shouldn't drink so much wine, he thought.

supporting studies, the research samples were mainly taken from these cultures.

Some studies have shown that there may be a consistent rank ordering of needs in each culture, however. In his study of clusters of needs in several countries, Ronen concluded that there is a support for Maslow's contention that groups of needs appear in a sequence rather than simultaneously.[48] Adler suggested a similar support for the existence of a need hierarchy in developing countries, but one which emphasizes security and self-esteem needs.[49] Recently, other writers have used the two clusters of developing and developed countries to study motivation. They suggest that while higher order needs (like achievement) are more valued in developed countries, lower order needs (security and affiliation) are more important in developing na-

Andean Preference

When a rich vein of ore was found in the Andes, Americans rushed in to develop the mining. But it was hard to get workers. Although the Americans offered all kinds of perquisites—good meals, hot water, housing, movies, and so on—the workers flocked to the French, who seemed to offer them nothing. The workers for the French lived in the roughest housing, had no movies, none of the comforts offered by the Americans. Baffled, the U.S. company sent in a stream of senior executives and conducted a series of studies, and eventually figured out what was happening. The French offered no perks but paid workers by the hour. The people of the Andes cared more about their time off; it was important for them to be able to come and go without question. When the Americans switched to an hourly basis they were able to lure the workers.

Source: T. F. O'Boyle. "Bridgestone Discovers Purchase of U.S. Firm Creates Big Problems." *The Wall Street Journal* (April 1, 1991), 1.

tions. Some have gone as far as to suggest that this difference is responsible for differences in economic prosperity (see the discussion later on the McClelland theory.) Grouping of countries into two such large categories may signal a recurrence of the universality assumption, however.

Finally, according to Maslow lower level needs have to be "reasonably satisfied" before the higher level is activated. While the idea of "reasonable satisfaction" and how it is comprised has been the subject of virtually no study to date, it seems logical to expect that what composes a reasonable level of satisfaction varies across cultures as well.

Motivators and hygiene factors Herzberg identified two groups of factors, hygienes and motivators, that influence individual performance in work organizations.[50] Hygiene factors could only create discomfort if they were not met but have no effect on motivation. These factors are external to the job (extrinsic) and include technical supervision, working conditions, pay, relations with peers, etc. Hygiene factors correspond to the lower level needs in Maslow's hierarchy. Motivators include job-related (intrinsic) factors such as the work it-

self, achievement, responsibility, and recognition. Motivators corresponded mainly to the highest needs in Maslow's hierarchy. We can portray this theory as a simplified, two-level version of Maslow's need hierarchy as depicted in Figure 7.5.

One major criticism of this theory is that it addresses satisfaction instead of motivation. Herzberg assumes that those things that satisfy employees will motivate them—not necessarily a correct assumption as many managers have learned through hard experience. A second criticism is that it treats pay as only a hygiene factor and ignores the effects of pay on motivation. Moreover, Herzberg emphasizes achievement as a strong motivator; therefore, the problems associated with its cross-cultural validity as previously discussed, become shortcomings of this theory. (See also the discussion of this issue with McClelland's theory.) Additionally, studies have found little evidence in support of a universal list of hygiene factors or motivators. In a study in the Panama Canal zone, Crabbs found that some hygiene factors satisfied employees.[51] Hines tested the theory in New Zealand and found that interpersonal relationships and supervision, both considered hygiene factors by

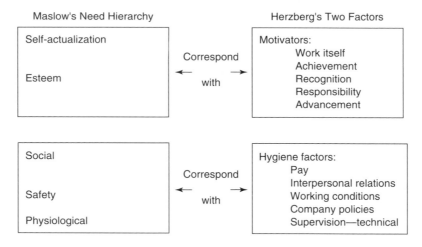

Figure 7.5 The Correspondence Between Herzberg's Two Factors and Maslow's Need Hierarchy

Herzberg, contributed to employee satisfaction.[52]

Research findings from several countries, including New Zealand,[53] Israel,[54] Zambia,[55] and the United Kingdom,[56] suggest that although there may be a clustering of two distinct groups of factors with functions similar to what Herzberg suggests (hygiene and motivators), their components vary across cultures. Interestingly, this conclusion is similar to the idea expressed when discussing Maslow's theory.

McClelland's three motives This theory identifies three important individual drives (needs): achievement, power, and affiliation. McClelland[57] suggested that the need for achievement was the most important factor leading to economic success. At the national level, the aggregate level of this need was related to the rate of economic development, he proposed. Achievement-oriented individuals seek responsibility and concrete feedback, take moderate risks, and are loners. In contrast to Maslow and Herzberg, and of interest from the perspective of this text, McClelland believed that the need for achievement, and related attributes, could be taught and in fact that the culture played an important role in socializing individuals toward the motives.[58]

Cross-cultural studies of McClelland's theory have produced conflicting results. Early support for this theory came from a study by McClelland in which he trained a group of entrepreneurs in India and later measured their achievement in terms of increased profits, starting new businesses, and investigating new products. He reported that as a result of his training, the rate of achievement-oriented activities among this group almost doubled.[59] Note, however, that a number of researchers since that time have questioned McClelland's findings. Bhagat and McQuaid have cited a number of studies in both developed and developing countries supporting this theory.[60] Hofstede found a positive correlation between the need for achievement and the need to produce and willingness to accept risk. On the opposite side, many studies have not found a link between this need and the rate of economic growth. For instance, Iwawaki and Lynn found similar levels of need for achievement between their Japanese and English samples despite a higher rate of economic growth for Japan.[61] Two studies found unusually low levels of this need among Chinese and Czechoslovakian managers inconsistent with the level of economic growth.[62]

While McClelland's idea does permit cross-cultural theorizing, it assumes only one path to economic development manifested through high need achievement, which is characteristic of Western individualistic societies. Recent economic progress in some Asian countries indicates the existence of alternative paths. Moreover, the lack of a common definition for "achievement" restricts research on McClelland's theory. While achievement is measured in financial terms in the American culture, in Japan, it is determined by other factors, such as affiliation. As stated earlier, some argue that the word *achievement* does not even translate to some languages. Moreover, Bond's summary of several studies leads to a conclusion that, for Chinese, achievement need is socially defined, with the ultimate goal of meeting expectations of in-group members.[63]

The implications of the conflicting findings are clear. Many training and organization development programs exported to other countries to boost employees' achievement needs prove useless. In a study in India, McClelland and Winter reported that their achievement training program had little effect.[64] A follow-up study revealed that the program had instead increased the participants' need for status, which is highly important in that culture.[65] For a program to be successful, it should be designed for the importing culture. Moreover, the link between the increase in need for achievement and performance has to be established in that environment. Furthermore, characteristics that are culturally conditioned as *early* in a person's life as these motives are probably cannot be changed in a brief training course.

Process Theories of Motivation

As noted earlier, limited cross-cultural research on the context (process) theories has been done and most of the research that has been done is U.S. based. The following section briefly examines two context theories and their applicability to cross-cultural management.

Expectancy theory   Mostly associated with the works of Victor H. Vroom, this theory proposes that motivation is a deliberate and conscious choice to engage in a certain activity for achieving a certain outcome or reward (see Figure 7.6). The logic of expectancy theory has prompted some to call it the thinking person's motivation theory.[66] Mathematically expressed, motivation (*M*) is the product of three variables:

1. *Valence (V):* The *value* (attractiveness) of the *potential reward* or outcome to the individual. Potential outcome includes pay, job security, fringe benefits, job satisfaction, companionship, and the opportunity to demonstrate and apply talent and skills. In short anything that a person can get from the job is a potential reward.
2. *Instrumentality (I):* The *performance-reward* link, which is the expectation that performance will lead to receiving the reward. Past experience forms a foundation for this linkage.
3. *Expectancy (E):* The linkage between the *effort* and *performance,* which deals with the belief by the individual that exerting a certain amount of effort will lead to accomplishing the task: $M = V \times I \times E$. The multiplicative nature of the relationship indicates that if any of the three variables is zero, motivation will be zero.

The expectancy theory has an appeal for researchers because it expresses the motivation process as a simple mathematical relationship among three possibly measurable variables. Furthermore, its logical nature makes it appealing for those who look for a universal theory to explain motivation independent of cultural differences.

Cross-cultural research on the expectancy theory involves answering two questions. First, does the multiplicative relationship between the three determining variables ($V \times I \times E$) hold for various cultures? Second, what effect does a given culture have on these variables?

Cross-cultural studies that attempted to test the validity of the relationships among various variables of the expectancy theory are rare. We can cite only one reported case, a study by Eden,

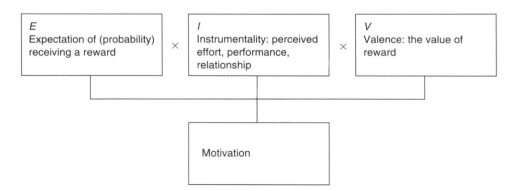

Figure 7.6   Expectancy Theory

which provides supports for the first question. Eden analyzed data collected from 375 male members of an Israeli kibbutz in regard to the relationship among intrinsic, status, and material rewards and motives. He concluded that the effect of externally mediated rewards on intrinsic motivation was explained on the basis of the expectancy theory.[67] To answer the second question, we need to examine variables individually for cultural effects. Valence, the value of the reward, varies across different cultures. In collectivist societies, social groups play an important role in determining the value of reward and the expectation of achieving it. It should not be surprising if, in such societies, people prefer spending more time with family and friends over an increase in pay. In those societies, work is not the central point in life, and employees usually prefer to spend more time on family and social activities. Using Adler's terms: "Expectancy theories are universal to the extent that they do not specify the type of reward that motivates a group of workers."[68] Instrumentality and expectancy are based on the individual's evaluation of his or her abilities, past experiences with supervisors and the organization, and the belief about what role he or she can play in determining his or her destiny. While Protestant cultures promote the belief that an individual is in charge of his or her destiny, Catholic and Moslem cultures encourage submission to the will of God. The belief that an individual does not have much control over his or

her life should lead to lower expectancy scores in these cultures. In Hindu and Buddhist cultures, the emphasis on social relationships and harmony, instead of materialism and competition, is probably the reason for the lower value of individual achievement and the belief in luck.

Equity theory   According to Adams, the individual's perception of inequity is a motivating force.[69] More specifically, a person compares the ratio of his or her compensation—what they get from the job (outcomes)—to his or her contributions to the job (input) with that of others in a similar situation. Compensation comes in many different forms including pay, job security, opportunity for advancement and promotion, good working relationships, and a safe and pleasant work environment. Inequity in either direction generates tension. People, however, are usually more sensitive to a lower ratio (underreward). They respond to the perception of inequity in many different ways. These responses include filing complaints, working less, or even changing their perceptions to reestablish the equity. Figure 7.7 illustrates this process.

Culture influences our perception of the value of the job outcomes as well as our contributions to the organization. Culture also provides the frame of reference for comparison of ratios. The sensitivity of people to inequity, and the avenues which they may pursue to remedy the problem, is also influenced by culture. For instance, if a less qualified peer receives a pay raise, a Japanese employee is more likely to

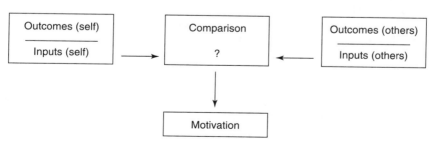

Figure 7.7   Equity Theory

reevaluate his or her perception of his or her outcome/input ratio compared to that of peers (refer to our discussion on "Cultural Definition of Self" in previous pages). Conformity to group and organizational norms would inhibit more severe actions. In a similar situation, an American employee would be more willing to file a formal complaint or even leave the organization.

In their research in an Israeli kibbutz, Yuchtman and Seachore found support for the equity theory.[70] More research is needed, however, to establish its cross-cultural validity. One practical bit of evidence for the validity of this theory is the worldwide practice of pay secrecy. Many organizations follow this policy to avoid unwanted comparisons and unnecessary complaints.

Motivation and Learning

Energizing, directing, and sustaining employee behavior are the major challenges of managing employee motivation. Motivation calls for the use of positive and negative incentives, or positive reinforcement and punishment, and scheduling them in a way to achieve desired results. In this sense, motivation and learning become closely related. B. F. Skinner and other learning theorists assert that behavior is a function of its consequences. Behavior that is followed by desirable consequences tends to be repeated. In contrast, undesirable consequences have the opposite effect. In this way, we learn to change our behavior to experience desirable consequences and avoid the undesirable (punishment) ones.[71] Like motivation, the two major concerns in learning are finding the right incentives and the correct way, or schedule, to administer them. The values and attractions of rewards vary across cultures. Similarly, cultural factors influence the undesirability of negative incentives. Also, culture is a major determinant of the types of reinforcements and methods of their application. Although all cultures use a combination of positive reinforcement and punishment, some

tend to use more positive incentives, while others make more use of punishment. Positive reinforcement leads to longer lasting and more predictable results but acts only to continue behavior. Punishment causes behavior to stop but usually lasts only a short time if punishment is removed. Also, there are dysfunctional consequences to punishment, such as low self-esteem. While these ideas appear to be universal—consistent laboratory results have been obtained with animals using food as a reward and electric shocks as punishments—the challenge for us in a cross-cultural setting is to find which rewards *really* reward in a given culture and which punishments *really* punish.

The methods of scheduling reinforcements affect the speed of learning and the extent of maintaining a behavior. While studying the schedules of reinforcement goes beyond the purpose of this chapter a key point is that incentives must be continued over time and administered consistently or they will lose their impact.

How Do You Motivate Japanese Employees?

In recent years, Japanese management and motivation practices have received much attention. The success of the Japanese auto industry during the 1980s called much attention to the way Japanese businesses worked. According to William Ouchi there are three fundamental properties of the Japanese organizations that distinguish them from those of the American firms: lifetime employment, internal promotion, and nonspecialized career paths. Many large Japanese companies offer lifetime jobs to their employees. Lifetime employment, although desired by workers and a goal of employers, covers perhaps 35 percent of Japan's workforce. Promotions take place entirely from within the firm. The process of evaluation is very slow, and long-term oriented. Because of lifetime employment and internal promotions, employees receive broad-based training. Employees are moved between functions, offices, and geo-

How the Japanese Teach Success

*Deborah Fallows**

Our American family lived in a suburb of Yokohama. Our sons attended Utsukushigaoka Shogakko—"Beautiful Hills Elementary School"—with 700 Japanese children. The most important thing our boys learned was not the academic content of their courses, nor even the Japanese language. Instead, they learned something far more valuable: a deep sense of how Japanese children think, act, and view the world. Learning the culture's values—developing a sense of being Japanese—is a deliberate goal of the Japanese school system.

Japanese children learn a lifelong lesson that is the cornerstone of the efficiency and success of modern Japan: Each person has a role to fulfill as best he or she can. Just as it is their father's role to be at work from early morning to midnight and their mother's role to take care of them, the house and all the family matters, it is their role to be students.

Being a student, like earning a salary later in life, is a full-time job. Students go to school six days a week. The only long vacation lasts six weeks during the summer, and even then there is assigned summer homework.

The days can be long. On regular school days, classes were followed by "club" meetings or sports. After a quick supper with mom, many students joined their schoolmates again for evening juku, or cram school, to do remedial work, review regular class lessons or prepare for exams. After all this came the night's homework.

Even before academics become very rigorous (in about sixth or seventh grade), organizing yourself and your possessions presents students with a challenge of coordination and attention. Our sons were constantly trying to keep track of their regulation school bags, regulation indoor shoes, regulation sports clothes and all the other paraphernalia required for school—from lunch mats to calligraphy kits to earthquake helmets—not to mention ordinary books, uniforms and school supplies.

Our sons were impressed by how well their Japanese friends followed schedules, rules and instructions—producing model replicas of teachers' art work or playing the identical, flawless renditions of piano tunes. By contrast, they began to notice how lost their Japanese friends were at simply "hanging around." When groups of kids came to our house, they liked games with rules: cards, board games, ping-pong. But begin improvising with bins of Legos or building blocks and they drifted away.

Just as Japanese men pay more attention to their companies than to their families, Japanese children pay more attention to their school than to their homes. Japanese kids don't do many chores around the house (mothers tend to free them up to study), but they soji, or clean their classrooms every day after lunch. My younger son became very adept at mopping the floor with the zokien—the special heavy-duty washcloth every child brings from home and hangs under his desk. Daisoji, or "big cleaning," when students scrub down all the halls and major rooms of the building was done every few weeks, often on Saturday.

The all-consuming nature of school seems less onerous when you appreciate that school and home blend together in Japan in a way they don't in America. A sensei, or teacher, is charged with a child's moral upbringing as much as his parents are. Teachers make regular visits to each child's house to meet with parents, talk about what a child should be doing differently at home and check up on the general living situation.

* Used by permission of the author.

Another lesson my children learned along with their Japanee classmates was a keen sense of how to act as part of a group—to make group decisions, to sublimate one's self to the identity of the group, to judge success or failure on the performance of the group.

On the first day of school, each of our sons was assigned to a kumi, or class. Forever after, our children were identified as Tommy of Roku-nen-ni-kumi (sixth grade, second kumi), or Tad of ni-nen-ich'-kumi (second grade, first kumi). The 40-some students of a kumi and their teacher were a unit that stayed together for at least two years, often more. The mothers of the students met regularly with the teacher in marathon after-school discussions of dynamics of the classroom, social problems, developmental problems, class outings and parties. The first two meetings I attended for the sixth grade focused for nearly an hour on the effect of having Tommy join the kumi.

I was embarrassed at first about all the attention focused on my son, and wondered after 30 or 40 long minutes if some of the other mothers hadn't had enough of talking about someone else's child. But I realize now that they each had a personal stake in this. Like it or not, Tommy had become part of their group. How the group dealt with him was part of their children's lesson in group behavior and part of their success or failure as a group.

When Tommy's class was preparing for a spring outing to the Yokohama '89 Exposition, he came home several nights in a row describing the kumi's progress in dividing itself into buddy-groups for the day's trip. There were 41 kids in his class, and they had to arrange themselves into equal units of six.

The first step was easy; the kids simply split off voluntarily into cluster. But one group ended up with four kids and another with seven. Just move one student over, right? No. The students and their teacher all felt that it would be unkind to single out one child to move by himself; they felt it would be smoother to move two together. Then they agreed that not only would the movers have to agree, but each child in the four-member group would have to approve each of the pair being moved to join them. For three days, during hour-long meetings, the kumi, under the watchful but unintrusive eye of the teacher, bartered back and forth.

These cultural messages—to learn your place, to blend with the group, to follow the rules, to try your hardest—comprised the non-academic core of education taught to every Japanese child by mothers and teachers alike. As foreigners, we were especially sensitive to the processes that were at work in the school. It could serve us all well to consider the messages we and our schools are imparting to our own American children.

graphical locations so that they become familiar with the total organization.[72] In exploring the reasons for Japanese economic success, Americans have developed a fascination with the Japanese motivation system. This fascination has resulted in several misconceptions, however. Here are some common "misconceptions" about motivation in Japan and some "facts" about how their system really works:

Misconception: Individualism plays no role in the Japanese motivation. The lack of rules,

definition of individual responsibility, and job analysis is a testimony to this fact.

Fact: Individualism plays an important role in Japanese motivation. The Japanese approach to the work not only involves individualism but a means of preserving and developing it, according to Brown. The Japanese have a different way of interpreting individualism, however. See the discussion under the next and the last "Fact."

Misconception: For Japanese, the only motivators are conformity pressure, and the need to belong. They do not worry about esteem and the work itself.

Fact: Japanese are very sensitive to both self-esteem and the esteem of others. Since work plays an important role in satisfying esteem needs, its meaning is very important to Japanese. Lifetime employment also makes the initial job choice more critical for many Japanese. Not all Japanese have lifetime jobs, however.

Misconception: Japanese workers enjoy much higher pay and benefits than American workers, and their standard of living is higher.

Fact: Although many Japanese workers enjoy better compensation than their American counterparts, the slight difference and higher costs make their living standards equal or even lower than American workers.

Misconception: Japanese managers have higher status and larger pay, and workers have to check with their supervisors before they do anything.

Fact: Japanese management is based on self-discipline rather than external control. Japanese children are raised to accept responsibility and be competitive. Only important matters are brought to the attention of supervisors and most problems at work are resolved at the lower level. The pay difference between the lowest paid workers and the CEOs is much lower in Japan than in the United States.

Misconception: Japanese workers are more interested in working and less interested in leisure time. They spend all of their waking hours working.

Fact: Some management experts have attributed characteristics of Japanese motivation to the country's high population density and a homogeneous cultural make-up. Rapid changes brought about by economic prosperity are creating a shift toward the Western values, however. The stereotype of Japanese workers who devote their life to work is only a superficial representation of reality. Even though they spend more time at work, they do not necessarily spend all the hours working at full speed. Many Japanese office workers spend more time at work because Japanese culture obligates them to be at work in the company of others, and because of a sense of loyalty to their company. It is expected that men return home late. "Some complain that they're trapped in a vicious circle: Because they put in such long hours, they can't work flat out all day long, but because they don't work flat out they need to put in long hours."[73] While office workers have opportunities for loafing, in Japanese factories there are many fewer opportunities for slaking off. "A Japanese factory worker rarely finds himself with a second between tasks to catch his breath; the time-study engineers usually find the second first."[74]

There are indications that the younger Japanese seek more leisure activities, and are more willing to express their opposing views. The sight of teenage gangs in American T-shirts and leather jackets riding motorcycles may surprise tourists in Tokyo but not the local residents. The children's love affair with Mickey Mouse led to the opening of Tokyo Disneyland. Will these changes have a dramatic effect on employee motivation in Japanese organizations? Only time will tell.

Global Trends In Motivation

Rapid change has been a reality of the latter part of the twentieth century. Dramatic technological changes and political restructuring around the world have created new problems as well as opportunities. Acceleration of the rate of change in recent years has made the prediction of global trends in motivation difficult. Two major questions have been raised regarding the changes in the management of motivation and human resources.

First, would the collapse of the Soviet system result in the integration of the socialist cultures into the Western cultures, and consequently lead to more emphasis on social needs (employee centered) in Western organizations? Some scholars of international management believe this will happen. They argue that there will be more emphasis on relationships in Western companies and more attention to work and production in the Eastern societies. So far, there is little evidence to support this contention. American companies have been reducing their staffs and lowering employees' benefits despite increases in reported profits. Traditionally, increased profits have led to more hiring and increases in employee benefits. Recent practices, however, have been contrary to historical trends. This "getting lean and mean" strategy has left unemployment and the employee benefit problems for the individual or the government to solve. On the other side, with the easing of restrictions on businesses in socialist states, there is a noticeable rise in entrepreneurial attitudes and behaviors. Freed from the Communist yoke, these societies have witnessed an explosion of emerging small businesses and privatization of government-controlled industries. Transformation to a market economy has caused new political and economic problems that have yet to be resolved.

Second, will the expansion of global business and advancements in telecommunication technology lead to more uniformity among cultures? There are some signs of this development. The popularity of the American culture overseas and Americans' rising interest in learning about other cultures are early indications of such a trend. There are some indications to the contrary as well. For example, in a study of macro-environmental characteristics of 18 industrialized nations over the 1960–88 period, Craig, Douglas, and Grein found a diverging pattern. Contrary to the popular assumption, they found that countries were diverging rather than converging.[75] Global economic problems and resulting protectionist attitudes are major obstacles in the road to a global culture.

Adler believes that employees bring their ethnicity into the workplace and promote or enhance their culture in their work organizations. In her words, Germans become more German, Americans become more American, Swedes become more Swedish, etc.[76] If the tendency to emphasize one's ethnicity and heritage is on the rise, the future may hold more problems for international managers. The management of the multicultural workforce is fraught with problems and difficulties. An example is the experience of Bridgestone, the Japanese tire company, which bought Firestone of Akron, Ohio, to gain a foothold in the U.S. market. Soon after the purchase cultural differences between Akron and Tokyo surfaced. Besides the language difficulty, adjusting to styles of work proved to be an obstacle to smooth operations. "The Japanese who work until 9 P.M. or later, won't fathom why their American colleagues won't stay that late, too. And the Americans complain about Japanese arrangements such as open offices and desks facing each other."[77]

Convergence or divergence of cultures will have a significant impact on how cross-cultural motivation is managed. Research findings are pointing in both directions.[78] Today's rapid changes call for continuous monitoring of cultural differences for effectively managing motivation.

Conclusion

Culture plays an important role in managing motivation in work organizations. Culture affects employee perceptions and the way employees respond to rewards or punishments. For managers who plan to work overseas or have employees from other cultures, cultural understanding is a prerequisite to success. Motivating the people without the knowledge of their culture is an impossible task. For example, when followers of Herzberg suggest that money is not a motivator, it may be because in Western societies most basic needs are reasonably satisfied. In some developing countries, where most people are less prosperous by Western standards, money is still an important motivating factor. Money, however, may not be a motivating factor in other cultures for a different reason. "Money is not an incentive everywhere—it may be accepted gladly, but will not automatically improve performance. Honor, dignity and family may be much more important. Imposing the American style of merit system may be an outrageous blow to a respected and established seniority system. Merit which must be defined: "May the best person win" can mean "the most popular person" or "the person from the most aristocratic family."[79]

The cultural diversity of MNCs poses a problem for the universal application of motivation theories. Studies suggest that the need to belong and associate is a strong motivator in societies that emphasize the value of social relationships. In these cultures the American concept of individualism is not a strong base for motivation. Although the individuals follow a hierarchical order to satisfy needs, this hierarchical order apparently varies across cultures. Unfortunately, the grouping of countries in large categories, such as developed and underdeveloped, without paying attention to cultural attributes, does not provide a good solution to understanding motivation. Understanding important needs and their rank order in a given society requires research designed for that specific culture. To be applicable in international settings, the traditional psychologically based motivation models should also take an anthropological orientation. An anthropological orientation allows the consideration of cultural influences on motivation, and provides international managers with an additional tool for understanding the idiosyncracies of human behavior.

Discussion Questions

1. Discuss the way ethnocentric tendencies affect our lives as well as the way we run businesses in the United States.
2. Do you know of any example of ethnocentrism in another country? If yes, describe it.
3. Explain how variation in the concept of "self" could affect a person's motivation.
4. Individualism is a well-known attribute of Americans. Americans are also known to help their neighbors in times of need. Are these two traits in conflict?
5. Work by itself could be a motivating factor for Americans. Do other cultures consider work as a motivator or a necessity? Discuss the meaning of work from the perspective of another culture.
6. Why is Maslow's hierarchy of needs considered ethnocentric? Is there a universal hierarchy of human needs?
7. Are motivators and hygiene factors universal?
8. Compared with the people of other countries, Japanese tend to work longer hours. What cultural characteristics of Japanese could you use to explain this tendency?
9. In your opinion, what are the reasons for the Japanese younger generation's interest in more leisure time?
10. What are the cultural implications of the expectancy theory of motivation? Does individual willingness to take risk make a difference in a person's motivation?

Endnotes

1. K. L. Miller. "Now, Japan Is Admitting It: Work Kills Executive." *Business Week* (August 3, 1992), 35.

2. H. Sisk and W. J. Cliffton. *Management and Organizations* (Cincinnati, OH: South-Western Publishing Co., 1985), 315.

3. I. Harpaz. "The Importance of Work Goals: An International Perspective." *Journal of International Business Studies*, 21 (1990), 75–93.

4. S. Ronen. *Comparative and Multinational Management* (New York: John Wiley and Sons, 1986).

5. E. J. Kolde. *The Multinational Company* (Lexington, MA: D. C. Heath and Co., 1974), 78–9.

6. R. G. D'Andrade and C. Strauss. *Human Motives and Cultural Models* (Cambridge, UK: Cambridge University Press, 1992), 4.

7. S. M. Lipset. "Culture and Economic Behavior: A Commentary." *Journal of Labor Economics*, 11, no. 2, pt. 2 (1993), S330–S347.

8. W. Nord. "Cultures and Organizational Behavior." In W. Nord, ed. *Concepts and Controversy in Organizational Behavior* (New York: Goodyear Publishing Co., 1972), 205–6.

9. F. Derakhshan and R. Kahan. "Attitudes Towards Older Employees in PRC and Taiwan: A Cross-Cultural Comparison," *Proceedings of Pan Pacific Conference* (1989), 216–19.

10. W. F. Whyte and P. R. Braun. "Heroes, Homework, and Industrial Growth." *Columbia Journal of World Business* (Spring 1966), 51–7.

11. M. Haire, E. E. Ghiselli, and L. W. Porter. "Cultural Patterns in the Role of Management." *Industrial Relations,* 2 (1963), 96–117.

12. J. S. Black and L. W. Porter. "Managerial Behaviors and Job Performance: A Successful Manager in Los Angeles May Not Succeed in Hong Kong." *Journal of International Business Studies,* 22 no. 1 (1991), 99–113.

13. L. Copeland and L. Griggs. *Going International: How to Make Friends and Deal Effectively in the Global Marketplace* (New York: Random House, 1985), 13.

14. W. H. Newman, "Cultural Assumptions Underlying U.S. Management Concepts." In J. L. Massie, J. Luytjes, and N. W. Hazen, eds. *Management in an International Context* (New York: Harper and Row, 1972), 347.

15. Copeland and Griggs. *Going International.* 13.

16. MOW International Research Team. *The Meaning of Working* (London: Academic Press, 1985).

17. J. Misumi. "Attitudes to Work in Japan and the West." *Long Range Planning,* 26, no. 4 (1993), 66–71.

18. I. Harpaz. "The Importance of Work Goals," 75–93.

19. E. E. Sampson. "The Challenge of Social Change for Psychology: Globalization and Psychology's Theory of the Person." *American Psychologist,* 44 (1989), 914–21.

20. U. Neisser. "Five Kinds of Self-Knowledge." *Philosophical Psychology,* 1 (1988), 35–59.

21. H. R. Markus and S. Kitayama. "Culture and the Self: Implications for Cognition, Emotion, and Motivation." *Psychological Review,* 98 (1991), 224–53.

22. Markus and Kityama. "Culture and the Self." 226.

23. Markus and Kitayama. "Culture and the Self." 227.

24. Markus and Kitayama. "Culture and the Self." 227.

25. R. P. Dore. *City Life in Japan* (Berkely, CA: University of California Press, 1958), 385.

26. T. Parsons, E. Shils, and J. Olds. "Categories of the Orientation and Organization of Action." In T. Parsons and E. A. Shils, eds. *Toward a general theory of action,* (Cambridge, MA: Harvard University Press, 1951), 81.

27. Markus and Kitayama. "Culture and the Self." 228.

28. E. Hamaguchi, "A Contextual Model of the Japanese: Toward a Methodological Innovation in Japan Studies," *Journal of Japanese Studies,* 11 (1985), 289–321. Cited in Markus and Kitayama. "Culture and the Self."

29. Dore. *City Life in Japan.* 389.

30. Markus and Kitayama. "Culture and the Self." 237.

31. F. L. K. Hsu. *Iemoto: The Heart of Japan* (New York: John Wiley and Sons, 1975), 215.

32. H. A. Murray. *Explorations in Personality* (New York: Oxford University Press, 1938).

33. Markus and Kitayama. "Culture and the Self." 240.

34. M. H. Bond. *The Psychology of Chinese People* (New York: Oxford University Press, 1986).

35. L. Festinger. *A Theory of Cognitive Dissonance* (Palo Alto, CA: Stanford University Press, 1957).

36. A. H. Maslow. "A Theory of Human Motivation." *Psychological Bulletin,* 50 (1943), 370–82. Also, A. Maslow, *Motivation and Personality* (New York: Harper and Row, 1954).

37. G. Hofstede. "The Cultural Relativity of the Quality of Life Concept." *The Academy of Management Review.* 9, no. 3 (1984), 396.

38. S. G. Redding. "Some Perceptions of Psychological Needs Among Managers in South East Asia," in Y. H. Poortinga, ed. *Basic Problems in Cross-Cultural Psychology* (Amsterdam: Swete and Zeitlinger, 1977), 338–43.

39. E. C. Nevis. "Using an American Perspective in Understanding Another Culture: Toward a Hierarchy of Needs for the People's Republic of China." *The Journal of Applied Behavioral Science,* 19, no. 3 (1983), 249–64; see also E. C. Nevis. "Cultural Assumption and Productivity: The United States and China." *Sloan Management Review,* (Spring 1983), 17–29.

40. F. L. K. Hsu. "Psychological Homeostasis and Jen." *American Anthropologist,* 73 (1971), 23–44, as was cited in E. C. Nevis. "Using an American Perspective." 261.

41. Ibid.

42. Ibid.

43. O. H. M. Yay. "Chinese Cultural Values: Their Dimensions and Marketing Implications," *European Journal of Marketing,* 22, no. 5 (1988), 44–57.

44. G. Hofstede. "Motivation, Leadership, and Organization." *Organizational Dynamics* (Summer 1980), 42–63.

45. D. C. McClleland. *The Achieving Society* (Princeton, NJ: Van Nostrand Rienhold, 1961).

46. Haire, Ghiselli, and Porter. *Cultural Patterns.*

47. H. J. Reitz. "The Relative Importance of Five Categories of Needs Among Industrial Workers in Eight Countries," *Academy of Management Proceedings* (1975), 270–3.

48. S. Ronen, "Cross-National Study of Employees' Work Goals." *International Review of Applied Psychology,* 28, no. 1, (1979), 1–12.

49. N. J. Adler. *International Dimension of Organizational Behavior* (Boston, MA: Kent Publishing, 1991), 152–53.

50. F. Herzberg, B. Mausner, and B. S. Snyderman. *The Motivation to Work,* (New York: John Wiley, and Sons, 1959); see also F. Herzberg. "One More Time, How Do

You Motivate Employees?" *Harvard Business Review* (January–February 1968), 54–62.

51. R. A. Crabbs. "Work Motivation in the Culturally Complex Panama Canal Company." *Academy of Management Proceedings* (1973), 119–126.

52. G. H. Hines. "Achievement, Motivation, Occupations and Labor Turnover in New Zealand." *Journal of Applied Psychology*, 58, no. 3, (1973), 313–7.

53. G. H. Hines. "Cross-Cultural Differences in Two-Factor Motivation Theory." *Journal of Applied Psychology*, (December 1973), 375–7.

54. D. Macarov. "Work Patterns and Satisfactions in an Israeli Kibbutz: A Test of the Herzberg Hypothesis." *Personnel Psychology* (Autumn 1972), 483–93.

55. P. D. Machungwa and N. Schmitt. "Work Motivation in a Developing Country." *Journal of Applied Psychology* (February 1983), 31–42.

56. R. N. Kanungo and R. W. Wright, "A Cross-Cultural Comparative Study of Managerial Job Attitudes." *Journal of International Business Studies* (Fall 1983), 115–29.

57. D. C. McClelland. *The Achieving Society* (Princeton, NJ: Van Nostrand Rienhold, 1961).

58. D. C. McClelland. "Business Drive and National Achievement." *Harvard Business Review* (July–August 1962), 99–112.

59. D. C. McClelland. "Achieving Motivation Can Be Developed." *Harvard Business Review*, (November–December 1965), 120.

60. R. S. Bhagat and S. J. McQuaid. "Role of Subjective Culture in Organizations: A Review and Directions for future research." *Journal of Applied Psychology Monograph*, 67, (1982), 635–85.

61. S. Iwawaki and R. Lynn. "Measuring Achievement Motivation in Great Britain and Japan." *Journal of Cross-Cultural Psychology*, 3 (1972), 219–20.

62. Ronen. "Cross-National Study." 153.

63. Bond. *The Psychology of Chinese People*.

64. D. C. McClleland and D. G. Winter. *Motivating Economic Achievement* (New York: Free Press, 1969).

65. U. N. Pareek and V. K. Kumar. "Expressed Motive of Entrepreneurship in an Indian Town." *Psychologica*, 12 (1969), 109–114.

66. D. R. Hampton, C. E. Summer, and R. A. Webber. *Organizational Behavior and the Practice of Management* (Glenview, IL: Scott, Foresman and Co., 1982), 6.

67. D. Eden. "Intrinsic and Extrinsic Rewards and Motives: Replication and Extension with Kibbutz Workers." *Journal of Applied Social Psychology*, 6 (1975), 348–61.

68. Adler. *International Dimension*. 159.

69. J. S. Adams. "Inequities in Social Exchange." In *Advances in Experimental Social Psychology*, vol. 2 (New York: Academic Press, 1965).

70. E. Yuchtman and S. E. Seashore. "A System Resource Approach to Organizational Effectiveness." *American Psychological Review*, 32 (1967), 891–903.

71. B. F. Skinner. *Beyond Freedom and Dignity* (New York: Alfred Knopf, 1971); see also B. F. Skinner. "Operant Behavior." *American Psychologist*, 18 (1963), 503–15; B. F. Skinner. *Contingencies of Reinforcement: A Theoretical Analysis* (Englewood Cliffs, NJ: Prentice-Hall, 1961); Also for a description of the conditioning process see B. M. Bass and J. A. Vaughn, *Training in Industry: The Management of Learning* (Monterey, CA: Brooks/Cole, 1966).

72. W. Ouchi. *Theory Z: How American Businesses Can Meet the Japanese Challenge* (Reading, MA: Addison-Wesley Publishing Co., 1981), 11–38.

73. U. C. Lehner. "Is It Any Surprise the Japanese Make Excellent Loafers?" *The Wall Street Journal*, (February 28, 1992,) 1

74. Ibid.

75. S. S. Craig, S. P. Douglas, and A. Grein. "Patterns of Convergence and Divergence Among Industrializing Nations: 1960–1988." *Journal of International Business Studies*, 23, no. 4, (1992), 773–87.

76. Adler. *International Dimension*. 58.

77. T. F. O'Boyle. "Bridgestone Discovers Purchase of U.S. Firm Creates Big Problems." *The Wall Street Journal* (April 1, 1991) 1.

78. D. A. Ralston, D. J. Gustafson, F. M. Cheung, and R. H. Terpstra. "Differences in Managerial Values: A Study of U.S., Hong Kong and PRC managers." *Journal of International Business Studies*, 24, no. 2 (1993), 249–75.

79. L. Copeland and L. Griggs, *Going International*. 14.

MANNERS EUROPE

JOSEPH J. DISTEFANO

John Wilman, Managing Director of Manners Europe, was reviewing the progress he had made since his arrival in the Netherlands two and a half years earlier. The building supplies and home improvement retail outlets for which he was responsible had expanded rapidly in the four years the company had operated in Europe. Now as he thought about the problems and opportunities that he faced during the balance of his assignment in Europe, he set high priority on solving current operational problems and planning future expansion. He knew that both of these objectives would involve increasing the efficiency and effectiveness of the finance and control aspects of the business, an area to which he and Tom Steiger, Director of Finance, had been devoting a fair amount of attention. In addition, there were business problems in several countries with which he had to deal. He looked forward to the challenge of the next several months.

Background of the Company

Manners Europe is part of a large United States corporation. Although the parent company operates worldwide in several different industries, a large percentage of its several hundred million dollar annual sales comes from manufacturing, wholesale, and retail activities in the United States involving lumber and forest-related products. In this main area of its business the company is one of the largest of its kind in the world.

This case was prepared by Joseph J. DiStefano of the Western Business School. Copyright 1974, The University of Western Ontario.

As the company's main business matured in the United States top executives became interested in the possibilities of entering the European market. Because of previous activity in the Netherlands involving the Manners agricultural division, they sent a person experienced in retailing to assess the potential. Taking advantage of a capability in four languages, this person made a two-month study culminating in a recommendation that European operations be started with the Netherlands as the base. The decision was made and this same person was soon named to direct the start-up. He spent the first year and a half establishing the legal requirements, choosing a site for the head office and generally dealing with time-consuming business-government relations. With these preliminaries completed the first store was opened. A second outlet was added nearby just before John Wilman took over. John explained the relatively slow pace of development by noting, "United States management was cautious because they understood that European patterns of business were different. They knew that Sears had experienced unexpected difficulties in Spain and that J.C. Penney had problems in Belgium. Wanting to avoid the errors of overestimating the transferability of United States business practices made by these experienced retailers, Manners' home office management was initially conservative about the rate of growth in Europe."

Current European Operations

Since John arrived, sales volume had risen from $1.5 million (United States) to $10 million from four stores in the Netherlands, three in Belgium, and three in the United Kingdom (operated on a joint venture basis with a British firm). In keeping with the company policy of hiring employees and managers from the country where the stores were located, only two of the 225 employees were American. Happy with the autonomy granted from home office, John noted that he had complete freedom over site selection and personnel matters and much greater authority in capital expenditures than his United States counterparts. With the rapid growth of the parent corporation, John's reporting relationship to the United States had varied. Most recently his superior had been changed from the Vice President for Financial Services to Mr. Ralph Jennings, Executive Vice President of the Manners Corporation.

The retail outlets for which John was responsible were self-service stores featuring some 10,000 lumber, building supplies, and home improvement products usually organized in eight groups over 20,000 square feet of interior space. Cashiers and an information counter were located in the front of the stores with an outside storage area for masonry supplies and heavier building materials. In describing their operations John said, "The idea of a one-stop outlet for all do-it-yourself home improvement products is key. The large variety of items combined with lower prices give us the competitive edge. Our size allows us to buy directly from manufacturers or importing agents," he went on, "thereby cutting out the middleman in cases where he is not providing a valuable service. In addition, our competitors here are more specialized and look for higher margins. By the way," John added, "tradesmen and small contractors are an important market segment besides the regular do-it-yourself customers."

Except for the first store all the outlets on the continent were modern, newly built structures with paved parking lots. They each averaged 20 to 25 employees.

It was at these individual stores where the annual planning cycle started each August. Describing this process John said, "Preparation of our objectives and budget is on an M. B. O.-like basis starting with individual salesmen on the floor and working up. For each outlet general objectives such as market share, store climate, and development of management are included as well as quantitative financial targets. These are all correlated here at headquarters."

The fifteen staff members for the European operations were located in a house that had been converted to offices, which was located next to the first outlet. In addition to the two Americans, this group included the Directors of Operations and Administration (personnel, insurance, credit, etc.) and their staffs together with two Merchandise Managers who served the individual stores and coordinated marketing activities. Figure 1 is an organization chart for Manners Europe.

Growth of the European Operations

Sales volume in the two Dutch stores was about $700,000 when John arrived in March. A third store was added and the fourth was scheduled to be opened in June. John decided that his early emphasis would be on getting these stores operating efficiently as a base from which to expand (the tentative target was to have twenty stores in Europe by the end of three years). At the time he arrived, sales volume was good, but there were no profits. Start-up expenses were high and there were operating difficulties.

As he started to address the problems, he soon realized their gravity. The Controller could not balance the books and there had never been an audit or physical inventory taken. John had the first inventory taken the moment he arrived and it indicated a shrinkage of 5 percent. In May he asked the division he reported to for help, and in September internal systems consultants spent two weeks going over the problems. Tom Steiger, who subsequently became Director of Finance, was among those who did the study summarized in Figure 2. Figures 3 and 4 provide background data about John Wilman and Tom Steiger, respectively.

Based on this study the company decided that it was important to have internal accounting

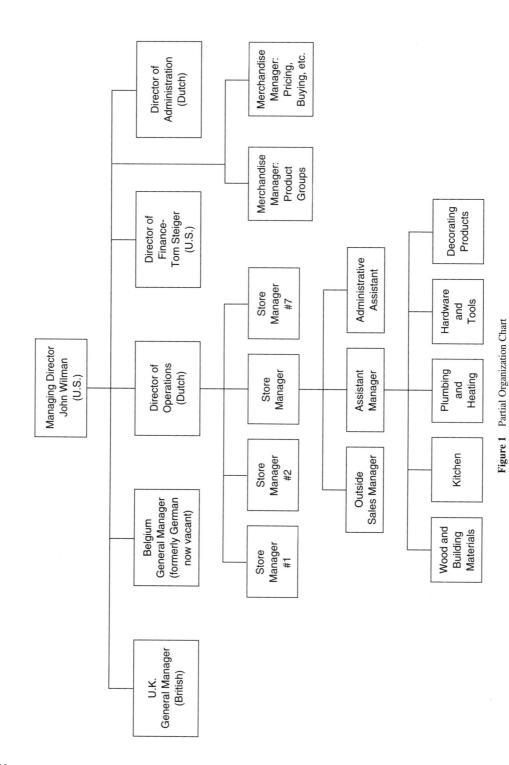

Figure 1 Partial Organization Chart

Figure 2 Systems and Procedures Review Summary

(Prepared by three corporate systems consultants including Tom Steiger, dated September 21.)

SECTION I
I. *Evaluation—Existing System*
  A. *Accounts Payable*
    • Lack of control over receivers vendor's invoices and open accounts payable balance.
    • Delayed match-up of payables documents and disbursements to vendors.
  B. *Margin Determination*
    • Lack of procedure for recording the effect of markdowns.
    • Lack of controls over physical inventory cut-off and processing.
  C. *Physical Inventories*
    • No control over cut-off (received sales, vendor's invoices, etc.).
    • Delay in updating book inventories and lack of control over accounts payable function.
  D. *Reporting of Sales (Sales Ticket Cash Register Operation)*
    • Group codes not entered on sales tickets. Cashier must decide correct codes for entry into register.
    • No group distribution made for sales tickets.
    • Sales discounts not always sales tickets.
  E. *Daily Sales Audit*
    • No home office audit function connection with Daily Business Report.
  F. *Accounts Receivable*
    • No daily or monthly control.
    • No bad debt reserve.
    • No formal procedure for credit or approvals.
  G. *Purchase Order System*
    • Many uncoded items distorts in determination
  H. *Procedures*
    • No written branch operating procedures, i.e., operation of cash registers, preparation sales tickets, etc.
  I. *General*
    • Disorganization of office function due to:
    • Lack of experienced personnel
    • Absence of priorities and work schedule
    • Varied demands or Chief Accountant's time
SECTIONS II–IV
Section II contained recommendations, modifications to the existing system in outline form matching items A through Section I. It also listed recommendations regarding personnel gave a list of priorities. Section III contained recommendations regarding organized systems. Section IV made longer-range recommendations assuming total of twenty stores in two and one-half years.

and control systems similar to those in the United States. They felt that the Dutch personnel in the company at that time were inadequate for implementing the systems without long-run assistance. The Executive Vice President and Senior Vice President also visited the Netherlands in November and recommended organizational changes which resulted in separate Directors for Finance, Operations, and Administration. After weighing the costs,

United States management with John Wilman's concurrence asked Tom Steiger to take on the finance job.[2]

Tom arrived on January 1 and soon found that the situation was worse than he had thought the previous fall (see Figure 5). In particular, the controller about whom Tom had been skeptical during his September study now appeared completely inadequate. "Rather than work on an important problem like reconciling our accounts

Figure 3 Background Data: John Wilman

Career with Manners
- Eight years with Manners.
- Training program for management development in lumber and building supplies division as follows.
  - Six months in field operations (lumber yard).
  - Six months in head office.
  - Seven months as assistant manager at a supply center.
  - Seven months as buyer in lumber merchandising.
- One of two-person corporate planning (a new function in company).
- Controller in new corporate activity: land development (recommended by corporate planning).
- Then named as head of European operations (after five years with company).
- John described his jobs in Manners as emphasizing operations management (lumber and store experiences), marketing (store experiences), finance (planning job), and control (land development responsibility).

Personal Background
- International experience: Visited parents during summers of college years (father was President of United States firm in Antwerp). Three months working construction in Switzerland. Speaks some Spanish, and Dutch, the latter through course work since arrival in the Netherlands.
- Family: Married, two children, one in Dutch school and one in international school. Wife very favorably inclined to taking European position. Wife has good language capacity in Dutch and French.
- Education: Undergraduate liberal arts in midwestern college. M.B.A. earned part-time while working for Manners . . . marketing and finance emphasis.

receivable with customer invoices, I'd find him sorting pop bottles!" said Tom. "And he was a compulsive talker; he'd spend hours chatting in the halls and offices. After several reviews and attempts to alter his behavior, I had to fire him when he wouldn't change." However, he brought his dismissal before the Labor Bureau. After seven months of bureaucratic procedures and negotiations between employer, employee, and the Labor Bureau, a satisfactory termination time was agreed to.[3] "But in spite of these difficulties, we have made progress," Tom added.

Systems and Procedures

Of the several internal and external problems faced by John and Tom, actual compliance with systems and procedures once they had been set up seemed to be difficult to accomplish. "Operating a business by numbers and controls just doesn't seem to be part of the orientation of the managers or employees," Tom noted. "Following a procedural manual for pricing, or reporting timeliness or accuracy is second place. Getting things done on time is a big headache . . . and it shows outside the business too. It takes 10 minutes to get a hamburger at McDonald's; they prepare them to individual orders instead of on a fast-food basis! And the 'starter' at the golf course sometimes simply doesn't show up on a Saturday morning."

Tom gave several examples of problems that concerned his department. "Receivers are an important tool for controlling payment to suppliers. It was taking from several days to weeks for us to get receiver notices from the stores, so we set up inventory receipt procedures and put a 48-hour limit on reporting receipt of goods to headquarters. It's taken a whole year to get the stores to comply and even now it isn't unusual to experience one or two week delays. We watch their accuracy and push for updating when stores fall behind. But they seem to *talk* more than to *do;* it sometimes takes five or six requests before we get action."

Another example had to do with the Chief Accountant for Belgium. Tom worked out a plan to shift the individual store bank balances (which were positive and drawing a low interest

Figure 4   Background Data: Tom Steiger

Career with Company
- Twenty-two years with Manners, successive positions as:
  - Internal auditor,
  - General books supervisor,
  - Controller, agriculture and lumber division,
  - Management Systems and Programs,
  - Internal Systems Consultant—Manners Europe,
  - Director of Finance—Manners Europe,
- Tom's comments about his career: "The company has always treated me right. As long as they do, I'll always work hard to the best of my ability."

Personal Background
- Tom and wife born, raised, and lived in same city in northwestern United States their whole lives. Had not moved in 16 years. Built own home in a big field with woods in the back.
- Wife always willing to move with the job. Children (boy and girl both 12) cried and had problems initially . . . now O.K. Extremely happy at prospect of vacation back in United States, but not unhappy in the Netherlands.
- Family weighed the disadvantages (second-class citizens, fewer material conveniences, no summer cottage, loss of friends) vs. the opportunity to see Europe and favored latter.
- Views of the Dutch people are quite different. Personally they are extremely polite (much more so than Americans), but outside the office in public settings (crowds, supermarkets, highway, golf course) if they do not know you, watch out!
- Language: Biggest problem is language barrier. Company should insist on three months of Dutch courses. Cannot read paper for local news where we live, wait anxiously for English-speaking TV shows, difficult to make friends. If you do not have language before arriving, low incentive to learn since you can get by. But for business and personal life, should do it before.

---

rate) to the main corporate account in Belgium (which often had a negative balance that was costing the company $11\frac{1}{2}$ percent interest). The stores' banks were not cooperating on the overdraft arrangements, and Tom requested the accountant to contact them to correct it. "I talked to him in the morning," Tom said. "He called our Director of Administration at headquarters but still hadn't taken any action to call the bank. After a few rather heated comments from me, he replied, 'I need to understand everything clearly before I do something.' I guess language difficulties are part of it," Tom said, "but sometimes I have to act the part of the 'bad guy from the States' to get any action. They're great in theory and talk, but there seems to be a gap when it comes to action."

He also had similar difficulties in the Netherlands. One of the store managers whom Tom described as "a fairly good manager, but an extremely strong-willed man" was deliberately not following procedures. "On three different occasions in the past few months, he deviated from important policies. We have a policy of no credit except to contractors, but we found that he was selling to his employees and using C.O.D. arrangements to carry them. This is used normally to handle accounts for a day or two where a customer might not be home, but he was stretching it to one or two months for some employees, effectively making it a charge account. I called him on the phone and John called him in. He was told to clear all these from the C.O.D. account, collect from the employees, and stop the practice. Two months later he had made additional sales to employees the same way.

"One of the men he sold to was our Director of Operations who happens to live near the store. I was shocked to find this out when I was reviewing the records, and since his office is right next to mine I told him so. He just laughed

Figure 5   Summary of Administrative Report

Prepared by Tom Steiger for U.S. Senior Vice President, dated March 6.

Problems: The problems listed on the September 21st report (Figure 2, Section I) were described in detail. The summary paragraph read as follows:

"To sum up the problems, there has been no control of activities, either at the stores or at the head office, no real account system, and therefore no accurate financial reporting except by accident. Some of the manipulations in the books and on the financial statements lead us to suspect fraud, but as yet we find no real evidence of that. We will watch for it as we continue to check everything out."

REASONS FOR PROBLEMS (Verbatim from report)
The basic problem seems to be that, from the beginning of operations, the personnel and equipment necessary for even a minimum of controls and for an adequate accounting system were considered an expense that this company could not afford. Working in this atmosphere, it has become a way of life for everyone that the preparation of documents, their accuracy and timeliness, and finally their recording on the books is something to be done only when and how it is convenient. This is by no means an overstatement, as the facts prove. Consider the keeping of a general ledger system having six profit centers and a total of between four and five hundred accounts. With the manual system being used, one single error in posting, adding, bringing balances forward, etc. results in an out-of-balance condition which is next to impossible to find. The installation of a simple bookkeeping machine a year or two ago would have made that job and its accuracy many times easier. Consider also, the problem of an accountant in establishing a cutoff for physical inventory when the stores prepare and send in receivers when it is convenient and with little regard for accuracy. And he had inadequate manpower, so that he is months behind in his regular work and therefore has not time to really dig into the problems. He soon throws up his hands and only goes through the motions.

Changing this way of life will undoubtedly be our biggest problem. It will be a long and hard educational process to make everyone, especially store personnel, realize the importance of doing things accurately and promptly.

The other major problem is the Controller. As stated above, probably no one could have done the job expected of him with the manpower and equipment provided. And yet there seems to be an inability on his part to regulate his own and his peoples' activities so as to get the most out of what he has. Scheduling has been nonexistent. Many things that he has done, such as some of the statement adjustments, have taken much more of his time in the long run than if he had booked the proper entries in the first place. His people are doing things which, with only a few minutes thought, could be improved upon so as to save 50 percent or more of the time spent on a particular job. Offsetting these deficiencies, though, is the acknowledgment by all that he is a very intelligent man. (But intelligence in speaking seven languages and in accounting principles might not mean intelligence in managing an accounting department.) For the time being we are giving him the benefit of the doubt because of the extenuating circumstances, and also because so much information is not recorded but is only in his head, so his leaving now would be a setback in straightening things out. We are watching this situation closely.

Plans for Solving Problems: This section of the report is summarized as follows.

The former manager of our first outlet was appointed Director of Administration—Europe. The appointment was described as "the real key in quickly bringing order out of the present chaos." His assignment in addition to personnel, insurance, and expansion was to work with me in designing and implementing controls and better procedures both in head office and in the stores. Other staffing changes were noted.

Plans for preparing for automation and running the automated system in parallel with the existing one were described. Details such as speeding up the processing of vendor invoices in order to take discounts were included. This was estimated to add $1/2$ to $3/4$ of a percent to the margin.

Detailed accounting adjustments to correct old errors in order to present accurate financial statements and reports were described.

The controller was given target dates for completion of specified activities and was warned that failure to meet deadlines would jeopardize his continued employment. Some pessimism was expressed regarding the probability for his success.

The report concluded with the following list of long range plans.
"a. Continued evaluations of procedures in head office and stores to provide better controls and more efficiency.
  b. Procedures for taking physical inventory and cutoff of accounting records.
  c. Investigation of different handling of collections of customers accounts receivable.
  d. Installation of full retail system of accounting.

e. Preparation of procedure manuals for other countries and implementation of procedures there.

f. Functional audit procedures for all stores and other countries' head offices.

I hope that all of this has given you some idea of what the problems are here and how we are attacking them. When you are here in person we can discuss them in detail and will, of course, welcome any suggestions you might have."

---

saying, 'Those rules don't apply to everybody, only regular employees.' I tried to explain what a difficult position that put the store manager in. It meant that he had to disobey me and the policy or offend his boss (the Director of Operations). He just mumbled without any admission that he shouldn't have done it nor with any promise to stop. His attitude seemed to be that it was nice to have procedures, but they really weren't important and didn't apply to him!

"But getting back to the store manager . . . he also ignored our instructions that any equipment purchase of over a specified amount must be cleared at headquarters. Last week he bought a pricing machine costing well over his limit without checking with us and in a month it will be useless because we're switching over to new procedures.

"His third offense was to ignore our inventory procedures. We recommend that all stores start to prelist their merchandise one month prior to the actual inventory. By listing all the items by name on the inventory sheets in advance, this saves a lot of time on inventory day. He started the prelisting the morning of the inventory and when I asked him why, he gave an excuse about having too much sickness among his employees. We checked his records and he had had only four employee-days of absence during the previous month.

"With these three incidents happening one right after another, I decided to raise the issue at the next administrative clinic we had (a periodic meeting called by Tom to review procedures). I recalled the events and said that I got the impression he followed only procedures that he agreed with or liked. He replied, 'Maybe so.' I

spent a fair amount of time explaining the reasons for the procedures and showing the serious implications of their not being followed as we add more stores. He then promised to do better, but I still have problems getting the cooperation of the Dutch managers."

Motivation to Work

In talking about other problems John Wilman noted that the achievement and production orientation in the United States was just not the same in the Netherlands. After the first two years of operating an M.B.O. kind of system, he had tried to tie it to compensation and felt that it had failed. "The incremental tax rate kills incentive," he explained. "A person may only take home 20 percent of an increase. Besides, many Dutch have a different view of compensation. They argue from an assumption that everyone gives 100 percent of their effort all the time, so they should be paid 100 percent as a normal exchange, not given a bonus."

Tom was concerned about obtaining the commitment of employees to work overtime on the few occasions when it was necessary. He cited an example from the previous week when they were trying to meet the time schedule for accounting reports to the United States office. The computer services company delivered the data at 9:00 PM on Friday (Tom said they were often late in spite of his complaints), and Tom and two of the employees worked into the evening and agreed to return at nine the next morning. After working for two hours on Saturday, the more junior of the two, who had only been with the company a few months, said that he had to leave for a tennis lesson since he had missed the previous week's lesson. He returned some time after two o'clock that afternoon. Later Tom asked the Dutch Chief Accountant about the incident, noting that it was the first overtime requested of the man in two months. He answered that it had puzzled him too and cited a similar experience with the employee. So on the following Monday Tom decided to ask about it. The following exchange took place.

Tom: "You know, you shocked me greatly when you left for tennis on Saturday. We needed you to get that report out and relied on you. I want you to develop."

Employee: "Yes, I realize that. But my wife is also taking lessons and she won't go without me. I want her to get over her shyness and am trying to encourage her to get out."

Tom: "It's understandable that you want to help her, but the chips were down. That report had to be finished. Social life has to take a second place in emergencies. I like to enjoy life, too . . . golf and bridge are my favorites, yet I missed my golf game on Saturday without any questions."

Employee: "Yes, yes, but my wife was involved."

Tom: "Well, if you had a family emergency, the company would understand and take second place. So when the company has an emergency, we expect you to help us. We need to rely on you."

Employee: "O.K."

John cited another example saying, "It's not just internal operations that get affected by this attitude. We have problems with the contractor in building our new stores, too. And this is true even though we've used the same contractor on all the jobs and might be able to expect a little extra consideration. Although we've put all the buildings out for bids, he's the only one who will agree to meet our time specifications of three months from start to completion. The nearest another bidder has come has been five months. We were concerned about his last job and were especially anxious to get the parking lot paved. It had been delayed by eight straight days of rain. We got one day of good weather for laying the asphalt and what happens? He and his workers went to the beach!!"

Tom gave another example. "We're releasing the Accounts Payable Manager (who was at the end of a six-month trial period). He's forty-five years old and can't find a job, but still has priced himself out of the market. He's unreliable; I have to check everything. I can't even trust him to balance out the check totals with the invoice totals each day."

Three or four months ago it was necessary to work on a Saturday morning, so I warned the people involved on the previous Thursday. He simply said, 'No, I won't be in the city Saturday.' He didn't tell me what I already knew—that he goes horseback riding every Saturday. He's one that has always taken the employees' part on this issue claiming that it is against Dutch customs to work overtime."

We had a run-in over a religious holiday too. For many businesses it was a holiday, but our stores were to be open for half the day. So John sent a memo to the headquarters staff saying that as long as the store employees had to work, it would be good for all of us to come in the half day, too. After all, they could see if we weren't here and how would that look? Anyway, this Accounts Payable Manager and two of his people didn't show up. The next day I asked about it. He said, 'They took it as part of their holiday allowance, and as for me, I marched in the parade with the band.' When I asked if he had seen John's memo, he gave me a cold stare, said 'Yes,' and walked away. To him personal life came first."

Compensation

John also discussed the relation between motivation and compensation. "As I mentioned, we've had difficulty linking pay with achievement of objectives. At the store manager level I first had difficulty when I introduced the idea. But I found that if I talked about it as an increase, as an add-on basis, it was more attractive. We link it to the sales and income of the particular product groups in their stores. But there is still the feeling that a bonus is demeaning, since it suggests to them that we think they weren't working up to 100 percent at their regular pay level. This is so strong that I've had some of our best Dutch sales personnel refuse commission arrangements and work for less on a nonincentive basis."

"For the sales personnel in charge of product groups, we relate their monthly bonus half to the overall sales of the store and half to their meeting the product group objectives. We added the cashiers, outside sales representatives, and warehouse staff to the bonus scheme and initially got a good response. The hourly employees have a fixed potential bonus. The outside reps' bonus is a percentage of sales, but their base salary is larger than it would be in the United States. But so far, I'm not satisfied with the way we're using it, nor do I think it's producing tangible results. Of course, much depends on how the individual manager uses it . . . on the quality and frequency of feedback to these people."

Belgium was more oriented to financial incentives according to John. The bonus scheme had been installed there and the repsonse had been encouraging.

Salary increases were a problem, too. John told of a recent incident involving two accountants. Accountant A was married and in his late twenties and was considered a low producer. Accountant B was single, aged seventeen, and produced at least five times the work of A. His salary was 25 percent less than A's. Yet when salary review came up, the Chief Accountant and the Director of Administration recommended a greater increase for A than for B. Tom refused their advice, gave A only the mandatory cost-of-living increase and added the remainder of the increase recommended for A to B's raise. Both the Director of Administration and Chief Accountant were visibly upset and voiced their disapproval. When A came in and angrily asked why he hadn't gotten an increase, Tom flatly told him he wasn't worth it. He had done poor work and refused to work overtime. Then A questioned B's raise saying that since he was single, he didn't need it. John indicated that A seemed to think that if he were paid more, then he would work harder. "It contradicts the assumption that we hold," John concluded, "that you get rewarded after you demonstrate your accomplishments. Education, age, marital status, and financial need have more influence on salary here than in the United States."

Recruiting

With the expansion of operations and employee turnover, recruiting was an issue that concerned both managers. Part of the problem came from the very low rate of unemployment in the Netherlands, which averaged 2 percent across the country but was virtually zero in several of the regions where stores were located or planned. Newspaper ads for clerks or cashiers went unanswered. Job titles were inflated to add status and prestige. For example, the accounts payable supervisor was listed as "manager" and people with little or no office experience would apply for the position. Tom commented that the Controllers for both the Netherlands and Belgium probably had had no supervisory experience at all.

Another reason for recruiting problems had to do with Manners being a United States company. Tom estimated that only about 10 percent of the Dutch aggressively sought employment with United States firms. Some wanted to learn United States business methods, while others liked the less dictatorial climate. But he thought that the vast majority viewed United States companies as too heartless, too demanding, and requiring too much hard work. The new Accounts Payable Manager told Tom openly that his family had criticized him for joining a United States company.

John agreed that it was difficult to find people willing to work for multinational companies. He thought they were viewed as being different from local companies in vague ways and were generally stereotyped as expecting more from people than did European firms.

But John noted that this varied within Europe, too. He said that the Belgian operations had been started with a German as General Manager. But soon letters directed to him from Belgian employees arrived with complaints about the autocratic practices of the German General Manager. They were resentful of German supervisors. Some Belgian customers even complained about a "German firm" being in Belgium. Differences in national attitudes contributed to the complications of recruiting.

It was also difficult to obtain people with the level of education desired by the company. There wasn't the supply of generally educated B.A.s as in North America. Some people had higher status degrees in which case they usually refused supervisor's positions as "beneath" them. Others had attended night classes and received "business school" diplomas which were hard to judge and generally meant minimum training in a narrow area such as bookkeeping.

Hiring experienced people from other firms was also subject to uncertainties, partially influenced by Dutch laws. An admittedly extreme example was described by John who told of receiving a request from a Dutch bank for a reference about a former Manners employee who had been fired for stealing. But according to the law, John was forbidden to say anything negative or to refer to the discharge. "I simply replied that the person worked for us from date x to date y," John said. "But it gives you some idea of the problem we face in screening people for jobs."

Besides the problem of finding skilled people in a situation of a limited and underqualified supply, other government regulations added to the risks. They prohibited the company from firing anyone with more than two months' seniority except with clear proof of fault for a limited number of offenses (such as theft). Because of this John had directed that all new employees at the supervisory level or above be required to sign a six-month contract which, in effect, lengthened this trial period by four months.

Other Problems External to the Company

But not all the operating or planning problems dealt with internal activities. One critical dimension involved supplier relations. John remarked about the "organized" nature of the supply situation with cartels, informal agreements, etc. "Ironically," he noted, "what was a strength at the sales end of our business—that is, our low price—turned out to be a distinct handicap at the supply end. Suppliers balked at shipping to a low-price retail organization that would force a cut in margins among their established customers. The fact is that we threatened two sets of the large suppliers' clients: both the traditionally smaller, more specialized, Dutch retail merchants and the middlemen vendors who we bypassed because of our large quantity buying. In addition to 'breaking the rules,' as newcomers we were hardly 'members of the club.' This is still a problem that I have to stay on top of.

"The supply issue in Belgium is a bit different," John added. "Initially we had trouble even getting vendors to talk with us, much less supply our stores. Slowly we realized that the way of doing business there was quite different. It meant being less direct, more informal, and entertaining more. We changed our manner of dealing with them and saw a dramatic improvement in both price and delivery. It was amazing.

"Business and government relations and the political environment represent another area where we have to adapt. This is particularly important to our plans for expansion. With the scarcity of land in the Netherlands building permits are *very* tightly controlled. Permission to build a store requires elaborate zoning regulations and a series of approvals. There's no under-the-table action either. And although we don't suffer any more than Dutch firms, the procedures are heavy and the red tape often causes delays that hurt us. On top of that, the city council of most local governments is controlled by small business people, shopkeepers, and other retail merchants from the center-city. Our kind of store directly challenges all that these people value and prize. That hardly helps us," John understated wryly.

"In Belgium it's very different from here . . . more like the United States. You can be driving along and see property that looks good and in a reasonable time get favorable zoning and buy it. It's less bound by fixed rules and regulations; much more political. The flexibility is reflected by a more rapid growth there. Of course, our competitors grow more quickly, too."

Shifting from this subject, John turned to some of the characteristics of the Manners Europe sales that concerned him. One item was that of product mix. He noted that plumbing and carpeting had shown strength in the Netherlands and Belgium but had been the slowest portions of their product line in England.

He was also concerned about the relative proportions of sales between consumer sales versus contractors and professionals. While the do-it-yourself acceptance of the Manners concept was encouraging, the contractors and professionals represented a definite problem. Traditionally in the Netherlands these people bought from special wholesalers called builders' merchants. Manners had broken this distribution channel and the professionals were resisting the change. They resented the fact that Manners wanted to sell both to them and direct to the consumer on a do-it-yourself appeal. In fact, this new pattern not only disrupted their long-standing relations with the builders' merchants, but also created new competition for the contractors and tradesmen—namely, the do-it-yourself consumer who would now use professionals less frequently.

John knew from direct experience that it was hard to sell the contractors on the merits of the Manners outlets and it was even tougher to sell the store managers on developing this market segment. Examining the comparative sales data he had assembled (see below), he felt that further action was necessary.

Percentage of Sales by Market Segment and Country

Market Segment	U.S.	Netherlands	Belgium	United Kingdom
Professional	50%	20%	5%	40%
Do-It-Yourself	50%	80%	95%	60%

In citing the discrepancies across countries John noted that the General Manager's position in Belgium was still vacant, though he was leaving for Belgium the very next day to continue work on finding the right person. The relative success of the English operation with small builders was partially explained by the fact that Manners' partner in the joint venture there was one of England's largest builders' merchants.

In comparing the countries on other dimensions, he stated that the Dutch stores were characterized by a smaller average sale per customer, but a larger number of customers relative to Belgium where fewer people bought more goods per stop. In England both figures were smaller than either the Netherlands or Belgium data, but their success in tapping the smaller builder market more than made up for this. John said that one survey at a store in the Netherlands indicated that 20 percent of their customers did not own a car. Eight percent shopped at the store by bicycle. Closing the review with a grin, John chuckled, "You ought to see the stuff they tow away on a bike . . . the most amazing scene I've witnessed is a man who bought a bathtub and managed to cycle away!"

Some Pressures to Act

One of the facts that added to the pressures for John to establish some priorities among these problems and start to deal with them was top management's policy of limiting United States executives to three years overseas. This meant that Tom Steiger's experience and expertise was available to the European operation only for an additional twelve to eighteen months. Yet future expansion depended on sound accounting and control systems. In addition, it meant another decision for John to make—whether to recommend an American or European as Tom's successor. At this time he couldn't see an inside candidate of the necessary caliber, and the market conditions made the price of obtaining the right outsider in Europe so high as to offset the cost disadvantages of bringing over a younger American. He also wondered if an American might be more willing and able to fight the battle of implementing change and obtaining cooperation than would a European.

On the other hand, he knew that a European would be more acceptable on several grounds. First, there was the publicly stated policy of being a fully European operation. This was generally known to the Manners' employees. John also knew that his boss, Ralph Jennings, was committed to the notion of European management. Then there were the cultural problems of adapting home office practices to the foreign op-

erations. This, he knew, could be used to argue either side of the choice. He wanted to have a recommendation ready on this question prior to his next scheduled return to the United States in early August. He would be meeting with Mr. Jennings then to review the European operations and wanted to be prepared if asked about this issue.

Perhaps of even greater urgency was the question of his own status. The three years limit on being overseas was a well-established policy about which the United States executives felt rather strongly. The Dutch employees were sensitive to this, too, and John neither wished to be a "lame duck" director, nor did he want to alienate them by leaving the issue unresolved. While he obviously wished to avoid antagonizing top management, he wasn't beyond lobbying tactfully for an extension for a year or two to consolidate into a firm base the expansion he had spearheaded since his arrival.

As he thought about his own career with Manners and about the lengthy list of issues turned up by his and Tom's review of their work in Europe, he knew he faced a busy period of analysis, decisions, and action in the next two months before his trip back home.

Notes

1. Names of the company and people have been disguised.

2. Tom estimated that it cost the company from two and a half to three times as much to have an American in the position than a local person. The difference was due to the basic salary difference plus foreign location bonus, travel, moving expenses, and education, cost of living, and housing allowances.

3. Approval of the Labor Bureau must be obtained and termination times and payment can be quite large (two years' salary). Also when a person is fired, he or she may receive 80 percent of his or her salary for up to three years as unemployment compensation paid by the government.

E I G H T

MANAGERIAL LEADERSHIP IN AN INTERNATIONAL CONTEXT

An important aspect of the managerial job is leadership. The attainment of organizational goals depends on the provision of direction and guidance to the members and on the securing of proper performance from them. Effective managers lead their followers to perform their jobs successfully. Put simply, successful managers are effective leaders. The ability of a manager to lead affects his or her ability to manage. Because organizational performance is based on the collective contributions of all members, without an effective leader to combine these contributions, organizational performance may suffer.

Although leadership is not an easy task, it is much easier in domestic firms than in an international enterprise. Providing direction and purpose for a culturally diverse workforce in a multinational company (MNC) is a very challenging task. Although many aspects are similar to its domestic counterpart, as many more of the MNC's operational requirements are different. In a domestic firm, because managers and workers share the same cultural values and heritage, many issues do not require much elaboration and explanation by the managers. Cultural norms provide a basic framework for the fulfillment of duties and a simple means for control. Such a vehicle is not available to an international manager who works with a culturally diverse workforce. In this chapter we learn about the difficulties that international managers may experience in leading.

This chapter introduces the readers to major theories of leadership. The basic premises and assumptions underlying these theories are examined. Through this examination, the chapter elaborates on their relevance under different cultural settings. A presentation of leadership practices in Europe and Japan concludes the chapter.

South Africa has been the venue of two world renowned leaders, Mahatma Gandhi and Nelson Mandela, each with different means to a broad common end—freeing their people from oppression and injustice. Included among the means used by both of them to promote their cause were business and economic actions aimed at hurting the purses of their tyrant rulers.

Mahatma Gandhi was born on October 2, 1869, in Porbandar, a city in the present state of Gujarat, in India. While he was a legal advisor for an Indian firm in South Africa he witnessed the widespread denial of human rights to Indian immigrants. It was in South Africa that Gandhi formed his philosophy of passive resistance and noncooperation as a strategy for opposing tyranny and human rights abuses. When he returned to India, Gandhi began teaching and practicing passive resistance and civil disobedience, which Indians called ahimsa (a Sanskrit word meaning "nonviolence"). He led Indians in a long and difficult struggle for independence from Britain. Knowing the importance of economic pressure, he ordered the complete boycott of all British goods. Finally, under his leadership India gained its independence in 1947.

Gandhi lived a spiritual and ascetic life. He wore the loincloth and a shawl common among the lowliest Indians. He responded to abuses, beatings, and jail sentences inflicted on him by British authorities by fasting, prayers, and meditation, and he urged his followers to do the same. Gandhi was revered by Indians as a saint, and they called him Mahatma ("great-souled"). He is the symbol of free India, and the spiritual leader of the nonviolent movement globally. His teachings and philosophy have influenced and inspired nonviolent movements everywhere.

Nelson Rolihlahla Mandela, who in 1994 was elected the first black president of South Africa, was born on July 18, 1918, at Mbhashe in the Umtata district. His father was a chief and his mother was one of the chief's four wives. In 1942 Nelson obtained his BA degree and became a student at the Witwatersrand University in the Faculty of Law. In 1944 Mandela joined the African National Congress (ANC), the political party aimed at eradicating the segregationist practices of the South African government. In 1947, he was elected the ANC's secretary, and its president in 1951. At first, he followed the nonviolent resistance against the apartheid policy of South Africa, but dismayed by its apparent failure, soon joined the armed struggle.

In 1960, police fired at unarmed pass-law protestors, massacring thousands. Consequently, civil strikes ensued and a state of emergency was declared. Thousands were arrested and the ANC was banned. Mandela was forced to go underground in April 1961. He organized the military training for armed operations against the apartheid regime. Soon, he was arrested and sentenced to imprisonment for five years. In 1963, following the arrest of other ANC leaders, Mandela, who was already in prison, was tried again, this time for sabotage and for attempting to overthrow the state. He was convicted and

sentenced to life imprisonment. While in prison he received many awards, honorary degrees, and even honorary citizenship from other nations. To force the dismantling of the apartheid regime, he pleaded with Western governments to impose economic sanctions against the government, and urged the MNCs to withdraw their investments from South Africa. Finally, the economic measures and worldwide condemnation forced the abandonment of apartheid practices.

When Mandela was released on February 11, 1990, some wondered whether he would be ready for compromise after spending more than a quarter of a century in prison. Some have argued that if he was bent on vengeance and had taken a personal position he could have caused mass riots and massive civil strife. But he, as the leader of South African blacks, set aside his personal feelings. He concluded his first speech after his release from the prison by saying, "I have fought against white domination, and I have fought against black domination. I have cherished the idea of a democratic and free society in which all persons live together in harmony and with equal opportunities. It is an ideal which I hope to live for and achieve. But if needs be, it is an ideal for which I am prepared to die."

Sources: J. M. Brown. *Gandhi: Prisoner of Hope*, (New Haven: Yale University Press, 1989); M. Fatima. *Higher Than Hope—The Authorized Biography of Nelson Mandela* (New York: Harper Collins, 1990); *Nelson Mandela Speaks—Forging a Democratic Nonracial South Africa* (New York: Pathfinder, 1993); C. S. Wren. "Mandela Sees Negotiations Soon over Political Rights for Blacks." *The New York Times* (February 13, 1990), A16.

Introduction

Many business failures can be traced to functional deficiencies, such as poor planning or marketing. Many more are due to the managers' inability to lead. Effective managers are those who can lead their subordinates toward the accomplishment of organizational goals. This is a feat not easily attained. Among the managerial skills, leadership competency is very difficult to master. Managers can rely on assistance from others in technical matters, but they have to resolve leadership problems through personal initiative. Leadership skills, therefore, are critical to managerial success.

If leading is an important determinant of success in a domestic business, it is much more important in an international operation. What constitutes a good leader in one culture may not constitute a good leader in other cultures. Most Americans, for example, prefer democratic leaders who seek input from their subordinates. In other cultures, such a leader may be regarded as naive or incompetent. To some cultures, a leader should always know how to take charge and lead the subordinates without needing much assistance from them. Any failure to take charge would be interpreted as a sign of incompetence.

Besides having technical expertise, international managers must possess the ability to organize and lead a workforce of diverse cultures, and to achieve cross-cultural collaboration in spite of multicultural difficulties. They need to be proficient in coaching, mentoring, and assessing the performance of people with different values, beliefs, and attitudes. The requirements for managerial leadership in international contexts extend well beyond functional management practices to encompass a sensitivity to, and empathy with, cultural diversity. The task of leading under demanding conditions requires an understanding of leadership concepts and the ability to apply them to different cultural circumstances.

In the following, we present the major leadership theories. As was the case with motivation theories, we will see that they have been developed and tested almost exclusively in the West. In turn, they have shaped managerial thinking and philosophies in the West. Even though these theories are based on Western cultural values and assumptions, they are often implicitly presented as universal theories. Consequently, practicing managers have applied them, along with other Western managerial concepts, to international situations without considering the need to apply them to the new contexts. Not surprisingly, the results have been less than stellar. While the available theories may not be fully applicable to other cultural settings, they can be useful. By reviewing these theories we will be able to examine their applicability to different cultural situations. The knowledge thus gained is also useful for the non-Western MNCs operating in the West.

Major Leadership Theories

Two streams of research at The Ohio State University and the University of Michigan fueled a modern debate on leadership that has persisted until today. Modern theories of leadership depart from the traditional trait theories, which propose that certain people are "born leaders." According to trait theories, leaders are endowed with certain characteristics—physiological, psychological, and intellectual—that set them apart from others. All we have to do is identify the persons with these traits and assign them to leadership positions. Years of research, however, have shown that while certain traits increase the likelihood of a leader's success, they do not guarantee it. Researchers have found that the leader's behavior, rather than his or her traits, is most important in determining leader effectiveness. More recently, attention has shifted toward situational demands and followers' characteristics and influences in determining leadership effectiveness. The initial ideas were highlighted in the studies that took place at The Ohio State University and the University of Michigan during the latter part of the 1940s and early 1950s.

The Ohio State University and the University of Michigan Studies

Two separate research efforts at The Ohio State University and the University of Michigan produced similar results. The Ohio State researchers identified two dimensions of leadership behavior that influence the followers' work performance. These two dimensions are *consideration* for workers and the *initiating structure,* or task orientation. Comparable dimensions were reported by the researchers at the University of Michigan and were labeled *employee oriented* and *production oriented.* Supportive leaders who create a friendly environment for workers and establish their relationship on the basis of mutual trust and respect are demonstrating concern for workers. Examples of consideration (employee-oriented behavior) are closer relationships between employees and their managers, treating subordinates as equals, doing favors and promoting the welfare of employees, giving advance notice of changes in the organization, and explaining managerial decisions. Leadership behavior that is related to task accomplishment and the efficient use of resources is termed initiating structure and production-oriented behavior in the respective studies. Close supervision of work activities, allocation of tasks, scheduling of work, supplying work instructions and generally providing the workers with direction and assistance in doing their jobs represent different aspects of this dimension.

A synthesis of concerns for production and concerns for people   The studies at The Ohio State University and the University of Michigan served as a springboard for further leadership research. In a departure from the trait theories, these studies brought to our attention that the leader's behavior makes a difference in the subordinates' work performance and attitudes.

While early research findings regarding the effects of these two dimensions on workers' performance have not been consistent under all conditions, certain patterns have been identified. The researchers at these universities found that often high consideration and employee-oriented behavior was associated with employee satisfaction, low turnover, and low absenteeism. The impact of consideration on performance, however, was low. Higher productivity and lower employee satisfaction were frequently related to high initiating structure and production-oriented behavior.[1]

Since concern for people and concern for production are two separate dimensions, it appears that leaders can employ a combination of both. Such a combination is actually proposed by scholars of leadership under the title of a *managerial grid.* Robert R. Blake and Jane S. Mouton have suggested that by combining a concern for people and a concern for production, managers can achieve the best results.[2]

Figure 8.1 depicts the results of combining the two dimensions of leadership behavior. The four quadrants in Figure 8.1 illustrate four extreme variations of leadership behavior. At the lower left-hand side of the figure, quadrant 1 represents low concern for production and low concern for people. This is the stereotypical ineffective manager who does not show much concern for either the workers or the work. The upper left-hand side, quadrant 2, showing a combination of low concern for production and high concern for people, represents the people-oriented behavior without much concern for the work. Quadrant 3, the lower right-hand side, is a combination of high concern for production and low concern for people, which typifies a taskmaster style. The upper right-hand side, quadrant 4, is a mixture of high concern for workers and high concern for work. Some management scholars have suggested that this is a very effective leadership style.

Likert's Managerial Systems

Managerial leadership takes place in the organization, and it is influenced by the prevailing

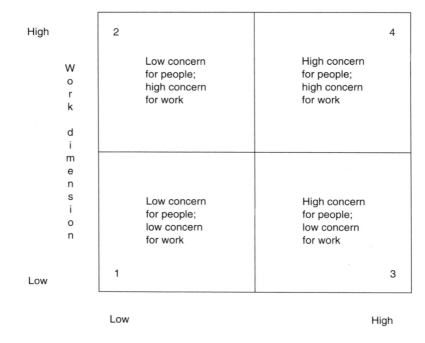

High

W
o
r
k

	2	4
	Low concern for people; high concern for work	High concern for people; high concern for work

d
i
m
e
n
s
i
o
n

	Low concern for people; low concern for work	High concern for people; low concern for work
	1	3

Low

Low   High

People dimension

Figure 8.1   A Synthesis of Two Leadership Dimensions

managerial practices. Therefore, it is not sufficient to study individual leadership behavior without a consideration of organizational norms and practice. Leadership behavior that is contrary to the prevailing managerial practices of an organization will not produce the desired results. Rensis Likert developed a questionnaire that measures the organization's management system. He proposed that there are four management systems: (1) exploitative authoritative, (2) benevolent authoritative, (3) consultative, and (4) participative. These systems are based on varying degrees of trust and confidence that each exhibits toward the subordinates. The following is a brief description of the four systems.[3] Research results have been varied, but there has been some evidence of support in U.S. settings.

System 1: exploitative authoritative   This system has no confidence and trust in subordinates. It relies on centralized decision making from the top of the organization. Subordinates are not involved in any important decision making. In system 1 management, fear, threats, punishments, and occasional rewards are major instrument of motivation. The superior–subordinate relationship is limited to and is based on mistrust and fear. An informal organization develops that parallels the formal organization. It usually resists and opposes the goals of formal organization.

System 2: benevolent authoritative   The relationship between superior and subordinate in system 2 resembles that of master–servant. Managers express a condescending confidence and trust toward subordinates. A superior–

subordinate relationship is characterized by patronizing behavior by superiors and cautious approach by subordinates. Although most decisions are centralized at the top of the organization, within a prescribed framework some decisions are made by the people at the lower levels. Rewards and punishment are used for motivating subordinates. An informal organization may develop within system 2 that does not always oppose the formal organizational goals.

System 3: consultative While managers have a substantial amount of confidence in subordinates, they still prefer to maintain control over most decisions. Strategic decisions are made by the top-level managers. Subordinates, however, are allowed to make many of the decisions affecting the lower levels. Communication flows in both directions, upward and downward. Rewards, some occasional punishment, and involvement in decision making are major motivating tools of system 3. The informal organization that usually develops within the formal organization may have an ambivalent attitude toward the formal organizational goals.

System 4: participative The participative management system is characterized by complete confidence and trust in subordinates. Decentralized decision making differentiates this system from the other three systems. Communication flows freely between all levels of organization. Subordinates participate in setting economic rewards, establishing goals, determining the methods of improving performance, and appraising progress toward goals. Substantial and friendly interaction between subordinates and superiors creates a high degree of confidence and trust. Control is decentralized throughout the organizational hierarchy. There is a great overlap between formal and informal organizations. Often, they are one and the same.

Likert proposed that system 4 is an effective managerial leadership approach. Research studies, again based primarily in the United States, tend to support his contention that participative

Authoritarian Leadership in a Matrilineal Society

The matrilineal Khasi society in northeastern India, one of the few surviving female bastions in the world, is making a fervent effort to keep men in their place.

Though an all-male organization that is battling the centuries-old matrilineal system has yet to make any significant dent, the rebels claim to have enlisted the support of some prominent Khasi women. Their struggle to break free, they say, has resulted in small victories; some have begun to have a say in family affairs and are even inheriting property. . . .

The men say the Khasi women are overbearing and dominating. "We are sick of playing the roles of breeding bulls and baby sitters," complains Mr. A. Swer, who heads the organization of maverick males. Another member laments: "We have no line of succession. We have no land, no business. Our generation ends with us."

The demand for restructuring Khasi society in the patriarchal mold is a fallout from the growing number of women who are marrying outsiders. . . . Following the custom, the youngest daughter inherits the property and after marriage her husband moves into the family house . . . .

While some men would like to end female domination, they do not support Mr. Swer's movement to abandon the deeply held tradition. . . . Mr. Swer admits that the Khasi men's demand is still a distant hope.

Excerpted from S. Zubair Ahmed "What Do Men Want?" *The New York Times* (February 15, 1994), A21. The article originally appeared in *The Times of India*, January 28, 1994.

management is associated with favorable attitudes toward the leader, open channels of communication, and group cohesiveness. Productivity and employee job satisfaction tend to be higher among system 4 organizations.

Situational Leadership

As attention turned away from the search for leadership traits, and moved toward efforts to find the best leadership behaviors or style, another set of factors emerged. Specifically, researchers discovered that no one particular style was effective under all situations. They concluded that the effectiveness of leader behavior is a function of the situation at hand. Situational factors such as the followers, the work, organizational culture, and other environmental factors influence the leader's effectiveness. This re-

alization was expressed in several situational theories of leadership. Several of the most popular situational theories are the leadership continuum and the contingency models.

The leadership continuum   According to Robert Tannenbaum and Warren Schmidt,[4] leadership is viewed as a continuum. At one end of this continuum is the total control by the boss (leader-manager) through the exercise of authority, and at the other end is the subordinate's autonomy to make decisions within prescribed limits. As Figure 8.2 illustrates, as we move from the left to the right along this continuum, the authoritarian role of leader-managers decreases and the autonomy, power, and influence of subordinates increase. At the extreme right side of the continuum, authoritarian leaders tend to use their power to influence their subordi-

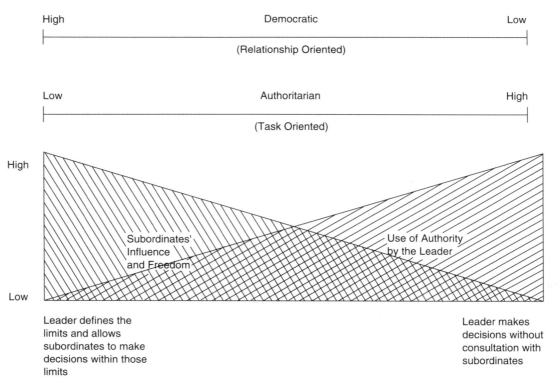

Figure 8.2   Leadership Continuum

nates. They make the decisions alone without consultation with their subordinates. At the other extreme left of the continuum, democratic leaders define the limits within which subordinates can make all the decisions, and allow them the full participation in decision making. A middle-ground approach is followed by the leaders who combine inputs from subordinates with the authority of the position to make decisions. Authoritarian leaders tend to be task oriented and democratic leaders tend to be relationship oriented.

Tannenbaum and Schmidt suggested that there is no one best way to lead. Leaders should use their power according to the situational demands. Four situational factors could determine the appropriate use of power by a leader-manager: (1) the personality of subordinates, (2) subordinates' expectations about the leader behavior, (3) the willingness of the subordinates to accept the responsibility, and (4) the ability of the group to accomplish the tasks. A combination of the situational requirements may dictate the full use of power by the leaders. If individual subordinates are not self directed and require close supervision, if the work group does not have the ability to solve the problems, if they are not willing to take the responsibility, and if they expect the leader to take charge, then the task-oriented leadership style may be more productive. In the opposite situation, a relationship-oriented leadership style would be more appropriate. Situational factors such as time pressure, the nature and scope of the problem, and organizational circumstances also impact the manager's behavior.

House's contingency model of leadership
The leadership continuum as proposed by Tannebaum and Schmidt is an acknowledgment that leadership behavior is similar to other types of behavior. It does not take place in a vacuum. Forces outside the leader have a bearing on his or her behavior. It brings to our attention the fact that leaders are not fully autonomous and totally oblivious to their surroundings. There are po-

tential forces that influence leadership behavior. Robert House has pulled together elements of a number of theories to propose a contingency model of leadership called path-goal theory.[5] House proposes that three major categories of factors impact the style the leader adopts. These factors are the nature of the subordinates, the organizational setting, and the group. The leader's style, then, changes in response to these factors. An effective leader assists the followers in reaching their goals and assures that the followers goals are compatible with the overall organizational objectives. In other words, effective leaders clarify the path for individuals to reach their goals and at the same time contribute to the attainment of overall organizational objectives. Let us briefly take a look at these forces.

Subordinates' characteristics and response
The subordinates' characteristics influence the leader. A leader may be inclined to supervise closely subordinates who are ill trained, lack experience, or are unwilling to assume the full responsibility of their jobs. Conversely, a leader may prefer to delegate responsibility and grant autonomy to those subordinates who have demonstrated the ability and the willingness to do the job without much external control. Like other people, leaders tend to like and trust those whose background and characteristics are similar to theirs. Therefore, the amiable relationship which may exist when the leader and the subordinates have something in common may result in more democratic leadership behavior.

Organizational settings
The task.   An important factor affecting employee performance is the nature of the task. Certain task characteristics reduce or eliminate the need for guidance and directions by the leader. Those who work on tasks that are interesting and intrinsically satisfying may not require much external motivation and persuasion. They may perform their jobs even in the absence of a leader. Under time pressure most people, including the leaders, become directive and task oriented. Faced with ambiguity, crisis, and

looming work deadlines, subordinates look up to the leader for direction and expect instruction and guidance. In those situations a leader may exhibit more autocratic behavior without too much resentment and resistance from the subordinates.

Organizational climate. The organizational climate and the leadership philosophy of the top management have a great bearing on the rest of the employees. Some organizations are known for a bureaucratic climate in which adherence to strict rules is expected. Such a climate may encourage tendencies toward a more centralized, directive, and autocratic leadership behavior. Conversely, where top management demonstrates a preference for informal relations, managers are more apt to rely on such behavior in their dealings with subordinates.

We are all subject to influence by our peers. Leader-managers are not immune from this rule. Individual managers are affected by the managerial style and behavioral pattern of other managers. Years of association with peers tend to create some degree of similarity in attitudes and a predominant leadership style among the managers. Deviations from norms are frowned on, and adherence to standards is promoted. A manager who treats his or her subordinates relatively leniently, for example, may hear objections by other managers who fear their subordinates may demand a similar treatment.

Work group Groups are the primary work units within most organizations. Very seldom can individual job assignments be performed independently and outside a group setting. These assignments are usually carried out within a work group structure. The members' characteristics and resources that they bring to the work group determine the group's characteristics. The nature of the work group influences the quantity and quality of the work performed by the individuals and the effectiveness of leadership behavior. For example, when there is a high level of conflict within the group, a directive leadership behavior (i.e., providing work guidelines

and a work schedule) would be effective. By recognizing the nature of the work group and providing the type of assistance, guidance, and coaching that may be required, the leader can influence the group and individual performance.

Leadership characteristics Leadership behavior and the person of the leader are inseparable. Personality differences result in people behaving differently under different conditions. In Chapter 7 we learned about many motivating forces. Motivating forces, we learned, could be external or internal to the individuals. Those high on achievement or power, for example, may be more comfortable giving orders and emphasizing task accomplishment. Others who are high on affiliation need may be more interested in forming friendly relationships with people. These managers may not directly push for higher performance. Instead, they may rely on personal relationships in fulfilling their responsibilities. The leader's philosophy regarding human nature greatly influences leader relations with followers. As Douglas McGregor[6] proposed, some managers, called *Theory X managers,* assume that people, by their very nature, are lazy, dislike to work, and avoid responsibility whenever possible. Such people, therefore, need to be controlled directly, and coaxed to work hard with whatever measure necessary, including coercion and threats of punishment. Some other managers, called *Theory Y managers,* believe the engagement in mental and physical work is very natural to people—like playing and resting. They assume that people generally like work, do not shy away from assuming responsibility, and under the right conditions will perform to the best of their abilities. Therefore, the use of external control and the threat of punishment are not the best ways to improve work performance. These two different philosophies, naturally, result in two different approaches to leadership behavior. Theory X managers tend to be more work oriented, while Theory Y managers tend to be more relationship oriented.

This discussion of the influence of situational factors on leadership behavior highlights the interactive nature of the leadership process. It also implies that effective leaders exhibit flexibility in directing their followers, and select leadership styles to fit the situations. When the appropriate leader behavior matches the primary demands of the situation (i.e., where subordinates are trained, the job is clear-cut, and the group supports the organizational goals), a participative style can be used. In contrast, where the opposite conditions exist, a more directive or authoritarian style is appropriate. House's path-goal theory of leadership proposes that there are many forces impinging on the leaders' relationship with the subordinates. The understanding of these forces can assist the leader-manager in selecting a proper course of action that meets the challenge of managing.

Fiedler's Contingency Model

Fred Fiedler[7] has proposed a different contingency model. He proposed that both leadership styles of concern for work (task oriented: similar to The Ohio State University's "initiating structure") and concern for people (relationship oriented: similar to "consideration" from The Ohio State University research) could be effective under certain conditions. The conditions that influence the effectiveness of these leadership tendencies depend on a combination of three elements: task structure, leader's position power, and leader–member relations. Various combinations of these elements produce situations that are favorable or unfavorable to the leader. As is described shortly, leadership effectiveness depends on a match between the leader's behavioral inclinations and the favorableness of the situation.

Leader–member relations   The situational favorability is strongly influenced by the leader–follower relationship. A situation is favorable to the leader if the group's acceptance of him or her is high, if the group and the leader are getting along, and if there is a high degree of regard for the leader. In such a favorable situation, the group and the leader can work together, and the leader has no difficulty in leading them. A leader who is liked and respected can influence the group far beyond the limits of his or her authority.

Task structure   A task is structured if all of the requirements for performing it are known to the members. The leader has no problem determining what should be done, who should do it, how it should be performed, and the reason for doing it. Such a task leaves less room for misunderstanding and disputes. The more a task is structured, the higher the situational favorableness.

Position power   Position power refers to the amount of power and influence that the leader has. A strong power position enables the leader to lead the group with no difficulty. No one would question his or her authority. Four types of power—legitimate (authority), expert, reward, and coercive—are the basis for the leader's position power.

Various combinations of these elements could create conditions that are either favorable or unfavorable to the leader. A favorable condition is when the task is structured, the power position is strong, and the leader–member relationship is good. An unfavorable condition is a combination of unstructured tasks, weak position power, and poor leader–member relations. Leaders who are task oriented are more effective under both extremes of either favorable conditions or unfavorable conditions (see Figure 8.3). Relationship-oriented leaders are more effective under moderately favorable conditions. An example of a favorable situation is a well respected and highly qualified head of an engineering firm. The tasks are structured, the power position is strong, and the leader–member relationship is good. A task-oriented leader would be able to get his or her group to work hard because they like him or her, they know the requirements of the tasks, and the leader has sufficient power to influence them. In an unfavorable situation, the

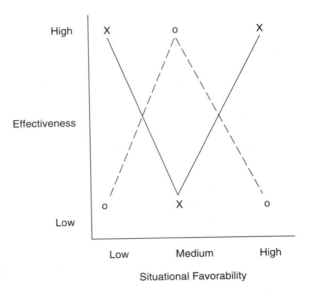

X = Task Oriented
o = Relationship Oriented

Figure 8.3   Effective Leadership Behavior under Various Situations
Based on Fred Fiedler and M. M. Chemers. Leadership and Effective Management *(Glenview, IL: Scott, Foresman and Co., 1974).*

only way to get the group to work hard is to demand it by setting goals, providing instruction for doing it, and guiding and controlling the work.

Compared with task-oriented leaders, relationship-oriented leaders are not very effective in the very favorable or very unfavorable situations. Their relative ineffectiveness is probably due to their lack of emphasis on production and minimum pressure they apply for higher performance. The relationship-oriented leaders are more effective in situations that are moderately favorable. In the moderately favorable situations, the more directive attitude of task-oriented leaders may lead to anxiety and conflict within the group. The nondirective and permissive attitude of a relationship-oriented leader is more effective.

Among the theories of leadership, situational theories have the best potential for application in cross-cultural settings. While these theories do not specifically consider national cultures as a situational variable, the underlying theoretical framework allows for such inclusion. Moreover, since they do not advocate a particular leadership style for all situations, the situational leadership theories accept that various leadership styles can be effective in different cultures. They also indicate that leadership effectiveness can be improved by modifying the contingent situational variables such as the group, the task, the followers' skills, and organizational policies. Still, imbedded in all these theories are certain assumptions. By learning about these assumptions, MNCs' managers will be able to modify them to fit the work environment in different cultures.

Assumptions Behind Leadership Theories

The leadership theories presented in the preceding section assume that the leaders and the followers have a great amount of commonality in their value systems and culture. They assume that the roles of leaders and followers are universal. These theories, implicitly if not explicitly, advocate democratic-participative leadership behavior as the preferred choice. Almost all were developed in the United States and are based on the American cultural values. As Reitz asserted, the American ". . . culture has traditionally placed higher values on democratic than on authoritarian leadership, certain biases can be detected in the research on the effects of these leadership styles. A great deal of research is designed to prove that democracy is superior to autocracy, rather than to test that proportion."[8] Recent research is questioning the validity of these assumptions. We could claim that democratic behavior is "nicer" than authoritarian behavior, but it is not necessarily more productive.[9] Other leadership behavior, under different circumstances and in different cultures may be more productive. "A single normative leadership style does not take into consideration cultural differences, particularly customs and traditions as well as the level of education and the standard of living."[10] In developing countries, for example, where most people are preoccupied with scratching out a livelihood, there is less concern for participation in decision making than in earning a living.

Cultural Relativity of Leadership

Cultural differences have a major influence on the effectiveness of various leadership behaviors. Norms, role expectations, and traditions governing the relations between various members of the society are a strong determinant of effective leadership behavior in a society. These differences are manifested in the MNCs whose employees comprise multicultural backgrounds. The challenge is for international managers working with multicultural employees to recognize these differences and adapt their relationships accordingly. To learn about these differences, we review two cultural dimensions: acceptance of authority and dealing with uncertainty. In previous chapters, we presented these two dimensions along with other cultural dimensions. While all cultural values influence the behavior of leaders, these two are of particular importance. Here we focus on their influence on leader-follower relationships. Using these two dimensions as a reference, we present the predominant leadership practices in Europe and Japan.

Acceptance of power and authority   The use of power and authority is central to management and leadership. Power and authority are universal to all cultures. Hierarchical relations are the mainstay of social interactions. The importance, emphasis, scope, and application of power and authority, however, vary among societies. Hofstede called this variation *power distance*.[11] In societies where power is more evenly distributed among the members, the difference between the more powerful members and the least powerful members is small. In others, there is a wide variation in power distribution and the difference between the most powerful and least powerful is large. To all the members, the large differences in power are legitimate and acceptable. Often, members feel uncomfortable if the distance is knowingly violated. For example, if a superior, in a large power distance society, attempts to reduce the distance by acting more accessible and friendly, his or her subordinates may not willingly accept such openness. They may attribute some ulterior motives to this overture.

In small power distance societies, people believe in equality and will attempt to minimize inequality. Superiors do not see themselves much different from subordinates and vice versa. With minimum distance among them, superiors are accessible to subordinates. Powerful people do not flaunt their power; they attempt to appear less powerful. Changes in small power distance societies take place incrementally through the redistribution of power.

People of large power distance societies believe in a hierarchical power distribution where everyone has a rightful place and everyone is protected by this order. Superiors consider themselves different from subordinates and vice versa. The difference between superiors and subordinates leads to inaccessibility of superiors. Power entitles people to certain privileges that include obedience and respect from others. Powerful people will not hide their powers and, in fact, use various trappings to signal their power. Officeholders can be identified by the mode of their dress, type of office, and their entourage. Meaningful changes take place only through dethroning of the powerful. Since other people are seen as a potential threat to one's power, they can rarely be trusted.

Avoiding uncertainty   To live is to deal with uncertainty. To manage is to deal with uncertainty in running an organization. A critical aspect of managing and leading is dealing with uncertainty by providing subordinates with direction and instruction for task performance. The orientation of society toward the handling of uncertainty is reflected in the management of its institutions and organizations. *Uncertainty avoidance* is "the extent to which a society feels threatened by uncertain and ambiguous situations and tries to avoid these situations by providing greater career stability, establishing more formal rules, not tolerating deviant ideas and behavior, and believing in absolute truths and the attainment of expertise."[12] Cultures with a strong uncertainty avoidance consider the uncertainties of life as a continuous threat that must be fought. They avoid conflict and competition and strive for consensus. Security in life is valued greatly, which leads to the search for ultimate truth and values. People in these countries take less risk, worry more about the future, and rely on seniority for advancement in the organizations. To avoid uncertainty, there is a heavy reliance on written rules and regulations.

Matters of importance are left to the authorities, which relieves subordinates from assuming the responsibility. Hofstede found that in countries high on uncertainty avoidance, loyalty to employers is considered a virtue.[13]

Cultures with a weak uncertainty avoidance accept uncertainty as an inherent aspect of life and take it in stride. They are contemplative, less aggressive, avoid expressing their emotions, and are tolerant of dissent and deviant behavior. There is less emphasis on rules and regulations and people are more willing to take risks. They believe that a certain amount of conflict and competition is constructive for the society, and devise various mechanisms to promote competition. Authorities are there to serve the people and if rules cannot be kept they should be changed. Loyalty to employers is not seen as a virtue, and people do not hesitate to change their jobs if there is opportunity for advancement.

A clustering of 40 countries according to their position on these two dimensions of power distance and uncertainty avoidance is depicted in Figure 8.4, where we see that the United States, Canada, and most Northern European countries are low in power distance and weak on uncertainty avoidance. Asians, Mediterraneans, and South Americans are high on both dimensions. A few Asian countries are high on power distance and low on uncertainty avoidance (upper left-hand side quadrant), and a few European countries are low on power distance and high on uncertainty avoidance (lower right-hand side quadrant).

It is important to recognize that the leadership theories reviewed in this chapter were all developed in countries low on power distance and low on uncertainty avoidance. It is not surprising that these theories usually lead to advocating the democratic-participative type of management style. Both superiors and subordinates in these countries value power sharing. These cultures have a more receptive environment for the practice of democratic-participative man-

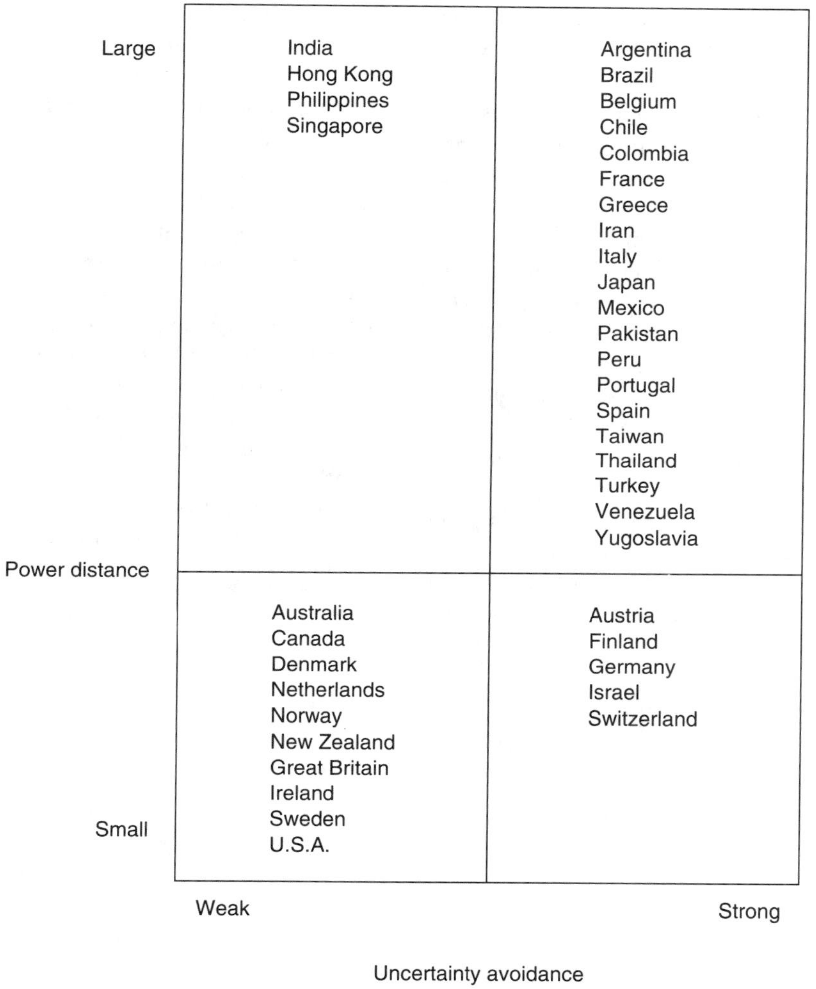

	Weak — Uncertainty avoidance — Strong	
Large	India Hong Kong Philippines Singapore	Argentina Brazil Belgium Chile Colombia France Greece Iran Italy Japan Mexico Pakistan Peru Portugal Spain Taiwan Thailand Turkey Venezuela Yugoslavia
Small	Australia Canada Denmark Netherlands Norway New Zealand Great Britain Ireland Sweden U.S.A.	Austria Finland Germany Israel Switzerland

Power distance

Uncertainty avoidance

Figure 8.4   Country Clusters Based on Power Distance and Uncertainty Avoidance
Note: In each cluster, countries are listed alphabetically, not according to their scores on the two dimensions. Also note that proportionally squares should be viewed as being equal in size.
Source: G. Hofstede. Culture's Consequences *(Beverly Hills, CA: Sage Publications, 1984).*

agement. Subordinates' participation in decision making brings about more autonomy and freedom. Those on low uncertainty avoidance are better suited to deal with the autonomy thus gained. In these cultures, superiors are comfortable with the subsequent uncertainty associated with the granting of autonomy to their subordinates. Similarly, subordinates are not uncom-

fortable assuming the risk and uncertainty associated with participation in decision making. The lower power distance between members of these societies allows for a closer relationship between leaders and followers.

Where power distance is large, subordinates may not feel quite comfortable with closer relationships between themselves and the managers.

Since leadership is an interactive process that requires subordinateship, the followers' expectation of a ideal leader greatly influences the feasibility of certain leadership practices. To most subordinates in large power distance cultures, for example, a benevolent autocrat or paternalist is an ideal superior. Hofstede's research indicates that subordinates in larger power distance countries tend to accept authoritarian leadership more readily. Table 8.1 depicts subordinateship at three levels of power distance. At each level of power distance subordinates accept certain leader behaviors as appropriate and, at each level, superiors also feel that certain leadership behaviors are more appropriate. A mismatch poses problems. Managers moving to large power distance cultures learn that they can be more effective by behaving autocratically. This is borne out by the Colonial history of most Western countries. Interestingly enough, among the ex-Colonial powers, France, with a larger power distance, enjoys a much better relationship with its old colonies.[14] Among the European countries, it was in France, too, that the application of management-by-objectives (MBO) failed.[15] MBO requires an agreement between managers and subordinates on a set of objectives and the means to reach them. This necessitates sufficient independence and autonomy on the part of subordinates for negotiation with superiors. Low power distance cultures more readily meet those requirements. Both managers and subordinates of high power distance cultures, however, have difficulty coping with those arrangements. Hofstede quotes French management scholars asserting that DPO (Direction par Objectifs, the French equivalent of MBO) does not work in France because:

> French blue- and white-collar workers, lower-level and higher-level mangers, and 'patrons'

Table 8.1
Subordinateship for Three Levels of Power Distance

Small Power Distance	Medium Power Distance (United States)	Large Power Distance
Subordinates have weak dependence needs.	Subordinates have medium dependence needs.	Subordinates have strong dependence needs.
Superiors have weak dependence needs toward their superiors.	Superiors have medium dependence needs toward their superiors.	Superiors have strong dependence needs toward their superiors.
Subordinates expect superiors to consult them and may rebel or strike if superiors are not seen as staying within their legitimate role.	Subordinates expect superiors to consult them but will accept autocratic behavior as well.	Subordinates expect superiors to act autocratically.
Ideal superior to most is a loyal democrat.	Ideal superior to most is a resourceful democrat.	Ideal superior to most is a benevolent autocrat or paternalist.
Laws and rules apply to all and privileges for superiors are not considered acceptable.	Laws and rules apply to all, but a certain level of privileges for superiors is considered normal.	Everybody expects superiors to enjoy privileges; laws and rules differ for superiors and subordinates.
Status symbols are frowned on and will easily come under attack from subordinates.	Status symbols for superiors contribute moderately to their authority and will be accepted by subordinates.	Status symbols are very important and contribute strongly to the superior's authority with the subordinates.

Source: G. Hofstede. *Culture's Consequences* (Beverly Hills, CA: Sage Publications, 1987), 259. © 1984 by Geert Hofstede. Reprinted by permission of Sage Publications, Inc.

all belong to the same cultural system which maintains dependency relations from level to level. Only the deviants really dislike this system. The Hierarchical structure protects against anxiety; DPO, however, generates anxiety. . . .[16]

Cultures high on power distance and uncertainty avoidance are not fertile ground for participative management. Underlining this point is the French experience with MBO and the failure of recent attempts by the French government at democratization of the workplace. During the 1980s, the French government implemented laws that were designed to promote workplace democratization from the bottom up. The goal was to promote a new citizenship in the workplace, and to make the worker the agent of change. It mandated the creation of the "direct expression groups," where employees could freely express their concern and raise questions about the operation of the firm. The government felt that French management had lagged behind managers elsewhere in developing productive relations with employees and that it needed reform. Neither management nor workers showed much interest in the reforms, however, and the French business community adamantly opposed the reform. It saw the expression groups as a potential threat to their authority. Likewise, employees were not interested in the democratization of their workplace. They were more concerned with job security, higher wages, and shorter work weeks.[17] As Hofstede noted, where both power distance and uncertainty avoidance are high, having a powerful superior whom we can both praise and blame is one way of satisfying a strong need for avoiding uncertainty.[18]

Not only do managers of low power distance cultures find it easy to act autocratically in large power distance cultures, but they find it difficult to operate in an environment with a lower power distance than their own. U.S. managers, for example, have difficulty in fully accepting industrial democracy as it is practiced in Sweden or Germany. Power sharing and participation in decision making take on a whole new dimension in industrial democracy. From the American perspective, industrial democracy impinges on the prerogatives of management. American managers do not accept a power sharing scheme that cuts across all levels of the organization and in which the lower levels have a major role.[19]

An essential aspect of leadership is the role and behavior of subordinates. Subordinate employees use various strategies to influence their superiors. Table 8.1 summarizes subordinateships for three levels of power distance. The choice of these strategies is dependent on their perceived appropriateness in a given culture. What an American subordinate may find appropriate may not be viewed similarly by an Asian. This difference was observed in research among Chinese and Americans working in Hong Kong and Americans working in the United States. It was found that a difference exists between Eastern and Western styles of upward influence. Americans preferred overt tactics involving image management that permit them to showcase their individual skills and abilities. They preferred, for example, to manage an independent project or to make sure that important people in the organization heard of their accomplishments. In contrast, Hong Kong Chinese preferred a more covert approach that works behind the scenes, one that may involve using their family and trusted friends to obtain information and influence that may help them to succeed.[20]

Managerial Leadership in Europe

Managerial leadership centers around the relationship between the manager and the followers. The manner of relating to employees, the style of projecting and using power, and the method of dealing with conflict and crisis set the stage for managerial leadership. The boundaries within which these issues are dealt vary among cultures. Americans prefer informality and a moderate use of power. They are pragmatic and practical. While they are conscious of projecting

Cultural Prism: Authority and Leadership

The respect of subordinates depends on appearance of strength and competence, but what comes across as strong and competent is not the same everywhere. In Mexico, machismo is important. In Germany, polish, decisiveness and breadth of knowledge give a manager stature. This is not to say that you should adopt without restraint any of the more blatant symbols of power in a country; it is foolish to appear arrogant or superior to local subordinates. The point is, you should behave appropriately for your role, or your employees may be confused.

Americans are peculiar in their concentration of interest and effort into a few activities. With few exceptions, industrial leaders in the United States are known only for their corporate identity. Latin American management emphasizes the total person. Leaders are respected as multidimensional social beings who are family leader, business leader, intellectual and patron of the arts. . . . French and Italian industry leaders are social leaders. . . . In Germany, power can be financial, political, entrepreneurial, managerial, or intellectual; of the five, intellectual power seems to rank highest. Many of the heads of German firms have doctoral degrees and are always addressed as "Herr Doktor."

. . . To communicate rank or to estimate the power of a foreigner you have to know the local accouterments of success or position. . . . Appearance and clothing are extremely important to the Latin Americans. Arabs and American businessmen seem to value large offices. . . . Ostentatious displays of power are considered bad form by the Germans.

Source: L. Copeland and L. Griggs. *Going International: How to Make Friends and Deal Effectively in the Global Marketplace* (New York: Random House, 1985), 120..

a proper image, they do not sacrifice the results for the proper appearance. They allow participation by the lower levels of organization when such participation can lead to improved performance and productivity. Assuming that the Europeans, due to a shared cultural heritage, have the same preferences can lead to disappointment.

England

On the two dimensions of uncertainty avoidance and power distance, British are very similar to the Americans. Their high tolerance for ambiguity and low power distance is reflected in their industrial relations practices. Labor–management relations are less codified in England than in all other Western European countries, not surprising in a country that does not even have a written constitution. While the French managers believe in a rigid separation of professional and private life, the British executives perceive a fluid and much less clear boundary between the two spheres. The British are more passive and empathic, spending time relaxing, doing chores, and simply being together. While the career strategy of the French executive is more defensive, that of the British counterpart is more aggressive and risk-taking. The British see the most positive characteristics of the boss as persuasive-paternalistic or consultative.[21]

Probably due to a high tolerance for ambiguity, the British prefer a generalized, nonspecialized education for managers. A British manager was quoted as saying "the more difficult it is to plan, the less you need full-time professional planners."[22] Centuries of class conflict have left their mark in the workplace. Often, British workers consider their employers to be exploitative, since employers have exploited their ancestors for centuries. Over the years, British la-

The British

An American executive advising a young manager who was being assigned to England:

> Remember, the United Kingdom is a polyglot of ancient cultural influence—Anglos, Saxons, Normans, Vikings, Celts, Picts, Romans, and others. Today this so called homogeneous isle is becoming more pluralistic with the influx of immigrants from the commonwealth nations. . . . Normally, you will find them reserved, polite, and often friendly, but don't take them for granted. For all their simulated modesty, the British can be tough and blandly ruthless when necessary. They are masters at intelligence gathering, political blackmail, and chicanery, as a reading of book *Intrepid* will illustrate. Despite how quaint and eccentric they may appear to you at times, don't sell them short. They are a game people who built an empire with a handful of men and women. Although England and Wales are only the size of Alabama, and the population density is close to the size of France, the British once ruled 14 million square miles and more than 500 million souls. I remember reading once: "Because their Union Jack once flew over a good portion of the globe, the people have an empire ethos that gave meaning to those who served it." . . . It explains their effortless superiority in world affairs, and their inward, invisible grace as a people. It produced a tradition of public service and an education and class system that was dedicated to the needs of the Empire. It also spawned a credo that natural leaders, not low-born self-made men and women, should rule among the multitude.

Source: P. R. Harris and R. T. Moran. *Managing Cultural Differences* (Houston, TX: Gulf Publishing Co., 1991), 458.

bor has developed a socialistic attitude that at times even advocates the public ownership of corporations. It has produced a class-war outlook in which workers are not enthusiastic about toiling for the "boss class."[23] The elitist and hierarchical organizational systems prevalent in Britain are not much concerned with nurturing the people in the factories. By and large the workers carry out what they are told to do.[24]

The British are very protective of their "space." Outdoor cafes common in some parts of Europe are absent in Britain. Phillips attributes this to the dislike of British for close proximity to other people. "The worst thing that can happen to a Briton on holiday is for someone else to come and sit next to them on the beach."[25]

France

French people tend to favor formal and ritual activities over informal activities.[26] They are idealistic and concerned with the essence of values. While the motto of the French republic is Liberté, Egalité, Fraternité (Liberty, Equality, Fraternity), the importance of social classes cannot be ignored. The French social classes are the aristocracy, the upper bourgeoisie, the upper-middle bourgeoisie, and the middle, lower-middle, and lower classes. The French are very status conscious. Social status depends on one's social origin. While Americans can aspire to the highest level of society through their own accomplishments and hard work, the best that the French can do is climb one or two stages of the social ladder. Education, knowledge of litera-

Managerial Leadership in France

French managers see their work as an intellectual challenge, requiring the remorseless application of individual brainpower. They do not share the Anglo-Saxon view of management as an interpersonally demanding exercise, where plans have to be constantly "sold" upward and downward using personal skills. . . . The design of French organizations reflects and reinforces the cerebral manager. France has a long tradition of centralization, of hierarchical rigidity, and individual respect for authority. French company law resembles the country's constitution in conferring power on a single person. . . . the *president-directuer-general* (PDG). . . . is chairman of the board and chief executive rolled into one. . . . The PDG is not answerable to anyone.

Source: J.-L. Barsoux and P. Lawrence. "The Making of a French Manager." *Harvard Business Review* (July–August 1991), 58–67.

ture and fine arts, a tastefully decorated beautiful house, and the proper ancestral social origins are outward signs of social status.[27]

The top French managers are an elite group, very much aware of their "grandes écoles" roots. Grandes écoles supply almost all top positions of the well known and large public and private organizations. The military influence and tradition is very much evidenced in these schools and, therefore, they have maintained their strong male tradition. Mostly engineers by background, the graduates of grandes écoles excel in quantitative thought and expression and in the numerical dimensions of strategy. They have a great affinity for written communication, which reinforces a formality that permeates their relationships. To them, the manager should be able to grasp complex problems, dissect and synthesize them, manipulate ideas, and appraise solutions. They would rather be considered intellectuals than practicals and are obsessed with grammatical rectitude. French managers tend to have a bias for thought and intellect rather than action. In this vein, the witty detractors of French inclination for theory have one French civil servant telling the other: "That's fine in practice, but it'll never work in theory."[28] French organizations are highly centralized and hierarchical, and decisions are made at the very

apex. Educational credentials are the basis of a finely graded distribution of positions and offices. Unlike U.S. companies, in French organizations, such highly credentialed managers are allowed to accumulate all the responsibilities they feel capable of handling.[29]

French workers are very much concerned with the quality of life. Very seldom are they willing to sacrifice free time and vacation for the sake of work. They cherish their two to four weeks of annual vacation, one of the longest in Europe. The French managers' leadership style is predominantly autocratic. However, they tend to avoid face-to-face confrontations and conflicts in organizations. Perhaps the social class distinction that separates the workers from the ruling executives leaves less room for face-to-face relationships. Therefore, impersonal rules are devised to protect both the superiors and subordinates. "From below, one obeys the rules and thus does not submit to the absolute authority of an individual and as a result protects one's independence. From the top, edicting the rules affirms the capacity of sovereign power."[30]

Germany

Large power distance and strong uncertainty avoidance are two characteristics of German society. According to Hofstede,[31] societies that are strong on uncertainty avoidance are intolerant of deviant persons and ideas, and consider them dangerous. People of these societies are nationalistic, aggressive, consensus seeking, have an inner urge to work hard, are concerned with security, and are strong advocates of law and order. Almost all of these characteristics are stereotypical of Germans. Germans are known for their industriousness and efficiency. They are an inward people who tend to be very private. Compared with Americans, Germans seem to take a long time to develop friendly relations with others. Germans are status conscious and idealistic. They are reserved and to outsiders appear to be cold. They are detail oriented and meticulous. When Ford Motor Company started its *World Car* concept, integrating the worldwide production of automobiles, they learned firsthand about the German precision. The Germans made components that required very fine fitting. Other countries, however, were not accustomed to producing, for example, doors and body parts with the precision of few millimeters. The result was incompatibility.

While Americans are satisfied with partial models that leave many questions unanswered, such as various motivational models, control mechanisms, and delegation, Germans have tried to develop more systematic models. This approach to management has produced the so-called "Harzburger model." This model considers managing by means of defining tasks to be performed, creating job descriptions for the tasks, and defining behavioral roles for their performance.[32] Such a bureaucratic model approaches leadership and motivation from an institutional and economic perspective. It views the firm as operating in an economic free enterprise system that "motivates" it to seek profit. Within such a system, individuals are considered rational persons who seek to maximize their personal profit or utility in a manner consistent with the firm's objectives.[33] Viewed from an institutional perspective, leadership is there-

---

Leadership Succession in a German Company

I look carefully at the young people who are brought to my attention by my colleagues. I spend a lot of thought on these people. . . . I invite these young men to my home for dinner. Often I give garden parties for perhaps 60 or 90 people in honor of some visiting foreigners. Then I can see how they behave, how their wives behave, how well they get along with foreign people, the quality of their education. . . . We don't like people who can't behave properly. . . .

We invest a lot in these people. If they have language deficiencies, we train them. If they are to work in Latin America, we send them to Spain for three months so they speak a really good Spanish.

At the moment, I do not know that there is a member of corporate management whom I could propose as my successor. So I look (around) the world a bit, and we have identified two or three people who could qualify. So I might arrange a golf game with some of my fellow chief executives . . . . As we play, I might say to one chief executive: "There is a chap in your organization who, we think, can do things for us. What are his chances with you?" He might respond: "Well, his boss is only three years older, so I can't offer him anything like your opportunity. You can have him."

Source: R. Shaeffer. *Developing New Leadership in a Multinational Environment* (New York: The Conference Board, 1985), 10.

fore considered a phenomenon of the acquisition, possession, and use of power. This view of leadership, however, is tempered with the institutional participation of employees in the management of the firm through *codetermination*. In addition, it considers the responsibility of leadership to improve employer–employee relationships on the basis of voluntary socioethical obligations. The aim is to develop a new relationship between capital and labor on a voluntary rather than a legal basis. It advocates a consensus-based partnership between unions and management.[34]

German managers are predominantly from the engineering disciplines. With very few exceptions, these managers have middle- or upper-class backgrounds.[35] German workers are among the highest paid and best treated in the world. They have one of the shortest work weeks and among the longest paid vacations. Although only about 42 percent of the German workforce is unionized, contracts negotiated by labor unions cover both unionized and non-unionized employees. This is due to the fact that about 90 percent of employers are members of an employers' association, and collective agreements are on regional and industry levels.

Managerial Leadership in Japan

The nature of the decision-making process at the higher levels of organizational hierarchy influences the type of leadership employed throughout the organization. In the United States, of the two components of the decision-making process, decision formulation is the domain of top management and implementation of those decisions is relegated to the lower levels. In the American system of decision making, fewer levels and smaller numbers of people are involved. Therefore, a shorter time period is needed for decision formulation. To implement these decisions, however, organizations are compelled to secure the commitment and support of the lower levels and a larger number of

people. When successful, this method produces quick results. Securing the commitment and support of lower levels in implementing these decisions requires certain leadership characteristics and skills very akin to selling and marketing. To produce results, the leader has to be very persuasive and has to command resources that the subordinates desire, or have the personal traits (charisma) that make them follow his or her directions.

In contrast to the U.S. decision-making process, the Japanese employ a consensus-building method known as *ringisei*, or *ringi* for short. In fact, Japanese have no equivalent for "decision making."[36] *Ringiseido* literally means "a system of reverential inquiry about a superior's intentions." In this context, the term means obtaining approval on a proposed matter through the vertical, and sometimes horizontal, circulation of documents to concerned members in the organization.[37] In the ringi system, everyone who will feel the impact of a decision will be involved in making it.

The system originated in the government offices and national enterprises at the beginning of industrialization. In a ringi system the business plan or proposal about important problems that require a budget must be sent from the lower to the higher positioned staff and finally be decided by the president. The business plan or proposal must be sent from the lower group head to the head of the next level, and finally to the department head. If at each succeeding level, the superior cannot consent to the plan, it must be sent back to the original lower level manager for modification or total revision and be sent to the upper level again.[38]

In a ringi system, the demand for information pulls down the decision toward the implementation level. At the same time, the requirement of decisions to match the corporate strategies pulls it upward. The equilibrium of these two conflicting demands usually takes place at the middle level. The success of the system depends on the competency and leadership of middle-level

Ringisei: The Japanese Decision-Making

When an important decision needs to be made in a Japanese organization, everyone who will feel its impact is involved in making it. In the case of a decision where to put a new plant . . . (for example) will often mean sixty to eighty people directly involved in making the decision. A team of three will be assigned the duty of talking to all sixty to eighty people and, each time a significant modification arises, contacting all the people involved again. The team will repeat this process until a true consensus has been achieved. Understanding and support may supersede the actual content of the decision, since the five or six competing alternatives may be equally good or bad. . . .

When a major decision is to be made, a written proposal lays out one "best" alternative for consideration. The task of writing the proposal goes to the youngest and newest member of the department involved. Of course, the president or vice-president knows the acceptable alternatives, and the young person tries like heck to figure out what those are. He talks to everyone, soliciting their opinions, paying special attention to those who know the top man best. In so doing he is seeking a common ground. Fortunately, the young person cannot completely figure out from others what the boss wants, and must add his own thoughts. This is how variety enters the decision process in a Japanese company.

Source: W. G. Ouchi. *Theory Z* (Reading, MA: Addison-Wesley Publishing Co., 1981), 44–45.

management who have to serve as a bridge between the upper and lower levels of the organization. The effectiveness of middle managers depends on their personal relations with other managers. Unless they can obtain the required information from all corners of the organization they will not be able to perform their job successfully.[39] Under the ringi system, managerial leadership at the top entails coping with crisis situations or charting new directions for the organization. The chief executive does not alter or disapprove the decisions reached through ringi. The lower levels will take every precaution so that no ringi decision reaches the top that will not be approved. After the general direction and strategy of the firm is communicated to the middle and lower levels, operational decisions and methods of implementing those decisions are entrusted to them. In Japanese firms, chief executives spend most of their time on establishing and maintaining close relationships with government officers and other corporate heads.[40]

High on both power distance and uncertainty avoidance, the Japanese culture favors consensus and shuns deviant behavior. Japanese tend to favor authoritarian-paternalistic leaders. Respect for authority is central to Japanese society. From an outsider's view, the ringi system of decision making appears to connote an egalitarian practice. Taken in the context of Japanese culture, however, it is another way of removing uncertainty and abiding by the power of authorities. As Prakash Sethi and his associates assert, "The controlling and motivating mechanism in Japanese organizations are not humanism and egalitarianism, but hierarchy, authority, power, and domination . . . egalitarianism as a cultural trait does not exist in Japan."[41] Hierarchical authority relationships are not confined to the corporation, but extend to all aspects of Japanese society. The use of authority and submission to it governs all interactions. Managers rely on the use of authority and its by-product, discipline, to achieve what American managers try to attain by other techniques such as power sharing and management-by-objectives. As Bruce-Briggs asserts, Japanese labor discipline was not created by skillful corporate management. Of course, discipline and hierarchy are Western terms. The Japanese speak of "expected behavior" and "harmonious relations."[42] The discipline and respect for authority have been there all along as parts of Japanese cultural character. Japanese do what is expected of them. They are expected to respect authority, work hard, work right, and not block productivity improvement. Consider the ordinary observation of the visitor to Japan:

> Early in the morning in Tokyo: Along the curb sanitation men carefully polish their tiny Isuzu garbage truck. Imagine the response of American garbage men to such a directive. . . . Just before opening time at a little middle-class shop in Kyoto: Before the main counter stands a young man in a business suit—obviously the manager. To his left and two steps to his rear, a slightly younger man—the assistant manager—listening intently. Lined up before them, in better formation than . . . (any) Army squad, the uniformed shopgirls, the No. 1 girl one pace forward, all in "respect" position—hands clasped before them, head slightly bowed, eyes fixed on the managers, receiving the orders of the day.[43]

While the use of authority is at the center of Japanese leadership, the desire for consensus and the subordination of the individuals to the group minimize its abuse.

Conclusion

A critical factor that determines the success of an organization is the leadership ability of its management. A review of leadership theories reveals that there is no one best way of leading. Many situational factors contribute to the effectiveness of managerial leadership. These factors include the leader's characteristics, the followers' characteristics and expectations, the task, organizational policies, and the top management values and philosophies. An ever-present factor that influences other situational factors is the national culture. Most leadership theories have ignored the influence of national culture on the ef-

fectiveness of managerial leadership. The reason for this oversight is the researchers' ethnocentric tendencies. The major leadership theories in use today have all been developed in the United States to be used by American managers. These theories have avoided any discussion of the national culture, yet have implicitly assumed American middle-class cultural values as a framework. Based on the American values, most of these theories have advocated a participative-democratic leadership style. While the application of these theories could be effective in the United States, it is doubtful that they would be equally effective abroad. Without a consideration of cultural differences, the application of all leadership theories will be limited to their original home culture. Therefore, international managers should consider cultural differences in leading the multicultural workforce of the MNCs. Since learning about individual country differences is very demanding, we have discussed cultural differences among several regions of the world.

While there are cultural differences among various regions of the world, such as Asia, Europe, and North America, there is a diversity of cultures within each region as well. Some of the differences are very subtle, yet can significantly affect behavioral responses and leader–follower relationships. Although we certainly appreciate the cultural differences between the British, the French, and the Germans, we may neglect the differences between some smaller nations. Similarly, it would be a big mistake to label all Asians under the Oriental cultures. The difference between Indonesia and Korea, for example, is greater than that between Japan and the United States. According to Maruyama, for example, the Danish culture is closer to the Indonesian culture than to the Swedish culture in terms of the way people organize thoughts and behavior. In the Danish culture, the main purpose of communication is maintenance of a familiar atmosphere and maintenance of affection. In contrast, in Sweden the purpose of daily interpersonal communication is the transmission of new information or frank feelings.[44]

At the present time, there is no leadership theory broad enough to cover cultural values. The existing theories, however, can be useful to international managers if we take into account cultural origins. Armed with an understanding of cultural differences, we may be able to chart a safe passage in the sea of international management. Taking such a perspective we advise international managers of a few caveats. First, the use of authority varies by cultures. The conspicuous use of power and authority is frowned on in some cultures and encouraged in others. Second, cultures vary in their practice of delegating authority and responsibility. Subordinates in some cultures are not comfortable in participating in decision making. Third, the meaning of work varies by cultures. For some, work is a necessary evil; for others, it is a source of pride and purpose. Dealing with each requires a different leadership approach. Finally, when abroad, observe the native management practices for cues as to what works well.

Discussion Questions

1. What leadership characteristics of Mahatma Gandhi and Nelson Mandela do you consider to be similar?
2. Why should an international manager learn about the leadership theories developed in the United States?
3. Tannenbaum and Schmidt suggested that there are three forces influencing a manager's actions. Describe these forces.
4. How could a leader's philosophy regarding human nature effect his or her relationship with the followers?
5. By using Fiedler's contingency model, elaborate on the contention that leadership effectiveness depends on a match between the leader's behavioral inclinations and favorableness of the situation.

6. What is the meaning of the phrase "the cultural relativity of leadership"?
7. Leadership theories reviewed in this chapter favor democratic leadership style. Do you think these theories are valid for non-Western cultures?
8. What are the differences between the managerial leadership practices of the United States and France?
9. This chapter refers to the difficulties that the Ford Motor Company experienced when it integrated its European car manufacturing operations. What cultural differences were causing those problems?
10. Briefly explain the Japanese decision-making process called ringi. In your opinion why is ringi effective in Japan?
11. Elaborate on the statement "there is a functionality in the host country managerial practices."

Endnotes

1. R. L. Kahn and D. Katz. "Leadership Practices in Relation to Productivity and Morale." In D. Cartwright and A. F. Lander, eds. *Group Dynamics*, 2nd ed. (Evanston, IL: Row, Peterson, 1960), 554–570; and R. J. House. "A Path-Goal Theory of Leader Effectiveness." *Administrative Science Quarterly,* 16 (1971), 321–38.

2. R. R. Blake and J. R. Mouton. *The Managerial Grid* (Houston, TX: Gulf Publishing Co., 1978).

3. R. Likert. *The Human Organization* (New York: McGraw-Hill Book Co., 1967).

4. R. Tannenbaum and W. H. Schmidt. "How to Choose a Leadership Pattern." *Harvard Business Review* (May–June 1973), 162–75.

5. House. "A Path-Goal Theory of Leadership Effectiveness"; R. J. House. "Path Goal Theory of Leadership," *Journal of Contemporary Business* (Autumn 1974), 81–98.

6. D. McGregor. *The Human Side of Enterprise* (New York: McGraw-Hill, 1960), 33–34.

7. F. Fiedler. *A Theory of Leadership Effectiveness* (New York: McGraw-Hill, 1967).

8. H. J. Reitz. *Behavior in Organizations* (Homewood, IL: Richard D. Irwin, 1977), 524.

9. Reitz. *Behavior in Organizations.* 526.

10. P. Hersey and K. H. Blanchard. *Management of Organizational Behavior* (Englewood Cliffs, NJ: Prentice-Hall, 1972), 79.

11. Hofstede, *Culture's Consequences* (Beverly Hills, CA: Sage Publications, 1984).

12. G. Hofstede. "Motivation, Leadership, and Organization: Do American Theories Apply Abroad?" *Organizational Dynamics* (Summer 1980), 42–63.

13. Hofstede. *Culture's Consequences.*

14. Hofstede. "Motivation, Leadership, and Organization." 57.

15. J Rojot. "Human Resource Management in France." In R. Pieper, ed. *Human Resource Management: An International Comparison* (Berlin, Germany: Wlater de Gruyter and Co., 1990), 98.

16. Hofstede. "Motivation, Leadership, and Organization." 57–9.

17. F. L. Wilson. "Democracy in the Workplace: The French Experience." *Politics and Society,* no. 19 (Dec. 1991), 439–62.

18. Hofstede. "Motivation, Leadership, and Organization." p. 53.

19. K. Fatehi-Sedeh and H. Safizadeh. "Labor Union Leaders and Codetermination: An Evaluation of Attitudes." *Employee Relations Law Journal,* 12, no. 2 (Autumn 1986), 188–204.

20. D. A. Ralston, D. J. Gustafson, and R. H. Terpstra, "The Impact of Eastern and Western Philosophy on Upward Influence Tactics: A Comparison of American and Hong Kong Chinese Managers." Paper presented at the Academy of International Business, October, 1993.

21. Hofstede, *Culture's Consequence.*

22. M. Marks. "Organizational Adjustment to Uncertainty." *Journal of Management Studies,* 14 (1977), 1–7, in Hofstede, *Culture's Consequence,* 118.

23. P. R. Harris and R. T. Moran. *Managing Cultural Differences* (Houston, TX: Gulf Publishing Co., 1991), 458.

24. N. Phillips. *Managing International Teams* (Burr Ridge, IL: Richard D. Irwin, 1994), 6–9.

25. Phillips. *Managing International Teams.* 9.

26. Rojot. "Human Resource Management in France." 95.

27. Harris and Moran. *Managing Cultural Differences.* 465–71.

28. Phillips. *Managing International Teams.* 12–13.

29. J.-L. Barsoux and P. Lawerence. "The Making of a French Manager." *Harvard Business Review* (July–August 1991), 58–67.

30. Rojot. "Human Resource Management in France." 95.

31. Hofstede. *Culture's Consequences.*

32. R. Wunderer. "Leadership." In E. Grochla and E. Gaugler, eds. *Handbook of German Business Management* (Stuttgart, Germany: C. E. Poeschel Verlag, 1990), 1390–1400.

33. G. Reber. "Motivation." In E. Grochla and E. Gaugler, eds. *Handbook of German Business Management,* (Stuttgart, Germany: C. E. Poeschel Verlag, 1990), 1490–1500.

34. Wunderer. "Leadership." 1309.

35. K. Bleicher. "Management." In E. Grochla and E. Gaugler, eds. *Handbook of German Business Management,* (Stuttgart, Germany: C. E. Poeschel Verlag, 1990), 1395.

36. Hofstede. *Culture's Consequence.* 27.

37. S. Prakash Sethi, N. Namiki, and C. L. Swanson. *The False Promise of the Japanese Miracle* (Boston, MA: Pitman Publishing, 1984), 34.

38. Y. Takahashi. "Human Resource Management in Japan." In R. Pieper, ed. *Human Resource Management: An International Comparison* (Berlin, Germany: Wlater de Gruyter and Co., 1990), 218.

39. Prakash Sethi, Namiki, and Swanson. *The False Promise.* 39.

40. Ibid., 41.

41. Ibid., 267.

42. B. Bruce-Briggs. "The Dangerous Folly Called Theory Z." *Fortune* (May 17, 1982), 41–4.

43. Bruce-Briggs. "The Dangerous Folly." 41.

44. Maruyama. "Changing Dimensions." 92–5.

BILL KEANE

JOHN BARNETT

Bill Keane faced three issues in managerial and personal ethics during his assignment as managing director and chairman of Szabo Diamond Company, S. A. Before describing the incidents and issues of these three ethical decisions, Bill and Szabo Diamond are described.

Bill Keane

Bill was born in New York, in March 1950. His parents both worked in the business his father owned, and the family was upper middle class. Bill attended Lawrenceville School and studied government at Williams College. Following military service in the Army Signal Corps, from 1970 to 1972, Bill completed his studies at Williams. He became active in mountain climbing, an activity he still pursues.

Bill entered the M.B.A. program at Stanford University, graduating in 1976. His initial job was with an international consulting firm. One of his first assignments was with Lyon, Churchman and Associates, West Coast importers of diamonds. After 9 months of this consulting effort, Bill joined the diamond operations of Lyon, Churchman and Associates in Los Angeles. He also was married during this period.

The wholesale distribution of diamonds is significantly controlled by DeBeers. The digging, processing, and exporting of diamonds is somewhat more open, although increasingly less so as one moves toward the wholesale customer through the DeBeers distribution system. Nonetheless, occasional opportunities arise, and

Bill found himself undertaking various assignments in Brazil, Zaire, Australia, and Indonesia.

Szabo

In early1981, Bill became the managing director and chairman of Szabo Diamonds. Szabo, on the northeast coast of South America, became a sovereign state within the British Commonwealth on May 11, 1968, and became a republic in 1978. Its capital, Luna, then had a population of 280,000 and the country a population of 3,200,000.

Diamonds were first discovered in Szabo in the early 1930s by prospectors from the Consolidated Minerals Trust (CMT). CMT subsequently formed Szabo Trust (ST) Limited in the mid-1930s and ST negotiated a series of agreements with the government in which ST paid the government a percentage of net profits and a mineral rent in exchange for a monopoly in the mining and exportation of diamonds. The Universal Diamond Corporation (UNDICO) participated in diamond exporting and, in various ways, in CMT and ST. UNDICO sorted, graded, and marketed diamonds.

One way for the outsider to enter the diamond industry is as a diamond processor. A local Szabo processing company offered several things. First, to the outsider, it might be the only means of entry into the diamond fraternity, although one would also have to ensure a source of supply by making CMT/ST and the government of Szabo partners. Second, the processing stage would be a further means of controlling smuggling, a rampant problem throughout many stages of the diamond business. Toward this end, the Szabo government should clearly be made a partner.

Thus, Szabo Diamonds, S.A.—a partnership of international interests and the Szabo government with Lyon, Churchman and Associates (LCA) as the managing partner—opened and operated a diamond-processing factory in Szabo as a foothold toward securing a portion of the overall exportation of diamonds or other natural resource development projects.

LCA made the Szabo government an interest-free long-term loan, which the Szabo government used to acquire a majority interest in Szabo Diamonds, S.A. Factory operations and all managerial decisions were controlled by LCA for a fee. Bill oversaw all the financial controls of Szabo Diamond. He stayed out of day-to-day factory operations, which were supervised by an English factory manager.

Decision One—March 1981

Bill's first ethical decision came in his early weeks in Szabo. Part of his duties included calling on all the government ministers connected with mining and exporting. LCA made contributions to schools and hospitals, which could be the reason for a visit to a minister or to the premier. Friendship with the ministers, partially based on mutual favors, was most helpful in both the short and long terms. LCA wanted Bill to have considerable influence with the government of Szabo.

During his second visit to a particularly important government minister, after polite conversation about Bill's new home, tennis, and the weather, the minister said: "I have a large, 60-carat yellow diamond. On one of your trips, would you be interested in taking this out of the country for me for a fee?"

Decision Two—May 1982

In New York, Szabo Diamond Company had hired an excellent manager, Manuel Ramon, a native of Szabo. He was the number two manager in Szabo, reporting directly to Bill Keane, who was most impressed with Manuel Ramon's ability. Bill and Manuel Ramon came to Szabo together in 1981 after both had undertaken international assignments for LCA. As typically was done by companies hiring expatriate managers, Szabo Diamond leased a local residence for use by Bill Keane and another for use by Manuel Ramon.

The political situation in Szabo was active. Occasionally, a group of politicians in and/or out of the government would put together a leadership alternative and would try to convince some of the army and others to help them overturn the existing government. While the current premier had kept control for almost a decade, there nevertheless were ongoing coalitions and plans for a coup d'état surfacing every 2 or 3 years.

A year after Bill got to Szabo, rumors of a plot to overthrow the premier began to circulate in Luna. In January 1982, Manuel Ramon's brother, Jose, who had been living outside Szabo while undertaking an assignment for the World Health Organization, returned to Szabo and to Luna. As often was done with the extended families within Szabo, Jose and his family moved into the house occupied by Manuel Ramon and rented by Szabo Diamond Company.

Jose had been a leader of the opposition to the premier, although he had never been directly proven to be a conspirator. A few of his associates had been, and they were subsequently tried and hanged for treason. Jose was widely respected and well known throughout Szabo. From Jose's return in January until May 1982, the rumors of his involvement in a plot to overthrow the premier were an increasing topic of conversation among close groups and trusted individuals. Further, the house occupied by Manuel Ramon, and now by Jose, was increasingly the site of evening meetings which were presumably political.

Bill knew Manuel Ramon was important to him, to Szabo Diamond, and LCA, and that he was close to Jose. Accordingly, he was most disturbed when the minister of internal affairs, who was very close to the premier, said to Bill during his visit to the Government House:

> We, the Government of Szabo, are the majority shareholders in Szabo Diamond Company, which you manage. We are most disturbed to see our investment being used to pay rent for a house inhabited by an enemy of this government. Our house is being used for meetings plotting against us. The house is too close to a military installation. What are you going to do to correct this unacceptable condition?

Decision Three—December 1983

Just before Christmas 1983, Bill was compelled to participate in a smuggling investigation being conducted by a witch doctor or shaman.

The diamond factory procedure involved the Szaboan workers, of whom there were about 115, coming to a glass-enclosed area called the bench. There the worker would receive a packet of diamonds of a specified grade, never larger than one carat, to be either cut along a mark (sawed), rounded (girdled), or polished. The worker and one of the European administrators (the English manager, his English assistant, or a Dutchman also supervising operations) would count the number of diamonds (usually six to eight), agree on a total, and the Szaboan would perform the necessary step, returning the diamonds for checking.

General labor problems arose because the workers specialized as polishers, sawyers, or girdlers, and they were paid on a piecework basis. This piecework rate meant that they were relatively well paid by Szabo standards. There were frequent times, however, when the various stages of the process would become uneven. That is, there would be no girdled stones to be polished or no cut stones to be girdled, because workers in one group were slow or had been absent due to personal or tribal reasons. The workers resented these frequent shutdowns of one or more sections of the production process.

A more specific labor problem was when a difference arose between what the bench said a worker should have and what the worker said. Differences could arise because of (1) bench error; (2) worker error, such as a diamond actually flying out of the polisher as the worker failed to control the gem and the machine; (3) smuggling; and (4) substitution, in which an inferior stone is brought into the factory and exchanged for a superior stone.

Just before Christmas the number of differences increased. The workers were unhappy about being suspected of stealing. One day the Szaboan head of the labor union came to Bill with a request that a tribal shaman investigate the matter.

Bill, who had seen shamans perform various rituals in Szabo, including healing and exorcism, agreed to the use of the shaman. Bill reasoned that such an investigation might reduce the workers' dissatisfaction and the "differences," and that it would also show some respect for tribal customs and procedures.

Thus, shortly before the end of the next work day the shaman arrived. All European and Szaboan employees participated in the investigation, led by Bill. Bill had anticipated that this shaman would follow the practice Bill had seen other shamans use, namely, going amongst the employees with a "magic" stick or broom that would only strike the guilty. This investigation, however, consisted of a different procedure, which was described to everyone beforehand by the shaman. Bill and then every other employee lined up single file, walked up to a pot full of palm oil placed over a stone. The oil was heated to a rolling boil. Then a large rock was dropped to the bottom of the pot. Each person was to pick up the stone, lift it out of the boiling oil, and put it back in the pot. The shaman assured everyone that only the guilty persons would be burned.

Bill went first, picked up the stone, and replaced it in the boiling oil. He felt nothing. Only two persons were burned, one Szaboan and the

Dutchman (they both wore bandages for several weeks). Bill was certain that some out-of-the-ordinary phenomenon occurred, and he wondered what to do. He commented:

> I was and am totally convinced that there's something behind all of this. The boiling oil wasn't even hot to my touch, nor to over one hundred other people's touch. While I don't go to church, and we have not had our three children baptized, I still consider myself a Christian. I've always believed in some power, and this experience probably showed some aspect of that power.

NINE

INTERNATIONAL HUMAN RESOURCE MANAGEMENT

Chapter 9 proposes that the expansion of the firm to international markets should be accompanied with a commensurate change in its human resource management (HRM) practices. A transition from domestic to international HRM is predicated with the change in managerial attitudes and corporate culture. As firms progress from a domestic to an international posture, appropriate changes in managerial philosophy should take place to accommodate the cultural diversity of multinational company (MNC) personnel.

Certain managerial characteristics are known to increase the probability of success in a foreign assignment. It is argued that these characteristics should be used as recruitment and selection criteria. The application of these criteria would help in staffing overseas subsidiaries with the right personnel. Predeparture training and preparation will also improve the chances of success in a foreign assignment. Besides expatriate managers, MNCs employ host country and third country nationals. HRM practices for dealing with foreign personnel are discussed. A discussion of remuneration and compensation concludes the chapter.

More than 100 years ago Kipling said, ". . . East is East and West is West, and never the twain shall meet." Today, however, Motorola Corporation is proving otherwise and the meeting is providing Motorola with considerable sales growth in Asia's booming telecommunication and semiconductor markets. To assure continuous growth, Motorola has established more than a dozen factories in several East Asian countries including new factories in China, Malaysia, and Singapore. These countries not only produce a variety of Motorola products including high-end walkie-talkies and digital cordless

phones, but they are also the source of new products. Handie-Talkie, a miniature two-way radio, for example, was designed and manufactured in Penang, Malaysia. With the exception of one U.S. research manager, Malaysians run the entire operation. At the persistent urging of Ms. S. K. Ko, the Penang plant manager, Motorola also allows the Malaysians to design new software for cellular conference calls.

Motorola's success in Asia could be attributed to its ability to tap the human resources and brain power of the East. It has integrated Asian managers into the corporate power structure and has granted them a considerable amount of decision-making authority. Tam Ching Ding, the president of the Asia-Pacific semiconductor division, is the most visible of Motorola's Asian managers. These managers often combine Asian cultural beliefs with modern management practices. Knowing that cultural factors are the critical elements of East–West meeting, Motorola is going to great lengths to safeguard its investment and assure continued success by practicing the old adage, "when in Rome, do as the Romans do." In so doing, it is accepting cultural practices that would raise eyebrows in the United States. For instance, as a $400 million Silicon Harbor complex in Hong Kong was nearing completion, Tam asked his 87-year-old geomancer, or diviner, to double check the new facility's feng shui— literally, its wind and water—for good luck. The soothsayer proclaimed the omens were favorable, the complex had water—a symbol of wealth—on three sides and was ringed by mountains—a source of power. The executive suite's layout, however, was wrong. Tam ordered a major renovation to achieve the proper alignment. Now, he can gaze over his *desk, across the cobalt bay, to the towering face of Horse Shadow Mountain and boast that his office has about the best* feng shui *in Hong Kong.*

Tam's influence extends beyond the Asian markets and into Motorola's corporate home office. When the new semiconductor headquarters was built in Phoenix, Arizona, a few changes were made at Tam's insistence. Two waterfalls were installed in the entrance to counter the forces of the city's landmark Camelback Mountain. Competitors may snicker at these practices, but they also may acknowledge that Motorola may have learned how to profit from the secrets of the Orient.[1]

Sources: P. Engardio, L. Therrien, N. Gross, and L. Armstrong. "How Motorola Took Asia by the Tail." *Business Week,* (November 11, 1991), 68; G. P. Zachary. "High-Tech Firms Shift Some Skilled Work to Asian Countries." *The Wall Street Journal,* (September 30, 1994), A1 & A2.

Introduction

The Motorola story portrays an organization that has adopted a global perspective. It illustrates some of the HRM practices of a firm that utilizes the capabilities of its human resources globally. The change in perspective that enables the organization to exploit fully its worldwide human resource capabilities is an evolutionary process. The process begins when an organization takes its first step in expanding beyond the home market boundaries.

The Transition from a Domestic to an International Position

As discussed in previous chapters, most firms begin as domestic corporations. Their operations are geographically limited to the boundaries of their own home markets. They serve the domestic market and the customers of their home country. A saturated domestic market and intense local competition cause many firms to resort to export.

Exporting and gaining familiarity with foreign markets result in willingness and increased interest in expanding operations abroad. The firm may establish branches, offices, and production facilities in foreign countries in an attempt to better serve those markets and take advantage of foreign market opportunities. To bolster the market share and earnings, such a firm would recognize the need for a long-term commitment to host countries and their economic aspirations. As the markets in host countries expand, the firm prospers, grows, and gets more involved with the host countries' institutions and people. In a way, the firm integrates with host countries. From expansion abroad and integration with host countries, the firm may emerge with the view that national boundaries are mere demarcations that identify culturally and politically diverse consumers. In other words, cultural and political diversity do not imply limitations and restrictions to business opportunities.[2]

The evolution from a domestic corporation to a multinational enterprise is a continuum. As Figure 9.1 shows, at one end of the continuum is the local/national orientation, in which the firm is exclusively devoted to serving the home country market. At this position, the firm's business philosophy and mission reflect its home country environment. Its managers and employees alike share the predominant culture of the country. Therefore, problems arising from cultural misunderstanding are not as pronounced as those at the other end of the continuum.

The other end of the continuum comprises the multinational phase of the firm when it operates in many national markets and is influenced by the cultures of those countries. Consequently, managing the corporation becomes much more difficult and demanding.

During its evolution, the corporation not only develops its corporate culture, but it also establishes its basic HRM policies. These policies encompass employee selection, training, evalu-

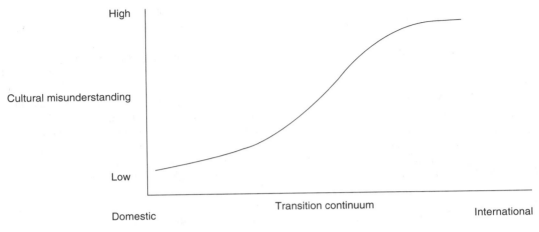

Figure 9.1   Organization Type and Cultural Problems

ation, rewards and compensation, and termination. Similar to the company's culture, the type and tone of these HRM policies will be an outgrowth of the cultural environment of its markets. The management–employee relationship and view of each other are strongly influenced by the firm's culture. The firm's culture, in turn, is determined by the national culture. Since management and labor usually share the same culture, in the early stages of the firm's evolution, misunderstandings are at a minimum. As it evolves, the MNC must adopt a multicultural or cross-cultural perspective in its operations and in dealing with its employees. Managers from different cultures have different assumptions about the "ideal" way of managing and "ideal" management policies.[3] Similarly, employees from different cultures have different views about the proper job-related behavior and expected management behavior. These culturally based differences in management and employee expectations can lead to conflicts and misunderstandings. Managerial practices that acknowledge the cultural diversity of the firm can reduce this conflict.

Because MNCs operate in a culturally diverse environment, their management practices, such as employee selection, career planning, performance appraisal, and compensation policies, should be adapted to fit specific countries and their cultures. For example, in some cultures, career management systems represent formal, long-term human resource plans. Central to such a position is the assumption that human beings control the environment and nature. In cultures that believe human control over the environment is minimal, such an approach is inappropriate. Common appraisal methods in the United States are based on employee performance and accomplishments. Such systems are ineffective in societies where lineal and personal relationships are more important than individual achievements. In the same vein, in collectivist societies, where the emphasis is on the group and not the individual, the individual's concern with affiliation may outweigh the desire for recognition. Under such circumstances, a promotion that singles out an individual and separates him or her from the group may be viewed as a punishment rather than a reward.[4] There are similar variations among cultures regarding selection, hiring, training, compensation, and recognition practices.

Recruitment and Selection

To maintain market leadership in any country, it has become increasingly vital for a firm to attain a leadership position in the world market. In other words, international competitiveness is becoming a requisite for domestic success. The ability of a firm to compete in the world market, among other factors, may be determined by the quality of its human resources. In turn, the quality of a firm's human resources primarily depends on its HRM practices. The human resource practices are shaped by the organization's staffing philosophy, which serves as a screening mechanism, allowing only certain types of people to join the firm.

Recruitment Philosophy

An international corporation has the option of hiring from a global pool of applicants. An objective selection process would result in choosing the best qualified applicant. Most international staffing decisions are purportedly based on objective criteria. Research has shown, however, that the attitudes of the top executives toward the people of the host cultures will have a strong bearing on those decisions. Managers' attitudes determine whether expatriates are selected for management positions in foreign subsidiaries. According to Heenan,[5] the underlying motivation behind these key decisions is the MNC's level of trust in the host country nationals and managerial perceptions of their competence. MNCs may follow any of the four recruitment approaches: home country, host country, regional, and global.

Home country approach Managers using the home country approach tend to staff all key positions, at the home office or abroad, with home country executives. They feel that this group is the most intelligent, capable, and reliable. Saying this does not imply that these decisions are based on prejudice. In fact, their basis may be a lack of knowledge and experience with foreign persons and cultures. This type of attitude is most evident in firms that are highly centralized[6] and rely on low-cost production of commodity-type products for international markets.[7] There is also evidence that where the political power of the host country is seen as a

threat, MNCs will be more inclined to use expatriate managers. The aim is to ensure that the objectives of the firm are not subordinated to those of the host country.[8]

Host country approach Managers in a host country approach have the attitudes that the host country management should be left to the host country nationals. They believe that the natives are better able to understand the requirements of the assignment. The same principle is followed in staffing the home country positions with the home country nationals. To the MNC executives, the foreign operation is a mysterious undertaking that is best left to foreign executives. As long as the firm remains profitable, or the objectives are achieved, host country executives are allowed to operate the organization in any way they feel is appropriate. The resulting low- profile approach of headquarters results in absolute authority for the host country manager over the foreign organization.[9]

Regional approach Managers who use the regional approach believe that the global market should be handled regionally. For example, all European markets would be coordinated through a headquarters in France, all markets in North and South America through a headquarters in the United States, and so on. Consequently, personnel selection is carried out regionally. Although information flow and personnel transfer is high within each region, there is little or none between the regions.[10] This staffing style is used when products are similar all over the world but the marketing must be tailored to meet the needs of different cultures.[11] This is often a result of strong competition from smaller, more localized organizations.[12] While such an attitude will result in a performance appraisal based on regionwide criteria, it is not a global perspective.

Global approach This approach is evident by a global systems approach to management. Managers with this perspective believe that top qualified people can come from any background and culture. They also believe that the whole world is their market. Therefore, resource allocation, staffing, manufacturing, and marketing should be done within the framework of the global economy.[13] Consequently, staffing requirements are fulfilled based on overall competence rather than ethnicity. The result is an HRM system that is most appropriate for the complex and dynamic global market. In such a market competition is not regional, but consists of other MNCs that operate on a worldwide level and have similar characteristics.[14]

Selection Criteria

The quality of home country managers who are assigned to a foreign business operation is an important factor that can make a difference between the success and failure of the operation. This is true not only for firms new in the international market, but also for established MNCs with extensive experience in foreign countries. To host country personnel, these managers represent the MNC and the home country. The image they create lasts long after the initial assignment is over and they have departed for home. Therefore, only the best qualified managers should be sent abroad.

In the past, it has been quite common for firms to use managerial and technical expertise as the sole criterion for selecting expatriate managers for foreign assignments (expatriate managers are home country managers on assignment to host countries). Technical and managerial expertise, however, is not enough for today's international assignments. To select managers only on technical and managerial expertise could result in disappointing outcomes. MNCs must work to make the expatriate assignment a positive experience, for both the company and the manager. In doing so, it is imperative that the selection criteria for foreign managers encompass all aspects of work, and respond to the social, political, and cultural situation.

To succeed abroad, what characteristics should a manager possess? What criteria should be used in selecting managers for foreign assignments? In general, all of the characteristics that make a good domestic manager are necessary for an international executive, too. However, there are certain additional attributes that are essential for success in global operations. There are many opinions regarding the full range of desirable and required characteristics for an international executive. The following are the more frequently mentioned characteristics.

Technical and managerial skills For a manager assigned to a foreign operation, basic technical and managerial skills are very crucial. All of the technical, administrative, and managerial skills that make a manager succeed at home would be necessary in a foreign assignment as well. A person's past performance is usually a good indication of his or her managerial and technical abilities. We should, however, acknowledge that not all managers who are successful at home do equally well on foreign assignments. The novelty of physical environment, and political, social, and cultural differences make experiences gained at home less applicable in a foreign country. Quite often, an international assignment involves novel problems that only a very astute manager can solve successfully. Usually, an international manager is expected to train local employees. It is entirely possible that these employees are being introduced to a new method, a new process, or the use of new machinery. In a foreign assignment, the support that other colleagues can offer may not be readily available. Therefore, it is essential that expatriate managers be able to function with minimum support. Moreover, in such assignments where the expatriate is the only expert in the organization, innovative ability and insight are very crucial.

Similar to domestic operations, characteristics and attributes needed abroad also depend on the hierarchical position of the manager. There are four categories of assignment for an expatriate. These are the chief executive officer responsible for an operation abroad, the head of a functional department in a foreign subsidiary, the troubleshooter whose responsibility is to solve a specific operational problem, and the operator.[15] For each of these positions a different set of attributes is needed. Skills required for an operative who is in regular contact with host country nationals are maturity, emotional stability, and respect for the laws and people of the host country. A troubleshooter needs technical knowledge of the business, initiative, and creativity. The head of a functional department requires maturity, emotional stability, and technical knowledge of the business. For the position of the chief executive officer of a foreign subsidiary the most important skills are communication skills, managerial talent, maturity, and emotional stability.[16]

While different characteristics are needed for various managerial assignments, all successful expatriates share certain common characteristics. In addition to managerial and technical expertise, the "ideal" expatriate must possess the right combination of interpersonal skill, intelligence, and emotional stability. To succeed, the expatriate should have a family that is supportive of the assignment and able to adapt to the new environment.[17] The following are the most important characteristics for any foreign assignment.

Motives and desire   A very important factor for selecting a manager for a foreign assignment is his or her personal motive for seeking and accepting the assignment. The best candidates for a position in a foreign country are individuals who possess a genuine interest in foreign countries, their people, and their cultures. Individuals who seek the assignment solely for the extra money they might earn, the added prestige they might gain, or the "boost" that such an assignment might give to their careers are not as likely to be successful in expatriate situations.[18] A good indication of a manager's interest is past experience. If a manager knows foreign languages, has taken international business courses, and has traveled extensively or lived abroad, he

or she has demonstrated an interest in foreign countries and cultures.[19]

Social skills   Probably the most important success factor for the international manager is social skill. Social skills for international managers are not necessarily the same as those that create success at home. A socially skilled person in a domestic operation is a person who has learned the rules and norms for developing and maintaining relationships with people. A socially skillful person has learned the proper behavior for various circumstances. Because we acquire these skills by practicing them under specified rules of our own cultures, going beyond the familiar boundaries of home culture may render our skills less effective. Naturally, understanding the host country's culture and politics, and the knowledge of the host's history and geography are very helpful, but may not be sufficient.

In international situations where rules and conditions are different, managers should be flexible, adaptable, and able to accept the unfamiliar. For example, unlike the United States, in other cultures the relationships between individuals typically develop slowly and cautiously over time. Once established, these relationships are permanent and the obligations would not be dissolved even with the dissolution of the relationship.[20]

Among the many social skills that international managers should have is the ability to understand why foreigners behave the way they do. To understand people, an understanding of their culture is necessary. We perceive and interpret others' behaviors using our cultural cues and models. The ability to understand and to make the correct attribution to the behavior of people from other cultures enables managers to predict more accurately and to anticipate others' reactions to their actions. This reduces the element of uncertainty in interpersonal and intercultural relations. A very important element of any culture is the language. Although we can study and learn about a culture without speaking the language, knowing the language immensely facilitates learning.

The ability to speak the host country language not only allows for better communication, but creates a more informal and friendly communication environment and minimizes the differences. Even when a manager is not proficient in speaking the language, the willingness to use the language suggests to the host nationals that the manager is interested in interacting with them. It also indicates the manager's confidence and trust in them by taking risks and being vulnerable.

There are many cultural activities that provide opportunities for socializing with local people and learning of their culture. Some of the most popular cultural activities are playing or attending sports events, listening to or playing music, and eating out. Participation in these cultural activities allows a manager to ease the difficulty of moving into a new environment and provides the chance for establishing long-lasting friendships with host nationals. Enjoying the local sports and music and demonstrating flexibility and openness in culinary choices allows a manager to act as an "insider" and not a foreigner. Developing friendships with locals who could act as mentors in providing guidance through the maze of cultural complexities makes life much easier. Host national friends can help the manager to understand people's attitudes and expectations—at work and away.[21]

Diplomatic skills   On foreign assignments, international managers interact with business associates, government agencies, and political leaders. In most developing countries, the government assumes a larger role in business and trade than is customary in the United States. The ability to relate to government officials properly and to conduct business transactions under unfamiliar conditions requires diplomatic skills. The manager serves as an ambassador in representing the company to other businesses and to host government bureaucrats.[22] To negotiate favorable terms and create a positive impression, the negotiation skills and the patience of a diplomat are required.

Maturity and stability   Venturing into a strange environment, facing unfamiliar conditions, and dealing with unexpected situations are all part of going abroad and conducting business transactions in a foreign country. Emotionally and intellectually mature persons more readily handle the burden of foreign assignments. Mature persons recognize their own assumptions, values, motives, needs, and shortcomings. Consequently, they are in a better position to understand the attitudes and behaviors of other people, to appreciate cultural differences for what they are, and to be able to suspend judgment when there is insufficient understanding of circumstances. They are also able to understand the inherent logic in different ways of life in various cultures. Mature persons do not overreact when they encounter unfamiliar and potentially threatening situations. These characteristics enable managers to maintain emotional equilibrium under the most demanding and difficult conditions. Therefore, they can cope constructively with adversity and handle the stresses of daily life under an unfamiliar environment.[23]

Family factors   When evaluating candidates for foreign assignments, it is very important to review not only the candidate, but the candidate's family as well. The family influences the individual's chances for success in a foreign country. The inability of spouses or children to adapt to their new surroundings is a major reason for failure in overseas transfers, including premature returns and job performance slumps.[24] While the expatriate manager has the relative security of a familiar work and office routine, the family must cope with an unfamiliar new environment on a daily basis. To prevent failures due to family difficulties, MNCs have begun to address family-related issues. For example, Ford Motor, Minnesota Mining and Manufacturing, and Exxon include spouses in their screening process for foreign assignments, and/or offer educational and predeparture preparation assistance.[25]

Locally contingent attributes   For assignments to some countries, certain attributes such as the candidate's age and gender must also be considered. Older people are respected and seniority is emphasized in many countries. In these cultures, youthful representatives may have a great deal of difficulty gaining access to important personnel and key decision makers.[26] Some countries deny women access to key decision-making situations. In these countries, women also encounter a great deal of resistance from superiors, subordinates, colleagues, and clients. These people not only question a woman's professional competency, but also doubt the very legitimacy of her authority in the executive role.[27] The following incident is an example of the type of situations that women may face when they go abroad:

> An American female executive was given the responsibility of negotiating a business deal with a Japanese firm because she was the most qualified person. Properly dressed in an elegant suit, she arrived on time in the board room of the Japanese corporation and was prepared for a very serious negotiation. The Japanese senior executives kept asking politely where was her husband. She answered that her husband was at home in New York, taking care of their daughter. At this point the Japanese thought they finally had discovered that she was a secretary. Therefore, they asked to see her boss. To their amazement she made it clear that she was the boss! The meeting proceeded, but not with an ideal opening. Halfway through the meeting, taking a break, she asked for directions to the Ladies' Room. There was no Ladies' Room.[28]

Personnel Selection Options

As it prepares to staff its foreign-based offices, the multinational firm must decide if it will fill managerial positions with expatriate, host country, or third country managers. We argued earlier that the attitudes of top executives toward the

people of other cultures influence personnel selection. Often, at the early stages of internationalization, the firm follows a home country approach in staffing decisions. As the firm gains international experience and learns about other cultures, it may move through the other three approaches to personnel selection and finally arrive at the global approach in staffing.

The selection and hiring process of MNCs is a very complex and difficult task. The staffing requirements and the needs of each foreign office are different. Besides these differences, there are a multitude of other factors, such as local laws and contractual obligations, that have to be considered. In addition, the MNC's management philosophy regarding staffing plays a pivotal role in the personnel selection. The prevailing managerial philosophy influences the choice among the three alternatives.

Expatriate manager   The MNC may choose expatriates to fill managerial positions in its foreign offices. The selection of expatriates for foreign assignments is influenced by the ethnocentric attitudes and philosophy of the MNC's top executives. It may also be due to some operational needs. For example, home country managers may have a long history of service with the parent company. They possess an in-depth knowledge and understanding of the policies and procedures of the firm, and are familiar with the business and industry. They may also have technical training or possess functional expertise that local managers lack. Sometimes, due to a shortage of well-trained local managers, expatriates are the only logical choice.[29] MNCs may also select expatriates to fill foreign positions as part of their corporate managerial training program. Many MNCs view foreign-duty assignments as an indispensable part of an executive's "global" development training.[30] General Electric, for example, is now sending its brightest stars abroad rather than the run-of-the-mill managers it once picked for foreign posts.[31]

Before accepting the assignment, the prospective manager should have an intensive and in-depth meeting with the manager's superior(s). The purpose of this meeting would be to agree on such issues as the expatriate's level of remuneration, the parameters and responsibilities of the assignment, and the projected home office position after the foreign assignment is over.[32]

Instead of prolonged assignments for the expatriates and their families abroad, a MNC may decide to consider alternatives of short-term duration. For example, expatriate managers may make prolonged visits to foreign subsidiaries. In this way expatriate managers could share their problem-solving talents and technical expertise with foreign subsidiaries, while the expense and disruption that accompany expatriate relocation are avoided.

An MNC may also select individual managers or teams of managers to undertake temporary project assignments in foreign countries. Project assignments are typically associated with start-up of a special project, such as the introduction of a new product line or getting an information system on line. These assignments usually last from three weeks to six months and are an excellent way of providing the necessary management personnel to introduce new products, build new facilities, or introduce new management information systems.[33]

Host country national manager In the past, many multinational firms displayed an ethnocentric view, staffing foreign offices almost exclusively with expatriate personnel. As MNCs have evolved and assumed a more global perspective, their policies for staffing foreign managerial positions have also undergone an evolutionary progression. Today, many MNCs are selecting more host country and third country nationals to fill managerial positions in their foreign subsidiaries. MNC selection of host country nationals to fill managerial positions in foreign countries is due to the increasing costs and the high failure rate of expatriate assignments.

The cost of relocation can be very high for the company and for the expatriate. Expatriate assignments often fail because the expatriate manager and the family are unfamiliar with the host culture or because they fail to adapt. The failure rate for expatriate assignments can range anywhere between 30 and 50 percent, and can climb as high as 70 percent in less developed countries.[34] The hiring of local managers saves the MNC the cost of relocating the expatriate manager and the costs associated with their failure. By using local personnel, the MNC is also spared the higher salary that must be paid to an expatriate working in a foreign country. Besides their base salaries, expatriate managers also receive medical insurance, pension benefits, foreign currency adjustments, and foreign service incentives. Moreover, housing costs, relocation and transportation expenses, cost-of-living compensation, and educational allowances increase the burden on MNCs. According to one estimate, for example, the typical first-year expenses of a U.S. executive with a family of four in Britain would be about $302,000.[35] The host country personnel may resent and envy the expatriate's higher pay scale. This may eventually affect the productivity and the morale of local employees who receive a lower level of compensation.

A host country national may also be selected because of knowledge and understanding of local markets, consumers, and governments. Local managers may provide the company with valuable governmental contacts. These contacts may be especially helpful when dealing with governmental red tape and bureaucracy. They are also useful when host governments do not trust or are uncertain about the presence of a foreign corporation within their borders. Some foreign governments may have regulations requiring the use of indigenous managerial personnel.[36] In these situations, host country managers are a better choice.

For some markets that have stringent business requirements, such as Japan, hiring host country nationals is one way of breaking into those markets or being competitive. To recruit in such a market, MNCs may be forced to pay higher salaries than local companies and offer other benefits. For example, in Japan, foreign employers on average pay 10 percent more than Japanese firms and have shorter working hours, more flexibility, and merit-based promotions. The MNCs are paying premium salaries in Japan because most Japanese view foreign employers as unstable, unfamiliar, and nonprestigious. An alternative, however, is available to MNCs. Since Japanese firms are reluctant to hire women, MNCs have started to hire women in larger numbers. Consequently, foreign firms, and especially the Americans, have been successful in attracting some top graduates of Japanese universities.[37]

Host country managers can help MNCs to have a more harmonious relationship with local employees, customers, and the community. Integrating these managers into MNCs, however, is difficult. Conflicts may arise because of differences in national and corporate cultures. Certain steps can be taken to smooth the integration of these managers into MNCs and reduce the potential for conflict. MNCs should identify talented host-country managers early in their careers and prepare them for future positions. The prospective candidates should be rotated to home country positions for a few years, enabling them to absorb the home country and corporate culture. They also can develop a network of friends and colleagues who can be very helpful to them in the future. An alternative is to appoint a home country manager as a "shadow manager" for a host country candidate. The role of the "shadow manager" is to acclimate the host country manager to the MNC's corporate culture, and to ease the communication link to the home country. NCR, Fuji-Xerox, and many other firms have used this approach.[38]

Host country staffing has many benefits. There are, however, certain caveats with this practice, particularly for smaller firms. The legal consequences of hiring a host country citizen are often complicated and costly. For instance, labor laws in many European countries require employment contracts with generous termination benefits.[39]

Selection criteria for host country national managers are similar to those used for third country nationals. Therefore, the discussion of these criteria will have to wait until the review of the third country national managers.

Third country national manager   Sometimes, local managers do not possess the requisite managerial expertise or do not wish to work for the MNC. In those situations, third country managers may provide a viable staffing alternative. For example, because of the political tensions in Iran during the early 1980s, American firms doing business in Iran often used British or Canadian personnel to represent their interests inside Iran.[40]

It is possible that irrespective of political situations or availability of home country personnel or host country nationals, the third country national may be the best person and the right manager for the job. Third country executives often speak several languages, and know the region and its industry well. The use of third country nationals is a common practice among international hotel firms. Recognizing the qualifications of these managers and their usefulness to the firm, American MNCs have started to increase the number of third country nationals in their foreign affiliates. For example, the ranks of third country managers at Scott Paper leaped from 3 in 1987 to 13 in 1991. Another example is Pioneer Hi-Bred International, which employed 29 such managers in key positions in their foreign operations in 1991, triple the number for the prior five years.[41]

Host Country or Third Country Staffing Criteria

The criteria for selecting host country and third country national managers are much the same as those used for selecting expatriate managers.

Technical expertise, adaptability, flexibility, and communication and decision-making skills are among the key desirable characteristics. If the local or third country manager is to operate successfully in the global environment of the MNC, these managers should also possess an international attitude and perspective.[42]

In addition to the desired personal and professional expertise, host country and third country managers should be able to speak the language spoken in the MNC's home country. Managers in the host country typically have extensive contacts with home office staff. The home office staff, however, often lack the ability to speak the language of the host country. If an effective communication link between the home office and the foreign subsidiary is to be established, it is essential that local and third country managers be able to speak the corporation's home country language.

Making the decision to hire a local manager may be much easier than finding a local citizen who has the qualifications for the job and/or who is willing to take a job with the MNC. Qualified national managers may be difficult to find for a variety of reasons. In the past MNCs selected primarily expatriate managers to fill foreign positions. Consequently, host country personnel may not have received the professional training that would allow them to assume managerial roles. As a result, a shortage of managers with the proper training may exist in many countries. The problem of finding a qualified manager may be even more pronounced in less developed countries (LDCs). A combination of poor educational opportunities and depressed economic conditions may limit the number of talented and qualified people available for employment. Individuals who do possess the proper educational credentials often have no desire to enter the MNC workforce.[43]

In areas that have abundance of qualified managerial talents, MNCs may still experience difficulties in attracting and then hiring these individuals. In Japan, for instance, employees pledge complete allegiance to their employers, promising that they will not seek employment elsewhere. Moreover, Japanese workers often do not want to work with "foreigners," preferring instead to work with people from their own culture.[44]

Before hiring a particular local manager, the MNC must consider the host country's cultural norms regarding superior–subordinate relationships. For example, managers in many less developed countries (LDCs) are expected to be highly responsive to requests from subordinates. Since managers with this background may have difficulty saying "no," performance appraisals, reward, and control situations may be particularly difficult for them.[45]

The MNC must also consider the expectations that these managers may hold about their position with the corporation. The managers' career expectations and job performance will be a function of their cultural background. The MNC should be aware of these expectations and take them into account when hiring local or third country managers. They should also adopt personnel management policies that offer incentives and rewards that are appropriate to specific cultural settings.

Product Life Cycle and International Human Resource Management

So far we have used managerial philosophy and orientation to explain HRM practices at MNCs. Earlier in the chapter we propose that the MNC evolves from a domestic to a multinational enterprise. During this evolution it establishes its basic HRM policies and practices. We propose that these policies and practices are the outgrowth of the cultural environment of its diverse markets. As the MNC expands to different markets, it gains experience in dealing with different cultures. The imperatives of accommodating to market requirements shape the MNC's managerial philosophy and its HRM practices. In effect, we implicitly present a historical view of

MNC's HRM practices. There is, however, an alternative explanation. Based on the concept of product life cycle, it is suggested that each stage of MNC life requires the application of certain HRM strategies.

Vernon[46] proposed that international trade and investment go through three phases. Adler and Ghadar[47] have expanded Vernon's concept by adding a fourth stage. The four stages that MNCs go through are (1) high tech or product orientation, (2) growth and internationalization or market orientation, (3) multinationalization or price orientation, and (4) globalization. Adler and Ghadar argue that the impact of culture on organization and the management of human resources is a function of environmental imperatives of each stage.[48] In the next few pages, the four stages of international product life cycle are discussed, followed by a presentation of corresponding HRM practices.

International Product Life Cycle

In phase 1, firms produce new and unique products that command a high price relative to direct costs. They depend on research and development and apply advances in science and engineering for product development. At this stage there are only a few firms capable of producing these products. Phase 2 begins with the entrance of competition. Competition forces firms to focus on expanding to new markets. International expansion is an option they may choose. Initially, foreign markets are supplied by exports from the home country. Later on, assembly operations are established in countries with large domestic markets. As the emphasis shifts from product development to market development, marketing replaces research and development as the most important function. Increased competition and standardization of products at the end of phase 2 drives prices down and creates a need for further cost reduction. Since the market is saturated with competitors, the price falls to barely above costs. The realization that a competitive advantage can be achieved only by

managing and controlling costs marks phase 3. To reduce and control costs, production is shifted to countries with the lowest production costs. By phase 3, home country production is drastically reduced and the home market is supplied with imports from low production facilities abroad.

The first three phases have their own special features and characteristics. Phase 4, however, is the culmination of the previous three phases. It is the result of dramatic changes in market forces. These changes can best be described as a progression from one stage to another.

For a couple of decades following the second world war, American firms enjoyed a monopoly power and an undisputed leadership position in the world markets. For them phase 1 was characterized by the absence of foreign competition and a long product life cycle. A typical product life cycle then was 15 to 20 years. A salient characteristic of this phase was the dominance of the product development function. In the meantime Europe and Japan rebuilt their economies and began to challenge the U.S. dominance. Movement from phase 1 to phase 2 resulted in increased worldwide competition, a shortened international product life cycle, and increased prominence of the marketing function. Technology transfer and price competition, which are characteristics of phase 3, followed. By the 1980s, an international product life cycle was reduced to 3 to 5 years.

Today, we are at the beginning of phase 4. This phase is characterized by mass customization of products designed to meet individual needs. These products are produced by assembling components sourced worldwide. Product life cycles have been shortened further, and for some products, the life cycle is now only a few months. The emphasis is on both top-quality products and services at the least cost. Accurate identification of consumer needs and quick response to them are hallmarks of phase 4. Firms succeed in phase 4 by both becoming highly differentiated and highly integrated, and by combining the local responsiveness of phase 2 with the global integration of phase 3. In other words, firms are forced to compete simultaneously in phase 1, phase 2, and phase 3 market conditions.

At each phase the influence of cultural diversity on the firms varies. Figure 9.2 depicts the four stages of the product life cycle and the influence of culture on organization at each stage. In phase 1, technological superiority, product uniqueness, and monopoly power allow the firm to operate with an ethnocentric perspective and ignore the cultural differences between home and host markets. In phase 1 firms export their products and push the cost of absorbing cultural differences to foreign buyers. In a way, these firms send a message to foreigners that says, "We will allow you to buy our products."[49]

A phase 2 firm cannot operate with an ethnocentric perspective. The competitive pressure of phase 2 does not allow firms to ignore the cultural differences and expect the cost of cross-cultural mismatch between sellers and buyers to be absorbed by foreign customers. To succeed, phase 2 firms need to consider cultural differences and modify their operating styles to match those of their foreign customers and clients.

The undifferentiated products and price competition of phase 3 reduce the importance of

sensitivity to most cultural differences. While in phase 2, there might be many different ways of designing, producing, and marketing products for diverse markets; in phase 3, only the least-cost method can succeed. In the market of undifferentiated products, the importance of market segmentation based on culture or national considerations diminishes. In other words, price competition makes the impact of cultural differences negligible.

In phase 4, the minimum criteria for success are top-quality, least-cost products and services. Firms gain a competitive advantage by designing sophisticated mass-customization global strategies. Successful market segmentation based on culture becomes a winning strategy. Phase 4 firms compete in a global market, with research and development, production, and marketing networks that are spread all over the globe and serve very discrete market niches. Consequently, managing cultural diversity within the organization and with their suppliers and customers becomes a requisite for success.

HRM Practices

Product life cycle indicates the impact of culture on the firm. It can be used to suggest corresponding HRM practices for each phase.

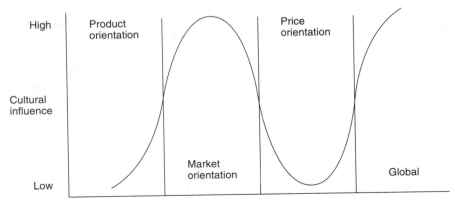

Figure 9.2   International Product Life Cycle and Cultural Influence

Firms operating in phase 1 that produce unique products and sell them primarily to a home market do not require much international sophistication from their employees. The firms' monopoly power insulates them from the impact of cultural differences and forces the buyers of the product to absorb the cost of cross-cultural mismatch. Foreign customers must speak the language of the MNC, accept the MNC's cultural and managerial practices, and, after the purchase, modify products and services themselves to match their needs and requirements. Firms in phase 1 get away with using the ethnocentric approach because their buyers and clients do not have an alternative. Personnel selection for foreign assignments, therefore, is based solely on the ability to get the job done. There is no international career and international and cultural training. For firms operating in phase 1, international experience not only is not important, but also, in many cases, it may hinder the executive's progress in the hierarchy. These firms do not send their most qualified employees to a foreign subsidiary. An executive accepting a foreign assignment falls outside the mainstream of the executive network and quite often is overlooked for promotions.

Cultural adaptability and sensitivity are important to phase 2 firms. Personnel selection, however, is still mostly based on technical competence and willingness to accept foreign assignments. In phase 2, firms could gain competitive advantage by producing culturally appropriate products and services and tailoring their marketing programs to host countries' cultural requirements. These firms, besides the expatriate managers, quite often employ host nationals in some host country positions such as marketing and personnel. Expatriate managers of the phase 2 MNCs perform well only if they know the host country's language and understand the culture. To perform well, the expatriate managers need to acquire appropriate skills and knowledge about the host culture. They also gain unique and valuable experience. The skills,

knowledge, and experience thus gained, however, are not valued much when they return home. Going abroad is not a very good career strategy for ambitious managers of the phase 2 firms. For the same reason, and because of a lack of understanding of international operations, very seldom do foreign nationals ascend in the hierarchy of the home country organization. Membership on the board of directors of phase 2 firms, and top executive positions, are exclusively reserved for home country nationals.

Survival for a phase 3 firm in the global market depends on price competitiveness. For geographically dispersed MNCs with a worldwide network of suppliers, manufacturers, and distributors, integration becomes an important undertaking. They achieve integration primarily through standardization of their products and services, and centralization of their operations and structure. International assignments are given to the best employees, and the search for managerial talent is expanded to include other nationals from the worldwide operation. While international experience is valued for career advancement, cultural sensitivity and language skills diminish in importance. Phase 3 firms attempt to integrate by creating or assuming similarity. They assume similarity by producing generic products and services to take advantage of economies of scale and scope. They create similarity within the firm by using the home country language and by imposing home country values and cultures on their managers. They attempt to mold foreign managers in the image of home country executives. Home country or third country national managers who assimilate into the headquarters' corporate culture can ascend to higher level positions. They assume that cultural differences can either be ignored through the corporate culture or minimized to reduce their impact.

Phase 4 MNCs produce and sell top-quality, least-cost, differentiated products for local tastes globally. The need for global integration and national responsiveness forces phase 4 firms to select their best people for the assignments scattered all over the globe. The home country market no longer is dominant and boundaries between home country, host country, and third country managers vanish. Internally and externally, firms are faced with cultural diversity that they cannot ignore and have to manage. Successful phase 4 MNCs are those that can identify situations when cultural differences could be used as an asset. Phase 4 firms serve culturally differentiated market segments worldwide. To identify and respond quickly to local needs, managers need to be culturally sensitive and speak more than one language. Successful firms recognize that cultural diversity cannot be ignored and are able to identify situations where cultural diversity can be managed as an asset and those where such diversity is a liability.

International Management and Intercultural Training and Preparation

In spite of the fact that corporations devote a great deal of time and attention to selecting the proper candidates to undertake foreign management positions, 30 to 50 percent of all expatriate placements do not work out as anticipated. Besides the direct financial costs involved with a failed expatriate assignment, the firm may incur other costs, including voided business deals, loss of valuable employees, the break up of joint ventures, and poor relations with the host government.

The primary reason for the failure is the inability of the employee or the family to adjust properly to the new environment and the new culture.[50] The failure, however, begins with selecting the wrong person. With adequate screening and proper selection procedures, managers with a higher probability of success are selected. The screening process includes interviews, tests, and assessment centers. While some psychological and technical skills tests are available, these tests are not widely used by MNCs.

Two reasons limit the use of these tests. First, specific criteria for overseas success is lacking. Second, psychological tests have the potential for cultural bias and have relatively low validity.[51] Interviews are very common for selecting prospective candidates for foreign assignments. Assessment centers are the most promising method of selecting international personnel. The centers include individual and group exercises, individual interviews with managers or psychologists, and perhaps some mental ability tests. After selecting a manager, predeparture preparation and training further enable the expatriate to adjust to the host country culture. Figure 9.3 illustrates the many factors that could influence an expatriate's adjustment and consequently contribute to the success of assignments abroad. As Figure 9.3 suggests, many reasons for the failure of the expatriate could be eliminated with a proper selection process. A proper selection process alone, however, is not sufficient. Predeparture preparation and cultural and international management training are necessary for improving the chances of the expatriate's success. Predeparture preparation and training help managers prepare for most of the problems they may encounter in a foreign country. The preparation and training could be particularly helpful for a manager going to a culturally tough environment. The cultural toughness of the host country is measured by the distance and dissimilarity of home and host country cultures. The larger the cultural distance, the more difficult the adaptation process. Individuals may find that some cultures are far more difficult to adapt to than others.[52] American executives, for example, have an easier time in England than in China. For the Americans, Chinese culture is tougher than British culture.

Predeparture Preparations

To lessen the possibility of foreign assignment failure, most companies provide employees and their families with predeparture briefing programs. Predeparture preparations serve to re-

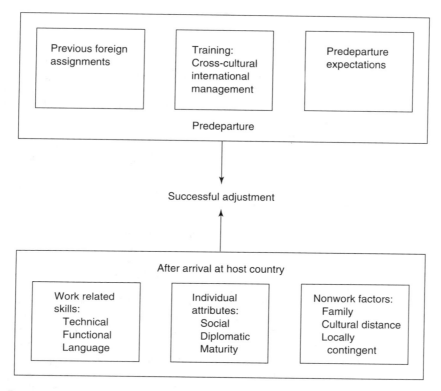

Figure 9.3 Factors Influencing Expatriates Cultural Adjustment

duce the cultural shock that foreigners experience when entering a new culture. In particular, spouses and family benefit from participating in workshops that introduce them to the host culture. The family needs more help because the impact of cultural shock on managers is typically less severe than on their families, because the work environment, even in a foreign country, is more familiar to managers and they spend most of their time working at first.

Predeparture workshops may include language training and typically provide information on practical considerations such as health, safety, and medical needs, as well as information on how to handle and manage the daily routine of a household including grocery shopping, transportation, international mail, and communication. Such information reduces predeparture apprehension and eases the entry into a new environment.

Providing employment information and helping career-oriented spouses to secure a meaningful job has an enormous positive impact on the family. Instead of viewing them as the employee's aggravating chattel, spouses should be considered a company's unexpected bonus. As a resource they should be utilized to the benefit of both the employee and the MNC. For example, some MNCs emulate governments and universities and establish preferential employment policies for spouses.[53]

Mentors at home and host country offices can be very helpful to expatriates. Matching the expatriate manager and the family with a host country mentor helps their entry into the foreign culture. A mentor at the home country corporate

Japanese in London

International expansion of Japanese firms has brought a large number of Japanese expatriates to England. The typical Japanese expatriate is still a company man spending three to five years abroad. Most commonly he (rarely she) will be a banker in his 20s or 30s; a small minority will be senior executives sent over to run a London headquarters or (less often) a plant in Wales or the northeast.

The biggest snag for a Japanese expatriate with a family is providing an education for his children. Stepping off the exams escalator at home risks sacrificing a job-for-life in a prestigious company. Parents with no option but to bring their children to Britain with them scramble for places in schools that teach the Japanese national curriculum. The best known is the Japanese School in Acton, West London. Britain now has eight private Japanese schools, and six Saturday schools attached to Japanese-owned factories in Wales and the north-east.

A mini-industry has developed to make the Japanese feel at home. Those moving to Britain can choose among eight Japanese estate agents to find them a house. Once here, they look for a location that reflects their position in the social pecking-order. Around London it is St. John's Wood and Hampstead for bosses; Finchley, Golders Green and Ealing for middle managers; Croydon for the lower ranks.

The unadventurous can live as though they have never left Tokyo: reading Japanese newspapers, buying their spectacles from Japanese opticians and suits from Japanese tailors, playing mahjong in Japanese clubs and singing "New York, New York" in karaoke bars. London has more than 60 Japanese restaurants and eight Japanese food shops to stave off the torments of English food. In the provinces there are regular food parcels from relatives in Japan and weekly lorry loads of supplies from London shops.

As they become more established, the Japanese are also growing more adventurous. There is plenty that they like about Britain: huge houses and (relatively) easy commuting, cheap and readily accessible golf courses. And the women enjoy their freedom and status. Japanese firms have recently started to worry that company wives may not want to go home. Perhaps Britain will change Japan as much as Japan is changing Britain.

Excerpted from "Island-hoppers." *The Economist* (September 14, 1991), 68. © 1991. The Economist Newspaper Group, Inc. Reprinted with permission. Further reproduction prohibited.

office assists in the repatriation program and reentry into their home culture when the manager and family are ready to return. This action could make the entire expatriate experience easier for the manager and the family, and will increase the chances of success.[54]

International and Intercultural Training

The attitudes and behaviors of managers are influenced by their culture. This influence quite often creates cultural biases. To overcome their cultural biases and achieve a truly global perspective, international managers should receive international and intercultural management training. Such training helps managers develop the skills they need to function in a variety of cultural settings and geographic locations. International management education and intercultural training may also help managers develop "global" perspectives, and be more receptive to and have empathy toward the cultures and customs of other nations. They also learn not to blindly accept their own cultural norms as universal standards. Such training can provide these managers with the understanding that no one culture, or method of managing, can consistently produce superior solutions to international managerial problems. They could also learn how to adapt their management styles to fit the many cultural situations they may encounter.

The purpose of international management education and training is to provide MNC managers with an awareness of the diversity of management practices around the world. The aim is also to improve their understanding of business and management philosophies and practices that exist in different countries and cultures. Through documentary programs, participation in business games, and role-playing scenarios, managers can develop a better understanding of culturally based differences in managing.

International management training and education programs can be arranged either as an in-house service or conducted at educational and training institutions. These programs could be designed to develop understanding and skills pertinent to a specific country and culture or a region. For example, managers could learn about the basic tenets of Japanese management and how those are different from the American practices. Alternatively, training programs could focus on East Asian cultural factors influencing the management of firms. Ideally, the faculty of international management programs are comprised of professional and business personnel who represent a wide variety of nationalities and cultures. A culturally diverse staff helps to ensure that MNC managers are exposed to many different cultural philosophies and value systems.

Besides international management education and training, managers that are expected to have extensive contact opportunities with people of other cultures should receive some form of in-depth intercultural training. Intercultural training is useful for all MNC managers operating abroad, whether they are expatriate, host country, or third country nationals.

Intercultural training intends to develop a set of skills that will be useful to international managers. Most intercultural training programs hope to develop in managers the following attributes and skills[55]:

Self-awareness: The recognitions of personal assumptions, values, needs, strengths, and limitations, and the understanding of personal response in different cultural settings.

Culture reading: The ability to discover and understand the inherent logic in cultural norms and expectations.

Multiple perspectives: The ability to suspend judgment about other cultures and appreciate others' perspectives.

Intercultural communication: To send and receive verbal and nonverbal messages accurately in different cultures.

Cultural flexibility: The ability to adjust and change expectations and plans in accordance with the host country cultural requirements.

Cultural resilience: The skill to handle culture shock, and recover and rebound from setbacks arising from cultural differences.

Skills in building interpersonal relationships: The ability to develop and maintain interpersonal relations with host country people.

Intercultural facilitation skills: The ability to manage cultural differences and use these differences constructively.

During the course of an intercultural training program, managers are provided with a wide range of information about foreign countries, their cultures and customs, and the anticipated roles that the managers may be expected to assume in these cultural settings.[56] Such intercultural exposure enhances a manager's ability to deal with the routine, as well as the unexpected and unusual situations that interactions with other cultures may present.[57] The nature and length of each individual's intercultural training is a function of several factors. These factors include the type of involvement and interaction the manager will have with host cultures, the manager's position in the company's hierarchy, and the cultural toughness of the other cultures.[58]

A typical intercultural training program most commonly provided by many MNCs follows a documentary approach. The program provides managers with printed materials on a country's history, geography, sociopolitical and economic systems, and cultural practices. This documentary information may be supplemented by lectures or films that provide practical information on such day-to-day concerns as local transportation, housing, shopping, schools, and finances.[59] For managers who will have extensive contact with foreign cultures, a documentary program alone may not provide the higher level of intercultural sensitivity and awareness that may be needed.

To develop an in-depth sensitivity to a culture's mores and behavioral patterns, managers need specialized training that goes beyond a review of reports and instructions in foreign languages. The scope and depth of the training should match the extent and frequency of interaction and involvement with the people of different cultures. As the need for interaction with different cultures increases, training programs should assume a more interactive or affective-immersion-oriented perspective.

A promising approach to intercultural training is intercultural assimilator or intercultural sensitizer (ICS). The origin of ICS goes back to the efforts of Fielder, Osgood, Stolurow, and Triandis during the early 1960s to develop a computer program that could be used to give cultural training to people from different cultures. The purpose of ICS is to teach individuals to see situations from the perspective of members of the other culture.[60]

Initially, Osgood called the program "culture assimilator." The term *assimilator,* however, conjures up images of assimilationist intentions that are definitely not the intentions of the program. As Albert has suggested, the term *ICS* is a more appropriate name for the instrument. There is no one definitive format for constructing ICSs. Some have emphasized the major customs of the target culture, others have attempted to present the value contrasts between the two cultures, and still others have dealt with differences in interpersonal attributes between the cultures. Despite the variations, ICSs attempt to provide the learners with extensive information about a target culture in a two- to six-hour time span. The information chosen for the ICS portrays the very important and significant differences between the two cultures. In other words, the ICS focuses on critical problems and on key differences. The basic requirement for constructing an ICS is to identify two situations or critical problems and to provide the learner with an active experience from which they can learn the behavior, norms, perspectives, attributes, values, and customs of other culture.[61]

During affective intercultural training, managers spend a good deal of time interacting with citizens of the host country. Alternatively, they may associate with individuals who have extensive, firsthand knowledge of the host country. As a result of these interactions, managers move beyond an objective, generalized knowledge of foreign countries and gain an understanding of the subtle nuances of their cultures. For example, they will learn the proper way to listen, to scold, or to praise in a given cultural setting. This type of information can be invaluable to managers as they deal with people from other countries and cultures.[62]

European and Japanese managers are better trained than Americans to deal with cross-cultural relationships. Many American firms have realized the need for global understanding and experience among their managers and are trying to close the gap. A few have already installed elaborate training and career-tracking mechanisms. Colgate-Palmolive Company, Procter and Gamble Company, General Electric, Raychem Corporation, and PepsiCo Inc., to name just a few, are among the firms that have instituted screening, selection, and training programs geared to identify young managers, early in their careers, for global operations. For example, a typical participant in Colgate's global marketing-management training program holds an MBA degree from an American university, speaks at least one foreign language, has lived outside the United States, and comes with both strong computer skills and prior business experience.[63]

Training Host Country or Third Country Nationals

In addition to generalized international management education and specific intercultural training, host country or third country national managers who are new to the MNC should also undergo a period of introduction and orientation to the firm and its corporate culture.

In the orientation phase the new employees are introduced to, and educated about, the general aspects of the corporation's operations. They are instructed about the firm's overall purpose and mission, its management policies and philosophies, its marketing/sales strategies and tactics, and its financial management practices.

The second phase of the training process consists of a combination of socialization and indoctrination programs. The purpose is to make the new employees a part of the MNC by introducing them to the norms and values of the firm's corporate culture.[64] How successful the MNC will be at implanting its "view of the world" within its new employees depends on several factors. Formal and informal organizational practices such as salary increases, promotions, job assignments, and superior–subordinate relationships are the most conspicuous organizational factors. The less obvious are personal factors such as the importance of the managers' culture to them, how closely they adhere to the dictates of their culture, and the degree of differences between host country national culture and the MNC's corporate culture. These factors

could affect the acceptance of corporate culture by host country or third country nationals. The more important the managers consider their own culture, the more they adhere to their own cultural norms, and the more different the MNC's corporate culture is from the host country national culture, the more difficulties these managers will experience in their socialization efforts. I should add, however, that while the MNC's culture may affect and even change the way the managers behave in work/business settings, this change in behavior may be only superficial. On a deeper level, the managers may cling to the mores and norms of their own culture.[65]

Training Host Country Nonmanagerial Employees

The pressure by host countries is forcing MNCs to hire and train an increasing number of local people. While the MNCs may be able to manage their foreign operations with few or even no local managers, it will be impossible for them to run their foreign subsidiaries without local labor. Often, in developing countries, training shop-floor employees is equivalent to managing technology transfer. Successful technology transfer requires a major commitment to train the local labor force in the use of equipment and machinery.

In training local labor, a few issues require careful consideration. First, most developing countries are short in skilled labor. An adequately trained employee may be lured away by other MNCs or by host country employers. Training employees without adequate measures to maintain them is a waste of time and resources. Second, MNCs should observe cultural factors and differences in religions. Training a supervisor from one ethnic group to oversee the work of another ethnic group may not be a wise choice. In India, for example, Muslims may not be willing to work for a Hindu supervisor. Third, training methods that are useful in developed countries may require extensive modifications to make them fit the needs of developing countries. Where most local labor is not literate, training should take the form of coaching. In those situations, instead of printed material and written instructions, videos, films, and personal demonstrations should be used. Fourth, the trainer should know the cultural idiosyncrasies of training. Whereas a frank confession of personal limitations and admission of gaps in knowledge may be appreciated by Americans, such admissions in some cultures result in the loss of respect and diminish the authority of the confessor. Finally, the teacher–student and trainer–trainee roles are not universal. While Americans are comfortable with active learning by participating in the learning process, and by expressing personal opinions, the people of some other cultures are more comfortable with passive learning.

Repatriation Problems

When the expatriates return home, they face problems and cultural shock that are similar to what they encountered on assignments abroad. This is particularly true after a prolonged stay abroad. Not many expatriates are prepared to deal with reentry difficulties. Repatriation issues are quite often ignored by MNCs. It is assumed that coming back to the home country environment should be a very easy task that does not require much preparation. Contrary to this assumption, expatriates not only may find themselves feeling like foreigners in their own country, they may face many unpleasant surprises at work. They have to adjust and adapt to changes that have taken place during their absence.

Many factors cause anxiety and stress for expatriate managers returning home. The most important concern of the returning expatriate is career and job assignments. Many find that they have been left out of promotion opportunities and are treated as outsiders. To their surprise, experience and expertise gained on international assignments may not be valued at the home office. Upon return, even if promoted, they may

experience a loss of autonomy and feel a sense of status loss. The worst case is if they have been less than successful in their foreign assignments. Although the foreign assignments are much more difficult and challenging, to most firms, a failure is a failure, and it is not accepted very easily. Expatriates returning home may face financial difficulties when the cost of living differences and the extra benefits granted to them made living abroad much more comfortable.

These problems, of course, could be minimized by a well-planned predeparture strategy. For example, financial burden could be eased by special agreements on real estate. Job, position, and status issues should be addressed and agreed to in advance. Symbolic events, such as holding board of directors meetings abroad, or arranging frequent meetings among expatriates and home office executives could reduce job-related problems.

Compensation

Executive compensation is a very important and complicated aspect of HRM. The complexity and importance of executive compensation increases as an organization expands beyond its home market. In formulating a compensation package, a domestic business has to deal with only one set of cultural, legal, financial, and structural considerations. In the construction of an international compensation package, these considerations multiply. Besides the issue of compensation for the executives who serve the global operations, compensation of local host country employees poses additional difficulties for MNCs.

An equitable and adequate compensation package is critical in motivating and maintaining highly qualified international executives. The expatriate managers are in no position to assess the adequacy of the compensation package before arriving in the foreign location. An inadequate package can be expected to produce less than satisfactory performance from a disgrun-

tled expatriate. Even worse, it may result in expatriates returning home, leaving the organization with serious staffing problems.[66] A deficient
compensation system may create similar problems with host country or third country managers. Most of these problems could be avoided
with a compensation package that has the following features[67]:

1. When considering the differences in the cost
   of living, additional taxes, currency fluctuations, and an incentive for going abroad, it
   should not result in a siginficant gain or a
   loss for the manager.
2. The package should be comparable with the
   compensation packages offered by other
   MNCs in the industry.
3. The package should be equitable in comparison with domestic compensation system and
   policies.
4. The firm should be able to freely transfer expatriates between various foreign operations.

The first three criteria deal with the cost of the
package, external equity, and internal equity.
The fourth criterion is concerned with the relationship between the compensation and other
HRM policies. For example, in a large MNC
where international assignments are requisites
for promotion to higher positions, an expatriate
may not be overly concerned with the exact
amount of remuneration. As long as the incentives are built into the assignments, and each is
perceived as a sign of progress on the way to the
top corporate job, managers feel secure and accept minor inadequacies.[68] Of course, compensation creates fewer problems for an MNC that
has few expatriates and operates in an industry
with limited competition. In such a case, each
expatriate assignment and the associated compensation package could be negotiated individually.

Compensation Methods

There are different methods of expatriate compensation. Over the years, three standard approaches have emerged[69]:

1. The headquarters scale, plus an MNC's affiliate differential
2. The citizenship scale
3. The global scale.

***Headquarters, and affiliate differential
scale***   Under this system the salary scale of the
home office for a particular job is used as the
base. A foreign service allowance is then added
to this base to cover the differences between
home and host countries. The affiliate differential may include the following:

1. Cost of living allowance for housing and
   consumer good differentials
2. Tax equalization adjustment for host country
   taxes
3. Education of children, periodic family home
   leaves, language training, medical care, and
   so on
4. Differentials for inflation, currency devaluation, and work-related legal fees
5. Expenses to comply with customary professional and social obligations
6. Hardship bonus for working abroad.

The concept of differentiating salaries based
on host country conditions and requirements
could be taken one step further. An equitable
compensation system may be devised that considers not only the hardship and extra costs, but
the gains and extra benefits of an assignment.
This method is called a balance sheet method. It
is predicated on the belief that discounting for
the premium that is paid for going international,
a person should neither gain nor lose from accepting the assignment.[70]

Citizenship compensation scale   This compensation system was developed to deal with
third country expatriate managers. An expatriate's remuneration is paid based on the standards of the country of the manager's origins.
An affiliate differential is added to this salary
base. A German manager, for example, working
for an American MNC in France is paid based
on the German scale plus an additional affiliate
differential. This system creates difficulties when

managers of more than one nationality are assigned to similar jobs and the same subsidiary. Some have suggested using one system for all third country personnel by employing the balance sheet concept.[71] Such a system may create equity between third country nationals, but may create another problem. Offering different pay for the same job to home country and third country employees creates resentment toward home country personnel. In the eyes of third country nationals, it may also be seen as discriminatory and be the source of dissatisfaction.

Global compensation scale MNCs that have committed themselves to a global strategy and that have an executive rank comprised of many nationalities are attempting to convert to this method. They offer the same salary for the same job despite the executives' country of origin. An affiliate differential is added to the base salary to account for the differences between countries. The global pay scale requires a global job classification and ranking. Preparing global job classifications for a large company is a formidable task. The identification and measurement of internationally comparable job elements that are applicable to various cultural settings seems an impossible task. The technical aspect of a job may be universal and measurable, but role expectations and behavioral requirements are not. The problem is compounded when we attempt to calculate the affiliate differential. There are no reliable data sources for determining some items included in the affiliate differential. The difficulties of using a global compensation system are many; however, the logic and appeal of equal pay for equal jobs seem to make this system the wave of the future.[72]

Host Country Employees

Compensation of local employees in various host countries is another HRM practice that requires careful consideration. Traditionally, host country employees have been paid prevailing local wages and salaries. However, some posi-

tive differential was typically used to attract the best of the host country labor force. This differential, however, was kept at a minimum in an attempt to cause no serious upward pressure on the prevailing host country salary standards. The nondisruptive concept of compensation for host country personnel was defended on two grounds.[73] First, it was claimed to be the morally correct approach. Second, any upward pressure on host country standards would inevitably lead to increased costs. Overall this philosophy seemed equitable, because often the quality of host country personnel was not comparable to the MNC's staff from the home country or from other countries. In a buyer's labor market the use of local compensation standards worked well. With the expansion of MNCs and the proliferation of technology transfer, however, there is a growing pool of qualified personnel in many host countries. In a seller's market, which characterizes most of the industrializing countries, and where there are government pressures for hiring more host country managers, the application of local compensation standards is problematic.

MNCs have grudgingly recognized the indefensibility of a salary system that pays the same job different remuneration based on nationality. In response they have experimented using alternative methods. Some examples are as follows.[74]

One method allows host country personnel who meet certain performance standards to be shifted from local to international status. The reclassification is accompanied with compensation adjustment to match the international scale. This means a qualified host country manager receives the same salary as other international managers, including the home country staff. In return, the host country manager agrees to a career as a third country expatriate manager. Another alternative shifts all local managers above a certain level to the home country salary scale. All other managers at lower levels remain on host country compensation standards. The objective here is to motivate host country employees for self-improvement and better performance.

Despite the methods used, the process of industrialization and economic growth are causing a strong upward pressure on MNC wages and salaries paid to host country personnel and these pressures are expected to continue.

Conclusion

A successful evolution from a domestically oriented firm to a multinational or globally oriented enterprise necessitates that a firm abandon its original unicultural viewpoint and adopt a multinational or global perspective. It should also accept that there is no "ideal" way to select and evaluate personnel, and no perfect way to staff foreign offices. Managerial policies have to be formed and managerial decisions have to be made considering the cultural and environmental influences that affect the MNC's foreign operations. Managers who have a global perspective are sensitive to, and comfortable with, cultural differences. They can function effectively in different cultural settings. To maintain their sensitivity, they must receive international management education and intercultural training throughout their careers.

As a firm progresses from a provincial, parochial outlook to a global perspective, its managers need a corresponding change in attitudes and orientation. An ethnocentric approach that assumes the universality of HRM practices for all cultures is inappropriate for a global enterprise. To succeed in the global market, managers of MNCs should act as corporate citizens of the world. They should adopt management styles that are transnational and cosmopolitan, lacking a national identity or an ethnocentric prejudice.[75]

Global competition requires human resources that are broad based, multilingual and understand the complexity of the multicultural global market. The development of human resources to meet the challenge of global competition requires careful planning and preparation. Prospective candidates, from whatever cultural background, should be identified early in their careers. The recruits should be trained and groomed for global operation. For example, in Coca-Cola company, to create such a pool of global talent, every one of their 21 operating divisions is expected to seek out, recruit, and develop a small group of people beyond their current needs. The excess talent can be tapped whenever there is a need for a global opportunity that requires such talent. Coca-Cola takes the position that the company not only needs capital to invest in the global market, it needs people to invest too.[76]

The first choice of many firms, for foreign assignments, is still an expatriate. But for emerging firms that view themselves as the global companies, the whole world is their talent market. These firms weave an international personnel thread into their organization at the entry level. They identify prospective managers for a global career from many countries and train them for these tasks. Most of the training takes place in the host country. Some of these candidates are selected from the host country for the specific goal of host country assignments. The cost of identifying, recruiting, and training global talents at the entry level is much less than recruiting and hiring senior-level foreign executives.[77]

Many factors influence the choice of staffing foreign operations. The most important factors seem to be the need to understand the uniqueness of each local market, and the ability to respond to their cultural requirements. The need for local responsiveness and global competitiveness is forcing MNCs to select more cosmopolitan managers. Today, an increasing number of major U.S. firms are appointing foreign-born managers to top executive positions. In 1991, between 7 and 10 percent of high-level assignments went to foreign executives, compared with only 1 percent in 1986. Examples are a vice president of worldwide purchasing at

General Motors, an executive vice president at Xerox, a vice chairman at Citicorp, a chief executive officer at Compaq Computer, the president at Unisys, the chief financial officer at AT&T, and a chief executive officer at Apple Computer.[78]

Consequently, a new breed of executives is emerging in the global arena. These managers have a global perspective, are multilingual, and have extensive experience in more than one culture. Ben Makihara is a representative example of the new cosmopolitan managers. In 1992, he was appointed as the president and chief executive officer of Mitsubishi, the giant Japanese trading company with $123 billion in assets. Mr. Bernard Makihara was born in England and is an alumnus of St. Paul's School and Harvard. He spent two years as a counselor at a summer camp in Vermont, and has 22 years of experience in Seattle, New York, and London. His daughter is working for *Time* magazine and his son for Goldman Sachs. His friends include James D. Robinson III, CEO of American Express, and Gerald Brinstein, CEO of Burlington Northern.[79] In Japan, as a rule, only the graduates of prestigious Japanese universities, with extensive experience at the home office are promoted to top managerial positions. The appointment of Mr. Makihara as the top executive of Mitsubishi is an indication that even in Japan, where tradition and customs play a significant role, the new reality of the global market is changing long-established HRM practices.

Discussion Questions

1. The transition from a domestic to an international posture creates additional problems, particularly, in HRM for the firms. Discuss the sources of these problems.
2. Some argue that MNC recruitment philosophy is based on the level of trust and perceived competence of the host country nationals. On that basis, MNCs may follow four recruitment practices. Explain these recruitment practices.
3. What skills should a manager possess to succeed abroad?
4. What is the role of family members in the success of an expatriate manager?
5. Describe locally contingent factors that influence the success of a foreign assignment.
6. Should a different set of criteria be used in the selection of host country or third country nationals? Explain your answer.
7. Elaborate on the application of the international product life cycle to HMR practices.
8. Elaborate on the attributes of a good compensation system for an international firm.
9. Identify different international compensation systems presented in this chapter.

Endnotes

1. P. Engardio, L. Therrien, N. Gross, and L. Armstrong. "How Motorola Took Asia by the Tail." *Business Week* (November 11, 1991), 68; G. P. Zachary. "High-Tech Firms Shift Some Skilled Work to Asian Countries." *The Wall Street Journal,* (September 30, 1994), A1, A2.

2. S. H. Rhinesmith, J. N. Williamson, D. M. Ehlen, and D. S. Maxwell. "Developing Leaders for the Global Enterprise." *Training and Development Journal* (April 1989), 26–34.

3. A. Laurent. "The Cross-Cultural Puzzle of International Resource Management." *Human Resource Management* (Summer 1986), 91–102.

4. S. C. Schneider. "National vs. Corporate Culture: Implications for Human Resource Management." *Human Resource Management*, 27, no. 2 (Summer 1988), 231.

5. D. A. Heenan. *Multinational Management of Human Resources: A Systems Approach* (Austin, TX: University of Texas at Austin, Bureau of Business Research, 1985), 5–9.

6. D. J. Lemak and J. S. Bracker. "A Strategic Contingency Model of Multinational Corporate Structure." *Strategic Management Journal*, 9, no. 5 (1988), 521–6.

7. B. S. Chakravarthy and H. V. Perlmutter. "Strategic Planning for a Global Business." *Columbia Journal of World Business*, 20, no. 2 (1985), 3–10.

8. Ibid.

9. Ibid.

10. Heenan. *Multinational Management*. 8.

11. Chakravarthy and Perlmutter. "Strategic Planning," 3–10.

12. Lemak and Bracker. "A Strategic Contingency." 523.

13. Heenan. *Multinational Management.* 9.

14. Chakravarthy and Perlmutter. "Strategic Planning." 9–10.

15. R. Tung, "U.S. Multinationals: A Study of Their Selection and Training Procedures for Overseas Assignments." *Academy of Management Proceedings* (1979), 298–9.

16. Ibid.

17. S. Overman. "Shaping the Global Workplace." *Personnel Administrator* (October 1989), 41–4.

18. A. V. Phatak. *Managing Multinational Corporations* (New York: Praeger, 1974).

19. A. V. Phatak. *International Dimensions of Management* (Boston, MA: Kent Publishing Co., 1989), 115.

20. G. Fontaine. *Managing International Assignments: The Strategy for Success* (Englewood Cliffs, NJ: Prentice Hall, 1989), 126.

21. M. Mendenhall and G. Oddou, "The Dimensions of Expatriate Acculturation: A Review." *Academy of Management Review,* 10, no. 1 (1985), 39–47.

22. Phatak. *International Dimensions of Management.* 114.

23. Mendenhall and Oddou. "Expatriate Acculturation." 41.

24. S. Shel. "Spouses Must Pass Test Before Global Transfers." *The Wall Street Journal* (September 6, 1991), B2.

25. Ibid.

26. E. R. Koepfler. "Locating and Staffing Offices Abroad." *Systems 3X and AS World* (July 1989), 124–6.

27. W. Q. Kirk and R. C. Maddox. "International Management: The New Frontier for Women." *Personnel* (March 1988), 46–9.

28. G. Schwartz. "Timely Tips." *The Wall Street Journal* (September 21, 1990), R22.

29. R. L. Desatnik and M. L. Bennet. *Human Resource Management in the Multinational Company* (New York: Nicols, 1978), 156.

30. Schneider. "National vs. Corporate Culture." 240.

31. A. Bennett. "GE Redesigns Rungs of Career Ladder." *The Wall Street Journal* (March 15, 1993), B1.

32. N. J. Adler, "Expecting International Success: Female Managers Overseas." *Columbia Journal of World Business* (Fall 1984), 79–84.

33. Desatnik and Bennet. *Human Resource Management.* 166.

34. Ibid., 171.

35. J. S. Lublin. "Companies Try to Cut Subsidies for Employees." *The Wall Street Journal* (December 11, 1989), B1.

36. Destanik and Bennet. *Human Resource Management.* 171.

37. R. Neff. "When in Japan, Recruit as the Japanese Do–Aggressively." *Business Week* (June 24, 1991), 58.

38. W. J. Best. "Training Japanese Leaders for Western Firms." *The Wall Street Journal* (May 11, 1992), A12.

39. M. Selz. "For Many Small Firms, Going Abroad Is No Vacation." *The Wall Street Journal* (February 27, 1992), B2.

40. C. Oakes. "Multinational Requirement: Stick with the Basics." *Management Review* (September 1988), 55–6.

41. "Firms Woo Executives From 'Third Countries'." *The Wall Street Journal,* (September 16, 1991), B1.

42. Phatak. *Managing Multinational Corporations.* 197.

43. Desatnik and Bennet. *Human Resource Management.* 169–70.

44. P. Lansing and K. Ready. "Hiring Women Managers in Japan: An Alternative for Foreign Employers." *California Management Review* (Spring 1988), 112–27.

45. Desatnik and Bennet. *Human Resource Management.* 144.

46. R. Vernon. "International Investment and International Trade in the Product Cycle." *Quarterly Journal of Economics,* 80, no. 2 (1966), 190–207.

47. N. J. Adler and F. Ghadar. "International Strategy from the Perspective of People and Culture: The North American Context." In A. M. Rugman, ed. *International Business Research for the Twenty-First Century,* (Greenwich, CT: JAI Press, 1990), 179–205.

48. Ibid.

49. Ibid., 187.

50. P. C. Earley. "Intercultural Training for Managers: A Comparison of Documentary and Interpersonal Methods." *Academy of Management Journal* (December 1987), 685–96.

51. S. Ronen. *Comparative and Multinational Management* (New York: John Wiley and Sons, 1986), 536.

52. Mendenhall and Oddou. "Expatriate Acculturation." 43.

53. R. Pascoe, "Employers Ignore Expatriate Wives at Their Own Peril." *The Wall Street Journal* (March 2, 1992), A13.

54. Mendenhall and Oddou. "Expatriate Acculturation." 163.

55. G. Shames. "Training for the Multinational Workplace." *The Cornell H.R.A. Quarterly* (February 1986), 25–31.

56. Earley. "International Training." 686.

57. Mendenhall and Oddou. "Expatriate Acculturation." 79.

58. Ibid., 78–9.

59. Earley. "International Training." 686–96.

60. R. D. Alert. "The Intercultural Sensitizer or Cultural Assimilator: A Cognitive Approach." In D. Landis and R. W. Brislin, eds. *Handbook of intercultural training* (New York: Pergamon Press, 1983), 186–217.

61. Albert. "The Intercultural Sensitizer." 189.

62. Earley. "International Training." 686.

63. J. Lublin, "Your Managers Learn Global Skills." *The Wall Street Journal* (March 3, 1992), B2.

64. Desatnik and Bennet. *Human Resource Management.* 113.

65. Schneider. "National vs. Corporate Culture." 233.

66. S. W. Frith. *The Expatriate Dilemma* (Chicago: Nelson-Hall, 1981), 35.

67. Ibid., 36.

68. Destnick and Bennett. *Human Resource Management.* 209.

69. E. J. Kolde. *The Multinational Company* (Lexington, MA: Lexington Books, 1974), 175–82.

70. Frith. *The Expatriate Dilemma.* 34.

71. Ibid., 88.

72. Kolde. *The Multinational Company.* 180.

73. Ibid., 180.

74. Ibid., 181.

75. R. T. Moran. "A Formula for Success in Multinational Organizations," *International Management* (December 1988), 74.

76. J. J. Laabs, "The Global Talent Search." *Personnel Journal* (August 1991), 38–44.

77. Ibid.

78. J. Lublin. "Foreign Accents Proliferate in Top Ranks as U.S. Companies Find Talent Abroad." *The Wall Street Journal* (May 21, 1992), B1.

79. R. Neff and W. J. Holstein. "The Harvard Man in Mitsubishi's Corner Office." *Business Week* (March 23, 1992), 50.

PT MULTI BINTANG INDONESIA (A)

ROBERT W. HORNADAY

Selling beer in an Islamic country is not easy. But that is exactly what PT[1] Multi Bintang[2] Indonesia (MBI) has done for over 60 years. Founded in 1929 and taken over by Heineken of the Netherlands in 1951, the company has survived depressions, wars, and revolutions.

Heineken still holds over 75% of MBI stock. Today the company's flagship brand, Bintang, controls nearly 60% of the Indonesian beer market, selling over 50 million liters annually. Further, Bintang is good beer. Western tourists are pleasantly surprised to find excellent beer when they visit Indonesia. MBI intends to defend and, if possible, improve its market share. The company plans to remain the market leader in the Indonesian beer market.

The Beer Industry in Southeast Asia and Indonesia

Members of the Association of Southeast Asian Nations (ASEAN)[3] protect their domestic beer producers with high tariffs. Even so, the Southeast Asia beer market is quite competitive.

[1] PT abbreviates "Perseroan Terbatas," meaning Incorporated or Limited in English.

[2] Bintang means "star" in English.

This case was written by Associate Professor Robert W. Hornaday of The University of North Carolina at Charlotte, while a visiting professor at the Program Magister Management, Gadjah Mada University, Yogyakarta, Indonesia. Research assistance was provided by Djoris and Handoyo Prasetyo. The case is intended as a basis for class discussion rather than to illustrate either effective or ineffective handling of an administrative situation.

Send correspondence concerning this case to: Director, Program Magister Manajemen, Universitas Gadjah Mada, Yogyakarta, Indonesia. Refer to UGM Case 1693.

[3] Brunei Darussalam, Indonesia, Malaysia, Philippines, Thailand, and Singapore.

The regional leader is San Miguel, the largest manufacturing company in the Philippines. San Miguel holds 90% of the Philippine market, 60% in Hong Kong, and is the largest foreign beer producer in China. Singapore's Asia Pacific Brewery (APB) is the next largest, with breweries in Singapore and Malaysia. APB has licensing agreements with Heineken of the Netherlands. APB brands (Tiger, Heineken and Anchor) are the unchallenged market leaders in Singapore and Malaysia. Because of tariff barriers, San Miguel has only a tiny market share in the two countries. To meet the challenge posed by San Miguel's expansion, APB plans to build a brewery in Vietnam.

Indonesians consume 100 million liters of beer annually, barely .5 liters of beer per person per year. That's not much compared to 7 liters for Malaysians. Chinese beer consumption jumped from .5 liters per capita annually in 1979 to 7.3 liters in 1991, reflecting China's rising standard of living. The Filipinos are

Southeast Asia's biggest beer drinkers, consuming 1.5 billion liters per year, about 25 liters per capita. However, 40 to 50 million Indonesians are occasional beer drinkers—more than the entire Filipino adult population. They will likely drink more beer as their incomes rise. Analysts expect beer consumption in Indonesia to increase at a rate of about 3%–4% per year.

MBI is the dominant brewer in Indonesia. Bintang Beer controls over 55% of the market (Exhibit 1). Its market share exceeds 70% in East Indonesia and North Sumatra. Heineken owns over 75% of MBI stock and the company uses Heineken technicians and managers. MBI cooperates with APB, Heineken's ally in Singapore. In addition to Bintang, MBI makes Green Sands Shandy,[4] Tiger Beer (licensed from APB), and Guiness Stout (licensed from the Irish

---

[4] Shandy is a mixture of ginger beer and beer that contains about 1% alcohol. Most beers, by comparison, contain about 4% alcohol.

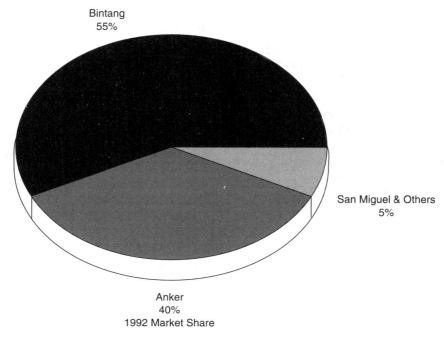

Bintang
55%

San Miguel & Others
5%

Anker
40%
1992 Market Share

Exhibit 1   PT Multi Bintang Indonesia: Indonesian Beer Market.

brewer Guiness). MBI also owns the Coca-Cola franchise for the province of North Sumatra and Aceh Special District for Coca-Cola, Sprite, and Fanta soft drinks.

Next in market share is Anker Beer, brewed by PT Delta Djakarta, a publicly listed company. Very strong in West Java and the Jakarta[5] area, Delta Djakarta also produces Carlsberg (under Danish license), Anker Stout, and Shanta Super Shandy. Considered a well-managed company, in 1990 Delta Djakarta had the highest earnings per share (567 rupiah)[6] of any stock listed on the Jakarta Stock Exchange. In 1993, San Miguel purchased 49% of Delta Djakarta from Mantrust Group, an Indonesian conglomerate. San Miguel Beer, produced under license by another Indonesian brewer has only a small market share in Indonesia.

Company Background

Founded in Medan, North Sumatra, in 1929, the company that became MBI moved to Surabaya[7] in 1936. During World War II, the Japanese took over the company. The Dutch returned after the war and Heineken purchased the company in 1951, calling it Heineken's Indonesian Brewery and using the Heineken grand name. During the final confrontation with the Dutch over Indonesian independence, the Indonesian government nationalized the company in 1962. In the process, the brand name changed from Heineken to Bintang.

After an aborted communist coup attempt in 1965, the company reverted to Heineken ownership in 1967 with a new name—The Indonesian Beer Company (PBI). Heineken changed the brand name slightly—to Bintang Baru, meaning

---

[5] Jakarta is Indonesia's capital with a population of about nine million people.

[6] Indonesia's currency is the rupiah (Rp) valued at about 2070 to the U.S. dollar in early 1993.

[7] Surabaya, a major port located in East Java, is Indonesia's second largest city with a population of three million people.

new star, a signal to beer drinkers that the old Heineken quality had returned. Major expansion occurred in 1971 with the construction of a new brewery in Tangerang near Jakarta. In 1981, PBI bought out a small brewery and soft drink bottler in Medan, North Sumatra. When the Indonesian government allowed companies to publicly list their stock, PBI changed its name to PT Multi Bintang Indonesia (MBI) and sold 16.7% of its shares to the public. It was the eighth Indonesian company to go public.

MBI operates breweries in Surabaya and Tangerang (Jakarta). It sold the Medan brewery in August 1992. The company is very closely tied to foreign brewers. MBI pays Heineken .08 guilders (US $.045) in technical fees for each liter of Bintang. Arthur Guinness & Son (Dublin, Ireland) receives 6% of the value of Indonesian Guiness Stout sales. APB in Singapore receives 4% of Tiger beer net sales in Indonesia. Although the MBI's Coca-Cola franchise in North Sumatra and Aceh Special District are profitable, other efforts to diversify away from beer have not been successful. Frezzy Malta, a malt based non-alcoholic drink introduced in 1985 was withdrawn from the market in 1987.

Corporate Governance

The objectives of the company as stated in the corporate charter are:

1. The production of beer and soft drinks as approved by the authorities in Indonesia.
2. The marketing of these products in local and international markets for the company and for third parties within the laws and regulations of Indonesia.

MBI takes special efforts to be a good corporate citizen in Indonesia. It prides itself on its skilled workforce. The company offers a wide range of employee benefits. Annual labor turnover is less than 1%. MBI corporate officers engage in monthly dialogues with workers at each facility. Twice each year, national meetings, called *Musyawarah Bersama*,[8] allow workers to present their views on company policies and conditions. Concerned about environmental matters over the past few years, the company has installed modern waste water treatment equipment and is exploring ways to reduce water consumption. Plastic crates introduced in 1990 will reduce usage of tropical wood. In 1991, MBI launched a major public relations program in conjunction with its 60th anniversary. Company officials held seminars in all major cities extolling the virtues of modern management techniques. These appearances received positive coverage in the press and on television, further enhancing MBI's image as a good corporate citizen.

Every January the CEO of Heineken in Amsterdam issues a *President's Letter* containing the parent company's view of world economic conditions. The *President's Letter* also contains Heineken's goals and a description of special and general problems. Based upon the *President's Letter* the top executives of MBI develop two plans. The first is an operational plan containing the annual budget. The second, a policy plan, outlines the objectives for three years and provides guidance for all long range planning activities. The company uses SWOT analysis as a framework. Company executives believe that MBI's strategy should be to differentiate itself from competitors in a positive way in order to fulfill customer needs, an idea borrowed from Kenichi Ohmac's *The Mind of the Strategist.*

A Board of Commissioners represents MBI shareholders. At present the President Commissioner is Tanri Abeng, former President Director of MBI. Three of the other four commissioners are Dutch citizens representing Heineken (Exhibit 2).

The Board of Directors provides executive guidance to the company. Four of the six direc-

[8] An Indonesian method of deliberation where anyone who wishes to speak may do so. Decisions are reached by consensus.

Exhibit 2
PT Multi Bintang Indonesia

Board of Commissioners[1]

President Commissioner
  Tanri Abeng, Indonesian
Commissioners
  J. B. H. M. Beks, Dutch, Heineken
  J. B. P. Maramis, Indonesian
  W. A. van den Wall Bake, Dutch, Expatriate Jakarta
    Banker
  Bernard Sarphati, Indonesian

Board of Directors[2]

President Director
  Erik J. Korthals Altes, Dutch, Heineken
Finance Director
  Soedjono Christantyo, Indonesian
Technical Director
  Freddy G. R. Lefebvre, Dutch, Heineken
Commercial Director
  Sedyana Pradjasantosa, Indonesian
Heineken Directors (both are Southeast Asia regional
  executives)
  Maarten Hendrik Rijkens, Dutch
  P. W. Kamphuisen, Dutch

---

[1] Similar to a U.S. Board of Directors.

[2] Similar to a U.S. Executive Committee.

tors are *executive directors,* meaning that they have line management responsibilities. The other two directors serve in staff advisory positions. Erik J. Korthals Altes has been President Director since 1991.

Tanri Abeng

No discussion of MBI is complete without mention of the role of Tanri Abeng. In 1979, MBI hired Tanri Abeng, a former Islamic student activist, as President Director. After his undergraduate days at Hassannudin University in Ujung Pandang, Tanri went to the United States on a scholarship. He received his MBA from the State University of New York at Buffalo and became a management trainee with Union Carbide, a large American chemical firm. Returning to Indonesia in 1969, Tanri helped manage the construction of a new Union

Carbide plant in Indonesia. At that time he was the Deputy Finance Director. By 1976 he had moved to the Principal Director's office, but he was still deputy. In 1977 he moved to Singapore to take over the Marketing Division. Union Carbide's Singapore plant supplied markets in 62 countries. Tanri got a good introduction to global marketing. From 1977–1980, his division produced record profits for Union Carbide in Singapore. For these efforts, Tanri expected to be named Principal Director of Union Carbide Indonesia. But another Union Carbide executive (an English citizen) was named to the post instead. Union Carbide asked Tanri to serve as Deputy Principal Director in Indonesia for about a year. After that he would become Principal Director. Tanri was disappointed. He felt he had earned the post of Principal Director. He didn't want to be anyone's assistant. He was ready to be the boss. To Union Carbide's surprise, Tanri quit the company and accepted an offer from Heineken to take over MBI (at that time still named the Indonesian Beer Company–PBI).

The Situation

PBI was not doing well. Market share slipped from 57% in 1976 to 49% in 1978. The company was losing money. Heineken had used expatriate managers (mostly English) since its return in 1967. But the management culture was basically paternalistic. All major decisions were made by expatriates who kept themselves separate from the Indonesian staff. Efficiency suffered. Morale among Indonesian employees was low.

Heineken was searching for an outsider who could turn the company around. Tanri Abeng looked like a good choice. Heineken wanted Tanri to attend a training course in Amsterdam for five months, but he thought it would be a waste of time. His first task was to *stop the bleeding*—to stop losing money. First step: increase efficiency in transport, production, sales, and distribution. How to do it? Tanri scrutinized

all costs. He examined the costs of company policies. For example, private use of company vehicles stopped. High level staff received transportation allowances. Only sales staff used company vehicles. This saved Rp 300 million the first year.

Cutting costs was not enough. Revenues had to increase. Tanri returned to the basics: *product, price, place,* and *promotion.* He decided that Bintang was a good product, probably superior to its competitors. Price was not an issue. Except for special promotions, the market price for Indonesian beer was the same. There is no price competition because of government tax policies. As for promotion, Bintang was the best known brand in Indonesia. It had a higher brand recognition than any of its competition. That left only place. Place, in the beer industry, meant distribution.

Improving Distribution

Tanri took a hard look at PBI's distribution system. To get better market coverage, he reduced the number of distributors from 112 to 12. These twelve *stockage* distributors became the focus of distribution efforts. Spread throughout the archipelago, they provided inventory support and promotional services to smaller distributors and retail outlets. In the process of changing its distribution system, PBI had to write off Rp 300 million in bad debts. However, since that time, the distribution system has not lost one rupiah to bad debts.

Tanri personally explained his campaign to PBI's sales people. After three generations, he was the first President Director to meet face to face with salesmen. This happened at the 1980 national sales meeting. The President Director, Tanri told his salesmen, is also a salesman. He sells ideas—ideas about strategy, about goals, and what the organization will become in the future.

Every year Tanri met with his salesmen. Before, company headquarters in Jakarta set sales strategy. There was no deviation. If a salesman in Ambon[9] wanted to try a different promotional technique, he couldn't. The centralized system provided no motivation for creativity. Regional distributors did not try innovative sales techniques. They were afraid to violate company promotional policies. Tanri decentralized the system. Local distributors ran their own promotions. The goal was to increase sales, not to blindly follow policies set in Jakarta.

In the space of one year the new strategy showed positive results. While profits lagged due to bad debts and expenses associated with the new distribution centers, revenues increased and market share climbed 2%—back to 51%.

New Directions

Tanri presented a new strategic plan to the Heineken family[10] and Board of Directors in 1980. He described the changes he had made in the Indonesian operation. To achieve future success in Indonesia, Tanri argued that the company should diversify its product line. Selling beer was not enough for two reasons. First, the majority of Indonesians, because of their Islamic faith, felt that beer drinking was wrong. To avoid criticism from religious leaders, MBI had to aim its advertising at non-Islamic market segments—mainly Christians, Buddhists, and Hindus, which comprise about 15% of the population. Second, beer is too expensive for the average Indonesian. He recommended that the company diversify into non-alcoholic beverages.

Heineken executives approved Tanri's recommendations. When the company filed for listing as a public corporation in 1981, the name of the company became PT Multi Bintang Indonesia (MBI), dropping the word "beer" from the title. Tanri spent about two million dol-

lars to design a new corporate logo and change the corporate identity with advertising and promotions. The company took on other products such as Green Sands and Guiness Stout. Sales of Coca-Cola products in North Sumatra and Aceh increased. MBI began research and development work on a new malt based non-alcoholic drink.

Introduced in 1985, Frezzy Malta was Tanri's major effort to diversify away from beer by producing a cheap drink that could be enjoyed by Indonesia's Islamic majority. Unfortunately, despite two years of major promotion, the product failed. Indonesian consumers did not like the taste. For the best taste, the drink had to be served cold. Many retail outlets in Indonesia have no cooling equipment. MBI withdrew Frezzy Malta from the market in 1987.

The Frezzy Malta episode showed Tanri how good marketing ideas often fail. MBI plans to be cautious in any major diversification efforts. New products must be able to generate adequate returns to justify the assets expended in their development.

Culture and Efficiency

In his eleven years with MBI, Tanri brought an Indonesian philosophy to its management culture. He firmly believes that successful management is a combination of science and art. Science is the same everywhere. But art depends upon culture. Tanri, when he was MBI President Director, told interviewers that the company uses its "competitive culture to compete in a dynamic business." It tries to anticipate changes in the marketplace and turn those changes into strategic opportunities. But the company's market focus does not exclude other considerations, such as the company's human resources. Human resources are the "basic resources behind the concept of competitive culture," according to Tanri. MBI expects its employees to have a good attitude and respectable private lives. On the job they should display a high level of dedication,

---

[9] Ambon, a predominantly Christian city in the Moluccu Islands, is located 1800 miles east of Jakarta.

[10] The Heineken family still controls the business.

professionalism, and knowledge so they can carry out their duties effectively and efficiently.

Tanri attributes MBI's success not to clever managers, but to its open culture, where each employee feels responsible for the company's future. But an open culture is not an end in itself. It must lead to a competitive attitude that fosters professionalism. MBI strives for professionalism at all levels. New employees are selected carefully and receive the opportunity to broaden their experience so that they understand how they fit into the company's competitive culture. Since top down authoritarian management soon dissipates managerial energy, the company uses a decentralized system of management. Lower level managers have decision responsibilities. This requires a high degree of professionalism at all levels of management. Each individual is expected to work toward the common goal. The company offers scholarships to qualified employees who wish to improve their skills.

Tanri's Style

As President Director, Tanri did not duck issues. In his view Indonesians value openness and compromise. An example of his public relations style occurred in 1991 when Islamic factions in the Aceh Special District caused an uproar over Green Sands Shandy. Green Sands tastes like a sweet soft drink, not like beer, alleged the protestors. Devout Muslims were being tricked into buying a drink that contained alcohol. The leaders of the protests demanded that MBI either stop selling Green Sands, or take the alcohol out.

This was an important issue for MBI. Although the company does not sell much beer to the Acehnese who are strict Muslims, it does sell Coca-Cola products in Aceh bottled by its Medan plant. MBI did not wish to alienate the Acehnese. On the other hand, MBI's main product is beer. If the company backed down in the face of Islamic protests over Green Sands it could probably expect similar complaints about beer.

Tanri met the issue head on. He strongly defended his product. He refused to change the ingredients of the Green Sands. Since the product was launched nine years before the protests, Tanri pointed out that everyone knew that the drink contained alcohol. Although he stood his ground, he was not confrontational. He conducted his defense of Green Sands in an Indonesian style. He spoke softly, he was open, and he listened. The furor over Green Sands subsided.

Well aware of his reputation as an ethnic Indonesian corporate executive, Tanri took a major interest in management education. He was an active promoter of the Indonesian University of Economics and Banking (STEKPI) and the Indonesian Management Development Institute (IPMI). When it came to the careers of young managers he recruited and trained at MBI, he encouraged them to prepare themselves to climb the corporate ladder. If that meant that they left MBI for opportunities with other companies, Tanri wrote letters of recommendation and wished them well. He felt that the need in Indonesia for professional managers was so great that it was in the long term interest of MBI to help its young managers to move up, even if it meant that they left the company. Tanri was not angered when other companies "hijacked" his managers.

By the time Tanri stepped down as MBI President Director in 1991, he was clearly the most successful professional manager in Indonesia. Without family wealth or influential political backing, he had become a leading corporate executive. He was a successful ethnic Indonesian swimming in a commercial sea dominated by ethnic Chinese. While staying on as President Commissioner at MBI, Tanri went on to become President Director of PT Bakrie Brothers, a major Indonesian conglomerate. He serves as a commissioner on several other corporate boards. He is also active in volunteer organizations such as the Tourist Promotion Board.

Taxes

Indonesian brewers face special problems. In addition to overcoming the difficulties of marketing beer in an Islamic culture, they must import raw materials (mainly malt and corn) from Europe and Australia, increasing transportation costs. The government protects Indonesian agricultural commodities with duties and tariffs, so import taxes must be paid on these imports. Direct taxes are the major cost item for Indonesian brewers.

There are three taxes on alcoholic beverages. The first is the value added tax (VAT) of 10% applied to all manufactured goods. Next is a luxury tax (beer is considered a luxury item in Indonesia). In 1992 the luxury tax increased to 35% of the factory price of luxury goods. The third tax is an excise tax on alcoholic beverages. In 1992, this tax increased to Rp 500 per liter. MBI expects another increase in 1994. In total, MBI pays out over 50% of its revenue in taxes. The same is true of other brewers.

Tax increases over the past seven years have drastically increased the cost of brewing beer in Indonesia. Since 1991, taxes amount to more than all other costs combined (Exhibit 3). These tax increases could not always be passed on to consumers. The demand for beer in Indonesia is elastic. Generally, if the economy is growing, sales of luxury items, including beer, go up. During periods of uncertainty, beer sales stagnate or decrease. In the face of tax increases in

1985 and 1986, brewers could not increase prices because of poor market conditions caused by a decrease in the world price of oil (Indonesia's major export) and a drastic devaluation of the rupiah. In 1990, when the excise tax on alcoholic beverages increased by 25%, brewers were only able to increase the retail price of beer by about 8.5%. Other major tax increases occurred in 1992. Again retail prices could not keep up. The total 1992 tax increases amounted to about 30%, while retail prices increased only 11%.

Taxes are the major uncontrollable cost faced by Indonesian brewers. Most of the efficiencies and cost cutting programs at MBI have not contributed to more profits, but to counteracting the effects of increased taxes. As taxes increase, other costs must decrease to maintain the same level of profitability (Exhibit 4). Experts expect the so-called "sin" taxes on beer to increase. Beer taxes are easy to collect and popular with Islamic leaders.

MBI Financial Situation

With revenue growth that has kept up with the expansion of the Indonesian economy, MBI has carefully improved efficiency because of the necessity to absorb tax increases rather than increase retail beer prices. The company's financial statements show a steadily profitable firm with conservative management (Exhibits 4 and 5). The financial statements now show new equity injections since 1981. The price of MBI stock has varied between Rp 10,050 per share and Rp 8,200 per share between January 1992 and March 1993. Average 1992 price earnings ratio was 12.4 although such ratios mean little since the stock is so infrequently traded. The company's stock traded on only 17 out of 247 days in 1992. These transactions involved 158,000 shares valued at Rp 1.191 billion (about $5.8 million). Many analysts believe that this illiquidity is caused by sellers' beliefs that the company is in good shape and potential buyers'

Exhibit 3
PT Multi Bintang Indonesia Distribution of Revenue

Year	Costs	Taxes	Profit
1985	50%	40%	10%
1986	52%	40%	8%
1987	51%	38%	11%
1988	49%	42%	9%
1989	49%	42%	9%
1990	50%	41%	9%
1991	43%	47%	10%
1992	37%	54%	9%

Exhibit 4
PT Multi Bintang Indonesia Balance Sheets[1]

Accounts	1992	1991	1990	1989	1988	1987	1986	1985	1984
Assets									
Current assets	49,089,888	44,611,094	52,028,150	37,810,937	33,350,867	30,002,653	24,656,629	20,577,890	20,242,749
Fixed assets	43,177,573	45,421,683	39,490,940	30,751,723	24,488,981	25,484,987	28,446,947	28,331,999	27,034,580
Intangible assets	2,563,811	2,563,811	2,354,690	2,274,038	2,266,670	1,783,550	—	—	38,276
Other assets	13,173,573	11,889,048	7,090,099	7,175,806	7,772,346	3,391,841	1,700,445	2,016,145	556,088
Total Assets	108,004,679	104,485,636	100,963,879	78,012,504	67,878,864	60,663,031	54,804,021	50,906,034	47,871,693
Liabilities and Shareholders' Equity									
Liabilities									
Current liabilities	41,274,259	41,414,848	43,371,907	28,624,454	19,737,226	16,714,339	16,586,692	12,748,831	11,660,885
Long term liabilities	264,940	1,583,357	3,537,149	1,628,193	3,418,037	1,237,500	290,682	1,406,250	1,342,500
Other long term liabilities	11,355,385	9,857,377	7,478,295	5,618,512	4,494,547	3,992,491	5,246,059	4,838,446	4,118,134
Shareholder's Equity									
Share capital	21,070,000	21,070,000	21,070,000	21,070,000	21,070,000	21,070,000	21,070,000	21,070,000	21,070,000
Premium on share capital	1,802,340	1,802,340	1,802,340	1,802,340	1,802,340	1,802,340	1,802,340	1,802,340	1,802,340
Retained earnings	32,237,755	28,757,714	23,704,188	19,269,005	17,356,714	15,846,361	9,808,248	9,040,167	7,877,834
Total Liabilities and Equity	108,044,679	104,485,636	100,963,879	78,012,504	67,878,864	60,663,031	54,804,021	50,906,034	47,871,693

[1]Stated in 000s of rupiah.
Source: PT Multi Bintang.

Exhibit 5
PT Multi Bintang Indonesia Income Statements[1]

Accounts	1992	1991	1990	1989	1988	1987	1986	1985	1984
Sales	172,858,768	159,258,976	143,720,632	106,583,982	92,556,058	81,803,394	66,774,244	58,659,881	50,968,294
Sales and excise taxes	79,932,735	67,179,800	62,347,666	44,260,579	26,075,544	31,157,807	25,263,689	21,419,911	17,154,204
Net sales	92,926,033	92,079,176	81,372,966	62,323,403	56,480,514	50,645,587	41,510,555	37,239,970	33,814,090
Cost of goods sold	51,958,529	52,908,576	50,318,871	38,597,437	36,648,511	30,649,982	25,884,821	20,674,704	17,980,816
Gross profit of sales	40,967,504	39,170,600	31,054,095	23,725,966	19,832,003	19,995,605	15,625,734	16,565,266	15,833,274
Operating expenses	16,119,593	16,852,704	13,032,391	10,346,982	9,936,165	10,149,718	9,252,190	8,572,808	8,594,438
Operating profit	24,847,911	22,317,896	18,021,704	13,378,984	9,895,838	9,845,887	6,373,544	7,992,458	7,238,836
Other income (expenses)	1,707,621	1,041,623	1,660,106	324,744	1,305,988	1,885,599	1,475,242	617,457	690,112
Income before extraordinary loss	26,555,532	23,359,519	19,681,810	13,703,728	11,201,826	11,731,486	7,848,786	8,609,915	7,928,948
Extraodrinary loss	(1,232,469)	.00	.00	.00	.00	.00	.00	.00	.00
Income before income tax	25,323,063	23,359,519	19,681,810	13,703,728	11,201,826	11,731,486	7,848,786	8,609,915	7,928,948
Corporate income tax	9,201,022	7,244,243	6,248,027	4,391,305	2,738,373	2,867,942	2,234,605	2,601,482	1,907,842
Net Income	16,122,041	16,115,276	13,433,783	9,312,423	8,463,453	8,863,544	5,614,181	6,008,433	6,021,106
Earnings per share	765	765	638	442	402	421	266	285	286

[1]Stated in 000s of rupiah, except earning per share.

Source: PT Multi Bintang.

views that there is not much room for rapid growth.

An analysis of the financial performance shows that a major corporate objective is to return profits to shareholders. Since becoming a public company in 1981, MBI has maintained a payout ratio of about 80% (Exhibit 6). MBI initial equity holders who contributed Rp 21.070 billion have received a 313% return in dividends alone, an average of 26% per year—a payout of Rp 87.190 billion in dividends. An additional Rp 55 billion of owner equity remains in the firm. Heineken's share of the dividend payments totaled Rp 66.277 billion. MBI also paid Heineken annual technical assistance fees amounting to .08 guilders per liter of beer produced. These technical fees amounted to about Rp 5 billion in 1992. The preceding figures have not been adjusted for the devaluation of the rupiah that occurred over the same time period. Nevertheless, it is clear that MBI has maintained a relatively high rate of dividend payout and retained only 20% of earnings for increasing the capitalization of the firm. Whether the company will be able to continue this policy in the face of anticipated tough competition from San Miguel remains to be seen.

The Threat from San Miguel

As previously mentioned, San Miguel purchased 49% of the stock of Delta Djakarta, the second largest Indonesian brewer. This purchase gives San Miguel access to the Indonesian beer market and constitutes a serious challenge to the dominance of MBI.

San Miguel set up a joint venture to brew beer in Indonesia in 1976, but withdrew when it failed to gain significant market share. In the early 1980s, the Indonesian government closed the beer industry to foreign investment. The only way San Miguel could re-enter Indonesia with equity capital was to purchase an existing company. Currently San Miguel holds only a meager share of the Indonesian beer market through a licensing agreement with Gunung

Agung Group. The alliance of San Miguel with Delta Djakarta provides Indonesia's second largest brewer with financial and marketing resources that easily match those of Heineken, MBI's parent. MBI can no longer outspend its opponent. Perhaps of more importance, the City of Jakarta continues to own 30% of Delta Djakarta stock. This gives added political clout to the company that can't be matched by MBI. The coming of San Miguel presents a major threat to MBI.

Founded in 1890, San Miguel ranks among the ten largest brewers in the world. It is the largest manufacturing company in the Philippines, accounting for 4% of GNP and 7% of all tax revenue collected by the government, reporting $2.2 billion in 1992 sales. It has diversified into processed foods, agribusiness, and packaging. San Miguel has 90% of the Philippine beer market, producing 1.9 billion liters of beer annually. San Miguel entered the Hong Kong market in 1948 and now holds 60% market share. It is the largest selling foreign beer in China with an investment of $3.5 million in Guanzhou Province (Canton) where annual beer consumption is 12 liters per person. San Miguel has a 30 year lease and exercises management control over the Chinese plant. It is making a major effort to export San Miguel Beer to Vietnam and Nepal. Even so, because of huge sales in the Philippines, only 3% of San Miguel beer revenues come from foreign sales. San Miguel sells practically no beer in Singapore or Malaysia.

Some observers believe that the Delta Djakarta deal clinches San Miguel's position as Southeast Asia's dominant brewer. With 60% of the market in Hong Kong, 90% in the Philippines, a strong foothold in China and Vietnam, and now access to the Indonesian market, San Miguel has isolated the region's second largest brewer APB (an ally of MBI) to the Singapore and Malaysian markets. In the future, a new regional free trade agreement might lower local tariffs that ASEAN countries use to protect local beers. San Miguel managers expect

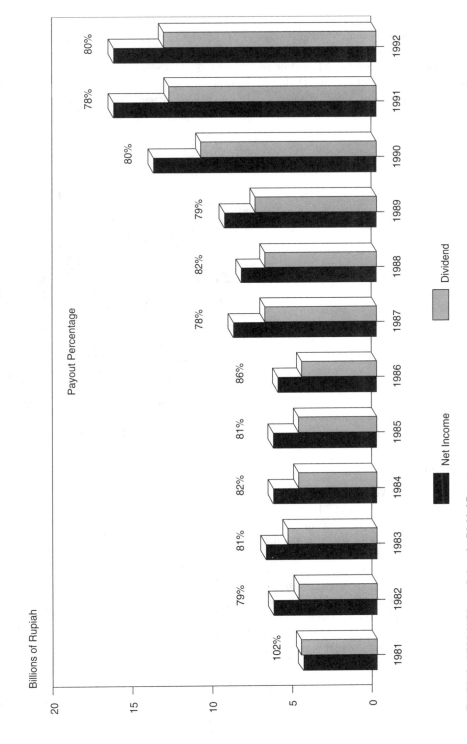

Billions of Rupiah

Payout Percentage

Exhibit 6 PT Multi Bintang Indonesia: Divided Payout

335

that such an agreement would give them increased sales in Singapore and Malaysia.

It is not clear exactly how San Miguel plans to exploit its purchase of Delta Djakarta. Spokesmen for the company say that for now, both Anker and San Miguel brands will be sold in Indonesia. San Miguel processed food products will be distributed through Delta Djakarta's existing distribution network. MBI planners have little doubt, however, that San Miguel's long range goal is to become the largest brewer in Indonesia.

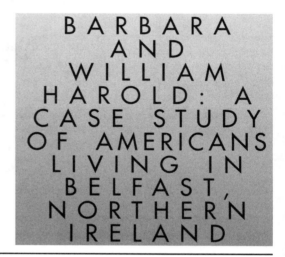

BARBARA AND WILLIAM HAROLD: A CASE STUDY OF AMERICANS LIVING IN BELFAST, NORTHERN IRELAND

RAE ANDRE

Part A: William Harold

When you first meet William Harold, he is likely to tell you that he is from Minneapolis, that he has been in the airplane business ever since he got out of the army in the '50s, and that he is an engineer. "We don't know how long we will be staying here. The airplane business is like that. We have just been put back on reduced time. That means three days a week. Management, too, will be on three days a week. As it is, the Government picks up the fourth day of my salary anyhow, so that my compensation will

Reprinted with permission from Professor Rae Andre, College of Business Administration, Northeastern University.

not be drastically reduced. Our company is under some scrutiny for going to a three-day week. The issue for the people in Northern Ireland is, are you here on a permanent basis. Yes, I think most American companies are here to stay. At the same time, everyone is here on an approximate ten-year tax relief. Most companies, after they have run out of the tax incentive, do tend to leave." William Harold is married and has two kids going to the Belfast schools, an eight-year-old boy and an eleven-year-old girl. They speak with Belfast Irish accents after living in Belfast for two years.

When you see William among his Irish friends, you can see that he is well assimilated. There is much laughter and poking fun. William will talk about the "wee nip" that he is going to have after work. He describes the neighborhood that he lives in as "all Irish," except for themselves. "We are very happy," he says. "Most of my friends are Irish. In fact, I don't pal around with the other Americans in Northern Ireland. There are about forty at the managerial level in other companies here.

"They call this a war zone, but it doesn't feel like a war zone. The only time the violence has struck me is when the University was bombed this fall. I should have been in the classroom right below it, when the bomb went off. Barbara was in the building at the time and said that the whole building shook and that someone told her that the University had been bombed." The University had previously been bombed, before he arrived in Northern Ireland. "I do avoid certain areas of town. There are certain areas of town that I would not drive into. I would not go anywhere locally unless I know someone or am going to someone's house. I don't pay any attention to it. I don't worry about it."

Barbara and William live in a large home leased for them by the company. In many ways it is a typical Irish home of the upper middle class. What is different about it is that when you walk in the front door you are toasty warm right away. The family walks around constantly in bare feet or slippers. The doors between the hall and the living room and the hall and the kitchen are open—unlike the same situation in other Irish households, where heat is being conserved. The television, showing video tapes, is on nonstop. It is on all through the day and during dinner. There is an electric fire in the grate, whereas the Irish would have a coal fire. The house is quite nice and William likes it very much, but there are some things that they miss. For instance, in their house in Reno the family had three televisions, one for William and Barbara, one for the children and one for the den. If anything one wanted to watch was on, each of them could scatter to their different televisions. Coming over, they had a nine-thousand pound transportation limit, but of course they could not

bring any of their electrical appliances. So here they all have to debate who is going to get to watch what on the television.

The house has an especially large refrigerator, and there is a freezer in the garage as well. Nevertheless, Barbara complains that they can never store enough or make enough use of their leftovers. Barbara is an excellent cook. Serving a meal to an American guest, she prepares spareribs. William suggests that the pork in Northern Ireland is absolutely superb. In fact, the local bacon is one of his favorite things. Barbara typically makes several different types of salad, much like one would have in the United States. She makes a potato salad into which she puts the local shrimp. For her guest she also makes carrot salad and cucumber salad. A good German wine is served. Barbara comments that they cannot get California wines here, with the exception of perhaps Paul Masson or Gallo. They drink the German and the French wines.

The family has two cats and a long-haired chihuahua. The house is constantly full of action and talk.

The following are excerpts from a conversation with William:

What is there that I miss about the States? Nothing.

I belong to a private club. Private clubs are very popular here. I go there to play golf and squash quite a bit. It is hard to get into these clubs. This club I am in, in fact, has a one-year waiting list. It is associated with the telephone company; it's their plant club.

I am taking my Master's of Science and Management at the University one day a week from one p.m. until nine p.m. They give us a lot of work. It has a three-year program. I probably won't finish it, but I'll transfer the credits to the States. Right now I'm studying Taylor and right brain/left brain differences for a paper for a course. There really isn't that much to do around here. So I am glad to have the opportunity to go to school. And of course the company is paying for it.

Most people just stay home at night and watch videos. We belong to two video clubs. We go out to the movies also, but the movies only change once a fortnight or once a month. On the weekends we just mostly watch videos. I can watch an American football game every week. Just last week we got the entire Superbowl.

We do like to take advantage of the travel. We go all around, and we are planning to take a cruise on the Nile soon. All four of us.

There is one American restaurant in town, the only American restaurant. It is the only place you can get a hamburger and other American foods. It is quite good. The Irish food is just very plain; they do not put many spices on their food. I always eat my lunch out. I never eat in the plant cafeteria.

Every Sunday I buy all the papers.

When we first arrived here we had two cars. Both were stick shift and Barbara was having trouble learning how to drive a car with a stick shift, so we traded them in and got one big car instead. Barbara makes good use of the buses.

What are the prospects for economic stability here, over the long term? Not very good, unless they get some industry in. Not big industry but small shops—eight people. That is what they need most.

It is difficult for me to get even my suppliers to come over here from England. The Irish don't like the Brits and the Brits hear so much bad publicity—and that's just what it is, just publicity about Northern Ireland—that they are just frightened to come here. So I pick them up at the airport and I take them to the office and I take them to lunch and then I take them back to the airport. That's it.

Part B: Barbara Harold

We have been here a little over a year. We came on December 1, 1982, so we have been here now fourteen months. There is not a lot to do here.

Some time ago, we formed the Ulster American Women's Group, just because there were so many of us here and we wanted to have something to do. So we would tour the national historic sites or go down to Dublin and meet with the American Women's Club down there.

This year I'm taking a one-year course in health education at the University because at a certain point you just must get on with your life. I didn't want to come here and just waste my time. That is what I would have felt I was doing if I hadn't taken this course. I am a nurse and I am able to work here, so that when I finish my one-year program I could take a job if I wanted to. I quit work back in 1976 and haven't worked since.

When I first came here I had trouble finding things, things you want. I learned that you can call around and find sour cream or other things you are used to cooking with, but it takes time. When you do find it, you will only find one little bit of it. It took me three months to find Parmesan cheese, and when I could find it, it was only in two-ounce containers. Everything here is small.

When we arrived here my daughter was ten. At age eleven-and-a-half they make the children take examinations to be tracked into what is in America the equivalent of the secondary school system. She can either go into a grammar school, which is your college prep, or into the equivalent of a high school, which is less advanced. When you send your child to grammar school or high school, you have to choose which school you want to send them to. They arrange open houses at these schools to allow you to select them. How can you select a school on the basis of a two-and-a-half hour presentation? I fought to get her exempted from that exam because she had only been in their school system for seven months. They are allowing her to take a four-hour psychological test instead. She is taking it next Tuesday. She is a little worried about it. But I'm not worried about her. Naturally every American child is one year behind when they start school here in Northern Ireland because they start school one year earlier. They work the children very hard. Typically, they will have four or five hours of homework a night in grammar school. They put a lot of pressure on them that I don't think is necessary.

I don't mix very much with my neighbors. To some extent, yes. But there seem to be limits. My daughter Claire at one point took me down to meet the mother of one of the children that she had been playing with for months. I had a frank conversation with the woman, who said, "Well, yes, I am very pleased to meet you but to tell you the truth, I am just as happy staying at home in the evenings and not going out. And I probably wouldn't take the time to come up and meet you specifically." I don't think it has always been this way, but since The Troubles people just keep to themselves more.

I was surprised at how advanced the women are in this country. Women are very aware and very eager to make something of themselves beyond being just a homemaker. But the men, sadly enough, seem to want to keep them down.

It's unusual to be invited into their homes, in my experience. At first I thought it was me, but now I think it is them. I had been warned about this, that someone who would spend an hour on the phone talking to you would never accept your invitation back to your home to have coffee. Recently, the students at the University in my class decided that they would have a little party and since my home is right on the edge of the campus I offered it. It took me a great deal of time and effort to convince them that I was serious, that I really wanted people to come into my home. I don't know why that is, it just is.

I don't know how long I will be staying here. The airplane industry is unpredictable; it just depends. We have been moving around quite a bit. Before we came here we were in Reno for a year. [Note: William says that Barbara really misses her true hometown, which is Savannah. All their furniture is being stored there, and their permanent home there is being rented.]

The Irish are not very spontaneous. I would be bopping in and out of my friends' homes if I were in the States. Here I met a woman who was telling me about her travels with a friend and said that she hadn't spoken to that friend for six months. I wouldn't have done that. I would have at least phoned up my friend during that six months time. But that's just not the way they are here.

I think most American women here are bored. This is an outpost, there isn't much to do. If you go to the club with William . . . I don't go there because I don't like that sort of thing. You would walk in and see the women sitting together on one side of the main room and the men sitting together on the other side.

There are some people—it is a shame—who won't let themselves take advantage of me, they won't let me be of use to them. There just seem to be barriers between me and them. Sometimes I just think it is because I am Black. There are just some people who can't deal with that. I'm Black and intelligent, but they don't understand that. They just don't relate to that. I judge people by who they are and how they talk to me, not by the color of their skin.

I've got used to the moving, but here I just feel like I'm camping out. There are no comfortable chairs to sit on in this house. If you go into that room there, you'll see all the chairs are just not comfortable. The refrigerator is large by Irish standards but too small for me; I can't keep any leftovers in it. They say this is an upper middle class area but I'm not impressed, and not just because of American standards.

Part C: Background on the Harolds

Barbara is originally Jamaican and was brought up in London. She said she was not at all frightened to come to Northern Ireland. She had been warned that she might not get along with the Irish. She had been warned about The Troubles, but because of her previous experience in England she said these things did not scare her. She is a nurse and midwife.

William was formerly with the U.S. Army. Now he is an aircraft engineer with an American company. First the Harolds spent a year in Reno with this company, and then they were sent to Northern Ireland. The division in Northern Ireland is going to be the production facility for a jet which is currently being built in the United States. The prototypes are being built and tested at this point. Supposedly, the plant was put on three days as opposed to four days because the testing is not going quite as perfectly as planned.

Barbara and William have some disagreement over the extent to which he has assimilated to the culture.

Both of them speak fondly on their house on an island off the Georgia coast. Their children also speak fondly of the States. The children both complain that there is nothing to do here, especially the older girl, who says that the sports for girls are very poor. She only has gym on Wednesdays. The food is terrible, she says. If she were in Georgia, her daddy would drop them off to rollerskate two days a week, Friday and Saturday. The boy, on the other hand, is into soccer and rugby and his team has won several championships.

Discussion Questions

1. What are the issues of cross-cultural adjustment for Barbara and William? For their children? How do the problems of adjustment differ for the wage earner and the non-working spouse?
2. What adjustment issues are especially important because these people are *Americans?*
3. What safety issues must the family be concerned about in this situation? In other situations living or travelling abroad? How should their company become involved with these issues?

HIGH TECHNOLOGY INCORPORATED: THE INTERNATIONAL BENEFITS PROBLEM: A SEQUENTIAL CASE STUDY

RAE ANDRE

Part A

At High Technology Incorporated (HTI) the benefits policy for international assignments states that:

> Wherever legally possible, HTI will attempt to provide the employee with Home Country benefits under the Life Insurance, Disability Pension and Social Security Plans during temporary international assignments.

HTI employees typically spend one to three, and sometimes as long as four years overseas. Historically, during this time many employees have received benefits equalling or surpassing those of the home country. Recently, company policy has shifted towards equalizing benefits across countries. The system has been less than perfect, however, with some employees finding that their stay overseas has reduced their benefits. At a 1984 conference for the corporate personnel managers of local companies, Jack Cooke, HTI Corporate International Benefits Manager, commented on HTI's difficulties in fairly compensating its U.S. employees abroad. During his discussion he made the following points.

Reprinted with permission from Professor Rae Andre, College of Business Administration, Northeastern University.

Home Country Coverage

In 1984 HTI carried out an audit of employees and inventoried people for the purposes of determining offsets—the benefits given to overseas employees to offset loss of home country coverages for pensions, insurance, and similar benefits. The issue was to examine offsetting benefits to determine:

(a) if there was enough funding, and,
(b) if the funding was allocated to the appropriate areas.

HTI gathered pension and benefits data for each employee on overseas assignment. A benefits book was published for each individual. The audit revealed that there was a considerable amount of overfunding (in the plans of 4 countries) and some underfunding—people with no plans at all. Cooke believed that HTI was not fulfilling its promise to provide equitable contracts to employees sent overseas. The audit pointed up the fact that whereas HTI was providing adequate funding, the money was being put in the wrong buckets—it was not being well distributed among the countries and individuals who needed it.

Cooke noted that the employees' main fear concerns the security of their coverage. He vividly recalls the old saying "Don't worry . . . but don't die or get sick on assignment!" and how it applied to a Canadian employee in Scotland. The employee died on the last night of his assignment. When his wife was questioned by Scottish authorities shortly after the death it was discovered that the man had been covered by Canadian Social Insurance (federal social security), and so was ineligible for death benefits in Scotland. The Scottish social security agency refused to pay a death benefit and returned all HTI contributions to the wife, saying the employee should not have been covered in the first place.

The Scottish case highlights the need to review the current local policy to determine when coverage should apply and what steps should be taken to ensure continuity of coverage. Currently the company does not cover the employee under foreign programs when an employee cannot be maintained in a Home Country Plan. A lack of coverage results in one of two major ways.

First, the home country legal requirements or plan documents may not permit participation by non-residents. For example, a citizen and resident of Country A is transferred to Country B. Country A does not provide certain coverages, retirement income coverage for example, to its citizens if they live outside of Country A. HTI does not provide this coverage either.

Second, non-nationals in the home country are not allowed to stay in home country programs. For example, a citizen of Country B is working in Country A. In Country A he is only covered for health insurance for a specified period, after which, unless he becomes a citizen, he will not be covered. Again, HTI has no policy to cover him.

To give a real life example, "What about my pensions in the U.K.?" is a question often asked by 'permanent' British employees living in the U.S. From the company's viewpoint, it may be difficult to decide what 'permanent' means. Cooke pointed out that any American citizen on a United States payroll is covered by U.S. Social Security anywhere in the world. This type of problem only arises with HTI employees from nations other than the United States.

Additional Issues

Cooke identified several other problems that he felt needed to be addressed. One was that the permanent relocation policy did not address past service: What happens if a person relocates permanently out of their home country? How should their benefits, especially their pension benefits be calculated? Another problem was that company and employee sometimes differed about how to define "home country." If an employee had been in a country other than their country of origin for ten years or more, which was their home country? Also, there were some employees with *no* evident home country.

Cooke sent questionnaires to the personnel heads in the various countries concerned, asking them to tell him what problems they would face in attempting to make the international benefits program more equitable. Three major issues were identified.

(1) LEGAL. The first issue was complying with legal requirements in the various host countries. Of the three issues, this was considered to be the most serious. For example, sometimes employees found themselves involuntarily vested in host country plans by law, when HTI would have preferred them to be covered in the United States. Cooke pointed out that to date corrective action on this particular problem has involved alerting line management of the situation and developing recommendations.

The home country law sometimes excludes non-residents from coverage in their home country. As an example, if a U.K. (English) resident is outside of the U.K. for more than 3 years, they have to leave their retirement plan. Extensions are possible, but only for the fourth year. The non-residents can buy back into the U.K. plan later on. But in the meantime the company has chosen to provide coverage for subsequent years.

(2) FINANCIAL. Two issues arise here. The first is liability for past service. For example, with the case just mentioned, who pays for the uncovered years? The host country? The individual? HTI? Also, individuals may lose coverage due to local fiscal requirements. For example, a country might not have a sliding scale for social security benefits, thus putting the well-paid individual at a disadvantage relative to his home country peers.

(3) ADMINISTRATIVE. Not all HTI facilities even *have* pension plans. And among those that do, there are different requirements. Some have a minimum age of 25, some do not. Some have a one year waiting period for eligibility, some do not. Some have voluntary participation, some do not. And some are benefit plans, while some are contribution plans.

At the time of Jack Cooke's talk, these issues at HTI were far from solved. The policy was that when HTI moved someone permanently, the employee would get the sum of the benefits from the country left and the new country. However, because of high inflation in many countries, this often meant that the employee was losing money.

Discussion Questions

1. What are the most important issues facing Cooke?
2. How would you define "home country" and "permanent employee"?
3. How should past service be handled?
4. What steps should be taken to address overfunding?
5. Recommend a revision to the policy in order to address these issues.
6. Does inflation impact any of your recommendations?
7. Cooke jokes that the three most commonly told lies are: "The check is in the mail"; "Of course I'll love you tomorrow"; and, "I'm

from home office and I'm here to help you." What will be the international reaction to Cooke's plan?

Part B: Do Not Read This Part Until Told To Do So. HTI: Cooke's Recommendations

HTI's Corporate International Benefits Manager, Jack Cooke, feels that the company's benefit policy should be revised. The problem is summarized by him as follows: "If HTI moves someone permanently, they get the sum of the parts, and the money left in the other country is often losing money for them due to inflation. This is all they get and it's not adequate." Cooke recommends that the HTI policy be revised to read:

> Assignments shall not result in loss of retirement and retirement-related benefits to the employee, whether compulsory or voluntary, calculated inaccordance with the program in effect in the Home Country.

Cooke believes that for temporaries—people on international assignments of up to 4 years—the problem should be fixed locally. "Whatever the component—risk insurance, annuity or pension plan—we should sit down with local counsel to provide substitute coverage that equals what they had at home." This may not lead to double coverage since HTI tries to get temporary people excluded from local plans wherever possible. Sometimes HTI chooses to live with the double coverage.

Cooke weighed the pros and cons of providing the employee with the sum of the parts earned in their different countries of employment plus vesting them and updating them in their home country. The advantages are that this policy:

- reflects the employee's HTI career in each country

- updates vested benefits so that total benefits are current
- provides equitable treatment with employees in the home country
- allows the company to retain control
- is undertood by employees
- is simple to administer and provides more company flexibility than the alternatives (i.e. moving people from country to country, changing their benefits each time, which employees resist).

The disadvantages of this policy are that it:

- is administratively complex
- may not recognize continuous service for survivorship and disability benefits
- will be affected by exchange rates, i.e. severe inflation
- may not achieve retirement income objectives

Cooke noted that through their research HTI found that other companies had not solved the problem either.

Discussion Questions

1. Discuss the pros and cons of Cooke's plan. Why do you suppose that other companies had not solved the problem either?
2. What alternatives can you suggest?

Part C: The Bandits

HTI faces an additional problem, one faced by most international companies. The problem is reclassifying people from temporary to permanent. Cooke noted, "We have 13 to 14 American 'bandits' living in Geneva, Switzerland. Their kids can't even speak English, and they own ski chalets. They have home leave benefits that are more generous than others. But they are 'temporary' and they are so powerful we can't get them to change to permanent status." The same problem is found among some employees who live in the United States. The following table indicates how many bandits of various nationalities are employed by HTI:

Employees on Extended Assignments
(Source: Sample of 550 expatriates)

Assignment Years	4–5	5–7	7–10	10+	TOTAL
To Switzerland	13	18	11	7	49*
To U.S.	9	18	6	1	34

* From Germany, $n = 11$; Netherlands, $n = 8$; U.K. $n = 17$; U.S., $n = 13$.

On the other hand, if HTI does change the bandits' designated home country, the new home country must give them benefits as if they spent their entire career there. This can be costly to the company in some instances but it can also be an inducement: "Come over to Switzerland at age 63 and we'll fix you up. If the company does not do this, it reduces its flexibility to move people."

Discussion Question

1. Make a recommendation as to how the bandits should be treated.

PART THREE

FUNCTIONAL ASPECTS OF INTERNATIONAL MANAGEMENT

T E N

INTERNATIONAL LABOR RELATIONS

In this chapter we address major problems that the expansion of international business creates for both the multinational companies (MNCs) and national labor unions. The chapter opens with a discussion on how the MNCs divide international industrial decisions between the headquarters and the subsidiaries. One of the major issues of international industrial relations is the power and flexibility of the MNCs. Often, national labor unions face a dilemma when negotiating with the MNCs in that they cannot cross national borders but the MNCs are not restricted to a particular location. Restricted to operate within the boundaries of national markets, labor unions are at a disadvantage against the MNCs. Labor unions complain that while they are negotiating with the local subsidiary, the real decision maker is the headquarters. There is some truth in this contention. While the MNCs typically assign to the subsidiaries most operational decision making for local industrial relations, strategic decisions such as locating a plant and increasing employment levels at various sites are reserved for the headquarters.

National laws do not permit labor unions to establish formal alliances beyond national borders. We discuss how labor unions deal with this limitation. Specifically, to counter the negotiating power of the MNCs, national labor unions increase their informal alliances. These informal alliances involve activities such as coordination of contract negotiations, cooperation, sharing of information, and exerting pressure on the MNCs on behalf of each other. Informal arrangements among the national labor unions are organized through international labor institutions. These institutions are regularly employed to advance the cause of labor unions worldwide.

To learn about the diversity of industrial relations globally, the chapter describes a sample of the practices in different countries. The discussion of diversity of industrial relations begins with a presentation about U.S. labor unions. From among the European countries, the industrial relations of England, France, and Germany are examined. Japanese enterprise unions stand in contrast with the labor relations practices of other industrialized countries. The chapter ends with an explanation of the cultural and historical roots of Japanese labor relations.

On Valentine's Day, the 500 employees of Hyster Company's forklift-truck factory in Irvine, Scotland, were introduced to the labor unions' predicament in dealing with MNCs. They faced a dilemma: Accept a cut in their wages or lose their jobs. Hyster Corporation, headquartered in Portland, Oregon, had a message for them. With a grant from the British government, it was ready to invest $60 million into the plant, which would create another 1000 jobs. This would create an overcapacity in Hyster's European facilities, however. To reduce overcapacity, Hyster was willing to close two production lines at its Dutch factory and move them to Scotland. In return, Hyster workers and managers would have to take a 14 percent and 18 percent pay cut, respectively. They had only 48 hours to decide.

Next day, each employee received a letter from the company. It indicated that Hyster was not yet convinced that Irvine was the best of the many available alternatives for a leading plant in Europe. At the bottom of the page, there was a ballot asking them to vote. Only 11 people voted "no." In the words of some employees, "It was an industrial rape. It was do-or-else." Hyster's workers in Irvine were not unionized. A union would not have made a difference.

The following day, Hyster broke the news to the manager of its plant in Nijmegen, Holland. It was the first official word of Hyster's decision to reduce the workforce in the Nijmegen plant.

Source: B. Newman. "Single-Country Unions of Europe Try to Cope with Multinational." *The Wall Street Journal* (November 30, 1983), 1.

Introduction

The dilemma that Scottish workers at the Hyster plant were facing is one of the many complexities of international labor relations. International trade makes it possible to move capital and equipment across national boarders. Therefore, capital is considered mobile. For three reasons, however, labor does not enjoy such mobility. First, the movement of labor across national borders is restricted by immigration laws. Trade agreements such as NAFTA and EEC, however, will influence cross-border labor movement. Second, even without those restrictions, labor is not as mobile as capital. Searching for new jobs in a foreign land is difficult for most workers. Also, relocation is very difficult for people. Uprooting and leaving behind family and friends is not easy and is often impractical. Third, the demand for unskilled and semiskilled workers is very low globally. Starting up in a new place is much more economically feasible for well-educated workers who have special skills.

There are exceptions, however. Recent trends in some developing countries point to an increasing movement of labor across national borders. In particular, prosperous countries of East Asia mirror demographic characteristics that first were observed in Europe and North America. The economic gains of these nations are followed by lower birth rates and urbanization. Lower birth rates and better living conditions create an aging population. To cope with a shrinking labor force, these countries draw immigrants from less developed countries. Good wages in these countries also attracts workers from other countries. Rapid industrialization of these countries is resulting in demographic changes that will challenge their labor relations practices and immigration laws. Already, examples of these changes can be seen in Singapore, Taiwan, and Malaysia. Singapore, which limits immigration of foreigners, is forced to relocate many industries to its neighbors. Taiwan is recruiting thousands of foreign workers from other Asian countries. In Malaysia, foreigners already hold more than 50 percent of construction and plantation jobs.[1]

Compared to unskilled labor, immobility is not a serious problem for skilled labor. As the skill level improves, labor mobility increases. Indeed, at the higher levels of skills the market for labor is global. Most nations welcome highly educated and skilled workers. Some labor relations experts argue that with the increasing level of education among the people of the world, and the rising need on the part of industry for more skilled workers, the globalization of labor is inevitable.[2] With the globalization of labor comes the standardization of labor relations practices.

Two forces will drive workplace standardization: companies responding to global labor markets and governments negotiating trade agreements. For a global corporation, the notion of a single set of workplace standards will eventually become as irresistible as the idea of a single language for conducting business. Vacation policies that are established in Germany to attract scientists will be hard to rescind when the employees are relocated to New Jersey; flexible hours of work that make sense in California will sooner or later become the norm in Madrid; health care deductibles and pension contributions designed for one nation will be modified so that workers in all nations enjoy the same treatment. Typical of most innovations in corporate personnel practices, the benefits which are of most importance to high-wage, highly valued employees (who will be the most often recruited internationally) will be standardized first.[3]

Workplace standardization may be inevitable in some distant future. Today, however, diversity in workplace practices is a norm of international business. While there are some industrial relations practices common to most Western nations, no two countries are alike. Cultural, political, legal, and economic diversity among nations have resulted in dissimilarities in workplace practices. Understanding of these practices is very crucial for the success of foreign operations. MNCs, particularly at the early days of entry into a market, are vulnerable to mistakes. Several Japanese firms entering the United States, for example, quickly learned that the ignorance of discrimination laws and labor practices could lead to disputes and be costly. During the 1970s and early 1980s several Japanese companies operating in the United States, including Sumitomo Shoji and C. Itoh, were sued by their American employees for race and sex discrimination. The Itoh and Sumitomo cases reached the U.S. Supreme Court and judgments were rendered against both of them.[4] In these cases, the Japanese subsidiaries had engaged in employment practices in the United States without serious considerations of their legal implications. In other words, they were the victims of the "innocent abroad syndrome." Their problems were caused by their unfamiliarity with the host country (U.S.) laws and practices.

Locus of Control in International Workplace Practices

A critical issue for any firm, be it a domestic or multinational firm, is its relationship with labor. No organization can survive without a healthy relationship with its employees. Labor relations practices are particularly vital to MNCs because of the cultural, political, and legal differences among the host countries. Historical precedents, traditions, and cultural norms establish employment practices and superior–subordinate relationships unique to each country. This diversity makes international labor relations more difficult and complex than domestic practices. On the one hand, due to the uniqueness of each country's environment, host country managers need the authority to handle their own labor relations. On the other hand, to function as a corporation, some form of centralized control is necessary. There are many arguments in support of each position.

Headquarters–Subsidiary Relationships

Because of the diversity of the workforce and labor management relationships, MNCs treat each subsidiary as a separate entity. Each domestic operation sets its own labor relations policies and negotiates its own labor contracts. The home office, however, maintains overall control and keeps various labor relations programs in line with corporate policies. Since the MNC subsidiaries are interdependent, work disruption in one subsidiary affects others. This interdependency necessitates some uniformity in labor practices among the subsidiaries and the integration and control of these practices from the home office. Also, the implementation of MNC corporate strategies requires the integration of various labor relation programs throughout the firm. The need for uniformity, integration, and control, therefore, compels MNCs to coordinate various labor relations programs and labor union contracts. To counter the flexibility of MNCs, labor unions have begun cooperation across national borders. In turn, the movement by labor unions to cooperate internationally enforces the need for control from the home office.

National Unions' Quandary

The nature of MNCs and their vast resources offer them flexibility and power in negotiation with national unions. They can shift production across national boarders and play one national union against the other. Production and manufacturing facilities are opened or closed at the headquarters discretion with little or no involvement by the labor. In pursuit of corporate goals, they allocate resources to each subsidiary according to corporate strategies. They establish and direct these strategies from the home country corporate headquarters. These actions are carried out while very little or no information is shared with national labor unions. Therefore, the labor unions argue, the welfare and interests of national labor unions are of secondary importance to MNCs. National labor unions feel handicapped in dealing with MNCs. They cannot match the resources of MNCs and do not have their flexibility. Realizing their handicap, the U.S. labor unions long have been in search of ways to counter the MNCs' apparent advantages. At first, the U.S. labor unions, through legislative initiatives, attempted to curb any MNC operations that were considered detrimental to the unions. In 1970, Charles Levinson, the secretary general of the International Chemical Foundation, for example, asserted that "trade unions have no choice but to provide the countervailing force which is badly lacking to keep MNCs within permissible bounds."[5] Years of effort, however, have not brought about many gains.

Besides leading the legislative offensive aimed at limiting the operations of the MNCs, labor unions have indicated an interest in worldwide collective bargaining with the MNCs. Many years ago, Victor G. Reuther, the United Auto Workers' (UAW) international affairs director, made the following prediction:

[In the future,] we will see a very significant change in the whole character of collective bargaining. To deal with MNCs the trade unions are going to have to look beyond their narrow national views and embrace an international approach. This doesn't mean we will sit down in one room with General Motors and sign one agreement for the world but it means we need the machinery to coordinate negotiations internationally.[6]

Although Reuther's prediction has not fully materialized, it has not been totally false either. Global labor negotiation covering the operations of one company located in different countries is a dream of the labor unions and a prospective nightmare of the MNCs.[7] Knowing that negotiating global contracts with the MNCs has not been feasible, labor unions instead realistically aimed at increasing cross-border cooperation among national unions. The aim was the coordination of national labor negotiations with the MNCs. Over the years, labor unions have had some success promoting international labor causes.

Cross-border labor tactics   In supporting the labor agenda, international labor unions employ several tactics. These tactics include sharing information with and providing financial assistance to each other, coordinating and synchronizing activities, and finally persuading and pressuring the MNCs into cooperation. In employing these tactics, national unions utilize the services of international labor organizations such as the Organization for Economic Cooperation and Development (OECD) and the International Labor Organization (ILO).

Coordinating and synchronizing.   Labor unions have tried to use the timing of contract negotiations for various national subsidiaries of integrated MNCs, such as Ford Motor Company, to their advantage. To the extent that they can succeed in standardizing contract expiration dates regionally, such as Western Europe or North America, they could chip away at the MNCs flexibility. Such coordination brings the prospect of a regional strike into a labor negotiation contract. Standardization of contract expiration dates weakens the MNCs' temptation to play one national union against the other. But there are many obstacles in the way of common expiration dates for international labor contracts. Among them are differences in the national union structures, collective bargaining approaches, and national labor laws.

Sharing information and financial assistance. While the goal of contract negotiation timing has not been realized, labor unions have succeeded in other areas. As early as 1970, labor unions began collecting and sharing data on employment practices of the MNCs. Examples of cooperation between the U.S. labor unions and their foreign counterparts are the United Steel Workers informing union members in Jamaica of the financial structure of aluminum companies, assisting Liberian workers in their negotiation with the local affiliate of an American steel company, or lending a Jeep and a boat to a little union in South Africa.[8]

Such informal cooperation may increase in the future, and MNCs may find the global labor market to be a much smaller arena. In Mexico, General Motors and Volkswagen already have tasted a sample of the future to come. Mexican government officials have attributed the labor strikes of the early 1990s in the GM and Volkswagen subsidiaries to the help Mexican labor received from the UAW. While denying any involvement in those strikes, the UAW has acknowledged providing financial assistance to the Mexican labor unions.[9] Of course, the UAW has self-interest in those strikes. The successful negotiation of higher wages by Mexican labor benefits the UAW members too.

Pressuring MNCs to cooperate. Besides the sharing of information or financial assistance, American labor unions have explored other avenues of helping their foreign counterparts. To help labor unions in Costa Rica, the U.S. labor unions attempted to put the financial squeeze on the Costa Rican government by targeting its $300 million in annual exports to the United States. The American Federation of Labor and Congress of Industrial Organizations (AFL-CIO), for example, filed a complaint with the U.S. trade representative, requesting the suspension of Costa Rica's benefits under the Generalized System of Preferences and the Caribbean Basin Initiative.[10] It claimed that Costa Rica does not provide sufficient legal protection for labor unions.

Labor unions realize their inherent limitations as national organizations facing powerful MNCs. They understand that, at the present time, it is not possible to expand beyond their national borders. In some distant future, regional trade agreements, such as NAFTA, may provide labor unions with such opportunities. They have, however, been successful in pressuring intergovernmental organizations, such as the OECD and the ILO, to adopt a voluntary code of conduct for MNCs. Through the informal cooperation across national boarders, labor unions sometimes succeed in promoting their cause. For example, when in 1990, Ravenswood Aluminum Corporation replaced its 1700 workers permanently, United Steel Workers enlisted the help of foreign labor unions. The union discovered that Marc Rich, the billionaire, controlled Ravenswood Aluminum. With help from the labor unions in Europe, Rich's business deals came under scrutiny, and some ran into trouble. For instance, Czech unions pressured the government to reject his offer for Slovak State Aluminum. The union also persuaded Anheuser Busch, Miller Brewing, and Stroh Brewery not to buy Ravenswood's aluminum sheet for use in their cans.[11]

European labor unions have employed cross-border cooperation and assistance to their advantage too. In the early 1990s, workers at British Aerospace (BA) went on strike demanding working hours in parity with their French counterparts at Aerospatiale, BA's French partner. The British strikers of Amalgamated Engineering Union (AEU) received financial and other tangible supports from IG Metal, the German engineering union. Their strike was coordinated by the Federation of European Metalworkers (FEM). After the strike lasted four months, BA granted its employees a 37-hour work week with productivity agreements. This proved that national unions can cooperate and pursue a common goal. Now, the FEM aim is to standardize the working week for its six million members in 16 European countries.[12]

National unions need to cooperate with one another, but are unable to do it formally. In almost all countries, labor strikes in support of other national unions are illegal. While national unions are restricted in their actions, multiple sourcing of labor could effectively be used by MNCs to undermine the power of national labor. In 1993, for example, several MNCs decided to relocate their operations primarily from France to England. This caused an uproar by the European labor and governments alike, and demonstrated that the ability of MNCs to pit one national union against the other is a powerful tool. During this period, Hoover, a subsidiary of the American Maytag Corporation, announced a plan to close a vacuum-cleaner plant in Dijon, France, and move the work to a plant near Glasgow, Scotland. Scottish workers had accepted changes in working conditions in exchange for job guarantees and the prospect of gaining 400 new jobs. As a consequence of this move, the French would lose 600 jobs. There was other bad news too. Moore Corporation of Canada revealed a 25 percent workforce reduction. Grundig AG of Germany disclosed a plan to move thousands of jobs to Austria. A unit of Rockwell International Corporation, U.S.A., indicated they were going to move 110 jobs from Nates, France, to Britain. These announcements caused outrage in France. French labor unions

and government officials contended that Britain was offering unfair incentives and taking advantage of looser labor laws and lower wages to lure away French jobs.[13]

Host Government Involvement

International industrial relations practices are made more complex by host government involvement. Regulations and legislation covering workplace practices are the basis for government involvement. In the late 1970s, for example, the failure of J.C. Penney's expansion into Europe had been partly attributed to labor problems. J.C. Penney had acquired outdated and inefficient retail chains in Italy and Belgium in the hope of turning them around. Slashing bloated payrolls proved to be almost impossible. In both countries, government regulations and labor laws made layoffs prohibitively expensive and time consuming. J.C. Penney was forced to get out of both countries by selling these stores at a loss. The divestiture of the Belgian chain of 52 stores alone cost J.C. Penney $16 million.[14]

The Badger Company, Inc., owned by Raytheon Company, had a similar experience. In 1976, the Belgian subsidiary of the Badger Company, due to financial difficulties, closed its operation and dismissed its workers. The Belgian government demanded indemnification

---

Immigrant Workers

Globalization of business creates opportunities, as well as problems, for both MNCs and labor unions. Recent economic expansion in South East Asia, for example, has resulted in the opposition by labor unions to immigrant workers. From Malaysia to Hong Kong to Japan, labor unions have expressed strong opposition to imported workers. They fear that with the availability of cheap migrant workers, employers who are interested in short-term quick solutions will not upgrade the salaries and working conditions of local employees. Expressing the labor unions' disapproval of the imported labor, G. Rajasekaran, a leader of the Malayan Trade Union Congress, asks "How can you develop a country by flooding it with foreign labor?"

Source: R. Pura. "Many of Asia's Workers Are on the Move." *The Wall Street Journal* (March 5, 1992), A13.

for those workers from Badger but were told that funds for indemnification were not available. The lack of indemnification money in the Belgian subsidiary, the government claimed, was because the parent company had deliberately bled the Belgian operation of its finances. Therefore, it was the responsibility of the parent to make up the shortfall in indemnification funds. When several OECD governments threatened to not grant any future business to Badger Company, the company was forced to comply with the Belgian demand.[15]

Host government involvement in MNC workplace relations can be direct and formal, or indirect and informal. In formal and direct cases, the MNCs are obligated to comply with specific laws and to follow certain procedures, as was the case with J.C. Penney. Indirect and informal cases involve demands and pressures by the host government where there is no legal basis or precedence for them. Often, for example, the MNCs are forced to include more of the host country nationals in managerial positions. In some cases, the MNCs are obligated to hire personnel from a pool designated by the host governments. International hospitality groups that entered China in the 1970s experienced the difficulty of running their hotel operations under those circumstances. They were not allowed directly to tap the local labor market for their personnel needs. The government would supply them a list of applicants from which they had to make their selections. Often, the only qualification of these workers was their membership in the Communist party.[16]

International Labor Organizations

International labor organizations, in their varied structures—as we discuss later—have attempted to create some form of uniformity in their practices for dealing with the MNCs. Because of cultural, political, and economic differences among the nations, they have failed to create uniformity in wages and working conditions in various subsidiaries of MNCs in different countries. International union delegates in their many meetings have not been able to agree on the priority of many work-related issues. Agreements on these issues have been made more difficult due to the differences between the Japanese attitudes toward work methods and the rest of international labor unions. Except for wages, which are considered universally important, there is disagreement on all other issues. Besides the legal obstacles, the differences of priorities among national trade unions is a major impediment to the standardization of employee relations practices globally. Surveys of labor union members in different countries have revealed varying priorities. For example:

> . . . among Latin American delegates trade union rights have ranked just as high (as wages). A share in determining or controlling the speed of the assembly or production line has been their number two demand. The forty-hour week was third.
>
> By contrast, in Western Europe the main interests of English and French production workers after wages have been job security and shorter working hours. This is also the case in the U.S. today, but until very recently health care and pensions were of very high priority and may again become important. West Germany places the most emphasis on the job environment, stressing more relief periods. A few years ago the German metalworkers made much of their significant breakthrough in winning five minutes' relief time in each working hour and another three minutes for personal needs, thus beating the American autoworkers' forty-six minutes per eight-hour shift at that time. There was also a gain in controlling the pace of the production line: a minimum time allowance of one-and-a-half minutes was set for any job operation in the new plant.[17]

At the present time, standardization of workplace practices seems an unattainable goal. Progress in other areas, however, keeps labor's hopes alive. By disseminating information and publicizing the gains made by the unions in one country, others are encouraged to emulate them. Also through informal agreement among national unions of different countries, labor negotiation contracts have been more successfully negotiated. The British Aerospace strike, which was described in the previous pages, is a sample of successful cooperation that international labor unions would like to repeat.

International organizations concerned with labor issues can be divided into two groups. The first groups are the affiliations of national unions through the international labor organizations. These organizations are formed and run by the labor unions. They are managed and directed by the personnel drawn from the national labor union members. Among the first group are the International Confederation of Free Trade Unions (ICFTU), the World Federation of Trade Unions (WFTU), the World Confederation of Labor (WCL), the European Trade Union Confederation (ETUC), and International Trade Secretariats (ITSs). The second group is established by national governments for political and economic purposes. This group includes the ILO, the OECD, and the Centre on Transnational Corporations (CTC).[18] We should note that these organizations do not have any legal authority over national labor unions. While national labor unions cannot cross national borders, through these organizations they attempt to cooperate informally with one another.

International Affiliations of Labor Unions

With the membership from national labor unions worldwide, these labor organizations are concerned with improving the wages and working conditions for their members. They are independent of the national governments and other nonlabor institutions. Through regular communication and cooperation with each other, they join forces in pursuit of labor objectives. They employ the various tactics explained in the preceding pages, including the appeal to the national governments.

International confederation of free trade unions (ICFTU)   In 1949, the issue of communist domination through the representatives of Eastern bloc countries caused a split among the WFTU members. National trade unions that withdrew from WFTU formed ICFTU. While the recent history of ICFTU begins with the split in WFTU, its roots go back to the 1913 Secretariat of Trade Union Federation. Surviving the two world wars, in 1945 it emerged as the World Federation of Trade Unions. It included labor unions of communist countries too. After the split it adopted the title of ICFTU. The inclusion of the word "free" in the title is an intentional reference to the members' autonomy and the lack of control by governments. ICFTU is headquartered in Brussels, Belgium, and has 140 affiliated national centers in 99 countries with approximately 82 million members.[19]

The world federation of trade unions (WFTU)   A counterpart to ICFTU and covering the national unions of Communist countries, WFTU is headquartered in Moscow. It, however, has affiliated members in some Western bloc countries, such as France and Italy, and maintains offices in Asia, Africa, and Latin America. Along with other institutions that were formed by the Soviet Union to handle the affairs of the satellite countries, the future status and the direction of WFTU is doubtful.

The world confederation of labor (WCL)   Membership in the WCL consists of Christian trade unions. Similar in political philosophy to ICFTU, WCL is the smallest of the international confederations of trade unions. It originally was established in 1920 under the title of International Federation of Christian Trade Unions. It recently changed its name to broaden its membership and avoid confusion with the ICFTU. With support from the Catholic church, the WCL was formed to counter the liberal and socialist unions gains among urban workers. The headquarters of WCL is in Brussels, and it has regional centers in Asia, Africa, and Latin America.

The european trade union confederation (ETUC)   As a regional international labor organization, the ETUC primarily deals with the European Economic Community (EEC). It is the outgrowth of the European Regional Organization (ERO) that was formed to deal with labor problems arising from the implementation of the Marshall Plan.

International trade secretariats (ITSs)   The International Trade Secretariat organizations are set up along major industry lines to assist the affiliated national unions. They provide help within the same industry and within a specific MNC across national boarders. They supply members with data, coordinate communication, and provide financial assistance for collective bargaining purposes. Excluding those in the Communist bloc, and within the Christian confederation, there are 16 major secretariats independent of, but associated with, ICFTU. Three of the 16 have been in the forefront of confrontation between labor and the MNCs. These secretariats are the International Metalworkers' Federation, the International Federation of Chemical, Energy and General Workers' Unions, and the International Union of Food and Allied Workers' Associations.

Intergovernmental Organizations

These institutions are established by national governments to deal with international labor problems. The most active and well known of these organizations are the ILO, the OECD, and the CTC.

International labor office (ILO)   ILO was established by the League of Nations in 1919, and was charged with the responsibility to develop international minimum standards for industrial relations, and to draft international labor conventions on human rights, freedom of association, wages, hours of work, minimum age for employment, working conditions, health and safety, vacation with pay, and other work-related concerns.[20] At the present time it is one of the agencies of the United Nations whose primary objective is to protect the fundamental rights of workers. It also strives to promote cooperation between the workers and their employers. It encourages and supports programs by the members that benefit workers. The highest priority is given to achieving full employment, improving the standard of living, enhancing health care and safety in the workplace, and improving working conditions.

Each member nation appoints four delegates to the ILO, two from government, one from labor, and one from business. The 56 members of the Executive Council, which governs the ILO, is elected every three years. Membership in the council is comprised of 14 each from labor and management, and 28 from government representatives. Of the 28 government representatives, 10 are from the United States, Canada, the Soviet Union, China, Japan, England, Germany, France, Italy, and India.[21]

ILO periodically compiles and reviews the International Labor Code, which it sends to members for their ratification. Ratification of these standards by the governments is voluntary, but they have been very useful, especially to developing countries. Another noteworthy accomplishment of the ILO is the Tripartite Declaration on Multinational Enterprise and Social Policy. It covers recommendations on working conditions, training, health and safety, and other labor relations concerns. Although adherence to these recommendations is voluntary, labor unions have relied on them for curbing labor abuses.[22]

The organization for economic co-operation and development (OECD)   An agency of the United Nations, OECD is centered in Paris, France. It was established in 1961 to promote economic growth and employment and to achieve a rising standard of living in member countries.[23] In 1976, OECD issued the Guidelines for Multinational Enterprises. Many issues pertinent to the MNCs, such as investment, technology, taxes, and industrial relations, are covered in the guidelines. Among the stipulations of the guidelines are four major issues of interest to labor. First, labor has the right to unionize and labor should be free to form or join a union without the fear of reprisals. Second, MNCs should negotiate labor contracts with the unions representing the workers. Third, in contract negotiations, MNCs should not intimidate workers with the threat of transferring its operations to other countries. Fourth, in addition to matters that are covered in the collective bargaining document, MNCs should regularly consult with the labor unions and provide them with information on issues of mutual concern.[24]

National labor unions have used the guidelines in their contract negotiations with MNCs. Often, labor unions try to include a clause in the collective bargaining contracts that would stipulate compliance with the OECD guidelines.

The centre for transnational corporations (CTC)   The CTC is an autonomous agency of the United Nations (UN). Based in New York, CTC is established to assist host countries, and particularly developing nations, to deal with MNCs. It also examines the impact of MNCs on host countries' social, political, and legal environments. Of major interest to the CTC is the role of MNCs in the economic development of developing countries. Whenever needed, the CTC assists developing countries in their negotiation with the MNCs with the aim of improving their economies. The CTC has been involved in the development of a code of conduct for the MNCs. Among all the activities of the CTC and the work of the UN, labor has an especially keen interest in the issue of a code of conduct for the MNCs. Such a code could establish standards for working conditions, provide procedures for settling disputes, and protect MNC workers. The labor unions hope that, whenever it is finalized and approved by the UN members, the code will strengthen the workers' positions against the MNCs.

Diversity in International Labor Relations

International labor relations practices, as one would expect, are characterized by diversity. It is apparent that labor unions, organizations, and collective bargaining practices are as varied as the diversity of the nations. Not only are the worldwide industrial relations practices different, the degree of unionization varies as well. The size of national unions, however, is not a reflection of their impact on the labor market. In Germany, for example, while union members constitute a minority of the labor force, collective bargaining agreements cover almost the entire economy. Statistics on union membership in selected countries are shown in Table 10.1. While union membership has been declining in the United States, in other countries unionization either is stabilizing or rising. Not shown in Table 10.1 is data on union membership for developing countries. Statistics for unionization in these countries are either unavailable or unreliable. Given the historical patterns of unionization in industrialized countries, it is generally expected that union membership will rise in these countries.

In the following pages, we present a sample of the diversity in international labor relations by discussing the labor unions in Europe, Japan, and the United States (referred to as triad nations). Our selection is based on the fact that the bulk of foreign direct investment (FDI) around the globe is made by the triad nations. Also, the labor relations practices of the triad are often used as models for other countries. Therefore, an understanding of these practices is very useful for international managers. We will begin with the United States and move next to Europe. More than any other nation, the West German model of organized labor has influenced the European labor unions and collective bargaining practices. We, therefore, devote more attention to the German model. In addition to Germany, our coverage of the Europeans in-

Table 10.1

Labor Union Membership in Selected Countries
(in thousands)

Year	U.S.	Canada	Japan	France	Germany	U.K.
1955	16,802	1,268	6,286	2,554	7,499	9,738
	(33)	(31)	(36)	(21)	(44)	(46)
1960	17,049	1,459	7,662	2,592	7,686	9,835
	(31)	(30)	(33)	(20)	(40)	(45)
1965	17,299	1,589	10,147	2,914	7,986	10,325
	(28)	(28)	(36)	(20)	(38)	(45)
1970	21,248	2,173	11,605	3,549	7,958	11,187
	(30)	(31)	(35)	(22)	(37)	(50)
1975	22,361	2,884	12,590	3,882	8,623	12,026
	(22)	(34)	(35)	(23)	(39)	(53)
1980	20,095	3,397	12,369	3,374	9,261	12,947
	(22)	(35)	(31)	(19)	(40)	(56)
1985	16,996	3,666	12,418	2,944	9,324	10,821
	(17)	(36)	(29)	(17)	(40)	(51)
1988	17,002	3,841	12,227	—	9,388	10,238
	(16)	(35)	(27)	—	(39)	(46)
1989	16,960	3,944	12,227	1,970	9,463	—
	(16)	(35)	(26)	(11)	(39)	—
1990	16,740	4,031	12,265	—	—	—
	(16)	(36)	(25)	—	—	—

Note: Numbers inside parentheses are percentages of total civilian wage and salary employees.

Source: Figures are taken form C. Change and C. Sorrentino. "Union Membership Statistics in 12 Countries." *Monthly Labor Review* (December 1991), 46–51.

cludes Britain and France. Our discussion ends with Japan.

Industrial Relations in the United States

Two pieces of legislation, the National Labor Relations Act (1935), commonly referred to as the Wagner Act, and the Labor–Management Relations Act (1947), usually called Taft–Hartley Act, form the legal foundation for the organization of labor unions in the United States. These and other labor statutes gave workers the right to form, join, or assist labor organizations, and to bargain collectively through their representatives with the employers. While organized labor is an integral part of the American business, it does not enjoy the legal status offered to the German and some other

European unions. The legal status of representing the workers is bestowed on a union only if it gains the majority support of the workers. Therefore, employers are not legally obligated to negotiate with a minority union. Without a majority union, there is no collective bargaining. This is in contrast with Germany's collective bargaining, which covers almost the entire industry even though the majority of German workers are not unionized. This is a reflection of the American culture that emphasizes individualism and advocates free enterprise.

The objectives of the U.S. labor unions are very similar to those of other national unions—to improve the welfare of the workers and serve as their economic agents. To accomplish these objectives, the U.S. unions have mainly relied on the business and industry level activities. At this level, organizing labor unions and using collective bargaining have been the major instruments of goal accomplishment. The political route, a favorite of the European labor, has not been abandoned, however. Although the U.S. unions have been politically active and have sought the protection of law, they never have aspired for political prominence. There is, for example, no American equivalent of the British Labor Party. While, traditionally, the European unions have been a mainstay of politics, their American counterpart has played a supporting role.

One of the major differences between the American labor movement and those of other nations is the U.S. approach to industrial relations. More than any other nation, the U.S.'s industrial relations practices are adversarial. While the United States has been a fertile ground for some of the most enlightened and progressive management theories, such as participative management, job enrichment, and management-by-objectives, there is no legal-formal instrument in the United States for joint decision making by management and labor. The works councils of Europe, for example, are totally absent from the American scene. American businesses go to extremes to prevent unionization of their operations. Even when a business is unionized, decertification efforts, aimed at removing the union, are not uncommon. Also, unlike the Europeans, the American unions insist on their independence in collective bargaining and lack a centralized decision-making authority.

Typically, in a collective bargaining situation, unions negotiate with a company at local or national levels. Also, some industrywide bargaining occurs at the national level, such as is the case in the steel industry, and at the regional level, such as occurs in trucking. Usually, these labor contracts cover union recognition, management rights, job classifications, and wages. Other items included in these negotiations are seniority rights, standard work periods, length and number of work breaks in an eight-hour work period, holidays, vacations, medical insurance and retirement benefits, grievance procedures, and the commitment to no-strike and no lockout provisions during the contract period.

European Industrial Democracy

In the United States, since the Hawthorne studies, participative management has been the subject of most management literature. Although both participative management and industrial democracy deal with the sharing of decision making and power between management and labor, their approaches are quite different. Even within each approach there are different variations of power equalization and sharing of decision making between management and labor. The European approach, however, deals with a more formal-legal approach of workers' representation on the board of directors of firms as compared to the United States' informal style.

Differences between participative management and industrial democracy   The following is a summary of the basic differences between the American participative management and European industrial democracy[25]:

1. The two methods have been adopted with different fervor and different results in different countries. Thus, industrial democracy has appeared most often in Europe and participative management is practiced in the United States.
2. Industrial democracy is a formal, usually legally sanctioned arrangement of workers' representation at various levels of management decision making. Participative management, on the other hand, is an informal style of face-to-face leadership.
3. Industrial democracy is a structural approach aiming at equalizing power by joint decision making through workers' representation on ad hoc committees, permanent committees, councils, and boards at various levels of the

management decision making. Participative management is a voluntary behavioral approach advocated by the management for informal sharing of decision making with subordinates at the workplace. Organizations try to achieve this goal through indoctrination, training, organizational policies, social pressure, and other means.

Industrial democracy has taken several forms in different European countries. The German model of worker participation, however, has exerted a powerful influence on labor movements elsewhere in Europe.[26] In particular, the German model has influenced the industrial relations of the Northern European countries of Denmark, Sweden, and Norway; furthermore, the former Soviet Eastern European countries are likely to feel increasing influence from this model as well. The content of today's European industrial democracy movement, if not its context, is slowly but steadily, becoming similar to the German.[27] Therefore, in the following, we examine the German model in detail.

Industrial Democracy in Germany

Decision making in any organization can be considered a hierarchy consisting of four major levels. At the top of this hierarchy lies the institutional level dealing with policy making, which is concerned mainly with the direction and the future of the organization. The middle management level deals with the implementation of decisions made at the institutional level. At the technical level, decisions are related to the actual production of the organization's outputs and the day-to-day operations. The workers' level, which is at the bottom of the hierarchy, implements all decisions made at the technical level (Figure 10.1).

The four levels of organizational hierarchy in actual practice overlap. Usually, participation in decision making takes place between the two adjacent levels. The extent and the nature of participation, however, are always determined by

the higher level. In the United States, examples of this kind of participation are committees, job enrichment programs, management by objectives (MBO), and so on, all of which involve adjacent levels (i.e., job enrichment usually involves the technical level and the workers, while MBO involves middle management and technical level). However, there is a spillover effect, and the decisions made at the institutional level will have a long-lasting effect on the other levels, particularly at the workers' level. Institutional decisions require more information than the decisions made at other levels of the hierarchy. Furthermore, the information received from the lower levels of the organization is very crucial for the quality, accuracy, and, if needed, the modifications of these decisions. These ideas argue for a change in the more typical adjacent-level influence-sharing processes and suggest, at least for the German model, that top management needs to find ways to share decision making with those at the worker level. Therefore, the inclusion of the lower level employees in the decision-making process of the institutional level not only is a democratic action, but also can be considered an appropriate act for the sake of organizational efficiency and effectiveness.

This type of involvement in decision making has been called participation at the board level or *codetermination* in Europe. The term *codetermination* more specifically is used to indicate the German model of industrial democracy. This model is basically the participation of representatives of all employees, blue collar as well as white collar employees including managers, on the two-board system of German industries. The two-board system is discussed later in this chapter.

Labor Unions in Germany

Industrial relations in Germany are governed by two closely related yet separate institutions of codetermination and collective bargaining. While codetermination allows labor to participate at the highest level of the organizational

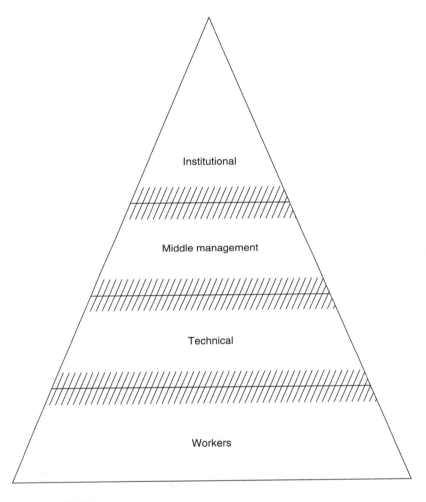

Participation Area //////

Figure 10.1   Decision-Making Participation and Organizational Hierarchy

decision-making process, the German constitution provides a very general and broad framework for collective bargaining. It guarantees collective bargaining rights for labor to negotiate with the employers over wages and working conditions. German labor laws impose restrictions and limitations on labor strikes and plant lockouts. Wildcat strikes, particularly in recent years, are not uncommon. They are, however, mostly related to economic issues and not labor rights. The law has established minimum requirements for many workplace practices such as working hours, vacations, and safety regulations. Through collective bargaining these minimums can be augmented.

Industrywide labor contract negotiations take

place regionally. Some of the problems that in other countries are subject to collective bargaining are handled by works councils in Germany. Works councils, however, are not allowed to bargain for remuneration and other work-related issues that are the domain of collective bargaining. While the majority of German workers are not union members, almost all employers are members of employers' associations. In 1988, for example, unionization was approximately 42 percent, and the coverage of employers' associations was 90 percent. More than 80 percent of unionized workers belong to a branch group of the Dutch Gewerkschaftsbund (DGB), which in 1988 had about 7.8 million members in 17 unions.[28]

Although union members are in the minority, collective bargaining contracts encompass more than 90 percent of workers. This is due to the widespread membership in employers' associations and industry-wide contract negotiations. Collective agreements are negotiated on a national or area-wide industry basis and establish wage patterns for the whole industry. These contracts cover both unionized and nonunionized workers if the company is a member of the relevant employers' association.[29] Moreover, both unions and employers are strongly centralized, and because collective bargaining covers almost the entire German labor market, through collective bargaining, labor is included in national economic planning.[30]

Background and structure of codetermination   Germany's experience with codetermination can be thought of as the product of two separate and independent forces. The first force was the Germans' desire for democratization of the workplace. The second force was the policy of the Allied forces after World War II, particularly the British, of strengthening the German labor movement. Allied forces wanted to prevent the resurgence of Fascism, which they believed was aided by the powerful coal and iron industrialists in Germany.

The Germans' sentiment for codetermination can be traced to the social unrest and workers' demands for a greater voice in the design of the work situation in the first part of the nineteenth century. By 1905, for example, in all mining enterprises employing more than 100 workers, "workers' committees" had gained recognition. The mines were legally obligated to establish workers' committees and consult with them before the introduction of any work rules or guidelines.[31] Democratization of the workplace gained additional momentum when the Workers' Council Act of 1920 gave workers' councils managerial and bargaining power. The workers, through the workers' councils, were given the right to have two representatives on the supervisory board. Furthermore, the handling of grievances and the establishment of work rules as well as wage agreements, within contracts negotiated by the unions, became the domain of workers' councils.[32]

Workers' councils were suppressed during World War II. They came to life again after the war, and were given legal recognition and expanded authority by the Western occupation authorities. At the Potsdam Conference, the Allied powers agreed to break up the steel and coal industries. These industries exemplified Germany's military and industrial might, and had aided Hitler in his quest for world domination. To curb the power of the managers in these industries, the Allied forces agreed to give more voice to the labor.

It is ironic, in a sense, that the total collapse of the German political and economic systems aided the fulfillment of an old demand of the German workers. The attempts to prevent the emergence of a military industrial system on the one hand, and the desire for a new start and consensus by all the parties in Germany on the other hand, provided the setting for the development of codetermination. It was the convergence of the two fundamentally different forces that resulted in the Co-Determination Act of 1951, which was amended in 1956. The Workers Constitution Act of 1952 extended workers' participation to all business organizations but gave workers only one-third of all the seats on the supervisory boards.[33]

Since the policies of the occupation authorities reinstated workers' representation on the supervisory board, many changes have taken place. Germany no longer is an occupied country. The economy and the political system of Germany have emerged as one of the strongest in the Western bloc. The unions and workers have been a potent political force, constantly renewing their demands for parity with management. Finally, the Co-Determination Law of 1976 was passed, which was designed to grant workers full parity on the supervisory board and, through this board, on the operational system of enterprises.

Today, the 1976 legislation is in force, side by side with earlier laws, for companies with more than 500 employees. The workers and shareholders are given parity representation on the supervisory boards of these companies, but the numbers vary with the size of the firm. The big companies, for instance, are divided into three categories of 2000 to 10,000, 10,000 to 20,000, and more than 20,000 employees. The supervisory boards of these companies consist of 11, 17, and 21 members, respectively.[34]

Although the law has given the workers more power over the management of larger companies than ever before, it has fallen short of giving full parity representation to workers. If disagreement arises between the representatives of workers and shareholders, the law stipulates that the shareholders' position would prevail.[35] The structural arrangements of codetermination as it stands now in Germany are depicted in Figure 10.2. The main features of codetermination are as follows[36]:

a. All private companies, profit or non-profit organizations with five employees or more are subject to the "Work Constitution Law" of 1972. This law makes provision for formation of workers councils in each firm or in each independent unit within a company. The size of

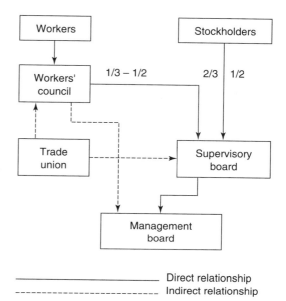

Figure 10.2   Structural Arrangement of Codetermination

the council depends on the number of employees and can vary from one to thirty-five. Where the size of the council is at least three, blue collar and white collar workers vote separately and are represented on the council proportionately to their numbers. Employers and councils are encouraged to cooperate and are bound by the framework of the collective bargaining.

The functions of work councils include the areas that are not regulated by collective bargaining such as handling grievances, agreements on piece rate and wages, and working conditions that are not covered by a union contract. Furthermore, a work council is entitled to negotiate with an employer on matters such as hiring, firing of large numbers of employees, establishing plant rules, and making changes in the plant location. Also, it supervises the application of work laws and administers the welfare agencies in the plant. The members of the work councils need not be trade union members. However, in practice more than 80 percent of the members of all work councils belong to trade unions.

b. Companies with more than 500 employees are governed by two boards, the supervisory board and the management board. The supervisory board is the equivalent of the board of directors of American corporations and is a policy-making body. The supervisory board appoints the management board. The management board is responsible for the day-to-day operations of the firm. The appointment of the labor director on the management board—which represents the labor viewpoints and promotes their cause—needs the approval of the majority of workers' representatives. The workers elect one-third to one-half of the supervisory board, depending on the size of the firm, and the employers elect two-thirds to one-half.

c. The election of representatives on the supervisory board is governed by an intricate and elaborate set of procedures. For example, in the case of a ten-member board, of the five workers representatives, two are elected by the workers' council, two by the union federation approved by the union of the firm and the workers' council, and the fifth member is an outsider designated by the union federation. The chairman and the vice-chairman of the board must be elected by two-thirds majority of board members. If a two-thirds majority cannot be reached, the stockholders' representatives elect the chairman, and the vice-chairman is elected by the workers' representatives.

The chairman has been given the tie-breaking vote.[37] The supervisory board meets at least quarterly and, besides having the policy-making power and the power to select the management board, its consent is required on matters such as the purchase of land and property, mergers and acquisitions, new plant location, important investment decisions, long-term loans, and the purchase or sales of stocks of other companies.

Opposition to codetermination   Opposition to codetermination comes from three sources.[38] The first source of opposition is employers or their representatives. They fear that codetermi-

nation may result in the loss of management control and the dilution of power and authority. They also fear that inefficiency may follow and profits may suffer if high-level decision making becomes subject to labor approval. The second group opposing workers' participation at the board level, interestingly enough, comes from the labor unions. The labor unions would prefer to achieve industrial democracy through the institutionalization and strengthening of collective bargaining rather than participation and representation on the board of directors. The Communists and Socialists are the third source of opposition. They see participation in high-level decision making as a delay in the final victory of the proletariat. From this perspective, collaboration with capitalists will not advance the labor cause. The weakening of Communism in the post–USSR era may impact the strength of this source of opposition.

Whatever the arguments are against codetermination, the opposition cannot ignore some of its benefits and impacts on the German economy. Furthermore, the management fear of dilution of their authority because of representation of workers on the supervisory board so far appears not to be valid. The workers' representatives on the board have shown an understanding of "economic necessities" and a consideration for long-term objectives of the firm. There is also no evidence that these representatives have exploited their position to obtain unreasonable pay raises for the employees.[39]

Moreover, in response to the criticisms of codetermination, Mazzolini has argued that management fears that codetermination may result in the dilution of management authority and control has no basis. Based on an extensive series of interviews with leading executives throughout Europe, Mazzolini provides the following explanation[40]:

> contrary to common belief, especially in countries where there is no tradition of participation, systems such as German co-determination do not imply the downfall of the free

enterprise system. . . . Experience shows that labor generally worries only about those issues which have a clear bearing on working class, leaving administrative and overall policy decisions to management. While labor's influence causes firms to be more socially responsible, fears of more fundamental changes are unwarranted.

Except for the UAW, most American labor unions are opposed to the board level workers' representation because they see it as a potential threat to the union power and existence. They fear that the workers' representative on the board of directors might be independent of the union. Codetermination might also undermine the "adversary relationship" image between the U.S. unions and management. American labor leaders consider codetermination rather superfluous compared to what U.S. labor has achieved through collective bargaining.[41] They believe that unions influence more issues through collective bargaining than they could hope to affect by worker representation on the board of directors of corporations. In the words of one union officer, if unions were to share decision making with management as partners, the unions would be "most likely the junior partner in success and the senior partner in failure."[42] Other objections of unions to codetermination stem from the fear of losing power, the possibility of creating conflicts of interest, and disturbing the existing economic orders. Traditionally, Americans favor minimum or no government involvement in business. They are reluctant to invite government into an already complicated setting.[43]

Evidently, this skepticism is not shared by European unions. The advocates of codetermination and industrial democracy claim that the union strength can be supplemented through workers' representation on the board of directors of firms. For example, "in a system of collective bargaining alone, contract enforcement is difficult since management must be relied upon for implementation. A system of workers

councils and board representation, in contrast, provides alternative institutions for contract enforcement."[44] According to many European labor relations analysts, collective bargaining and workers' participation at the board level are each essential to the other's continued expansion.[45] Additional opposition to codetermination comes from the critics who assert that cultural differences would impede the application of codetermination in the United States.

French Labor Unions

According to Pieper, certain cultural characteristics of French society are reflected in its industrial relations[46]: The French value rationality and order, and view authority as absolute and omnipotent. Because of its absolute nature, authority cannot be shared or compromised. Both in practical terms and symbolically, it must remain sovereign. Checks and balances of due process and countervailing institutionalized power common to American society is foreign to the French. These values have greatly influenced the fate of organized labor. Viewed from the upper levels of the hierarchy, to be rational and bring about order and harmony, the imposition of substantive rules from the top is necessary. Viewed from the lower levels, the authority is threatening and should be avoided. Achieving independence, autonomy, and security necessitates keeping a distance from the superiors and not dealing with them directly. Directly dealing with the superior leads to the acknowledgment of one's total dependence. The solution is to avoid face-to-face relationships between superiors and subordinates and to create rules. The only other alternatives are either total conflict or absolute submission, neither of which is culturally acceptable. To protect one's independence and not submit to the absolute authority one obeys the rules. In the words of Peiper:

> From the top, edicting the rules affirms the capacity of sovereign power. Those rules are impersonal, which from below reinforces the

sense of following an abstract order and not bowing to absolutism; and from above follows the rational model of "one best way" of ruling absolutely over one's domain without having to be bothered to make unnecessary allowances for individual peculiarities. . . . Thus the power is centralized at the top; and below, the impersonal rules define strata of subordinates with precisely defined borders . . . [in which] . . . individuals enjoy total protection and independence. . . . Therefore the power recedes higher and higher, farther and farther from the knowledge of the element necessary to make decisions. It must decide without knowing. . . . and it is in the interest of the subordinates to hide or manipulate information.

A preference for formal, ritualistic activities and the absence of cooperation between various levels within the hierarchy produces a general climate of apathy. The training of the French elite administrators and executives confounds the problem. Most elite French managers are from grandes écoles, the selective and prestigious universities that act as a clubby network, which doles out top positions only to their own members.

A combination of the French cultural characteristics just discussed and a variety of historical reasons have resulted in very low unionization in France. The large number of small firms, which are usually not unionized, also contributes to low unionization. Moreover, French unions have held onto a society-changing agenda much longer than most unions in the United States and Northern Europe, instead of concentrating on economic issues.[47]

Among the major European countries, union membership is the lowest in France. By various estimates, 7 to 10 percent of the labor force is unionized.[48] The leading amalgamation of the French union is the Confederation Generale du Travail (CGT), with an estimated membership of 1.2 million workers in 46 unions. The second largest union group is the Force Ouvriere (CF), with an estimated membership of 1.1 mil-

lion in 36 unions. Three other large union groups, Confederation Francaise Democratique du Travail (CFDT), Confederation Francaise des Travailleurs Chretiens (CFTC), and Confederation Generale des Cadres (CGC), have combined membership of 1.25 million.[49] Both the CGT and CFDT are strongly influenced by Marxist views of class conflict. They hope through political means to bring about a general societal change and the victory of the proletariat.[50]

French labor unions are highly political, ideologically oriented, and weak in the private sector. They are, however, strong in the public sector. The low level of membership does not reflect the real power of French unions. Union strength comes indirectly through the election of union candidates onto the firm-specific representative institutions, particularly the works councils.[51] Their strength becomes evident when labor strikes in the public sector disturb electricity supplies, transportation services, and civil organizations. Unions, however, enjoy public support. Even those workers who are not union members fully support the unions in a crisis or when they are called on to strike.

Labor Unions in Britain

Labor relations and collective bargaining in the United Kingdom have been described as "formal" and "informal" systems coexisting in a context of legal abstentionism.[52] In contrast to the United States and Germany, industrial relations in Britain are characterized by relatively no legal restrictions and structure. Voluntarism, a social philosophy of undisputed pursuit of self-interests, is a hallmark of industrial relations in the United Kingdom.[53] Voluntarism and the lack of restriction means that there are no limitations on wildcat strikes or lockouts. There are also fewer restrictions on layoffs or hiring part-time workers or subcontracting. Collective bargaining agreements are considered "gentlemen's agreements," which are binding in honor only and not subject to legal enforcement. The tradition of collective bargaining reflects the "grass-roots" character of British labor organizations. The shop steward has a very significant role in the workplace bargaining, and is as important in making and administering the rules as the unions. This is in contrast with the European system where the pattern and overall regulation of collective bargaining is influenced from the top.[54] The shop steward is a unique feature of English labor relations.

> . . . shop stewards are elected by fellow union members in the plant. Today they play a central part in helping to determine the likely reaction there to the eventual terms for a settlement. Their influence in this respect is very great and it is equally powerful at the bargaining table. The national union officials may lead the contract negotiations with employers but the stewards, by virtue of their everyday ties to the rank and file, wield almost as much, if not more, influence in the bargaining.[55]

Since British labor has traditionally relied on "self-help," and has preferred minimum or no legislative interference, it is not surprising that unlike other European labor movements, British labor has opposed the institutional forms of labor representation, such as codetermination. In recent years, however, the state has been getting more involved in industrial relations. The Employment Protection Act of 1975, for example, grants certain rights to unions, including access to information and consultation with management in the case of workforce reductions. It granted certain rights to unions and workers and established government agencies to provide arbitration, mediation, and conciliation for resolving industrial disputes.[56]

A unique characteristic of labor unions in Britain is their participation in politics. The historical roots of labor involvement in politics goes back to the 1906 election when a newly formed Labor party won 29 seats in the House of Commons. Over the years, the Labor party has become the political counterpart of the union movement. While in other European countries left-wing political parties sponsored the trade unions, in Britain, the unions created the socialist political party. While the relationship between the unions and the Labor party is very strong, labor unions have not attempted to dominate the party and the government. They have always worked pragmatically with the government of the day. Even within the Labor party, major initiatives comes from what might be called the intellectual rather than the union side.[57]

The Trade Union Congress (TUC) has taken the leading role in the British labor movement, with the 1985 membership exceeding 9.5 million in 88 unions. The largest union is the Transport and General Workers' Union, with 1.4 million members. Other large unions are the Amalgamated Engineering Union, with a little less than 1 million members, and General, Municipal, Boilermakers, and Allied Trades Union, which has more than 820,000 members.[58]

Japanese Enterprise Unions

Japanese labor relations practices are quite different from the other industrialized countries. Historical precedents and cultural attributes have created a unique set of relationships among labor and management in Japan. Unlike the labor unions of other nations, Japanese labor unions are not separate entities independent from the firms. As "enterprise unions," they could be regarded as extensions of the organizations. While Japanese labor unions are not totally independent, nonetheless they represent the workers and play an important role in the economy.

Management practices and attitudes toward workers are important factors that shape the nature and the type of industrial relations in an enterprise. The distinguishing features of Japanese management practices are lifetime commitment (employment), a seniority-based wage system, and collective decision making (ringi). These practices and the historical developments have created enterprise unions and industrial relations that are uniquely Japanese.

Historical factors   After the second world war, with encouragement from the Americans, a trade union law was enacted that assured labor the right to organize, to bargain collectively, and to strike. The economic hardships following the war made it very urgent for the labor unions to safeguard the workers' living standards. To achieve this objective, unions found it necessary to launch a joint effort combining white and blue collar workers at the enterprise or plant level. Similarly, employers wanting to restore the balance of power to their own favor exerted considerable efforts to create just such an enterprise union. To prevent the establishment of an all-powerful labor organization, however, they undertook three measures. First, they established vertical labor organizations. Second, to bring about order in the workplace, radical workers were removed from the workplace. Third, they set up a new industrial relation system in every company. These measures, particularly the vertical character of the unions, weakened their horizontal solidarity. Various levels of union organizations were established parallel to the corporate structure, such as at the head office, plant, department, and section levels. At each level, the unions were in constant interface with their corresponding management counter-parts. Facilitating the establishment of this unique labor–management relationship was Article 2 of the labor law. It stipulated that all employees below the section heads, regardless of their jobs, may organize into unions. Therefore, in some large plants, it is typical that supervisors are elected as union representatives. This adds to the unions' fragmentation and increases management's influence.[59]

Management practices   Lifetime employment and the no-layoff policy practiced by large Japanese firms increase the loyalty of workers to the firm and reduce the cost of training and turnover. Long-term relationships among employees foster an attitude of cooperation and trust and minimize conflict. Slow and orderly promotion based on seniority emphasizes the individuals and not the job titles. Knowing that they will work together for a lifetime, and that there is ample time for the firm to recognize their contributions, employees learn to work for mutual benefits. Permanent employment makes rotation of workers to different jobs in the firm a practical choice. While time consuming, the ringi system of collective decision making and consensus building produces quality decisions that those affected by them understand and accept. The slow process of collective decision

---

Japanese Enigma

As far as outsiders can tell, most Japanese accept with equanimity all the daily demands that they subordinate individual desires to those of the community. This striking communalism is, however, the result of political arrangements consciously inserted into society more than three centuries ago by a ruling elite. . . . For centuries statecraft in Japan has resulted from a balance between semiautonomous groups that share power. . . .

At the most basic level of political life Japan is no different from any country. The Japanese have laws, legislators, a parliament, political parties, labor unions, a prime minister. But don't be misled by these familiar labels. The Japanese prime minister is not expected to show much leadership; labor unions organize strikes to be held during lunch breaks; the legislature does not in fact legislate (bureaucrats in ministries write the laws); laws are enforced only if they don't conflict too much with the interests of the powerful.

Source: "The Enigma of Japanese Power." *Fortune* (May 8, 1989), 150.

making allows enough time for everyone to adjust to the emerging decisions and commits them to the implementation of those decisions.

More than any other industrial country, labor relations in Japan are based on the realities of the labor market condition rather than on an open contest of power. Permanent employment and seniority-based promotion procedures enable Japanese workers to anticipate, with a high degree of certainty, how they will advance in jobs, wages, and other amenities. With assurances of job security and near certainty on career prospects, wages are the remaining major bargaining issues that could cause occasional conflict. Also, until recently, in an environment of continuous and rapid economic growth, conflict over wages could be resolved with a win–win outcome.[60]

The unique Japanese labor relations have evolved in a cultural framework of collectivism and paternalism. While modernization and global competition are eroding the foundation of lifetime employment, still most large Japanese firms follow this tradition. These firms continue to offer the welfare benefits that were established at the beginning of modernization and benefits that were established after the first world war to eliminate the turnover of skilled employees. Now the typical benefits offered by these firms are housing, medical and health care, recreational and sport facilities, daycare for children, commuter subsidies, and meals at work.

Since employees are expected to stay with the firm for a long time, they are also expected to be team players. Instead of seeking individual gains, each member is expected to strive for collective benefits. The Japanese attribute of collectivism stands in sharp contrast to the Western ideal of individualism. While modernization and global competition are changing labor–management relationships, Japan has maintained its unique paternalistic character. Again, these relationships have cultural and historical roots.

Because industrialization was originally sparked by a dynastic elite, the idea of paternalistic concern for the welfare of subordinates is strongly rooted in Japanese management. Although the government has intervened to regulate the manager in the field of labor relations, it has nevertheless given strong encouragement to the paternalistic approach.[61]

Almost all unions in Japan are enterprise unions. Because they are company-specific, there are more than 74,000 of them, in 94 federations. The largest of labor organizations, the General Council of Trade Unions of Japan or Sohyo, has more than 4.36 million members in 50 federations. The second largest is the Japanese Confederation of labor or Domei, which has 2.16 million members in 29 federations. In third place is a federation of 10 unions called Churitsuroren, the Federation of Independent Unions of Japan, and the fourth is Shinsanbetsu, the National Federation of Industrial Organizations, which has five labor federations.[62]

With the tradition of enterprise unions and the collectivist orientation of the Japanese, the labor unions take a less adversarial posture against the firms. Compared with most other industrial countries, except for Germany, the incidents of labor strikes are lower in Japan. Many strikes do not last long, and some are even only a few hours in duration. Most contract negotiations, and about half of the strikes, take place during shunto, or the annual Spring Labor Offensive. Regardless of the union's affiliation or the lack of it, negotiations take place at the company level, and in their negotiations and demands for wage increases, unions consider the good of the company. In 1987, for example, when the economy was slowing down, labor unions decided to soften their demands. Steel workers accepted the smallest raises in history, and the largest shipbuilding unions did not even ask for a raise. With cooperation from the labor unions, companies were able to resist the urging of the government to boost wages and spur the economy. The sharpest public expression of conflict could be seen in the Shinichi Tsuji, the leader of the smallest and most radical of the three unions at the Japanese affiliate of Shell Oil Company. He told a newspaper reporter that his union is getting tough. The day before, they had gone on strike for 45 minutes, and they were planning a lunchtime multi-union demonstration so that workers would not have to miss any work.[63]

Conclusion

International industrial relations pose problems for both labor and management. Managerial problems are due to the differences in legal practices, labor laws and customs, host government interference with market forces, and cultural characteristics among various national markets. Problems facing national labor unions center around the erosion of bargaining power. In collective bargaining, the balance of power has shifted in favor of the MNCs. The worldwide variations in wages, benefits, and industrial practices provide the MNCs with the opportunity to reallocate works to places that offer more favorable business conditions. Obviously, such moves will result in the loss of jobs in areas where wages are higher and business conditions are less conducive to profit making.

While the increasing internationalization of business and the consequent interdependencies create problems for the MNCs, they pose a much more difficult challenge to labor unions. National borders limiting workers into separate national labor markets restricts labor options in contract negotiations with the MNCs. The borders, however, have much less restrictive power against the MNCs. Competition among nations to attract FDI offers multiple opportunities to the MNCs for investment and additional munitions for fighting the national labor unions' demands. With the gradual removal of trade barriers, these problems will intensify. Because capital is much more mobile than labor, with the lowering of trade barriers capital can relocate in

low labor cost countries, while labor mobility is hampered due to political, social, economic, and cultural factors. Low trade barriers provide more opportunities to capital than labor. Even with the total removal of trade and business barriers, labor cannot readily take advantage of opportunities in other labor markets. Empirical evidence suggests that the removal of trade barriers undermines the power of unions in setting higher wages. While reducing barriers may eventually lead to an improved economy, initially at least, it reduces the welfare of national labor unions and increases the incentives to international cooperation among these unions.[64]

Faced with the reality of decreasing trade barriers, national labor unions are searching for ways to counter the increasing bargaining power of the MNCs. While national laws do not permit formal labor cooperation across national borders, informal methods are still available. Through international labor organizations such as ICFTU, ILO, and ITS, national labor unions are expanding their informal cooperation and coordination of negotiations with the MNCs. A few successful examples of these types of activities have encouraged national labor unions to search for additional measures. The ultimate goal of conducting collective bargaining with the MNCs at the international level, however, has to wait for the distant future. Given the present circumstances and developments, we can safely predict that the future of international collective bargaining will be much more contentious and volatile.

Discussion Questions

1. What is the major problem of national unions negotiating with the MNCs?
2. Why, for collective bargaining, do the MNCs treat each subsidiary as a separate entity?
3. Why do host countries get involved in international labor relations?
4. Elaborate on cross-border tactics that are

used by national unions for promoting the labor agenda.

5. What is the ultimate goal of international labor unions? Do you find this is an attainable goal?

6. What is the objective of the International Labor Office (ILO)?

7. Explain the major features of the German industrial democracy (codetermination).

8. In the United States, the relationship between management and labor is called adversarial. Why?

9. French labor unions have the lowest membership rate among all Europeans. What cultural characteristics are attributed to this low membership rate?

10. What are major characteristics of the British labor relations?

11. Distinguish between the European industrial democracy and the Japanese "enterprise unions."

12. Northern Europeans claim that their model of industrial democracy provides for smoother industrial conflict resolution than the adversarial labor relations of the United States. Elaborate on your acceptance or rejection of this claim.

Endnotes

1. R. Pura. "Many of Asia's Workers Are on the Move." *The Wall Street Journal* (March 5, 1992), A13.

2. W. B. Johnson. "Global Work force 2000: The New World Labor Market." *Harvard Business Review* (April–March 1991), 115–27.

3. Ibid.

4. S. P. Sethi, N. Namkiki, and C. L. Swanson. *The False Promise of the Japanese Miracle* (Boston, MA: Pitman Publishing, 1984), 55–60.

5. "Multinational Unions: International Organized Labor Tackles the Corporate Octopus." *The Washington Post* (November 11, 1970).

6. J. P. Gannon. "Worldly Hard-Hats: More U.S. Unions Help Foreign Workers Pressure American Companies Overseas," *The Wall Street Journal* (December 7, 1970), 30.

7. B. Bendiner. *International Labour Affairs* (New York: Oxford University Press, 1987), 89.

8. Gannon. "Worldly Hard-Hats." 30.

9. S. Baker. "Free Trade Isn't Painless." *Business Week* (August 31, 1992), 38–9.

10. "Costa Rican Unions Brought Back to Life by AFL-CIO." *The Wall Street Journal* (September 10, 1993), A17.

11. M. Mallory and M. Schroeder. "How the USW Hit Marc Rich Where It Hurts." *Business Week (*May 11, 1992), 42.

12. J. Parry and G. O'Meara. "The Struggle for European Unions," *International Management* (December 1990), 70–3.

13. C. Forman. "France Is Preparing to Battle Britain Over Flight of Jobs Across the Channel." *The Wall Street Journal* (February 3, 1993), A18.

14. B. Ortega. "Penney Pushes Abroad in Unusually Big Way as It Pursues Growth." *The Wall Street Journal* (February 1, 1994), A1.

15. R. G. Blainpain. *The Badger Case and the OECD Guidelines for Multinational Enterprises* (Deventer, The Netherlands: Kluwer, 1977).

16. Interview with the White Swan Hotel manager, Bejing, China, June 1985.

17. Bendiner, *International Labour Affairs.* 66.

18. Readers interested in a comprehensive discussion of international labor organizations should consult A. P. Coldrick and Philip Jones. *The International Directory of the Trade Union Movement* (New York: Facts on File Inc., 1979); and Bendiner. *International Labour Affairs.*

19. J. P. Windmuleer. *American Labor and the International Labor Movement* (Ithaca, NY: The Institute of International Industrial and Labor Relations, Cornell University, 1953); and *Labor Confronts the Transnational* (New York: Labor Research Association, 1984).

20. P. R. Baehr and L. Gordenker. *The United Nations: Reality and Ideal* (New York: Praeger Publishers, 1984), 33–6.

21. Bendiner. *International Labour Affairs.* 57.

22. W. J. Feld. *Multinational Corporations and U.N. Policies* (New York: Pergamon Press, 1980), 93–6.

23. *OECD: History, Aims, Structure* (Paris, France: OECD Publication Office, 1971).

24. Bendiner. *International Labour Affairs.* 68–9.

25. B. M. Bess and V. J. Shackleton. "Industrial Democracy and Participative Management: A Case for a Synthesis." *Academy of Management Review,* 4, no. 3 (1979), 393–7.

26. D. G. Garson. "The Co-Determination Model of Workers' Participation: Where Is It Leading?" *Sloan Management Review,* 18, no. 3 (Spring 1977), 65.

27. Ibid.

28. P. Conrad and R. Pieper. "Human Resource Management in the Federal Republic of Germany." In Rudiger Pieper, ed. *Human Resource Management: An International Comparison.* (Berlin, Germany: Walter de Guryter and Co., 1990), 107–9.

29. Ibid.

30. C. Summers. "An American Perspective of the German Model of Worker Participation." In A. Gladstone, R. Lansbury, J. Stieber, T. Treu, and M. Wiess, eds. *Current Issues in Labor Relations* (Berlin, Germany: Walter de Gruyter and Co., 1989), 113–28.

31. J. H. Lux and B. Wilpert. "Co-Determination: Worker Participation in Federal Republic of Germany." In B. Wilpert, A. Kudat, and Y. Oxhan, eds. *Workers' Participation in an Internationalized Economy* (Kent, OH: Kent State University Press, 1978), 56.

32. A. Sturmthal. *Works Councils* (Cambridge, MA: Harvard University Press, 1964), 53–4.

33. "The Mitbestimmung Mess-Up." *Management Today* (August 1978), 49.

34. Ibid., 50.

35. Ibid., 50–2.

36. Lux, Joachim, and Wilpert. "Co-Determination." 58–60.

37. J. E. Hebden and G. H. Shaw. *Pathways to Participation* (New York: John Wiley and Sons, 1977), 53–5; and Jenkins, *Job Power*, 117–8.

38. "The Mitbestimmung Mess-Up." 50–2.

39. Hebden and Shaw. *Pathways to Participation.* 57.

40. R. Mazzolini. "The Influence of European Workers over Corporate Strategy." *Sloan Management Review,* 19, no. 3 (Spring 1978), 80.

41. J. C. Furlong. *Labor in the Boardroom: The Peaceful Revolution* (Princeton, NJ: Dow Jones Books, 1977), 108.

42. Ibid., 110.

43. K. Fatehi-Sedeh and H. Safizadeh. "Labor Union Leaders and Codetermination: An Evaluation of Attitudes." *Employee Relations Law Journal,* 12, no. 2 (Autumn 1986), 188–204.

44. Garson. "The Co-Determination Model of Workers' Participation. 74.

45. Ibid.

46. Pieper, *Human Resource Management.* 94–5.

47. "Unions in France: Yesterday's Men," *The Economist* (February 18, 1989), 71–2.

48. Comparative Politics (January 1992), 191. C. Howell. "The Contradictions of French Industrial Relations Reform." 191.

49. Bean, ed., *International Labor Statistics* (London, UK: Routledge, 1989), 218–9.

50. Y. Delamotte. "Changing Life at Work: Current Trends in France." In B. Martin and E. M. Kassalow, eds. *Labor Relations in Advanced Industrial Societies* (Washington, DC: Carnegie Endowment for International Peace, 1980), 172–83.

51. Howel. "The Contradictions of French Industrial Relations Reform." 181–97.

52. A. C. Neal, "Co-Determination in the Federal Republic of Germany: An External Perspective from the United Kingdom." In A. Galdstone *et al.,* eds. *Current Issues in Labor Relations,* 128–45.

53. D. Kujawa. "International Labor Relations." In I. Walter and T. Murray, eds. *Handbook of International Management* (New York: John Wiley and Sons, 1988), 11/3–11/25.

54. Neal. "Co-Determination in the Federal Republic of Germany." 128–45.

55. Bendiner. *International Labour Affairs.* 123–4.

56. A. W. J. Thompson and L. C. Hunter, "Great Britain." In J. T. Dunlop and W. Galenson, eds. *Labor in the Twentieth Century,* (New York: Academic Press, 1978), 85–148.

57. Ibid.

58. Bean. *International Labour Statistics.* 251.

59. Y. Takahashi. "Human Resource Management in Japan." In Pieper, ed. *Human Resource Management,* 212–32.

60. S. B. Levine and K. Taira. "Interpreting Industrial Conflict: The Case of Japan." In B. Martin and E. M. Kassalow, eds. *Labor Relations in Advance Industrial Societies,* 61–88.

61. C. Kerr, J. T. Dunlop, F. H. Harbison, and C. A. Myers. *Industrialism and Industrial Man* (Cambridge, MA: Harvard University Press, 1960), 131.

62. Bean. *International Labour Statistics.* 231.

63. E. S. Browning. "Japan's Firms Have a Friend: The Unions." *The Wall Street Journal* (April 28, 1986), sec. 2, 24.

64. J. Driffil and F. van der Ploeg. "Monopoly Unions and the Liberalisation of International Trade." *The Economic Journal,* 103 (March 1993), 379–85.

NEGOTIATING LABOR DISPUTES WITH SAS CABIN ATTENDANTS

ROBERT C. HOWARD

"It never fails. Just when you think you have another dispute-proof agreement, some one reinterprets the rules or finds a discrepancy. It happens every year." Eddie Settergren, Manager of Flight Administration at Scandinavian Airline Systems (SAS) in Frösundavik, Sweden, was referring to recent disputes at SAS between management and labor over the company's annual collective agreement or Kollektivavtal. From January to August of 1989, Eddie had taken part in over 40 dispute negotiations at SAS pertaining to rest periods, check-in and duty times, breaches of the Kollektivavtal, salaries, and aircraft staffing. Eddie hoped a review of the more tense disputes would lead to a future problem-solving profile and, ultimately, savings of at least Skr20 million.[1]

Scandinavian Airline Systems

Scandinavian Airline Systems (SAS) was founded in 1946 by the merger of the three national airlines of Denmark, Sweden, and Norway. Along with other European carriers,

This case was prepared by Research Associate Robert C. Howard under the direction of Professor Werner Ketelhöhn as a basis for class discussion rather than to illustrate either effective or ineffective handling of an administrative situation. Copyright © 1990 by International Institute for Management Development (IMD), Lausanne, Switzerland. IMD retains all rights. Not to be used or reproduced without written permission from IMD, Lausanne.
[1] In 1988, the average exchange rate was $1 equaled 6.1 Skr.

SAS grew and prospered in the three decades following World War II, with the assistance of cartels and protectionist measures. Yet, following the rapid rise in oil prices during the 1970s and worldwide deregulation, the company came under increasing pressure to contain costs. After suffering a 20% decline in its global market share and a $30 million deficit, Jan Carlzon was appointed Chief Executive Officer of SAS in 1981. Over the next three years, Carlzon transformed the company from a production driven business to a customer oriented, market driven service company.

Unions

In Sweden, two parties represented the collective views of the nations' unions: the Swedish Employers Federation (SAF) acted on behalf of private employers while the Federation of Salaried Employers in Industry and Services (PTK) represented the interests of Sweden's private employees. Across the country, unions were further organized by company size, industry, or job function. Thus, the Commercial Employers Association (HAO) represented large private companies in Sweden including the airlines, while the Commercial Employees Union (HTF) represented Scandinavia's cabin attendants. Within the Commercial Employees Union, members were organized by country of origin. Thus, SAS cabin attendants belonged to the Danish Cabin Attendants Union (CAU) in

Copenhagen, the Norwegian Cabin Attendants Union (NKF) in Oslo, or the Swedish Cabin Attendants Union (SCCA) in Stockholm or Malmö.

Each of these country organizations had a board plus a number of area specialists. The Stockholm-based union, for example, and a board of 14 people, elected by the Swedish cabin attendants, and were specialized in areas including recruitment, vacation, pension insurance, and per diem allowances. In addition, the SCCA had seven elected representatives on environmental safety, four people overseeing the group's finances, and four people assisting in union elections. In Denmark and Norway, the local unions were organized similarly, although the size of the boards and the number of area specialists differed. More importantly, the members of each local union, from board members down were employees of SAS. Therefore, in addition to paying the travel and related negotiation expenses of its executives, SAS also covered the expenses of the employees' union representatives. (See Exhibit 1 for the relationships among these various organizations.)

Participants and Types of Disputes

At SAS, the parties present during a negotiation depended on the issue, and consequently, the mechanism via which an issue was being resolved. That is, negotiations at SAS were of three types: Kollektivavtal (Collective Agreement), Codetermination Law, and Dispute.

Kollektivavtal

In its simplest form, the Kollektivavtal used in Sweden dated from 1928 when the right to make such an agreement was signed into law. At SAS, the annual Kollektivavtal was the third and most comprehensive type of negotiation and included numerous regulations on flying conditions like cabin attendant flight times, length of rest periods between flights, number of days off after flights, and salaries. What the Kollektivavtal did not include, however, were rules and regulations

about service on board such as the number of meals to be served, whether they should be cold vs hot, and whether a flight included cocktails.

For scheduling purposes, the management of SAS classified their flights into three types of travel patterns: long, short, and mixed. By definition, long flights utilized DC-10s or 767s, short flights DC-9s, while mixed used a combination of both. Each travel pattern also described the nature of on-board service, flight conditions specified in the Kollektivavtal and crew requirements.[2] For example, a DC-9 on a domestic flight required a crew of only two hosts/hostesses. The same plane, when flying an inter-Scandinavian flight, had a crew of two hosts/hostesses and one purser. An intercontinental flight in a 767 on the other hand, required one purser, three stewards, and four hosts/hostesses.

Within the Kollektivavtal, there were two agreements on flight regulations and how much time off one had after flying. The first agreement, used exclusively for short flights, was known as the 5/4 and signified five days' "production" followed by four days off. The second agreement, known as the Bilaga B or Annex B to the Kollektivavtal, was more comprehensive than the 5/4 and covered both short and long flights. The Bilaga B dated from 1946 and, with the growth of SAS and the worldwide airline industry, had become increasingly complex. As a result, management and the unions began to develop the 5/4 as a separate document for short flights at the end of the 1970s. In 1989, however, both agreements were still in force and

---

[2] Cabin attendants began as a host, hostess or steward. Hosts and/or hostesses main functions were to ensure the comfort of all passengers, particularly the elderly and those with children and infants. Additional responsibilities included: giving medical aid, keeping the cabin and toilets clean, making public announcements, and carrying out duties delegated by the purser. The steward was responsible for preparing and heating meals, securing the galley before takeoff and landing, and carrying out the orders of the purser. As the manager, the purser assigned working areas and saw that all inflight duties were performed.

Exhibit 1

Working Relationship Among Unions in Sweden

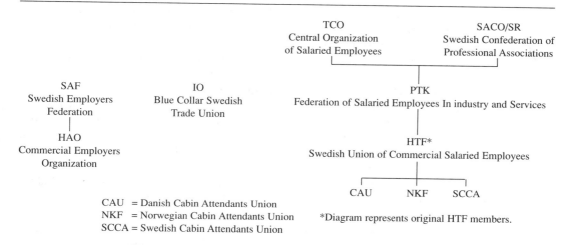

1. The above diagram represents the working relationships among Sweden's various unions. Analagous organizations and relationships existed in Norway and Denmark.
2. As of October 1989, the SAF represented 42,000 private companies employing over 1,200,000 workers.
3. As of December 1987, the Swedish Trade Union Confederation (ILO) had 24 affiliated unions with a total of 2,279,908 members, most of them manual laborers.
4. As of June 1986, the Central Organization of Salaried Employees (TCO) had 20 affiliated unions with a total of 1,211,506 members in both the public and private sectors.
5. The Swedish Confederation of Professional Associations (SACO/SR) consisted of 26 professional associations, graduate organizations, and organizations of government officials. The organization was founded in 1975 through the merger of the Swedish Confederation of Professional Associations and the National Federation of civil Servants. Doctors, dentists, pharmacists, architects and certain teaching groups were among the principal occupational groups.
6. The Federation of Salaried Employees in Industry and Services (PTK) represented 544,000 members of eight TCO unions and 48,000 members of 14 SACO/SR unions.
7. As of December 1988, the Union of Commercial Salaried Employees (HIF) represented 122,000 salaried employees in the private sector including the wholesale and retail, transportation, trade union and non-profit organizations, media companies, the health and medical care sector, hotels and restaurants, the farmers' cooperative movement and certain other sectors.

Source: Company Records

were used by SAS cabin attendants, depending on their operating base, as follows:

Country:	Denmark[3]	Norway	Sweden
Short Flight:	Bilaga B	5/4	5/4
Long Flight:	Bilaga B	Bilaga B	Bilaga B

Codetermination Law

In Sweden, the Codetermination Act of 1977 required employers to advise and consult employ-

ees before making any significant changes in company operation. Depending on which country was involved, local[4] negotiations began in Oslo, Copenhagen or Stockholm. For example, if SAS wanted to appoint a new Swedish manager, Eddie Settergren and one assistant would negotiate with two SCCA union representatives that an individual was the best person to fill the

---

[3] Also applied to Swedish cabin attendants based in Malmö.

[4] Only SAS managers and SAS union representatives were present during a local negotiation.

position. Provided the union spokesmen agreed, the manager was appointed and the process was complete. For more detailed issues such as pension insurance or environmental safety, area experts were present and offered their insight.

If, on the other hand, the union preferred a different manager, they could request a central negotiation to be held at HAO in Stockholm. In a central negotiation, one representative from the HAO led the SAS management team, while one representative from the Commercial Employees Union (HTF) led the labor team. Should the two parties fail to agree at the "central" level of the Codetermination Law, the issue was decided by SAS. If unions believed the SAS decision were unfair, they could start the process over in a dispute negotiation, provided they could identify a legitimate violation in working conditions.

Dispute

As with Codetermination Law negotiations, issues discussed in a dispute had three possible steps, the first two steps being identical for both processes. However, the third step in a dispute negotiation was settled in a Workers' Court or Arbetsdomstol in Stockholm. Typically, the Arbetsdomstol consisted of seven representatives. Two of these were chosen by the Swedish Employers Federation (SAF) and, depending on the issue, two were chosen by labor from either the Federation of Salaried Employees in Industry and Services (PTK) or the Blue Collar Swedish Trade Union Confederation (LO). Lastly, two judges from the court and one judge from a ministry, well versed in legislation, were chosen by the government.

Prior to appearing in court, management and labor met with the Arbetsdomstol chairman who ensured that both parties were familiar with the case. Thereafter, representatives for each party presented their clients' case to the Arbetsdomstol and the panel of seven judges. Normally, one to two months passed from the initial meeting with the Arbetsdomstol chairman to the trial before the panel of judges. After a case

was presented, the court recessed for up to two months before reaching a settlement. Throughout the entire process and until a judgment was reached, the previous SAS or union ruling was applied.

In summary, the single most important difference between Codetermination Law and Dispute negotiations was *who* initiated the issue. In other words, when management sought union approval on an issue, information sharing was conducted via the rules of the Codetermination Law. When the unions sought to implement a change, however, they normally began via the dispute mechanism. (See Exhibit 2 for a diagram contrasting the two types of negotiations at SAS and the parties involved.)

The Mixed Flight Dispute

As described on Page 3, there were two agreements in the Kollektivavtal regarding flight regulations and time off after flying. Procedures for short flights which used DC-9s were contained in the 5/4 agreement, while regulations on long flights which used DC-10s or 767s were contained in the Bilaga B. Typically, cabin attendants flying short flights had at least two days off before switching to the long flight travel pattern. On occasion however, it was necessary for SAS' planning department to schedule cabin attendants to work a short flight one day, followed by a long flight the next. And, although no agreements existed on linking short and long flights, SAS had, since the late 1970s, limited mixed flights to standby crews—about 10% of the cabin attendant work force on a day. In the mid-1980s, union leaders began to object to mixed flights and claimed that SAS had to schedule days off between travel patterns. Furthermore, without an agreement specifically linking the 5/4 and the Bilaga B, labor claimed that SAS was violating two agreements.

Round One

As Eddie walked with Ulf down the corridor of SAS's "glass palace" in Frösundaviks, Sweden,

Exhibit 2

Types of Negotiations and Their Participants at SAS Codetermination Law

LOCAL If Disagreement then ⟶	CENTRAL If Disagreement then ⟶	SAS MAKES DECISION
Begin in Copenhagen, Oslo, or Stockholm Representing Management: 1 SAS Flight Administration Manager 1 Assistant Plus experts if needed	Held in Stockholm 1 SAS Flight Administration Manager 1 Assistant 1 Commercial Employers Organization spokesman (HAO) Plus experts if needed	
Representing Labor: Depending on the issue, 2 to 8 spokesmen as follows: from the CAU, and/or 2 from NKF, and/or 2 from each of the SCCA chapters. Plus experts if needed	1 Commercial Employees Union spokesman (HTF) Depending on the issue, 2 to 8 spokesmen as follows: 2 from the CAU, and/or 2 from NKF, and/or 2 from each of the 2 SCCA chapters. Plus experts if needed	If labor disagreed with management's ruling, they could start the process over in a dispute negotiation. To do so, however, the unions had to identify a legitimate violation in working conditions.
Begin in Copenhagen, Oslo, or Stockholm Representing Management: 1 SAS Flight Administration Manager 1 Assistant Plus experts if needed	Held in Stockholm 1 SAS Flight Administration Manager 1 Assistant 1 Commercial Employers Organization spokesman (HAO) Plus experts if needed	Held in Stockholm Panel of seven judges representing management and labor.
Representing Labor: Depending on the issue, 2 to 8 spokesmen as follows: 2 from the CAU, and/or 2 from NKF, and/or 2 from each of the SCCA chapters. Plus experts if needed	1 Commercial Employees Union spokesman (HTF) Depending on the issue, 2 to 8 spokesmen as follows: 2 from the CAU, and/or 2 from NKF, and/or 2 from each of the 2 SCCA chapters. Plus experts if needed	2 from Swedish Employers Federation (SAF) 2 from the Federation of Salaried Employees in Industry and Services (PTK) 3 judges; 2 court appointed plus 1 judge from a government ministry

Source: Company records.

they reviewed the events of a dispute on linking the short and long flight agreements. "As I recall, in 1986 the agreement linking short and long flights expired before we were able to conclude a new agreement. We then prepared instructions for the scheduling department on how to plan mixed flights," Ulf said. Eddie agreed and added, "And because the issue involved a change in company operations, we had to advise all employees of these changes as required under the Codetermination Act. Then, the union

leaders objected and requested a central negotiation." At the central negotiation, SAS restated its opinion that its proposal on linking short and long flights was within its right. Again, union leaders objected but, realizing that SAS had the final say in a Codetermination Negotiation, started the process over in a local Dispute Negotiation.

The basis for the dispute, one union representative claimed, was that by mixing short and long flights, SAS violated two individual agreements—the Bilaga B and the 5/4—and therefore owed the unions and the cabin attendants Skr5 million. SAS disagreed with the unions, whereupon the latter requested the problem be settled via a central Dispute Negotiation. During the central negotiation, SAS again restated its position, as did the unions, and the matter remained unsolved. Although the issue could have been pursued further in the Arbetsdomstol, neither party took the initiative to file the necessary paperwork and the issue died.

Shortly thereafter, in January 1987, Ulf Cederwall asked union representatives if they would be willing to discuss a new mixed flight policy within the ongoing Kollektivavtal Negotiations. Labor leaders agreed and, in February 1987, discussions resumed on how to link the Bilaga B to the 5/4 agreement.

Round Two

Despite good intentions, renewed discussions aimed at linking the two flight agreements soon broke down and, in the spring of 1988, the unions initiated a second Dispute Negotiation. Unlike their efforts of 1986, however, labor spokesmen were now asking for a guarantee of two days off between short and long flights. This was not possible, Eddie pointed out, because there were times when bad weather or mechanical difficulties might require an attendant to fly short haul one day and long haul the next. Union leaders were not willing to compromise, however, and insisted on a guarantee of two days off between flights.

Not surprisingly, the parties failed to reach agreement at a local level and, in May 1988, the issue was elevated to a central negotiation. Yet again, no agreement was reached. This time however, rather than letting the issue die, in August 1988 the unions requested that the Arbetsdomstol try the case. Although the court agreed to hear the case, they were unable to start until January, 1990. (See Exhibit 3 for a summary of the steps in the disagreement over linking short and long flights.)

Possible Outcomes

If the court ruled in favor of the unions, SAS would lose at least Skr5 million annually. More important, such a ruling would pose a serious challenge to SAS after 1991. Until then, the 5/4 and Bilaga B guidelines were to be applied exclusively to short and long flights, respectively. Thereafter, however, SAS intended to replace its DC-10s with 767s and use the latter on both long *and* short flights. Thus, a ruling in favor of the unions would jeopardize SAS's long-term strategy as well as its short-term profitability. As Eddie reviewed the case with Ulf, they wondered what arguments they could prepare to secure a ruling in SAS's favor. On the other hand, the court might rule in SAS's favor in which case the situation would remain unchanged.

Exhibit 3
Summary of Disagreement on Linking Short and Long Flights

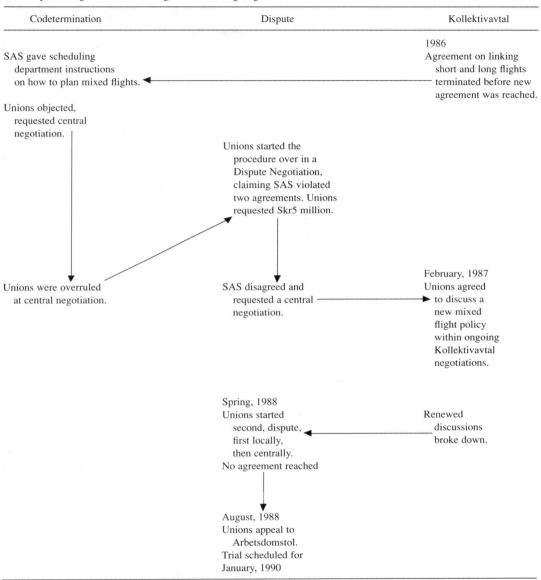

Codetermination	Dispute	Kollektivavtal

THE EL AL STRIKE IN NEW YORK

ARIE REICHEL
JOHN F. PREBLE

It was a cold and snowy day in late March 1984 when those passing by the El Al[1] offices at 850 3rd Avenue in Manhattan and at JFK International Airport saw picketers standing by the barriers and carrying placards. On a summer day, some six months later, picketers were still there. Was this the same strike or a new one?

From Los Angeles to New York City to Miami to Tel Aviv, potential El Al passengers kept calling the reservation desks expressing concern that they might not be able to fly because of the strike. Reservations agents indicated, rather matter-of-factly, that El Al service had not been affected by the strike.

The Situation

After 12 months of negotiations between the management of El Al Israel Airlines, Ltd., New York, and union representatives for the 225 employees of El Al, members of District 100 of the International Association of Machinists and

---

[1] El Al, the national airline of the State of Israel, was incorporated November 15, 1948. Its charter objective was and remains "to secure and maintain a regular airlink at all times and under all conditions within a framework of maximum profitability" (El Al At A Glance). The principal shareholder is the government of Israel. During the time of the case, the Chairman of the Board was Mr. Nachman Perel, and the President was Mr. Rafael Harlev. The main office for North and Central America, located in Manhattan, is directed by the General Manager, Mr. David Schneider. The General Manager for Marketing is Mr. Adi Zecharia.

A. Reichel and J. F. Preble. "The El Al Strike in New York." Journal of Management Case Studies, 1987, 3:270–276. Reprinted by permission of the publisher. Copyright © 1987 by Elsevier Science Publishing Co., Inc.

Aerospace Workers (IAM), negotiations had reached an impasse.[2] Subsequent efforts by the National Mediation Service failed to break the deadlock (Village Voice, Jul. 10, 1984; New York Times, Mar. 17, 1984). After a 30-day cooling-off period had passed, the old contract expired on March 31, 1983 (AFL-CIO News, Apr. 7, 1984), and El Al implemented a new contract. The employees then voted on two issues: (1) to accept or reject the firm's proposals; and (2) whether or not to strike. Ninety-four percent of the rank and file voted to reject the firm's proposals, and 89% of union members voted to go on strike. The strike commenced on March 16, 1984, and continues as this case is being written.

Throughout the negotiations, the style of El Al management was somewhat inflexible. For example, several weeks before the strike broke out, Mr. Rafael Harlev, the airline's President, visited New York to meet with employees. He asserted that the union would have no choice but to accept all of management's proposals and he added, "if you don't accept these proposals we will close the New York office and move to another city in North America." But labor–

---

[2] According to the Railway Labor Act (which includes employees of airlines as well as trains), a contract is open for negotiation according to a preset date. A contract is in effect either until a new one is signed or until the Federal Mediation Board releases the firm and the union from the mediation process. This release can take place after 30 days of a cooling-off period that is necessary after a failure in negotiations. After this period, the firm has the right to implement its latest proposal for a contract. The union, in turn, has a right to strike.

management relations turned bitter when El Al, just a few days after the walkout, flew in 90 workers from Israel (many with dual citizenship), housed them at a Manhattan hotel, and escorted them to work and back in armed limousines (*Village Voice,* Jul. 10, 1984; *Business Week,* Jul. 23, 1984). In addition, management made two trips a day to the airport to ensure the smooth operation of incoming and outgoing flights. The management personnel were seen carrying suitcases and handling agent-related issues such as ticketing. It all looked like a well-planned military operation, which, from a management perspective, had been very successful.

Since then, relations have worsened, with charges being made back and forth between the union and the management. The IAM, as noted in a letter dated July 25, 1984, from the Union Label and Service Trades Department (AFL-CIO) to the National and International Unions State and Local Central Bodies Union Label and Service Trades Councils Labor Press, has charged El Al officials with refusal to bargain in good faith, walking out of meetings, and demanding wholesale concessions with a take-it-or-leave-it-attitude. The IAM feels that El Al is trying to "bust" the union (*Village Voice,* Jul. 10, 1984). However, management strongly denies what has been said about them in the press.

For its part, El Al has charged in the Israeli press that strikers had anti-Semitic motives—even though almost half are Jewish (*Business Week,* Jul. 23, 1984). In the same article in *Business Week* it was reported that IAM headquarters failed to renew a $1 million Israeli bond that matured in June, due to their negative feelings toward El Al's actions. Further, El Al's management stated that some of the strikers who considered returning to work were threatened and harassed by union activists. The AFL-CIO has demonstrated support for the union position with the endorsement of a boycott against El Al Israel Airlines as of July 20, 1984. There were reports of clashes between guards hired by El Al and the strikers. The atmosphere was one

of confrontation rather than cooperation. One possible solution to the situation was the use of binding arbitration, should both sides agree to it.

With regard to Israeli labor relations, it has been reported (*Business Week,* Jul. 23, 1984) that in the late 1970s eight unions were representing El Al employees. This created a chaotic environment resulting in 69 strikes over a ten-year period. Chronic losses at El Al, a major drop in the Israeli tourist trade in late 1982, and a wave of strikes caused a four-month shutdown of the airline. El Al reemerged in January, 1983, with only one union (Histadrut), whose members would have no right to strike. A two-year wage freeze was imposed, as well as a 20% cut in the workforce and the elimination of many union work rules. Losses were consequently cut from $46 million in fiscal 1983, to approximately $15 million for fiscal 1984. Additional cost-saving measures were then to be imposed on the U.S. employees through a set of concessionary demands mentioned earlier. For 20 years preceding this development, El Al's labor–management relations in the United States had been excellent.

Management Proposals

The management of El Al in New York had demanded, as part of a larger package to save the ailing state-owned company, that the IAM make a large number of concessions:

1. agree to a three-year freeze in hourly wages;
2. give management the right to contract out commissary and auto-repair jobs (essentially eliminating these departments);
3. make overtime mandatory, at a reduced rate of pay;
4. give management the right to hire an unlimited number of part-time employees (threatening job security);
5. cut vacation days by five days, across the board;
6. allow supervisors to do the work of unionized employees for up to four hours per day;

7. give management the right to impose the concept of crossutilization, whereby workers could be assigned to work in numerous job classifications;
8. give El Al the unilateral right to contract out all the work involving maintenance, catering, and dispatching of aircraft;
9. give the right to lay off various units; and
10. abolish the lifetime employment guarantee given recently to 37 employees.[3]

Mr. Schneider, the general manager in New York, felt that these proposals were fair in light of the severe financial problems of the airline and the sacrifices already made by other union members in Israel and around the world. Further, he emphasized that many of management's proposals were necessary to maintain around-the-clock service to passengers at JFK International Airport in New York.

Union Response

The IAM[4] was divided in its response to management's demands. Some 80 IAM members have returned to work since the strike began (*The Jewish Week,* May 11, 1984). The union believes that it has compromised a great deal by offering these counterproposals:

1. accept a one-year wage freeze;
2. eliminate the commissary and auto-repair shops;
3. accept a reduced rate of pay for overtime and a maximum of two to three hours of overtime in unusual cases;

4. allow part-time workers to be hired for up to 8% of the workforce as long as this does not cause full-time employees to be laid-off;
5. cut two vacation days per person per year;
6. a "Tour Desk," comprised of employees who will do both reservations and ticket issuing (less rigid job classifications; but the IAM disagreed on the additional demand by El Al that ticket agents be freely transferred from one location to another).

Although the union has offered the above concessions and counterproposals, management has declined to accept most of these and is taking an even harder line with respect to the 140 remaining strikers. El Al is willing to take back only 10–20 of these employees, recalling others only when any of the 70 replacements leave (*Business Week,* Jul. 23, 1984). The union is insisting that El Al take back all 140 members out on strike.

Solidarity

Support for the union came early on in the strike when Lane Kirkland, President of the AFL-CIO,

---

[3] These proposals, as well as the union's reactions and counterproposals, have been reported in the popular/trade press, including *Business Week,* Jul. 23, 1984, *Village Voice,* Jul. 10, 1984, *The Jewish Week,* May 11, 1984, and *AFL-CIO News,* Apr. 7, 1984 and May 12, 1984. Interviews were also conducted with Mr. David Schneider, General Manager for North and Central America, El Al Israel Airlines, Ltd., and Mr. Motti Horovitz, an employee of El Al, and a trustee for Lodge 2656, which represents clerical workers at El Al's Manhattan office.

[4] At the beginning of the strike all 225 strikers were members of the IAM. The union headquarters is in Washington, D.C., and the current membership is 600,000 down from 1,000,000. The next level below headquarters is the district level. El Al employees are represented by District 100, where Mr. Gene Hoffman is the general chairman and the union's chief negotiator in the El Al talks. Within the district, El Al employees are in two different locals: 2656 (New York City) and 1894 (airport). Other employees of various airlines and travel agencies are also members of District 100. The main communication between management and the union is maintained through the district representative. Under this representative, there are "locals," who are responsible for administrative tasks such as collecting dues, updating membership lists, etc. Managers and supervisors are not members. Union officials are elected in a democratic way. The general chairman of a district is elected every four years. Each department has one or two shop stewards. A chief shop steward, who is elected every two years, deals primarily with grievances.

wrote a letter to Mr. Meir Rosenne of the Israeli Embassy in Washington, D.C. In the March 20, 1984, letter Mr. Kirkland asked Meir Rosenne to intervene and to try and do something about the "take-it-or-leave-it" attitude of El Al. Later on, the Executive Council of the AFL-CIO sent a cable to Israel's Prime Minister Shamir and to the opposition Labor party in Israel "to call upon the Israeli government to instruct El Al to enter negotiations in good faith and stop its attack on the union."

On March 29, 1984, Secretary general Yerucham Meshel of Histadrut, the Israeli Labor Federation, sent a cable to Mr. Kirkland expressing solidarity and support with the striking employees of El Al Israel Airlines. The cable read as follows:

> Have cabled yesterday to our minister of transport condemning in the strongest possible terms El Al's handling of dispute with the company's employees in the U.S. and demanded that strike-breakers be immediately called to Israel and that negotiations with the union be resumed in keeping with accepted trade union procedures and in strict adherence to prevailing collective agreement.
>
> Histadrut expresses its full solidarity with striking El Al employees members of the International Association of Machinists and Aerospace Workers and will continue pressing for speedy resolution of conflict in accordance with free democratic trade union principles.

On April 5, 1984, Mr. Frank J. Barbaro, the head of the Labor Commission of the New York Assembly, sent a letter with 59 assembly member signatures to Prime Minister Yitzhak Shamir expressing grave concern over the way in which El Al Airlines was conducting itself in its collective bargaining with District 100. Mr. Chaim Korfu, Minister of Transport for Israel, responded to the letter to Mr. Shamir on May 6, 1984. Mr. Korfu pointed out that El Al has been under receivership in Israel and has been directed by the court to effect substantial cost sav-

ings, ensure continuous operations, and, failing that, liquidate the company. The general tone of the letter to the legislators was not supportive, and Mr. Korfu insisted that the company never tried to break the union.

At least two additional requests for support and solidarity were made by high-level IAM representatives. On April 12, 1984, Mr. R. L. Rapp, General Chairman, sent a letter to Mr. Edward J. Cleary, President of the New York State AFL-CIO, explaining the situation at El Al and asking for support and assistance. Mr. William W. Winpsinger, International President of IAM, sent a letter on April 17, 1984, to Mr. Harry Van Arsdale, President of the New York City Labor Council, detailing the actions of El Al management and asking for support and solidarity. Evidence that these calls were heeded is contained in a letter dated April 24, 1984, from Mr. Morton Bahr, Vice President of the Communications Workers of America AFL-CIO, District 1, to Ms. Carol G. Creamer, President of IAM Local 2656. In this letter, Mr. Bahr indicated that, in response to a request from the NYC Labor Council, he had recently met with representatives of a major U.S. Jewish organization and an Israeli official who had just arrived in the United States and that he articulated all important points, on behalf of the strikers, to these individuals. Additionally, on May 22, 1984, Mr. Martin Lapan, Executive Director of the Jewish Labor Committee, sent a letter to friends of the committee discussing El Al's attempts to break the union and its charges of anti-Semitism against the U.S. strikers. He urged Jewish leaders to call on the Prime Minister of Israel to instruct El Al to settle the dispute before greater damage was done to Israel's image and interests.

As a result of mounting pressure from labor organizations and Jewish organizations, on July 18, 1984, there was a high-level meeting between the employees' leadership and El Al management, including Mr. Rafael Harlev, the

President of El Al. He asserted that El Al would not accept back a considerable number of the strikers. This resulted in a deadlock, and soon afterward the AFL-CIO declared a general boycott against El Al, sending cables to numerous labor organizations in Europe asking for their help.

The Anti-Semitism Issue

The striking U.S. employees have been accused several times of anti-Semitism. These accusations were made in various places, including the Israel daily, *Davar* (the Histadrut paper). The article claimed that El Al employees accused Israel of being ruthless and declared the strike to be part of the Palestinian's struggle for self-determination.

The strikers argue now that it never happened. "We are not leftists, we have been avid supporters of Israel. We have organized many donation parties and bought Israeli bonds."

In an article in the *Village Voice* (Jul. 10, 1984), it was noted that strikers were deeply offended by the charges. During several of Israel's wars, many of these white-collar, middle-class, Jewish employees worked overtime without compensation, in some cases donating their paychecks to the effort. The strikers emphasize that they are not against the country, but rather the tactics of El Al's management. "You have to separate your feelings and know what you're striking for."

Local Lodge 2656 of IAM is so concerned about the anti-Semitism charges that at their general membership meeting held on Tuesday, April 24, 1984, they passed the following resolution:

> We, the members of Local Lodge 2656, District 100, International Association of Machinists and Aerospace Workers, AFL-CIO, hereby condemn El Al Israel Airlines for lying to the Israeli media by labeling our Union and its leadership as anti-Semitic. This is a despicable tactic being used by El Al Israel Airlines to try and justify their union-busting actions.

Recent Trends in Labor–Management Relations

Yost (*Sunday News Journal,* Sep. 1, 1985) detailed a number of reasons why unions are facing an unsure future in the United States. For the last two years, nonunion pay raises were greater than the pay raises for union workers (3% per year average). Major strikes for the first six months of 1985 totaled 18, down from 235 in 1979. Many believe that unions have priced themselves out of the market, particularly in mature industries. The combination of deregulation in several industries, increased foreign competition with vast, inexpensive labor forces, a conservative president, the recent recession, and a large unemployed labor pool (ready to be strikebreakers) has weakened labor's strength. Management's stance has been problematic, as well, with its demands for two-tier contracts, plant-closing threats, and filing bankruptcy to cancel labor contracts (Continental Airlines). President Reagan's firing of 11,500 striking air traffic controllers only served to emphasize the declining power of unions. This decline is reflected in recent union pay concessions. For example, Braniff airline's unions agreed to a 10% employee pay cut (Pearce and Keels, 1985).

Burdetsky and Katzman (1984) argued that surefire strikers are more than likely a thing of the past. Unions are competing with automation, imports, high unemployment, and public opinion. In order to be successful, these authors argue that a union needs both public support and the ability to inflict pain on the employer. These conditions are rare in today's labor environment. El Al strikers are currently discovering these realities. El Al's ability to hire replacements for the strikers and to fill in where necessary with supervisors and managers has allowed it to maintain all scheduled service on time. Additionally, high levels of public support have been difficult to achieve because of the potential problem of damaging close ties between the United States and Israel. This situation is made clear in the following statement from *Village Voice* (Jul. 10, 1984):

> For some of the Machinists, the strike has been what one called a "rude awakening" to the realities of political life. Despite a number of interviews and visits by the press, no coverage has appeared in city papers or local television—an absence perceived by many as reluctance to criticize Israel.

Current Developments

The circumstances surrounding this strike and the tactics of El Al were being carefully noted by other offshore airlines (*Business Week,* Jul. 23, 1984). Mr. Martin Seham, a New York lawyer who has been negotiating for El Al, will represent Aer Lingus (Irish carrier) and Varig (Brazilian state-owned company) in demanding future concessions from the IAM. District 100 representative Hoffman is concerned with the dangerous precedent that could be set at El Al. But the question remains, can anything be done to avert these dangerous developments?

On March 3, 1985, Arie Egozi, New York correspondent for the Israeli daily *Yedioth Aahronot,* reported that some 80 El Al employees are still on strike. Attempts to resolve the strike have been met with a strong reluctance to move from initial positions. Additionally, the IAM has introduced new financial demands and ultimatums.

Throughout the strike many people have expressed the opinion that a "political" solution is needed to resolve the strike. This would involve the Israeli government playing a major role in the settlement. A step in this direction took place recently. It was reported in *Davar* (Jun. 19, 1985) that Mr. Amos Eran, the general manager of Mivtachim (Histadrut's pension fund) had been appointed by Israeli Prime Minister Peres to be his personal representative in an effort to end the strike. After meeting with the union representatives, Mr. Eran reported back to Mr. Peres that the American union is prepared to take most of the areas in dispute to arbitration. As of October 1985, the strike continues and its final resolution does not appear close at hand.

References

AFL-CIO News, April 7, 1984.

AFL-CIO News, May 12, 1984.

Burdetsky, B. and Katzman, M. S. "Is The Strike Iron Still Hot?" *Personnel Journal,* July 1984, 48–52.

Business Week, July 23, 1984, 71–72.

Davar, June 19, 1985.

El Al At A Glance. Public Relations Department, El Al Israeli Airlines Ltd.

New York Times, March 17, 1984, 27.

Pearce II, J. A. and Keels, J. K. "The fall and rise of Braniff." *Journal of Management Case Studies,* 1985, 1, 4–12.

Sunday News Journal, September 1, 1985, E1–E2.

The Jewish Week, May 11, 1984.

The Village Voice, July 10, 1984.

E L E V E N

INTERNATIONAL MANUFACTURING MANAGEMENT

G. H. Manoocheri
California State University, Fullerton

Global competition has dramatically changed the nature of competition in manufacturing. It has created great opportunities for some companies and industries, but has also created major threats for others. Global competition has changed the manufacturing environment, which has altered manufacturing goals and priorities and consequently changed the role of manufacturing operations. To compete effectively in the global environment, many companies have adopted the world class manufacturing practices. Also, global competition and global markets have encouraged multinational companies (MNCs) to spread their operations around the globe. However, coordination of the scattered operations is a challenge. These issues are discussed in this chapter.

In the 1950s and 1960s, Xerox had a monopoly on a key industrial process: copying documents. Xerox was very successful, profitable and growing. However, Xerox copying machines malfunctioned or broke down regularly, and the Xerox executives knew it. Instead of redesigning the machines so they would not fail, Xerox created a field service force to repair the failures. This set the stage for the entry of competition, and the Japanese rushed in. They designed machines that did not fail as often, cost less, and made better copies. Soon they captured a significant market share, which drastically affected the Xerox revenues. In the late 1970s, Xerox nearly went out of business.

But Xerox fought back. It created a world class manufacturing operation that could match the best in the world. In the early 1980s, it launched a major quality improvement program. The program

encompassed all aspects of the operation including closer attention to customer needs, better design of the products, closer ties with the suppliers, a more streamlined process, fewer defects, and much higher employee involvement. In addition to quality efforts, Xerox focused on the use of technology and just-in-time (JIT) methods. State-of-the art equipment was used to enhance quality and improve flexibility of the operations. JIT methods such as setup time reduction, pull systems, electronic kanban links to suppliers, cross-trained workers, and manufacturing cells were used to improve the efficiency, quality, and flexibility of the manufacturing operation. In 1989, as a result of these programs, Xerox won the prestigious Malcolm Baldrige National Quality Award. Customers have noticed the improvement as well. Xerox has been able to recapture some of the lost market share.

Having successfully defended the erosion of its market share in copying machines, Xerox is now confronting a revolution in technology that has altered the office environment; and is again trying to rejuvenate itself by emphasizing new technology, new products, and new markets. To succeed in the fast-changing environment, Xerox is abandoning its insular culture and forming strategic alliances with other high-tech companies, such as Sun Microsystems, Microsoft, and Compaq Computer, to develop new products.

To compete in a highly competitive global economy, Xerox is integrating its operation into a tightly coordinated network of plants around the globe. Since the early 1980s, it has been

creating international design teams,
developing communication systems,
coordinating purchasing, streamlining
the flow of inventory between plants, and
developing a global forecasting system.

Information for this vignette was gleaned from M. E.
McGrath and R. W. Hoole. "Manufacturing's New
Economies." *Harvard Business Review* (May–June 1992),
94–102; J. H. Sheridan. "America's Best Plants." *Industry
Week* (October 15, 1990), 27–9. T. Smart. "Can Xerox
Duplicate Its Glory Days?" *Business Week* (October 4,
1993), 56–8.

Introduction

Increased global competition in recent years has
created a new manufacturing environment and has
changed manufacturing priorities. As a result, we
have rediscovered the importance of the role the
manufacturing function can play in the success
of a firm. Consequently, the manufacturing function is viewed as a competitive weapon. These
changes are not unique to any particular country; similar changes in the manufacturing role,
priorities, and management practices are taking
place all over the world.

The focus of this chapter is on manufacturing, as distinct from services. Manufacturing is
in the arena of global competition because manufactured products are typically more standardized and can be more easily transported to other
markets than can services. Service operations
produce intangible products that generally require high customer contact; therefore, they have
to be located close to the customers. Also, services, at least at the present, account for a small
portion of international trade.

The chapter is divided into three parts. First,
to appreciate international manufacturing management concepts and issues, we start the chapter with a discussion of the impact of global
competition on U.S. manufacturing. In the second part, we review the popular manufacturing
practices that seem necessary for success in the
new environment. Some of the more prevalent

practices such as total quality management
(TQM), just-in-time (JIT), factory automation,
employee involvement, and outsourcing are discussed. Finally, we focus on managing the geographically scattered manufacturing operations
of MNCs. Alternative approaches on where to
locate facilities and how to coordinate them are
presented in the last part of the chapter.

Manufacturing and Global Competition

The most significant factor affecting the manufacturing function in recent decades has been
the increase in global competition. It has created
new opportunities as well as major threats. It
has given manufacturers access to foreign markets and resources overseas, but it has also
opened domestic markets to very tough foreign
competitors. Some of these foreign manufacturers have had great success in meeting customers' needs and have developed a large market share in a short period of time. For example,
in the United States, many foreign brand names
that were totally unknown just a decade ago
have become common household names. Of
course, such success has come at the cost of
American manufacturers.

The American Experience

Nowhere is the impact of global competition
more evident than in the manufacturing sector.
A case in point is U.S. manufacturing. U.S.
manufacturing has lost the dominance it enjoyed in the decades following World War II. In
some industries, such as steel and auto, it has
lost its industrial and technological leadership.
The results have appeared on the U.S. balance
of trade. In the 1980s, for example, the U.S. imported some $920 billion more in merchandise
than it exported. American companies have virtually abandoned the production of certain products. For instance, the consumer electronics industry is now dominated by foreign firms.
Detroit's auto makers now supply only 62.5 percent of the U.S. automobile market from domestic factories versus 71.3 percent in 1980. A

decade ago American factories made 94 percent of the computers sold in the United States, now they make 66 percent. The U.S. share of the world semiconductor market has decreased from 57.2 to 36.5 percent.[1]

Why is the United States losing ground? Many explanations have been offered. Some argue with a good deal of justification that U.S. manufacturing lacks the government support that is provided to its competitors. A shift from manufacturing to services is another explanation. It is argued that service firms are not as productive as manufacturing firms. Also, a comparatively low net investment rate in new equipment and facilities by U.S. companies is considered to be a main contributing factor. In the last decade, the net investment rate for U.S. industries was 6 percent of total output, as compared to 18 percent for Japan. High wages, stringent unions, changing attitudes toward work, and a dysfunctional education system all have been considered as partial causes of low competitiveness.

These explanations, however, are incomplete. Despite various contributing factors, ultimately the management of companies and their employees are responsible for gaining the competitive advantage. This is evident by the success of the Japanese firms, such as Honda and Toyota, which have set up shops in the United States and operate under the same conditions as the American manufacturers. Until World War II, the manufacturing function was of prime importance and typically had top priority in the allocation of resources within a company. However, after the war, its significance started diminishing in many U.S. companies. One major cause of this descent was that U.S. manufacturing did not face worthy competition in the years following the war. During the war, the industrial capabilities and economic infrastructure of Japan and the European countries were largely destroyed. Meanwhile the United States was at the peak of its industrial and technological capability, comfortably away from all of the destruction of war, and enjoying a well-developed and efficient mass production system. The global demand for manufactured products exceeded U.S. manufacturing capacity. The great success of U.S. manufacturing and the fact that no nation was in a position to challenge the U.S. dominance made the U.S. companies complacent. The U.S. firms felt they had mastered all of the manufacturing problems, and that there were no more challenges in manufacturing. Therefore, no further gains were expected from the additional allocation of resources into manufacturing. So, companies started focusing on other functions of the business and ignoring manufacturing as a focus of innovation.

After the war, as Europe and Japan built their industrial base, the world manufacturing capacity gradually caught up with the demand. In the mid-1960s capacity started exceeding demand. This led to the prominence of marketing as companies tried to explore new opportunities in the market to utilize their capacity. As a result, many companies became totally marketing-oriented. New product introduction and product proliferation became the dominant strategic focus without much regard for manufacturing capabilities. Increased product proliferation without a corresponding upgrading of the manufacturing capabilities can have a devastating impact on manufacturing performance. It increases the variety and complexity of manufacturing tasks, which can consequently lead to lower quality and efficiency. Coupled with this marketing orientation was the development and popularity of financial measures to boost profitability. In turn, these changes in emphasis contributed to the descent of manufacturing. The use of financial measures such as rate of return and payback period typically favors short-term projects over long-term ones. However, the attainment of manufacturing strategic capabilities requires long-term resource commitments to R&D and capital expenditures. Hence, the resulting short-term horizon mentality starved manufacturing and led to the loss of its capabilities. In short, overemphasis of marketing and finance and underemphasis of manufacturing led to the loss of the U.S. manufacturing competitive edge.

A final problem was a shortage of expertise in manufacturing at the CEO level. Due to the lack of appreciation for and attention to manufacturing in the past several decades, not many manufacturing managers could reach the top-level management positions. Thus, in many manufacturing companies, top managers had for the most part marketing, financial, or legal backgrounds. This, in turn, resulted in further neglect of manufacturing, because these managers did not understand the significance of manufacturing, the impact of marketing and financial strategic decisions on manufacturing, and the contributions of manufacturing to the corporate strategies.

In summary, in the several decades following World War II, in U.S.-based firms, manufacturing was neglected. The imbalance of world manufacturing demand and supply, product proliferation, popularity of financial tools, and top management's lack of technical background all contributed to the manufacturing problems we have reviewed. However, since the mid-1970s, as a result of global competition, particularly from the Japanese, American firms have started to appreciate and rediscover manufacturing's importance.

The American experience has demonstrated the value and importance of manufacturing. To succeed in the world market MNCs need to develop and maintain a manufacturing capability that can compete against the best in the world.

The Changing Global Environment of Manufacturing

The changing manufacturing environment is intensifying global competition. The current manufacturing environment is becoming much more dynamic and complex than has been the case historically. Increasing global competition and the fast pace of technological development are the main factors shaping the new environment.

Global competition   Higher global competition means more competitors. The number of players has simply increased. For example, General Motors has to compete with many more auto manufacturers today compared to the three primary U.S. manufacturers of the early 1970s. In addition to Ford and Chrysler, for example, GM has to compete with Toyota, Nissan, Honda, and several European firms. Similarly, General Electric has to compete with Sony, Philips, Siemens, Goldstar, and a host of others, in addition to Westinghouse and Whirlpool. Not only are there more participants in the game of global competition, the rules of play are different too. Foreign manufacturers operate under different conditions than U.S. manufacturers and may face fewer limitations and have access to cheaper resources. The result may be a competitive advantage for the foreign firm, which forces the domestic manufacturer to either eliminate the source of disadvantage or to compensate for it by becoming more efficient in other areas. In the past, for example, if GM granted a raise to its workers through a labor contract negotiated with United Auto Workers (UAW), Ford and Chrysler would follow GM. They would all then pass their higher costs to consumers via corresponding price increases. Thus, none of the companies would have an advantage. Today, however, Toyota and Honda have nonunionized factories in the United States and can also tap their factories outside the United States; therefore, they do not have to follow the lead of the U.S. firms. This puts additional pressure on U.S. manufacturers to become more competitive or lose additional market share.

Technological development   Another factor shaping the new manufacturing environment is the increased pace of technological development. Technological developments impact manufacturing through changes in product design and process improvements. Higher technological development means more frequent product and process design changes. Developments in technology are expanding exponentially. They

AT&T in China

After initial miscues, AT&T has recently reentered China. It has opened offices there, and in 1993, signed its largest foreign business venture ever, to help modernize China's creaky phone system. AT&T's past records in China, however, have left a lot to be desired. Very seldom has a savvy corporate giant so completely missed the boat as AT&T did in China a decade ago. China is widely expected to have the biggest market for telephone switching equipment in the world. Nevertheless, AT&T treated the country as an insignificant market.

In the early 1980s, China was interested in upgrading its telephone network, and was shopping for advanced digital switching technology. It was considering AT&T as a prospective supplier. At the time, however, AT&T had a protected monopoly in the U.S. market and was not interested in transferring its advanced technology to a suspected market. In contrast, European and Japanese competitors were eager to do business with China, and soon became China's primary equipment suppliers.

In the mid-1980s, when AT&T was broken up and was looking outside the U.S. for additional business, it sold some switching equipment to China. But because AT&T was totally unfamiliar with the Chinese telephone market and their telephone habits, the initial foray was a disaster. Unlike the Americans, average Chinese had limited access to the phone and, therefore, the phone lines—already in a bad shape—were overused. Moreover, Chinese tended to stay on the phone much longer than Americans. Special switches were needed that could handle the heavy use of the telephone lines. Oblivious to the differences between the United States and China, AT&T simply shipped them off-the-shelf products. Needless to say these switches were quickly overwhelmed by the volume of telephone traffic. Since AT&T did not have an office in China, the problems were handled by its Hong Kong office. Parts and technicians had to be shipped from the United States. This resulted in unusually long delays and much frustration. Disgusted by the poor service and unhappy about the whole business, the Chinese eventually cut off AT&T from their market. AT&T now is trying hard not to repeat the past mistakes and is serious about winning their business.

Sources: B. Ziegler. "AT&T Reaches Way Out for This One." *Business Week* (March 8, 1993), 3; D. P. Hamilton. "After Initial Fuzziness, AT&T Clears Up Signal to Asia." *The Wall Street Journal* (June 30, 1993), B6; C. S. Smith. "Learning from the Past." *The Wall Street Journal* (December 10, 1993), R3.

have created new products and even new industries. Developments in computers, telecommunications, and consumer electronics are but a few examples. These developments have also had a major impact on the manufacturing process. Automation, through the application of new technologies, has dramatically improved the capability of many manufacturers. Although technological developments create many opportunities, they also lead to challenges. Taking advantage of new technologies and developing new products or processes typically requires a major investment and is fraught with risks.

Taken together, increased global competition and faster technological developments lead to a very complex and dynamic manufacturing environment. Greater global competition increases the need to introduce new products into the market or improve existing ones. At the same time technological developments enhance the ability of the manufacturers to produce new products and improve processes. Consequently, product life cycles are getting shorter in many industries. Competitors, motivated by conquering the world market, try to outperform others by introducing new models more frequently. For example, Sony, which first introduced the Walkman in 1979, has marketed more than 160 models[2] to stay ahead of its competitors. The result is that the average life of a Walkman is less than 18 months. In the competitive market of low-end personal computers, the product life cycle has shrunk from several years less than a decade ago to only several months today.

Changing Manufacturing Priorities

To survive and prosper, MNCs need to adapt to the changing global environment of manufacturing. Primary indicators of this adjustment need are changes in the priorities (goals) of the manufacturing operations. Traditionally, the manufacturing function was considered a cost center, absorbing and consuming a large portion of the firm's resources without much contribution to its success. It was viewed as a necessary evil. Its primary goals were to meet the schedule and minimize cost; that is, to produce the products on time at the lowest cost. As a cost center, manufacturing could not provide any competitive advantage. Under the more stable environment of the past, when competition was primarily based on price, a firm with that view of manufacturing could have survived. However, in today's global environment, the manufacturing function can play a variety of roles in contributing to the achievement of the firm's strategic goals. Strategically, manufacturing can provide an MNC with a competitive advantage. In addition to minimizing cost, manufacturing can maximize product quality, operation speed, and flexibility.

Product quality Tough international competition has made quality a competitive weapon. Many Japanese companies that have gained a significant market share in the United States have done so through emphasis on quality. They positioned themselves as the provider of higher quality products at competitive prices. Toyota is a good example of a company using this approach. Quality is a necessary element in winning international markets. Many American firms, including Xerox, Motorola, and Harley-Davidson have made quality their top priority and successfully expanded their market share.

Operating speed In a dynamic environment where the window of opportunity (product life cycle) is very small and remains open for only a short time, a firm needs speed and flexibility. When the product life cycle is very short, a firm has to get the product to the market fast if it is to be successful. If the life cycle of a product is only one year, a delay of three months in product introduction to the market could be the difference between success and failure. In highly dynamic environments delay in bringing products to the market is detrimental. A good example is that of Lotus Development, a software company. Lotus was late introducing a new version of its spreadsheet, Lotus 1-2-3, allowing Microsoft's Excel software to gain a solid market share. Another aspect of speed is fast delivery time. It is generally referred to as lead time, the elapsed time between receiving the order and filling it. Reducing lead time is a top priority for many firms because it enables them to react to the needs of the market faster. Shorter lead time increases customer satisfaction, decreases the cost, and increases the quality and flexibility of the firm. Table 11.1 presents several examples of the firms that, by emphasizing speed, have been able to reduce the time needed to develop and produce products.

Flexibility Flexibility is another top priority for international manufacturing. MNCs need to focus on two types of flexibility: product flexibility and volume flexibility. Product flexibility refers to the ability to accommodate ever-changing product designs and unique custom-made products by switching from production of one product to another quickly and without additional cost. Volume flexibility is the ability to accelerate and decelerate the production rate in reaction to the demand. Both types of flexibility depend on the manufacturing capability to produce different products in the same facility. For example, Toshiba's computer factory in Ome

Table 11.1
Speed in Product Innovation Production

Product Innovation Company	Product	Old	New
AT&T	Phones	2 years	1 year
Hewlett-Packard	Computer printers	4.5 years	22 months
Honda	Cars	5 years	3 years
Navistar	Trucks	5 years	1 year

Product Production Company	Product	Order-to-Finished-Goods Time	
Brunswick	Fishing reels	3 weeks	1 week
Hewlett-Packard	Electronic testing equipment	4 weeks	5 days
General Electric	Circuit breaker boxes	3 weeks	3 days
Motorola	Pagers	3 weeks	2 hours

Source: B. Dumaine. "How Managers Can Succeed Through Speed." *Fortune* (February 13, 1989), 56.

assembles nine different word processors on the same line and, on an adjacent one, 20 varieties of laptop computers. This allows Toshiba to handle the increasing demand for the new models and decreasing demand for the old models quickly. It does not run out of a popular model or overproduce one whose sales have slowed.[3]

In short, the new environment is changing the role of the international manufacturing function in many MNCs. The job of manufacturing is no longer merely one of minimizing cost; rather it can make a significant contribution to achieving some strategic priorities such as quality, speed, and flexibility that have a major impact on the success of the company. Thus, many firms are rediscovering the importance of the role of the manufacturing function. They are investing in manufacturing assets to build and sustain the manufacturing capabilities required to compete globally.

World Class Manufacturing

This section covers some of the popular practices of the world class manufacturers. Most of these practices are influenced by the Japanese approach to manufacturing. But the popularity

of these practices is not due to the fact that they are Japanese; rather it is because they are needed to meet the challenges created by today's global environment. A world class manufacturer should be able to meet market needs very quickly. It should have flexibility and speed in producing the products the customers need with high quality and efficiency. A world class manufacturer embraces such practices as total quality management, just-in-time systems, factory automation, employee involvement, and outsourcing.

Total Quality Management

Japanese competition and the Japanese success in the world market made it clear to American manufacturers that quality is imperative for global competition. The primary reason that U.S. auto makers lost such a large market share to their Japanese competitors during the 1970s and 1980s was the superior quality of the Japanese-made cars. The same was true in other industries such as copiers, machine tools, computer chips, TVs, and many others. In an about face, American firms have begun emphasizing quality manufacturing. This new emphasis has resulted in the popularity of total quality management (TQM) among American manufacturers. More recently, European managers and others have also felt the pressure for quality improvement, because they now have to compete with Japanese as well as improved American MNCs. The development of the European quality standard, ISO 9000, and its worldwide acceptance clearly indicates the importance of quality in world trade.

In recent years, TQM has created significant changes in the way we manage our organization, including manufacturing operations. The quality movement started on the manufacturing shop floor; but it quickly became evident that achieving high quality goes beyond the manufacturing function—it embraces the whole organization. The TQM approach is significantly different from the traditional quality control (QC) approach. The difference starts with the way quality is defined. Under QC, quality is defined as "defect free," while with TQM, the quality definition is much broader. It focuses on "fitness for use"; that is, how well the product meets the needs of the customer. So, quality starts with the customer. The needs of the customer are sought and translated into product specifications, and then every unit is to be produced to those specifications.

The QC approach is passive. It assumes that defects are caused by variations in the production process. Excess variations can lead to defects. The job of QC is to "find it and fix it," detecting the bad ones through inspection. The focus is on product quality and weeding out defects, but no effort is targeted at finding the sources of the variations that cause the defects. At best, it is a standard maintaining approach that tries to meet the acceptable quality level. However, the TQM approach is an active one. It focuses on finding and eliminating the causes of the variations that create defects, so they will not be repeated. Thus, it prevents production of defects. It emphasizes process control. If processes are under control, you will not get defec-

tive products. By focusing on process control and identifying and eliminating the sources of variations, TQM can achieve continuous improvement of the process itself, leading to continuously improving products.

Also, with the QC approach, quality is considered to be the job of the quality control department only. Production managers and workers do not consider quality as one of their primary concerns. In fact, they see quality in conflict with their primary goals of minimizing cost and meeting schedule deadlines. Typically, quantity, producing to the schedule, has a higher priority than quality. Such a setting creates conflict between quality and production people. It creates a situation of "us against them," where the quality control department plays the role of the police, monitoring the performance of the production workers, and production people try to hide quality problems or do just well enough to pass the inspection so that they can meet their cost and schedule targets. However, under the TQM approach quality is the job of everyone in the organization from the top floor to the shop floor. Quality is a companywide concern. It is assumed that everyone in the organization is impacting quality. The machine operator, the planner, the buyer, the design engineer, the accountant, the shipping clerk—all are responsible for quality. Everyone is involved in building quality into the product. Achieving effective employee involvement for quality improvement requires major changes in the job design, organization structure, compensation systems, and organization culture.

Another major difference between the two approaches is with regard to the cost and quality relationships. Managers believing in the QC approach maintain that quality costs money and thus they cannot afford it. Under TQM, it is assumed that higher quality means lower costs because the high costs associated with poor quality more than offset the costs associated with preventing quality problems. Higher quality decreases the costs of inspection, and internal and external failure. Internal failure costs such as scrap, loss of yield, and rework can be very expensive, but external failures can be much more expensive. Costs of field service, warranties, lawsuits, and loss of goodwill and market share can be extremely high. In the United States, the costs associated with poor quality have been underestimated in the past.

In summary, TQM basically involves the pursuit of four objectives[4]:

1. Ever better, more appealing, less variable quality
2. Ever quicker, less variable response—from design and development through supplier and sales channels, offices, and plants all the way to the final user
3. Ever greater flexibility—in adjusting to customers' shifting volume and "mix" requirements
4. Ever lower cost—through quality improvement, rework reduction, and non–value-added (NVA) waste elimination.

Just-in-Time Production System

Another popular practice of world class manufacturers is adoption of the just-in-time (JIT) system. JIT was developed and perfected by Toyota during the 1960s and 1970s. Its adoption spread very rapidly in Japan. In the early 1980s, some American companies started experimenting with it. At the beginning it was received with disbelief and resistance; however, after the success of some American companies, its popularity has exploded. Today, almost all Fortune 1000 manufacturing companies are implementing some aspects of JIT. This popularity is earned because of the significant benefits that the application of JIT can bring a company. Hewlett-Packard, for example, implemented JIT in its Boise, Idaho, plant and enjoyed the following benefits: lead time cut from five days to one, work in process (WIP) cut from seven days to less than one day, raw materials cut from one month to ten days maximum, and units per person per day doubled.[5]

The primary objective of JIT is reduction of cost through elimination of waste. Waste is defined as anything other than the minimum amount of equipment, materials, and workers that are absolutely essential to production. To meet this objective in the dynamic global environment, JIT advocates that each process should produce the needed parts in the needed quantities just in time to be used or sold. The ideal is an operation design in which each process produces only one piece, inspects it, and passes it to the next process, with only one piece of inventory between each two processes. The application of JIT leads to a drastic reduction of inventory. In fact, JIT considers inventory as "the root of all evil" that hides operations problems and causes inefficiencies and poor quality.

Achieving the JIT objective requires operations practices that are very different from the conventional practices. Implementation of JIT could mean a major overhaul of the production system. Also, it necessitates changes in other organizational systems, such as improving the company's information processing capability, cross-training of workers, and decentralizing of the decision-making process.[6] The core elements of JIT are given in Table 11.2.

Pull system   One of the most distinctive elements of JIT is the *pull system,* as compared to the conventional push system. Under the pull system, the final assembly line pulls the required items for its production from the preceding processes when needed, at the exact quantity. The preceding process would produce the

Table 11.2
Elements of Just-In-Time Production

---

* Pull system
* Uniform scheduling
* Small lots production
* Setup time reduction
* Group technology and multifunction workers
* High quality
* Dedicated workers
* Reliable suppliers

---

exact quantity to replace the withdrawn parts. The preceding process, for its production, pulls the required parts from its own preceding process. This pulling of the requirements goes back upstream through all the processes and, in some companies, even continues to the vendors. The pull system requires a minimum amount of inventory between the processes, but the WIP inventory is much smaller than the inventory typically held by the conventional production system. The pull approach is accompanied by an information system known as *kanban*, which is typically a card that has the information regarding the type of item withdrawn and its quantity. This card is circulated between a user station and its feeder station, to inform and authorize the feeder station of what to produce. The kanban system connects all of the stations in the shop. With the use of the pull system and kanban, each process produces just what is needed immediately based on up-to-date information. For example, if for whatever reason a part is not needed anymore, it is not withdrawn from the station; and the station will not produce any more. It is assumed that it is better for a station to be idle than to produce a part that is not needed.

Uniform scheduling Considering the low level of inventory, for the pull system to work smoothly the production requirements should be leveled and matched with the available capacity. High fluctuations in production requirements can cause high inventory buildup of some components and shortage of some others. To minimize the fluctuation in production requirements, a level and uniform final assembly schedule should be developed and maintained. With uniform scheduling, we try to produce every part everyday and to repeat the same schedule everyday. Such a final assembly schedule creates predictability and results in a level load for all upstream production processes.

Small lots and short setup time Uniform schedules along with the JIT goal of producing only what is needed result in small lots produc-

tion. In the JIT environment the ideal lot size is one. JIT companies continuously work on reducing production lot size, because a lower lot size leads to reduction of waste. However, producing in small lots is not economical as long as setup times are long. The term *setup time* refers to the time needed to set up machinery and equipment for a production run. Therefore, setup time has to be reduced. Reduction of setup time is typically one of the early challenges of companies implementing JIT. In the past, American firms were not concerned with shortening the setup time. It was not a priority, because setup was done infrequently. But with the popularity of JIT, many firms have successfully focused on setup time reduction. The JIT literature provides many examples of companies that have reduced setup time dramatically.

Group technology and multifunction workers Another distinctive component of JIT is the use of group technology. Group technology involves the grouping of parts produced in a shop into families of parts based on the similarity of their production processes. Separate manufacturing cells are designed and each is dedicated to the production of a family of parts. A cell is a grouping of machines with different functions needed to complete production of all members of a family. Thus, all the parts in a family are run through the required processes and machines, which are located close together, in very small lots. Associated with the manufacturing cell is the use of multiple-skill workers. Workers are trained to operate different machines in a cell. Group technology and multifunction workers provide a great deal of production capacity flexibility. As production requirements of a cell change, workers can be assigned in and out of the cell in order to adjust the production capacity of the cell. In addition, this arrangement results in drastic reduction of WIP inventory, production lead time, required manufacturing and storage space, as well as improvement of quality.

Implementation of the multifunction worker concept has faced some opposition from labor unions. To protect their members' jobs, traditional union bargaining practices emphasize fixed and narrow duties for each job title. Such narrow job descriptions lead to very inflexible, wasteful, and inefficient operations. In industries that face stiff global competition, unions are gradually giving in and accepting the concept of multifunction workers as a necessity for improving competitiveness, and ultimately for protecting the union members' jobs which could be lost if the firm goes under. They have realized that global competition has eliminated borders and that, say, an American auto worker is ultimately in competition with Mexican, Japanese, or German workers. American workers have to be competitive or they will lose their jobs. One example of the unions' change of attitude is the cooperation of the UAW with New United Motor Manufacturing, Inc. (NUMMI), a GM–Toyota joint venture in Fremont, California. In 1984, NUMMI took over the GM–Fremont plant. Toyota, which is in charge of operations management, implemented JIT in the NUMMI plant, after extensive efforts to ensure worker cooperation. NUMMI has a radically simplified job classification system. Where GM–Fremont had 18 skilled trades classifications, NUMMI has only 2, but those 2 have much broader job specifications.[7]

High quality   The JIT system does not rely on buffer stock to smooth the flow of material and make up for production disruption. Therefore, internal problems such as equipment breakdown, poor quality items, unacceptable worker performance, system problems, and so on, have to be eliminated. The production requirements at each workstation have to be met exactly for the system to work smoothly. That is, all the items produced have to be of good quality; in other words, zero defects. Therefore, high quality is very essential to the implementation of JIT. To communicate the importance of quality

to workers, for example, at Toyota assembly plants, workers have the authority to stop the production line when they notice a quality problem, their own or somebody else's. To achieve the high quality required for JIT, many manufacturing companies consider JIT and TQM complementary and implement these two together.

Dedicated workforce   A prerequisite to JIT implementation is a cooperative and committed workforce. Because buffer stock is not available, WIP is minimal, and the production lot size is small, a quick response is needed to changes in the market and disruptions in the production process. Therefore, the JIT firm has to rely on the high performance, dedication, and multifunctional skills of its workers. Only a company that has a good worker–management relationship can successfully adopt a JIT system. JIT requires workers who are dedicated, knowledgeable, and motivated problem solvers, team players with interpersonal and communication skills and who are disciplined. "The JIT production system will not work without the highest level of worker loyalty. The JIT organization depends on its employees to help isolate and eliminate the source of production problems and to complete the daily schedule regardless of those problems if at all possible."[8] In the NUMMI plant discussed earlier, by the end of 1986, after about two years of operation, productivity and quality were higher than that of any other GM facility; and absenteeism had dropped from between 20 and 25 percent at the old GM–Fremont plant to a steady 3 to 4 percent. Also, worker participation in the suggestion program increased from 26 percent in 1986 to 92 percent in 1991.[9]

Reliable suppliers   To achieve the full benefits of the JIT system, a company needs to expand the system to its vendors. This requires cooperative vendors that are willing to implement JIT. Many large manufacturers with JIT systems have asked their suppliers to adopt it, too.

JIT implementation has a major impact on the vendor–customer relationship. The relationship should be based on mutual benefits, trust, information sharing, and good cooperation. The conventional practices are not appropriate and a major modification in the relationship is needed. For example, instead of the common practice of granting annual contracts based on the lowest cost bid, a manufacturer should grant long-term contracts based on the supplier's overall capabilities as a business partner. In essence, the company and its vendors form a manufacturing family whose fates are closely linked.

Factory Automation

Emerging types of automation, benefiting from the developments in electronics and microprocessing, can enhance many different aspects of manufacturing operations. Continental Can Company, a division of Continental Can Systems in Chicago, had many operating and administrative problems and was losing money. The firm decided to invest $10 million in factory automation including CIM (computer-integrated manufacturing), CAD/CAM (computer-aided design/computer-aided manufacturing), and CNC (computer numerical control) machines and robots. As a result, WIP was cut in half, overall lead time was reduced by 30 percent, and on-time delivery rate was increased from 50 to 90 percent.[10]

There are two basic types of manufacturing automation: fixed and programmable. Fixed automation is a system in which the sequence of processing operations is fixed by the equipment configuration. The operations in the sequence are usually simple. It is the integration and coordination of many such operations into one piece of equipment that makes the system complex. Mechanized assembly lines and conveyors are examples of fixed automation. Fixed automation is designed to produce one type of part or product. Thus, its use is appropriate for products with high production volume, stable product design, and a long product life cycle. These characteristics are needed to compensate for fixed automation's two main drawbacks: high initial investment cost and relative inflexibility. Specialized complex equipment is expensive to design and build; and because it is designed for the production of a particular product, it cannot be used in the production of other products. Fixed automation, however, results in high efficiency and low per unit variable costs when producing high-volume products.

In programmable automation, the production equipment is designed with the capability to change the sequence of operations to accommodate different product configurations. A program controls the operations sequence. The system can be reprogrammed to produce new products. This type of automation is used for low- and medium-volume production. The products are typically made in batches. To produce a new batch of a different product, the system must be reprogrammed. Examples of programmable automation include numerically controlled machine tools and industrial robots.

Flexible automation is an extension of programmable automation. A flexible automation system is capable of producing a variety of parts or products. The system can have product programs stored in its memory; and with a signal from the operator it can change over from one product to the next with virtually no time lost. Consequently, the system can produce various combinations and schedules of products in very small lot sizes. Although there are limits to the variety of products that can be produced on a flexible automation system, it has a significant advantage over fixed automation. It can provide efficiency without a dramatic loss of flexibility.

The primary benefit of programmable automation and flexible automation over fixed automation is higher flexibility. Flexible automation, especially, eliminates the traditional trade-off between efficiency and flexibility. A large volume of production is not required to take advantage of the efficiency offered by automation. Nor will obsolescence of a product make the equipment obsolete. This flexibility makes programmable automation very desirable for today's manufacturing environment since speed and flexibility are necessary to compete in a market that is dominated by high variety products with very short life cycles.

Computer-integrated manufacturing To enhance competitiveness, many manufacturing companies have applied computer automation in major manufacturing functions. While these computer automation applications make improvements through so-called islands of automation, the maximum potential is achieved only through linking and coordinating these islands in an automated system. Such an integrated, linked automated system is referred to by names such as the factory of the future, the paperless factory, and CIM. CIM includes computer-aided engineering (CAE), CAM, computer-aided assembly, automated storage and material handling, and automated production planning and inventory control.

CAE, which includes CAD, is an engineering process for designing new products. In interaction with graphic software, an engineer can design a new part or modify an existing part. The designer can get the computer to create drawings of the part on a display monitor, rotate the part, present different views, and zoom in on a specific area. A computer can also run some simulations and test some characteristics of the part, such as conducting stress tests, if needed. Once the design is finalized, it is stored electronically in the computer. This electronic image is available to other modules. If drawings are needed, a plotter can efficiently produce them. Compared to the traditional manual system, CAE has increased the productivity of the design process dramatically.

CAM is the application of computer automation to the fabrication process and includes some technologies such as CNC machines, flexible manufacturing systems, and computer-aided inspection. Basically, CAM involves a computer controlling a machine so that it performs specific activities. For example, a CNC machine can drill, bore, mill, or turn many different parts in many various sizes and shapes based on the instructions it receives from a computer. CAM can be linked to CAE. This integration gives CAM access to the final design specifications stored electronically in CAE. CAM can translate the product specifications into detailed machine instructions for manufacturing the part. This leads to higher efficiency and better quality.

In computer-aided assembly a computer controls robots and other equipment to assemble products. Like CNC machines, robots are programmable machines. Through program instructions, a computer can control the movements of a robot's arm to provide specific operations. Auto manufacturers use robots in welding, and computer makers use robots to insert components in computer boards. Advanced generation robots equipped with sensors that simulate touch and sight can perform more complex tasks. For example, General Motors uses robots to assemble and insert dashboard components.

Automated storage and material handling cover the process of moving, packaging, and storing parts, materials, and products. The system includes two basic technologies: automated guided vehicles (AGVs) and automated storage and retrieval systems (AS/RS). AGVs are typically small, driverless battery-driven vehicles that move materials around in a shop. Some AGVs have the capability to load and unload specific materials. They could be used to pick up materials at a specific station and drop them off in another station. Their movement is guided by a computer along cables installed below the floor. AGVs reduce material handling costs and provide much higher flexibility compared to a fixed conveyor. AS/RS is a computer-controlled system for storing and retrieving materials. To store parts, a computer guides AGVs and cranes to load the part and store it in a specific bin designated by the computer in a high-rise rack structure. When needed, the computer finds the address of the bin where the part is stored and guides a crane to retrieve it. Through the use of AGVs and AS/RS, material handling and storage can be almost totally automated.

Automated production planning and inventory control manages the production schedule. Based on forecasts and customer orders, the system indicates the production schedule of finished goods and their components, schedules operations, schedules the required purchased materials, and schedules the shipments of finished goods. Connected to an accounting system, it can serve as an information system linking critical functions and facilitating factory management.

In summary, CIM applications can lead to significant benefits. It results in higher flexibility and speed in reacting to market trends and customizing products to specific customer needs. It reduces inventory and costs. It provides more consistent quality. For example, beginning in 1988, Fuji Electric, Japan's fourth largest maker of electrical machinery, installed flexible, computer-integrated lines where setup, part selection, and assembly are all automated. Now Fuji uses one-third fewer workers, one-third less time, and almost one-third less inventory to make about 8000 varieties of products—three times more than before.[11] Competing in today's environment requires the manufacturers to keep up with and take advantage of appropriate technologies.

One interesting contrast between JIT and factory automation is with regard to the workers' role in the production system. As discussed earlier, JIT relies heavily on the workers' performance. A dedicated and skilled workforce is a critical element of JIT. In the past, a primary goal of most factory automation projects has been the replacement of workers with machines. However, more recently, many American manufacturers who spent millions of dollars on building "workerless" automated factories have come to the conclusion that replacement of workers by reliance on automation, fixed or flexible, can be costly; and it leads to building large complex systems that are inherently vulnerable to failure. As a result, a new approach to automation is emerging. Mammoth automated facilities are broken down into more manageable cells, which are just as versatile but less apt to fail. Workers with their unmatched dexterity and judgment are back in assembly jobs where robots floundered. The new approach relies extensively on information technology and uses software and computer networks to facilitate workers' tasks as well as to improve their efficiency, quality, speed, and flexibility. "The new automation paradigm . . . involves an ingenious balancing in which software and computer networks have emerged as more important than production machines, in which robots play a mere supporting role if they're present at all—and in which human workers are back in unexpected force. Call it the digital factory, for its dependence on information technology, or the soft factory, for its mix of the human and the mechanical. Whatever you call it, it's likely to set the tone of manufacturing for years, even decades, to come."[12] The new approach to automation, like JIT, emphasizes the workers' role in the production system and it is used to enhance, rather than to replace workers.

Employee Involvement

Employee involvement is one of the main components of world class manufacturing operations. It is referred to by a variety of names such as workers' participation, participative management, quality circles, quality of work life, self-managed teams, and employee empowerment. Whatever the name, the basic concept is involving employees in managing and decision making by sharing information and power. It is hoped that higher employee involvement will result in workers' greater understanding, better decisions, higher dedication and commitment, and ultimately better performance.

Employee involvement is becoming very popular in many industries. There are several reasons for such popularity. A primary factor is greater global competition that has led to a tougher competitive environment. In such an environment only companies that can get the best use out of their resources, including human resources, can survive and prosper. Also, in an environment where speed and flexibility are critical for success, organizations need to be adaptable. A trained and dedicated workforce is a primary resource that gives an organization adaptability. Finally, the application of emerging manufacturing practices and technologies such as TQM, JIT, and CIM require a highly skilled and committed workforce. These practices depend greatly on workers' performance; and the full potential of these practices will not be achieved without a committed workforce.

Considering these environmental factors, application of employee involvement can lead to the following specific benefits:

- Greater understanding and acceptance of decisions by subordinates
- Greater commitment to implementation of decisions
- Greater understanding of objectives
- Greater fulfillment of psychological needs and, therefore, greater satisfaction
- Greater social pressure on all members to comply with decisions
- Greater team identity, cooperation, and co-ordination
- Better means of constructive conflict resolution
- Better decisions.

Many experts see employee involvement as a key factor in increasing U.S. competitiveness and its ability to succeed in the global market. Paul Allaire, CEO of Xerox, maintains, "We're never going to outdiscipline the Japanese on quality. To win, we need to find ways to capture the creative and innovative spirit of the American worker. That's the real organizational challenge."[13] Through employee involvement, workers' creative and innovative spirit can be reached. Moreover, as global manufacturing moves to developing countries, capturing the innovative potential of a culturally diverse workforce becomes a more challenging task.

How to make it work   To get active employee involvement, most companies have to go through a major overhaul of their management system. Many different aspects of the organization are affected. Experts emphasize attention to the following:

1. Define employee involvement clearly. How much involvement and in what areas are desired? You can prevent misunderstandings by providing a clear definition, and formal manuals and procedures. You can't let the zealous worker or the reluctant supervisor rely on his or her own interpretations.

2. Define the organizational mission, goals, and objectives. The need for clear organizational direction is greater when decision making is dispersed. If employees are to make good decisions, they should know the goals and plans. When you agree on an overall mission, you can be more flexible about the means for achieving it.

3. Modify the organization design. To foster employee involvement you need to change the traditional organization design by moving toward more decentralization and delegation, a wider span of management, flatter organization structure, fewer management levels, and more reliance on expert authority as compared to position authority.

4. Provide training. Most companies need to provide an extended amount of training to the workers to turn them into effective problem solvers. In addition to basic oral and written communication, math, and technical training, companies need to provide behavioral and problem-solving training. Workers need to learn how to operate effectively in teams.

5. Share information. If workers are to make decisions, they need to have access to the required information. Management needs to open up. It should share information about the com-

pany's competitive environment and its competitors' performance, the company's performance, the costs of operations, limitations, and constraints.

6. Establish effective two-way communication. In many companies there is only one-way, top-down, communication. To have an active employee involvement program, an effective bottom-up communication channel has to be established; a suggestion box does not suffice.

7. Adopt appropriate compensation plans. Compensation plans should be consistent with the goals of the organization. If the company is encouraging involvement and teamwork, the traditional individual incentive plans are not appropriate. Even though intrinsic rewards are a source of motivation, ultimately if employees are putting more effort and making greater contributions, they should be paid accordingly.

8. Build around trust. If the employees are to give up the known and safe way of the past and follow management into the new world of employee involvement, they should be able to trust management. Eliminating the status symbols, such as reserved parking spaces, separate cafeterias, and sharing information and productivity returns are ways to increase trust in management.

9. Provide job security. If employees feel that their greater involvement can lead to higher productivity, which in turn may result in the elimination of jobs, there will be very strong resistance to the involvement program. Management has to assure workers that no jobs will be eliminated because of involvement programs.

World class manufacturing status cannot be achieved without an effective employee involvement program. So, employee involvement deserves special attention; and it should be a primary top management goal.

Outsourcing

Traditional industrial wisdom encouraged higher vertical integration; that is, a company should try to control a larger number of processes in the supply chain. For example, if IBM buys Intel, a supplier of chips, or Computer City, a computer retailer, it becomes more vertically integrated. The logic for support of higher vertical integration is that the company can gain more control over its fate. It assures availability of raw materials and components. It also results in tighter control over cost and quality. General Motors, for example, buys internally 70 percent of the parts it uses, including spark plugs, headlights, windshield wipers, and batteries.[14]

The recent changes in the competitive environment have made companies change direction with regard to vertical integration. The primary reason for this change of direction is the need for flexibility, fueled by the greater global competition and ever-increasing pace of technological changes. Highly vertically integrated companies are slow to change, and the business environment is changing so fast that no company can do it all alone. The cost and investment requirements for research and development, product design, process transformation, and retooling are too high to allow a vertically integrated company to maintain its competitiveness in all the activities it performs. The trend is to shun vertical integration and to focus on what you do best. The idea is to nurture a few core activities, ones that are crucial to your competitiveness, and outsource the rest of the activities. Through strategic alliances and joint ventures, a company can get outside specialists to do the noncore activities.

The primary advantage of outsourcing is greater speed and flexibility in responding to the changing marketplace. Rather than going through the lengthy process of in-house development of a component, service, or technology, the company can buy it from the specialists. In addition, outsourcing allows the company to focus its resources on its core competency. It directs the company's scarce capital and talents to components and activities that are critical to the product and that the company is distinctively good at making. Under this philosophy, it is a mistake to tie up the company resources on non-core activities and components. It dilutes the company focus and could lead to neglecting the development and improvement of core activities that are the firm's primary source of competitive advantage. Moreover, outsourcing can lower costs where the supplier has a distinct comparative advantage such as greater scale, lower cost structure, or stronger performance incentives. For example, at a Livonia, Michigan, General Motors factory that produces suspension components, a UAW contract pays an average of $37 an hour, including benefits, far more than many independent suppliers.[15]

Outsourcing has some real risks as well. Successful outsourcing requires (1) alliance with cooperative and able suppliers and (2) choosing the right specialty, core competency on which to focus. By depending on the outsiders, the company can lose control of the activities it cedes to its partners, as Intel experienced when it relied on a Japanese partner, NMB Semiconductor, to make products called flash memory chips. Just as the market was taking off, NMB had trouble getting its line up and running. As a result, Intel's market share dropped 20 points in one year.[16] Critics also are concerned that outsourcing can turn companies into hollow corporations, referring to companies that abandon manufacturing in order to improve profits and outsource production to plants in low-wage countries. It is argued that this approach will lead to a loss of engineering and manufacturing expertise and ultimately the downfall of the firms. According to Bettis, Bradly, and Hamel, improper use of outsourcing is playing an important role in the continuing competitive decline of many Western firms. It has enabled Japanese and other Asians to gain virtual control of the consumer electronic industries.[17]

Another risk of outsourcing is associated with the decision on what to keep in-house and what to outsource. Outsourcing a core activity can be disastrous, as IBM experienced. In producing its first personal computer, IBM relied on a pair of outsiders for key technologies: Intel for microprocessors and Microsoft Corporation for the operating software. These partnerships resulted in accelerated product development and market success for the IBM personal computer. But it also meant that IBM's system was not proprietary. Soon personal computers turned into a commodity, with hundreds of clone makers producing a better machine at a lower cost than IBM. The winners were Intel and Microsoft who ended up with the core activities.

Even though there are some risks associated with outsourcing, many companies are moving in that direction, particularly, in industries that face a fast changing market, such as apparel and electronics. Dell, Nike, and Liz Claiborne have effectively used outsourcing. Even companies in more traditional industries find outsourcing beneficial. A notable example is Chrysler. It buys 70 percent of its parts from outside suppliers, as compared to the industry's past practice of buying about 30 percent from outside.[18]

The extension of outsourcing is seen to lead to "the virtual corporation."[19] The virtual corporation is a temporary network of companies, including suppliers, customers, and even competitors, located around the world, coming together quickly to exploit fast-changing opportunities. Each partner brings its core competence in an effort to create an excellent operation, an excellence that cannot be matched by any single company. Information technology plays an important role in the development and operation of the virtual corporation. It is foreseen that a national information infrastructure will link computers and companies across the United States and ultimately the world. This communication superhighway will permit people in different companies to work closely and routinely via computer networks in real time.

Manufacturing in the Twenty-First Century

In a recent Japanese study involving some major corporations and universities, experts tried to identify what changes the twenty-first century will bring for manufacturing and what are the essential characteristics of manufacturing required to maintain their competitiveness.[20] It was concluded that the future will bring major changes in the business environment. In the future, competitiveness will depend on the development of "a new type of make-to-order manufacturing." The key ingredient will be flexibility—the ability to respond quickly to changing markets, to accommodate customization, to introduce new products rapidly, and to implement new production processes. Electronic links, flexible production systems, and the breakdown of corporate bureaucracy are considered essential. The study has identified a number of desired characteristics:

- A shift away from large, complex manufacturing plants toward smaller factories capable of responding quickly to local market demands
- Abandoning of mass production methods in advanced industrial nations in favor of low-volume production of an increased variety of customized products
- Greater emphasis on flexibility
- Continued shortening of product life cycles
- Products featuring higher value-added content, including an increase in the amount of software relative to hardware
- More intellectual input from all employees
- Increased "networking" of manufacturing resources, including materials, information, and capital
- Greater emphasis on "amenities" for workers—to make manufacturing jobs more appealing.

As you may notice, these characteristics are very much in-line with what has been discussed previously in this section.

Globalization of Manufacturing Operations

To compete effectively in today's global competitive environment, an MNC has to use an ap-propriate global plant configuration; this requires considering where to locate plants, what each plant should produce, and how to coordinate their activities. Multiple-plant MNCs should decide whether to establish or expand their international manufacturing base. This is a strategic decision, because it binds the company for a long time and impacts the company's revenues and costs significantly. It is also a very complex decision because of the many factors involved. Variations in tariffs, costs of inputs, proximity to markets, fluctuation in currencies, and access to foreign technology are but some of the factors to consider. A company has to determine how and what network of global plants will help to achieve its strategic goals.

Basic Approaches to Plant Location

Plant location decisions are strategic in nature and commit the MNCs to long-term direct investments. A firm may choose to locate all of its manufacturing facilities in the home country or it may locate some of its operations abroad. The most common reasons for establishing factories abroad are access to low-cost production input factors, proximity to market, and access to technological resources. In the following we will elaborate on these choices.

Located in home country   The simplest approach, of course, is to produce everything at home and then export to other markets. In the past, Japanese firms followed this strategy very successfully in product lines ranging from TV sets to automobiles. The advantages of such an approach are that it is simple to manage and that the manufacturing firm does not have to face the pitfalls of overseas operations. In the initial stages of growth, when the size of the market and the firm's market share are relatively small, such a strategy will work better.

Located in host country   As the firm grows, often it has to establish an international manufacturing base to compete effectively. Moreover, protectionist pressures can force the firm to establish operations overseas, as Japanese auto makers had to establish manufacturing fa-

cilities in the U.S. Consideration of protectionist pressures is one of several reasons for establishing manufacturing operations in host countries.

Access to low-cost production input factors
The low cost of production has motivated many
MNCs to establish some operations in foreign
locations. Although proximity to cheaper raw
materials and energy have been the incentives
for some firms to relocate, the primary reason
for most companies has been the access to
cheaper labor. To use this strategy, companies
typically produce the core products and components that are considered essential to their
success in the home country close to their headquarters, engineering, and R&D, with the peripheral components being produced overseas.
The core components are generally capital and
technology intensive, and the peripheral components are labor intensive. In the 1970s and 1980s,
many American companies moved some, or
even all, of their operations to Far Eastern and
Latin American countries to take advantage of
lower production input costs. More recently,
through the maquiladora (companies that are located along the U.S. border in Mexico) operations, U.S. companies use this strategy to establish plants close to the U.S.–Mexico border.
Then they produce more technology-intensive
components in the United States and send the
components to the Mexican sister plants for the
more labor-intensive operations.

Of course, the primary advantage of this approach is the lower cost of production. It is argued that to compete with foreign companies,
U.S. manufacturers should try to lower their
costs by locating some operations overseas.
Also, consumers will benefit, because this approach will result in lower costs of final products. To relocate the operations for a product or
a component successfully, certain requirements
must be met. First, the production input cost differential should be large enough to justify the
move. It is important to account for all relevant

Manhole Covers for America

In an industrial warren of narrow dirt alleys, fetid swamps and festering slums so clogged
with people, cows, goats, pushcarts, rickshaws, trucks and honking buses, not far away from
the lights of Calcutta, enterprising Indians are doing their part in international business.

Under the watchful eyes of Biswa Karma, the Hindu god of industry, that adorns each
factory, hundreds of small foundries churn out thousands of different iron castings. Here,
workers earn one-tenth their U.S. counterparts and are happy that their wages can pay for a
meager living for the whole family. Jaidev, a skinny, dark-eyed, energetic man is one of
them. He makes manhole covers for America. Around him in a gritty, tinroofed foundry,
hundreds of other workers are molding, chipping, grinding, brushing, polishing and painting manhole covers labeled "City of Dallas," "Fresno County Sewer," "Hartford County,"
"City of L.A.," and "Austin Texas Sanitary Sewer."

Mr. Jaidev's foundry along with a whole host of other Indian foundries are locked in a
fierce competition with the foundries from Brazil, China, Canada and Mexico, to win the
hearts of American buyers of manhole covers. "It is a tough business," complains Raj
Katawala, a foundry manager, "we have to put up with many restrictions to do business with
the U.S. Not only are we barred from certain segments of the U.S. market, such as the federal highway projects, we have to compete with Chinese who do not know the cost of anything. They just find our prices and lower theirs."

Source: J. P. Sterba. "The Manhole Cover Is a Thing of Beauty to Howrah, India." *The Wall Street
Journal* (November 29, 1984) 1, 29.

costs, including the cost of additional transportation required. Second, as the product is removed from the headquarters, R&D, and the customers to a distant location, the customer contact and engineering support diminish. Therefore, further improvement of the product or the manufacturing process will be very limited, if any. Thus, the component or product should be a mature one with high-volume demand and stable product design and manufacturing process.

Some experts, considering more recent trends, argue against manufacturing offshore. In fact, in a reversal of the earlier trend, some companies are bringing their operations back to the United States. Several factors explain this new trend. The savings in labor cost is no longer substantial. Adjusted for inflation, the U.S. workers' wages have essentially stood still since the late 1960s, while pay has increased elsewhere. According to the Bureau of Labor Statistics, Germany's wages have increased from 74 percent of America's in 1985 to 144 percent in 1990, and Japan's have moved from 50 to 87 percent.[21] If we consider the fact that workers in less developed countries are typically less productive, need more training, and lack the industrial culture, the wage difference becomes even less important. Furthermore, productivity improvements in manufacturing operations have made labor costs less significant. Because of more automation, better product and process design, and continuous improvement, the labor content in most products is shrinking. According to a survey of manufacturers, labor represents only 15 percent of the cost of making a product. For most electronic items it is 5 to 10 percent.[22] Therefore, wage savings are unlikely to have a major impact on total cost. Moreover, as discussed before, speed of production and quick response to the customers' needs have become key competitive advantages. Having part of the operations offshore clearly slows the company's ability to respond quickly to the customers. Also, a related factor is the popularity of

JIT. With JIT, it is more desirable to have suppliers located close to the factory, so they can make frequent deliveries of small shipments. Similarly, fast product development is a key competitive factor in today's highly dynamic manufacturing environment. Locating engineering in Silicon Valley and the factory in Taiwan does not allow for the close and frequent interactions needed among the designers and manufacturing engineers to accelerate product development. Finally, patriotism plays a role. Concerns for the large U.S. trade deficit and decrease in U.S. manufacturing employment have encouraged some companies, such as Wal-Mart, to favor U.S.-made products. While some U.S. firms are moving operations back home, many Japanese firms, recently, have moved their manufacturing operations abroad because the costs of manufacturing in Japan have markedly increased due to the highly elevated value of the yen.

Proximity to the market. Many manufacturers establish operations overseas to be closer to their customers. Spreading the international manufacturing base often leads to better customer service. It enhances their long-term business relations with the customers. It is a clear sign of their commitment to that market. This proximity leads to greater interaction with customers that will increase the manufacturer's ability to respond quickly to the customers' needs and to better customize the product to their exact specifications. It also improves deliveries and reduces transportation costs. Proximity to the customers is essential, particularly for bulky or heavy products, such as construction materials.

Companies can satisfy some demands of local government and gain certain benefits by locating manufacturing plants in their country. For example, some companies have received subsidies to locate in a particular area, others have received tax exemptions, and still others have received protection from imports. Furthermore, manufacturing inside a country eliminates the trade restriction risk. In fact, the rise of trade barriers will enhance the position of the company as it limits the competition from those companies located outside. Moreover, when a market is served from a manufacturing operation inside the country, production costs and sales revenues are denominated in the same currency. This reduces the risks related to currency and price fluctuations. The significant increase in the value of the yen since 1986 has reduced the ability of many Japanese companies to compete overseas.

Finally, by locating manufacturing operations in small but developing markets, a company can preempt the competition. Through accumulating local experience, gaining customer confidence and loyalty, and favorable treatments and permits from local government, the company can maintain a high barrier to entry for others. As the company grows with the market, it does not entice others to risk raiding such a stronghold. Many tobacco factories, tire factories, and breweries have used this strategy effectively.

Access to local technological resources. This factor has become increasingly important in the last decade, due to changes in the international business environment. The United States is no longer the undisputed industrial and technological leader of the world. Japan and Western Europe have caught up with and, in some cases, have surpassed the United States. As a result, in some industries, American manufacturers can learn from their competitors in those countries. Therefore, it is argued that world class manufacturers should operate in all three major industrial centers of the world; i.e., Western Europe, North America, and Japan and the newly industrialized countries of the Far East. Companies operating in these three centers have technologies and employees of comparable sophistication and will simultaneously and independently be developing new products, innovations, and technologies as by-products of meeting their local customers' needs. By being present in these three centers and having access to the sources of improvements, a manufacturer can almost surely have superior products and

operations compared to those companies operating only in one center.[23] Some American manufacturers were caught by surprise when they faced Japanese competition, because they were totally ignorant of the technological developments in Japan. Experts believe that the U.S. auto industry would be very different today if the auto manufacturers had had an earlier presence in Japan as they did in Europe.

Integrated Manufacturing Operations

The majority of the companies with an international manufacturing base, using the approaches discussed in the previous section, run their manufacturing operations located in different countries fairly independently of each other. More recently, many have argued for the use of an integrative approach. Such an approach defines the strategic role of each factory in the network and coordinates overall operations to take advantage of their synergies and thus leads to higher performance. There are three types of integrated approaches: rationalized, coordinated, and strategic.

Rationalization
"Rationalization means shifting from a set of local-for-local plants, each serving its own national market with a broad product range, to an integrated network of large-scale production-specialized plants serving the world market."[24] Instead of multiproduct-multistage plants independently serving a national market, production becomes centralized; and plants become specialized in manufacturing only a certain component, model, or product line for the worldwide market. Only a few components or products are manufactured in each plant, but in very large volumes. Rationalization requires development of a single worldwide product line.

The primary benefits of rationalization are greater efficiency and lower costs resulting from taking advantage of economies of scale, more efficient use of resources, and the elimination of the duplication of efforts and units. Rationalization is most appropriate in mature industries with highly standardized and stable products. The more similar the competitors' products are, the more important the price will be in influencing the customer's choice. High standardization and stability of the product will increase the desirability of the rationalization approach, and will lead to lower prices that are crucial in such an industry. Rationalization must seriously be considered if the production process is highly sensitive to scale economies; that is, higher production volumes will yield much lower production costs. Ford Motor Company, for example, is moving in the direction of higher rationalization. It is reorganizing its decades-old structure, in which Ford North America, Ford of Europe, and, more recently, Ford Asia/Pacific operated as quasi-independent car companies. It will put major functions such as product development, sales, and purchasing under one executive with authority to think and act globally. This move centralizes the authority and greatly diminishes the autonomy of the geographic groups. Alexander J. Trotman, Ford's CEO, maintains: "We want to be a global company in primarily product development, manufacturing and purchasing to optimize the strength Ford has in various parts of the world."[25] The new structure is designed to avoid costly duplication of efforts in different parts of the world and to improve efficiency.

However, rationalization is not recommended for all companies, particularly when the company operates in an industry where customers' needs and preferences are substantially different between countries, transportation costs are disproportionately high, or a higher operating scale does not lead to significant cost savings.

Coordinated global manufacturing   As we have noted, many companies with an international manufacturing base might find rationalization inappropriate for their operations. However, to achieve and maintain their competitiveness they need to coordinate all their global operations. Proper coordination can result in higher efficiency of operations and effectiveness in taking advantage of global opportunities. The key challenges are to meet the need for rationalization and the need for expanding the manufacturing base in order to meet specific local market requirements.

Greater coordination improves the ability of the company to share information and resources among its operations in different countries. Sharing information about technology, manufacturing, products, and markets is essential. Proper coordination enhances the ability to transfer technology improvements developed at one plant to other similar plants, to adopt a product developed in one market to other markets, or to copy an effective manufacturing practice in other plants. Improved coordination enhances resource utilization. For example, the ability to schedule one plant to ship products to customers of similar plants in other countries requires a high level of coordination. Unless the plant has the flexibility to produce a variety of products, a key requirement is that the products made in different plants be interchangeable to customers. Achieving the interchangeability of the products, considering local market differences, is only possible through cross-border product development and manufacturing engineering team efforts. Cross-border teams allow employees from facilities in different countries to come together and share their goals, requirements, capabilities, and limitations. This sharing of information can lead to more compatible and coordinated designs for products and plants.

One company that has had great success in moving toward coordinated global manufacturing is Whirlpool. In 1987, Whirlpool was primarily a North American company. In an effort to go global, it purchased the Philips's floundering European appliance business in 1989. Today, it manufactures in 11 countries and markets its products in 120 locations. Many companies have a global manufacturing presence, but Whirlpool through concentrated management efforts has achieved coordinated global operation. Whirlpool's CEO, David Whitwam, states: "Our vision at Whirlpool is to integrate our geographical businesses wherever possible, so that our most advanced expertise in any given area isn't confined to one location or one division. We want to be able to take the best capabilities we have and leverage them in all of our operations worldwide."[26] One example of Whirlpool's success in integrating its global expertise is the development of an award-winning super-efficient refrigerator. To create this refrigerator, Whirlpool used insulation technology from its European business, compressor technology from its Brazilian affiliates, and manufacturing and design expertise from its U.S. operation.

Based on the experience of Whirlpool, to achieve coordinated global manufacturing, a company needs to create a unifying vision. Whirlpool's vision is to be one company worldwide. To keep people moving toward that vision, the company has to create the proper process and structure. At Whirlpool, employee involvement and empowerment were seen as the vehicle to move people with different cultures and backgrounds toward the one-company vision. Line people and managers in different regions are brought together to work on coordination projects. Every year, Whirlpool brings together about 150 of their senior managers to work on the company's vision and strategies and develop coordination projects, called One-Company Challenges. Cross-border committees are set up to work on these projects. Whirlpool's goal is to have cross-border product teams. For example, one team designs strategies for refrigerators, one for ovens, and one for washing machines. Such teams will run operations throughout the world. These teams develop functional and brand objectives and identify the best opportunities and strategies to achieve them.

Communication and interaction among the employees in different countries is essential for effective coordination. Today's telecommunication technologies have facilitated the task. As discussed earlier, development of the informa-

tion superhighway, which is underway in the United States and other developed countries, will permit employees scattered in different countries to work closely and routinely via a computer network in real time. People don't need to sit next to each other to work together. Global competition and technology are changing the way organizations work.

Strategic role of the factory   In an effort to coordinate multisite manufacturing operations, Kasra Ferdows focuses on identifying and explaining the role of a particular factory in the competitive strategy of a firm. He has developed a framework that is presented in Figure 11.1.[27] The framework is based on two dimensions: the primary reason for establishing an overseas site, and the extent of technical activities at that site. Using these two dimensions, six types of factories have been identified.

Offshore factories.   These factories are established to take advantage of cheap local production inputs. The basic characteristic of these plants is that managerial investment in the plant is kept to the minimum needed to run the plant. Not much product or process engineering goes on at the site. The operation data is reported to the headquarters and headquarters basically makes the strategic decisions. Maquiladora plants set up in Mexico are examples of offshore factories.

Source factories.   The primary reason for establishing these factories is also to have access to cheap production resources. But they house more managers, engineers, and technical staff. They become the technical center for a specific activity, process, or product; and a provider of information to other factories. For example, the Apple Computer's plant in Singapore is a source factory. It supplies assembled printed circuits to other Apple factories. It is specialized in production of these components, and some advanced engineering work for this process is done there.

Server factories.   These factories are set up to supply a local market. Like the offshore fac-

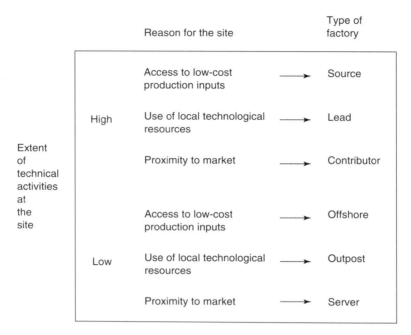

Figure 11.1   The Role of International Factories

tories, the investment in managerial and engineering talent is kept to the minimum essential. However, they have more autonomy for managing the flow of material and information between the factory and its suppliers and customers. A good example is a soft drink bottling plant in a developing country.

Contributor factories. These factories are set up to serve a specific regional market. But their role is broader than a server factory; and they have more managerial, engineering, and technical staff. Like source factories, they become the focal point for the company's efforts for specific activities, components, technologies, or products. They contribute to the company's know-how in that specific area. Nestle's plant in Singapore is an example of a contributor factory.

Outpost factories. These factories collect information for the company. They are located where the technologically advanced competi-

tors, suppliers, and customers are located. The assumption is that presence in such markets provides an efficient means of information gathering. In practice, however, most companies that seek an outpost factory either acquire an existing one or go into a joint venture. Ford's purchase of 25 percent interest in Mazda in Japan was primarily for the purpose of establishing an efficient mechanism for collecting technological information.

Lead factories. Lead factories have a significant role in building the strategic capabilities of the company. They gather technological information not only for the headquarters' use, but for their own use as well. Proximity to technological resources and ample availability of engineers gives these factories a favorable position for the development of specific manufacturing capabilities. Lead factories often have responsibilities for the development of a certain product or process technologies for worldwide application. Hewlett-Packard plants in France, Germany, and the United Kingdom are good examples of lead factories. Each plant has responsibilities for many technical activities beyond production.

This model provides management with a framework for identifying and tracking the strategic role of the factories. It can also guide management in the choice of an appropriate organizational design and communication system for the factory network.

The Factory as a Campus

What are the future trends in factories established abroad? The strategic role of the factory discussed earlier may imply the singularity of purpose for a given factory. On the contrary, an MNC may assign more than one strategic role to a given factory. The factories of the future may have an expanded strategic role. Given such a scenario, what will be the mission of such factories? What do the MNCs expect from these factories? Ferdows suggested that, in the future, factories established abroad will resemble a "campus" more than a factory.[28] These factories aggressively build direct links to suppliers, the distribution chain, engineering, research and development, labor unions, and environmental agencies. Although these factories are a very important part of the MNC operation and produce key products, they are more than manufacturing outlets. In Ferdows' words:

In one way or another, more than production seems to be going on at these sites. The organizations in these factories seem to be more extrovert than the typical factory—with more direct links to outside the factory. More process engineers, development engineers, sales technicians, computer experts, production planners, purchasing managers, maintenance mechanics, human resource professionals, distribution and shipping managers, quality management professionals, cost accountants, and other "overhead employees" seem to be working on these sites. The atmosphere is dynamic, interesting and challenging—precisely the conditions needed to attract

highly qualified individuals . . . . [T]he scope of what they can do in the factory is not limited . . . neither the factory's strategic charter nor the culture in the company is putting tight constraints on their potential value in the company.[29]

The factory aims to remove the barriers between itself and its environment, both inside and outside the company. IBM, NCR, Fujitsu, and Sony, to name just a few, already have such factories around the globe. Of course, the mission of these factories involves building a world class specialty—a useful competency. The exact nature of this competency ideally should be kept fluid and self-correcting, so that the factory can grow into its chosen area of competency gradually. A global manufacturer must have well-run factories, but these factories can be regarded as "campuses" where both production and learning take place, and where production assignments serve as learning opportunities, and the knowledge thus amassed buttresses the MNCs' competitive position.

Conclusion

Global competition has significantly altered the manufacturing environment. As a result, the manufacturing environment is much more dynamic and complex. To succeed, a manufacturing firm needs to develop and maintain operational capabilities that are flexible enough to meet the customers' needs quickly, efficiently, and with high quality. Many firms develop such capabilities through the adoption of world class manufacturing practices such as total quality management, just-in-time production systems, employee involvement and empowerment, factory automation, and strategic outsourcing.

A key challenge for companies such as Xerox, Ford, and Whirlpool, which have manufacturing bases in many countries, is to meet the need for scale and specialization as well as the need for flexibility and adaptability to the local market requirements. Such companies need to integrate and coordinate their scattered manufacturing operations in order to achieve the highest level of efficiency and flexibility.

Discussion Questions

1. American manufacturers no longer command the dominant position they held for a couple of decades following World War II. Why?
2. What are major changes in the global manufacturing environment that have affected U.S. firms?
3. World class manufacturing involves certain practices. Briefly describe these practices.
4. Differentiate between total quality management and just-in-time production.
5. Explain the "pull system" in a just-in-time production system.
6. What is *kanban*?
7. Briefly describe the role of group technology and multifunctional workers in just-in-time production.
8. Some have argued that outsourcing results in the hollowing of American companies. Explain your position regarding this argument.
9. What are the benefits of locating factories in the host countries?
10. What integrative choices are available to MNCs that locate their factories abroad?
11. According to Kasra Ferdows, factories located abroad can contribute to the competitive strategy of the MNCs in several ways. This creates six types of factories. What are the six factory types?
12. What are the characteristics of a factory that resembles a campus more than a factory?

Endnotes

1. T. A. Stewart. "The New American Century—Where Do We Stand." *Fortune* (Spring–Summer 1991), Special Issue, 12–23.

2. R. B. Chase and N. J. Aquilano. *Production and Operations Management* (Boston, MA: Irwin, 1992), 61.

3. T. A. Stewart. "Brace for Japan's Hot New Strategy." *Fortune* (September 21, 1992), 64.

4. R. J. Schonberger. "Is Strategy Strategic? Impact of Total Quality Management on Strategy." *Academy of Management Executive*, 6, no. 3 (1992), 80–7.

5. R. J. Schonberger. *World Class Manufacturing* (New York: Macmillan Free Press, 1986), 229–36.

6. K. Fatehi-Sedeh. "Conversion to Just-In-Time Production System." *The Journal of Behavioral Economics*, 13, no. 2 (1984), 111–33.

7. P. S. Adler. "Time-and-Motion Regained." *Harvard Business Review* (January–February 1993), 97–108.

8. Fatehi-Sedeh. "Conversion to Just-In-Time Production." 130–1.

9. Adler. "Time-and-Motion Regained." 99.

10. M. Attarian. "The Automated Factory." *Business Horizons* (May–June 1989), 81.

11. Stewart. "Brace for Japan's Hot New Strategy." 68.

12. G. Bylinsky. "The Digital Factory." *Fortune* (November 14, 1994), 92.

13. B. Dumaine. "The Bureaucracy Buster." *Fortune* (June 17, 1991), 38.

14. S. Tully. "The Modular Corporation." *Fortune* (February 8, 1993), 114.

15. Ibid.

16. J. A. Byrne. "The Virtual Corporation." *Business Week* (February 8, 1993), 102.

17. R. A. Bettis, S. P. Bradley, and G. H. Hamel. "Outsourcing and Industrial Decline." *Academy of Management Executive*, 6, no. 1 (1992), 7–22.

18. Tully. "The Modular Corporation." 114.

19. W. H. Davidow and M. S. Malone. *The Virtual Corporation* (New York: Harper Collins Publishers, 1992).

20. J. H. Sheridan. "A Look at the 21st Century?" *Industry Week* (November 20, 1989), 38–9.

21. E. Faltermayer. "U.S. Companies Come Back Home." *Fortune* (December 30, 1991), 107.

22. C. C. Markides and N. Berg. "Manufacturing Offshore Is Bad Business." *Harvard Business Review* (September–October 1988), 117.

23. T. Flaherty. "International Sourcing: Beyond Catalog Shopping and Franchising." In K. Ferdows, ed. *Managing International Manufacturing* (Amsterdam, The Netherlands: Elsevier Science Publishers, 1989), 96.

24. Y. L. Doz. "Managing Manufacturing Rationalization Within Multinational Companies." *The Columbia Journal of World Business* (Fall 1988), 82.

25. P. Ingrassia. "Ford Realigns with a System of Global Chiefs." *Wall Street Journal* (March 31, 1994), A3.

26. R. F. Maruca. "The Right Way to Go Global: An Interview with Whirlpool CEO David Whitwam." *Harvard Business Review* (March–April 1994), 136.

27. K. Ferdows. "Mapping International Factory Networks." In *Mapping International Manufacturing*. 3–21.

28. K. Ferdows. "Why Manufacture Abroad: Moving Beyond the Production Benefits." Working Paper, School of Business, Georgetown University, July 1993, 12–13.

29. Ibid.

SONY IN AMERICA

WILLIAM A. STOEVER

Akio Morita and a friend founded Tokyo Telecommunications Company (name translated) in Tokyo in 1945 and incorporated it in 1946. It manufactured communications equipment for Japanese telephone and telegraph companies and for the national railroad. From the beginning it stressed quality production and heavy investment in R&D. It started research on consumer goods in 1947 and brought out its first product, a tape recorder, in 1950. It brought out a transistor radio in 1955 and a pocket-sized version in 1957; the latter became its first export product and was quite successful in the U.S. and Europe. It introduced the world's first fully transistorized television set in 1959.

International Expansion

The company's early successes in exporting, combined with the Japanese government's drive to increase exports, stimulated its efforts to internationalize. It changed its name to Sony in 1958 because it wanted a shorter name that would be easier for foreign customers to remember. It began establishing overseas subsidiaries and joint ventures in 1960 and expanded rapidly. Among the most important were:

- established Sony Corporation of America (originally a marketing company) in 1960 (U.S.A.)
- incorporated Sony Overseas S.A. in 1960 (Switzerland)
- established Sony Tektronix Corp. in Japan as joint venture with Tektronix Inc. to produce oscilloscopes in 1965 (U.S.A.)
- set up Sony (U.K.) Ltd. in 1968 (U.K.)
- established CBS/Sony Group Inc., a 50–50 joint venture with Columbia Broadcasting System (CBS) in 1970 to manufacture and market musical equipment in Japan (U.S.A.)
- set up Sony G.m.b.H. (1970) (which became Sony Deutschland G.m.b.H. in 1980) (West Germany)
- established Sony Trading Company in 1972 to identify products manufactured in the U.S.A. and Europe and market them in Japan
- established its first manufacturing facility outside the Orient in San Diego, California, in 1972 to assemble television sets (U.S.A.)
- set up Sony France S.A. in 1973 (France)
- established Sony Eveready, Inc. in Japan in 1975 as joint venture with Union Carbide

Corp. to import and sell Union Carbide's high-performance dry cells (U.S.A.).

- acquired Wega Radio and Wega Hi-Fi, a highly reputed manufacturing group in 1975 (West Germany)

- established Sony Prudential Life Insurance Co., Ltd. in 1979 as joint venture (51% owned by Prudential Life Insurance Co. of America) to sell life insurance in Japan

- established Sony/Wilson, Inc. in 1979 as joint venture with PepsiCo, Inc. (U.S.A.) to import and sell Wilson sporting goods in Japan

- acquired hard disk technology and operations from Apple Computer Inc. (U.S.A.) in 1984 to produce hard disks in Japan and market them in the U.S.A.

- Sony Corp. of America acquired Digital Audio Disc Corp. from CBS/Sony Group Inc. in 1985 (U.S.A.)

- entered joint venture agreement in 1985 with Vitelic Corp. (U.S.A.) to obtain Vitelic's proprietary CMOS memory technology in exchange for agreement to manufacture Vitelic products for sale by Vitelic

- acquired CBS Records Inc. and CBS Inc.'s share of CBS/Sony Group Inc. for approximately U.S. $2 billion in 1988 (U.S.A.)

- acquired (bought out) Materials Research Corporation in 1989 (U.S.A.)

- purchased all the outstanding common stock of Columbia Pictures Entertainment, Inc. and of the Guber-Peters Entertainment Company (a Columbia affiliate that produced movies and TV fare), for approximately $3.6 billion and assumption of $1.5 billion of Columbia's debt (1989) (U.S.A.)

- Sony Music Entertainment Inc. (SMEI; formerly CBS Records) established Columbia House Company as 50–50 joint venture with a subsidiary of Time-Warner Inc. (U.S.A.) to market music and home-video products in the U.S. and Canada (1991)

Over the years Sony also set up 100% subsidiaries or joint ventures in Australia, Austria, Belgium, Brazil, Canada, Denmark, Hong Kong, Italy, Korea, Malaysia, Netherlands, Panama, Saudi Arabia, Singapore, Spain, Taiwan and Thailand.

These companies show an evolution in Sony's strategy over the years.

- Its first overseas subsidiaries were marketing organizations to sell products manufactured in Japan.

- Its early joint ventures were for the purpose of obtaining technology for its home plants.

- It set up its *sogo shosha* (Sony Trading Company) partly to diversify and partly because its overseas representatives found some good-quality foreign products it could sell back home. It could channel these products to its growing chain of retail outlets (which eventually reached 8,000) and eliminate middlemen's commissions. This move also helped it deflect growing criticism of Japan's closed market.

- Its first overseas manufacturing facilities were necessitated because upward revaluations of the yen, a reaction against the flood of Japanese goods, and the possibility of protectionism threatened to make exports from home uncompetitive. Later overseas manufacturing was to get closer to its markets and to find the lowest-cost production locations.

- Many later acquisitions and joint ventures were for product diversification.

- Some later acquisitions of foreign companies were to gain additional returns on technology it had developed. Materials Research Corp., for example, had been foundering until it obtained an infusion of capital, technology, R&D and market credibility from Sony's buy-out.

In 1991 Sony had a total of 16 manufacturing plants: nine in Japan, four in Europe, and three in the U.S.A. Its sales breakdown was 29% in the U.S., 28% in Europe, 26% in Japan, and 17% in the rest of the world.

Marketing Philosophy

Sony has always been product-driven and indeed has no market research facility. It allows its R&D and product people to follow their heads and develop the products they want to develop; it believes these are the products that will sell. One such product developed without any prior market research was the Sony Walkman, a small radio with earphones that could be carried in a person's pocket or belt and played in public places while doing other activities; it was a notable success. Morita once said, "We don't market products that have already been developed; rather, we develop markets for the products we make." The company is willing to sell off (or write off) investments in products that "don't work."

Sony has several times demonstrated its willingness to cut prices and profit margins in order to build market share. For example, in Fall 1990 it cut prices on automobile compact disk players, which had been a major profit generator. An executive of an American competitor surmised that this was preparatory to pruning its line to make room for new products. Another said it should also help solidify Sony's brand name and image.

Long-Term Perspective

Sony has been willing to take a long-term view of its investments in both R&D and production facilities. Sometimes its thoroughness and deliberate pace have worked to its disadvantage, however. For example, it started developing its betamax system for video-cassette recorders (VCRs) in 1960 but didn't bring it to market until 1976. Then it hoped to reserve the market for itself and so it failed to license the tape technology to other manufacturers. Soon thereafter its archrival Matsushita Electric Co. brought out

VCRs using the VHS system, which it licensed widely and which eventually became the industry standard. Although many observers considered Sony's system superior, it never captured more than about a sixth of the market and ceased production in 1986. The company ended up having to write off a large portion of its R&D investment in the product.

The Question of Cheap Labor

An ongoing question at Sony was whether to open production facilities in less-developed countries (LDCs) in order to take advantage of cheap labor. Mexico was one of the countries that had approached the company to offer subsidized plant sites, tariff exemptions for components for products to be re-exported, and subsidies for training of labor. Such an offer would be especially attractive for products that had reached life cycle maturity, such as Sony's core of consumer electronics. But the company's top management was concerned about difficulties in rapidly imparting its product and technology innovations, maintaining its quality edge, and preserving its top-market image. It was especially concerned that products manufactured or assembled in Third-World countries might damage the reputation of the ones originating in Japan and other industrialized countries. Thus when it announced plans in 1990 to expand existing capacity and open new plants in Singapore, Malaysia and Thailand, these were mainly to serve internal markets in Southeast Asia. Sony also wasn't convinced that LDC assembly plants would insulate it from the harmful effects of currency fluctuations, especially at times when the yen was strengthening. As a generalization, its Japanese managers were more reluctant than its foreign managers to entertain the possibility of LDC production.

Management Problems

Sony's overseas top management was all Japanese until 1972, when the company concluded it would have to internationalize its outlook and management practices. One of its first foreign top executives was an American, Harvey Schein, who became president of Sony Corp. of America. However, this and other non-Japanese appointments created some problems. The foreign executives had been accustomed to taking charge and making rapid, more-or-less unilateral decisions, and they chafed when they had to clear their major moves with Tokyo headquarters, especially since decisions there were made by the slow collegial *ringi* process. There were also communications problems between headquarters and the foreign subsidiaries, due partly to difficulties of getting timely translations and partly to failures to understand what executives of the other nationality really *meant* by what they said. At any rate, Harvey Schein resigned in 1977. Akio Morita selected another American to replace him, a man considered to be more amenable to cooperating with Japanese executives.

A 1990 survey identified factors causing dissatisfaction among senior American executives in Sony and other Japanese and other foreign-based companies:

- lower compensation than their counterparts in American-based companies;
- less upward mobility—the "bamboo curtain" keeping them out of the top ranks;
- less true decision-making power than their high public profiles would seem to signify—i.e., a concern not to become mere tokens or figureheads;
- the reluctance of Japanese top managers to allow their American middle managers to design and carry out statistically sound market assessments before commiting large sums to development and production of new products;
- the feeling that there was always a Japanese in the shadows double-checking every move by the Americans;
- cultural barriers that are seemingly insur-

mountable regardless how much effort the American executive makes to learn the language and customs of his corporate overlords.

In the late 1980s Sony began trying to create a hybrid Japanese-American structure based largely on personal rapport. It believed the new style could correct deficiencies typical of American managers such as a lack of communication with workers and poor management of pay scales. It also declared that its policy was to be "global localization," under which local companies were to obtain a global perspective on their operations while operating largely on their own and preserving their internal cultures. Materials Research Corp., for example, retained most of its American top management after it was bought out. However, almost all the American executives of Columbia Pictures left their positions shortly after Sony purchased it in 1989. One who remained was the chairman of the television division, Gary Lieberthal, who signed a highly lucrative long-term contract and was appointed a Columbia director in 1990. However, he unexpectedly announced his retirement at the end of 1991 at age 46. Sony officials said the retirement was voluntary.

In 1991 all 18 of the parent company's Senior, Representative and Managing Directors were still Japanese nationals. (These are different classes of directors provided under Japanese law.) Sixteen of its 19 Directors were Japanese, two were American, and one was Swiss. Its highest-ranking American executive was Michael P. Schulhof, vice-chairman of Sony-USA and a Director of Sony Corp.

Stockholders

Sony's stock is traded on the Tokyo Stock Exchange and also on the New York Stock Exchange (in the form of American Depository Receipts, or ADRs) and other foreign exchanges, and 37% of its shares were owned by foreigners. Its dividend payouts have been low by American standards, but American share-holders were willing to hold the stock as long as its growth prospects remained bright. However, American stockholders are quicker to react to the prospect of falling earnings than Japanese, and one disadvantage of having its ADRs traded on the NYSE is that it could come under heavier selling pressure in the face of a threat. In fact its stock fell from a high of 65 and 3/4 in 1989 to a low of 31 and 3/8 in 1991. (See Appendix.)

The Move into the Entertainment Industry

Sony began diversifying into entertainment-related companies in the latter part of the 1980s for several reasons:

- Competition heated up in the consumer electronics business, making it harder for the company to maintain sales and profit growth in its core businesses.
- Morita noted the example of Kodak, which has made much more money on its film than its cameras.

- Even after the market for VCRs and tape and disk players reached saturation, consumers would keep buying tapes and disks.
- Profit margins on those items could run up to 50%.
- The company believed it could find synergy by producing the tapes and compact disks to be played on its electronic hardware.
- It also believed it could create synergy between the Japanese and American entertainment industries by acquiring production companies in both countries, especially since American producers were acknowledged to be the world's leaders in entertainment.
- Finally, it viewed its move into Hollywood as an important test of American receptivity to an expanded Japanese role in U.S. culture.

At the same time Michael Schulhof was engineering the acquisitions of CBS and Columbia Pictures acquisitions, rival Matsushita was sim-

Appendix.
Sony Corporation Income Statements, 1989–1991 (millions of yen, except per-share data)

March 31:	1991	1990	1989
Net Sales	3,616,517	2,879,856	2,145,329
Other revs	74,259	65,386	56,143
Gross op'g revenues	3,690,776	2,945,242	2,201,472
Cost & exps	3,179,211	2,485,300	1,915,183
Op'g Income	511,565	459,942	286,289
Foreign cur. translation	cr37,209	dr39,724	cr4,818
Other income, net.	105,367	91,553	55,200
Total income	654,141	511,771	346,307
Deprec'n & amortization	214,116	164,751	125,790
Misc. deductions	72,753	48,708	22,451
Interest exp	102,681	70,883	32,550
Income tax	146,184	128,017	91,129
Deferred inc. tax	6,214	1,041	4,047
Equity in opers. of affil. cos	cr4,732	cr2,355	cr2,129
Net income	116,925	102,808	72,469
Dividends	16,890	14,155	11,339
Bal. after dividends	100,035	88,653	61,130
ADR Earnings:	$2.03	$1.77	$1.66

ilarly motivated to acquire MCA Corp., owner of Universal Studios, for $6.1 billion in 1990. Some observers criticized both Sony's and Matsushita's acquisitions, saying the Japanese parent companies grossly overpaid for them. They also said the companies were spreading themselves too thin and going beyond their areas of special competence. Sony's core of developing and manufacturing leading-edge electronics and other up-market products was a very different business from recruiting and managing artists and selling music recordings.

At least Sony recognized that its American entertainment business would have to be managed in the American way. Hence Peter Guber, the driving force behind Guber-Peters, was made CEO of a new entity, Sony Pictures. His management style was much more tumultuous and free-spending than that of the buttoned-down engineers and accountants who ran the parent company and most of its subsidiaries. He spent over $1 billion on movie and TV production in his first two years, gambling that such movies as "Hook," "Bugsy Siegel," and "Prince of Tides" would take in hundreds of millions, enough to cover the multimillion-dollar compensation to stars like Dustin Hoffman, Madonna, Jack Nicholson and Warren Beatty and still have something left over for the company to cover its costs and show a profit. He also started plans for a "Sonyland" theme park similar to Disneyland.

The Situation in Late 1991

As shown above, Sony's major commitments from 1988 through 1991 were almost all in the U.S., where it had invested almost $6 billion to acquire full ownership of CBS Records and Columbia Pictures and to set up its joint venture with Time-Warner. It took on more than $2 billion debt to finance these acquisitions.

Unfortunately much of the world entered a substantial recession just as these transactions were being completed. Demand for audio-visual equipment in Japan was sluggish, and the parent company's export competitiveness was damaged by the continuing high value of the yen, causing its revenues to decline at home. Consumer spending in the U.S. and Europe also fell off sharply, especially for discretionary items. The hoped-for synergy between Sony's Japanese and American entertainment businesses was very slow to materialize. Vigorous discounting by competitors in the U.S. and Europe drove down prices and profits. Sony was especially vulnerable to such declines because of its heavy debt service payments, and its net income fell 5% in the quarter ending in June 1991. The company's financial officers imposed measures designed to cut costs by 10%, and they told Guber to shelve the plans for the Sonyland theme park.

Discussion Questions

1. Sony's Viewpoint

   a. What are the pros and cons of Sony's international diversification strategy?

   b. Is Sony's marketing philosophy suitable in the U.S.? Should the corporation set up a formal market research facility in the U.S.? Should it adopt American-style market research techniques here?

   c. Should Sony start up manufacturing facilities in Mexico or another less-developed country (LDC)? Why or why not?

   d. Can the company successfully create a hybrid management style suitable for its American operations? What should it do about the problems of finding, acculturizing and retaining top executives in its American subsidiaries?

   e. Were Sony's acquisitions of CBS Records and Columbia Pictures a good strategic move? Did the corporation do an adequate assessment of the American entertainment market before making these acquisitions? What should it do about the financial problems related to the acquisitions?

f. What other problems was the company facing at the end of 1991, and what should it do about them?

2. The American Viewpoint
   a. Should American companies like Tektronix and Apple sell or license their technology to Japanese or other foreign companies like Sony who intend to use it to produce products at home for sale in the U.S.?
   b. Should companies like Vitelic be allowed to use their technology to produce products in Japan or other foreign companies for sale in the U.S.?

P I Z Z A   H U T
I N   M O S C O W:
T H E   P R E - C O U P
V I S I O N

SANDRA HONIG-HAFTEL
RONALD L. CHRISTY

Introduction

Pizza Hut opened two restaurants in Moscow in what was then the USSR in September of 1990. This was the outcome of a joint venture agreement with the Moscow City Council. Today, the venture is profitable despite operating in a volatile environment where political, monetary, social and economic infrastructures are continuously changing en route to free markets. Since the introduction of *perestroika* (the policies designed to adopt more market oriented approaches toward production and distribution of products and services) change has been progressing exponentially. The attempted political

Some of the data for the writing of this case was adapted and edited by the case writers from "Pizza Moscow," a study commissioned by Pizza Hut International from the London Business School in June of 1991 and co-authored by Assheton Don, Claire Don, Amy Stoner and Andy Rafalat. Additionally, data was collected through personal interviews, surveys, and observations of company documents and archival records. Prepared by Sandra Honig-Haftel and Ronald L. Christy, Wichita State University. Reprinted with permission.

coup which failed in 1991 ultimately resulted in the resignation of Mikhail Gorbachev and the rise of Boris Yeltsin as leader.

PepsiCo Background

Pizza Hut, which had gained the number one leadership position in the pizza food service market, was acquired by PepsiCo in 1977. PepsiCo had developed early formal business ties to the Soviet Union which dated back to 1972. At that time, an agreement was reached to trade Pepsi for Stolichnaya vodka which would be sold by PepsiCo in the West as a means of generating hard currency. Pepsi-Cola has become the major consumer product in the former USSR and is ranked as Pepsi-Cola's fourth largest national market worldwide.

PepsiCo's substantial interests in the USSR, and the company's contacts made at high levels within the Soviet political system, reflected the drive and commitment to the development of the Soviet market from the very top of the company. According to company reports, PepsiCo's Chairman, Donald Kendall, "was himself pushing hard for the opportunity to open restaurants in the USSR in the mid-1980's."

Kendall made some of his first visits to the USSR in the early 50's, introducing the concept of Pepsi Cola to Khruschev and initiating negotiations. The 20 or so years of negotiation and preparation that followed ultimately culminated in Pepsi Cola becoming the widest spread foreign product trademark in the USSR. This history was invaluable in helping the firm establish a full operating business and laid the groundwork for the Pizza Hut venture in Moscow (Exhibit I).

The Early Vision

The restaurant business as it is known in the West and in Europe was culturally alien to the USSR. Kendall had no rules and no recognizable ways of proceeding. There was only a vision and an intention that this thing had to be done. According to Steve Bishopp, Vice President of Finance for Pizza Hut International, Kendall really was the one who sparked the idea. "Don has always been involved with the Soviet Union in business, and saw opportunity to develop business with them, because Pizza Hut was one of the businesses in his corporation when he was Chairman."

An early letter from the Polit Bureau in the Kremlin suggested that the Soviet Union of the mid-1980's did not cater to families. Alcoholism was focused upon as a serious problem and officials were looking for ways to provide a family environment where families could be fed and entertained. Pizza Hut was determined to provide a wholesome non-alcoholic setting, one that could contribute to solving this social problem. The missionary work by Kendall was followed by invitations to Pizza Hut managers to see for themselves what was possible.

In 1985, a team was sent by PepsiCo to evaluate pizzerias in Moscow. A team member observed, "From that very first moment when we got on the plane, we recognized that the conventional rules of business had to be put to one side. We had to look at what we saw with objectivity and common sense to be able to react to it in an unbiased way."

According to Andy Rafalat, then Director of Technical Services for PepsiCo's Eurafme (Europe, Africa, and the Middle East) catering operation, "We all knew that potential customers were there, but we also recognized that the system really didn't allow free enterprise to take place. On that November day (in 1985) it really was the start of an adventure into the unknown, an unknown where there were no points of reference."

With the Pizza Hut team reporting a familiarity with and ready acceptance for pizza, particularly among young people in Moscow, PepsiCo

Exhibit I
Chronology of Events for Start-up Joint Venture

	1972	Agreement reached to trade Pepsi for vodka
September	1987	Letter of intent signed with Moscow city council
	1988	Feasibility studies conducted
February	1989	Contracts signed
	1989	Moscow general manager (Alex Antoniadi) employed
January	1990	Building work began
April	1990	$3 billion trade deal signed
June	1990	Staff fully employed; training began
September	1990	First two restaurants opened
April	1991	Andy Rafalat returned to London

Adapted from Pizza Hut, "Pizza Moscow," 1991.

chose Pizza Hut as the vanguard of the push into the USSR. According to a company document, "Its major attraction was the relatively simple, cheap and widely available nature of most of the ingredients." Flour, tomato paste, oil and many items for the salad bar could all be purchased from Soviet sources.

By early 1987, when joint ventures were permitted in the USSR, Kendall visited the Mayor of Moscow. In September of that year, a letter of intent was signed with *Mosobschepit,* the catering arm of the city council. This was the first joint venture agreement signed between the Soviets and a U.S. company.

Much of the foundation for the eventual success of the negotiations, which were concluded in 1989, is attributed to the single-minded way that Kendall developed his contacts in the U.S., and with Soviet and Eastern European politicians. A company executive observed, "He was a unique man, and the Chairman of a big international company. Yet he always found the time to regularly visit these market places, to make it his business not only to know the leaders, but also to gain an understanding of how those systems were actually working. He had a strong opinion, his own opinion, because he actually saw what was taking place. That was a unique perspective, a chief executive who actually spent time in those markets and understood the problems and really was able to lead his team from the front."

Skilled at networking and making business contacts, Kendall met the former Soviet Ambassador in Washington. "Don was able to meet the man, not only the Ambassador but the man who had a family with him, the man who enjoyed sidling down to the Pizza Hut on a Sunday morning and who was able to share his thoughts and deep perspective of the Russian psyche and mentality."

Contacts were essential and Kendall ensured that invitations were forthcoming from a number of organizations. In the early and mid-1980's few Western business people knew how to establish business contacts in the Soviet Union, then the world's largest government bureaucracy. Kendall secured those contacts and reminded PepsiCo and Pizza Hut executives that they should visit these countries. Kendall's persistence, demonstrated through meetings, extensive contacts and letters to organizations, resulted in the creation of a plan of action for how to do business with the Soviets.

Plan of Action

By 1987, the laws had changed and joint ventures were now permitted. According to Rafalat. "It was now feasible for an organization to work with a Soviet organization and develop something resembling a private enterprise. We started to recognize the importance of having locally driven businesses. . . . We also recognized the importance of 'living off the land,' which meant using local facilities and resources to maximum effect."

In 1987, a letter of intent was signed delineating each partners objectives and expectations for the new joint venture. Early in the planning process, two Moscow restaurants were conceptualized, one taking rubles and the other hard currency. It was planned that the joint venture would maximize local sourcing and would possibly be expanded at a later date.

The operation would generate both a positive ruble and hard currency cashflow. Although rubles could not be converted into the firm's home currency for the benefit of shareholders in the short term but hard currency could, it was thought that the first restaurants would give the company a toehold in a potentially huge market and that "rubles could well become convertible in the longer term." Furthermore, opening the two restaurants was seen as a valuable learning experience of how things actually work in the USSR. The company would be building contacts with Soviet authorities and training a core force of local employees. According to company reports, the media coverage was also an added benefit to Pizza Hut's worldwide operations. PepsiCo's primary motivations were to initiate actions towards "the long-term goal of a significant restaurant presence in this potentially huge market."

Negotiating the Contract

Negotiations begun in 1987 took almost two years to complete. The partners were eager to explore the new opportunities offered by the joint venture, which they regarded at the time as "almost a fashionable thing to do." They were content to be led by Pizza Hut and had little desire to control the business. Yet culture and language became a barrier toward completing negotiations in a timely manner.

"We were talking two different languages whose words conveyed different meanings because we were from different systems where everything was incomparable . . . even dictionaries became to an odd extent useless, . . . Negotiation took close to two years, eighteen months. I think we recognized that they were going to take a long time. . . . How we progressed, how we learned, how once we were negotiating [with] Moscow was changing around the thinking, the laws, the gradual acceptance of pizza *Perestroika* and the market forces."

After the letter of intent was signed in 1987, things did not go smoothly. The partners failed to keep the many timetables set, delayed their planned visit to the UK, neglected to arrange supplier visits for Pizza Hut representatives, failed to arrange translations of many necessary documents, and even told the firm that previously confirmed restaurant sites were now unavailable. There seemed to be a complete lack of willingness or knowledge of how to overcome obstacles. This was viewed as symptomatic of a lack of understanding of how a market-based business worked.

"We had a small, flexible negotiating team. There was Scott, a lawyer who was able to detail the structure of an agreement, presenting op-

tions and scenarios for both us and the Soviets. There was David Williams, our Vice President who was able to bring in his tremendous experience in negotiating joint ventures in different countries. I was very much the local element, spending time in Moscow looking at various sites, learning how Russian operations work, trying to understand the supply structures and what we needed to do. We also brought in our Finance Director when required to produce numbers and calculations. Between us, we had a good balance.

"We found, however, that the Russians approached negotiations very differently. There seemed to be no real seriousness attached to the operation. The negotiating team was frequently being changed. This was so new to them that they really didn't know how to handle a structured negotiation. One of our biggest problems was always negotiating through an interpreter. It really was only through the many days and weeks that we were spending on these negotiations that we really started to appreciate the huge differences and gaps which we would have to recognize and overcome.

"We spent weeks and months negotiating details which in hindsight proved to be totally useless. For example, we negotiated for the number of telephone lines we ought to have for days. When we actually moved to Moscow, these efforts proved useless because there was no power to get a telephone line. None of us really knew how to get these things done. That's just part of doing business in that part of the world. We were all learning."

Restating Problems as Opportunities

Problems were not considered insurmountable by the Pizza Hut team. According to Andy Rafalat, "Failure is not a word used with us. Problems may occur if management in a given venture is weak or inexperienced." Generally, new business opportunities were viewed as arising from technological or market changes. The company viewed itself as more oriented towards developing existing resources than towards the pursuit of new opportunities.

After the Pizza Hut team learned more about the Moscow market, team members felt that success was assured. What may have been perceived as problems by others was constantly restated as an opportunity by Pizza Hut. This consistent philosophy propelled the venture forward. Eventually, the Soviets fulfilled all of the required commitments and the two parties moved towards signing a legal contract. Contracts were concluded in February of 1989. The first two restaurants were planned to open at the end of 1989. The joint venture was to have a Board of six members, three nominated by each partner, and a Soviet Citizen as Director General. The Director General and a Deputy Director General would jointly decide all major issues.

The contracts detailed the partners' roles. Pizza Hut would provide personnel and training and the partners would deal with negotiating local matters such as visas, customs, utilities and supplies. By-laws were also drawn up stating how the partnership would resolve disputes and how the chain of command would operate. A standard franchise agreement was also signed between Pizza Hut and the new joint venture detailing the initial franchise fee at $25,000 and the monthly service fee (royalty) at 4% of gross sales.

Two feasibility studies ran in parallel with the joint venture negotiations. Although many of the early assumptions turned out to be false, these studies succeeded in formulating the basic operating conditions for the venture.

"Pizza Hut was to provide experienced personnel and training, their partners would deal with the local matters such as utilities, visas, customs, and suppliers. The contract also stipulated in what order claims could be made on any hard currency earned in the business. Royalties to Pizza Hut came first, followed by other pay-

ments . . . to PepsiCo before the Soviet party could make claims."

Financing the Venture

The foundation for financing the initial joint venture between Pizza Hut and the Moscow City Council relied upon earlier agreements made by PepsiCo. In 1990, a $3 billion counter-trade arrangement (see Chronology of Events) between PepsiCo and Soviet authorities was finalized. This extended the trade of vodka and Pepsi to the year 2000, called for 25 additional Pepsi plants for a total of 50, and introduced a new component: the building of ten Soviet commercial ships for sale and lease internationally. This barter arrangement set the scene for financing the first two Pizza Hut restaurants.

At market exchange rates, the upfront cost of the project was very low. Pizza Hut was able to pay for the hard currency costs in rubles, acquiring them through a Soviet bank loan and converting them into hard currency at the official exchange rate. The new business was capitalized at $2.96 million, contributed by the partners as follows:

Soviet Party	$000	Pizza Hut	$000
Land/building	1200	Equipment	856
		Plans & drawings	184
Start-up expenses	120	Start-up expenses($)	200
Reconstruction	200	Reconstruction	200
TOTAL	1520 (51%)		1440 (49%)

Strategy and Organization

Andy Rafalat was assigned to Moscow in 1988 as a full-time chief executive. As stated by Rafalat, "By now, I had been with this project three and a half years. Once the realization came that it was going to happen, I think the truth dawned on me that a project has to have a person behind it. Somebody has to lead it, and it was also an automatic that for it to be transformed to reality, I would have to lead it and really own it. Then the realization came that . . . relocation to the Soviet Union would be required.

"We then gave thought to the hiring of key people, how they would be trained both in London and the Soviet Union, and how systems would have to be developed. We would have to tackle supplies and logistics in an area where there was a total lack of any infrastructure that made sense in any commercial way of thinking. There was no business structure in Moscow.

"I told my family that we would be moving to Moscow in the wintertime. The kids had to change schools, we had to find living quarters and learn how to adapt to an environment where shopping and services were unavailable. Finally in February, 1990 the actual move to Moscow took place."

The management strategy was to staff the venture with Soviet personnel. As their abilities strengthened, Rafalat would withdraw and return to London where he was based, focusing more on the potential expansion of the business rather than overseeing day-to-day operations.

A management team was recruited, with Alex Antoniadi as General Manager to instill Pizza Hut's management theory into the system with hands-on responsibility of daily business management. (See Exhibit II.) Alex Antoniadi formerly ran five restaurants in Moscow and brought this experience into the new venture along with his industry contacts and high food and staff quality standards. His mission was to convey the Pizza Hut culture of high standards for cleanliness, quality, staff performance, and service.

Antoniadi accepted a proposal to come to London for training only after he was assured the General Manager's position and allowed to select his own restaurant managers—Boris

Paiken and Sacha Youdin. Antoniadi's high personal work standards helped to permeate Pizza Hut's management standards throughout the venture. A hard worker, Antoniadi quickly became a local celebrity. His long-term associations and Rafalat's persistence in pursuing the venture in combination with ongoing open communications with the partners provided the strategic foundation for effectively managing the partnership relationship. Antoniadi's contacts were also invaluable in helping to obtain approval documents from various state agencies and authorities.

Pizza Hut pursued a *laissez faire* strategy with Rafalat, empowering him with full entrepreneurial operating responsibility. This seemed to be the general style of the firm. As stated by one executive, "While the company tends to carry out as much homework as realistic on new ideas and markets, once they are established, these projects are handed over to small teams or to individuals to guarantee ownership and provide freedom of action for the relevant individual in charge. This ensures that projects have definite sponsors on whom success or failure rests."

Consistent with *laissez faire* philosophy, Rafalat was empowered with the management of the venture and with the objective of moving out as quickly as possible by empowering local people with a sense of ownership and management.

Site Location and Construction of the First Two Restaurants

In 1988, recognizing that site selection was critical, proposed locations for the first two restaurants were evaluated according to the following ideal features:

1. Size—250–300 square meters
2. One level
3. Frontage—10 meter minimum
4. Corner with return frontage

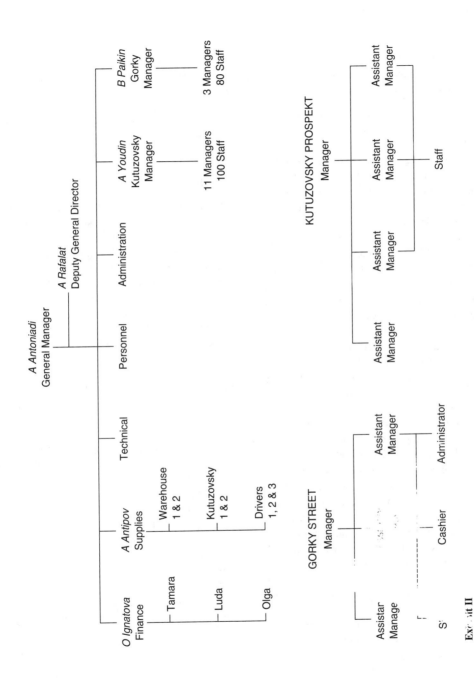

A Antoniadi
General Manager

A Rafalat
Deputy General Director

O Ignatova
Finance

— Tamara

— Luda

— Olga

A Antipov
Supplies

— Warehouse
1 & 2

— Kutuzovsky
1 & 2

— Drivers
1, 2 & 3

Technical

Personnel

Administration

A Youdin
Kutuzovsky
Manager

11 Managers
100 Staff

B Paikin
Gorky
Manager

3 Managers
80 Staff

GORKY STREET
Manager

Assistant
Manager

Assistar
Manage

S

Cashier

Administrator

KUTUZOVSKY PROSPEKT
Manager

Assistant
Manager

Assistant
Manager

Assistant
Manager

Assistant
Manager

Staff

Exhibit II

425

5. Heavy pedestrian flow
6. Parking capacity for automobiles
7. Proximity to offices, shops and apartments
8. Proximity to tourist hotels for hard currency

Early identified sites were rejected and the Soviets pursued tours of low-grade sites. This suggested a lack of will to move the project forward or a genuine ignorance as to the nature of the project. Finally, detailed Pizza Hut location maps were provided and suitable sites for the two proposed Pizza Huts in Moscow would be finalized—one on Gorki Street and the second on Kutuzvosky Prospekt. Preliminary drawings of the restaurants were rendered for both sites and were included in the 1988 Feasibility Study.

Construction began in January, 1990. Both restaurants, although conversions of existing buildings, required considerable work. Soviet builders were initially employed but with little performance success. Forced to turn to a West European contractor with multi-national experience, the partners gave the 6 million dollar construction contract to Taylor Woodrow, a UK company.

"The quality of work demanded by Pizza Hut necessitated a large proportion of imported materials and labor; only 10% of the building materials and none of the finishing materials were sourced locally. The Soviet partners found it hard to understand why the operation should need to import cement, for instance, but delivery times were as much of an issue as the quality of materials. None of the local suppliers were able to respond quickly to demands or to guarantee delivery dates. Local supplies of equipment were also very unreliable. Taylor Woodrow was unable to ensure that a crane, for instance, would be available on a certain date, and the workforce was obliged to flag down drivers of passing machinery and pay them to lift the heavy loads."

Construction crews consisted of people from six countries: the United Kingdom, Sweden, Italy, Portugal, Poland and the USSR. The Western crew members assisted the Soviet builders, training them on various building techniques.

After about eight months of building, the two restaurants opened on September 11, 1990. Considerable fanfare and celebration brought extensive free media coverage of the event.

Sourcing

Although Pizza Hut committed early on to "living off the land," this was sometimes quite difficult. For example, the kitchen equipment had to fit in with Pizza Hut's unique production system and was therefore imported, as were the crockery and restaurant furniture. There simply was no Soviet supplier able to make the product to Pizza Hut's specifications.

"We were told how important it was to get local people involved at each step of the way. The phrase 'living off the land' was very much overused in our negotiation strategy, but every time we said it, it conveyed to us an image of where we were going to find local managers and local people to work in our new venture. We were going to try to localize the supplies as much as we could. And we were going to finalize the concept to every extent possible to get it to run in the country. That really shaped our thinking.

"We started focusing on the sole issue of local supplies. I think that if there was one area that frightened us, it was how to get local sourcing to work. Having seen the disastrous state of most Soviet food factories, the poor controls, storage and distribution, we knew that we were going to have to get right into the food production network. Yet we did not want to do the food producer's job.

"We sent out a clear message to suppliers that we would be willing to pay market prices for their goods in rubles, whatever that market price was. We wanted to negotiate with them. We sent signals of encouragement to the supply community at large that Pizza Hut was open for business, paying market prices for goods.

Pizza Hut gained agreement to initially import all food items with no customs duty, although the intent was to source most of the required products locally over time. This would reduce importation costs over 5 years and increase generation of hard currency. These products would also be marketable as export goods and would generate more hard currency for the USSR. Using local food supplies as much as possible would put the inconvertible ruble currency earned in the ruble restaurants to good use. Aligning costs and sales in the same currency would also minimize the operation's future margin exposure to exchange rate swings. Antoniadi's network of local supplier contacts became crucial to the venture and also made it difficult to recreate the operation outside of Moscow. Outside of Moscow, local recruits would be needed to establish local supply networks to replicate the Moscow structure.

Some suppliers negotiated long term contracts to supply Pizza Hut. Vegetables came from co-operatives. Other products, such as flour, were allocated to Pizza Hut on a centralized basis through the state plans. Although a cheese factory had been identified to produce Mozzarella to Pizza Hut specifications, by winter the quality of the cheese became unacceptable. All cheese supplies had to be sourced from the West, along with some of the meat products, proprietary in-house dough and spice blends. Other products, such as the wooden tables and chairs and Turkish cooking oil, were imported.

The Future

Envisioning the future as one with a possible 5000 units, Rafalat dedicated the success of the venture ". . . to all the visionaries who knew it was possible." Describing the world behind Soviet borders during the mid-1980's, Rafalat said, "It was a world of secrecy, of relatively unknown languages and of cultures that we knew very little about." It was ". . . the unpredictable Wild East, to be avoided by all but the most daring. There were, however, individuals, visionaries, who realized that despite the current situation, the region presented huge opportunities for future generations. These opportunities would yield enormous payback, not only in commercial terms, but also in providing bridges between two cultures, bridges which would bring these contrasting cultures and unknown systems closer."

Now, after the pre-start negotiations and construction, the task ahead was to develop and implement the major operating systems. Employees had to be recruited and trained. Management and control systems had to be developed, and a new financial system—a hybrid accounting system—had to be developed to reflect doing business in two currencies—hard currency and rubles. Rafalat and Antoniadi went to work to put in place systems for employee compensation and rewards, pricing, purchasing, warehousing and distribution, marketing and tracking of sales performance. They were propelled in their mission by ". . . a powerful vision of a chain of restaurants stretching across the Soviet Union, from Odessa to Vladivostok."

T W E L V E

INTERNATIONAL MARKETING MANAGEMENT

Firms can succeed only if they offer the types of products and services that customers want at acceptable prices. Marketing management should enable the firm to accomplish this feat. Similar to other activities of the international operation, international marketing is much more complex than its domestic counterpart. An effective international marketing strategy is built on the knowledge of foreign markets and an understanding of cultural differences among countries. Although modern communication and ease of traveling is shrinking the physical and cultural distances between countries, considerable differences among markets still remains. In this chapter we learn how an international firm can seize the opportunities that these differences could provide. We will learn how activities of market assessment, product development, pricing, promotion, and distribution can be handled on an international basis.

One of the delights—and dangers—of foreign travel is shopping, and nowhere are its pleasures more alluring and its pitfalls more hazardous than in the bazaars, or souks, of the Middle East. Souks are seductive, and it's a rare traveler to any Mideast city who can resist the siren call of the labyrinth of little shops, the friendly greeting of the merchants, the romance of it all. It's the rarer traveler still who, once seduced into the souk, can resist the temptation of a bargain.

For one thing, many bargain hunters have heard the triumphant talk of a friend or acquaintance. A sample story is that of a businessman who told how he purchased a dozen dirty metal plates in the Mecca souk for 30 cents apiece. They turned out to be Napoleon Bonaparte's dinner service, lost since the Egyptian campaign of 1798. But the wary traveler will keep in mind that for every tarnished plate that turns out to be silver there are hundreds of silvery plates that turn out to be tin. Bargaining stories always sound better in the retelling.

Aside from the unfamiliar currencies and multiple exchange rates, the biggest burden on the bargain hunter is the simple problem of desiring the object for which he or she is bargaining. The first axiom of bargaining is that the more you long for an object the more you are likely to pay for it; the less anxious you are to own it, the better price you will get. If the traveler understands these realities— and enters the souk willing to pay a reasonable price for the entertainment value of the bargaining process—souk shopping can be fun. The sport then lies in trying to match wits with the seller, realizing all the while that the house almost always wins.

The souk merchants of the Middle East are always gracious hosts. You may expect that within minutes of entering a shop you will be offered coffee or tea and asked if you know the shopkeeper's cousin, who once worked in Cincinnati. This hospitality is often no less disinterested than that of the wolf who enticed the three little pigs. Still, it's pleasing.

Having made his sale, the souk merchant almost surely will insist on introducing you to his "uncle," who happens to have a shop in the next lane and who will provide merchandise at particularly low prices, for such fine newfound friends.

The merchant will walk you to his uncle's shop himself and make a personal introduction. It is most generous. It is also known as selling a sucker. You have just made the metamorphosis from shopper to merchandise. You may expect to be sold a number of times during an afternoon in the souk, with each merchant collecting a commission from the next.

Here is some bottom-line advice: Enter the souk with no more money than you can afford to lose; bargain as long as you can for every purchase, because the longer the bargaining lasts the fewer bargains you can make and the less money you will lose, and never, ever, admit to anyone what you really paid for anything in a souk.

Excerpted and adopted from P. R. Kann. "Soaked in the Souk: A Sucker's Guide to Bargain-Hunting in the Middle East." *The Wall Street Journal* (January 9, 1985), 25. Reprinted by permission of *The Wall Street Journal*, © 1985 Dow Jones & Company, Inc. All rights reserved worldwide.

Introduction

Visitors to the Middle East who are not familiar with the art of bargaining in bazaars may pay much more than local people would pay for the same items. There is no resemblance between the retail outlets of the United States and the souks of the Middle East. U.S.-based marketing practices, which include fixed prices, self-service, and open spaces in retail outlets, are absent from the corridors of bazaars. For an exotic shopping adventure, visitors may not mind if the prices of the few souvenirs they buy are inflated, as long as the experience is regarded as an entertaining episode. To do the same bargaining on a daily basis, however, could become annoying and be considered a waste of time for the same individuals.

Like foreign visitors caught off guard by charming shopkeepers and bewitched by the se-ductive ambience of the souks, firms may find the environment of foreign markets equally bewildering. Unprepared firms may find it confusing to operate in a foreign environment where most business practices are unfamiliar to them. Unfamiliarity with environmental conditions is a common feature of foreign markets. For many facets of marketing, however, there are considerable differences between developed countries and developing countries. Supporting services that, in most developed economies, are taken for granted do not exist in many developing countries. In most developing countries, market information and economic data either do not exist or are unreliable. Channels of distribution are not fully developed and the infrastructure for marketing promotion is inadequate. Understanding foreign market characteristics can reduce the initial shock that venturing abroad may cause. Advance knowledge of the major similarities and differences of foreign markets is the basis of realistic expectations and fewer disappointments.

Internationalization of Markets

American, European, and Japanese products are found in many places around the world. Regardless of their geographic location, customers have the choice of selecting from a cornucopia of products with many similar features. Traditionally, we have stereotyped countries according to their product specializations. Although some reminiscence of this kind of stereotyping still lingers, we can no longer assume that good quality watches are made only in Switzerland, that the best wines come only from France, or that the Germans make the best cars. Proliferation of technology has created an environment where new products and new competitors emerge from all regions of the world, from developed as well as developing countries. Nowadays, these products are not the exclusive domain of any one country. Excellent watches are made everywhere in the world, including the

United States, Japan, and European countries. Many people who only a few years ago would not have accepted anything but the best French wines, are now finding California wines just as palatable. Both luxury and economy cars are produced in Japan, in the United States, and in many European countries, in direct competition with Germans and with each other.

It also used to be easy to identify a particular multinational company (MNC) with a particular country. The country of origin made a difference between the American, European, and Japanese MNCs. At present, however, many MNCs have outgrown their countries of origin. They are more similar than dissimilar, regardless of "home" country. They use the same technology, produce similar products, and compete in the same markets serving the same customers. They produce products in the location that provides them with the most favorable factors of production, and market their products to customers worldwide. To most large MNCs, national borders do not represent the separation of markets, but inconvenient demarcations on the map. These MNCs have penetrated deeply into the national markets to neutralize the impact of fluctuations in currency exchange rates as well as the possibilities of protectionism by host governments. In the words of Akio Morita of the Sony Corporation, they have achieved "global localization." They are as much insiders as the local companies, and still enjoy the benefits of world-scale operations.[1] In other words, successful MNCs manage their foreign operations in any specific area in very much the same way that local businesses operate in the same area. Often, the only indication of their foreignness is the composition of their board of directors.

No market is an island by itself, and no country has a monopoly on information and technology. Gone are the days when an MNC could sell its leftover inventory of products from its home market to uninformed and eager customers in less developed markets. Today MNCs are catering to a generation of consumers all over the world who are more educated, and therefore more informed, than the previous generations. Telecommunication technology and fast and convenient transportation have the potential to provide consumers with adequate and timely information about global markets. They are aware of the lifestyle, consumption patterns, and product quality and availability in the rest of the world. In the United States, Japan, Europe, and everywhere else, sophisticated, educated, and informed consumers demand quality products at reasonable prices. Customers everywhere reject products that do not meet their expectations of functionality, quality, and price. Increased global competition among firms provides the customers with more choices and alternatives. Because choices and alternatives are available to them, they can demand that products meet their tastes and expectations. Global competition and the pressure to offer quality products at lower prices can be met only if the MNCs' understanding of the markets matches their worldwide flexibility in production and sourcing.

In the midst of cultural diversity among nations, easy access to information and technology are moving world markets toward ever-increasing similarity. The divergent forces of cultural differences are set against the converging forces of technological development and material gains resulting from industrialization. People are using the same products produced by the same MNCs around the globe. The same products that are sold in New Delhi, Lagos, and Tangier are available in New York, London, and Tokyo. These converging forces are not only creating similarities in product availability, they are also moving consumers toward commonalities in preferences. In the world of ever-increasing convergence, firms face competition from the MNCs of developed countries as well as from newcomers from newly industrializing countries. To achieve success in the world of rapid technological changes and intense competition, all the resources and capabilities of the firm must be marshalled. Although there are certain inherent values in product innovation and new product development, success in world markets depends increasingly on an effective marketing program. Technological diffusion has the potential to render most new product development problematic, because imitators can quickly duplicate products and new product features. As a result, marketing management assumes critical importance. In the words of Levitt "success in world competition turns on efficiency in production, distribution, marketing, and management, and inevitably becomes focused on prices."[2] While technological innovations secure a competitive position, effective use of marketing management activities such as sourcing, product positioning, product promotion and distribution, and pricing can permit MNCs to gain a competitive advantage.

International Market Assessment

The first step in international marketing is a determination of the most appropriate foreign markets for the firm's products and services. Where in the world can the firm successfully sell its products and services? What are the major forces that may help or hinder the firm's operations and activities in these markets? What are the potential benefits of entering these markets? What are their sizes and rates of growth? What entry strategies would be most appropriate? What are the similarities and differences of these markets when compared to the MNC's home market? In the following we address these and similar questions regarding international marketing activities.

Environment of International Marketing

Many changes are taking place in world markets. The most profound change is in the pattern of world trade and economic growth. At the present time, most world trade takes place between the developed markets of North America, Europe, and Japan. However, trade between developing countries and developed countries is

growing. Specifically, trade between a number of Asian countries in the Pacific Rim region and the markets of developed countries is rapidly increasing. Moreover, these economies are growing at a faster pace than the rest of the world. The impetus for growth and expansion in these markets began with the emphasis on lower production costs. American and European countries abandoned production of certain products, such as shoes, garments, toys, and television sets, in favor of purchasing them from the low-cost suppliers of Asia. Fueled by exports and foreign direct investment, and powered by technology transfer through MNCs, these countries are now emerging as promising markets of the future. Although, the mature markets of North America, Europe, and Japan offer many business opportunities for the MNCs, the emerging markets of industrializing countries offer potentially greater opportunities. Many developing countries, however, are poor in the infrastructure and support services that are taken for granted in developed countries. Success in these countries hinges on an understanding of the particularities and attributes of their markets and the ability to compensate for inadequacies in infrastructure and support.

In marketing their products and services around the globe, MNCs face cultural, political, and economic differences among the world markets. These differences determine the choice of marketing activities that can generate the best results. If a host market is very similar to the MNC's home market, minimum adjustments are needed in product offerings, promotion, pricing, and placement. Any significant differences, however, necessitate modifications in marketing programs.

Political factors International marketing activities are heavily influenced by political and legal systems. Unlike the United States, in most of the rest of the world, governments are actively involved in directing the economy and regulating business transactions. Firms venturing beyond the U.S. national market should be prepared to deal with bewildering sets of rules and regulations.

Moreover, there are differences among political systems regarding government involvement in business and government attitudes toward business competition. These differences influence MNCs and their marketing activities.

MNCs should also be on the watch for sudden changes in government policies toward foreign businesses. It is not unusual for a change in government—through normal transfer of power or a forced seizure—to result in new business restrictions or prohibitions. In extreme cases, a change in government may cause the total loss of business.[3] Political risks associated with operating in many foreign markets, therefore, necessitate special provisions and contingencies in marketing plans. These provisions may call for staying out of some markets, changing the mode of entry in some, and seeking protection against political risk in others. Protection can be obtained in the form of home government (U.S.) guarantees or private insurance.

In the United States, the role of government and legal systems is to provide protection against abuses to all market participants. Americans expect minimum government involvement in the running of business itself. The common belief is that government cannot handle business operations as effectively and efficiently as private firms. Therefore, it should leave the business to private enterprise. By contrast, in most other countries, irrespective of their political orientations, governments take an active role in business. In these countries, many industries are either controlled by the government or receive significant direction from the government. The differences we observe regarding the government role in business are largely the results of historical experience and market characteristics.[4] In the United States, private enterprise has been successful in providing the goods and services people demand at acceptable prices. At the same time it has generated attractive employment opportunities for society as a whole. Therefore, the public has largely been satisfied with business performance and its role in the society. This in turn has resulted in confidence in the efficacy of private enterprise and a belief that government should stay out of business.

The people of other countries have a different view of government participation in the economic system. In many developing countries, private enterprise has been mostly the domain of members of the rich upper-class and of foreign companies. Government participation in the economic system is seen as an equalizing and liberating force that generates employment opportunities for the masses, while providing goods and service that private business would have rejected as unprofitable ventures. Government is also the protector of the national wealth in some industries (e.g., the extractive industry) that otherwise would have been exploited by the foreigners. In most developed countries, government planning has been responsible for the economic growth of the post–World War II era. This has established a tradition of government involvement in the economy by providing direction and setting national goals. These countries view government participation in many industries as a legitimate role, and as a necessity to protect domestic industries from demise or domination by the foreigners.

With the failure of Communism in the former Soviet Union, however, the wave of privatization of government-operated industries is spreading to many developed and developing countries. Still, the rest of the world does not share the American view regarding the arm's-length relationship between business and government. To succeed abroad, American managers need to make a philosophical adjustment to the reality of the role of government in the economy. They need a realistic assessment of the government-business relationship, and need to recognize that not all government interventions are harmful to MNC operations. To encourage investment in designated industries or regions, governments often provide various incentives to foreign investors. Government involvement in business can also reduce some of the uncertainty and associated risk of doing business. By accepting the government's influence as another factor to deal with, MNCs will be less disappointed or discouraged when faced with restrictions and limitations that are a way of life in many host countries. As Fayerweather suggested:

> To be effective in countries where the role of the government is strong, the U.S. manager must make a philosophical adjustment in his notion of his function as a businessman. Rather than being essentially a private entrepreneur, he is to a degree the executor of government policy. . . .The philosophical adjustment is important . . . for it permits the manager to formulate a sound over-all concept of his relation to government action rather than regarding it alternately as a boon and an annoyance according to inappropriate U.S. standards.[5]

Americans also believe that a competitive mode of doing business is most beneficial to society. Two factors have contributed to the formation of this belief. First, the monopolistic abuses of the 1800s resulted in the passage of the Sherman Antitrust Act and other laws that followed to strengthen the Sherman act. The U.S. antitrust laws made it illegal for firms to carve out markets, set prices, and in any way collude. Second, the size of the U.S. domestic market allowed the efficient operation of several firms in almost all industries. Consequently, the belief in the efficacy of competition became ingrained in the American thought process and a cornerstone of U.S. economic policies. In the rest of the industrialized countries, especially in Europe, where national markets had traditionally been small, most industries could not support the efficient operation of several firms. Business agreements that enabled large-scale operations and economies of scale represented a logical alternative. Therefore, these areas devel-

oped a different view of business parameters. In short, the view that monopolies are not good for the consumers and that competition among businesses should be encouraged is purely American.[6]

Economic factors Because of their revenue-generating potential, international markets are of interest to MNCs. In assessing markets MNCs are interested in the size of the economy, the level of economic development, and growth potential. Paradoxically, however, while the more economically developed countries provide better opportunities for marketing, the growth potential in some newly industrializing countries is more promising. Assessing such markets is not a single process where the marketer considers only the population of the country. Although opportunities for sales are obviously higher in the more populated countries, population per se is not a sufficient measure of market potential. For example, a heavily populated country, such as India, with a low level of income may not be an attractive market for expensive products.

Population and gross national product (GNP) are two indicators of the market size. With some exceptions, GNP indicates the level of economic development. GNP, however, can also be a misleading measure in certain cases such as Kuwait or Saudi Arabia. Because of the huge oil revenues and small population, the GNP per capita figures for these countries are comparable to those of Western Europeans. Their economies are, however, far less developed than the Europeans. A more accurate measure of economic development includes not only GNP, but other indicators such as the infrastructure, literacy rate, and energy consumption. Comparative data on some of these measures for a selected number of developed and developing countries are provided in Tables 12.1 and 12.2. As can be seen from these tables, there is a large difference between developed and developing countries. The figures in Tables 12.1 and 12.2 are representative of market characteristics and the wide gap that exists between developed and develop-

Table 12.1
Economic Data for Selected Countries

	U.S.	U.K.	Japan	Germany	France	Mexico
GNP per capita (U.S. $)	21910	16020	25840	22360	19420	2610
TV per 1000 population	814	434	610	506	400	127
Radio per 1000 pop.	2122	1145	895	949	895	242
Telephone per 100 pop.	50.9	43.4	42.1	67.1	48.2	11.8
Newspaper per 1000 pop.	259	394	566	331	193	127
Cars per 1000 pop.	574.2	362.4	281.6	386.2	415.1	84.3
Energy consumption, kg per capita	10034	5000	4164	5576	3979	1788
Calories per capita per day	3680	3282	2926	3464	3618	2986
Protein, grams per capita per day	111	94	96	103	113	82

	Brazil	Egypt	India	China	Philippines
GNP per capita (U.S. $)	2710	610	360	370	730
TV per 1000 population	204	98	127	27	41
Radio per 1000 pop.	373	322	78	184	136
Telephone per 100 pop.	9.4	4.2	0.7	1.1	1.7
Newspaper per 1000 pop.	4.8	38	127		56
Cars per 1000 pop.	71.1	20.1	1.2		7.4
Energy consumption, kg per capita	780	703	317	837	308
Calories per capita per day	2723	3318	2243	2703	2452
Protein, grams per capita per day	61.7	84.5	55.7	66	56.5

Source: *U.N. Statistical Yearbook 1990/1991* and *World Tables 1993.*

ing countries. Developed countries spend more on food and energy, both in amount and as a percentage of total household expenditures. There are more cars, radios, televisions, telephones, and newspapers per capita in developed nations. These indicate the market potential in developing countries for many products, such as cars and appliances, that have reached the maturity stage in developed countries. The lower level of income, however, is a limiting factor for the sale of many high-ticket products. As the income level in these countries improves, presumably, more consumers will be able to buy these items. Consumers who earn $250 annually, for exam-

Table 12.2
Share of Household Consumption for Selected Developed and Developing Countries (in percent)

	U.S.	Germany	Poland	Iran	Kenya	Mexico
Food	10	12	29	37	38	35
Clothing/footwear	06	07	09	09	07	10
Rent, fuel, power	18	18	06	09	07	08
Medical care	14	13	06	06	03	05
Education	08	06	07	05	10	05
Transportation, communication	14	13	08	06	08	12
Other*	30	31	35	14	22	25

* Includes appliances and other consumer durables.

Source: *Fortune* (Autumn/Winter 1993), 69–72.

ple, can afford Gillette razors; at $500 they can move up to electric shavers; at $1,000, television sets and refrigerators are within their budgets. A $2,000 annual earning makes automatic washers potential purchase items, and at $10,000 they can afford the purchase of inexpensive cars. In China, for example, the most sought-after consumer products during the 1970s were bicycles, electric fans, and sewing machines. In the 1980s, Chinese consumers were buying televisions, refrigerators, and washing machines. The next wave of popular items may be VCRs, motorcycles, and telephones.[7]

Not only are many of these countries the future markets for the MNCs' products, some of them already are on the verge of rivaling developed countries. In the Pacific Rim region, excluding Japan, Citicorp bank of New York, for example, has found a tidal wave of growth that has enabled it to transfer marketing innovations from East to West and back again. Within five years, Citicorp increased its consumer deposits from $2 billion to $12.5 billion, while earnings grew at 40 percent annually. Among innovative products that Citicorp offered in the region are two services aimed at two different segments of the market. For the lower end of the market, it trained the clerks of a drug store chain to accept deposits for Citicorp. At the higher end of the market, for the people who have a minimum of $100,000 on deposit, it offered Citigold service, which provides the customer with separate tellers, swanky premises, and personal attention. It also provides them with many options, including multicurrency accounts that allow them to move deposits among currencies. A Citigold account holder from Singapore, for example, can cash a check in Hong Kong, Riad (Saudi Arabia), or Frankfurt.[8]

Cultural factors   The world markets are characterized by cultural differences and similarities. Religious beliefs, family structure, social relationships, superstitions, and aesthetics are major aspects of culture that impact interna-

tional marketing. Religions influence consumer behavior and marketing practices in two ways. First, religious beliefs profoundly influence moral and ethical standards. Buddhism and Hinduism, for example, emphasize spirituality over materialism. Material gain and earthly possessions, however, are not discouraged by some other religions. Moslems, for instance, consider commerce a noble undertaking. Second, religions determine specific consumer behaviors by prescribing certain purchasing practices, and by the designation of holidays and religious ceremonies. Moslems and Jews, for example, are not supposed to consume pork products. Hindus do not eat beef, and Sikhs (an Indian religious sect) do not shave their beards or cut their hair. Alcoholic beverages are prohibited by Islam. Christmas holidays are a time of high consumption, while market activities slow down considerably during the month of Ramadan in which Moslems fast.

Purchasing patterns are also partly determined by the social roles and relationships prescribed to the members of the society. The fundamental social unit in all societies is the family. Family size varies in different societies. In most developed countries, the nuclear family consists of parents and their children. Most traditional societies have extended families in which grandparents, parents, children, and grandchildren along with other close relatives live together. The purchasing pattern of such a large household is quite different from that of a small family. The extended family is the provider of some services that a nuclear family needs to secure in the open market. Nursing homes and babysitting, for example, are the products of living in the developed countries which are needed by the small nuclear family. Conversely, care for the elderly is the responsibility and obligation of extended family in developing societies. Also, in the extended family, relatives are always around to watch over the youngsters.

The relationship between old and young, male and female, and other members of the society varies by culture and by the level of economic development. In many traditional societies, the husband has the dominant role and the wife has a secondary position within the family. The proper place of the wife is in the home, and her role is to raise the children. Therefore, almost all purchasing decisions needed to run the household are made by the wife. The husband makes most other decisions for the family. Where there are enough employment opportunities for the women, and where working outside the home is not considered improper for them, women are more involved in major purchasing decisions. In most societies, however, certain household purchasing decisions are considered the exclusive domain of either gender. For those decisions, the other partner is informed, consulted, or totally left out of the decision-making process. There is no universal pattern for these types of purchases. To promote their products and target the customers, the marketers have to learn who makes the purchasing decision in each country.

Every culture has its own definitions of and standards for aesthetics. Although mass communication is slowly spreading the Western concept of aesthetics to the rest of the world, there are distinct cultural differences regarding what is considered beauty and good taste. Still,

beauty is in the eye of the beholder. This is especially true when the eyes of the beholders see everything through cultural looking-glasses. While there seems to be a universal appreciation for exemplary works of art and music from various cultures, such as Beethoven's fifth symphony, the architectural beauty of the Taj Mahal and Notre Dame, the paintings and sculptures of Michelangelo, and the Rubaiyat of Omar Khayyám, there are cultural differences regarding aesthetic aspects of many consumer products. Product design, packaging, and promotional programs need to be sensitive to cultural tastes for shapes, colors, music, and aroma. In the same vein, the choice of brand names should consider the cultural implications of names and the nuances of various sounds. General Motors learned a lesson in aesthetics of sounds when it introduced the Chevrolet name brand Nova (star) in Puerto Rico. It had disappointing sales. In search of the reason for the anemic sales of Nova, the marketers learned to their dismay that when pronounced with a Spanish accent, "Nova" sounds like " no va," which translates to "it does not go."[9]

In most cultures, colors convey certain meanings. While black is appropriate for a mourning ceremony in Western societies, white is considered the proper color in some Southeast

Lucky Numbers

Chinese people believe that similar sounds can produce similar outcomes. Therefore the "identity of pronunciation" has become the foundation of many allegedly lucky numbers. Numbers that are pronounced identical to other words are treated similarly. For instance, in Cantonese Chinese, "eight" is pronounced *ba,* which is very similar to *fa,* the prefix of the verb meaning "to become wealthy." So, to them, eight is the most preferred numeral. In an auction of telephone numbers, someone paid 40,000 yuan ($7,200) for one particular seven-digit phone number. It probably included the numerals 168, which sound like "good fortune the whole way." Likewise, in Taiwan, a company spent over $23,000 to buy the license plate ending with 8888.

Sources: *Global Studies: China* (Harrisonburg, VA: The Dushkin Publishing Co., 1993), 210–5; N. Berliner. "Party lines." *The New York Times Magazine* (September 5, 1993), 16–7.

Asian countries. American brides wear white, while their counterparts in China wear red. Indonesians use various colors of ink and stationary to convey unwritten messages of affection and anger. Black ink on white paper is formal and is used for business and official correspondence. Blue ink on white paper is emotionally neutral, while red ink on white paper is a sign of anger. Blue paper means affection, and green paper suggests that the writer hopes for a favorable amorous reply.[10]

While sensitivity to cultural aesthetics is prudent business, it runs contrary to standardization. It may create multiplicity of name brands, design characteristics, and promotional programs. Nonetheless, the desire for efficiency and cost control should not overshadow the sensitivity toward culturally based aesthetics.

Not all daily decisions have a logical basis. Sometimes, our choices are based on superstitions and illogical inclinations. Every culture has its own share of superstitions. Although the rising level of education everywhere reduces superstitions, it does not eliminate all such beliefs. Industrialization, modernity, and improved literacy rates, however, are weakening the foundation of superstitious beliefs everywhere. Nevertheless, international marketers should be aware that certain names, numbers, locations, and actions could have connotations of bad luck that may, in the opinion of the believers, provoke evil spirits.

Most societies have a fascination with numbers. To them, some represent good luck and others are bad omens or symbols of evil. Of course, similar to other cultural phenomenon, the significance and meanings of numbers are not universal. American hotels, for example, very seldom use the numeral 13. In numbering hotel floors, they skip from 12 to 14. While 13 is an unlucky number in many Western cultures, it is considered a lucky number in China. The numeral 4 has the dubious distinction of being a bad omen in China. It is pronounced similar to another word, *sei*, which means "die." In Taiwan, hospitals and hotels normally have no fourth floor, and elevators skip from three to five, excluding number four.

Knowing that illogical beliefs influence people's attitudes, experienced MNCs sometimes take careful steps to appeal to them. To please a senior Asian executive at Motorola, a new building in Hong Kong was designed with the aid of a geomancer (a diviner and soothsayer). The geomancer made sure that the building's *feng shui* (literally, the wind and water) were proper for good luck.[11]

Cultural differences influence MNC marketing in other ways as well. Because the MNC employs people of diverse cultures, cultural variations in decision making and interpersonal relationships impact the internal conduct of its marketing function. Dealing with colleagues in joint marketing decisions is easier if we understand cultural differences. The differences between Oriental and Western styles of decision making, for example, have certain implications for international marketing. A few Oriental cultural characteristics that are pertinent to marketing decisions are[12]:

1. *The importance of "face saving":* It is very important to respect and defend the dignity of individuals, even in trivial matters. In the marketing context, a product represents the extension of a person. Therefore, an executive who initiated a product may insist on going forward with it even if its weaknesses become apparent. Any direct criticism of the product is not taken lightly.

2. *Panethical approaches that emphasize social objectives in decisions:* Utilitarianism is an important decision guideline to Westerners. Cost-benefit analyses are an example of a utility-based decision-making model. Conversely, the teachings of Confucius emphasize social justice above any utility considerations. The marketing implications are that concerns for consumers may surpass cost and benefit considerations. It also implies that a "moral" prod-

uct warranty is more binding and stronger that any legal requirements. In backing its products, a firm may go beyond the legal obligations to maintain its reputation.

3. *Intergenerational time perspectives:* People of all cultures attempt to make life easier for their children. Beyond this, however, Orientals have a longer and broader intergenerational perspective. In marketing decisions they consider the rights of both current and future generations. To them, consideration for the future generations is a valid decision-making criteria. The traditional revolving-credit societies that Asian-Americans brought from their homelands to the United States are good examples of an intergenerational time perspective in operation. Access to capital markets is usually difficult for small entrepreneurs, and especially for the members of minorities. Therefore, many Japanese-Americans and Chinese-Americans rely on *Tanomoshi* and *Hui,* respectively.

> A *Tanomoshi* or *Hui* typically consists of about one dozen individuals, each one wanting to own his service station, a one-truck hauling service, or other such small businesses. Once each month, the group gathers at one member's home for dinner, and each person brings with him a prespecified sum of money, perhaps $1,000. The host of the evening keeps the whole sum—say, $12,000—which he then uses to buy a second truck or open his service station. The group meets in this fashion for twelve successive months until each person has put in $12,000 and has taken out $12,000. In this manner, people who would have great difficulty saving the whole sum of $12,000 are able to raise capital.[13]

There are two features of these societies that are characteristically Oriental. First, the emphasis on the intergenerational perspective and the concern for abiding by moral obligations make them possible. As a result, there are no formal contracts or use of collateral to protect the loan. These societies are usually limited to those within the kinship network. Therefore, if a member fails to fulfill his obligations, members of his family will certainly make up for him. Otherwise, all branches of the family will be shut out of the economic and social network of the community, a price that none of the members would want to pay. Second, note that earlier recipients of the lump-sum money effectively pay a lower interest rate. On rational grounds, it would seem that the later recipients should not accept this inequity. This would be true if the relationship was short term. Over the long run, however, there is an understanding that the arrangement may extend over more than one generation, and the apparent inequities wash out. There will be many opportunities to repay past debts by taking a later position in the subsequent *Huis* or *Tanomoshis.* In such a long-term relationship, children may pay back the obligations accrued by parents, and likewise they may reap the benefits due them.

Cultural understanding benefits the MNC in its external relationships to the industry as well. Understanding the impact of culture on marketing decisions enables the MNC to predict its competitors' moves and responses more accurately. Armed with the knowledge of cultural attributes impacting its markets, and based on market assessment information, the MNCs may decide on certain market entry strategies. These entry strategies are made based on overall corporate strategies that consider the firm's capabilities and market opportunities.

Market Entry Strategies

The firm's capabilities, its knowledge of foreign markets, and its experience marketing abroad are the basis for selecting the proper mode in which to enter a market. There are three basic entry strategies: exporting, franchising and licensing, and direct investment. Each strategy can be carried out with a variety of options, which may include a combination of more than one strategy. We examine these strategies next.

Exporting

The first and least complicated option that a firm can choose for going abroad is exporting. By exporting, the manufacturing facilities at home could be fully utilized. Often, in a saturated home market, where overcapacity causes inefficiency, through exporting the firm can utilize the excess capacity, thereby improving its cost position. While exporting does not require manufacturing operations abroad, it involves significant marketing effort and expenditure. Through exporting, firms can learn about international markets and gain experience in dealing with foreign customers. Also, exporting allows the concentration of manufacturing operations that can result in gains in efficiencies. Where transportation costs are negligible, or where they can be offset by efficiencies derived from manufacturing concentration, and where there are no import barriers in a market, exporting to that market is a viable strategy. Of course, to succeed by exporting into a market, the product has to suit the prospective consumers' tastes and preferences.

Exporting can be either direct or indirect, through another domestic firm that acts as an export agent. In direct exporting, the firm sells its product directly through a sales representative or agent to foreign customers. Direct exporting allows greater control over the marketing function and the development of marketing expertise. Firms that export directly provide all of the services needed for exporting, such as legal investigation and financial tracking, transportation, distribution channels, and promotion campaigns. Indirect exporting takes place through a domestic agent who acts as an intermediary between the firm and the foreign customers and earns a commission in the process. Indirect export could also take place through an export management company or a trading company. An export agent who purchases the products from the manufacturers and sells them abroad is called an export management company (EMC).

EMCs are usually small firms that concentrate on complementary and noncompetitive products. Therefore, they can offer a more complete product line to a small number of importers.[14] Export trading companies differ from EMCs in the size and services they offer. Export trading companies are usually larger, often take title to products, and can provide a broader range of services. Because of their international experience, export trading companies are well placed to expand into foreign markets. Japanese trading companies, *sogo shosha,* such as Mitsui, Mitsubishi, and Sumitomo, have been instrumental in introducing Japanese products to the world markets.

There seems to be a pattern of shifting positions among the world markets with regard to marketing and manufacturing. For several decades after World War II, the United States was the major exporting center from which manufactured products were supplied to world markets. As the Europeans and Japanese, with the aid of the United States, rebuilt their infrastructures and manufacturing capabilities, U.S. firms shifted their operations abroad. Cost advantages made offshore manufacturing more profitable than exporting from the United States. As additional countries develop their infrastructure and production capabilities, they are becoming attractive manufacturing locations and the source of exporting for the MNCs. Since the mid-1980s, for example, Asia's highly competitive producers in the Pacific Rim region have been increasing their exports to the United States and Europe, and the region has become a major destination for foreign direct investment from industrialized countries.

Licensing and Franchising

Licensing Licensing is an agreement between two firms for the exchange of something of value for a payment. The licensing contract may cover the right to use patents, trademarks, copyrights, blueprints, process or production technologies, and other proprietaries. It allows and obligates the licensee to produce a product or service for the local market. Licensing enables the MNC to supply a foreign market from local production, alleviating the cost of exporting.

There are several advantages to licensing. It requires very little additional investment and is a quick way to enter a foreign market. There is no need for costly investment in manufacturing and marketing facilities. It enables the licensor, which may not have the resources or the knowledge of foreign markets, to earn additional revenues without the commitment of substantial resources. Licensing may be used as a way of testing the market for future direct involvement and investment. Where the rate of technological advancement is fast, licensing can generate additional revenues from technology that potentially may quickly become obsolete. Also, where exporting into a market is restricted by the host government, or political risk of direct investment is high, licensing is a viable strategy.

While there are obvious benefits to licensing, there are certain reservations associated with it as well. Most licensing fees are small. Compared with other forms of marketing strategies, licensing does not generate much revenue. By licensing its proprietary advantage, the firm runs the risk of assisting the emergence of foreign competition. After the expiration of the contract, the foreign firm may continue marketing the product or service without making any fee payments. Having learned the technology, and having developed the capacity to provide the product or service to the market, the licensee may become a competitor.

Franchising Franchising is one form of licensing. Franchising can be defined as a form of marketing or distribution whereby a parent company grants another firm the right to do business in a prescribed manner for a period of time. The franchising agreement could be for the selling of a parent company's product, the use of its name, its trademark or, its architecture, and the adoption of its methods of production or marketing. In a survey of American franchising firms, Hackett found their motivations for expanding to oversees markets were very similar to those leading firms toward licensing. Above all, franchising firms were motivated by a desire to take advantage of markets with great potential.[15] Franchising has a number of specific benefits. It enables the firm to gain operating efficiencies and economies of scale. With franchising, it is possible to penetrate a market rapidly at a lower capital cost. The targeted consumer can be reached more effectively through the cooperative advertising and promotion permitted by franchising. It replaces the need for internal personnel with motivated owner/operators. Moreover, certain responsibilities are shifted to the franchisee. These include site selection, human resource management, and other administrative concerns. Of course on these matters, the franchising company provides guidance and assistance.[16]

Relative to licensing, a franchising company usually has more active involvement in the development and control of the marketing mix. Generally, however, the arrangement is established in a way that ensures that the franchisee adheres to a set of agreed-on standards in managing the franchised operation. McDonald's, for example, considers cleanliness to be the most important success factor in the fast food business, and has established cleanliness and hygiene standards and procedures accordingly. All franchisees are regularly inspected for compliance to these procedures. While it insists on strict adherence to such standards, McDonald's has learned that modifications to foreign cultures and tastes are necessary. When it began to franchise in Germany, for example, sales were much lower than expected. An inquiry revealed that adherence to the corporate policy of serving no alcoholic beverages had hurt sales. Consequently, for foreign operations, the policy was changed, and sales increased. By now, McDonald's is an experienced international firm that has more than 4,400 restaurants in foreign countries, and is willing to adapt its mode of operations and its menus to local tastes and preferences. In India, for example, where 80% of Indians are Hindus and do not eat beef, it has begun to introduce nonbeef hamburgers.[17]

Direct Investments

Direct investment is an alternative market entry strategy for firms with sufficient resources. While the costs of direct investment are higher than other entry alternatives, it provides a better control for the execution of corporate strategies. The firm may decide to enter a market through a 100 percent owned business, or to share the ownership with other investors in a joint venture. In a full ownership firm, the firm may establish a foreign subsidiary, acquire an existing firm in the host country, or merge with a host business. While in the past, developing countries imposed ownership restrictions on MNCs, many of them are following a more liberal position today. Most countries now allow MNCs full equity ownership of foreign subsidiaries. While complete ownership allows for greater control and flexibility, it is subject to a higher level of political risk. Sharing a minority equity with host country investors has certain advantages. Host governments are more hesitant in restricting the operation of a firm when local investors stand to loose. Furthermore, when doing business with the host government, a locally owned firm is typically in a more favorable position than a foreign company.

The problems and advantages of managing a foreign subsidiary were discussed in the previous chapters. Here it suffices to remind ourselves that establishing a foreign subsidiary means behaving like a local firm. While headquarters may maintain strategic control, day-to-day operational decisions are made by the subsidiary.

Joint ventures   In a joint venture, two or more firms share the ownership control and the risk of operating a business. International joint ventures are usually formed with host country partners. Joint ventures reduce capital requirements and combine the resources of partners. Having a local partner gives the MNC a local perspective, and reduces the mistakes that an outsider invariably makes. This is especially important in the early years of operation. A local partner can provide an insider's knowledge about the market, labor conditions, and competition. It can bridge the cultural gap between the MNC and the host country. It can also be an insurance against capricious host government policies that may hinder foreign businesses.

The benefits of joint ventures come at a price. The price of having a partner is sharing the revenues and the control, and the accompanying loss of flexibility. There may be differences in the objectives of the partners. MNCs' global strategies, for example, may call for more retained earnings to spend on R&D and the expansion of product lines. The local partner may prefer more dividends. In a joint venture, MNCs lose the flexibility of shifting production and expenses between subsidiaries worldwide. Therefore, in a joint venture, as in any relationship, the choice of partner can make a difference between success and failure. The MNC must be very careful to find a partner with complementary resources, similar objectives, and a compatible vision.

Marketing Mix

To sell products and services successfully in foreign markets, the firm needs a proper marketing mix. *Marketing mix* refers to strategic decisions regarding the four P's of marketing: *products,* the type of products and services offered; *price,* the price charged for these offerings; *place,* the distribution channels employed; and *promotion,* promotional programs utilized. A proper marketing mix is a winning combination of the four P's. Products should be those that customers demand, prices should be competitive and should generate good revenues, distribution channels should make available those products to target customers, and promotional programs should provide sufficient information about the products and generate interest in purchasing among potential consumers. Deficiencies in any one P could lead to failure. All four P's must fit together synergistically. While experience in the domestic market is helpful in making these decisions for international markets, such experience also may lead to a simplified notion of the functioning of international markets. Sometimes, a firm's successful marketing practices are duplicated abroad, assuming that what is good for the home market should be good enough for a foreign market. Of course, this may be far from the reality. Such a practice may result in the introduction of inappropriate products and services that ultimately will fail.

Standardization versus Customization

There are many similarities, as well as differences, among the world markets on which marketers can capitalize. A marketer who attempts to exploit the markets' similarities benefits from the standardization of the marketing mix. Diversity among foreign markets can be capitalized on by customization. Combining both marketing strategies of customization and standardization is very difficult.

Standardization is a very attractive strategy. Great cost advantages can be achieved if existing products that are sold in the domestic market can be sold abroad without modification. Standardization may not require new investment in machinery, equipment, and product development. Because existing production facilities are utilized for serving foreign markets, increased capacity utilization improves efficiency. Even if new investment is needed for product design and production facilities, standardization allows for a larger production run. The larger production runs produce efficiencies in the manufacturing operation. The cost savings resulting from the larger production run and efficiency gains allow lower prices. Moreover, efficiencies and cost reductions can be achieved through the standardization of other facets of the marketing mix. By extending the existing distribution channels and promotional programs, significant cost savings can be achieved. For firms that supply their global customers from various foreign subsidiaries, price standardization simplifies business transactions. It allows a single price quotation to important customers regardless of which foreign subsidiary supplies the product.

Europroducts

While politicians are scrambling to find an easy solution for the creation of a United States of Europe, manufacturers are trying to create standardized products for the European consumers. Euromanagers are finding that Europroducts are easier to imagine than to produce and sell to Euroconsumers. Mars Inc., the American candy firm, abandoned its successful European brand names in pursuit of making standardized global brands. Raider, the most successful chocolate biscuit in Europe was renamed Twix; the big-selling British chocolate bar, Marathon, became Snickers; and Bonitos, the French candies, were christened M&M with new coating colors. It has yet to solve the dilemma it faces with Milky Way and Mars bars. Both are sold worldwide but they refer to different products in different countries. In the United States, Milky Way has caramel and chocolate, in Europe it has no caramel. Similarly, the European version of the Mars bars has no almond.

Source: E. S. Browning. "In Pursuit of the Elusive Euroconsumer." *The Wall Street Journal* (April 29, 1992), B1.

Market and product characteristics, however, may inhibit standardization strategies. Host countries may establish certain product specifications that force MNCs to modify their products to local requirements. Consumer tastes and preferences vary across cultures. Local conditions and logistic problems may render certain products that are sold at home unsuitable for host markets. Chocolate candy bars that are sold in U.S. stores, for example, melt in the hot climate of tropical markets. The British and Japanese drive on the left side of the road. Automobiles that are destined for those markets should have their steering wheels on the right side. Television advertising is useless for many developing countries where most consumers cannot afford televisions. Consequently, in many situations, adaption and customization of the marketing mix may be the only viable strategy.

The argument for customization recognizes that while standardization is a very attractive strategy, not many consumer products can become universal in use. Only products with certain specific characteristics can have universal appeal. The characteristics of a universal product include global brand name recognition (achieved by huge financial outlay), minimal product knowledge requirements for consumer use, and product advertisement that needs low information content.[18] Some products that appear to have achieved universality status are Coca-Cola, McDonald's, Levi jeans, and Colgate toothpaste. Others such as Federal Express, Pizza Hut, and Domino's Pizza are in hot pursuit of such recognition.

Product

Successful marketing is customer driven. The focus of all marketing activities is the satisfaction of the customers' needs and wants. The main ingredient of the marketing mix is the product. Products that are designed based on the customers' preferences, tastes, and purchasing power are essential to the marketing mix. Without the right products, all other components of the marketing mix remain ineffective.

In marketing terminology, the term *product* refers to the physical design and cost, as well as the nonphysical factors, of the product that contribute to customer satisfaction. Customers are attracted to a product not only for its physical characteristics but for its nonphysical attributes as well. They buy the *total product*. The product image, the packaging, brand name, operating instructions, after-sales service, and warranty are all inseparable aspects of the product and ones that customers consider when making purchasing decisions. A television set not only satisfies the viewing pleasure of the consumer but it also represents the reputation of the manufacturer, the image associated with the brand name, the manufacturer's warranties, and the services offered by the retailer such as the credit and home delivery.

For some products the nonphysical aspects are more important to customers than the physical aspects. For many years IBM successfully dominated the mainframe computer market because of its superb after-sales service. Customers concerned with the smooth functioning of their mainframe computers were assured of timely service.

Products and services are either used by the general consumers or by industrial firms. On that basis products are classified as either *consumer products* or *industrial products*.

Consumer products   Consumers products require greater modification and adaptation than industrial products. Because of cultural, socioeconomic, and demographic differences among customers, MNCs are forced to modify products to local tastes and preferences. While many consumer products cannot be standardized, certain basic consumer staples do not require much modification. MNCs, such as Coca-Cola and Kodak, have been successful in offering the same product worldwide. Even for those products that appear to appeal to all customers globally, often some modifications are necessary. Coke's sugar content and taste, for example, varies by country. Similarly, the physical appearance of electronic products such as stereo components is not universal. Amstrad, an English electronic company, capitalized on the British preference for the appearance and the look of stereo equipment. The British were unhappy with the simplified and functional products made for the global market. They preferred teak furniture exteriors and complex control panels. By offering products with those features, Amstrad was able to capture market leadership in England.[19]

While Amstrad gained market share by differentiating a product that was supposed to be culture free, Whirlpool, with some success, has been standardizing a product that was assumed to be culturally differentiated. When in 1989, Whirlpool formed a joint venture with Philips Electronics NV it was told that there was a diversity in preferences among Europeans for washing machines. A year later, it acquired full control of the venture, and gained market share by courting what it referred to as a Euroconsumer, which was defined as someone wearing clothes that are washed in Whirlpool machines. Before Whirlpool entered Europe, manufacturers had always made narrow, top-loading machines for the French market. It was assumed that due to lack of space in the kitchen, those machines were the only types the French would buy. It was learned, however, that consumers across Europe would accept changes if a machine offered significant improvements.[20] Knowledge and understanding of consumer habits are essential for product modifications. Sometimes, a very small change can make a big difference in the consumer's acceptance of a product. Consider the following case.

In the early 1980s, Japanese manufacturers began selling automobiles in China. These cars tended to stall frequently. Chinese considered them of inferior quality and consequently sales began to suffer. An investigation of the problem revealed that Chinese drivers stop the engine while waiting for the traffic lights to change. The air-conditioning in these cars, however, kept running, and caused the battery to go dead. Restarting the car with a dead battery was impossible. The solution was simple. The wiring was modified to stop the air conditioning when the ignition key was turned off.[21]

Similar to other business decisions, modification of existing products should take into account the costs and benefits involved. The additional costs of changing product features and characteristics should be covered by the revenues thus generated. For this reason, in developing countries with a small market, some MNCs leave certain modifications of their products to their customers. The 250-volt electric current, for example, is common in many developing countries. In these countries, consumers buy electrical converters to use with any American electrical equipment that operates on 120 volts. For the larger market of Europe, however, which uses smaller washing machines, new sizes were introduced by Whirlpool.

Critics have long maintained that MNCs should consider the sociocultural impacts of modern products and technologies on developing countries. They have argued, for example, that labor-saving technologies that reduce production costs in developed countries are not fit for developing countries. Concerned about the cultural impact of modern products and technologies, the advocates of appropriate technologies have suggested that MNCs should carefully match transferred technologies with the sociocultural and economic conditions of importing countries.[22] Recently, however, the impressive economic gains of some developing countries resulting from the use of the most advanced technologies have dulled these critics' sharpest complaints.

Industrial products Industrial products are those purchased by manufacturers and producers. Such products include components, parts, and materials that are used by producers in the production of consumer products. Ball bearings, transistors, various fasteners, metal sheets, machine tools, and crude oil are examples of industrial products. While many consumer products require some alteration to fit the local market conditions, many industrial products do not need such modification. The bulk paper that is sold to all newspapers and printers, for example, is virtually the same. Each customer buys certain standardized grades of paper that are made to industry specifications. Sometimes industrial products are modified to fit the original manufacture's requirements. Internal and external rear view mirrors used in automobiles, for example, may need slight changes to match the overall design of different automobiles. These changes, however, have less to do with cultural differences than with manufacturing requirements.

There are three differences between industrial customers and individual consumers. First, industrial customers' purchasing decisions are more dictated by economic considerations than by feelings, attitudes, and the influence of social forces. However, the degree of influence of noneconomic forces on the purchasing decision of industrial consumers varies among cultures. Industrial consumers of traditional societies such as Japan have a tendency to restrict most of their purchases to home country products. Such tendencies may be due to the long-term orientation of traditional societies, where relationships may extend over more than one generation. Second, industrial consumers are generally more informed and knowledgeable than individual consumers. They understand the product, and look for products with certain specifications and characteristics. Product specifications are established well in advance of purchasing, and often are known by more than one individual. Third, industrial consumers are more similar in their purchasing behavior. The similarities among industrial consumers have economic roots. When purchasing decisions are influenced primarily by economic considerations, products that can reduce production costs are favored over other products. Therefore, labor-saving

machines and equipment have great appeal to high labor wage countries. Also, promotional programs that are designed to appeal to the psyche of individual consumers are far less effective for promoting industrial goods. Because of these characteristics it is feasible to standardize industrial products for culturally diverse global customers.

Service   International marketing of services is greatly different from the marketing of physical products. The difference is due to the characteristics of the service industry and a series of barriers to international service marketing. Nowhere is the difference between developed and developing countries more evident than in the service industry. By some estimates more than 60 percent of developed countries' gross national product (GNP) is attributed to services. For developing countries this figure is estimated at less than 30 percent.[23]

Four characteristics differentiate services from physical products (goods). These characteristics are inseparability, intangibility, perishability, and heterogeneity.[24] Inseparability means that the service producer is an inseparable part of the services produced. It also means that production and consumption of the services take place simultaneously. Teaching, banking, health care services, and orchestral performances are examples of services. The tellers interact with the customers while providing them with banking services, and health care specialists are in regular contact with the patients while dispensing their treatment. Services are intangible products. They cannot be felt, seen, or transported as physical products. The live performance of an orchestra, for example, cannot be transported to other places. Services are perishable. Unlike the physical products, services cannot be stored for future use. There are some exceptions. Programmed instructions, expert systems, and artificial intelligence, for example, can be used repeatedly. Even in these cases, however, we do not know how many people at various times will be using the service. Therefore, inventory of

Chinese Modernity

Consumers are benefiting from China's overtures to the free market in many ways. Some Chinese are getting their first experience with consumer products that are taken for granted in the West. The arrival of these products has a decidedly Chinese flavor. After five years of waiting the Xhenxian family has just received their first telephone. The Xhenxian family, which consists of the husband and wife, their oldest daughter and her husband with their two children, live together. The acquisition of the phone was not easy, nor was it cheap. Personal connections with a manager of the telephone company, 1,000 yuan ($175) worth of gifts, worth about five months' salary, plus the 5,000-yuan deposit brought in the telephone. The Xhenxian family has kept the news of their acquisition from spreading for the fear of the inconveniences it could bring. If everyone around the complex knows about it, they may want to use it. Worse yet, they may receive phone calls, in which case the Xhenxian family may spend all day running messages around the complex. When important guests pay them a visit, however, the telephone is displayed in a prominent position, suggesting the modernity of the family.

Source: N. Berliner. "Party Lines." *The New York Time Magazine* (September 5, 1993), 17–8.

---

these services is quite different from that of physical products. We consume services at the point of production. An empty seat on a passenger airplane flying from Dallas to Daralsalam, Tanzania, is lost for ever. It cannot be sold to future customers. The heterogeneity that is characteristic of the services means that no two services are the same. Two customers opening checking accounts in the same bank receive two different services from the same teller. It does not matter how hard and diligently the teller tries to act in the same manner with them, the services will still be different. These characteristics create unique problems for marketing of services. Production, quality control, pricing, and promotion of services are more difficult. Because of these features, services do not lend themselves to standardization.

We have drawn a sharp distinction separating goods from services, but in reality all products have tangible and intangible characteristics. Some products, however, are inherently more tangible, while others are inherently more intangible. The tangibility and intangibility of selected products are depicted in Figure 12.1.

Astute marketers, through promotional programs, enhance intangible attributes of their products and thereby gain a competitive advantage. A good example is Morton Salt's attempt to differentiate itself from others by the slogan "When it rains, it pours."

Because of their unique nature, most domestic services face limited foreign competition. The requirements of on-site production and producer-consumer interaction create cultural barriers to most services. Producers-sellers must be intimately familiar with the culture to succeed in service industries. Language, customs, unwritten rules, and the proper mannerisms of each culture put foreigners at a disadvantage for offering most services. Additionally, governments have raised tariff and nontariff barriers in service industries. Although free trade has facilitated global competition for most goods, services have not enjoyed a similar treatment. There is a general reluctance by host governments to open service industries to foreign firms. This reluctance stems from the close relationship between a society and the services offered that society.[25] Some service industries,

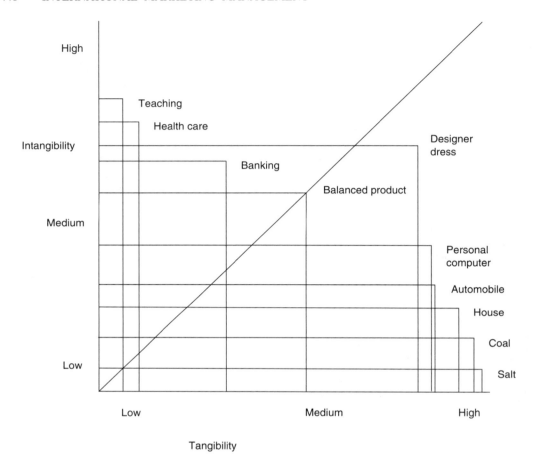

Figure 12.1   Tangible and Intangible Dimensions of Select Products

however, face additional restrictions. Certain services are considered strategically important to the society. Participation of foreign firms is severely curtailed or totally banned in such services. There are more trade barriers, for example, in banking, insurance, telecommunications, and aviation than in other service industries.[26]

There are both tariff and nontariff barriers restricting participation of MNCs in services. The challenge to international marketing is how to overcome these barriers. Tariff barriers are taxes that are imposed on imported services. Nontariff barriers include formal and informal restrictions, such as the policy of buying only from

national suppliers, prohibitions against the employment of foreign nationals, physical distance, and direct competition from host governments. New technologies in telecommunications and computers are rendering some service barriers less effective. Electronic fund transfer and reservation systems have overcome the effects of physical distances for banking, finance, and travel services, for example.

Some international barriers to services can be eased through marketing strategies of embodying, differentiation-customizing, and strategic alliance.[27] Through embodying, service features are made integral parts of the product. The design services, for example, can be embodied in clothes sold abroad. Because barriers to importing merchandise are much lower, embodying extends "style" and "fashion" services through products sold to retailers. Some consumers are always willing and able to pay for the desired high-quality goods and services that only a few producers can offer. The heterogeneity attribute of services allows customization and differentiation. Suppliers who differentiate themselves through customization can overcome barriers to services. Wealthy customers, for example, go to internationally known providers of health care services on a regular basis. Strategic alliances with domestic partners may be a key to entering some markets. Global hospitality firms such as Hilton and Hyatt have successfully entered the closed markets of the world by teaming up with local partners.

Price

On the surface it may appear that pricing a product is a very simple task. All a firm has to do is decide the size of the markup and add it to the cost of production. But because price serves other functions, the pricing decision represents a difficult task. Besides its obvious link to revenues, price can create a perception of quality. Coupled with other components of the marketing mix, price can be used as a strong competitive strategy. If a firm has a cost position lower than its competitors, a low price strategy could force the existing competition out, and keep potential entrants from the market.

There are interactions between price, other marketing components, and functional areas such as finance and production. Therefore, prices cannot be set without careful consideration of their impact on these other areas. The complexity of pricing policies becomes evident if we just consider the impact it may have on revenues. A firm may, for strategic reasons, lower its prices. Lower prices may, in turn, increase sales but the total impact on revenues might be negative. Lower prices may also create

the impression of lower quality, in which case both sales and revenues could fall.

International pricing is much more difficult. The difficulty arises from the additional factors that should be considered in making pricing decisions, including host government price controls, production cost differentials among markets, and the presence of other MNCs. Problems may also arise when setting prices for products produced in one market that are sold in another market. Cost factors vary among countries; therefore, MNCs with worldwide production facilities do not have uniform cost structures for the same products. For these MNCs the challenge is setting prices for products produced in different locations and sold in different markets.

MNCs encounter more pricing complications when they sell from their various facilities to a *global buyer.* A global buyer is a customer who makes large purchases for its multiple operations in many markets. Naturally, the buyer expects one price for the same product regardless of its origin. Since MNC subsidiaries have different production costs, depending on the area of origin, uniform pricing requires the intrafirm accounting procedures of *transfer pricing.* Transfer pricing is one of the most controversial issues between the MNCs and host governments. The accounting of intrafirm transactions by MNCs has the potential to reduce the reported revenues of a subsidiary and consequently to reduce its tax liability. In response, the host governments will typically want to investigate what is perceived as a suspicious mechanism to permit tax evasion.

There are other pricing issues that involve host governments. Many host governments impose price controls on specific products. They may set both minimum and maximum price limits. A minimum price limit is set to protect domestic industry against foreign competition, while a maximum price limit is set for the benefit of consumers. Similarly, subsidizing domestic producers of certain products represents a method to assure product affordability to the people of the country. In such cases, MNCs are forced to adjust their pricing policies to follow local requirements.

Another source of pricing difficulty and complexity results from the nature of international competition. Dealing with other MNCs makes pricing strategies a complicated undertaking because they are more flexible and resourceful than their domestic counterparts. The MNCs can support lower prices for certain products in one market from the revenues generated by other products sold globally. Artificially setting prices of exported products below home market prices is *dumping*. Dumping is an illegal act. Except for flagrant cases, however, it is often very difficult to prove that lower prices are dumping and not the result of the MNCs' competitive advantage.

Regardless of the considerations involving the host government involvement and market

characteristics, pricing decisions are based on product types. Products are either new ones having no competition, or existing ones that face competition from other similar and substitute products. MNCs have less discretion when pricing existing products. The prices of other competing products exert a major influence on the price of an existing product. There is, however, more flexibility and discretion for pricing new products. By combining pricing and promotion, four pricing/promotion alternatives are available: high profile, preemptive, selective, and low profile.[28] Depending on the objectives and product/market characteristics, firms may choose one of four possible options (see Figure 12.2).

High profile   By combining high price with lots of promotion, the firm intends to penetrate the market fast and recover its investment as quickly as possible. The strategy will be most

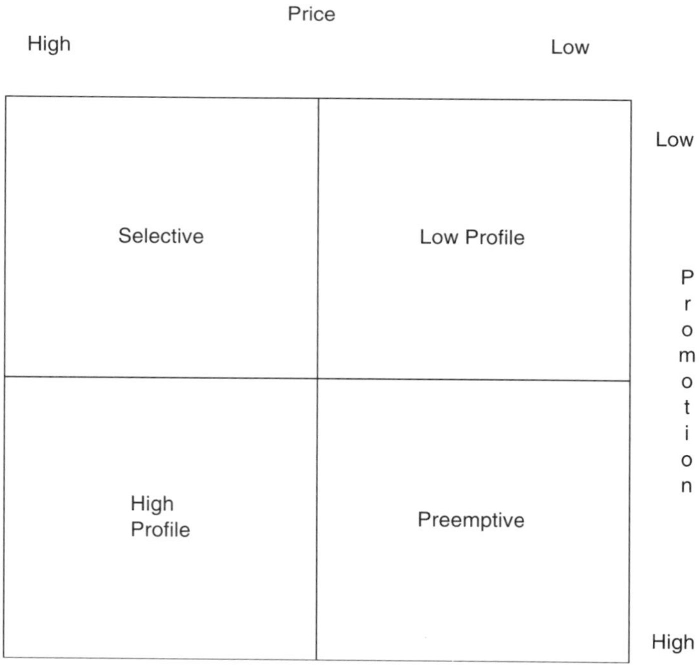

Price

High   Low

		Low
Selective	Low Profile	
High Profile	Preemptive	High

Promotion

Figure 12.2   Price/Promotion Options

effective if the competition cannot, in a short time, enter the market with a competing product. Polaroid employed this strategy in the pricing of its early models of the SX-70 instant cameras.

Selective In a high price and low promotion strategy, the firm is not concerned with the time that it takes to penetrate the market. The patent rights or technological sophistication imbedded in the product may not allow competition to duplicate the product. Secure in its unique position, the MNC spends little money on promotion. This strategy has been successfully employed by Intel in the marketing of its microprocessors around the globe. The resulting high profit margin enables the firm to lower prices when competition finally catches up. Lower prices limit the newcomers' market share. A variation of this strategy offers lower prices in a modified product that has distinctive features of the original. L'Oreal, a French cosmetic firm with a global reach, for example, has used this strategy effectively. L'Oreal was the first to use a wrinkle-hiding liposome in its Niosome face cream, at $50 a jar. For three years it enjoyed high profit margins. As competitors finally entered the market, it introduced a liposome product called Plenitude at supermarkets for $8 a jar.[29]

Preemptive In preemptive pricing, the goal is to secure a dominant market position without allowing the competition a foothold. With a high level of promotion and low prices, the firm tries to reach market saturation and establish brand loyalty in a short time. The hope is that high volume will make up for the low price. The low profit margin associated with this option may make the market less attractive for potential competitors. Some Japanese manufacturers have been employing this strategy in the United States. These manufacturers have been accused of dumping and some have faced legal actions by the U.S. Justice Department.

Low profile When market potential is not high, slow steady market penetration is proba-bly the best strategy. Low price when combined with low promotion is the least attractive pricing option. This option fits the low incomes and small size characteristics of many developing countries. The low level of income may leave consumers without much purchasing power. Therefore, many high ticket products will not sell well in these markets. A low profile strategy, however, keeps the MNC name and its products visible in these markets while waiting for future opportunities.

Channels of Distribution

Channels of distribution are the links between producers and customers which, in their final point, permit the means to offer products in their final form for the purchase by customers. This linkage involves transportation, distribution, warehousing, and retailing. Other services are provided along the distribution channel such as keeping inventory, providing financing to customers, delivery to homes, and post-sales repair and maintenance. Properly established, a distribution network often represents the difference between success and failure in a market. Because of the physical nature of distribution channels, once in place they are very difficult to change. Often, at least some of the channels are not under the control of the producer. Therefore, not only are changes very difficult, they require time and capital. Moreover, without access to distribution channels, it is impossible to reach customers and gain any meaningful market share. As an example, L'Oreal, the French cosmetic firm, is dominant in the European market, but has only a very modest share of the U.S. market. Its weak position in the U.S. market has been attributed to its difficulties with its channels of distribution in the United States.[30]

Most manufacturers do not own their channels of distribution. They establish a close relationship with them. A good relationship that is nurtured over a long time is as valuable as the outright ownership. The value of channels of distribution cannot be overstated. In the mid-

1970s Renault wanted to enter the U.S. market. Establishing its own distribution network was considered too costly. To gain access to a distribution network, in the mid-1970s Renault purchased a controlling interest in what then was American Motors. American Motors, however, proved to be a drag on Renault's earnings. Eventually, American Motors was sold to Chrysler.

While establishing the proper channels of distribution is very difficult in home markets, it is even more troublesome abroad. In some countries, such as Japan, established patterns of relationships between producers, wholesalers, and retailers represent major impediments to entry by foreign firms. The personal nature of these relationships excludes newcomers let alone foreigners. Faced with the entrenched and closed distribution system of Japan, direct marketers have recently succeeded in establishing beachheads in consumer electronics. Dell and Compaq have demonstrated that with quality products and right prices, a determined marketer can succeed in such traditional markets by means of direct contact.

The nature of the product and market characteristics dictate the choice of the channel. Some products are better distributed by a company agent. Others can best be sold through a distributor. The degree of control desired and the capital investment a firm is willing to make determine the choice of the channel. In countries with a poor infrastructure and insufficient established distribution channels the MNCs are forced to develop their own. Pizza Hut and McDonald's, for example, were forced to establish their own channels in Russia. They established their own vendors of raw materials, constructed their own warehousing capabilities, and put together their own delivery system of refrigerated trucks.

Promotion

Communication with the customer is the first step in selling a product. Before people buy a product, they have to know about its existence

and its characteristics. Often, the consumers' knowledge about a product is not sufficient to lead them to buy it. In a free market where many products are available to consumers, persuading them to buy a specific product is an important task of marketing. As we learned in the discussion of the product, consumers buy a product for its tangible as well as intangible characteristics. The prestige and reputation of a firm are important aspects of its products. Therefore, marketers not only attempt to generate interest in the products that the firm is selling but try to create a favorable image of the firm. To rely on and promote the firm's image as a part of the promotion and advertising effort is a double-edged sword for American MNCs. While in some places, such as South America, American products have an image advantage, in other places they do not. Some European countries are very conscious of American domination. In Sweden, for example, Heinz, the American ketchup, deliberately plays down that it is a typical American product. In its advertising, the theme made-in-America is so muted that the Swedes do not realize Heinz is American. They assume that because of the name Heinz is a German product.[31]

As product complexity increases, determination of its quality by mere physical inspection decreases. When it is impossible to judge the quality and durability of a product, such as happens with TVs or automobiles, the role of advertising and marketing promotion increases. In such a case, the name and prestige of the manufacturer and the retailer may be a deciding factor in consumer purchases. Also instead of direct advertising, indirect advertising (word of mouth) is substituted for personal judgment. In developing countries, due to the lower literacy rate, word of mouth and the firm's image are strong promotion mechanisms.

To promote a firm and its products, marketers can choose from a range of media and methods of promotion. Brochures, pamphlets, billboards, newspapers, radio, and television are the most common media choices. Of course, the choice of media depends on availability, costs, and potential benefits. As indicated in Table 12.1, developing countries do not have an abundance of news media. For many people of developing countries, television remains a luxury. Therefore, firms are forced to use print media and to rely primarily on newspapers and radio advertisements. In extreme cases, where news media is scarce, personal demonstration of the product to large audiences can effectively serve the purpose. The United Nations personnel working with lower income people of developing countries have been successful using this method. They were able to inform families about effective ways of dealing with a variety of health- and family-related issues.

Various promotional tools commonly used in developed countries are either unavailable in developing countries or are prohibitively expensive. Attractive food packaging such as is common in the United States is impractical for developing countries. Such packaging makes the final price beyond the reach of most consumers. Similarly, because of the lack of infrastructure and supporting services in these countries, certain promotional techniques are not feasible. Coupons, which are popular with most consumers in the United States, for example, cannot be used in developing countries because services to process them do not exist or are not reliable. Instead, a more appropriate promotion is free sample demonstration.[32]

Because for many products there are intermediaries between producers and consumers, often promotion and distribution interact closely. Therefore, the task of promotion becomes twofold. On the one hand, marketers have to persuade consumers to want the product. On the other hand, the wholesalers and retailers have to be convinced to carry the product and to make it available to the consumers. When trying to inform and persuade consumers, cultural differences cause many problems, but convincing the intermediaries is often even more

difficult. These intermediaries feel more comfortable dealing with the familiar local firms, and are suspicious of foreigners. The entrenched and closed distribution system of Japan, for example, has caused problems for the American firms trying to compete with Japanese companies.

Cultural differences surface more frequently in promotion and advertising than in the other components of the marketing mix. Since communication is at the heart of promotion, cultural differences in communication add to an already difficult task. Informative and persuasive messages from one language are very difficult to translate into other languages. Styles, tastes, and norms of doing business when combined with subtleties of the language and meaning require the tailoring of promotion materials for local audiences. What in one culture is considered an aggressive business practice may be considered phony in others. Local laws and restrictions often are major barriers to global advertising. General Mills, for example, could not run its commercials on German television by merely changing the language. Toy soldiers holding guns and driving tanks cannot be shown on German television. As a result, General Mills had to produce a totally new television advertisement.[33]

Advertising is an integral part of American life, and most Americans are reasonably receptive to promotional programs. Many Americans, therefore, would be surprised to discover that their perceptibility to advertising is not universal. To many people of developing countries, advertising is a wasteful practice. Their attitudes toward the advertisements can be summarized in a question: If a product is good enough for everyone to notice, why does it need advertisement? They may construe heavy advertisement, as it is practiced in the United States, as an indication of product flaws. Therefore, a careful consideration of differences in marketing promotions among countries is a prudent management practice.

Because of cultural differences and legal restrictions, MNCs have apparently been unsuccessful in developing global advertising. Some even assert that, unlike products or even distribution channels that can be deployed on a worldwide basis, advertising remains a local undertaking. Because of regional and global free trade agreements, however, it is expected that promotion programs will become more international in tone and converge.[34]

Conclusion

Two forces distinguish today's management of business operations. These two forces are internationalization of the markets and technological diffusion. In its many forms, technology transfer is accelerating the rate of industrialization globally. Nations that previously were major importers of many manufactured products are joining the ranks of exporters. Technological diffusion around the globe is creating new competition from all corners of the world. National markets are slowly but inexorably opening their doors to world trade. In the environment of expanding free markets, no firm can remain secure from the pressure of international competition. Although innovations and new product development can secure sufficient earnings, competition will quickly move in and crowd the market. Also, no national market can be secure from the pressure of foreign competition. In the game of business competition, firms that learn to compete at the global level are the future winners. Firms that are confined to their domestic markets limit their earnings and growth. To compete at home and abroad, firms need the knowledge of and expansion into foreign markets. International marketing management is the key to a firm's successful expansion abroad.

The first step in marketing abroad is the assessment of potential markets to enter. Learning about sociopolitical, economic, and cultural aspects of potential markets reduces the probability of failure. In particular, understanding cultural differences is a prerequisite for successful international marketing. Armed with knowledge about the foreign markets, the next steps are decisions regarding the choice of markets to enter and the modes of entry. Exporting, licensing and franchising, joint ventures, and direct investment are major modes of entry. The choice of entry depends on the nature of the product, the resources available to the firm, the amount of risk the firm is willing to take, and the amount of control it desires over the foreign operations. Considering all relevant factors of international marketing, exporting is least demanding and foreign direct investment is the most challenging.

The success of international marketing depends on the proper marketing mix. The marketing mix involves the right combination of product, price, channels of distribution, and promotional programs. Knowing what products foreign customers want, what prices to charge, how to get these products to them, and how to let potential customers know about them are the keys to success. International marketing management is torn between the desire to standardize and the need to customize the marketing mix. Some products can be standardized for global markets; however, most products have to be adapted to local tastes and preferences. Price standardization is extremely difficult. Similarly, channels of distribution are mostly local. While it is possible to standardize certain products for global markets, promotional programs remain local. Cultural differences impact advertising and other components of promotion. Attempts at creating global promotions so far have not been very successful. The ability to think, plan, and prepare globally and execute the plans according to local requirements are the keys to effective international marketing management.

Discussion Questions

1. Describe the two reasons given in the book for the confidence of the American people in the efficacy of the market competition.

2. Since American antitrust laws are not enforceable in foreign markets, what should American firms do when operating abroad?

3. What factors should be included in the assessment of foreign markets?

4. Describe the effect of culture on the purchasing behavior of the people.

5. What are the influences of religions on international marketing management?

6. Beauty is in the eye of the beholder. Therefore, for consumer products, no foreigner could effectively compete with local businesses. Do you agree or disagree? Support your position.

7. Elaborate on the relationship between superstition and international marketing management.

8. What characteristics of Eastern cultures do you consider most influential on international marketing management?

9. What are the benefits of international joint ventures?

10. Elaborate on the effects of technology transfer and telecommunications on standardization of the marketing mix.

11. What problems do MNCs face when attempting to market international services?

12. Why are promotion and advertising the most problematic of the international marketing mix components?

Endnotes

1. K. Ohmae. *The Borderless World* (New York: Harper Perennial Publishers, 1991), 8–9.

2. T. Levitt, "Globalization of Markets." *Harvard Business Review* (May–June, 1983), 92–102.

3. K. Fatehi-Sedeh and M. H. Safizadeh. "Sociopolitical Events and Foreign Direct Investment: American Investment in South and Central American Countries, 1950–1982," *Journal of Management* 14, no. 1 (1988), 93–107.

4. J. Fayerweather. *International Marketing* (Englewood Cliffs, NJ: Prentice-Hall, Inc., 1965), 27–9.

5. Ibid., 28.

6. Ibid., 27–9.

7. S. D. Goll. "From Soap to Luxury Cars, Consumer Tastes Develop." *The Wall Street Journal* (Monday, October 18, 1993), A10.

8. R. Jacob. "Citicorp: Capturing the Global Consumer." *Fortune* (December 13, 1993), 166–7.

9. D. A. Ricks. *Blunders in International Business* (Cambridge, MA: Blackwell Publishers, 1993), 35.

10. P. Just. "Brief Communications." *Human Organization* 42, no. 3 (Fall, 1983), 47.

11. P. Engardio, L. Therrien, N. Gross, and L. Armstrong. "How Motorola Took the Asians by the Tail." *Business Week* (November 11, 1991), 68.

12. D. K. Tse, K.-H. Lee, I. Vertinsky, and D. A. Wehrung. "Does Culture Matter? A Cross-Cultural Study of Executives' Choice, Decisiveness, and Risk Adjustment in International Marketing." *Journal of Marketing* 52, (October, 1988), 81–95.

13. W. G. Ouchi. *Theory Z* (Reading, MA: Addison-Wesley, 1981), 85–6.

14. J. D. Daniel and L. H. Radebaugh. *International Business* (Reading, MA: Addison-Wesley, 1992), 525.

15. D. W. Hackett. "The International Expansion of U.S. Franchise Systems: Status and Strategies." *Journal of International Business Studies* 7, no. 1 (Spring, 1976), 65–75.

16. A. J. Sherman. *Franchising and Licensing: Two Ways to Build Your Business* (New York: American Management Association, 1991), 4.

17. "Where Is the Beef?" *Fortune* (January 27, 1994), 16.

18. W. C. Kim and R.A. Mauborgne. "Cross-Cultural Strategies." *The Journal of Business Strategies* (Spring, 1987), 28–35.

19. C. A. Bartlett and S. Ghoshal. *Transnational Management* (Homewood, IL: Irwin, 1992), 113.

20. M. M. Nelson. "Whirlpool Gives Pan-European Approach a Spin." *The Wall Street Journal* (Thursday, April 23, 1992), B1.

21. M. Maruyama. "New Management Dimensions in International Business." *Technical Forecasting and Social Change* 43 (1993), 197–9.

22. K. Fatehi and F. Derakhshan. "Appropriate Technology, Appropriate Management and International Trade: An Integrative Proposal." *Approtech* 5, no. 1 (1982), 19–22.

23. L. D. Dahringer. "Marketing Services Internationally: Barriers and Management Strategies." *Journal of Service Marketing* 5, no. 3, (1991), 5–17.

24. V. A. Zeithmal, A. Parasuranam, and L. L. Berry. "Problems and Strategies in Service Marketing." *Journal of Marketing* (Spring, 1985), 33–48.

25. L. D. Dahringer. *Marketing Services* 7.

26. P. E. Fong and M. Sundberg. "ASEAN-EEC Trade in Services: An overview." In J. J. Waelbroek, P. Praet, and H. C. Ruger, eds. *ASEAN-EEC Trade in Services* (Singapore: ASEAN Economic Research Unit, Institute of Southeast Asian Studies, 1985), 48–9.

27. L. D. Dahringer. "Marketing Services." 5–12, Suggests six guidelines for overcoming international service barriers. Combining the three strategies offered here could provide similar results.

28. Y. N. Chang and F. Campo-Flores. *Business Policy and Strategy* (Santa Monica, CA: Goodyear, 1980), 272.

29. S. Toy, L. Zim, Z. Schiller, R. Neff, and P. Dwyer. "Can the Queen of Cosmetics Keep Her Crown?" *Business Week* (January 17, 1994), 90–2.

30. Ibid., 90.

31. G. Stern. "Heinz Aims to Export Taste for Ketchup." *The Wall Street Journal* (Friday, November 20, 1992), B1, B9.

32. K. Kashani and J. A. Qeulch. "Can Sales Promotion Go Global?" *Business Horizons* (May–June, 1990), 37–43.

33. R. Alsop. "Countries' Different Ad Rules Are Problem for Global Firms." *The Wall Street Journal* (Thursday, September, 27, 1984), B1.

34. K. Kashani and J. A. Qeulch, 37–43.

PT PRIMA COMEXINDO: AN INDONESIAN TRADING COMPANY

ROBERT W. HORNADAY

At the age of 38, Hashim Djojohadikusumo has put together an impressive entrepreneurial empire. He is an indigenous Indonesian able to compete in an economy dominated by the ethnic Chinese. Hashim[1] is also well-connected. His father, Sumitro Djojohadikusumo, the dean of Indonesia's Western-educated economists, has been a major force in Indonesian politics and economic planning since World War II. His elder brother, Lieutenant Colonel Prabowo Subianto, is married to the youngest daughter of the President of Indonesia.

Although he has interests in 22 companies, Hashim controls them personally, not through a holding company (Exhibit 1). He estimates revenues of these companies to be between $400 million and $500 million per year, mostly from cement and international trading. With his aggressive acquisitions Hashim has battled powerful competitors such as Mitsubishi and Mitsui and now controls both Semen Cibinong and Semen Nusantara, both giant cement companies.

Hashim's most famous takeover deal failed. In 1992, he put together a $500 million offer to take control of Astra International, Indonesia's premier industrial conglomerate. Complicating Hashim's bid was the fact that his father was Chairman of Astra's Board of Commissioners.[2] In the end the Soeryadjaya family, founders of Astra, selected another bid from a group of ethnic Chinese businessmen, but Hashim had clearly established himself as a major player in Indonesia's world of high finance.

[1] The Indonesian print media uses first names—a custom followed in this paper.

[2] Similar to a U.S. Board of Directors.

Exhibit 1
Holdings of Hashim S. Djojohadikusumo

Manufacturing:
  PT Semen Cibinong (Cement, Building Materials)
  PT Semen Nusantara (Cement)
  PT Gunung Ngadek (Cement)
  PT Tirtamas Majutama (Investment Holding Company)
  PT Cabot Chemical (Carbon Black Production)
  PT Aditya Nusa Bakti Indonesia (Petrochemical Investments)
  PT Plytama Propondo (Plypropylene Production)
  PT Rejo (Cigarette Production)
Coal and Power:
  PT Batu Hitam Perkasa (Coal Investments and Power Generation)
  PT Termina Batubara Indah (Bulk Terminal)
  PT Adaro Indonesia (Coal Mining)
Property Development:
  PT Aditya Toa Development
Trading:
  PT Prima Comexindo Trading (International Trading)
Consulting, Financial and Other Services:
  PT Bank Industri (Commercial Banking)
  PT Bank Universal (Commercial Banking)
  PT Indoconsult (Consulting)
  PT Redecon (Consulting)
  PT Prahabima (Financial Investments)
  PT Katena (Film Production)
  PT Era Persada (Investment Holding Company, Telecommunications)
Agriculture:
  PT Tidar Kerinci Agung (Palm Oil Plantation)
  PT Bima Sakti Mutiara

In spite of his takeover activities, Hashim claims he is mainly a trader. He likes to buy and sell. Many of his deals are small. While arranging commodity deals in Europe he doesn't pass up the opportunity to do some used car trading. He has already sold eleven used cars he bought in Germany to customers in the Ukraine.

One of Hashim's first ventures was PT[3] Prima Comexindo. Founded in 1986 with an initial equity investment of $50,000, the company has carved out a niche as an international trader specializing in trade between Indonesia and other developing countries. Hashim holds controlling interest in the company and there are

---

[3] PT abbreviates "Perseroan Terbatas," meaning Incorporated or Limited in English.

---

no foreign equity holders. Comexindo practices what Hashim calls "proactive countertrade." This means finding markets for goods that are available only through countertrade. Sellers are easy to find. The trick is to find buyers who can pay with cash or countertrade goods.

Countertrade

For developing countries with limited foreign exchange, countertrade offers a way to finance necessary imports by bartering exports. The basic idea is that if a company wishes to sell to a countertrade country, it must buy (or arrange purchase by others) enough products from its customer to finance the deal. Classical economists scoff at countertrade, calling it a reversion to the days of village barter which creates unnecessary inefficiencies in the international trading system. For developing countries seeking to increase exports, however, countertrade is an attractive policy. Trade within the Soviet Union and the Warsaw Pact was almost exclusively countertrade involving no cash transactions. Exhibit 2 contains general information on countertrade.

Indonesia became one of the first countries outside the Soviet Bloc to use countertrade, by announcing in 1981 that all imports funded by the Government must be financed by 100% countertrade purchases. The goals of the Indonesian countertrade policy were to promote exports of non-petroleum exports[4] and to develop new export markets. Although the policy was detailed, including substantial penalties for non-compliance, it did not achieve its primary objectives. Purchases financed by soft loans from the World Bank, the Asian Development Bank, and the Islamic Development Bank were exempt as were other special categories. Third-party countertrade specialists made large profits by assuming supplier obligations to buy Indonesian products, selling Indonesian products through traditional channels at discounted prices. The results were disappointing. Exports did not increase, new markets did not open, and Indonesian commodities are sold at discounted prices. Non-performance penalties are rarely enforced. Millions of dollars of countertrade obligations remain unfilled by foreign suppliers. Exhibit 3 contains a description of Indonesian countertrade activities.

In 1988, Indonesia improved coordination of countertrade activities by appointing a Director General for Countertrade within the Department of Trade to improve direct bilateral trade between Indonesia and other developing countries. In addition, the government provided low-cost bank financing to subsidize direct commercial agreements between Indonesian private sec-

tor firms and foreign government agencies. Indonesia does not have a state trading company as do countries such as India, Pakistan, and Egypt, so the support offered to private trading companies provided a boost to Indonesian trading activities. The emphasis shifted from forcing foreign suppliers to buy Indonesian goods to encouraging Indonesian traders to find new markets.

PT Prima Comexindo History

Comexindo is a full service trader, offering a full range of countertrade services including commodity trading, financing, and shipping support. In the short span of six years, the firm has set up a network of agents and representatives in Asia, East Africa, and Eastern Europe. Comexindo operates out of permanent offices in seven countries. It has a multi-national staff of 400 employees from 18 different countries. In 1992 the company generated a $250 million turnover in trading activities.

Comexindo considers itself an exporter of Indonesian goods. It seeks trading markets where Indonesian producers enjoy long-term comparative advantages. The company seeks to break the domination of Indonesia's foreign trade by offshore trading companies.

Comexindo does not limit its activities to large, well-publicized deals. The company is capable of handling all aspects of international trade. Its focus remains on the Southern Hemisphere, providing services to buyers and sellers who usually lack foreign exchange. Exhibits 4, 5, and 6 provide a good look at the depth and breadth of Comexindo's activities.

About 60% of Comexindo's transactions are countertrade agreements of which 65% involve third countries as importers of countertrade goods. The company operates as both a buyer and a seller in its countertrade operations, taking title to the goods it trades. It does not serve as an agent for others. The company buys in the source country (free on board) and sells in the destination country (cost, insurance, and

---

[4] Indonesia is a major oil producer and member of OPEC.

Exhibit 2
Countertrade

In a normal export transaction, the seller directs a flow of goods or services to a buyer. The buyer pays with foreign exchange currency, usually using a letter of credit (LC). Some countries that lack foreign exchange reserves or credits require sellers to engage in countertrade. In countertrade transactions, the seller helps the buyer to arrange a corresponding outflow of exports, to pay for the imports. Assume, for example, that a U.S. manufacturer wants to sell aircraft to a countertrade country. As payment for the aircraft, the seller would either accept or arrange to sell goods and services from the buying country in lieu of cash payment. McDonnell-Douglas, in a famous deal, swapped DC-10s for Yugoslavian hams as part of a countertrade arrangement. Ghana bartered $8 million in diamonds, and forest products in 1985 with Bulgaria for farm equipment and pharmaceuticals. In 1986, Caterpillar Tractor sent earth-moving equipment to Venezuela which sent iron ore to Romania. The Rumanians sold men's suits to England for cash that was passed back to Caterpillar. In practice, most countertrade deals involve some cash.

The former Soviet union created a vast countertrading network within its own republics and throughout Eastern Europe. When the Eastern Bloc began to trade with the West in the 1970s, most deals involved countertrade. The same continues today. After the collapse of the Eastern Bloc, foreign exchange is practically non-existent. Exporters wishing to sell to the CIS* and Eastern Europe must be prepared for countertrade deals. Even fast food companies use countertrade. McDonald's has major investments in food processing plants and retail outlets in Russia. But earnings are in rubles. Rubles are not convertible and nearly worthless. To get earnings out of Russia, McDonald's exports processed food products produced by its Russian plants to West Germany, where it sells the products for cash. All CIS states are good candidates for countertrade. They lack foreign exchange and the skills to sell their goods in international markets.

Common Countertrade Transactions

1. Barter.

One contract. Direct exchange of goods. No money involved. Pure barter exchanges are rare. It is difficult to value the bartered goods. Most deals require at least some cash flow to pay for transportation, storage, and agent fees.

2. Counterpurchase.

More than one contract. Seller assumes an obligation through a separate contract to purchase goods for export from the buying country. The counterpurchase contract can account for all or some portion of the original sale. Payment in counterpurchase arrangements is frequently made through clearing agreements. Under a clearing agreement, the parties exchange goods of equivalent value over a specified time period. Accounts maintained through inter-bank agreements keep track of sales and purchases. There are two common variations of counterpurchase agreements. In a "switch" agreement, the seller arranges exports to a third country. If the third country has trade surplus under a bilateral trade agreement with the import country, payment is made by reducing the surplus by adjusting clearing accounts. In the second variation, the seller uses blocked currency in the importing country to purchase goods for export.

This is the most common type of countertrade. Eventually, after all contracts are fulfilled, the contracting parties receive payment in cash.

3. Co-Production.

Seller agrees as part of the contract to set up production facilities in the importing country. The host country gains through a transfer of technology. In the case of petroleum and mining operations, the seller accepts payment in production sharing contracts rather than monetary royalties or commissions.

4. Offset.

Seller agrees to make purchases in the importing country to "offset" the foreign exchange used to pay for the imported goods. Manufacturers of heavy equipment and aircraft usually agree to purchase parts and components produced in the importing country as a form of "offset." Large military purchases often involve direct payments as "offsets" for exports, services, and financing directly related to the sale.

---

*Commonwealth of Independent States. A confederation including most of the republics formerly belonging to the Soviet Union.

Exhibit 3

Indonesian Countertrade

The use of countertrade in the Eastern Bloc spread to developing countries. In late 1981 Indonesia was one of the first noncommunist countries to issue comprehensive countertrade regulations. Under regulations in effect in 1992, government import contracts valued at 500 million rupiah* (Rp) must be linked to the export Indonesian goods of equivalent value. There is a hefty penalty (up to 50%) for non-compliance. Indonesian goods must be exported to new markets, not existing customers at existing levels. Petroleum and natural gas products do not qualify as countertrade goods.

Although Indonesia's countertrade rules sound quite restrictive, in practice enforcement is on a case-by-case basis. Most developing countries use countertrade as a method of reducing trade deficits and to conserve foreign exchange. By contrast, Indonesia considers countertrade an incentive to improve non-energy exports. In other words the purpose is to encourage exports, not to penalize imports.

The Indonesian regulations attempt to encourage non-petroleum exports (Table 1). They present a rather long and cumbersome process for suppliers (Table 2). The Government has approved early $5 billion in countertrade deals since 1982. About 34% remains unfulfilled (Table 3). Swiss suppliers have completed only 13% of their countertrade agreements. Suppliers from five countries account for nearly 87% of total Indonesian countertrade (Table 4).

Tables 1 through 4 contain more information on Indonesia's countertrade activities.

Table 1:

Indonesian Countertrade Policy

Implemental Directive on
the Linkage of Government Procurement from Import
with Export of Non–Oil/Gas Commodities from Indonesia[†]

I. GENERAL

1. These directives have been adjusted to the basic provision on the Linkage of Government from Import with Export of Non-oil/Gas commodities from Indonesia, issued by the Minister/Secretary of State in his capacity of Chairman of the Team for the Control on the Supply of Government Goods/Equipment under No. R-079/TPPBPP/I/1982 dated January 21, 1982.

2. Government Procurement is interpreted as the purchase/supply which is implemented by Departments/Non-Departmental Government Institutions and State Owned Business Agencies, the financing of which is derived from the State Budget of Income and Expenditure (APBN) and/or Export Credit.

3. a. A Department/Non-Department Government Institution or a State owned Business Agency which has done a purchase subject to linkage is obliged to comply with the stipulations contained in KEPPRES (Presidential Decree) No. 10/1980 in conjunction with KEPPRES No. 17/1983 on the Team for the Control on the Supply of Government Goods/Equipment and KEPPRES No. 14A/1980 in conjunction with KEPPRES No. 18/1981, of which the implementation is coordinated by the Minister/Secretary of State in his capacity of Chairman of the Team for the Control on the Supply of Government Goods/Equipment (The Team of KEPPRES No. 10/1980).

b. The Minister/Secretary of State in his capacity of Chairman of the Team for the Control on the Supply of Government Goods/Equipment would determine the purchases of the Government/supply for government purposes.

4. The purchase/supply of goods for government purposes of which the import component has a value of over Rp 500 million (five hundred million) is subject to linkage.

5. Exempt from linkage are the following:

a. If the source of financing is derived from a soft loan, loan from the World Bank, Islamic Development Bank and the Asian Development Bank.

b. Domestic components contained in the contract of the Foreign Supplier like component of services, goods and taxes/duties.

c. Services which are used by various government agencies related to specific expertise, for example: foreign accountant, lawyer, surveyor, consultant's services, purchase of technology (patent), etc.

d. Purchases or imports under the Joint Venture system between state companies or foreign companies.

*The Indonesian currency unit is the rupiah, exchanged at about Rp 2,070 to the dollar in early 1993.
†Unofficial translation provided the Directorate of Foreign Trade.

Exhibit 3
Indonesian Countertrade (continued)

II. STIPULATIONS ON LINKAGE

1. The Indonesian export commodities which are subject to linkage are agricultural products, industrial products and mining products except oil and natural gas. The Department of Trade will periodically publish a list of export commodities which are available, together with the names of the exporters/commodity associations.

2. The value of the goods linked must be similar to the value of the government purchase from abroad (in FOB quotation). Particularly with respect to the supply of contracted work of construction, the value subject to linkage is the total value of the components of material/goods to be imported. This value must be clearly indicated in the tender document.

3. The overseas supplier who has won the tender may comply with the obligation of purchasing Indonesian export commodities other than oil and natural gas by the:

3.1 Supplier himself;

3.2 Companies affiliated or having relationship with the Supplier;

3.3 Other company/third party; the Supplier delegated his obligation to a bona fide third party, to be confirmed by a recommendation and/or certificate of bonafidity issued by a Bank or another agency this delegation is to be made in the form of an Assignment Agreement (Annex 2). The Department of Trade is competent to approve or to reject such assignment.

4. The suppliers/overseas buyers/companies mentioned under point 3, would select one or several commodities to be purchased from Indonesia and make direct contact with the Indonesian exporters and sign the transaction contract in conformity with the form of contract normally applicable.

5. The purchase done by the overseas supplier must be an additional amount of the total transactions of trade previously affected.

6. The goods purchased under the linkage system, the export there of is to be directed to the supplier's, country of origin. If the government procurement mentioned is supplied from several countries, the export may be destined to the supplier's country that has won the tender or the country of origin of the goods. Export destined to a third country is only justified if such third country is not a traditional market for the export commodities concerned, whereas the export thereof shall not disturb the existing marketing channel.

7. The transaction of the Indonesia export commodities is to be effected in US-dollar currency or in any other foreign currency which is quoted in the Indonesian Foreign Exchange Market.

8. The contract between the Indonesian exporter and the overseas supplier in this case is not a Future's Buying, as an attempt to safeguard the position of the overseas supplier or the position of the exporter with respect to the future price development (hedging).

9. The purchase of Indonesia commodities other than oil and natural gas under the linkage system has to be shipped in stages and regularly during the validity of the contract on the government procurement, and the obligation has to be completed at the end of such purchasing contract. If at the end of the completion of the project/implementation of the purchase (government import), the export from Indonesia has not been completed, either partly or entirely, a penalty will be imposed on the winner of the tender or on whom such obligation has been delegated, to the extent of 50% (fifty percent) of the export value that has not been implemented yet.

Exhibit 3
Indonesian Countertrade (continued)

Table 2:
Administrative Process for an Indonesian Countertrade Deal

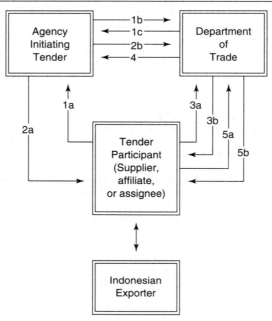

1. Letter of undertaking (LU)
   a. Transmission of LU and tender document.
   b. Transmission of LU to the Department of Trade.
   c. Approval of LU.
2. Announcement of the tender award.
   a. To the supplier(s).
   b. To the Department of Trade.
3. Draft Annex A (countertrade guarantee and/or assignment agreement).
   a. From supplier(s) to the Department of Trade.
   b. Endorsement from the Department of Trade.
4. Contract signature approval.
5. Annex B (export letter, bill of lading, invoice documents)
   a. From supplier or assignee to the Department of Trade.
   b. Confirmation letter or penalty from the Department of Trade.

Table 3:

Counter Purchase Obligations and Realization 1982–1992 (U.S. $)

Number	Supplier Origin	Obligation	Realization	Remainder	Surplus
1.	Japan	1,607,994,119	979,131,327	628,862,792	41,240,413
2.	USA	128,743,711	121,404,911	7,068,800	5,187,623
3.	West Germany	1,357,775,079	978,006,191	379,768,888	3,724,266
4.	Singapore	185,892,839	138,877,128	47,015,710	5,362,554
5.	Netherlands	50,771,646	43,079,180	7,692,466	14,471,426
6.	Canada	244,500,649	243,888,299	612,349	170,395
7.	South Korea	73,285,295	73,285,295	—	1,130,340
8.	England	135,328,929	134,329,178	999,751	6,165,145
9.	Rumania	81,701,131	61,946,839	19,754,292	18,587
10.	France	307,140,240	183,240,401	123,999,831	1,370,404
11.	Hong Kong	51,991,960	36,121,641	15,870,318	1,144,416
12.	East Germany	6,580,000	2,263,418	4,316,581	—
13.	Sweden	4,139,420	4,139,420	—	650,063
14.	Australia	89,802,582	89,038,483	764,099	560,521
15.	Italy	15,411,031	15,411,031	—	88,297
16.	Malaysia	2,357,545	2,357,545	—	25,444
17.	Austria	32,399,758	32,399,758	—	161,716
18.	Panama	1,012,489	1,012,489	—	16,209
19.	Mexico	1,255,170	—	1,255,170	—
20.	Yugoslavia	16,187,226	16,187,226	—	126,122
21.	Switzerland	507,816,742	65,356,343	442,460,399	1,777,359
22.	Belgium	1,540,814	1,540,814	—	36,762
23.	Poland	4,905,000	4,905,000	—	5,632,268
24.	Spain	428,368	—	428,368	—
25.	Finland	757,858	757,858	—	23,505
26.	Thailand	27,803,793	—	4,251,000	2,408,793
27.	Jordan	11,839,905	11,839,905	—	448,969,3310
	Total	4,949,114,097	3,263,993,267 (66%)	1,685,120,830 (34%)	91,901,331

Source: Department of Trade.

Table 4:
The Top Five Indonesian Countertrade Export Buyers 1982–1992 (U.S. $)

Number	Country	Obligation	Realization	Remainder
1.	Japan	1,607,994,119	979,131,327	628,862,792
2.	West Germany	1,357,775,079	978,006,191	397,768,888
3.	Switzerland	507,816,742	65,356,343	442,460,399
4.	France	307,140,240	183,240,401	123,999,831
5.	Canada	244,500,649	243,838,299	612,349
	Total	4,025,226,929	2,449,572,561	1,575,654,368

Source: Department of Trade.

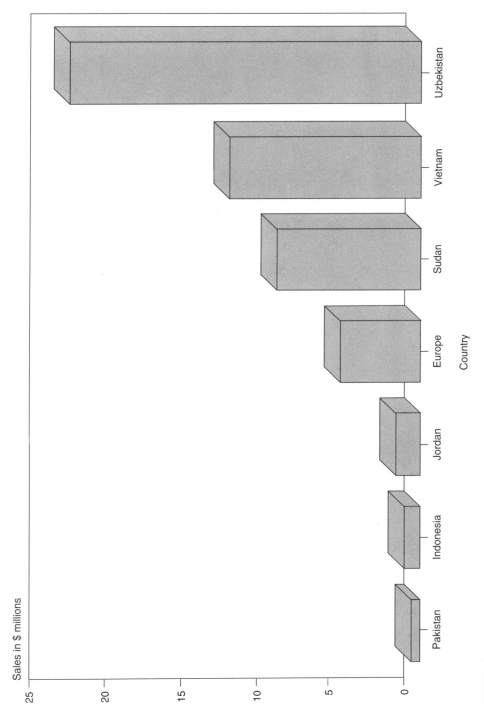

Exhibit 4 PT Prima Comexindo 1992 Sales per Country

466

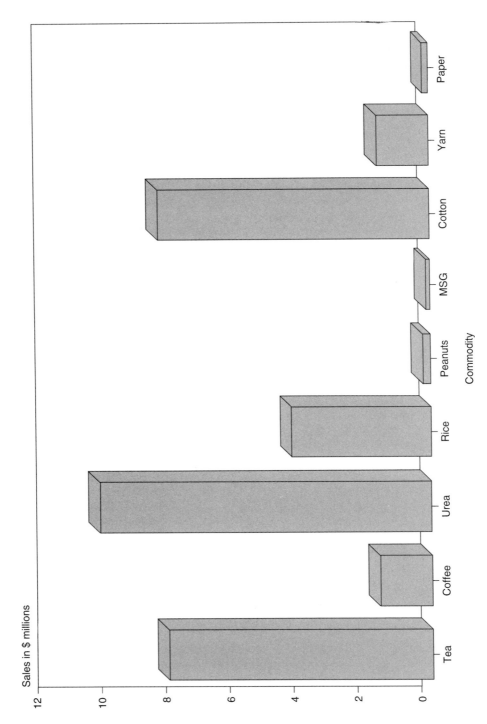

Exhibit 5 PT Prima Comexindo 1992 Sales per Commodity

Exhibit 6
PT Prima Comexindo Trading Flows

Commodity	Sources	Markets
Tea	Indonesia, Vietnam, China	Pakistan, CIS*, Middle East, Europe
Coffee, Cocoa, Palm Oil	Indonesia, Vietnam	Europe, Singapore
Rubber	Indonesia	Africa, Middle East, CIS
Maize	Vietnam, Indonesia	Southeast Asia
Rice	Vietnam, East Asia	Philippines, India, CIS, Middle East
Oil Seeds	Vietnam, China	
Peanuts	Vietnam, China, India, East Africa	
Pulp, Paper Products	Indonesia, CIS, Sri Lanka, Eastern Europe	Pakistan, East Africa, CIS
Cement	Indonesia	South and Southeast Asia
Coal	Indonesia	South and Southeast Asia, Eastern Europe
Chrome Ore	Pakistan, East Africa, CIS	China
Steel Scrap	Indochina, USA	
Synthetic Fibers	Taiwan, Indonesia, India	Vietnam, Europe
Cotton Fibers	Central Asia, Pakistan, India, China East Africa	Europe, Indonesia, Vietnam, Bangladesh, Taiwan, Korea, Philippines
Garments, Knitted Products	Indonesia	Europe, CIS, South America
Yarns	Indonesia	Europe, East Asia
Greige, Finished Fabrics	Indonesia	Eastern Europe, CIS, South America
Jute, Kenaf Fibers	China, Indochina, Bangladesh	
Urea (Fertilizer)	Indonesia, CIS	South and Southeast Asia, East Africa
Potash, Sulfur, Phosphates	CIS, Middle East	
Chemicals, Pharmaceuticals, Footwear, Leather, etc.	CIS, East Africa, South Asia	

*Former Soviet Union.

freight). It bears the risk of ownership and expects profits commensurate with that risk-taking. Exhibit 7 describes common export pricing terms.

The company got its start when Hashim teamed up with Asghar Mehdi, an experienced international trader. Both men saw bilateral trade opportunities between developing countries, particularly those in the Southern Hemisphere. They believed it was possible to bypass traditional trading arrangements that flow through developed countries. They wanted to avoid quota allocations applied by developed countries to goods like textiles. Indonesia, they knew, had great export potential. In bulk commodities, Indonesia continued to export agricul-

tural products, energy, and fertilizer, but had become the world's largest exporter of cement as well. In addition Indonesia produces tires, auto batteries, textiles, garments, shoes, and light machinery. To Hashim and Asghar, the problem was not having something to sell, it was to find buyers.

Asghar had good contacts in Pakistan (he is a Pakistani with Canadian citizenship). The first Comexindo bilateral contract was between Indonesia and Pakistan. Pakistan is the world's fourth largest importer of tea, and Indonesia is the third largest exporter of tea. Selling Indonesian tea to Pakistan was clearly a "win–win" situation. Comexindo arranged a $10 million deal to sell Indonesian tea to

Exhibit 7
Common Export Pricing Terms

---

1. FOB (Free on Board).

Price of goods loaded by seller on transport at a specific location. The buyer pays freight, insurance and other transportation costs. Title transfers to the buyer when the goods are loaded. For example:
FOB Factory—Buyer receives the goods at the seller's factory.
FOB Tashkent—Buyer receives the goods at an inland location (Tashkent).
FOB Odessa—Buyer receives the goods at a seaport (Odessa).
FOB Trans Pacific 5, Jakarta—Buyer receives the goods on a specified vessel
   at a specified port (Jakarta).

2. FAS (Free Alongside).

Price of goods includes delivery alongside a vessel for loading. The buyer pays other transportation costs as in FOB. Title transfers to the buyer when the goods are within reach of the vessel's loading equipment. Example:
FAS Trans Pacific 5, Jakarta—Seller delivers the goods within reach of the loading equipment of the Trans Pacific 5,
   docked in Jakarta.

3. CIF (Cost, Insurance, and Freight).

Price of goods includes insurance, freight, and associated costs to a designated destination. Title transfers when buyer accepts goods at destination. For example:
CIF Tashkent—Seller delivers the goods to their destination.
CIF Jakarta—Seller delivers the goods to a port of entry (Jakarta) near the
   buyer.

4. C and F (Cost and Freight).

Same as CIF, except that the price does not include insurance costs.

Pakistan, agreeing to be paid in Pakistani products of equivalent value. Indonesian banks financed the purchase and delivery of the tea to Pakistan. Unfortunately, a new government in Pakistan canceled the deal, but not before $7 million of trade had flowed between the two countries.

When opportunity knocked again, they were ready. In 1986, Vietnam was having difficulty servicing loans granted by the Indonesian Government. Comexindo knew that the Vietnamese had no money, but they had scrap steel (mostly war junk), a commodity used by the Indonesian steel industry and in short supply in Indonesia. The company arranged for the scrap to be shipped to Indonesia in partial pay-

ment of the loans. This was the beginning of a long-term relationship between Comexindo and the Vietnamese Government.

Trading with Vietnam gave Comexindo valuable experience in dealing with Communist countries. The Vietnamese knew little about international trade. They needed logistical assistance to move goods in and out of their country. Their banking system was not capable of financing large international transactions. In short, Vietnam needed the services of Comexindo.

In its dealings with Vietnam, Comexindo kept its eye on the long run. The company wanted to make a profit, but it also wanted a long term relationship. To further those ends,

Comexindo conducted itself in such a way that the Vietnamese were satisfied customers, likely to continue doing business with the company in the future.

Buoyed by its success in Vietnam, Comexindo began to look for other connections with Communist countries. Even before the break-up of the Soviet Union, the company had identified Uzbekistan as a promising trade partner. Uzbekistan produces one million tons of cotton per year and is always looking for buyers with cash. When the Soviet Union collapsed, Comexindo had agents in Moscow, Tashkent, and Odessa, working through the problems of buying Uzbek cotton.

In retrospect, the foresight of Hashim and Asghar has proved correct. In 1990, Indonesian trade with members of the Non-Aligned Movement (NAM)[5] totaled $7 billion, evenly split between imports and exports. By 1991 this had increased to $4.2 billion in exports and $4.4 billion in imports. Only a small portion of Indonesian exports to NAM nations are energy related. By contrast energy exports comprised 70% of the $10.9 billion exported to Japan in 1990.

International Trading

When negotiating an international trade agreement there are four risks to consider. These are country risk, commodity risk, financial risk, and operational risk. Country risk is the threat of political change or turmoil that might threaten an agreement. To reduce country risk, Comexindo maintains offices in countries with which it deals. Specialists keep an eye on local conditions that might cause trouble.

To be successful a trading company must have the technical and commercial expertise to trade in the products or commodities it is purchasing. Comexindo traders are professionals. They know their business. Each is expert in one commodity, familiar with pricing, the effect of

weather on crop yields, market conditions—all the factors that control the supply and demand for that commodity. This minimizes the company's exposure to commodity risk.

The payment arrangement is the cornerstone of any countertrade agreement. Herein lies financial risk. How and when does case flow? Monetary policies of the governments involved often cause difficulties. Indonesia, for example enjoys a freely convertible, relatively stable currency with few restrictions on movement of foreign exchange. Many developing countries, on the other hand, face foreign exchange shortages and use nonconvertible currencies. These countries rely upon clearing accounts for countertrade whereby a financial institution keeps track of a countertrade exchange in two currencies, neither of which is convertible into foreign exchange earnings. Comexindo usually structures its countertrade arrangements so that sellers are always paid in foreign exchange.

Small things sometimes cause difficulties. One Comexindo deal stalled because the Islamic Development Bank requires an instrument called a Letter of Guarantee from the Indonesian Government. Standard Indonesian banking practice is to issue a Letter of Credit (LC). The issue was resolved but it illustrates the need for experienced financial specialists.

To reduce the financial risks of non-payment, foreign exchange difficulties, and currency restrictions, Comexindo uses local banks with international reputations. For example, when dealing with countries that were formerly part of the Soviet Union, the company relies upon Moscow Narodny Bank, a British bank 100% owned by Russia (formerly by the Soviet Union).

After a countertrade deal is negotiated and signed, it must be executed. Here operational risk must be overcome. Comexindo employees are on the ground to accept the goods. They make sure that the company has the knowledge

---

[5] Most members of the NAM are developing countries.

and capabilities to take possession and move the goods. Besides physical handling, control and handling of documents is crucial. One missing certificate can hold up shipments worth millions of dollars. Many of the countries where Comexindo does business lack good communications. Things must be done right the first time.

Operations

Here are some examples of Comexindo operations:

A Multi-Country Deal

In 1992, Comexindo purchased $60 million in cotton from Uzbekistan in exchange for Indonesian tea and garments. Beginning in 1993, the company will participate in a three-way countertrade arrangement involving Uzbekistan, Vietnam and Indonesia. During the three years covered by the agreement, the government of Uzbekistan will deliver 50,000 to 60,000 tons of cotton per year to Comexindo. Some of the cotton will go to Indonesia. In return, Comexindo will supply the Interaloka Association, an Uzbekistan state-owned trading company, with tea from Indonesia and rice from Vietnam. For its part in the deal, Vietnam receives fertilizer from Indonesia.

This three-way trade arrangement is a counterpurchase transaction involving three contracts: a contract for the purchase of Uzbek cotton; a contract for the sale of Vietnamese rice to Uzbekistan, and a contract for the sale of Indonesia tea to Uzbekistan. The flow of commodities is shown in Exhibit 8. Comexindo must finance part of the purchase of Uzbek cotton until it receives payment from its cotton customers.

The key to completing the deal was financing the initial cotton purchases from Uzbekistan. The three-year contract is risky because Central Asia suffers from political instability. Banks in Singapore and Jakarta were reluctant to provide funding at reasonable rates. Comexindo turned to the Islamic Development Bank (IDB) in Jidda, Saudi Arabia, which specializes in loans to Islamic countries. Both Indonesia and Uzbekistan are Islamic countries, so the IDB was willing to fund the cotton and tea exchange between Uzbekistan and Indonesia. The IDB provided $15 million in soft loans to finance one third of the Uzbek cotton deal. Comexindo provided the balance of the financing. Indonesian textile producers could only purchase about 20% of the Uzbek cotton. The remaining 80% was sold through Comexindo traders in Singapore and Bremen, Germany.

Assistance to Vietnam

Deal-making is only part of successful international trading. Comexindo must also handle logistical problems. Vietnam is one of Comexindo's major customers, trading in fertilizer, tea, peanuts, and rice. The Vietnamese wanted to sell tea, but their tea was not up to international standards. Comexindo seized the opportunity by selling tea processing machinery to Vietnam in exchange for tea. The company handled both ends of the deal, providing quality control in Vietnam and selling on the international tea market.

To solve another problem, Comexindo built and operates a bulk loading and bagging facility in Vietnam. At first Comexindo had to ship packaged fertilizer because Vietnam lacked bulk loading facilities. Package shipment costs about $10 per ton more than bulk shipment, raising the price to Vietnam and cutting Comexindo's profits. The solution was obvious: build a bulk loading and bagging terminal in Vietnam. Accordingly, Comexindo proposed a joint venture to construct a $1.5 million bulk loading facility in cooperation with the Saigon Port Authority. Competition was tough. Firms from South Korea, Singapore and Europe also submitted proposals. Comexindo got the contract and now owns 60% of the venture. The new fa-

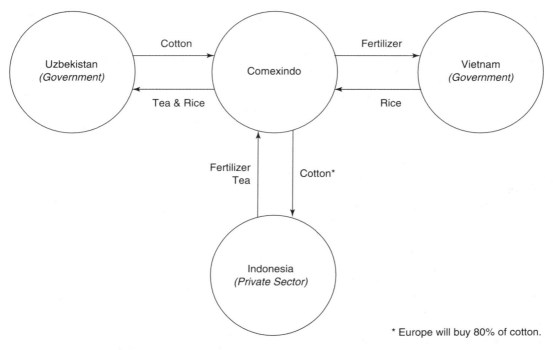

Exhibit 8   PT Prima Comexindo Three-Way Counterpurchase Plan

cility unloads bulk fertilizer from ships and bags it for ditribution in Vietnam. Indonesian fertilizer exports to Vietnam are expected to increase from 140,000 tons in 1992 to 200,000 tons per year.

Logistics in Central Asia

As previously mentioned, part of Comexindo's strategy is to buy FOB (free on board) and sell CIF (cost, insurance, and freight). This means that the company takes title to goods it purchases in the country of origin then transports them to the destination country where the buyer takes title. Trading with a land-locked country like Uzbekistan presents Comexindo with special problems. Comexindo agents monitor movement of the goods carefully. At railroad marshalling yards they check to make sure that railroad cars containing Comexindo goods are routed promptly with the proper documentation for international trade.

The company takes possession of the cotton in Tashkent, and agents then arrange rail transportation to the Black Sea port city of Odessa, Ukraine. The cotton travels over 2000 miles through Kazakhstan, Russia, and Ukraine, crossing the Volga, Don, and Dnieper rivers. The Soviet Union originally set up these rail routes between Central Asia and the Black Sea, but now rail traffic must cross three sovereign nations. Comexindo agents get the goods loaded on sea transport to Southeast Asia or Europe. The process is reversed for Comexindo goods destined for Uzbekistan. Title stays with Comexindo until the goods arrive at their destination.

Organization and Personnel

Top management of Comexindo consists of three officers. Hashim is President Director and Chief Executive Officer. Siswanto Sudomo is Director of Finance and Administration. The Executive Vice President for Trading Operations and Corporate Development is Asghar Mehdi.

Hashim is the primary deal maker. Asghar provides the operational trading know-how. Siswanto is a noted educator with a Ph.D. in economics from the University of Wisconsin. He handles financial problems and relations with Indonesia's banking community. Together, their skills complement each other to form an excellent executive team.

Although Hashim's excellent political connections are no handicap, the deals Hashim negotiates are successful because of economics, not politics. Sometimes the commercial arrangements lead to political relations, rather than vice versa. For example, the Uzbek cotton deal gave Ismail A. Karimov, the President of Uzbekistan, a reason to make a state visit to Indonesia to meet President Suharto, the father of Hashim's sister-in-law.

The key to Comexindo's growth is its professional staff (Exhibit 9). Respected by its competitors as an excellent company, Comexindo delivers on its promises. The company can execute countertrade deals. Comexindo understands that successful international trading requires foreign expertise and well-trained local executives.

Finances

Cash flow is always a concern in international trading. Although gross profit margins for Comexindo range from 3% on most commodities to 15% on manufactured goods, cash does not flow from a typical countertrade transaction until the buyer actually pays for the goods. This usually takes about 18 months.

To close counterpurchase deals, the company needs access to reliable sources of financing to cover the cash flow time lag. Unfortunately, it has great difficulty raising funds from Indonesian banks, the most likely suppliers in Comexindo's home country. Private banks in Indonesia are small and cannot afford to make major loans to one firm. The Government banks are short of funds and do not have the expertise to make the fast decisions required to support international trading. Comexindo has had to look outside Indonesian for financial support. It is the only Indonesian company that has been successful in getting loans from the Islamic Development Bank.

Future Plans

Comexindo plans to continue its growth. Although it does not limit its activities to certain areas or products, the main thrust of the company's efforts will center on finding markets for Indonesian exports. If buyers for those products desire counterpurchase arrangements, Comexindo will be ready and able to provide those services. The company has integrated backward by buying tea plantations to insure a reliable supply.

Hashim predicted that Comexindo will do $350 million in counterpurchase deals in 1993. He hoped to do $150 million worth of business with Russia and $100 million with Vietnam. Other business will come from the Uzbekistan deal and with smaller contracts with Sudan, Ethiopia, and India. In April 1993, Comexindo announced the signing of a three million dollar countertrade deal with Kazakhstan which borders on Uzbekistan. Kazakhstan will buy Indonesian tea, cacao, and spices. In exchange, Comexindo will purchase wheat and other commodities from Kazakhstan. Both parties expect the Islamic Development Bank to fund the arrangement. Like Uzbekistan, Sudan and Ethiopia will want to sell cotton. Russia, for its part, will most likely be interested in exporting

Exhibit 9
PT Prima Comexindo General Managers

I. Agribusiness I (Plantation Management)

General Manager: Andre Hughes (Dutch)
Active Commodities: Tea, coffee, cocoa, palm oil, rubber, and tobacco

II. Agribusiness II (Miscellaneous Commodities and Fertilizers)

General Manager: Praba Madhavan (Malaysian)
Active Commodities: Cereals, rice, oil seeds, animal feed, peanuts, spices, food additives
Fertilizers: Urea, potash, sulfur, phosphates, compound fertilizers

III. Industrial/Mineral Products and Raw Materials

General Manager: Permadi Soemarahatiano (Indonesian)
Active Commodities: Pulp, paper and paper products, waste paper, cement, coal, steel, chrome and iron ore, steel
                      scrap, steel products, non-ferrous metals, plant and equipment

IV. Textile Raw Materials and Finished Products

General Manager: Pradeep Dudaney (Indian)
Active Commodities: Synthetic and cotton fibers, garments, knitted products and piece goods, yarns, greige and
                      finished fabrics, jute and kenaf fiber

V. General Products and Trade Services

General Manager: K. R. Subramanian (Indonesian)
Active Commodities: Consumer goods, chemicals, footwear, pharmaceuticals, leather

VI. Shipping

General Manager: Mohammed Kassim (Pakistan/U.K.)
Services: Shipping, charter, and storage

---

capital goods such as heavy equipment and machine tools.

Comexindo is an excellent example of how a well-managed firm can compete successfully against giant international traders by finding the right niche. Other developing countries might well follow its example to break their dependence on traditional trading arrangements controlled by the United States, Japan, Western Europe, Hong Kong, and Singapore.

THIRTEEN

INTERNATIONAL FINANCIAL MANAGEMENT

A. Tourani Rad, University of Limburg,
The Netherlands
R. Khan, California State University,
San Bernardino

This chapter presents major issues of international financial management. We begin our understanding of this topic by studying the international monetary and financial system. Next, the foreign exchange market, the major factors influencing exchange rates, and various means and forms of hedging exchange rate risks are introduced. The following part studies international investments, diversification benefits, and the measurement and management of political risks. The final section reviews the international sources of finance available to MNCs.

Some say the dollar does not fall, it is pushed. They claim that the banks are the culprits, and they present a scenario in which the dollar is pushed down for big bucks. The setting is in Switzerland at the dinner table, Sunday night. Haans, the treasurer from the local branch of an American bank, and the chief traders from the Big Three Swiss banks are having dinner. In a passing remark one of the three chief traders turns to Haans and informs him that they had each decided to sell $2 billion during the coming week. This is a signal.

The next morning at 7:15 A.M. Haans proceeds to sell $6 million against Swiss francs two time zones backward to Bahrain while the rest of the speculative community finishes breakfast. In London, at 7:30 A.M. Jimmy Pritchard in his office picks up the phone. Haans is on the other end telling him the news. They agree to follow the lead of the Swiss bankers. Haans says that he will sell another $90 million and suggests $70 million to be more appropriate for Jimmy.

Finishing the phone call, Jimmy gives orders to his lieutenants. "We're going to hit the dollar again today. Henry, you take the lead. Mark, get ready, you must borrow everything Henry's going to sell today." Then he turns to the commercial chief. "Duncan, don't open your mouth before ten. Let Henry kick the hell out of the dollar. Then get your boys to go through the list of multinationals. Tell them the dollar might be a little soft. They'll watch the prices start to fall and by noon they'll run into your arms. We're counting on you to buy back this position for us from your commercials."

At this point, Mary Lou Jones, a trainee from New York, who has been sitting silently in a corner asks Duncan: "I heard you say that Mark has to borrow the dollars you are going to sell. How can you sell borrowed money?"

"Very simply. Mark borrows, say, $60 million in the Eurodollar market for four nights. We sell them today against other currencies and then place the pounds, marks, and francs on deposit. On Friday we buy $60 million at a lower price and use the sixty to pay back our loan. We keep the leftover pounds, francs, and marks."

"You mean you make money pushing the dollar down?"

"That's right. 'We' make money. You work for this bank too, Mary Lou."

Adapted from D. Edwards. "The Trading Room: It's Not a Gentleman's Game." *MBA* (June/July 1978), 13–23.

Introduction

As multinational companies (MNCs) search the world for opportunities, resources, and markets, they have to deal with an international financial climate that is in a constant state of flux. They must deal with exchange rates and interest rates along with political and environmental risks and, to function effectively, they must be able to analyze and adapt to changes quickly and efficiently. In selecting from the available alternatives, they must limit the risks of going overseas while maximizing the gains. Willingness to take on such risks and enter a new environment is not enough. To participate effectively in international business, a firm must have a clear knowledge of the functioning and the components of the international financial markets and the institutions that facilitate international business. International financial management is a fascinating and at the same time an intricate matter. It can dramatically affect the profitability of the MNCs. Unfavorable fluctuation in exchange rates may totally wipe out the operating profit of a subsidiary, if those profits have to be repatriated to the home country. While international financial management is the potential source of much frustration for the MNCs, it can provide many benefits, such as multiple sources of financing. Differences in the availability and costs of funds around the world can be used to the advantage of the MNCs. Whereas domestic firms are limited to the local domestic capital markets, MNCs have the benefit of financing their worldwide operations from alternative global sources.

International Monetary System

In today's world, a nation's economy is all too often dependent on its trade and financial transactions with the rest of the world. A clear trend that has been emerging in the past two decades is an increasing integration of domestic economies and financial systems into the global economy. Each nation has, however, its own economic objectives and follows policies resulting in fluctuations of its interest, inflation, and exchange rates. This has a direct impact on the flows of trade and capital among the nations. In

an effort to streamline the international trade and better manage capital flows, an international monetary and financial system has been devised.

This system is made up of an arrangement of rules, procedures, and various instruments for exchanging the one country's currency into the currency of another country. These arrangements and agreements among participating nations are known as the international monetary system. A knowledge of this system and its ever-evolving and ever-changing nature is necessary in order to understand and predict changes and how they will influence the foreign excahnge markets and, in turn, international transactions. This section briefly discusses the evolution of various exchange rate systems and the major exchange rate systems that currently coexist.

The Gold Exchange Standard— Bretton Woods[1]

Historically, international payments among trading nations have been made in gold and silver. When trade began to increase, a system came into being that was accepted by all trading nations. This system was known as the gold standard, and it defined national currencies in terms of a fixed amount of gold. Gold was chosen because of its ability to impose price stability and to bring about readjustments in trade imbalances. Once the exchange rates were fixed, the countries had to commit themselves, through pursuing a variety of economic policies, to maintaining the par value or a fixed price for their currency in terms of gold. Whenever there was an imbalance in trade, adjustments were made by flows of gold. For example, if a country imported more than it exported, it paid the difference from its limited gold and/or foreign currency reserves to other countries and the value of its currency depreciated (i.e., its value dropped against other currencies). The country, in turn, was forced to control its excessive purchases from overseas and had to undertake reforms to bring its currency back in line. The big disadvantage of this system was its effect on domestic economies, which moved up and down depending on the gold flows. Another problem with the system was that the supply of gold did not keep up with the rate of growth of international trade. This gold standard system was used from about 1880 to 1914 and broke down during World War I. The war considerably strained international trade and capital flows and countries imposed severe restrictions on gold exports. Many countries followed inflationary policies (i.e., printing more and more money) to finance the cost of the war. Doing this, however, lead to the collapse of existing currency parities.

The gold standard was reinstated in a modified form, known as the Gold Exchange Standard, from 1925 to 1933. At this time the United States and England could hold gold reserves, but other trading countries could hold both gold and dollars and pounds as reserves. However, in 1931 England quit the system in the face of huge amounts of gold and capital flows, the result of an unrealistic exchange rate. The coming years saw a decline in world trade related to currency devaluation, trade restrictions, export subsidies, and the resultant unemployment. These situations further contributed to the decline of the world economic system and led to the Great Depression. The interwar period was generally characterized by chaos in the international monetary relations, and the prevailing exchange rate regime was a mixture of widely fluctuating rates and rates maintained by an intricate exchange control apparatus.

In July 1944, representatives of world powers met in Bretton Woods, New Hampshire, in an attempt to find a solution to the crisis facing the international financial system. At this meeting, a system was hammered out that took into consideration the differing, and often desperate, needs of the various trading countries. It was a system that remained in place until 1971. One key element of the new system was that the value of the U.S. dollar was fixed in terms of gold and the United States pledged to buy and sell gold to central banks of other nations at $35 per ounce, without limitations or restrictions. The other nations agreed to establish the par value of their currencies in terms of the U.S. dollar, thus fixing their currencies indirectly to gold. They also agreed to maintain this par value within a 1 percent band. Should, for instance, a nation's currency fall in value against the U.S. dollar by more than 1 percent of its par value, that nation's central bank would then buy their pounds, or lira, with the U.S. dollar (selling dollars) to bring it back to the fixed exchange rate. Should the reverse happen and the currency rise by more than 1 percent of its par value, the bank would sell its lira or pounds for U.S. dollars (buying dollars) to prevent further increase. Thus, the goal of gaining stability in exchange rates was accomplished.

The Demise of Bretton Woods

The 1944 Bretton Woods Agreement depended heavily on the financial strength of the United States and the willingness of foreigners to keep the agreed on par value through purchase of dollars with their currencies. In 1945 the economic position of the United States was good. There was a dollar shortage after World War II and U.S. dollars were desperately needed to rebuild the devastated economies of Asia and Europe. However, by the late 1960s, the Asian and European economies had become competitors. They began exporting goods to the United States, thereby earning and accumulating the coveted dollars. Moreover, the Johnson administration financed the escalating war in Vietnam through inflationary monetary policies (i.e., printing dollars). Soon the dollars in the foreign exchange markets exceeded the demand from the rest of the world and to keep the agreed on par value the foreign countries had to buy dollars with their currencies. Many decided not to do so because buying the dollars had a direct impact on their money supplies. They had to print more money in order to buy dollars, thus fanning the fires of inflation. This refusal resulted in a loss of confidence in the dollar and the

United States experienced the so-called "Dollar Crisis" of 1968. Foreigners had three options: They could revalue their currency upward, exchange their dollars for gold, or pressure the United States to correct its economic policies. All the options were tried, but to no avail. The U.S. gold reserves began to dwindle as the foreigners exchanged their currencies for gold. Attempts were made by the United States to stop this conversion into gold, but they were unsuccessful and the U.S. gold reserves continued to decline. In 1971, President Nixon suspended the convertibility of dollars into gold, thus dealing the Bretton Woods Agreement its death blow. The president also imposed a surcharge on imports and launched wage and price controls in order to bring inflation under control.

In an effort to salvage the system and bring order to the foreign exchange markets, the major trading nations met in Washington, D.C., in 1971. They agreed to a change in the price of gold from $35 an ounce to $38, thus devaluing the dollar. They also agreed to increase the level of fluctuation to 2.25 percent, up from the 1 percent agreed on at Bretton Woods. This, however, did little to bring about the desired order. Inflation continued in the United States and the value of the U.S. dollar continued to decline. From the turmoil, there emerged a flexible exchange rate system, known as the *managed floating exchange rate system,* which is now in use.

Current Exchange Rate Arrangements

After the collapse of the Bretton Woods Agreement and President Nixon's action to stop convertibility into gold, the U.S. dollar floated freely against other nations' currencies. The floating exchange rate system is quite the opposite of the fixed rate system. Here the rate fluctuations depend on the supply and demand for the currency in question. There are no rigid established par values, and the countries are not obliged to intervene to defend their currencies. "Free float" is the purest form of the floating exchange rate system, where the value of the currency is es-

tablished by the market. The exchange rate (i.e., the value of that country's currency in terms of another country's currency) can change continuously. Factors such as interest rates, inflation, and economic growth will affect international flows of trade and capital and will thereby have an effect on exchange rates. Adjustment is automatic. There are no flows of gold or reserve currency; the exchange rates themselves change to reflect countries' respective purchasing powers vis-à-vis one another. If, in a particular country, imports are greater than exports, i.e., there is a trade deficit, the value of its currency will erode compared to the currency of other nations, and this will lead to an automatic depreciation of that country's currency in the foreign exchange market.

The pure free-floating system, however, lasted for only a short period of time, and then the managed-float system came into being with exchange rates allowed to fluctuate within a set band, and this is the system that prevails today. Under a managed-float, which is also known as a "dirty float," countries attempt to influence exchange rates and/or try to keep their currencies undervalued or overvalued compared to their true market values. Because exchange rate fluctuations can have a profound effect on the economic well-being of a country, countries attempt to keep their exchange rates at a level believed desirable by their economic policies. For example, if a country has an unemployment problem, it will pursue policies to reduce the value of its currency. This would cause its products to become cheaper in the world market leading to more exports, higher levels of production, and a higher level of employment.

The exchange rates of the U.S. dollar and currencies of other major industrial countries, which account for the bulk of international financial flows, are primarily determined by market forces. The majority of other countries, however, peg their currencies in one form or another against a single currency or composite of currencies. Moreover, in many developing countries, a multiple exchange rate system can be found. These countries require a considerable amount of foreign currency to buy from industrialized countries, but the amount they have is limited. In an effort to save the precious currency for developmental projects, these countries set a high rate of exchange, and so make the currency expensive in terms of local currency, for the importation of luxury items. A reduced rate of exchange is offered for those goods and services needed to aid in the development of the country. Thus, currently three major exchange rate systems exist: the floating, the fixed (or pegged), and the multiple rate systems.

Under the present exchange rate system there is no certainty regarding the future course of the dollar. The value of the U.S. dollar has been moving up and down against major world currencies since 1971. For example, the U.S. dollar was equivalent to 2.675 German marks in 1971, but only 1.8343 in 1979. This was primarily due to high inflation in the United States. In 1980, the dollar began to rise and continued this rise until 1985, when it was equal to 2.942 German marks. This increase in value was looked on most unfavorably by other nations, because it meant that the trading partners were unable to afford to buy the "expensive" U.S. goods and services. U.S. exporters were also unhappy because it reduced their exports. The dollar started a long downward slide during 1986 and 1987. It perked up a bit in early 1988, fell sharply in 1990 and was stable through 1991 to 1993. However, since then the value of the dollar has dropped again to about 1.6 German marks in 1994.

The European Monetary System

After the collapse of the fixed exchange rate system and the international monetary crisis that followed, several European countries sought to design a system that would give more stability to their exchange rates. In March 1979, members of the European Community (EC)—now the European Union (EU)—originally with the exception of Italy, established the European Monetary System (EMS). Full members of the EMS agreed, under the Exchange Rate Mechanism (ERM), to form a currency agreement to maintain exchange rates within a 2.25 percent trading band with respect to each other. These currencies were permitted to float jointly against the U.S. dollar. The object of EMS was to bring about monetary stability through closer monetary cooperation and common economic policies. To achieve this objective, a unit of currency known as the European Currency Unit (ECU) was created. The value of this currency unit is determined as a weighted average of the values of a "basket" of the currencies of the different member states. The par value of each EC nation's currency is defined in terms of ECUs. A European Monetary Cooperation Fund (EMCF) was established in 1982 to provide short-term credit to its member countries for support of their currencies in the foreign exchange market. The United Kingdom joined the EMS in October 1990 and in September 1992 it suspended its membership. Although the ERM helped to stabilize the exchange rates among countries with close economic ties, it was not a total success. Several member countries have had to realign exchange rates several times and, as recently as the summer of 1993, market forces led to an almost total collapse of the system. Member countries had to relinquish the old currency limits and allow their currencies to fluctuate within a 15 percent band, with the exception of Germany, Belgium, and the Netherlands, which agreed to a 6 percent band. For such a fixed exchange rate system to be successful, it is imperative that member countries subordinate their national economic supremacy to the common good that can follow from pursuing common policies. The EMS has had problems in this area.[2]

Fixed versus Flexible Exchange Rate Systems

A debate is still raging over which type of exchange rate system is best able to bring about stability in the foreign exchange market. There is no unanimous agreement. Some economists argue for the fixed exchange rate system to force nations to control inflation in their economies and keep the ambitions of local politicians in check. These economists claim that a floating regime leads to increased volatility in currencies and price uncertainty, which in turn lead to a reduction in international trade and a lowering of the world living standard. However, others favor a floating system and are of the opinion that the fixed exchange rate system imposes too rigid a financial discipline on national economies. They argue that a flexible exchange rate system allows for a smoother adjustment to external shocks. Central banks do not need to maintain the large, sterile reserves in gold or other currencies necessary to defend a fixed rate. Countries can follow independent monetary and fiscal policies, thus giving priority to domestic concerns rather than worrying about exchange rates.

The main cause of the problem of instability in the international monetary system, however, lies with the national governments themselves. Any or all of the aforementioned systems can be implemented successfully, but will achieve the desired goal only if all the countries involved are able to cooperate fully and coordinate and follow economic policies oriented toward this goal.[3]

International Financial Institutions

Several organizations have been established to facilitate the flow of international trade and financial transactions among nations. These organizations are usually managed collectively by a group of nations. Some of the more important ones are discussed next.

International Monetary Fund

The International Monetary Fund (IMF) was originally formed in 1944 by countries participating in the Bretton Woods monetary system for the express purpose of lending foreign currency to its member countries to further stabilize the exchange rates. All "free world" nations, except Switzerland, became members, each supplying capital to the fund in its own currency in amounts based on a quota determined by reference to the country's monetary reserves, volume of international trade, and national income. Part of this capita, generally 25 percent, was to be contributed in gold. In 1978, the IMF gold requirement was dropped and this portion of the contribution could then be made in currencies acceptable to IMF or in Special Drawing Rights (SDRs). Known also as "paper gold," SDRs are the units of account that the IMF issues to governments and they constitute a part of the countries' international reserves. SDRs were created in 1967 to supplement the international reserves of gold and foreign exchange. This was done in response to problems faced during the 1960s when the value of the U.S. dollar, which nations kept as the reserve currency, began to erode. At the same time world trade was experiencing a severe liquidity problem. (International liquidity is a term used to describe the world's supply of gold, foreign exchange, and other assets used between trading nations to settle their trade balances.) SDR is not a currency but rather an international reserve asset allocated to member nations depending on their quotas. SDRs are not used to settle private business transactions, but are employed by the central banking system of the individual countries to settle their balance of payment problems.

The IMF put into play certain functions designed to relieve some of the strains associated with international trade. In the event the exchange rates became truly strained, the IMF was empowered to provide the necessary funds and impose strict provisions designed to solve the causes of the exchange rate problems. Further, it attempted to coordinate and monitor economic policies of the various nations through research and consultation, offering solutions for correcting trade imbalances. It allowed devaluation (depreciation) of a nation's currency up to 10 percent, but anything above this required formal approval from IMF. Thus the main IMF function is the encouragement and aiding of free trade among nations. To this end, IMF provided financing to countries experiencing balance of trade problems during the 1970s and helped countries with debt repayment problems during the debt crisis in the 1980s.

The compensatory financing facility (CFF) is another important function of the IMF. It is available to countries having financial problems due to a reduction in exports. If the country can prove that the reduction is temporary, the IMF provides financing. Developing nations have benefitted from this service, particularly during 1982.

The financing carried out by the IMF is measured using SDRs. Initially the value of one SDR was set at $1, but more recently this value was based on the value of five major currencies: U.S. dollar, German mark, French franc, Japanese yen, and the British pound. The IMF uses a weighted average of a "basket" of these currencies, with the U.S. dollar receiving a weight of 42 percent, the mark 29 percent, and the franc, yen, and pound each receiving a weight of 13 percent.

World Bank

The International Bank of Reconstruction and Development (IBRD), also known as the World Bank, was originally established in 1944 to provide long-term funds to aid in the reconstruction of Europe after the devastation of World War II. Currently, the bank's loans are made to developing countries for implementation of development projects. Membership in the bank is acquired by purchase of stock. The bank is profit oriented and its principal activity is the provision to countries of partial financing of projects with various commercial banks and credit agencies joining the venture as cofinancers. In recent years, the bank has also helped to stimulate economic growth in some developing countries through the establishment in 1980 of the Structural Adjustment Loan (SAL) facility. The World Bank raises funds through sale of bonds and other debt instruments to private investors and governments. With borrowing amounting to U.S. $70 billion, the World Bank is one of the largest borrowers in the international capital markets. The bank carries a portfolio of loans that is well diversified among countries and currencies, and it has received the highest credit rating of AAA.

International Finance Corporation

The International Finance Corporation (IFC) was formed in 1956 to supplement the activities of the World Bank by providing capital and expertise to private enterprises in developing nations. It makes nonguaranteed loans to private businesses amounting to about 15 percent of the total cost of the project. The remainder has to be financed through other sources such as U.S. commercial banks, foreign commercial banks, and others interested in private enterprise development. Loans are made in U.S. dollars, German marks, Swiss francs, British pounds, or French francs.

International Development Association

The International Development Association (IDA) was formed in 1960 with the same goals and objectives as those of the World Bank, but it utilizes quite different methods. The IDA provides "soft" loans to the less prosperous nations, those who cannot qualify for, or afford, the conventional loans from the World Bank. These loans are much riskier and not always repaid. The IDA generally funds projects such as power, housing and education, thereby enabling the countries to stimulate development.

Regional Development Agencies

Several other agencies emphasize regional economic development. These include the Inter-American Development Bank (IDB), which is a Latin American version of the World Bank; the Asian Development Bank (ADB), which focuses on development of Asian countries; the Islamic Development Bank, which was established to increase social and economic development of Islamic countries; the European Investment Bank (EIB), which was formed to help achieve the internal and external goals of the European Community—now the European Union; and the African Development Bank (AFDB) with its goal of furthering development in Africa.

More recently, in 1990, the European Bank for Reconstruction and Development (EBRD) was set up with the prime goal of helping establish market-oriented economies for post-Communist Eastern European countries.

Islamic Finance and Banking

The Islamic religion considers interest payment or receipt usury. It is called *riba*, and is prohibited in any form. Today's business transactions, however, cannot be carried out without the use of loans. As a necessity, Islamic banks have emerged. The establishment and expansion of Islamic banks in Muslim and non-Muslim countries and particularly their growth in OPEC countries have attracted the attention of the business community. These banks provide a full spectrum of financial services. They make loans, accept deposits, and offer fee-based retail banking services that do not involve interest payments. These services include letters of credit and guarantee, domestic and international money transfer, traveler's checks, spot foreign exchanges, investment management, mortgages, and other services.

How can these banks operate without the use of interest? The answer is a profit-or-loss sharing system. This should not be confused with a whole host of legal fictions devised by some financial institutions to avoid calling charges interest or *riba*. One such legal fiction calls interest a service charge. In profit sharing, instead of guaranteeing a fixed rate of return (interest), the lender and the borrower enter into an agreement that spells out how profits or losses from the venture are to be shared between them. Therefore, in Islamic finance and banking, risk is shared by the lender, which then is encouraged to finance sound and secure ventures and avoid speculative ones. In this way, the joint ownership stakes encourage both the financier and borrower-entrepreneur to engage in productive investments. The following example illustrates the mechanics of financing a mortgage.

Aghaa Noor-ud-Din wants to buy a house that costs $200,000. He enters into an agreement with the Muslim Banking and Finance Corporation (MBF) for joint ownership of the house, and puts down $40,000 or 20 percent of the principal. MBF finances the remaining $160,000 and leases its portion of the house to him. Aghaa Noor becomes the resident owner and pays rent based on the portion of the home that MBF owns plus a little more to increase his equity. The value of the home could be reassessed every year and rental payments adjusted accordingly. If the market value of the property has increased the rent will increase and the amount Aghaa Noor must pay to obtain full ownership of the house increases. If the home's value falls, so does the rent, which reduces the MBF's income. In case of loan default, unlike in the conventional mortgage, Aghaa Noor does not lose his equity. MBF and Aghaa Noor split the proceeds from the sale of the property proportionately to their equity with the result that if the value of the house has fallen to, say, $100,000, Aghaa Noor will still get back 20 percent of that sum and the bank will therefore fail to recover its loan in full.

Sources: S. M. Abbasi and K. W. Hollman. "The Manager's Guide to Islamic Banking." *Business,* 40, no. 3 (July–September 1990), 35–40; M. A. Khan. "The Future of Islamic Economics." *Futures* (April 1991), 248–61; K. Brown. "Islamic Banking: Faith and Creativity." *The New York Times* (April 8, 1994), D1; M. Adacem. "Islam and the U.S. Banking Crisis." *The Wall Street Journal* (May 9, 1991), A10.

International Flow of Funds

International business is expedited by markets that permit the exchange of one currency to another and the flow of funds among nations. International transactions result in shifting money flows from one country to another. Here, balance of payments, which represents a measure of international monetary flow, is discussed.

Balance of Payments

A nation's balance of payments is a recording of its transactions with the rest of the world during a specified time period—generally one year. The balance of payment is a double-entry accounting system and is therefore always in balance because sources of funds must equal the uses of funds. The inflows, or sources, are recorded as credits or pluses. In the case of the United States, these include exports of goods and services, earnings on foreign investments, increases in foreign liabilities (purchase of U.S. dollars and dollar-denominated securities by foreigners), and liquidation of foreign securities by U.S. residents. The outflows or uses of funds are recorded as debits or minuses. These include imports of goods and services from the rest of the world by U.S. residents, payment of interest to foreigners on their borrowed capital, direct investment abroad, unilateral payments and grants to foreigners, and U.S. government purchases of foreign currency and foreign-currency-denominated financial assets.

The media often makes mention of balance of payment surpluses and deficits. Here the commentator usually has in mind specific sources of foreign exchange and specific uses of that foreign exchange. The difference between these two items constitutes a surplus if positive and a deficit if negative. Two such items receive the most attention in evaluating a country's balance of payments. These are the current account balance and the capital account balance.

Current account balance   The current account balance is a broad measure that includes both goods and services. The trade balance, the difference between exports and imports of merchandise, is its primary component. A surplus in the trade balance occurs when the value of goods exported exceeds those imported. Conversely, a deficit arises when the value of imported goods is greater than those exported. Other items in the overall current account balance include investment income and payments, unilateral transfers and sales and purchases of military equipment. If a deficit exists in this account, it has to be made up by the government's sales of dollar-denominated assets or U.S. dollars, and/or the sale of foreign currency reserves.

Capital account balance   The difference between foreign investment flows into a country and the investment by that country abroad is known as the *capital account balance.* Foreign investments include both direct foreign investment and purchases of foreign securities. Direct investment is investment in foreign companies as well as business investment in plant and equipment. An example of direct investment into the United States would be Hyundai, from Korea, building a plant in the United States. The purchase of foreign securities, of course, refers to stocks, bonds, bank loans, and so on.

What Do the Balances Tell Us?

The balance of payments is a compilation of the transactions between a country and the rest of the world. The current account balance is generally analyzed to see if the country is importing more than it exports, or living beyond its means, since large, persistent deficits in this account may drain currency reserves and so cause a loss in the value of the currency in the world financial markets. For example, critics are using these arguments when they contend that the negative U.S. balances can spell problems in the future.

It is possible to take corrective action after evaluating those factors that are affecting the trade balance. For a deficit, the implementation of policies tending to increase foreign demand for a country's goods and services would be an important step toward correcting the imbalance. For instance, low export prices spur demand for a country's goods, but export prices cannot be low unless domestic inflation is low and/or the value of the country's currency is lower when compared with that of the importing country. Theoretically, a country could also restrict imports to cure a balance of trade deficit; however, this has not been very successful in practice, since adjustment impacts other trading partners. If one country improves its trade balance by reducing imports, this action will have an impact on another country's balance of trade through a reduction in its exports and may lead them to take counteractions in retaliation.

In the United States, imports have been greater than exports and the difference is currently being financed by foreigners who buy U.S. Treasury obligations. Should foreigners stop buying treasury securities or should they, in general, find other more lucrative places to invest, the dollar will be in trouble and the differences, or in this case the deficit, will have to be made up by decreasing imports, increasing exports, or borrowing from foreign countries or the World Bank. Such borrowing often carries covenants that would impact the country's monetary and fiscal policies and so affect the quality of life in the borrowing country.

Foreign Exchange Market

The foreign exchange market is by far the largest financial market in the world. Daily foreign currency trading amounts to U.S. $1000 billion worldwide. The foreign exchange market is not a physical place. It is a worldwide network of foreign exchange dealers, brokers, and banks—all connected by telephones and computer terminals. This market is made up of spot and forward markets as well as foreign exchange futures and options markets. In the world today many business transactions require the exchange of one currency for, or into, another. If Honda Auto were to set up a plant in the United

States, they would first have to convert their yen into U.S. dollars to pay for the plant construction. If a U.S. firm decides to help a subsidiary in London build a plant, it will have to first exchange the U.S. dollars for the needed British pounds. The foreign exchange market functions to facilitate both of these exchanges or transactions.

The major banks such as Citicorp of the United States and Deutsche Bank of Germany constitute the heart of this market. In fact, these banks are known as "market makers," which means they stand ready to buy and sell foreign currencies at prices they quote. The market constituted by this group is also known as the "interbank market," and all others use this interbank market for their own specific reasons. Local banks, large and small corporations, brokers, and central governments are all involved. A local bank may be involved because its customer is an importer of perfume from Paris and therefore needs his bank to help him or her turn U.S. dollars into French francs. However, the central government may be buying/selling its own currency in order to keep its value stabilized in accordance with internal policies. Other financial institutions that deal with foreign exchange also participate directly in the interbank market. For example, the International Money Market (IMM), the Chicago Mercantile Exchange (CME), and the London International Financial Futures Exchange (LIFFE) are active in this market.

Spot and Forward Markets

Within the foreign exchange market are *spot* and *forward markets*. The spot market is a market where foreign currencies are bought and sold for immediate delivery, and the rate at which this immediate exchange takes place is known as the spot rate. The settlement for spot transactions usually takes two business days, which gives the banks the necessary time for transfer of funds.

Purchases and sales of foreign currency for future delivery are done in what is known as the *forward market.* This market is used when a business forecasts a need to either buy or sell foreign currency. In this market the rates are locked in today, but delivery will be at a specified future date. Common forward delivery dates are 30, 60, 90, and 180 days, and in some cases they are customized to suit the client.

This market is extremely important for MNCs wishing to make or receive foreign currency payments in the future. The corporation using this market will lock in the exchange rate now, thus protecting itself from adverse exchange rate changes over the length of the forward contract.

Bid/ask spread   Foreign exchange in both spot and forward markets is quoted as bid/ask. At any point in time a bid quote indicates the price the dealer will pay you for your currency and an ask quote is what he will charge you for the currency you want. The ask price will generally be higher than the bid price, the difference between the two prices being the return the dealer makes on the transaction. This spread will be small for large transactions between banks and large corporations, and will also tend to be small for currencies that are traded frequently. Conversely, it will be large for small transactions and infrequently traded currencies.

To illustrate the bid/ask spread, let us take the example of a corporation turning U.S. dollars ($100) into Japanese yen. The bank's bid quote is yen 104.25/US$ so the $100 will net 10,425 yen (100 × 104.25). However, if the corporation converts this 10,425 yen back into dollars at the ask rate of yen 105.25/US$, it will net only $99.05, (10,425/105.25) or $0.95 less, which is the spread or the cost of the transaction.

Exchange rate quotations   Table 13.1 is an example of foreign exchange quotations taken from the financial pages of a newspaper. For important currencies, there are up to four quotations. One is the spot quotation as we have discussed. It represents the "ask prices" for large transactions for immediate delivery. The bid prices, again, as discussed, will typically be less

than the figures shown on the table. These rates, which are for trades among the interbank market participants, are expressed either as "American quote" or "European quote." When the price of a currency is quoted as the number of U.S. dollars required to buy one unit of foreign currency, it is called an American quote. If the quote is given as the number of foreign currency units that would buy one U.S. dollar, it is referred to as a European quote. In most countries, when banks trade with nonbank customers, they use "direct quotation" (i.e., banks give the home currency price of a unit of the foreign currency). For example, banks in Belgium quote 35Bf/US $1. Banks mainly in Great Britain use "indirect quotation"; they quote the value of pound in terms of the foreign currency—for example, £1/US$1.65. Referring again to Table 13.1, and under the heading "Foreign Currency in U.S. $" (U.S. $ equivalent), for Australia, whose currency is the dollar, given in parentheses, the number 0.7335 indicates the American spot rate for the Australian dollar. This means the U.S. dollar price for the Australian dollar is U.S.$ 0.7335 ($ 0.7335/1A$). In the next column, under the heading "U.S. $ in Foreign Currency" (foreign currency per U.S. $), the entry 1.3633 indicates the Australian dollar price of one U.S. dollar or A$1.3633/1US$. It is the reciprocal of 0.7335 or 1/0.7335.

Major Determinants of Exchange Rates

Financial managers of corporations operating in the international environment must be concerned with exchange rate fluctuations and how they can affect the overall profitability of their corporations. Although the corporation may have undertaken a lucrative investment, exchange rate changes may result in this project offering negative returns. The currencies of major industrialized countries are traded freely in the exchange market. In such a market the exchange rate between two currencies is determined by the supply of and demand for the cur-

Table 13.1
Sample Foreign Exchange Quotations

Friday, May 27, 1994

The New York foreign exchange selling rates below apply to trading among banks in amounts of $1 million and more, as quoted at 3 P.M. Eastern time by Bankers Trust Co. Retail transactions provide fewer units of foreign currency per dollar.

Country	Foreign Currency in U.S. $	U.S. $ in Foreign Currency	Country	Foreign Currency in U.S. $	U.S. $ in Foreign Currency
Argentina (Peso)	1.01	0.99	Japan (Yen)	0.009592	104.25
Australia (Dollar)	0.7335	1.3633	30-day forward	0.009611	104.05
Austria (Schilling)	0.08654	11.56	90-day forward	0.009652	103.61
Bahrain (Dinar)	2.6522	0.3771	180-day forward	0.009728	102.8
Belgium (Franc)			Jordan (Dinar)	1.462	0.684
Commercial rate	0.02957	33.82	Kuwait (Dinar)	3.3523	0.2983
Brazil (Cruzeiro)	0.0005423	1844.03	Malaysia (Ringgit)	0.3862	2.5895
Britain (Pound)	1.5105	0.662	Mexico (Peso)		
30-day forward	1.5094	0.6625	Floating scale	0.3025719	3.305
90-day forward	1.5085	0.6629	Netherlands (Guilder)	0.5428	1.8424
180-day forward	1.5083	0.663	New Zealand (Dollar)	0.5885	1.6992
Canada (Dollar)	0.7209	1.3872	Norway (Krone)	0.1405	7.1196
30-day forward	0.7199	1.3891	Pakistan (Rupee)	0.0327	30.58
90-day forward	0.7182	1.3923	Peru (New Sol)	0.4726	2.12
180-day forward	0.7159	1.3968	Philippines (Peso)	0.03738	26.75
Czech Rep. (Koruna)			Poland (Zloty)	0.00004441	22517.0
Commercial rate	0.0344033	29.067	Portugal (Escudo)	0.00585	170.95
Chile (Peso)	0.002413	414.4	Saudi Arabia (Rival)	0.26665	3.7502
China (Renmimbi)	0.114943	8.7	Singapore (Dollar)	0.6513	1.5355
Columbia (Peso)	0.001187	842.64	South Africa (Rand)		
Denmark (Krone)	0.1554	6.4361	Commercial rate	0.2745	3.6428
Ecuador (Sucre)			Financial rate	0.2092	4.7800
Floating rate	0.000466	2148.04	South Korea (Won)	0.0012405	806.10
Finland (Markka)	0.18559	5.3882	Spain (Peseta)	0.007384	135.43
France (Franc)	0.17802	5.6175	Sweden (Krona)	0.1299	7.7007
30-day forward	0.17779	5.6247	Switzerland (Franc)	0.713	1.40251
90-day forward	0.17757	5.6315	30-day forward	0.7131	1.4023
180-day forward	0.17757	5.6315	90-day forward	0.714	1.4005
Germany (Mark)	0.6086	1.643	180-day forward	0.7166	1.3955
30-day forward	0.6081	1.6445	Taiwan (Dollar)	0.03723	26.86
90-day forward	0.6078	1.6453	Thailand (Baht)	0.03972	25.18
180-day forward	0.6086	1.6431	Turkey (Lira)	0.0000309	32325.0
Greece (Drachma)	0.004056	246.55	United Arab (Dirham)	0.2719	3.6778
Hong Kong (Dollar)	0.12942	7.7265	Uruguay (New Peso)		
Hungary (Forint)	0.0097494	102.57	Financial	0.206612	4.84
India (Rupee)	0.03212	31.13	Venezuela (Bolivar)		
Indonesia (Rupiah)	0.0004622	2163.52	Floating rate	0.0072	138.80
Ireland (Punt)	1.4848	0.6735			
Israel (Shekel)	0.3311	3.02	SDR	1.41516	.70663
Italy (Lira)	0.0006294	1588.79	ECU	1.1708	

Special Drawing Rights are based on exchange rates for the U.S., West German, British, French and Japanese currencies.
European Currency Unit is based on a basket of community currencies.

rencies themselves. As a result, exchange rates depend on many factors. Factors that lead to increasing the supply of or decreasing the demand for a certain currency will bring down the value of that currency in foreign exchange markets. In the same way, those factors that result in decreasing the supply of or increasing the demand for a currency will boost the value of that currency. Broadly speaking, exchange rate fluctuations can be attributed to the following factors: inflation rates, interest rates, balance of payment surpluses or deficits, government policies, and expectations.[4]

Inflation Rates

The theory that explains the relationship between inflation rate differentials and the exchange rate is known as the purchasing power parity (PPP) theory. According to this theory the exchange rate must vary so as to equate the prices of goods in two countries in terms of a single currency. In its simplest form: Prices of similar goods in both countries should be the same. If they are not, arbitrage (the purchase of securities in one market for immediate resale on another market in order to profit from a price discrepancy) will occur until their prices are once again brought into equilibrium. Suppose inflation is 20 percent in the United States compared with 10 percent in Japan. U.S. residents would then buy more Japanese goods and services and this would cause an increase in demand for Japanese yen. However, the Japanese would not be interested in buying goods from the United States because of inflationary prices. This in turn will reduce the supply of yen that would be bought by the United States to buy the Japanese goods. Now the increased U.S. demand and reduced yen supply will put upward pressure on the value of yen, and the yen will appreciate relative to the U.S. dollar until a new equilibrium price is reached, i.e., when the U.S. dollar depreciates sufficiently to counteract the 10 percent difference in rates of inflation.

Otherwise the price of identical products would not be the same, and profit opportunities would exist. There are obvious weaknesses in this version of PPP. It ignores frictions such as the costs of transportation, taxes and financing, and restrictions such as import quotas and exchange and capital controls. The main concepts underlying the PPP, however, are quite worthwhile, and remain at least approximately valid over the long run: If a nation's rate of inflation continues to remain higher than that of its trading partners for a long period of time, that country's currency will tend to depreciate.

Interest Rates

Another major factor that influences exchange rates is interest rates. Assume that the U.S. interest rates increase, while French interest rates remain constant. Then funds would move to the United States where they would earn a higher rate of return. This move would cause an increase in the supply of French francs followed by a demand for the U.S. dollar. The dollar will appreciate and the French francs will depreciate relative to each other. The interest rate parity (IRP) theory maintains that exchange rates will adjust to reflect parity between interest rate levels in two countries. Specifically, the IRP says that the interest rate differential must be the same as the differential between forward and spot exchange rates. Thus, the relative difference between interest rates on the two currencies must equal the forward premium or discount on the foreign market. The IRP relates interest rates to spot and forward exchange rates so that there is no advantage from investing in one or the other currency.

Balance of Payments Surpluses and Deficits

Another factor affecting exchange rates is a country's balance of payment position. If a country is importing more than it exports, it will be showing a balance of payment deficit. If this deficit is large and chronic, then the country's

Big Mac Currencies

The *Economist* has published Big Mac currency since 1986. Big Mac is a lighthearted guide to whether currencies are at their correct level. Burgernomics is based on the theory of purchasing power parity (PPP)—the notion that a dollar should buy the same amount in all countries. In the long run, argue PPP supporters, the exchange rate between two currencies should move toward the rate that would equate the price of an identical basket of traded goods in the respective countries. Our "basket" is a McDonald's Big Mac, which is produced locally in 68 countries. The Big Mac PPP is the exchange rate that would leave hamburgers costing the same in America as in, say, Japan. The first column of the table shows the local-currency price of a Big Mac. The second column shows prices in dollar terms. The cheapest is China, where a burger costs a bargain $1.03. Switzerland's Big Mac is the most expensive, at $3.96. These figures imply that the yuan is the most undervalued currency, the Swiss franc the most overvalued against the dollar.

	Big Mac Prices		Actual $ Exchange Rate 5/4/94	Implied PPP of the Dollar	Local Currency Under (−) Over (+) Valuation %
	In Local Currency	In Dollars			
U.S.	$2.30	2.30	−	−	−
Argentina	Peso 3.60	3.60	1.00	1.57	+57
Australia	A$2.45	1.72	1.42	1.07	−25
Brazil	Cr1,500	1.58	949	652	−31
Britain	£1.81	2.65	1.46+	1.27+	+15
Canada	C$2.86	2.06	1.39	1.24	−10
Chile	Peso948	2.28	414	412	−1
China	Yuan9.00	1.03	8.70	3.91	−55
Czech Republic	Ckr50	1.71	29.7	21.7	−27
France	FFr18.5	3.17	5.83	8.04	+38
Germany	DM4.60	2.69	1.71	2.00	+17
Greece	Dr620	2.47	251	270	+8
Hong Kong	HK$9.20	1.19	7.73	4.00	−48
Hungary	Forint169	1.66	103	73.48	−29
Italy	Lire4,550	2.77	1,641	1,978	+21
Japan	Y391	3.77	104	170	+64
Malaysia	M$3.77	1.40	2.69	1.64	−39
Mexico	Peso8.10	2.41	3.36	3.52	+5
Poland	Zloty31,000	1.40	22,433	13,478	−40
Portugal	Esc440	2.53	174	191	+10
Russia	Rouble2,900	1.66	1,775	1,261	−29
Singapore	$2.98	1.90	1.57	1.30	−17
South Korea	Won2,300	2.84	810	1,000	+24
Switzerland	SFr5.70	3.96	1.44	2.48	+72
Taiwan	NT$62	2.35	26.4	26.96	+2

+Dollars per pound.
Source: *The Economist* (April 9, 1994), 88.

currency is expected to be devalued. This has been the case with the U.S. dollar for some periods. Conversely, if the country is running a balance of payment surplus by exporting much more than it imports (i.e., selling to the rest of the world and receiving little from them), its currency will appreciate with respect to others. Germany, by exporting more goods than it imports, has been enjoying a trade surplus for quite some time. Thus, analysts may look at the components of balance of payments to predict exchange rate depreciation for countries with deficits in their international transactions and appreciation for those with surpluses.

Government Policies

A fourth factor affecting exchange rates is government policies. Governments often, by actually buying and selling currencies in the foreign exchange markets through their central banks, attempt to affect the value of their currency relative to others. Some countries follow a conscious policy of keeping an undervalued currency to increase their exports. Other countries, especially Third World ones, influence exchange rates by imposition of trade and foreign exchange barriers. These can take, among others, the following forms: import prohibition of what are considered nonessential items, restrictions on foreign direct investment, international portfolio investment, or owning deposits at foreign banks, and the requirement to surrender foreign currency income to the government. However, economic and political forces make sure that a country cannot artificially support a high or low exchange rate for any length of time. Sooner or later, it will have to put its house in order if it wishes to continue trading in the international marketplace.

Expectations

Essentially, it is through the medium of expectations that currencies' values go up or down. Expectations involve a future course of factors affecting exchange rates. Exchange rates move in anticipation of coming changes in economic conditions. For example, the news that inflation in the United States will go down may precipitate a buying spree of U.S. dollars and put upward pressure on the dollar. Such news affects financial transactions more than trade-related transactions, because financial transactions involve the holding of a specific currency for various reasons including investment, repatriation of income or dividends, and interest payments. Changes in expectations affect currencies' values very rapidly as traders and speculators using this news undertake profit-seeking transactions.

Over a short period of time, say, one to three years, changes in government policies and economic competitiveness can be important factors influencing currency values. Thus, predicting things such as movements in interest rates and the outcome of political elections can be useful in anticipating the short-term direction of changes in exchange rates. Over longer periods, however, inflation rate differentials are dominant factors.

Measurement of Foreign Exchange Risks

The risks involved in going international add new dimensions to the arena of finance. In addition to the usual problems of domestic inflation, and local regulations and restrictions, the multinational firm also has to deal with risks specific to international business. A major risk is that associated with exchange rates. It has long been axiomatic that the value of income derived from foreign operations remains uncertain until it is converted into the home currency. This being so, it can be seen that exchange rate changes have a direct impact on international operations affecting sales and investments made in the foreign country. Direct investments with fixed returns are often hardest hit. Over the years, managers have developed techniques to aid in the management of exchange rate risk. This is often known as *exposure management*. Exposure is the degree to which a corporation is affected by changes in exchange rates. There are three types of exposures when a business operates internationally—transaction, translation, and economic.[5] We first examine these types of exposures and then turn to the issue of their management.

Translation Exposure

This type of exposure occurs when the financial statements reported in foreign currencies are translated into the home currency to generate a consolidated statement. An example would be a U.S. corporation with subsidiaries in foreign countries all having their assets and liabilities denominated in the local currencies. For purposes of taxation, preparing consolidated financial statements, and so on, the subsidiaries' financial statements have to be translated into U.S. dollars and these translations can have an effect on the balance sheets and income statements. If a subsidiary is operating in a country whose currency has weakened relative to the U.S. dollar, the balance sheet items will appear to be worth less when compared with the last reported financial statement. The opposite is also true. If the subsidiary is operating in a country where the currency has appreciated relative to the U.S. dollar, the increase in the value of the foreign currency will translate as higher values.

These values are, however, not cash gains or losses, because no actual exchange has taken place. These financial translations are carried out to fulfill the reporting requirements demanded by all countries' governments and do not have a material effect on the economic value of the company. A number of procedures are used for translation purposes. Most U.S. corporations follow the current procedure outlined in Financial Accounting Standards Board (FASB) No. 52, adapted in 1981.

Transaction Exposure

This type of exposure stems from the possibility of incurring future exchange rate gains or losses by a firm on those transactions already entered into and which are denominated in foreign currencies. When a company in one country sells to a firm in another country, it has receivables and these may be denominated in foreign currency. The firm then has a transaction exposure. Similarly, a company with payables in foreign currency is also exposed. The exposed cash flows include accounts receivable or payable, principal, interest, dividend payment, and management fees, all denominated in foreign currency.

Suppose a firm in California exports its products to France and invoices in French francs. The invoice is for FF 1 million, and the current exchange rate is $0.20/FF. Now further suppose that immediately after the goods are shipped and the invoice received, the rates fall to $0.18/FF. The firm will now receive $180,000 (1 million × 0.18) and not $200,000 (1 million × 0.2), as originally invoiced. This loss of $20,000 is the result of transaction exposure.

However, the same firm buys manufacturing equipment from a German firm for 10 million German marks. If the marks rise from $0.50/DM to $0.53/DM, the firm would have to pay $5.3 million instead of the original $5.0 million or pay an additional $300,000 due to the rise in the dollar value of the mark (decrease in the value of the dollar).

A firm's transaction exposure has to be measured currency by currency and equals the difference between contractually fixed future cash inflows and outflows in each of these foreign currencies.

Economic Exposure

Economic exposure is the degree to which the firm's economic value can be affected by fluctuations in exchange rates. Economic exposure entails the current and future effects of unexpected exchange rate changes on cash flows generated by an MNC's subsidiaries, and on the earning power of the corporation as a whole. The impact of exchange rate changes can go far beyond the accounting period when those changes occur.

Transaction exposure can be considered as a part of economic exposure because it has cash flow implications. But the influence of shifts in exchange rates on a firm's cash flows is not solely due to currency transactions. Even a purely domestic firm can be affected by economic exposure, although the degree of economic exposure faced by a multinational firm is surely greater than that of a purely domestic firm.

Economic exposure is the probability that exchange rate fluctuations, accompanied by price changes, could result in transforming the expected amounts of a corporation's future revenue and costs. Theoretically speaking, however, the economic exposure can only be due to unexpected changes in exchange rates. Expected changes would be identified by the financial markets, and would be reflected in interest rate and inflation differentials between the country of the parent company and the country of the subsidiary and would have no impact on the running of a corporation.

The measurement of economic exposure requires detailed knowledge of a company's operations and their sensitivity to exchange rates. For example, economic exposure because of an unexpected depreciation of the currency of the country of the subsidiary against the parent company's currency requires tracing the impact of depreciation on its sales both in the domestic and international markets, as well as on its cost structure. For an operational measure of exchange risk, see the Appendix near the end of this chapter.

Management of Foreign Exchange Risks

Note that of the three types of exposures, the MNC will find it quite difficult if not impossible to perfectly manage economic exposure. In practice, subsidiaries have to be flexible enough to increase or decrease production and sourcing in countries that become low-cost producers due to changes in exchange rates. MNCs also should have internationally diversified sources of financing to take advantage in places where the real interest rate is temporarily low. Moreover, a number of techniques and procedures can be used to minimize or hedge the other types of foreign exchange risk. Hedging simply means taking a position in such a way that you neither win nor lose in a particular transaction. In the context of foreign exchange, it means that one is not affected by the exchange rate fluctuations. Specifically, transaction and translation exposure management focuses primarily on exposures that lead to identifiable foreign exchange gains or losses (i.e., on effects on contractual items). Hedging involves different strategies to minimize a firm's exposure. The popular ones are forward market hedge, currency option hedge, currency futures, and the currency swaps.

Forward Market Hedge

In a forward market hedge, the forward market is used to buy and sell foreign currencies forward. A U.S. company imports machinery from France and agrees to pay the company in French francs. The payment will be made at some future date depending on credit terms. If the company waited until the end of the credit period to pay its bills, the exchange rate between the countries could change and affect the transaction either positively or negatively. To avoid this uncertainty, the corporation can enter into a forward contract with a banking institution, agreeing to buy the French francs for U.S. dollars, at a specified time and at a specified rate of exchange. In this case the corporation has locked in a price today to buy French francs in the future.

Let's assume that a U.S. exporter sells equipment to a French firm for the amount of FF 5 million, the invoice to be paid in 90 days. The spot rate is $.1688/FF and the 90-day forward rate is $0.1674/FF. A simple hedge would be to sell French francs forward at the rate of $0.1674/FF. This will guarantee a receipt of $837,000 (FF 5 million × 0.1674) in 90 days when the French firm pays for the machinery. If the U.S. firm had not hedged, then it is exposed to the fluctuations of the foreign exchange market. However, by hedging it may be losing a certain amount to be obtained in the future. In our example, if the company did not hedge and the exchange rate stayed at the current spot rate of $0.1688/FF during the 90-day period, then the company would have received $844,000 (FF 5 million × 0.1688). By hedging the company actually received $7,000 less ($844,000 − $837,000), ignoring transaction costs, but avoided the risk of making a bigger loss had the exchange dropped below $0.1674/FF.

Currency Option Hedge

The forward market hedge removes uncertainty with respect to cash flows and offers the firm a fixed amount. But what happens if the value of the French franc declines against the dollar? Let's say that during the 90-day period, the rate falls to $0.1750/FF. If the company had not hedged it would have received a lot more dollars (FF 5 million × .1750), $875,000 to be exact. The option hedge remedies this problem and offers the firms both the protection and an opportunity to gain from favorable movement of the exchange rate. An option is a contract that offers a holder the chance to buy or sell something, in our case a financial asset, for a specific price during a specific period of time or on a specific date. Note, of course, that since the option represents something of value, the holder buys it for an agreed on price.

There are various types of options in finance—stock options, commodity options and foreign exchange options to name a few. Exchange-traded currency options were first introduced in 1983 by the Philadelphia Stock Exchange and they are available for the major currencies of industrialized countries. Customized or tailor-made options can always be arranged between banks and major corporations. There are two types of foreign currency options: call options and put options. A call option offers the holder the right to buy, and the put option offers the holder the

right to sell, the contracted currency at a specified price up to or on the expiration date. An American option can be exercised at any point of time to its expiration date; a European option can only be exercised at its maturity date.

There is an important difference between the forward contracts and options. With the options, a firm does not have to exercise its option if it feels that it is not advantageous to do so. It can simply let the option expire, and it only loses the premium paid to buy the option.

Returning to our example of the U.S. firm expecting FF 5 million in 90 days, if the firm anticipates that the French franc will depreciate against the dollar during the 90-day period, then it would buy a put option. This option will offer the firm the right to sell French francs for U.S. dollars at a given exchange rate. If the rate falls during the 90-day period, then the firm will exercise its option at the option exchange rate and receive a lot more U.S. dollars than what it would have received at the current spot rate. However, if the spot exchange rate moves up during the period and is higher than the option rate, the firm will simply not exercise the option and let it expire. It will simply buy dollars for French francs at the prevailing spot rate and will again be ahead.

Currency Futures Market Hedge

Exposure associated with foreign currency transactions can also be hedged in the futures market with use of currency futures contract. The Chicago Mercantile opened its International Monetary Market (IMM) currency futures market in 1972. Other markets have also developed around the world. A foreign currency futures contract entails the delivery of a foreign currency at the maturity date for an agreed price, which is set at the outset. On the delivery date, the foreign currency is received and the price of the contract is paid. The main corporate use of currency futures, like forward contracts, is for hedging. The futures market and the forward market are similar in concept, but they differ in their operations. The IMM currency offers contracts on only major currencies such as the British pound, Canadian dollar, German mark, Japanese yen, Swiss franc, and Australian dollar. Moreover, there are only a limited number of fixed maturity dates available. The futures market is an organized market and open to small investors. Moreover, futures contracts are standardized and can be executed rapidly. The forward market is a specialized market and contracts are negotiated between major banks and large corporations. In a forward contract, the currency is normally delivered at the maturity, whereas, in a futures contract, the physical delivery of currency rarely occurs. The vast majority are reversed before maturity by a sale or purchase of contracts that exactly offset the original purchase or sale.

Currency Swaps

Another technique to hedge against the exchange exposure is to undertake a swap. There are different types of swaps. A simple one is the currency swap. As the term indicates, it involves two firms exchanging one currency for another. Again they are used to protect future payments and/or receipts from exchange rate fluctuations. Suppose, a U.S.-based firm undertakes a long-term construction project in Germany, which will be paid on completion. During this long period of time, the economic conditions may change, thus affecting exchange rates. In an effort to overcome this situation, the U.S. firm will attempt to find a firm in Germany who has a long-term project in the U.S., ideally for the same period of time. These firms can then negotiate a currency swap whereby German marks can be exchanged for U.S. dollars at a negotiated exchange rate. In this way, both firms receive the payment in their own currencies regardless of the market rates. Further, they also know in advance the exact sum to be received because of the locked in swap rate. Swaps are usually arranged through the intermediation of a major bank.

Hedging is not the only tool available to companies to protect their overall earnings against foreign exchange risks. Many corporations match their foreign liabilities with foreign assets in an attempt to minimize exposure. Over the years MNCs have also set up sophisticated foreign asset management programs involving such strategies as converting liquid and current assets into strong currencies and gathering debt and other liabilities in weak currencies. Corporations also stimulate rapid collection of their receivables in depreciating currencies by offering sizable discounts, while extending generous credit in appreciating currencies.

International Investment and Diversification

Foreign investment can take two forms: portfolio and direct investment. Portfolio investment refers to the purchase of shares and loans in overseas firms, and it does not entail any control over the operation of these firms. Direct foreign investment occurs when an investor in a foreign country retains a lasting (partial) ownership and substantial control over an investment. The MNC is the standard example. Foreign direct investment by MNCs through the establishment of subsidiaries or acquisitions of existing businesses occurs because of greater cost-effectiveness and more profitability in finding raw materials and components, production facilities, and servicing markets through a local presence in a number of host countries rather than counting on home production and import and export activities to enhance their operations. Foreign investment has been growing rapidly since World War II. While U.S. corporations took the lead in establishing operations in other countries during the 1950s and 1960s, European and Japanese firms began these activities in the 1970s and have continued into the 1990s. More recently, large corporations located in developing countries such as Mexico and India are investing more and more abroad. During the last two decades, as we have noted, governments in many parts of the world have made progress in reducing the barriers imposed on foreign investments by treaties and law (i.e., the EU or NAFTA), and administrative practices and regulatory procedures. As a result, a positive environment has been created in which existing foreign investment opportunities are swiftly capitalized on and new ones are continually arising.

The rapid expansion in foreign investment also reflects relatively high expectations of foreign rates of return and the diversification benefits that such investment makes possible. The diversification benefits stem from less-than-perfect correlations among economic conditions in different countries. The latter is believed to be an important motivation for direct foreign investment. The basic premise of modern finance theory is that investors are risk averse and that they can reduce the risk level of a portfolio by diversification. There two types of risk: systematic risk and diversifiable risk. Systematic risk is that variation in an asset's return that is correlated with the performance of the whole economy. This is also known as market risk, and it is measured by "beta." Beta indicates the covariability of an investment's return with the market-wide (e.g., Standard and Poor 500 index), average return. Diversifiable risk includes all other types of variation. The latter risk can be eliminated through holding a well-diversified portfolio of stocks. As a result, little or no additional return should be demanded for bearing diversifiable risk. Systematic risk is the only risk that stockholders are exposed to and such risk has to be rewarded with a risk premium. An internationally diversified portfolio should be substantially less risky than a purely domestic portfolio. The growing internationalization of capital markets, the increasing activities of firms in the field of cross-border mergers and acquisitions, and extensive listing of firms' stocks on foreign exchanges have produced substantial opportunities for investors. In an integrated world financial market, an investor need not confine his portfolio choice to domestic securities since it is possible to combine foreign with domestic securities in his portfolio. For example, Solnik[6] has shown that holding a portfolio of U.S. stocks can reduce risk to 27 percent of that of holding only one stock, and by inclusion of non-U.S. stocks into portfolio the risk can be reduced by a further 12 percent. Findings such as these reveal that international diversification offers significant opportunities to reduce those risks that have national economy characteristics. Those risks that are systematic in a national economy can become diversifiable in an international context.

Sometimes it is maintained that institutional and political barriers, language and cultural differences, and lack of adequate information on foreign investments deters investors from diversifying across countries. It is argued that by holding shares of MNCs, an investor can derive benefits of international diversification. Fatemi[7] compares the performance of two portfolios: a portfolio of multinational firms, each with a minimum of 25 percent sales abroad, and a portfolio of purely domestic firms. He noticed that there was no significant difference in the rates of return for the two portfolios. There was, however, less fluctuation in the rates of return on the portfolio of the multinational firms. The beta coefficients of the multinational portfolio are significantly lower and more stable than those of the purely domestic firms. He also found that the higher the degree of international diversification, the lower the beta.

Investors, however, do not highly value diversified MNCs that have diversification as their main objective for international involvement. Diversification is cheaper and easier for an investor, through the purchase of an international portfolio of shares using a mutual fund, than for a firm. There are cases in which international diversification through purchase of MNC shares might be preferred to international portfolio investment. An extreme case is when the investor is not allowed to invest abroad. However, the growing globalization of capital markets will lead to lessening of such restrictions, and as they disappear it will become more beneficial to invest in the form of international portfolios rather than in the shares of multinational firms.

Measurement and Management of Political Risk

Another form of risk facing the MNC is political risk. Specifically, to assess the various alternative markets, MNCs need to determine the volatility of the political environments of the host countries. The ability to assess political risk could provide firms with a distinctive competitive advantage. Political risk has been defined in many different ways. Often, in management research and practice, political instability has been regarded as a synonym for political risk.[8] Frequently MNCs have avoided investing in politically unstable markets, considering such investment too risky. From a strictly financial perspective, however, a working definition of political risk refers to those unforeseen host government actions that may have a negative impact on the corporation's wealth. Political risks may manifest themselves through nationalization, currency controls, requirements for local partnerships, restrictions on repatriation of funds, increased regulations, and changes in taxation laws. It is important to see the difference between high tax rates and uncertain tax rate environments. When making an investment decision in the former environment, the investor simply takes high tax rates into consideration. In contrast, the risk that the tax rates will be raised substantially after the investment is made constitutes a political risk and cannot easily be incorporated into the firm's calculations. Generally speaking, political risks are due to government interventions into the functioning of the economy. But not all changes will have adverse consequences for the corporation. For instance, if the corporation is operating in an industry targeted by the host government for development, then it may not only escape any discriminatory

actions but also enjoy investment credits or tax concessions.

The expected consequences of political risk must be assessed and incorporated into the estimation of a project's cash flows. Several models to analyze and forecast political risk exist. Some of these models are based on opinion surveys and factors such as the frequency of government changes, conflicts with other countries, and the level of violence. These models try to provide political stability indices to show how long the government will remain in power and if it will be able to provide favorable conditions for foreign investments. Other models forecast the economic conditions of a country based on the level of inflation, interest rates, GNP, and balance of payment figures. Note, however, that while the forecasting performance of these models is rather good at the country level, it is quite weak at the corporation level. Moreover, these models suffer in that they implicitly assume that each firm in the foreign country faces the same degree of political risk.[9] Corporations react differently to the same political risk depending on their industry,[10] size, ownership structure, and the level of know-how. In addition, investments in natural resources or utilities are more apt to be expropriated than any other type of investments. Many corporations rely on consultants who specialize in predicting political risk, but it is apparent that even experts do not always come up with correct predictions. But this does not mean that the corporations should ignore political risk and invest and operate blindly. It is important to analyze the likelihood of any untoward activity that may affect the corporation and to have contingency plans.

The corporation can take several steps to manage political risk exposure. The most important one currently practiced is to invest in the countries through joint venture agreements. This type of direct investment involves local investors in ownership and management. While the corporation loses some freedom, it gains a local flavor. The company may even be perceived as being owned by locals, which may help the firm to obtain the necessary licenses and meet requirements and regulations that are not easily met by a foreign company. Further, this may also help avoid takeovers by the host government. There are other ways as well. The company may undertake investments primarily in those industries that are encouraged by the local governments and which fall into their national development plans. Another way would be to work with specialized technology, knowledge, and supplies that cannot be easily learned or duplicated. The local government would be hard put to take over such a firm, knowing that it would do no great harm to the corporation and no great good to the local government. Attempting to raise as much capital as possible from the local financial markets or through loans from a consortium of international banks is another way to overcome political risk. Lastly, the company planning foreign investments may purchase insurance. Several agencies offer protection against political risk and against expropriation, currency inconvertibility, war, and internal strife. These include Foreign Credit Insurance Association (FCIA), the Export-Import Bank (Eximbank), the Overseas Private Investment Corporation (OPIC), and, most recently established, the Multilateral Investment Guarantee Agency (MIGC). All of these agencies have their own unique programs and offer different premiums depending on the country and industry involved. Coverage fees for projects, under normal circumstances, range annually from 0.3 to 12 percent of the value of projects. The corporation should analyze the costs and benefits of these insurance policies before committing their funds to them. It is possible that the MNC could follow one or the other of the above-mentioned methods and not need the insurance at all.

Financing International Operations

For financing foreign operations, an MNC has access to a wide range of internal and external sources of funds. An important internal source of funds for a foreign subsidiary is its parent company or its sister affiliates. Funds provided to its foreign affiliate by the parent company can be in the form of equity capital or loans. MNCs usually have more leeway to repatriate funds in the form of interest and loan repayments than as dividends or reduction in capital. There are also tax advantages: interest payments are tax deductible in many countries, whereas dividend payments are not. These intercompany loans are often channeled through a financial intermediary, usually a large international bank, to a foreign affiliate.

Moreover, as multinational firms are represented in many nations, they have access to local banking facilities and securities markets in the different countries within which they operate. Some of the important ones are discussed next.

International Equity Markets

More and more multinational corporations tap foreign stock markets by placing new shares overseas. Major stock exchanges allow sales of foreign stocks provided the issuing corporations satisfy the listing requirements of the local market. This market is gaining in popularity because it provides access to European and Asian markets for many U.S. corporations in need of funds. The main advantage for U.S. firms listing overseas is the less stringent listing requirements, in terms of both cost and time, compared to those in the United States. However, large foreign corporations seeking large amounts of funds will often issue their stocks in the United States because the liquidity of the U.S. market permits it to more easily absorb the large issues. Some firms issue stocks in foreign countries to satisfy local ownership requirements, to increase a firm's international image, and to have a diversified shareholder base. Most of the large multinationals, however, offer their new stock in several foreign countries, with a portion being offered in the United States. This is done to ensure that the entire issue is subscribed and taken up by investors. American investors, instead of buying foreign stocks overseas, can buy American Depository Receipts (ADRs). When this is done, the shares of a foreign company that are intended to be sold to American investors are placed in a trust in a U.S. bank. The bank, in turn, will issue ADRs to American investors.

International Bond Markets

A bond is a debt instrument and in its simplest form provides for regular payment to its holder. Bonds are by far the most important vehicle of investment in today's world. World bond market capitalization far surpasses world equity market capitalization. The international bond market is an important source of longer term funds for multinational corporations. International bonds are sold to investors in countries other than the country of the borrower. There are two types of international bonds: foreign bonds and Eurobonds. A foreign bond is a bond issued by a foreign corporation or government in the domestic capital market of one country. They are usually sold through an investment bank operating within that country and are denominated in the local currency. Foreign bonds are subject to local security laws. An example would be dollar-denominated bonds issued by a French company and sold within the United States by a U.S investment banking firm. Major foreign bond markets are located in the United States, Switzerland, Japan, and Germany.

A Eurobond is sold simultaneously in more than one country other than either the country of the issuing corporation or the country in whose currency the bond is denominated. Eurobond issues are underwritten by an international syndicate of banks and securities firms. If the French company in the earlier example sold dollar-denominated bonds in Japan and Germany, the issue would be a Eurobond. The issue is not subject to U.S. jurisdiction, but is subject to the jurisdiction of each country where bonds are sold (i.e., Japan and Germany); however, since na-

tional currencies are not involved, such regulations are not very tight. Generally Eurobonds are denominated in a strong currency such as the German mark, U.S. dollar, or Japanese yen.

Eurocurrency Market

The Eurocurrency is a dollar or other currency deposited in a bank outside its country of origin. Thus, a Eurodollar is a U.S. dollar deposited outside the United States and hence outside the jurisdiction of U.S. authorities. Since the early 1960s, this market has established itself as a significant part of world credit markets for short-term needs of multinational firms and their foreign subsidiaries. Since these deposits of dollars overseas are beyond the regulation of the U.S. monetary authorities, they are not subject to reserve requirements and deposit insurance, leading to reduced costs for the banking institutions. The spread between the interest rate paid on Eurodollar deposits and charged on Eurodollar loans is rather narrow. The lower borrowing costs and greater availability of credit continue to attract more borrowers; for example, U.S. firms more than doubled their Eurodollar borrowings during the early 1990s. These deposits are usually placed in a foreign bank or a foreign branch of a domestic U.S. bank. The Eurocurrency market consists of those banks, Eurobanks, that accept deposits or make loans in foreign currencies. More than 80 percent of these deposits are in the form of term deposits for a specific period and at a rate set at a fixed margin above the London interbank offered rate, or LIBOR, which is a floating rate. At the end of each period, the interest for the next period is set at the same margin above the new LIBOR. The maturity of loans usually varies between three months to one year. The size of the margin typically varies from 0.25 to 0.5 percent, depending on the amount and maturity of the loan and the riskiness of the borrower. The Eurocurrency market is essentially a wholesale market where deposits and loans are typically $1 million or more per transaction.

Eurobanks also make up what is known as the Eurocredit market, which can be distinguished from the Eurocurrency market by the longer maturities on loans. The maturity of loans can vary from 3 to 10 years. Loans are again made on a floating rate basis at some fixed margin above LIBOR. The interest rate is reviewed periodically.

The Eurocurrency market is not limited to Europe however. It has since expanded to include banks in Asia that accept deposits and make loans in dollars. This is sometimes known as the Asian Market, with Singapore and Hong Kong representing predominant forces.

Conclusion

International financial management differs from its domestic counterpart because of the foreign sociopolitical uncertainty, foreign exchange risk, and different institutional and taxation environments. In this chapter, we first study the international monetary system and various exchange rate arrangements. Currently, the exchange rates of major industrial countries are determined rather freely. We summarize the factors affecting exchange rates: inflation rates, interest rates, balance of payments, government policies, and expectations. In the long term, however, inflation rate differentials are dominant factors.

We then analyze the operation of the foreign exchange market, its participants, quotations of spot and forward rates, premiums, and discounts on forward rates. We look at three types of foreign exchange exposure: translation, transaction, and economic. While economic risk is the most important one, it cannot be measured precisely and managed easily. We discuss ways to measure and minimize the risks associated with the other exposures through forward markets, option markets, futures market, and swap markets. We review how to manage political risks—unexpected events that might interfere with the normal operation of an MNC subsidiary.

We also see that international portfolio diversification allows investors to reduce the level of

risk they face and point out that it is a major reason for international investments. Financing international trade and investment is another major area of international finance. In the final section, we look at international sources of funds. Financial managers of MNCs have access to both the domestic and international financial markets. For their short-term needs, MNCs can borrow in the Eurocurrency market. For long-term needs, they may issue shares in the international stock market or sell bonds in the international bond market.

Discussion Questions

1. What is meant by a forward premium or discount?
2. Suppose the exchange rate between U.S. dollars and the French franc is FF 5.5/$, and the exchange rate between the dollar and British pounds is £ .60/$. What is the exchange rate between francs and pounds?
3. The respective market rates of interest in the United States and Germany are 12 and 8 percent. If the spot rate of exchange is 1.50 DM/$, what does this suggest about the forward rate?
4. What is the purchasing power parity theory and what are its main implications?
5. What is the interest rate parity theory and what are its main implications?
6. Differentiate between the spot exchange rate and the forward rate.
7. Explain what is meant by foreign exchange transaction exposure and economic exposure.
8. What are the major differences between forward contracts and futures?
9. What is an American type of foreign currency option?
10. Define a foreign currency put option.
11. Differentiate between systematic and diversifiable risks.
12. What are the major benefits of international portfolio diversifications?

13. Is it useful to invest in a portfolio of MNCs' shares?
14. Differentiate between Eurobonds and Euro-currencies.
15. What are ADRs?
16. What major risks does a U.S. corporation face in going overseas?
17. What is political risk and how can it be managed?

Endnotes

1. Historical information for this section was culled from J. Madura. *International Financial Management* (St. Paul, MN: West Publishing Company, 1993); D. K. Eitman. *Multinational Business Finance* (New York: Addison-Wesley Publishing Co., 1993); S. Sears and G. Trennepohl. *Investment Management* (Austin, TX: The Dryden Press, 1993); and F. Weston and B. Sorge. *Guide to International Financial Management* (New York: McGraw-Hill Book Co., 1977).

2. A detailed survey of the European monetary integration and the move from the EMS to EMU is given in D. Gros and N. Thygesen. *European Monetary Integration.* (London: Longman, 1992). See also H. Carre and K. H. Johnson. "Progress Toward a European Monetary Union." *Federal Reserve Bulletin* (October 1991), 769–83.

3. A classical and still interesting discussion regarding the different exchange rate mechanisms is the paper by M. Friedman and V. Robert. "Free Versus Fixed Exchange Rates: A Debate." *Journal of Portfolio Management* (Spring 1977), 68–73. Other relevant articles are D. B. Pauls. "U.S. Exchange Rate Policy: Bretton Woods to Present." *Federal Reserve Bulletin* (November 1990), 891–908, and M. D. Bordo. "The Classical Gold Standard: Some Lessons for Today." *Federal Reserve Bank of St. Louis Review* (May 1981), 2–17.

4. There have been quite a number of studies of the relationships between exchange rates, inflation rates, and interest rates. For the purchasing power parity see, for example, N. Abuaf and P. Jorion. "Purchasing Power Parity in the Long Run." *Journal of Finance* (March 1990), 157–74, and M. Adler and B. Lehmann. "Deviations from Purchasing Power Parity in the Long Run." *Journal of Finance* (December 1983), 1471–87. For interest rate parity, see K. Clinton. "Transaction Costs and Covered Interest Advantage: Theory and Evidence." *Journal of Political Economy* (April 1988), 358–70. For the relationship between the forward rates and spot rates, see E. F. Fama. "Forward and Spot Exchange Rates." *Journal of Monetary Economics* (1984), 319–38 and C. P. Wolff. "Foreign Exchange Rates, Expected Spot Rates and Premia: A Single Extraction Approach." *Journal of Finance* (June 1987), 395–406.

5. Various types of exposures and ways to manage them are thoroughly discussed in the finance literature. Among others, see R. C. Hekman. "Measuring Foreign Exchange Exposure: A Practical Theory and Its Application." *Financial Analyst Journal* (September–October 1983), 59–65; L. Jacque. "Management of Foreign Exchange Risk: A Review Article." *Journal of International Business Studies* (Spring–Summer 1981), 81–99; B. Cornell and A. C. Shapiro. "Managing Foreign Exchange Risks." *Midland Corporate Finance Journal* (Fall 1983), 16–31; E. Flood and D. Lessard. "On the Measurement of Operating Exposure to Exchange Rates: A Conceptual Approach." *Financial Management* (Spring 1986), 25–36. For a discussion on how the major U.S. companies manage their foreign exchange risk, see J. M. Westerfield. "How U.S. Multinationals Manage Currency Risk." *Business Review* (March–April 1980), 19–27.

6. B. H. Solnik. "Why Not Diversify Internationally Rather Than Domestically?" *Financial Analysts Journal* (July/August 1974), 48–54.

7. A. M. Fatemi. "Shareholder Benefits from Corporate International Diversification." *Journal of Finance* (December 1984), 1299–1314.

8. K. Fatehi. "Capital Flight from Latin America as a Barometer of Political Instability." *Journal of Business Research*, 30 (1994), 187–95.

9. For a detailed criticism of political risk models, see K. Fatehi and M. H. Safizadeh. "Sociopolitical Events and Foreign Direct Investment: American Investment in South and Central American Countries." *Journal of Management*, 14 (1988), 93–107.

10. K. Fatehi and M. H. Safizadeh. "The Effect of Sociopolitical Instability on the Flow of Different Types of Foreign Direct Investment." *Journal of Business Research*, 31 (1994), 65–73.

Appendix: An Operational Measure of Exchange Risk

Garner and Shapiro present a workable approach for assessing the economic exposure faced by a multinational corporation. This approach is straightforward in concept and easy to apply. Consider a U.S. parent company. It faces exchange risk to the extent that variations in the dollar value of its affiliate's cash flows are correlated with variations in the nominal exchange rate. To detect the existence of such a correlation, the statistical technique of regression analysis can be used. We regress actual cash flows from past periods, converted into their dollar value (CF_t), on the average exchange rate during the corresponding period $(EXCH_t)$.

$$CF_t = a + b \, EXCH_t + e_t$$

where e_t is a random error term. The regression model generates values for a and b coefficients, t-statistics, and the R^2 parameter. The regression coefficient b would indicate the sensitivity of the dollar cash flows to exchange rate changes. The larger the size of the regression coefficient, the greater the sensitivity of the firm's cash flows to movements in nominal exchange rates. In addition to the size of b, it is important to determine if it is statistically significant. This is measured by the t-statistic. A larger t-statistic means a higher confidence in the value of b. The magnitude of cash flow variability explained by variations in the exchange rate, i.e., R^2, is the most crucial factor for firm's exposure management policy. If the model produces a low value for R^2, say, 1 percent, then the firm should not devote much of its resources to foreign exchange risk management, even if the beta coefficient is large and statistically significant.

Because this method uses historical data, its validity explicitly depends on the sensitivity of future cash flows to exchange rate changes to be similar to past sensitivity. If the firm expects no substantial adjustments in its operating structure this method remains reasonable.

Source: C. K. Garner and A. C. Shapiro. "A Practical Method of Assessing Foreign Exchange Risk." *Midland Corporate Finance Journal* (Fall 1984), 6–17.

AMPAK INTERNATIONAL, LTD.

DAVID J. SPRINGATE

In early 1990, Robert Williams, the manager of the International Division of Rally Dawson Sports was seriously considering the possibility of opening a new subsidiary somewhere in the Middle or Near East. The countries that had come up for review included India, Pakistan, Syria, Egypt and Israel. Due to long term political instability and unpredictable economic policies of the various governments under consideration, the Middle Eastern countries had been placed on a list labeled as "potential future investment areas—not for present

This case was prepared by Dr. David Springate of The University of Texas at Dallas with the help of Mr. Aamir Niazi as a basis for classroom discussion. It is not intended to present either effective or ineffective handling of an administrative situation. Revision 1990 copyright by David J. Springate. Reprinted with permission.

action." Further, due to concern about new government nationalization policies in India, that country had been similarly classified. As a result, the focus had been turned to Pakistan. After extensive field research and several visits by the members of Rally Lawson Sports' international staff, the company had negotiated a tentative agreeement calling for a joint venture with Hamid Sports, Ltd., a local corporation. It was this tentative agreement that Mr. Williams was considering.

Rally Dawson Sports, headquartered in Houston, Texas, had been in the sporting goods business for twenty-two years. It had two manufacturing outlets, one located near Houston and the second one in Waco. The company's gross sales for 1988–89 were over $29 million (see Exhibits 1 and 2 for financial statements for the

Exhibit 1

Income Statement for Rally Dawson Sports for
Year Ended July 31, 1989 (dollars in thousands)

Sales	$29,503
Cost of sales	14,203
Gross Profit	$15,300
Sales salaries	802
Advertising	398
Delivery and freight	1,034
Depreciation	246
Office salaries	300
Business taxes and licenses	65
Rent expense, office space	200
Miscellaneous	162
Interest	105
	$ 3,312
Net Profit before taxes	11,988
Income taxes	5,754
Net Profit	$ 6,233

company.) Though there had been a short period of instability (1982–83), a steady growth of profits had been experienced since 1984 when a new management took over the operations.

A Pakistani site would be the third international location for Rally Dawson. In 1976, the company had moved to Spain and formed Compania Catalanade Desportes S.A., a manufacturing subsidiary. Rally Dawson's experience with the Spanish concern was very encouraging and in 1983 Bert Philips, the president of Rally Dawson, recommended Italy as the second international site. It took about eight months for the operations to start in Bologna, Italy.

Rally Dawson produced many types of sports goods used both by professionals and amateurs. Its major distribution channels led to retail sporting goods stores and to department store chains. It also sold directly to professional sports teams and to some major universities.

Link with Hamid Sports Company

Some of the reasons that prompted Rally Dawson to consider venturing abroad again in 1990 were:

1. To jump tariff and import barriers and regulations. These included local content regula-

Exhibit 2

Balance Sheet for Rally Dawson Sports, July 31, 1989 (dollars in thousands)

Current Assets			Current Liabilities	
Cash	$ 2,100		Bank Advances	$ 730
Marketable Securities				
(at Cost)	500		Unearned Fees	120
Accounts Receivable	2,500		Accounts Payable	1,400
Notes Receivable	650		Accrued Salaries	50
Inventory	3,100		Accrued Liability	700
Prepaid Expenses	700		Income Taxes	5,754
	$ 9,550			
			Long-Term Liabilities	
			Bonds (due 1999)	400
Fixed Assets			Shareholders Account	
At Cost	$ 4,550		Capital Stock	$ 4,500
Accumulated Depreciation	250		Retained Earnings	950
Land	450			
			TOTAL LIABILITIES	$14,800
	$ 5,250			
TOTAL ASSETS	$14,800			

tions and/or requirements that local exports be made in order to receive an import license.
2. To reduce or eliminate high transportation costs involved in serving Near and Middle-Eastern markets.
3. To obtain or use local materials available at a lower cost.
4. To obtain incentives (usually tax breaks) offered by the host governments.
5. To participate in the rapid market expansion in the Middle and Near-East.
6. To continue a strategy that called for the combination of Rally Dawson's advanced technology, reputation and managerial know-how with low-cost production inputs such as labor, capital and raw materials available in some countries abroad.
7. To diversify product lines and to some extent shield the company from cyclical developments in the American and European economies.

The primary reason for selecting Pakistan as a suitable location for investment stemmed from the facts that labor costs were extremely low and that suitable raw materials were available within the country at relatively inexpensive rates. In addition, Pakistani sporting goods had established a reputation of being long-lasting products of quality.

Mr. Williams had, however, not been in favor of joint ventures in the past. In the initial stages of the investigation, he advocated etablishment of a manufacturing subsidiary solely owned by Rally Dawson. Although it was legally possible to establish in a manner such that Rally Dawson would have no Pakistani partners, a practical perspective made the joint venture more desirable. The government of Pakistan encouraged private foreign investments where local entrepreneurs were given opportunity to gain know-how and to exercise some ownership control. With a local partner foreign investors found the investment approval process expedited. Subsequent government red-tape was also reduced.

Once Rally Dawson began to consider Pakistan as one of the probable areas for investment, it contacted the Pakistani Trade Office in Washington, D.C. The Trade Office maintained an active list of qualified Pakistani businessmen interested in joint-venture opportunities. The company was introduced to its proposed partner, Hamid Sports Company, through the Trade Office.

The Pakistani counterpart in the proposed joint venture had been in business for 18 years. Located in Sailkot (about 900 miles from Karachi) Hamid was the third largest producer of sports goods in Pakistan. Sixty percent of the annual sales for its fiscal year 1988–89 were in domestic markets and forty percent were exports. Most of the export sales were centered in the Middle East (Syria, Libya, Egypt) with these countries each constituting 30% of the exports. The remaining 10% was divided between Thailand and Sri Lanka. Total gross sales for Hamid for the fiscal year 1989 were almost $10 million. (See Exhibits 3 and 4 for recent income statement and balance sheet information for Hamid.) The Izmir Hamid family held 80% ownership interest in Hamid Sports. The residual 20% was divided among three other prominent families in Pakistan.

The management of Hamid Sports had not been able to keep up with current and timely strategies for maximizing the overall efficiency of production. This was due to the limited resources available in the country and the prohibitive cost of sending its managers abroad on a regular basis to attend management development programs. For this reason Hamid Sports was looking at the proposed joint Pakistan-U.S. investment as an opportunity to benefit from fresh technological and business management inputs. The venture would lead to expansion of Hamid's facilities in Pakistan. Hopefully, it would also lead to the capture of larger portions of the domestic market and parts of the export markets of Western Europe, U.S.A. and Canada. Hamid had wanted to expand sales into the latter area for some time.

Exhibit 3

Income Statement for Hamid Sports
Company for Year Ended October 31, 1989
(dollars in thousands)*

Sales	$9,700
Cost of Sales	4,850
Gross Profit	4,850
Selling Expenses	
Salaries & Commission	200
Advertising	100
Delivery & Freight	210
Automobile	40
Depreciation	178
	$ 728
Administrative Expenses	
Salaries	$ 505
Printing & Postage	50
Telephone & Telegraph	24
Business Taxes & Licenses	88
Sundry	63
Interest	25
	$ 755
Total Expenses	$1,483
Net Profit before taxes	$3,367
Income Taxes	$1,987
Net Profit	$1,380

To date Hamid Sports had specialized in field hockey, cricket, soccer, badminton and tennis equipment. The joint venture would also enable Hamid to introduce new product lines and help produce products for golf, skiing, football and baseball which would have market potential in Western Europe and North America.

Proposed Joint Venture

The joint venture, if consummated, would be called Ampak International, Ltd. It was to be a closely held corporation. The ownership would be 60% American (Rally Dawson) and 40% Pakistani (Hamid). The total initial capital investment was proposed to be the equivalent of $4,000,000.

The site for the proposed plant was selected when two representatives of Rally Dawson visited Pakistan in March, 1989. It was to be in Kotri, approximately 90 miles from Karachi. The latter was the largest seaport and the business center of the nation. In terms of availability of labor, Kotri had the reputation of having a substantial supply of unskilled, semi-skilled and skilled labor. Kotri was a highly industrialized area and locating the plant there was expected to be beneficial both in terms of communication facilities and labor. Another advantage compared to interior locations was the transportation cost saving. As mentioned, the port was relatively close to Kotri.

The investment proposal was put together in June 1989. It was decided that Rally Dawson would raise most of the capital needed for im-

Exhibit 4

Balance Sheet for Hamid Sports Company as of October 31, 1989 (dollars in thousands)*

Current Assets		*Current Liabilities*	
Cash	$ 750	Bank Advances	$ 400
Accounts Receivable	1,500	Accounts Payable	520
Inventory	1,600	Accrued Liability	275
Prepaid Expenses	400		
Total Current Assets	4,250		
Fixed Assets			
Cost	$1,900	Capital Stock	2,500
Less: Depreciation	178	Retained Earnings	2,277
Total Fixed Assets	1,722	Total Liabilities & Equity	$5,972
Total Assets	$5,972		

* Translated from rupees to dollars.

porting for importing the machinery and initial start-up capital needs. Hamid was assigned the chief responsibility of raising the local capital, customs duties on imported machinery, land and the actual structure of the plant, and a smaller amount of cash. In the initial proposal, it was suggested that the plant would have 500 workers working two shifts of eight hours each. The two shifts will enable Ampak to deduct a greater depreciation expense and also attain a higher level of production.

Machinery required was to be imported from the U.S. It was expected to have a higher level of efficiency and be more effective than equipment already in operation in Pakistan. Though Ampak was to be a labor-intensive project, a technologically sophisticated plant would go a long way toward increasing profits.

Managers of the two firms that would form the proposed joint venture had suggested a list of products to be produced by Ampak International, Ltd. The list was a result of market research done by a four-member team, consisting of two international staff executives from Rally Dawson and two members of Hamid's International task force. There was a possibility that in the final analysis, some of the products mentioned on the following list, put together in the fall of 1989 would be dropped.

1. Tennis equipment (For Western Europe, Canada and the U.S.)
2. Cricket equipment (For Pakistan, the U.K., and a small market in the Middle East)
3. Golf equipment (For Western Europe and the U.S.)
4. Soccer equipment (For Pakistan, Western Europe and the Middle East)
5. Baseball equipment (For the U.S. and possible to Japan)
6. Skiing equipment (For Switzerland, Austria and most of Scandanavia)
7. Football equipment (For the U.S. and possibly Canada)

8. Badminton equipment (For Thailand, Malaysia, Indonesia, Sri Lanka and Pakistan)
9. Field hockey equipment (For Western Europe, the Middle East, and Pakistan)

Although the products mentioned above were varied, it was considered feasible that a large manufacturing outlet could handle the production complexities. Many of the raw materials used to produce these products were common. In addition, not all items would be produced initially.

It was proposed to have the plant begin operations within one year. The tentative plan was that Ampak would issue 400,000 shares of common stock with a $10 (equivalent) par value. Rally Dawson Sports would exchange its machinery and start-up capital for 240,000 shares of Ampak's newly issued stock. Its total contribution would thus be $2,400,000, some of which it might borrow in the United States. Hamid would buy the rest of the shares.

Hamid Sports had assets it could use in the Muslim Commercial Bank in the amount of $1,600,000. It would also help the joint venture by raising a working capital loan through the Pakistan Industrial Development Bank. The terms anticipated were a six year loan at 10-1/2%, amounts to be drawn down as required up to $1,000,000 equivalent. The loan would be secured by Hamid's plant and equipment in Sailkot.

The proposed breakdown of the initial $4,000,000 capital of Ampak was:

Land	$ 200,000
Plant	900,000
Equipment	900,000
Start-up capital	1,900,000
Customs fees	100,000
	$4,000,000

Some start up capital would be used for market research and some to cover start-up costs in 1990 until the plant was operational. The estimated amounts involved were $100,000 and $200,000, respectively.

Managers

Staffing of Ampak was one of the major concerns for Rally Dawson. The general manager for the operations was to be Howard Adams. His present assignment was Operations Manager for the Spanish subsidiary. Prior to this he had been Manufacturing Manager for Dow Chemical in Brazil.

The administrative manager, Aamir Kohn, was selected from Hamid as he possessed skills which would be conducive to the local operations. As most of the skilled and semi-skilled labor would be Pakastani, fluency in the language and cultural empathy were important ingredients for this job.

The controller was to be a person who had extensive experience in the area of international accounting. Joe Sutton, previously associated with Clark Equipment Company, had been on Rally Dawson's staff for the last nine months and was very familiar with the company's international accounting practices.

The chief engineer, Khurshid Rakahmi, was a Pakistani who had worked in Pakistan with a sporting goods enterprise for the last eight years.

Some of the factors behind the selection of the U.S. managers were technical competence, managerial skills, cultural empathy, diplomatic skills, personal motives, emotional stability and business background.

An additional task was the finding of a person to serve as a liaison between Ampak and the Pakistani government. The importance of developing a good working relationship was felt to be crucial in Pakistan, a developing nation. The final choice was a Pakistanti who had an MBA from the Harvard Business School and an LLB (Law Degree) from the University of Panjals (a local university). He had worked for the Department of Commerce of Pakistan for four years. Prior to this he was associated with Proctor and Gamble in New York City and in various Western European locations.

Strategy in the Event of Failure

In the event that the new venture failed the proposed plan was to dispose of the assets and pay off the creditors first. If the sale of all the assets was not adequate to cover the funds needed to pay off the creditors, the two groups involved would then pay their share of the debt according to ownership interest. The government of Pakistan had no restrictions on foreign investors taking out the liquidation funds as long as all debts were paid and local stockholders were fairly treated.

Another situation that might arise was where the new plant did not turn out to be as profitable as anticipated. It was expected that if the plant barely broke even after two years Ampak would be dissolved. However, it was expected that Rally Dawson Sports would invest in another manner (a new joint venture or a new subsidiary of Rally Dawson Sports with some local capital participation) instead of transferring its remaining liquid funds back to the U.S. In this way, newly gained market knowledge and awareness of the economy and the area would not be wasted, but utilized in a constructive fashion.

Funding Sources and Profits

The major factor which led Rally Dawson Sports to resort to external sources of funding and not use the local Pakistani banks for all of the capitalization was the national government's hesitation. In discussion with government officials it became obvious the government was well aware of the fact that Rally Dawson Sports had other alternatives for raising capital, especially in the U.S. Officials stated that it would be more feasible for the Pakistani banks to finance only the local working capital needs. In this way they would not have to dip into their foreign exchange for machinery purchases outside Pakistan.

Exhibit 5

Profitability Calculation of Mr. Williams

Estimated Rates of Return before Tax (X)	Probability of Occurrence (P)	Weighted Values of the Estimated Rates $P \cdot X$	Deviation of Rates from Mean $X - \overline{X}$	Deviation Squared $(X - \overline{X})^2$	Variance $(X - \overline{X})^2 \cdot P$	Standard Deviation (Square Root of Variance)
(1)	(2)	(3)	(4)	(5)	(6)	(7)
22%	.1	2.2	+8	64	6.4	
18%	.2	3.6	+4	16	3.2	
14%	.4	5.6	0	0	0	
10%	.2	2.0	−4	16	3.2	
6%	.1	.6	−8	64	6.4	
	1.0	$\overline{X} = 14.0$			19.2	1.96
			$s^2 = 19.2/5 = 3.84$			

The standard deviation of a series of numbers may be written

$$s = \varepsilon \sqrt{\frac{(x - \overline{x})^2}{N}}$$

Exhibit 6

Projected Statement of Annual Cost of Sales for Joint Vetnture (1991–1995) (dollars in thousands)*

	1991	1992	1993	1994	1995
Inventory (beg. of Year)	$ 600	$1,200	$1,930	$2,540	$2,230
+Material purchases	600	800	1,000	600	650
+Direct Labor	200	350	400	375	360
Factory Overhead:					
Fuel	50	55	60	60	65
Insurance	115	115	115	120	120
Utilities	40	45	50	50	55
Maint. & Repair	30	35	60	50	50
Property Taxes	200	200	200	200	200
Trucks	30	20	15	25	20
Employee Benefits	60	60	60	60	60
Depreciation	175	150	150	150	150
+Total Overhead	700	680	710	715	720
Gives:	$2,100	$3,030	$4,040	$4,230	$3,960
−Inventory (end of year)	$1,200	$1,930	$2,540	$2,230	$ 960
Gives:					
Cost of Sales	$ 900	$1,100	$1,500	$2,000	$3,000

* Translated from rupees to dollars.

With reference to taking out profits, Mr. Williams knew that the Pakistani government allowed foreign investors to take out profits to the extent of the initial investment and any subsequent additions to capital. In other words, Rally Dawson Sports would be able to take out profits up to $2,400,000 plus half of any cumulative earnings. Such transactions would be coordinated by the State Bank of Pakistan, which assigned various remittance accounts to different commercial banks around the country.

Investment Considerations

There were several advantages which led Mr. Williams and the International team at Rally Dawson to look favorably on the proposed joint venture.

(a) A joint venture would protect the U.S. investment against nationalization. There was, of course, no guarantee that the government would not nationalize but the fact that a local interest would be involved could normally be expected to deter government take-over.

(b) The interest rate discussed between the Pakistan Industrial Development Bank and Hamid Sports was substantially lower than what Rally Dawson could get from the First National City Bank in Pakistan if it financed all the Pakistan working capital loan itself (10-1/2% as opposed to 12-3/4%).

(c) A joint venture would reduce the capital requirements of Rally Dawson. The manufacturing subsidiary in Spain, Catalanade

Exhibit 7
Projected Statement of Annual Earnings for Joint Venture (1991–1995) (dollars in thousands)*

	1991	1992	1993	1994	1995
Sales	$1,800	$2,300	$3,000	$4,000	$5,500
Cost of Sales	900	1,100	1,500	2,000	3,000
Gross Profit	900	1,200	1,500	2,000	2,500
Selling Expenses					
Salary & Commission	185	200	225	275	300
Advertising	40	50	75	100	150
Delivery & Freight	45	55	65	85	125
Automobile	30	10	8	15	25
	$ 300	$ 315	$ 373	$ 475	$ 600
Administrative Expenses					
Salaries	$ 120	$ 115	$ 120	$ 130	$ 150
Professional Fees	80	110	70	50	40
Printing & Postage	25	30	22	25	30
Telephone & Telegraph	30	40	35	45	50
Taxes & Licenses	50	70	80	100	125
Depreciation	50	50	50	50	50
Sundry	35	20	35	40	60
Interest	24	68	98	105	84
	$ 414	$ 493	$ 510	$ 545	$ 589
Total Expenses	$ 714	$ 808	$ 883	$1,020	$1,189
Net Profit					
before taxes	$ 186	$ 392	$ 617	$ 980	$1,311
Income Taxes	112	235	370	588	789
Net Profit	$ 74	$ 157	$ 247	$ 392	$ 522

* Translated from rupees to dollars.

Deportes S.A. had a critical need for additional capital equipment and the Spanish economy was currently experiencing an unusual period of credit squeeze. This fact had resulted in Rally Dawson being forced to resort to external sources of financing, namely the Import-Export Bank. With the lower capital requirements of a joint venture, such risks would be reduced.

(d) The international staff at Rally Dawson has no prior exposure to Asia or the Middle East. Mr. Williams felt that by going into a joint venture they would rapidly acquire needed skills and know-how of the local market place. Also, Mr. Williams knew that Hamid Sports had an effective distribution system which would facilitate the distribution of products produced by the new plant.

On the other hand, Mr. Williams had some reservations about the financing arrangements which meant that all of Rally Dawson's needed capital would have to be exported to Pakistan. He knew that the PIDB had made an exception earlier in a similar case for John Deere Corporation and had granted the firm a loan. John Deere had gone into a joint venture with a local enterprise and PIDB helped John Deere by financing one-third of the company's investment share. (John Deere had a 60% ownership interest in the fertilizer plant.) When asked, the bank responded that fertilizer was critical to the agricultural production of Pakistan and it had made an exception because that was a direct contribution to the national goal for self-sufficiency in food.

Exhibit 8

Projected Statement of Annual Cash Flows for Joint Venture (1991–1995) (dollars in thousands)*

	1991	1992	1993	1994	1995
Cash Receipts	$1,600	$2,400	$3,000	$4,000	$4,500
PIDB Advances	500	200	300	—	—
Depreciation	225	200	200	200	200
	$2,325	$2,800	$3,500	$4,200	$4,700
Cash Disbursements:					
Raw Material Purchases	$ 600	$ 800	$ 900	$ 550	600
Direct Labor	200	350	400	375	360
Factory Overhead	700	680	710	715	720
Selling Expenses	300	315	373	475	600
Admn. Expenses	414	493	510	545	589
Income Taxes	112	235	370	588	789
Plant & Equipment	225	200	220	200	200
Working Capital					
Debt Repayment	—	—	—	200	800
	$2,551	$3,073	$3,483	$3,648	$4,658
Cash over					
(short)	$ (226)	$ (273)	$ 17	$ 552	$ 42
Cash balance					
(begin.)	1,000	774	501	518	1,070
Cash balance					
(end)	$ 774	$ 501	$ 518	$1,070	$1,112

* Translated from rupees to dollars.

Project Evaluation by Rally Dawson Sports

Rally Dawson Sports usually looked for a five-year payback period, at least for domestic investments. Mr. Williams also knew he could think of a project's rate of return on investment as that rate that would discount all the amounts received as income or as repayment of principal to an amount equal the cost of the investment. But he felt payback to be a better measure of risk.

Mr. Williams felt that no one could know at the time an investment was made what rate of return would actually be realized. But some measures could be made. Rally Dawson Sports had tried in the past to measure risk by a proba-bility distribution of estimated rates of return on its investments. In one attempt Mr. Williams had gone so far as to estimate returns for the joint venture. This is shown in Exhibit 5. The probability measurement chart shown could be used to statistically describe Rally Dawson Sports estimate of risk. Calculations of the variance and the standard deviation of the distribution were possible. Exhibits 6–8 show additional projected financial statements for the joint venture that Mr. Williams had drawn up. At this point they were not considered to be final projections. They showed results from the point of 1991 when manufacturing operations were planned to start.

FOURTEEN

INTERNATIONAL INFORMATION SYSTEMS MANAGEMENT

Mohammad Dadashzadeh
Wichita State University

In this chapter the basic issues pertinent to international information systems management are introduced. The chapter first discusses the ramifications of internationalization on the information systems function. It examines various information systems options and offers alternatives available to multinational companies (MNCs). Based on the MNCs' requirements and the environmental limitations that the MNCs experience, the chapter makes several suggestions for deployment of specific information systems. Finally, the impact of the internationalization of the firm on the chief information officer's responsibilities and duties are discussed.

Exxon Computing Services Company (ECSC) is located in Houston, Texas. With a staff of 500 employees, it handles much of Exxon's general-purpose (nontechnical) computing, including processing of customer orders, customer invoicing, marketing terminal operations, refinery maintenance information, U.S. retail credit card operations, accounting, inventory tracking, payroll processing and human resource records. It also helps in coordination of Exxon's global telecommunications network for doing business in more than 80 countries. The ECSC Computing Center is a large, complex operation that can process more than 800 million computer instructions per second. This allows the center to provide computing services for more than 30,000 Exxon employees, and for 8,000 or more employees to use the center's computers concurrently at peak hours. To accomplish this, ECSC operates extensive telecommunications networks at Exxon locations around the world.

Exxon's mainframe computing consolidations are consistent with a "rationalization" movement among numerous large corporations in the past several years as telecommunications costs have declined and as networks have become more widespread and reliable. Satellite technology has improved, more fiber-optic cable has been laid worldwide, and new computer technology enables large corporate computing centers to partition their working environment to serve multiple operations located in different geographic areas around the world. In consolidation of its computing services, Exxon must work within the limits of the communications capabilities that are available in the countries involved. For example, Thailand currently lacks fiber-optic cable lines, which can carry both voice and data in large volumes. Satellites must be utilized to transmit data from Bangkok to the west coast of the United States, where fiber-optic lines are available, and back to Thailand. A backup route for Exxon's data leaves Bangkok in a different direction than the first to reduce the likelihood of both circuits going out due to weather or other problems. This alternate route goes from Bangkok to a satellite positioned over the Indian Ocean and back to earth at Hong Kong, where a leased fiber-optic cable runs under the Pacific Ocean to the west coast of the United States at Medford, Oregon. From there, buried fiber-optic cables carry data through California and the Southwest to Houston. The distance data now has to travel from Bangkok to Houston and back adds only about one second to the response time of the system, but has reduced computing costs at Esso Thailand by 10 percent.

Current telecommunications applications by ECSC range from international networks to satellite communications with Exxon ships at sea and with drilling rigs or production sites far removed from the existing communication infrastructure. With the use of modern telecommunications equipment, ECSC has been able to improve the quality and reduce the cost of ship-to-ship and ship-to-shore communications in Exxon's fleet. Ten years ago, in order to communicate with one of the ships in the Exxon fleet, the message would be delivered to an in-house communication center, and it would take two or three hours for that message to show up on the ship by radio. Then, the ship's radio operator would receive it, type it up, and deliver it to the captain. Now, Exxon ships are tied into a satellite network, so they can receive and initiate instantaneous telecommunications, including voice, data, and facsimile—just as if they were in a modern office building instead of thousands of miles from civilization.

Excerpted from D. A. Zwicker. *The Lamp* (Exxon Corporation), 75, no. 4 (Winter 1993), 9–12. Used with permission.

Introduction

We are living in the information age. Information and information technology (IT) govern every aspect of our lives. Information can be considered the lifeblood of business, a strategic resource that can provide a competitive advantage. The ability to gather, store, and process information is essential for making timely decisions. As much as 80 percent of the executive's time is devoted to receiving, communicating, and using information in performing a variety of tasks.[1] Because all organizational activities depend on information, systems must be developed to produce and manage them. No complex organization can function without an information system (IS). "An information system is a set of people, data, and procedures that work together to provide useful information."[2] Organizational success is greatly dependent on an effective IS. The need for an effective IS is particularly crucial for the survival and success of MNCs. Crossing national borders, the MNCs are vulnerable to uncertainties associated with multiple political, cultural, and economic systems within which they operate. Therefore, an effective MIS is very essential to the success of the MNCs.

The management information system (MIS) is a system of obtaining, processing, and delivering information in support of managing the organizations.[3] The mission of IS is to improve the performance of people in the organization through the use of information technology.[4] Before the advent of computers, due to technological limitations, the bulk of MIS consisted of paper reports generated by functional areas, such as accounting, manufacturing, and marketing. Accessing this information was very slow and time consuming. There was a time lag between the generation of information and its use. Depending on the physical distance between the source and the use of information, the time lag ranged from a few hours to weeks. As a result of the limitation in information management, geographic distances from the headquarters implied a higher degree of autonomy for the subsidiaries. Today, information technology comprises computers and telecommunications and allows instantaneous access to information regardless of the physical distance between the source and the use of information. The new-found MIS capability not only allows more timely decision making, it enables better control of distant operations. Such a capability is especially beneficial to MNCs.

Computer-based information systems (CBIS) play a vital role in today's business. The many benefits organizations seek to achieve through CBIS may be classified as (1) efficiency gains, (2) effectiveness gains, and (3) competitive advantage.

Efficiency gains are concerned with doing more with the same or fewer resources. CBIS can bring about efficiency gains by automating tasks in the factory as well as in the workplace. Effectiveness gains are concerned with doing the right things. CBIS can bring about effectiveness gains by improving internal as well as external communications and by facilitating superior managerial decision making. Competitive advantage is concerned with providing the organization with a significant and long-term benefit vis-à-vis the competition. CBIS can bring about competitive advantage by allowing the firm to differentiate itself from its competitors, or to become the lowest cost/price producer in the marketplace, or to carve market niches for itself through innovative services and/or products.

It is precisely because of the major impact that information systems can have on corporate strategy that today's managers must not only be computer literate but also information systems literate. Computer literacy is a knowledge of computer technology. Information systems literacy encompasses how and why IT is applied in organizations. A knowledge of organizations, managerial levels, information needs, and decision-making approaches are all important aspects of information systems literacy.

Today, no company of even modest size can operate without support from IS. But, at a time when business is increasing its dependence on information technology, technology is changing so rapidly that businesses are threatened by its pace. New developments arise before older ones can be assimilated, and systems purchased today are, at times, outdated even before they are put into use. It is, however, too late to stop. The use of any tool creates a dependence, and computers—one of the most enabling tools created by man—are heavily used already. Roach[5] has argued that 48 percent of all capital investment in the United States is being put into informa-

tion technology. To cease to invest, or even slow investment, is to accept the premise that new operations and opportunities can be developed without IT support, when old ones cannot be sustained without it! Therefore, management of the IT investment has become a critical concern, because there are real risks associated with inept organizational response to the rapid pace of developments in information technology.

The solution that emerged in the late 1980s to deal effectively with the rapid pace of change in IT was to build an *information architecture*, that is, to create a framework within which current as well as future organizational needs for information could be met with impunity from changing technology. The information systems architect, however, must often pay dearly for the mistakes of the past. Information systems, like buildings and streets, have had a tendency to grow haphazardly. As in a building, we do not like to break down an "outside wall," but, if we cannot modify the inside walls to make the architecture useful for today's context (i.e., information needs), then there is no other choice. A well-planned information architecture should, as much as possible, obviate the need for the demolition of outside walls.[6]

Figure 14.1 depicts a model information architecture. It is founded on providing infrastructures for communication integration as well as data integration *on which* the IT portfolio (i.e., the various application systems ranging from purchase order entry to R&D planning) would be developed.[7] Together, communication integration and data integration ensure that data is stored in a nonredundant fashion and that every authorized user can gain access to and update needed information from anywhere. These infrastructures must be provided to support the tactical deployment of IT, to assure that developing problems and opportunities can be addressed, and to guarantee that catch-up time would be short and thereby little ground would be lost to a competitor who leads with an innovative business idea based on IT. In addition, the model emphasizes four application portfolios

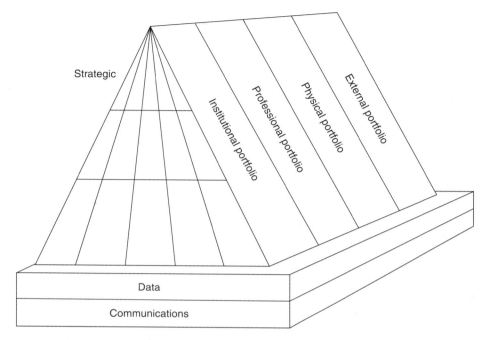

Figure 14.1 A Model Information Architecture
Source: J. A. Senn. Information Systems in Management. *(Lexington, MA: Nolan, Norton and Company, 1987). Reprinted with permission.*

that would comprise a mature information system:

1. *Institutional portfolio:* Information systems applications directed at recording and reporting on business activities. Examples include transaction processing systems such as payroll, order entry, purchasing, production scheduling, and accounting information systems.

2. *Professional support portfolio:* Information systems applications directed at managerial problem solving and decision making, competitive intelligence, and personal productivity. Examples include critical success factor reporting systems, decision support systems, expert systems, and such tools as are used for document preparation, computer-based messaging, electronic meetings, and work group computing.

3. *Physical automation portfolio:* Information systems applications directed at replacing manual work with information technology

both on the factory floor as well as in offices. Examples include computer-aided design and engineering, robotics, automated response units, and workflow automation.

4. *External portfolio:* Information systems applications directed at linking the firm with its suppliers, customers, or other firms for the purpose of creating a strategic alliance. Examples include electronic data interchange (EDI) with suppliers, order entry systems installed on customer premises, and interorganizational systems.

It is important to note that while the model acknowledges that the application portfolios must address the information requirements at all levels of management, it neither assumes a particular hardware or software architectural platform, nor advocates a centralized or decentralized approach to building the architecture. Those degrees of freedom are left to the eventual architect who must fit the suggested architectural form to the specific context of the organization. In the remainder of this chapter we use this model architecture as a backdrop to examine the ramifications of internationalization on the IS architecture.

Ramifications of Internationalization on the IS Function

The expansion of a company from a domestic corporation to a multinational one brings with it special problems for the IS function. Consider the following ramifications of internationalization on the IS function[8]:

- Although it is highly desirable to have common computer (e.g., PC) standards, local service issues and the level of support vary so widely that this seemingly straightforward issue becomes a complex one. The support and service issue notwithstanding, it may simply be overwhelmingly advantageous to improve government relationships by choosing a local brand even at the expense of system integration problems that this option may cause.

- Although it is highly desirable to have system developers located physically close to the end-users of the system being developed, the wide disparity between salaries abroad vis-à-vis the United States may make it overwhelmingly attractive to move portions of large development efforts overseas and risk the coordination problems.

- Expansion overseas also causes problems with scheduling and coordination. A business that crosses four time zones has five business hours that are supported in common by all portions of its operation, while one spanning more than eight time zones would have no common business hours at all. This shift in schedules can result in increased reliance on background transfers of information (such as e-mail), which

do not require human interaction in real time.

- In general, communications costs increase with distance. This creates an incentive to disperse data to reduce transmission costs, a strategy that can result in the loss of information control and increased security risks.

- The use of personal data generates a wide range of sensitivities in different countries. What is seen as a consumer micromarketing information system in one country may be regarded as quite intrusive in another. Moreover, existing legislation regarding computer privacy, computer security, software licensing, and copyrights remains substantially fragmented within countries.

- Expansion into other countries also causes problems with languages. Global information systems must be designed to support people speaking different languages, and data entry as well as report programs must be written to accommodate different alphabets and collating sequences.

- In some countries, the installation of new telephone lines still requires a lead time of two to three years, making the planning and implementation of an adequately redundant (fault-tolerant) communication infrastructure a time-consuming ordeal.

- Great unevenness in local technical support exists from one country to another. This can lead to considerable reliance on the parent company for troubleshooting, for system development efforts, and for scanning the emerging technologies that might impact their operations.

As can be seen from the items listed here, the IT function, like all other functional areas, is considerably affected by internationalization. Also, like all other functional areas, its response to internationalization will be affected by both country variables as well as company variables.

The IS Function Within the Multinational Corporation

Not surprisingly, MNCs have adopted different approaches for their IS functions. Some are centralized, some are decentralized, and some are distributed. Some are integrated, but most are not.

There are several classifications of international information systems. The following provides a useful starting categorization:

- *Multinational information systems:* This most prevalent model is characterized by essentially autonomous data processing centers in each nation-state in which the MNC operates. This approach suffers from problems of redundancy and duplication in data, applications, and operations. However, it historically represents the easiest solution available to the MNC given the conditions of national markets (i.e., regulations, language problems, facilities problems, etc., as discussed in previous chapters) that encouraged the autonomy of business operations in each country.
- *International information systems:* This model is characterized by a computer network that operates in more than one nation-state and in which data crosses international borders in support of completing a transaction.
- *Global information systems:* This relatively new model is fundamentally characterized by the integration of data. Support for manufacturing operations that must coordinate inputs and outputs of plants located in different countries on a real-time basis has been one of several driving forces toward such systems. Another impetus has been the desire to present a consistent face to a customer that may have dealings with the MNC in several countries in which it operates. However, it has been only the recent advances in distributed database manage-

ment and communication technologies that have made this model a viable alternative.

Using a concept that originally was developed by Perlmutter,[9] Roche[10] has proposed a more useful categorization of international information systems. Roche's proposal is based on the premise that a desired relationship exists between an MNC's global, regional, and national structuring and its information system. Accordingly, an *ethnocentric* MNC that pursues a global integrative business strategy should opt for centralized data processing at headquarters with a global database and on-line access from any location. A *polycentric* MNC that pursues a national responsiveness business strategy would most benefit from independent data centers in each host country with no data integration or real-time access with other locations. A *regiocentric* MNC that pursues a regional integrative and responsiveness business strategy should consider centralized data processing within regions with no data integration or real-time access with other regions. Finally, a *geocentric* MNC pursuing a global integrative and national responsiveness business strategy has basically no other option than to create a truly distributed database processing environment or, in other words, to build a global information system.

International IS Issues

Information technology is an important mechanism to facilitate, sustain, and promote international interactions. King and Sethi[11] have categorized IS issues as follows.

Intracorporate IS issues   Intracorporate interactions provide the interface between the corporate unit (and its IS function) and its overseas subsidiary (and its IS function). The IS issues in this category can be divided into (1) those pertaining to the IS function only and (2) those pertaining to the role of IS in supporting competitive strategy.

The issues pertaining only to the IS function emanate from the design of the *link* between the

IS function at the corporate unit and the IS function in the overseas subsidiary. The links are of three types: *organizational links, architectural links,* and *personnel links.*

Organizational linkage design must address the organizational structure of IS at the subsidiary, its control systems and reporting procedures, and its participation in the IS function of the corporation as a whole. Both company-level variables and subsidiary-specific variables must be taken into account in designing the organizational links. The former includes overall organizational structure and organizational strategy, while the latter involves the information dependency of the subsidiary, the importance (knowledge contribution) of the subsidiary, and the ownership of the subsidiary.

Architectural linkage design must address the issues of communication integration, data integration, application portfolio, and the hardware and software platforms. What is the desired level of connectivity? What is an acceptable level of standardization of codes (e.g., ethnic classification codes)? What is a tolerable level of redundancy in the databases? What is the desired degree of freedom in developing an application portfolio? What is an acceptable level of incompatibility of equipment?

Personnel linkage design must address the functions of selection, staffing, appraisal, and compensation of IS personnel in subsidiaries. What is the appropriate mix of local employees who speak the language, understand the culture and the political system, and expatriate employees who can emphasize firm-wide rather than local objectives?

The issues pertaining to the role of IS in supporting competitive strategy are influenced by industry-level variables as well as country-level variables. When MNCs in the same industry operate in the same countries, they cannot exploit comparative advantage sources (e.g., lower labor costs, raw material, etc., in one country vis-à-vis another). In such cases, the IS function must focus on maintaining a firm-specific competitive advantage; for example, by transferring systems (such as order entry terminals placed at customer premises) that have created such an advantage in the home country to the host country. On the other hand, when similar MNCs operate in different countries, the IS function should focus its efforts on exploiting sources of comparative advantage.

Intergovernmental IS issues The interactions between the IS function and intergovernmental units are concerned with either technical issues or regulatory concerns. There are several benefits from user participation in standard-setting organizations such as the International Standards Organization (ISO). Perhaps the most important of such benefits is remaining closely informed of directions in open systems (i.e., nonproprietary) standards and technologies and assessing their impact on the corporation's IS infrastructure.

While developing coherent international standards is important to any IS function, a consistent pattern of international regulatory practices is a prerequisite to information transfers required by the global firm. As a result, we find that telecommunications and IS issues have been prominent at various international negotiations including the General Agreement on Tariffs and Trade (GATT). Liberalization of global communications, in particular, can bring significant advantage to MNCs.

Host government IS issues The issues pertaining to the interactions between the IS function and the host government emanate from the MNCs' deployment of information technologies and the host government's reaction to it. These issues can be divided into (1) political, (2) economic, (3) technological, and (4) sociocultural.

Chief among political issues is the concern for ownership and the sovereignty of a nation over its resources, including the information resource. Information technology, in the form of satellite communications, for example, can render national control of information ineffective. Similarly, it is at times feared that MNCs headquartered in developed countries can, through the use of IS and transborder data flow, remotely control the physical operations of their factories and potentially bring operations in a less developed country to a halt.

Economic issues have typically surfaced in the form of restrictive policies against the use of IS for fear of displacement or unemployment of workers. In addition, host government policies for the development of indigenous IS industries can force an MNC's IS function into an unfavorable reliance on outsourcing in the host country and the deployment of less than optimal technologies. Technological issues relate to host government's IS-related policies regarding access to communication facilities and international networks and its interest in technology transfer. Sociocultural issues deal with the host government's stance on protecting the needs of the individual versus the needs of the society if and when an MNC's government-sanctioned IS practices meet opposition from groups or interests within the society.

Reactive international IS issues   National IS-related policies formulated in response to changes in similar policies in other countries have an enduring impact on the IS function of the MNC. As pointed out by the National Telecommunications and Information Administration (NTIA), "as direct beneficiaries or victims of many policy decisions, private firms have a critical stake in the nature and effectiveness of governmental decision making."[12] As a result we see that, for example, in response to the European Commission's Green Paper on the Development of the Common Market for Telecommunications Services and Equipment, American business interests rose to the occasion and suggested to the government a review of a number of revisions in the Open Network Provision proposed by the European Commission.

In addition to the preceding four categories of IS issues, King and Sethi[13] also examine intergovernment interactions as well as interactions between governments and intergovernmental bodies. They point out that these interactions primarily translate into bilateral, regional, and multilateral negotiations regarding issues that directly or indirectly impact the IS function of MNCs. As an example, the Canada–U.S. Free Trade Agreement includes computer and telecommunications services agreements to provide nondiscriminatory access, to maintain existing rights of access, to limit anticompetitive practices, and contains provisions for transborder data flows and access to data banks.

Global IS Management Issues

The model presented in the previous section provides one means by which to organize and discuss issues pertinent to global information systems management. Another approach is to undertake an empirical study to identify and rank important global IS management issues for MNCs. Two such studies are summarized in this section.

Deans, Karwan, Goslar, Ricks, and Toyne[14] report the findings of a study based on a mail questionnaire and follow-up interviews with top IS executives in U.S.-based MNCs. The study identifies "educating senior personnel as to the role and potential of MIS contribution on an international scale" to be the highest ranked issue, and "export restrictions on data processing equipment and software" to be the lowest ranked issue at the time of the study. Although such rankings of issues are clearly of interest, a somewhat more time-invariant insight is offered by classifying the issues along the dichotomy of what would and what would not be an issue of concern to the IS executive in a purely domestic arena. Table 14.1 presents such a classification for the issues identified in the Deans *et al.* study.

Based exclusively on the rankings, the list of 32 issues of concern are dominated by those that are also pertinent in the domestic IS arena. And, as characterized in Table 14.2, of the issues that pertain solely to operating in an international

Table 14.1
Classification of IT Issues Ranked by Executives

Not of Concern in a Domestic IS Arena (Pertinent to International Arena)	Ranking
International protocol standards	6
Telecommunications deregulation	9
Regulatory strategies of PTTs	15
Learning to conduct business in other countries	17
Vendor support in foreign subsidiaries	19
Local cultural constraints	22
Transborder data flow restrictions	23
Legal restrictions on hardware/software acquisitions	24
Level of IT sophistication in the country	25
Banned usage of telecommunications equipment	27
Language barriers	28
The national infrastructure	29
Currency restrictions and exchange rate volatility	31
Export restrictions	32

Of Concern in a Domestic IS Arena	
Educating senior personnel	1
Data security	2
Integration of technologies	3
End-user computing	4
Price and quality of telecommunications	5
Use of IT for competitive advantage	7
Data utilization	8
Changes in communications technology	10
Aligning the IS organization	11
Centralization/distributed processing	12
Recruiting and training	13
Software development	14
Integrated Services Digital Network	16
MIS planning	18
Use of value-added network services	20
External data	21
Interorganizational systems	26
Computer-integrated manufacturing	30

Source: P. C. Deans, K. R. Karwan, M. D. Goslar, D. A. Ricks, and B. Toyne. "Identification of Key International Information Systems Issues in U.S.-based Multinational Corporations." *Journal of Management Information Systems*, 7, no. 4 (Spring 1991), 27–50.

arena, technological issues dominate political as well as cultural concerns, which in turn dominate economic issues.

Another empirical study by Palvia and Saraswat[15] focused on identifying the relative importance of eight specific IT management issues to the IS executives of U.S.-based MNCs. The eight issues studied were (1) IT transfer, (2) cultural differences, (3) international standards, (4) IT infrastructure, (5) global IT applications, (6) global IT policy, (7) global IT marketing, and (8) transborder data flow. The study identified the problems faced with transborder data flow (restrictions on flow of data, data se-

Table 14.2
Categorization of IT Issues

IT Issues Pertinent Solely in the International Arena	Ranking
Technological	
International protocol standards	6
Telecommunications deregulation	9
Regulatory strategies of PTTs	15
Vendor support in foreign subsidiaries	19
Level of IT sophistication in the country	25
Political/Legal	
Transborder data flow restrictions	23
Legal restrictions on hardware/software acquisitions	24
Banned usage of telecommunications equipment	27
Social/Cultural	
Learning to conduct business in other countries	17
Local cultural constraints	22
Language barriers	28
Economic	
The national infrastructure	29
Currency restrictions and exchange rate volatility	31
Export restrictions	32

Source: P. C. Deans, K. R. Karwan, M. D. Goslar, D. A. Ricks, and B. Toyne. "Identification of Key International Information Systems Issues in U.S.-based Multinational Corporations." *Journal of Management Information Systems,* 7, no. 4 (Spring 1991), 27–50.

curity vulnerabilities, and telecommunications management) and the lack of international standards (telecommunications, software development, and computer architecture standards) as the top two issues of concern.

The studies in this section serve to point out the similarities between IT issues in both the domestic and the international arenas. In the next section, we present a guideline for building a global information system that addresses the special concerns raised in those studies.

Building a Global Information System

The challenge of setting up an information system spanning continents is no longer limited to the Fortune 500. The rank of firms operating internationally—either for production, distribution, or some other business function—is growing. The evidence indicates that multinational firms are earning more, and growing faster, than

firms without global operations. The IS directors of the firms venturing into foreign markets quickly realize that the challenges faced by IS range from the broadest organizational issues to the most detailed programming dilemmas[16]:

- When Toys R Us decided that the best way to begin its overseas expansion was to organize itself into separate national business units, its IS director realized that simply exporting the U.S. systems overseas would be an overkill. In the United States, Toys R Us systems are built with economies of scale in mind, where it might take 100 stores to justify a system or certain technologies. In Europe, Toys R Us has decided to keep information systems as simple as possible in order to get established and grow quickly. Therefore, in Europe, Toys R Us does not run the same kind of purchasing and logistic programs that it uses in the United

States. Instead it relies on manual clerical processes. Also, while advanced technologies are used for linking mobile workers and their hand-held terminals to store computers in the United States, they are not employed in Europe. Even the company's U.S. hardware infrastructure, consisting of Unisys mainframes to house corporate data, DEC VAX computers for the stores, and NCR point-of-sale terminals, is replaced in Europe by IBM AS/400 computers and point-of-sale (POS) systems.

- When Federal Express expanded outside the United States, the cultural nuances of billing resulted in revisions of their billing system. In Britain, customers do not pay from an invoice, but from a statement sent after the invoice. In Japan, the invoicing *protocol* calls for invoices to be sent within

a specific time period after the sale and to have a specific format.

- When bicycle and race-car helmet maker Bell Sports began exporting to Europe, the IS staff back in its Rantoul, Illinois, factory ran headfirst into European safety regulations requiring statements on packages and labels inside helmets. To get the right labels on the right helmets in an efficient manner, the IS department had to rewrite portions of its Material Requirement Planning II (MRP-II) systems.

- When Ikea, a $5 billion home-furnishing company from Sweden, opened its first U.S. store in 1986, the IS department had to make a variety of modifications to their store systems. For example, the IS staff had to do some "keyboard mapping" to allow the U.S. staff to prepare reports with um-

Esprit's Experience

Pete Bates, vice president of systems at clothing manufacturer Esprit de Corp in San Francisco, found out the hard way that sharing software on a global basis does not always work according to plan.

In 1992, Esprit's U.S. subsidiary adopted a production management system developed at the company's Far East affiliate. The software tracks where an item is manufactured, sewn, pressed, and so on. But the software was only a "moderate" success in the United States, Bates says, because "the ways of doing business are quite different in the two hemispheres." Similar to the experiences of virtually all major corporations that do business overseas, Esprit ran into a wall. It found that despite good intentions and the apparent benefits, sharing software across borders is not always the best choice. Work habits around the world are different.

Although many companies are going global and information systems groups are under increasing pressure to maximize technology investments, seasoned IS experts say not all software can or should be common everywhere. In the Far East, for example, it is standard for the shop sewing the garment to handle the other steps of finishing and washing. In the U.S., however, convention dictates that the individual steps be contracted out to different parties.

The end result, Bates says, was that "the system that Hong Kong put together did not have the features for us to manage effectively the transition from factory to factory." Consequently, Esprit's U.S. group abandoned software sharing with overseas units.

Source: J. Ambrosio. "Global Software?" *Computerworld* (August 2, 1993), 74–5.

lauts. Also, report programs had to be adjusted to deal with American-sized paper stock. More important, however, order entry/billing programs had to be rewritten so American customers could arrange to have furniture shipped to their homes. In Europe, the shipping company takes ownership of the order, and customers pay the shipper cash on delivery. In the United States, these procedures were unacceptable and the programs had to be rewritten to accommodate payment in advance of delivery.

As the preceding anecdotes illustrate, building a global information system presents a variety of challenges for the IS manager. Nevertheless, the experience of successful companies indicates that one key to success stands out: global operation demands global information, which in turn calls for a global infrastructure in planning, data integration, communication, and information resource management.

Planning Globally

Because of the wide geographic distances separating the MNCs' global operations from the headquarters and from each other, IS plays a critical role in strategic planning, implementation, and control of MNCs. Therefore, taking a reactive approach to building a global information architecture is nothing less than accepting a position of competitive defensiveness or possibly competitive disadvantage. Nevertheless, as several studies have indicated, most senior managers do not have a clear and personal business vision for IT. To help relate business integration and technology integration, Keen[17] suggests a framework that defines the business functionality of the firm's IT facilities in terms of two dimensions of *reach* and *range* (see Table 14.3). In this framework, *reach* determines the location the firm can link to, from locations within a single site, to the entire domestic operation, to locations abroad, to customers and suppliers domestically, to customers and suppliers internationally, and to anyone, anywhere. The *range* determines the nature of the information that can be shared directly across systems, from standard messages, to ad hoc access to data, to arbitrary single transactions to be completed by one party (node), to cooperative transactions to be completed by several nodes.

Reach and *range* together determine the extent of business options available to the firm.[18] In Table 14.3, for example, the shaded cells in the bottom row signify an integrated database within a single site, allowing various departments to share and update common data, while the absence of shading in the next to last row depicts the inability to process update transactions from remote locations even within the same

Table 14.3
Relating Business Functionality to Data and Communication Integration

Reach Whom?	Standard Messages	Access to Stored Data	Single Transactions	Cooperative Transactions
Anyone, anywhere				
Customers, suppliers, regardless of IT base				
Customers, suppliers, with same IT base				
Intracompany locations, abroad				
Intracompany locations, domestic				
Intracompany locations, single site				

Range (What Services Can We Deliver?)

country. Therefore, the *reach* and *range* framework serves to translate the IT integration issues for senior management as *what option is implied by our business plans?* A firm may opt to build an enterprisewide totally integrated IT infrastructure aiming for the maximum in *reach* and *range*. In so doing it needs to consider a variety of issues. One factor is the extent of the firm's centralization. In general, it is easier to put in place the rules and constraints of a global IT infrastructure when a corporate culture for centralization exists. Another factor is the availability of capital.

Because most companies are not well centralized or awash in capital, they must rely on multiple IT architectures (each signifying a different combination of *reach* and *range*) rather than the ideal totally integrated (global) infrastructure. These multiple IT architectures are too often determined first by geography and then by function. Unfortunately, such a traditional approach usually proves counterproductive, simply because a decision in one area of the organization quite often affects other areas. A better alternative is to take a business process perspective. This means viewing a business in terms of major processes such as order fulfillment and customer service rather than functional areas. The business process perspective enables us to overcome geographical boundaries in planning for information systems in a global concern.

Therefore, a company that wants to create a global information system must first come to terms with the processes that are essential to its business strategy. The identification and prioritization of such strategically important processes are critical to effective planning for a global information system.[19] Simply put, to compete effectively, such strategically important processes *must* be targeted for common global IT infrastructures, while other activities can be left to be supported by local (and even heterogeneous) IT architectures.

Communication Integration in the Global Organization

Regardless of the number of business processes that a firm chooses to support with a global IT architecture, there will be a substantial cost associated with establishing and maintaining the requisite communication infrastructure. It would be a serious mistake to assume that the only difference between building a global network and a domestic network is one of size.

Global communications networks, like their domestic counterparts, can provide both internal and external benefits to the firm. Internally, a global network can, at the very least, improve management control by facilitating communication among international business units, and, at best, support an on-line, real-time, integrated database for both transaction processing as well as managerial decision making worldwide. Digital Equipment Corporation, for example, reports that its global computer network helped it save $700 million in inventory-related costs over a two-year period by increasing control over the movement of inventory between its worldwide manufacturing plants.[20]

Externally, a global network can be used to advance a company's competitive strategy. Federal Express' global network connects the U.S. network with more than 60 subsidiaries worldwide in order to implement the company's differentiation strategy based on real-time tracking of packages. Marriott and Scandinavian Airlines have linked their global networks in order to create an interorganizational system focused on providing added value (convenience) to a shared customer by checking in customers' luggage for a flight at the hotel reception desk. Despite such benefits, global networks are far from widespread for the following reasons: (1) the high costs involved, (2) the existence of politically imposed constraints, and (3) technical problems.[21]

The costs of global networks can be substantial for a combination of reasons including the following:

• Telephone service in other countries is considerably more expensive than in the United States.

• Lower speeds of transmission lines in other countries means more time spent for data transmission.

• Cost of transmission may vary depending on the direction of data flow. For example, it costs four times as much to send data to the United States from Portugal than to send it in the opposite direction.[22]

• The arrangements between telephone companies for handling international calls are based on cost-sharing at each end of the link. The formulas penalize the low-cost U.S. carriers by paying, on average, 75

Designing Worldwide Systems

A multinational software firm, Cognos of Ottawa, Canada, faced various telecommunications problems when it was connecting its offices in 38 countries. First, Cognos tried to use the public X.25 packet-switching data networks—a worldwide standard. "The problem was that in every country it is a bit different," says Stewart Hamilton, manager of network services. "There's no question that each network decides on its own way to support X.25. You can't just go out and program all your gear and plug it into any network and have it work. It doesn't work that way. That's the theory, but in practice it just doesn't happen."

There were other problems too. "If a link is broken, there really is nobody to call. You can call the local telephone company or the international carrier, but there's just no accountability for the overall running of the network. We had outages between different networks for over two weeks that we couldn't do anything about."

Cognos also ran into regulatory problems. "If you want to plug a modem in a bunch of offices around the world, it's more the rule than the exception that you have to have that modem approved in that country. In certain countries, Spain in particular, we were having a lot of trouble getting certain gear approved for use. The approval process can take anywhere from weeks to years."

Then there were compatibility problems. "If we buy a piece of equipment from a company in Europe, it's made in the EC. If we buy it in North America, it's made in Singapore. Then the two pieces of equipment usually end up slightly different, and we get into problems when we put them into operation."

Cognos ultimately turned to two firms with worldwide telecommunications expertise to establish its networks. Infonet, El Segundo, California, took care of procuring leased lines in various countries. Motorola, Schaumburg, Illinois, agreed to supply Cognos with approved communications equipment in all the countries it operated in.

Excerpted from R. Brown. "Designing Worldwide Systems." *Systems 3X/400* (January 1992), 22–6. Used by permission.

percent of the call charge to the high-cost foreign PTT (Poste Telegraphe et Telephonique). In the case of Brazil, 99 cents on each dollar of telephone charges from the United States to Brazil is paid to the Brazilian PTT.[23]

- The PTTs are government or quasigovernment monopolies for telecommunications and are very unwilling to break up their cartels, which, in turn, have controlled international telephone pricing and revenue sharing.[24]

The high costs associated with global networks are compounded by the political constraints imposed on transborder data flow (TDF). Deans and Kane[25] have pointed out that although some of the TDF regulation problems encountered by multinational corporations increase the cost of communication between the parent and the subsidiary, their real impact is to create a control *barrier*. Examples of such barriers include the following:

- Required use of locally manufactured data processing equipment, communication services, and software

- Restrictions on the availability of flat-rate leased lines

- Restrictions on satellite transmission, for example, to receiving data only

- Requiring the processing of certain data locally

- Restrictions on the flow of data across national borders, for example, restricting the export of personnel-related data

- Threat of a tax on the value of data.

To deal with such TDF regulations, MNCs can resort to one or more of the following strategies[26]:

1. Decentralization of data processing on a geographic basis

2. Preprocessing of data to filter out restricted information

3. Alternative information channels to move data to the parent company

4. Database duplication and reprocessing at the parent company to obtain the desired level of reporting and control.

Table 14.4
European ISDN Offerings

Country	Name of Service	Date Available	Basic/Primary Rate	Service
UK	ISDN 2	1991	Basic	British Telecom
UK	2100 Premier	1988	Primary	Mercury
Germany		1989	Basic/primary	Deutsche Bundepost Telekom
France	Numeris	1987	Basic/primary	France Telecom
Austria		1993	Basic	PTT Austria
Belgium	Aline	1989	Basic/primary	Belgacom
Switzerland	Swissnet	1992	Basic/primary	Swiss PTT
Italy		1992	Basic/primary	SIP
Spain	Red Digital Service Integrados	1993	Basic	Telefonica
Sweden		1991	Basic/primary	Telia

Source: S. Fitzgerald. "Global Warming: ISDN Heats Up." *LAN*, 9, no. 6 (June 1994), 50–5.

In addition to the high costs and political constraints associated with building global networks, there are technical problems involving the quality of services and operability that must also be overcome. Simply stated, in order to build an efficient global network, a company must be prepared to mix a variety of technologies and deal with compatibility issues. The ideal "one-stop shopping" simply does not exist and future visions such as a *global information superhighway* or standards such as X.25 for public packet-switched data networks take many years to be fully implemented.

In Europe, the Integrated Services Digital Network (ISDN) is widely deployed (see Table 14.4) providing basic access to two full-duplex 64-Kbps (kilobit per second) channels from the desktop. Most PTTs also offer a Primary Rate Interface consisting of thirty 64-Kbps channels capable of handling digitized voice, video, and/or data. (The definition for the Primary Rate Interface differs in the United States and signifies twenty-three 64-Kbps channels.)

As in Europe, most major cities in the United States currently offer ISDN. Bell Atlantic (Philadelphia), Bell South (Atlanta), Pacific Bell (San Francisco), and U.S. West (Denver) are leading contenders in the deployment of ISDN. Although service offerings vary according to carrier, most services are aggressively priced (basic rate interface is generally offered for $25 to $50 per month plus usage charge). Therefore, it may not be unreasonable to expect that despite the current clamor over frame relay and asynchronous transfer mode (ATM) technologies, a great deal of telecommunication traffic between U.S. multinationals and their subsidiaries in Europe will traverse over ISDN. Where ISDN is not an option, traditional analog lines or digital lines (T1 services operating at 1.5 million bps) or optical fiber connections (OC-1 services operating at 45 million bps) can provide the needed connectivity even across oceans.

Then, of course, there are those situations where a company's only reliable means of data communication is through a wireless medium. Very small aperture terminal (VSAT) satellite networks, have had the same major impact on data communication as PCs have had on computing. Wireless networks, both spread-spectrum radio-frequency and infrared, are expected to provide a pathway in those places where a company must have a wireless link or no link at all.

Data Integration in the Global Organization

To understand the data integration issue, consider a global company that has determined order fulfillment to be its strategically important pacing process to be globally supported. Among other things, integrating these functions requires that information about stock availability be accessible from any of its business units around the world, and even though the customer's order has to be fulfilled by shipments from several sites, the customer is presented with a single invoice, and information about the customer is entered only once. To accomplish such data integration, a company has several alternatives:

1. *Centralized database/centralized processing:* In this approach, the database for order fulfillment resides in one location and all processing takes place in that location with remote sites acting as on-line data entry/update terminal nodes. This is similar to the traditional mainframe/dumb terminal computing model.

2. *Centralized database/decentralized processing:* A significant problem with the above alternative is that the centralized facility must be powerful enough to accommodate hundreds, or even thousands, of on-line terminals. In the centralized database/decentralized processing approach, although the database remains centralized, all of the processing, including the handling of issues related to concurrent update to

Reebok Tracks Athletes

To track more than 1000 athletes around the world Reebok uses Lotus Notes. These athletes' endorsements of its products constitute the heart of Reebok's promotional campaign. With Lotus Notes, a groupware application, Reebok maintains a global database of the results of their endorsements. These endorsements constitute a major investment in terms of payments to the athletes, which needs to be tracked and compared with products sales. Also tied into this system is the legal department which is attempting to standardize endorsement contracts. Similarly, the company's transaction processing systems is using the Notes database for near real-time reporting of the results of promotional activities around the world.

At Reebok, both regional and global specifications and standards are used in designing various products. With the help of Notes, Reebok designers can work collaboratively while serving their local markets. Notes enables designers to disseminate digitalized drawings and textual communications among all the company's design centers.

Source: M. Williamson. "Uniting Nations." *CIO* (June 1, 1994), 55–63.

---

shared data and backup and recovery, takes place at remote computers. This is similar to the local-area network computing model.

3. *Centralized database/distributed processing:* There are two problems with alternative two. First, because each remote computer must run the database management software as well as the order fulfillment application, there is still considerable computing power required of each node. Second, because the database is centralized, each remote query for, say, worldwide stock availability for a particular item, requires the *entire* stock file to be transmitted to the remote site for processing the request.

In a centralized database/distributed processing approach, the order fulfillment program is broken into the two components of database management system (DBMS) issues and user interface issues. The DBMS issues of concurrency control, backup and recovery, as well as searching the database to retrieve and/or update records matching specific criteria, are delegated to the *server* component of the program; while the user interface issues of displaying data and accepting keyboard input or responding to mouse movements is handled by the *client* component. Therefore, in our example, a remote query to obtain worldwide stock availability for a particular item is obtained by *the client program* from the user, which in turn forwards the query in a standard format such as SQL (Structured Query Language) to *the server program,* which processes the request and transmits only that portion of the stock file related to the requested item to the client program to display for the user. This is similar to the centralized client/server computing model.

4. *Distributed database/distributed processing:* A basic shortcoming of alternative 3 is the absence of fault tolerance. That is, should anything go wrong with the centralized database, all database access and processing comes to a halt.

In the distributed database/distributed processing approach, the database is logically and physically partitioned. For example, each site will have its own stock file and the customer file is divided (nonredundantly) among the various sites. As a result, there will be no single point of failure. Queries about enterprise-wide stock availability for a particular item are handled in a *location transparent* manner by the underlying distributed database management system. Distributed DBMS software such as Oracle and DB2 support such a distributed client/server computing model.

5. *Heterogeneous database processing:* All of the preceding alternatives assume that either the organization is initiating data processing operations at remote sites or that it is willing to scrap existing computing arrangements and reengineer them for the sake of supporting its strategically important pacing process. However, in those circumstances when a company acquires subsidiaries with established data processing and a dissimilar DBMS environment, an interim solution may be to create a heterogeneous distributed database processing environment. Unfortunately, commercially available software options for this alternative are quite limited. Nevertheless, it is possible to create a conceptual model of the overall database and allow users and programs to formulate their requests for enterprise-wide information against this view while translating each request, behind the scene, into a collection of cooperating transactions against various database management systems at different sites.

In general, retrofitting existing application systems in various countries to create a single system is more difficult than starting with a clean slate, but it is best to decide on a case-by-case basis.

IS Application Portfolio in the Global Organization

The cardinal rule in deciding what IS applications should be made global is that not every application needs to be a global application. Accounting and payroll systems are best left to local developers and maintenance program-

mers. Countries such as France impose a statuary chart of accounts,[27] and each country has its own taxation laws and its own version of the U.S.'s Internal Revenue Service with reporting forms such as W-2s, 1099s, and so forth. Therefore, it is a good rule of thumb not to globalize government-reporting applications. Nevertheless, there still remains a requirement for the consolidation of financial results as well as performance comparisons across subsidiaries that must be met by developing global applications.

As already pointed out, the decision as to which applications must be supported by a global architecture must emanate from global planning for IT. A company must start with its global strategy and identify those applications that are critical to its success. Those applications then comprise the company's initial global IS portfolio.

The traditional portfolio development has followed a chronological sequence of systems development and has moved from transaction processing to management reporting, decision support, executive information, and finally to workflow information systems. It is interesting to note that IS might find it easier to pursue the development of a global portfolio in the reverse chronological order (Table 14.5). That is, it appears that a greater chance of success exists if IS were to first bring electronic messaging and work group computing to the global organization. Next, it could target the development of a global executive information system, which does not have to deal with the more difficult problems of providing ad hoc access to, or update of, databases. At that point, IS can move into global decision support systems, which can employ historical data as well as more or less predefined snapshots of present databases. Next, it could support ad hoc access to enterprise-wide data for reporting purposes, which would, as a minimum, require the development of a conceptual model of the organization-wide integrated database. Finally, it can begin addressing

Table 14.5
Traditional Versus Global IS Portfolio Development Order

Traditional IS Portfolio Development Order
Transaction Processing Systems
Management Reporting Systems
Decision Support Systems
Executive Information Systems
Workflow Information Systems

Global IS Portfolio Development Order
Workflow Information Systems
Executive Information Systems
Decision Support Systems
Management Reporting Systems
Transaction Processing Systems

the rewriting of applications to support cooperative transaction processing and the real-time update of data at multiple sites.

Redefining the CIO as the Global Information Officer

The operational requirements of a truly global organization significantly increase the difficulties faced by its chief information officer (CIO).

IT investment and coordination issues for multinational corporations are vastly more complex than purely domestic ones, involving not only the domestic issues but also the added difficulties discussed in this chapter. As a global information officer (GIO), the CIO's responsibilities and performance expectations are transformed—both quantitatively and qualitatively.

What are the salient attributes of an effective GIO? Let us begin with those characteristics that one would expect to find in any CIO regardless of the global scope of his or her responsibilities. First, the CIO must provide the necessary guidance for developing an information architecture. On the one hand, this requires an in-depth understanding of information technologies: hardware and software platforms, telecommunications and networking strategies, centralized and distributed database management, open systems standards, and end-user computing tools and practices. On the other hand, it requires experience in managing IS personnel and the ability to administer complex, multifaceted projects. Second, the CIO must be

Programming for International Use

When writing a program to be used by an international audience, a variety of adjustments need to be made. Language on screen and on reports needs to be translated often to character strings longer than the English equivalent, and language-sensitive input needs to be modified. For example, if a yes or no input is needed, expecting a "y" or "n" will not work in France as "oui" does not start with a "y." The basic program design rule is to place all constant input and output strings outside the program in a language-specific data file.

There are also other problems. Some non-European languages such as Chinese and Japanese require special video support since they use double byte character sets. Other languages such as Thai use multi-byte character sets; sometimes, it takes one byte to get the character on screen, other times it may take as many as three bytes. Then, there are the Middle Eastern languages such as Arabic, Farsi, and Hebrew that are written from right to left. And in the case of Arabic and Farsi, the shape of a letter depends on its position in the written work (first, middle, last, or by itself).

Currency formats and date formats need to become country specific too. And, an important decision must be made regarding the stage in a transaction at which currencies are exchanged.

International Electronic Communication and Negotiation

Students participating in the International Communication and Negotiation Simulation (ICONS) Project at the University of Maryland experience the highs and lows of international negotiations during the course of a semester through a computer-assisted simulation model. In an ICONS simulation, cross-cultural awareness comes not only through the experience of playing the roles of high-level foreign policy decisions makers but also through the ability of the computer network to link the negotiators to peers at institutions around the world. Bringing technology to the classroom shrinks the globe.

ICONS links participants to a host computer at the University of Maryland, where the project facilitator employs global networks such as Internet to fashion a near universally available product. ICONS lets participants send and receive daily diplomatic communications. It also provides real-time conferencing, enabling country-teams to hold multilateral summits on such issues as cross-border pollution and ethnic conflicts.

Source: B. A. Starkey. "Negotiation Training Through Simulation: The ICONS International Negotiation Seminars Initiative." *Educators' TECH Exchange* (Spring 1994), 6–11.

especially responsive to evolving user requirements and changing corporate strategy. This demands staying informed about the business and operational requirements of the firm and positioning IS to respond to evolving needs quickly. Third, the CIO cannot afford to be hands-on all the time and thus the actual running of networks and data centers must be delegated to others. This, of course, requires effective delegation skills.

What is needed to transform the CIO to a GIO involves more managerial skills than technical expertise. The effective GIO must master how to manage the distributed resources of the parent company and its acquisitions to align the information systems with the company's strategic plan, and, to the extent possible, address the cultural differences, language issues, business practice variations, and technology limitations of the various host countries in doing so.

Kanter and Kesner[28] identify the following as critical success factors for the GIO:

1. *Management style and leadership:* The leadership qualities vital to the success of a GIO include (a) strategic focus, (b) flexibility in addressing tactical issues, (c) people-oriented and task-oriented project management style, (d) the

ability to delegate and manage through others, (e) ruling through consensus, and (f) a team approach to problem solving.

2. *Organization and structure of the IT function:* To be effective, the GIO and the IT function must be appropriately positioned within the larger organization. This means that the GIO must report to the chief executive officer and be an equal member in the top management team that deals with components of corporate strategy.

3. *Skill base:* The effective GIO must have a comprehensive knowledge of the corporation, its products and services, and its functional requirements. The GIO must understand the ramifications of emerging information technologies on the corporation. The GIO must have an understanding of the different countries and cultures in which the corporation operates in order to factor the impact of the work ethics and motivation of different nationalities in optimizing global IS projects.

4. *Commitment to total quality management:* The effective GIO must implement and enforce a total quality management program within the IT function. Viewing software as an engineered product subject to quality assurance

and market acceptance/viability is the fundamental cultural change that such a commitment brings to the IT function.

5. *Openness to outsourcing:* Instead of relying entirely on in-house solutions, the effective GIO practices the wisdom of outsourcing for specific expertise or relying on the cooperation of hardware and software vendors.

6. *Technology transfer and change implementation:* The effective GIO must facilitate the discovery of appropriate new technologies, fund pilot projects, and for those which look promising serve as the agent of change for successfully implementing them in the organization.

Conclusion

Technological changes and innovations affect all aspects of our lives and the conduct of business, both locally and globally. No technological change has had as profound an impact in a short time on modern enterprise as the advent of computers and telecommunications. The ability to send, receive, process, and otherwise manage an immense amount of information enables MNCs to exercise closer control over their foreign subsidiaries. Information systems management not only can be used to enhance internal operations, but also to create a competitive advantage. Instantaneous information exchange among the MNCs' worldwide operations drastically reduces geographical distances and brings dispersed subsidiaries closer to one another. While IS decreases barriers to centralization, it also creates opportunities for decentralization. The constant flow of information between the MNC headquarters and the subsidiaries empowers them to operate more locally and at the same time allows the headquarters to formulate strategies globally.

Discussion Questions

1. Why is information system management critical to the MNCs?
2. How do the information needs of MNCs differ from those of domestic firms?

3. What are ramifications of internationalization of the firm on the function of its information systems?
4. MNCs have adopted different IS functions. Elaborate on the reason(s) for the differences.
5. Describe intracompany IT issues.
6. Describe intergovernment IT issues.
7. Describe host country IT issues.
8. Elaborate on the internal and external benefits of communication integration to the MNCs.
9. MNCs have different options for data integration. Briefly describe these options and explain the reason for their use.
10. What are the differences between the role of chief information officer (CIO) and global information officer (GIO)?

Endnotes

1. J. A. Senn. *Information Systems in Management* (Belmont, CA: Wadsworth Publishing Co., 1990), 8.
2. Ibid.
3. V. Zwass. *Management Information Systems* (Dubuque, IA: William C. Brown Publishers, 1992), 6.
4. R. H. Sprague, Jr., and B. C. McNurlin. *Information Systems Management in Practice* (Englewood Cliffs, NJ: Prentice Hall, 1993), 14.
5. S. Roach. *The New Technology Cycle* (New York: Morgan Stanley, 1985).
6. J. Kanter. *Computer Essays for Management* (Englewood Cliffs, NJ: Prentice-Hall: 1986).
7. Nolan, Norton, and Company, 1987.
8. P. C. Deans and M. J. Kane. *International Dimensions of Information Systems* (Boston, MA: PWS-Kent Publishing, 1992); F. W. McFarlan. "Multinational CIO Challenge for the 1990s." In S. Palvia, P. Palvia, and R. M. Zigli, eds. *The Global Issues of Information Technology Management* (Harrisburg, PA: Idea Group Publishing, 1992), 484–93.
9. H. V. Perlmutter. "The Tortuous Evolution of Multinational Corporations." *Columbia Journal of World Business* (January–February 1969), 9–18.
10. E. M. Roche. *Managing Information Technology in Multinational Corporations* (New York: Macmillan, 1992).
11. W. R. King and V. Sethi. "A Framework for Transnational Systems." In S. Palvia, P. Palvia, and R. M. Zigli, eds. *The Global Issues of Information Technology Management* (Harrisburg, PA: Idea Group Publishing,

1992), 214–48; R. O. Keohane and J. S. Nye, Jr. *Transnational Relations and World Politics* (Cambridge, MA: Harvard Business School Press, 1972).

12. "Long Range Goals in International Telecommunications and Information: An Outline for U.S. Policy." *National Telecommunications and Information Administration,* Committee Print, S. Prt. 98–22, 25.

13. King and Sethi. "A Framework for Transnational Systems." 214–48.

14. P. C. Deans, K. R. Karwan, M. D. Goslar, D. A. Ricks, and B. Toyne. "Identification of Key International Information Systems Issues in U.S.-Based Multinational Corporations." *Journal of Management Information System,* 7, no. 4 (Spring 1991).

15. S. Palvia and S. Saraswat. "Information Technology and Transnational Corporation: The Emerging Multinational Issues." In *The Global Issues of Information Technology Management.* 554–74.

16. A. E. Alter. "International Affairs." *CIO,* 6, no. 5 (December 1992), 34–42.

17. P. G. W. Keen. "Planning Globally: Practical Strategies for Information Technology in the Transnational Firm." In *The Global Issues of Information Technology Management.* 575–607.

18. Ibid.

19. B. F. Mathaisel. "Managing IS Across Borders." *Chief Information Officer Journal* (July/August 1993), 33–7.

20. W. A. Hall and R. E. McCauley. "Planning and Managing a Corporate Network Utility." *MIS Quarterly,* 11, no. 4 (December 1987), 437–47.

21. P. J. Steinbart and R. Nath. "Problems and Issues in the Management of International Communications Networks: The Experiences of American Companies." *MIS Quarterly,* 16, no. 1 (March 1992), 55–76.

22. D. O. Case and J. H. Ferreira. "Portuguese Telecommunications and Information Technologies: Development and Prospects." *Telecommunication Policy,* 14, no. 4 (August 1990), 290–302.

23. Keen. "Planning Globally." 575–607.

24. Ibid.

25. Deans and Kane. *International Dimensions of Information Systems.* 484–93.

26. Ibid.

27. M. Williamson. "Becoming a World Power." *CIO,* 7, no. 16 (June 1, 1994), 40–52.

28. J. Kanter and R. Kesner. "The CIO/GIO as Catalyst and Facilitator: Building the Information Utility to Meet Global Challenges." In *The Global Issues of Information Technology* 465–83.

CARBON PRODUCTS, COLONIAL CORPORATION

WILLIAM R. KING
The Joseph M. Katz Graduate
School of Pittsburgh
VIKRAM SETHI
College of Business Administration,
Southwest Missouri State University

Jack Stack, IS manager, Carbon Products Division—Colonial Corporation, stepped out of the meeting with mixed feelings. "The business situation is too different in all three countries to have the same type of development approach," he thought.

To protect the identity of the company used in this case study, its name, industry, and its financial information have been changed. Reprinted with permission.

The meeting had been called by Bill Moll, IS Director of Colonial's Carbon & Inorganic Chemicals Business Group, as a strategy session to discuss the organization of the information systems groups in three of Colonial's subsidiaries in the United Kingdom, Brazil and Korea. The IS group in England had been quickly established, while the developmental effort had barely been started in the other two countries. Top management at Colonial felt that efforts in both countries needed to be accelerated. However, there was general feeling that the approach that had worked so well in the United Kingdom might not be appropriate for the other two countries.

Colonial Corporation

Colonial Corporation, headquartered in Columbia, Missouri, is a global producer of carbon, inorganic chemicals, and petrochemicals, with projected 1993 earnings in excess of $5.5 billion. Approximately 70% of the company's worldwide business is in the chemical and petrochemical industries.

Carbon and Inorganic Chemicals

Colonial's Carbon & Inorganic Chemicals Group had 1992 sales and operating profits of $2.25 billion and $376 million respectively, representing 43% and 48% of total corporate sales and earnings. The groups is comprised of two divisions which are essentially separate businesses: the Carbon Products Division and the Composite Materials Division.

Colonial is the largest producer of carbon products in North America and the second-largest worldwide producer behind Johnston Inc. The company produces commercial carbon fiber products for the automotive, aircraft, and other transportation OEM and after markets, commercial and residential construction and remodeling and industrial, mirror and furniture markets. Carbon products account for approximately 80 percent of Colonial's total group sales with the remaining 20 percent attributable to composite materials.

Colonial operates twelve composite material lines in North America, giving it an approximately 30–35% share of the North American market. While Colonial is not the lowest cost producer in the industry (Trellis Industries, the smallest domestic producer with an approximate 10–15% North American market share, is widely considered to be the low cost producer),

it does have a dominant market share position, is perceived by its competitors as being a good marketer, and has a reputation for supplying a high quality product. A significant portion of Colonial's composite material production, on the order of 35%, is upgradeable internally (through such steps as combining proprietary carbon fibers with other materials, including thermoplastic and thermosetting resins, cements, rubbers, carbons, and metals) for automotive, housing, aerospace, and specialty applications. The remaining 65% of material is shipped to independent contractors who supply similar markets.

Colonial's composite materials business has experienced strong sales and profit growth since troughing in the recession of 1982. During the early 1980s, the industry's results were negatively impacted by a recession-induced drop in demand, which coincided with the startup of incremental production. This, in turn, resulted in overcapacity and declining chemicals prices. As the economy expanded during the period 1983–87, demand for composite materials grew considerably and in fact outstripped increases in capacity. By 1985, supply and demand essentially returned to balance; in fact, during most of 1986 and 1987, the industry was sold out and deliveries were often delayed. Prices were raised an estimated average of 3–4% in each of these years.

Colonial derives an estimated $500 million in composite material sales from its European operations. Colonial has four carbon and composite material lines in Europe (two each in Italy and France) and ranks third in market share behind St. Johns and MNL Chemicals. These three producers have a combined market share of 75–80% in Europe, resulting in an oligopolistic industry structure. The European market for composite material is characterized by extremely tight supply/demand balance and rising prices. Carbon and related material supply in Europe is considerably tighter than in North America and prices there have risen 30–40% in the past three years. Currently, prices in Europe are roughly 20% higher than in North America. This pricing differential is sufficiently high to allow North American producers to export composite material to Europe and realize the same payback as on domestic business despite significant transportation costs.

In an effort to further its geographic diversification, Colonial recently formed a joint venture carbon fiber plant. Colonial owns 35% of the plant but retains operating control. The joint venture is targeted at the strong demand in China and other Pacific rim countries. Also, the joint venture establishes a toehold for Colonial in the Far East.

Inorganic Chemicals

Colonial is the world's second largest producer of inorganic chemicals behind Dallas Chemical Company (USA). Colonial produces polycarbonate resins for use in applications that include electrical, electronics, and automotive products.

Colonial's inorganic chemical sales were $490 million in 1992, 22% greater than expected. Sales benefitted from strong worldwide demand as manufacturers increasingly turned to inorganic resin products as replacements for traditional materials. Industry capacity is over 90%, and most producers claim to be sold out. However, there are presently no plans to expand U.S. industry capacity due to the fact that the industry leader Dallas Chemicals has substantial idle capacity which could be brought on line at a relatively low cost.

Geographic diversification is also contributing to Colonial's inorganic chemicals growth. The acquisition of Cyborg Chemicals Ltd. of the U.K. in 1987 gave the company a non-U.S. chemicals production capacity and will contribute an estimated $30 million to sales. However, Colonial intends to double the capacity of the U.K. plant and, in doing so, upgrade the product mix to allow for the production of electronic grade chemicals. Other steps Colonial is taking to increase its international presence in-

clude the establishment of joint ventures to produce resins in Korea and Brazil.

Coatings and Specialty Resins

Colonial's Coating and Specialty Resins Division accounts for 35% and 32% respectively of the corporate sales and earnings. Colonial is the second-largest manufacturer of paint in the world behind International Paints of the U.K. The company also produces automotive primers, finishes, refinishes, adhesives and sealants, factory-applied coatings for appliances, buildings, containers and a broad range of industrial applications, and consumer maintenance and other trade paints.

Colonial derives approximately 70% of its worldwide paint revenues from North America (U.S. 60–65%, Canada 5–10%) and the remaining 30% from Europe. On a global basis, 60% of the company's paint sales are derived from the automotive sector. Colonial has a very strong position in the automotive sector, which it revolutionized in the early 1960's with the introduction of electrodeposition technology, and has directly captured 70% of the domestic market. Moreover, the remaining 30% of the domestic market is protected since competitors use licensed Colonial technology.

In the area of automotive topcoats, Colonial has a number two domestic market share and has been gaining ground. In addition, Colonial intends to double its world market share in automotive coatings over the next 3–5 years. Management hopes that, given the company's already dominant position in primers, most of these gains will come in the topcoat area. In keeping with today's trends in auto manufacturing toward single-sourcing, Colonial's strategy for gaining market share focuses on becoming the sole coatings supplier to selected automotive assembly plants worldwide. Colonial also pioneered the concept of satellite coating centers, each adjacent to an auto customer's assembly plant. Colonial now has 14 such centers operating in North America, each dedicated to supplying coatings materials to a customer's plant on a "just-in-time" basis. Recently, Colonial was chosen to be the principal coating supplier to several Japanese car manufacturers in the United States.

The IS Group at the Inorganic Chemical Division

The Vice President of Technical Services has responsibilities over technical, research, engineering, and the corporate IS group. The corporate IS group is headed by the Director of IS, who is responsible for the corporate systems group, the corporate computer center, and the corporate communications group. The IS directors for all business groups report to the Corporate IS Director.

The IS manager in the Inorganic Chemicals Division is responsible for all application systems within the division, including manufacturing, financial, sales and marketing systems. The manufacturing area excludes the manufacturing floor and process control systems, which report to the corporate Director of Engineering, but includes functions such as order entry and inventory control.

IS Development at the Inorganic Chemical Division's Subsidiaries

The Inorganic Division has recently expanded in the following countries:

1. The U.K.—a wholly-owned subsidiary. A new furnace will add capacity for nylon resins and reinforcement products.
2. Brazil—50% joint venture to produce chemical reinforcement products.
3. South Korea—50% joint venture to produce resins for PCB's and reinforcement products.

While all three subsidiaries were acquired at the same time in 1987, the major IS emphasis has been on the development of the IS group at the U.K. plant. In a strategy session in

December, 1987, both Bill Moll and Jack Stack had expressed the thought that this subsidiary was critical to the long-term success of the European business. Jack Stack headed the strategy team that organized operations at this site.

The subsidiary in the U.K. was bought to meet the demand from European customers and the European facilities of U.S. multinationals who had previously been served from the two North Carolina plants. The advantages of doing so were several—better services to European customers, increased presence in the future 1992 market, and freeing capacity in the North Carolina plant for American customers. Another motivation for acquiring the U.K. plant was to enhance Colonial's role as a global competitor—a strategy that called for global products. This required that all plants make the same products, using the same technology and to the same manufacturing specifications.

The product mix at the U.K. plant remains the same as when the plant was bought and does not consist of Colonial-designed products. However, the migration to Colonial standards and specifications is under way. When Colonial bought the plant, it was not a computerized facility and had only remote terminals to its parent unit in Glouchester. In addition, there were no systems personnel on site. When discussing strategies to develop the IS function in the subsidiary, Jack Stack had proposed a quick changeover to Colonial's environment since the plant was bought to play a very integral role in the company's global strategy. It was decided, therefore, that an implementation of all of Colonial's systems on a realtime basis in the U.K. was the most appropriate step.

Financial controls have played an important role in Colonial's success as a world-class carbon products manufacturer. The effectiveness of the in-plant cost system, the mechanisms to cost products, and to know where variances lie is of significant advantage. Hence, the financial control system was implemented immediately in the U.K. plant. A System 36 was installed and, in a matter of one year, the plant had expanded from five CRT's to forty which routinized the collection and analysis of cost data.

All Colonial systems in the U.S. are realtime. Since it was decided to incorporate the U.K. plant completely into the Colonial network, a data line was installed to the U.K. to run realtime systems. The U.S. facility is now as much a part of the data network centered in Columbia, Missouri, as are the U.S. plants. Moreover, because of the time differences, the corporate computer can be run in slack hours, for example from 3 A.M. to 8 A.M., which , because of the time difference, are suitable hours for the U.K. plant.

All of Colonial's applications were transferred to the U.K. facility. This was considered to be the most efficient approach to ensure a rapid conversion to Colonial's method of doing business. Since all of Colonial's programs are interfaced rather tightly together, it was not feasible to pick up certain systems only. The complete transfer of applications was the fastest method to make the plant operational. However, because of substantial differences between U.S. and British tax laws, the only systems not totally transferred to the U.K. was payroll. Instead a payroll package was bought and installed on the System 36.

The reporting procedures and administrative functions of the plant are also very similar to those of U.S. facilities. The plant is on the same time schedule as other facilities, and essentially the data is required. Financial data is incorporated at the same level of detail as in the U.S. plants.

Much of the data content of the plant has been standardized, and the printing of forms is the same as in the U.S. Special consideration was given to managing different word usages and avoiding local colloquialisms. For example, dating routines in programs that are set to use the pattern of month/day/year in the U.S. are set to day/month/year in the U.K. Another case is pre-printed forms where the word "truck" had to be changed to "lorry." Most internal report formats were left unchanged while external reports were altered to suit different customers. Computer equipment is standardized for all plants, and any changes must first be approved by the IS function in the U.S.

During the transition, an extensive training program was undertaken. All managers and foremen and most workers were sent to U.S. facilities for training. In addition, several Colonial trainers were sent to the U.K. A special emphasis was placed on instructing the British financial officers on American financial statements and contracts. As each new system was brought on line in the plant, a user group and a system group arrived from the U.S. to help in training and setup.

Evaluation of IS Development and Other Subsidiaries

As described above, IS managers at Colonial had wanted a fast changeover of the new U.K. plant. Since the plant was strategic to the organization, the management team felt that it was critical to transfer all of Colonial's control systems to the plant as quickly as possible. The personnel in the U.K had at times expressed concern over the rapidity of this change.

Jack Stack described this by saying, "People are comfortable with old systems, they are like a pair of old shoes. That is the main issue—if it works, don't touch it." Extensive training programs succeeded in overcoming this resistance. While this rapid development worked at the U.K. plant, there were some reservations about whether the same strategies should be used at the Korean and the Brazilian plants.

Colonial's progress in Asia has been mainly through joint ventures as opposed to its 100% ownership ion Europe. The Korean partner is a global manufacturer of plastics and a large operation in its industry segment. The main contribution of the plant so far has been sales to the joint venture partner.

The Korean partner's outlook has been that it understands cost systems better, and therefore it has opted to use its internal cost systems. Colonial initially provided assistance in adapting their system to specialty chemicals. Most data transfers to Korea are batch. Data is transferred monthly to fulfill Colonial management reporting requirements. Most transfers occur via Hong Kong using Tymnet packet sharing.

Language is the primary problem in Korea. There are few American executives who can speak Korean. However, corporate IS managers have spent a considerable amount of time learning customs and culture. In contrast to the several programs with the U.K. subsidiary, no formal exchange programs have been initiated.

The Brazilian plant, although also a 50% joint venture, plays an important role in meeting the growing South American demand. The plant is expected to grow and be an integral part of Colonial's global diversification. As such, the emphasis is on meeting local demand through the joint venture. The plant, therefore, plays the role of maintaining and promoting presence in South America.

The plant originally did not have a mainframe to run the corporate applications software. An IBM System 36 was therefore installed. Although the System 36 connects to Colonial's corporate computer, all administrative controls are set up to the joint venture partner's standards.

The Brazilian plant is a small operation. Probably the biggest issue in Brazil is to adapt to the language, laws, and tax situations. For that reason, it was considered best for the Brazilian partner to be responsible for system operations, especially since systems expertise and a systems staff were already available as well as an accounting office. Colonial has also stationed two managers in the Brazilian plant in the finance and manufacturing areas.

Recently there has been considerable interest in a more active involvement with the two sub-sidiaries. It was thought that, as the European operations started to become active, more emphasis should be placed on developing the Brazilian and the Korean plants. Colonial's president John Carter felt that "If indeed we are to become a truly global organization, then we need to have integration across all subsidiaries. This means integration across all business processes including production, distribution, financing and sourcing." He also felt that information systems needed to be fully developed at all locations to support the integrated operations idea. Therefore, Bill Moll had been asked to prepare a strategy review on further developing systems support facilities at these subsidiaries.

Meeting with the IS managers in the Carbon & Inorganic Chemicals Group, Bill had asked for feedback on these sites. following these discussions, the question quickly became whether the same strategies that had worked in the U.K. would be applicable in Korea and Brazil. Several differences between the operations had quickly emerged as factors which would require examination if similar development were to be achieved.

Jack thought that organizational factors had helped the success of the U.K. operations. When the plant was bought, there were no IS personnel. It was easier to deal with the plant supervisors since they were familiar with the U.S. operations. This was not the case for the other two subsidiaries. In fact, the management of operations for the Brazilian plant was under a Common Board staffed by three VP's from Colonial. All decisions—strategic and operational—related to the joint venture had to be approved by this Board. All changes pertaining to IT—changes to hardware, software, and applications—also had to be approved. Jack felt that this administrative structure slowed decision making and implementation considerably and would be a major hurdle in the complete integration of the Brazilian operations.

Although cultural differences had never caused any major problems, Jack had sometimes expressed the thought that "It's often interesting and we do discuss among ourselves—what if they [IS personnel at the Brazilian subsidiary] had said no? And gone to their management and said—we can't do this. Those guys are out in left field. They are dreaming."

Jack had expressed these opinions at the weekend meeting and had proposed a slower approach to IS development at these locations as compared to the U.K. plant because of the differences between the cultures of the subsidiaries. Yet there was the directive from John Carter to examine the possibilities of fuller integration of the systems functions and therefore business processes.

PART FOUR

LEGAL AND SOCIO-ETHICAL ISSUES OF INTERNATIONAL MANAGEMENT

F I F T E E N

LEGAL ISSUES AND INTERNATIONAL MANAGEMENT

Dwight D. Murphey
Wichita State University

Although the twentieth century has witnessed the growth of an assortment of international agreements governing a variety of issues, the world remains primarily a community of nation-states, each with its own body of law, interests, and unique outlook. This situation makes it valuable to begin the discussion of international business law with a review of the relationship between culture and law in such diverse nations and national groupings as the United States, Europe, Japan, the Islamic nations, the developing countries, and the socialist and formerly socialist states.

Even this awareness of diversity will unavoidably involve an oversimplification, since the world is considerably more complex than such groupings suggest. Within the United States there exists, for example, the federal government and 50 different state governments—all with separate legal systems. If this is true for the United States, it holds with even greater force for the national groupings just mentioned, since the nations that make them up are by no means alike.

In any analysis of law, there is also a natural division between "substantive issues" and "procedural issues." Some of the major areas of discussion in this chapter are primarily substantive, in that they deal with the rules that actually govern international business conduct. It will be important, however, to remain aware of the many issues of process involving the mechanisms by which these rules are applied and by which parties seek a resolution of conflict. Even though the sections on national sovereignty, international legal issues, and multinational corporation operational disputes are largely substantive, procedural points will inescapably be intertwined with them, and it is worthwhile to pay attention to them as they arise.

Firms engaging in international business will find it indispensable to seek competent legal advice in each area of concern and for each country. No one professional will know everything there is to know. Nonlawyers will benefit from a review of international business law at the level in this chapter most directly by coming to recognize when to seek advice and by understanding the context to which the advice relates.

When MNCs establish branches or subsidiaries in a given nation, those extensions become subject to the municipal (local) law of the host nation. The unique qualities of that law will affect a number of practical issues, which will include the question of just where it is within that country that the firm will be subject to being sued.

If an American bicycle manufacturer set up a distributorship in Shanghai, could the distributor be subject to suit in a local court in a remote province of western China? A similar question was posed not long ago in the Supreme Court of the United States.

The case involved a suit against the German corporation that manufactures Audi automobiles; its importer into the United States; its regional distributor, which sold cars to dealers in three eastern American states; and its retail dealer, which had its place of business in New York. One of the cars was purchased in New York, and a year later was in an accident in Oklahoma. Alleging a defect in the automobile, the owners brought suit against the various companies in a state court in Oklahoma. Both the local trial court and the Supreme Court of Oklahoma upheld the right to bring the case in Oklahoma. The issue was eventually taken to the U.S. Supreme Court.

There, seven of the justices held that the Oklahoma courts had no jurisdiction (power) over the case. Two justices dissented. Both saw the controlling issue as one of domestic American Constitutional law: it has long been established that a state's courts are in violation of the Due Process Clause of the Fourteenth Amendment if they entertain cases against nonresidents in situations where the nonresident has not had at least "minimum contacts" with the state. The defendants in the Audi case had no contacts with Oklahoma, unless the sale of cars that might sometime find their way into Oklahoma was itself a sufficient "contact."

The majority of the justices focused on the concrete activity of the defendant companies. "Minimum contact" didn't arise from the mere "foreseeability" that cars would eventually be driven into distant states. "If foreseeability were the criterion," Justice White wrote, "a local California tire dealer could be forced to defend in Pennsylvania when a blowout occurs there." The dissenters, though, urged a broader view: that the defendant companies had sold Audis as part of a vast network of sales and servicing, and so shouldn't be surprised to be held accountable anywhere. The majority's view, of course, prevailed in the case, and the Oklahoma suit was dismissed.

Source: *World Wide Volkswagen Corp. v. Woodson,* 444 U.S.236 (U.S.SCt 1980).

Introduction

The Oklahoma decision discussed in the vignette has several facets. By illustrating how the law of international business often involves commonplace issues, it undercuts the natural but usually naive assumption that international legal issues, simply by being "international," are necessarily larger than life. Second, it shows how the municipal law of the host country can be controlling, both on such procedural matters as the place of trial and on substantive issues such as the product liability of sellers for harm caused by goods.

Third, the case points to how even the local law may not be fully settled. The presence of two dissenters among the U.S. Supreme Court justices demonstrates that even a question of court jurisdiction remained unclear almost two centuries after the United States was founded. Fourth, it is worth noting as an observation about law in general that the perspectives taken by the judges reflected not a difference over the facts, which were undisputed, but over how to organize the facts mentally. The question of "minimum contacts" turned on how the manufacturer's and distributor's business activity was to be seen: narrowly in its particularity or broadly in a larger context.

Finally, it is worth noting that there was no special tribunal for hearing the dispute. Recourse was had to the regular courts of the "host country." International tribunals exist for some purposes, but most of the world's legal business is done by the standard courts and administrative agencies of the country exercising jurisdiction.

Cultural Heritage and Business Law

The international scene, in its effect on law, involves a mixture of diversity, born out of widely varied cultural heritages and circumstances, with certain unifying themes and an increasing amount of joint effort.

The sections that follow illustrate the diversity by specific reference to certain nations and regions. More generally, however, it should be noted that countries differ widely over many aspects of law: Some have gone quite far in the area of environmental protection, while others impose relatively few constraints; some militate in favor of market competition, vigorously enforcing their antitrust laws, while others favor large-scale, protected industries; some have extensive social and labor legislation, such as that passed recently in the United States dealing with employee layoffs and plant closings, while others do not; and so on over a vast range of issues.

Many reasons exist for these differences. To illustrate, we consider the varied approaches to intellectual property rights (IPRs). IPRs represent one major form of property, the rights governing exclusive use of an intellectual contribution such as an invention or work of art. The principal reason for differences in the way IPRs are treated lies in the fact that developed and developing nations often perceive their interests in diametrically opposite ways. The developed nations, with their preference for economic dynamism, emphasize the importance of protecting inventors through strong patent, trademark, and copyright coverage as a way to encourage the constant improvement of technology. If IPRs are given weak protection in many parts of the world, the developed countries see this as a major loss of compensation and, hence, of incentive to creative persons and firms. Certainly this is the view taken by the United States, which has been the world's leading supplier of technology since World War II. The perspective of the industrialized nations has recently come to be shared by several countries such as Korea, Mexico, and Turkey, which are rapidly industrializing and whose perspective is accordingly beginning to match that of the technologically-advanced nations. By way of contrast, many poorer nations give little protection to IPRs, with the result that piracy in the form of unauthorized copying and imitation runs rampant. This difference has shown up starkly in the varied protection given to computer software. The intention of governments in the less developed nations is to benefit their own peoples, but the failure to protect IPRs sometimes produces

tragic results. This is apparent when those nations give little patent protection to pharmaceutical inventions, which leads to a diminished development or supply of drugs against tropical diseases.

Even in the face of differences, however, unifying themes bind the international community together. Legal systems can be classified into "legal families," since the nations in each "family" share a common legal heritage. One of these families stems from the Romano-Germanic Civil Law System, which has a long tradition of codification, i.e., of formulating law in extensive written codes. A subfamily of these nations bases its law on the Napoleonic Code, the French Civil Code of 1804. These include countries as diverse as Poland, Indonesia, and those of equatorial Africa. Another subfamily, which includes several continental European countries but also encompasses Japan and South Korea, bases its law on the German Civil Code of 1896.

A second legal family stems from the Anglo-American common law system. Here, the law was developed primarily through a gradual accretion of court decisions, built up over centuries by courts' reference to earlier precedents. A separate system of procedures and remedies known as "equity" was developed by a parallel set of courts, but "law" and "equity" were merged into a common system in most American states and in England in the nineteenth century. The vast influence of the Anglo-American system reflects the worldwide extent of the British commonwealth, since this family includes India, Australia, Canada, and New Zealand, among others.

The increasing role played in world affairs by Islamic nations makes it important to note the influence of Islamic law, based largely on moral precepts laid down by the Prophet Muhammad. This prevails in a large number of countries located primarily in the Middle East and southern Asia. Islamic law was frozen in content in the thirteenth century, and this rigidity leads to a rupture between Islamic fundamentalists, who wish to keep it as it is, and others who want to adapt it to the more secular modern world. The argument over law is merely part of the larger split among Muslims over the nature of Islam itself. The importance of Islamic law can be seen in the fact that by the end of this century one-fourth of the earth's population will embrace Islam.[1]

In addition to the links forged among the legal families, ties are established through the elaborate mechanisms of international cooperation. This is illustrated in the area of transportation: the International Convention Concerning Carriage of Goods by Rail (CIM) applies to railroading; the Warsaw Convention spells out the extent of international airlines' liability; and the Hague Rules define the liability exposure of international water carriers. Another example is the Convention on Contracts for the International Sale of Goods (CISG), drafted through the collaboration of eight different international organizations and 62 countries. The CISG is considered in a later section.

Efforts are made to bridge the gaps that separate nations. For example, the North American Free Trade Agreement (NAFTA) among the United States, Canada, and Mexico was approved by the U.S. Congress in 1994. In addition, since 1947 successive rounds of negotiations about tariffs and other trade barriers have been conducted under the General Agreement on Tariffs and Trade (GATT). The agreement arising out of the Uruguay round received Congressional approval in the United States within months after the approval of NAFTA. A major development has been the extension, among many nations, of most favored nation status, which spreads the reduction of barriers equally to the participating nations. The developed nations have gone beyond this to create a system of preferences for developing nations.

The heritage of different cultures bears strongly on the business law of the individual countries, as we see in the sections that follow.

The United States

Law in the United States has primarily grown up through court decisions, reflecting our British origin. On issues of federal Constitutional and statutory interpretation, the federal courts have developed their own body of decisions; but on issues of state law, both the state and federal courts apply the precedents built up by the courts of the state whose law controls. The separate court systems for law and equity were consolidated into a single system in virtually all states after New York took the lead in 1848. England followed in 1873. Later sections of this chapter explore several aspects of American law, but some are especially worth mentioning in this preliminary discussion of cultural differences.

Although practical and political considerations unquestionably play a frequent role, weakening any generalization, it is worth noting about American policy that idealistic considerations have often been a driving force. An example is the effort to assure the integrity of business practices. With the Foreign Corrupt Practices Act of 1977, the United States made it a criminal violation for any American company to bribe foreign governmental officials or political candidates. The legislation followed revelations that more than 400 American companies had made bribes. To assure compliance, large companies were required to maintain certain accounting systems and to have internal accounting controls that will give reasonable assurance that a company's representatives actually comply with the law and with company policy.

This idealism is not without cost. During the years since the act's passage, concern has been voiced that it has had a chilling effect on the ability of American firms to compete in cultures where bribery is rampant.[2] This concern, fed by the decline in the United States' competitive position, led Congress to amend the statute in 1988 to limit its scope and to make it clear that only intentional, not inadvertent, violations would be subject to prosecution.

This same idealism can be seen in the strong U.S. policy against insider trading. Such trading involves the buying and selling of securities by someone who has significant information about a company that is not known to the general public. Congress went so far as to strengthen the prohibition against insider trading in the federal Securities Exchange Act of 1934 after U.S. Supreme Court decisions in the early 1980s interpreted the statute narrowly. This reflects a prevailing view in Congress that such trading takes advantage of a less-than-level playing field, subjecting the average investor to an unfair disadvantage.

Subject to significant exceptions such as the Smoot-Hawley Tariff, which played so major a role in deepening the worldwide depression of the 1930s, the United States has been during much of the twentieth century a stalwart proponent of a legally assured competitive market. This has had two primary implications: an antitrust policy that is stricter than that of many other nations, and a commitment to free trade through lower tariffs and fewer barriers to commerce. This procompetitive stance reflects the powerful influence in American history of the promarket philosophy of classical and neoclassical economics.

American business law has during the twentieth century seen a strong movement toward uniformity, reducing the complexity that can arise if 50 different states enact separate rules, and toward flexibility. The Uniform Commercial Code (UCC) has been enacted in all states except Louisiana since the later 1950s, and codifies the rules relating to the sale of goods, negotiable instruments, stock transfers, and other commercial subjects. For the most part, the rules are more flexible than earlier law, allowing the parties more alternatives than they were previously given in a number of situations. For example, if a buyer unknowingly accepts defective goods, the acceptance can now be revoked under certain circumstances.

Europe

The law of continental Europe is based on the two major systems of codification, French and German, promulgated in the nineteenth century. The assumptions behind each code were fundamentally the same: private property, free-market economics, and individual self-sufficiency. European history during the nineteenth and twentieth centuries has, however, involved massive challenges to the classical liberal model on which these assumptions were based, through both nationalist and socialist critiques hostile to it. Since law reflects the enormous complexity of history and of thought in a society, it is not surprising that European legal systems today involve a significant mixture of ideologies.

This complexity has most recently been expressed by two diametrically opposed tendencies: toward European unification and toward resurgent nationalism. The latter is evident in the civil war among the Serbian, Croatian, and Muslim ethnic groups within the former Yugoslavia and in the protests within Germany against widespread immigration. However, despite the centrifugal tendencies of nationalism, Western Europe has since World War II engaged in a gradual process of unification, with the prospect of an eventual "One Europe." The Common Market, also called the European Economic Community or simply the European Community (EC), was formed through the Treaty of Rome in 1957. The purposes have been to eliminate tariffs and trade barriers among the member nations, unify the currency, bring about the free movement of people and investments, and to stand united vis-à-vis the rest of the world. A major step was taken on December 31, 1992, with the elimination of virtually all barriers among the member nations.

This new freedom of movement will be tested against ancient constraints. In Germany, for example, participation in business has traditionally required either membership in or some entree to the society of merchants known as the

"Handelskammer." In agriculture, several countries have a long tradition of protecting the small farmer. It remains to be seen how commercial freedom will work itself out within these contexts.

Japan

The history of Japan has been marked by relative isolation, cultural cohesion, a high level of energy, and a drive toward technological advancement. These factors are reflected even in so simple a thing as contract negotiation, where dignity, harmony, and social cohesion create an expectation for patient negotiation, long-term relationships, and few written formalities. Disputes are seldom litigated, and there are relatively few attorneys. Sellers are almost never sued for injuries caused by goods. Japanese family life is characterized by low consumption and high saving.[3]

The cohesion is illustrated further by the interlocking directorates and links among Japanese firms. No parent company controls the approximately 40 companies that make up the Mitsubishi Group; instead, each company owns part of the others, and direction is given by a "triumvirate" composed of the three leading companies. Top management from 26 companies meets at the Kinyo-Kai ("Friday Conference").[4] The effect of this cohesion is to make new entry by competitors extremely difficult. There is a general acceptance of insider trading.

The government plays a major role. When a Japanese firm wants to license technology from a foreign licensor, it does so through a central licensing agency, which gives it substantially greater bargaining power than it would have if it negotiated the license itself.

Islam

The Islamic legal system, or "Shari'a," prevails in several countries where there is a predominant Muslim population, such as in northern Africa, the Middle East, and southern Asia.

Countervailing tendencies exist between traditionalism and secularism, which impacts participation in a worldwide commercial system. Secular influences have in recent years led many Persian Gulf countries to enact commercial codes. But even where such codes exist, cultural-religious traditionalism affects virtually all aspects of life. Nonmarket values rank high: In Pakistan, for example, an Islamic court recently banned the charging or payment of interest; the concept of *riba* bars unearned or unjustified profits; and that of *gharar* considers it gambling to make any profit that was not clearly spelled out when a contract was entered into.[5] Not merely the economic system, but the entire social system, is molded by a nonsecular value system. Several Arabic countries bar women from driving cars and everyone from drinking alcohol.[6]

Developing Countries

The underdeveloped countries, categorized with varying degrees of optimism as the "developing nations," have long been caught in the tension between needing industrial and technological growth to provide for their rapidly expanding populations, while at the same time distrusting and resenting outsiders and market processes. Although these nations are participating to some degree in a worldwide move toward the *privatization* of enterprise, the main pattern has been central state control over societies that are often so diverse internally as to be only superficially governable.

Policies on most issues are formed out of a perception of national need. Since this need may be considerably at odds with what it takes to make a venture profitable, the policies can be self-defeating, except as judged by noneconomic criteria. To promote internal development, requirements are often placed on foreign investment, such as mandates to hire local managers, train native workers, reinvest profits, and build public utilities. Government policy is determined by a central development plan, together with what is often an intricate web of bureaucracy. In Brazil, for example, it takes an estimated 1470 legal acts to obtain an export license.[7]

Before an import license arrangement can be entered into with a firm in India, approval must be obtained from every government agency that will have anything to do with the product. Many requirements can seriously affect the commercial viability of the venture, such as the one that an Indian licensee must be free to export what it makes. This threatens the licensor with the possibility of "reexport," through which its own licensee becomes a competitor in the licensor's home market or in markets elsewhere around the world.[8]

Most developing nations place strict limits on foreign ownership and passive investments, and put restrictions on the payment of hard-currency royalties to foreigners. As noted previously, because they view innovation from their own standpoint, many of the nations believe that technology either is or should be a free good, and so they encourage or at least do not take measures against piracy.

Attitudes and policies become more open to international trade as a nation approaches the threshold of technical development. Until recently, Mexico fit the general pattern, but in early 1990 it went from being virtually closed to technology transfer agreements to being highly receptive. Mexico's participation in the North American Free Trade Agreement (NAFTA) can be expected to accelerate this liberalization.

Socialist and Formerly Socialist Economies

Partly because of their relative lack of development and partly because of their ideological insistence on central governmental control, the socialist nations have had several characteristics in common with the less developed countries. For example, any foreign ownership of a productive enterprise, in whole or in part, has generally been prohibited. There is variation, of course: Historically, Yugoslavia, while it existed

---

Business Contracts in China

The vast market of China is very attractive to MNCs. The potential profits are large, so are the risks, including unresolved contract disputes. If a dispute arises, the first option — and the practical one—is to resolve it informally, by using friendly relationships that you should have established with your Chinese partner. Taking your dispute to the courts is not the best choice. Because in China the role of the law is a tenuous concept, and the legal process is very slow. Moreover, the existing, outdated laws are no match for the changing business environment of China.

Chinese are not as legalistic and litigious as Americans. There are approximately 50,000 lawyers in China v.s. about 800,000 in the U.S. If you start your negotiations using lawyers, you may give the impression that you do not trust them. The advice to newcomers to China is to be patient, to take their time and to develop personal relationships with the Chinese partners. Once a trusting relationship is established, bargain hard, and put the agreement in a contract. However, before signing it consult a lawyer. While the courts may not be the best choice of enforcing the contracts and hearing the disputes, nonetheless there are legal recourses. An increasingly popular option is arbitration in the China International Economic and Trade Arbitration Commission. Through the Commission the parties in the dispute choose a panel to hear the case. Foreigners are allowed to sit in the panel.

as a Communist state, and China have both permitted American corporations to share ownership of businesses with an agency of government.[9]

Anyone dealing with one of these countries while they retain their socialist character is primarily doing business with its government. Most of these nations operate through foreign trade corporations that are authorized to handle all of the import or export of a certain item. Working out the details can be tedious, but the trade corporations usually perform well once the contract is reached. A danger to be evaluated in light of experience in each case arises from the contracts' generally requiring that any dispute be handled by arbitration in the socialist country. Potential profitability must also be judged in light of a frequent insistence upon trade conditions of various kinds. "Countertrade" conditions require a selling firm either to buy goods that are made with the technology or equipment that was sold (a buy-back transaction), or to buy unrelated goods (a counter-purchase). Under the latter, PepsiCo agreed to buy a given amount of Stolychnaya vodka as a condition to licensing Pepsi Cola bottling rights in the former Soviet Union. Payment under the contract is usually in the money of the socialist nation, and this frequently cannot be taken out of the country or has little worth outside it. Under these conditions, mutually beneficial relationships are difficult.[10]

Within the formerly Communist countries, the transition to a market economy offers both opportunities and dangers. Currency problems, inflation, the crumbling of the infrastructure, a lack of experienced managerial or entrepreneurial talent, breakdowns in supply, confused political and legal relationships, and potential civil disorder, including even potential civil war, must all be gauged by the firm that would enter the field. One of the great transitions in history is under way, if it can be made successfully; but it is a difficult time for firms and individuals.

National Sovereignty

With the League of Nations and later the United Nations, the world has in the twentieth century made tentative approaches toward world governance. A large number of treaties and conventions bind nations to a common policy on a multitude of subjects; and large-scale military efforts are becoming increasingly subordinated to joint effort through the United Nations. Nevertheless, national sovereignty continues as the central fact on the world scene. This section explores the varied manifestations of this sovereignty in the areas of taxation, currency exchange controls, trade restrictions, the government takeover of industry, and privatization.

Taxes

There are many forms of taxation. Much of the discussion here is about income taxation, but it is worth noting that value-added taxes (a form of sales tax imposed at each level of production and distribution) have become common. The political situation within the United States has been particularly volatile within recent years so far as a willingness to consider differing forms of taxation, such as a flat tax on income or a removal of all taxation on capital gains, is concerned.

Several small nations such as Bermuda, the Bahamas, and the Cayman Islands have made themselves tax havens by having no income tax. Others provide incentives such as tax credits, tax holidays, and favorable rates; Switzerland has long made itself a favorite by protecting the confidentiality of bank accounts (this was begun in the 1930s to shield the identity of Jewish depositors from inquiries by Nazi Germany). Since World War II, these havens have attracted a large volume of business activity. To combat this, several countries have copied the anti–tax-haven provisions, called Subpart F, of the United States' Internal Revenue Code, which applies the idea of "deemed income," imputing income to investors even though they have not received a distribution of the income from the business firm. Moreover, even where incentives are offered, business firms must scrutinize tax incentives carefully for pitfalls: Lebanon, for example, has required that if a firm receives tax benefits for five years, it must stay to conduct business for an equal period, a commitment that many firms would be wary to make in any event, much less under the strife-ridden circumstances within Lebanon not long ago.[11]

Countries differ in whom and what they tax. Three main systems are used[12]:

- Either to tax citizens or nationals of the country on all of their income, no matter where they made it and without regard to where they have their residence ("nationality principle"); or
- To tax legal residents within the country, regardless of where they earned the income ("residency principle"). The 66 countries that use this system also tax all income generated within their borders even by people who are living in other countries; or
- To tax any income earned from activities within the taxing country, but not income earned elsewhere ("source principle"). Nationality and residency are considered for some purposes. The source principle is used by more countries than any other.

All of this raises, of course, a considerable possibility of multiple taxation of the same income. The nations of the world have grappled with this in a number of ways.[13] One is for the home nation not to tax income that has been taxed by the host country (the exemption system). A second applies a tax credit, reducing the tax in one country by the amount paid in another (the credit system). A third does not give a credit, which reduces the tax dollar for dollar, but only a deduction, which reduces the declarable income (the deduction system). As seen by the taxpayer, the best is the exemption system,

the worst the deduction system. The credit system results in the taxpayer paying whichever is the higher rate between the two nations.

Tax strategy is accordingly important to those doing business internationally. In this context, the type of business entity (i.e., partnership, corporation, etc.) used is important, since tax treatment typically varies as to the different business forms, just as it does in the United States. A pitfall is that the host country may not treat the entity as being what it appears. Many have a central registrar that categorizes the firm in terms of local law.[14]

Most countries' income tax, like that in the United States, has a graduated scale of rates. But some, such as Jamaica and Iceland, impose a flat rate on personal income. Almost two-thirds of the world uses a flat rate as far as company income is concerned, varying the flat rate from industry to industry. A danger in less developed countries is that the government may impute a profit to a company and then tax it if the government believes the company did not report a reasonable profit.[15]

Currency Exchange Controls

Unless the parties use barter (an exchange of goods or services for other goods or services), payment under a contract will be in the currency of some agreed on nation. This gives rise, then, to the question of convertibility of that currency into a party's own money, and further to that of the repatriation of profits.

The world monetary and banking system consists of a marketplace with a number of firms, rather than a single comprehensive structure. People speak of a foreign exchange market, but it is not to be found in any one location, since the market exists instead in the millions of transactions conducted around the globe by a great many banks, brokers, and dealers. Custom plays a large role, as does each country's own laws and institutions, along with such world agencies as the International Monetary Fund and the Bank for International Settlements. Many of the relationships are governed by informal agreements.

A currency is considered convertible if, within this market, it can be traded freely for others at the ratios established by the market. This is done through either spot or future contracts. Most convertibility is done on a spot basis, where money is exchanged for another currency that will be delivered to the buyer within two business days. A future contract provides for a later delivery of money, normally within 30, 60, or 90 days. By locking in the exchange rate at the time the purchase is made, the buyer of the currency is able to hedge against the risk of future rate changes (see Chapter 13 for more details).

Problems exist in repatriating profits from a number of developing countries, which may require permission, place a percentage restriction on the amount that can be taken out, or specially tax such profits. If a foreign business liquidates its assets, anything it receives for them over the firm's initial investment may be considered dividends and treated accordingly. These difficulties point to the dangers of short-term investment in developing countries.

In the United States, the Overseas Private Investment Corporation (OPIC) sells insurance that applies where there is a legally existing right of convertibility. If the insured is confronted by a foreign government's denial of that right, or if conditions (such as banking procedures) change to block convertibility, OPIC will make it good. OPIC coverage is not available, however, for dealings with countries such as China that grant no legal right to convert.[16]

Trade Restrictions: Tariffs and Quotas

The impact of issues relating to national sovereignty on trade restrictions is well illustrated by the history of the United States. The United States was committed to free trade during the Jefferson–Jacksonian era prior to the Civil War, but was heavily protectionist under the leadership of the Republican Party from the Civil War

until the 1930s. The worldwide depression during the 1930s provoked a clamor within each nation to withdraw from world trade as a way to "save itself," but this was generally perceived as the world emerged from World War II as having prolonged and deepened the depression. This perception has led to continuing efforts since World War II to negotiate a removal of trade barriers. At present, the situation is characterized by movement away from both trade restrictions and governmental intervention into trade.

Governmental intervention into trade comes in many forms, including tariffs and other constraints on imports, export controls, state subsidies, limits on foreign investment, preferences in government procurement, and countermeasures against "dumping."

Imports As to the United States, law relating to imports is almost all at the federal level, because under the Constitution the states have virtually nothing to do with foreign commerce. Under the "import-export clause" of the Constitution, a state cannot tax an import. The U.S. Supreme Court has accordingly been called on at various times historically to establish tests for the point at which a good loses its character as an "import" and starts being just part of the mass of property that is subject to property taxes.

Some imports are prohibited. These include such things as illegal drugs, food that is considered dangerous, and obscene or insurrectionary published materials. Sometimes the prohibition is imposed not because the item is harmful, but to protect a certain industry, such as the United States' protection of its fur industry against competition from Russian furs. At other times the prohibition is retaliatory, such as the U.S. ban on fish from a country that seizes American fishing boats. Since 1917, the U.S. "Trading with the Enemy Act" has barred imports from countries engaged in armed conflict with the United States. Quotas are sometimes imposed on imports, and are less severe than outright prohibitions. The "voluntary" restrictions that

Japan has placed on its automobile exports to the United States have been a substitute for the quotas that the United States once imposed.

A tariff is an *ad valorem* tax, since it is based on the value of the import. Whether a tariff will apply depends on where the goods came from, how they are classified, and what value is given them. Various practical aspects, such as the rate to be used and whether any trade restrictions apply, depend on the country of origin. If more than one country has been involved in the creation and transport of the goods, rules of origin are used to determine which is the country of origin. The main rule is the "substantial transformation test," which looks to see where the product underwent a major change.[17]

Although procedures vary from country to country, it is helpful to understand the steps in the U.S. entry process.[18] The importer posts a bond to guarantee that the duty will be paid. Entry documents, with a complete commercial invoice telling about the shipment, are processed by the U.S. Customs Service, and the tariff is entered on an entry summary form. The importer is allowed to have the goods after a tentative duty is set. The final ruling by the Customs Service about the tariff, which by law must be made within one year of the goods' entry, is called *liquidation.* Appeals are available, first at an administrative level and then in court. If the importer wants to know ahead of time whether there will be a duty, the firm can ask for a binding ruling.

Exports   In the United States, the Constitution prohibits a tax on exports, which makes their treatment substantially different from imports. Just the same, the federal government has traditionally controlled exports. A rule of thumb is that it takes permission by way of an export license to send anything out of the country.

Some exports are prohibited ("embargoed"). The reasons include assuring the availability of goods that exist only in small quantity, the prevention of nuclear proliferation, and other foreign policy and national security goals. The

United States and 16 other nations belong to the Coordinating Committee for Multilateral Export Controls (COCOM). Violation of its constraints, such as against selling certain military technology to unfriendly nations, is a criminal offense. Such a prohibition arose as to Iraq after its seizure of Kuwait, and exports are banned from regimes like those of Cuba and North Korea that remain committed to Communism, or to international terrorism, like Libya. To know what is currently prohibited, an exporter should check with the Office of Export Administration, which carries out the Export Administration Act, to see what is on the "commodity control list." Other agencies can also play a role, such as the Nuclear Regulatory Commission for the export licensing of nuclear materials and the State Department for military hardware.

Because it would be easy to circumvent these prohibitions by sending the goods to an acceptable destination with the intention that they then be sent on to one of the prohibited destinations, an *end-user certification* is required. American law makes the exporter accountable for where the product is finally used, such as North Korea, even if the goods are sent to that location by someone else after the exporter has gotten them to a valid destination such as France.[19]

Most exports don't involve prohibited destinations. For exports in general, two kinds of licenses are issued. A general license is a blanket approval for the export of goods of a certain kind, and can be issued by the exporter to itself if it complies with certain rules. A validated license is governmentally issued, looks to the nature of the goods and where they will ultimately be used, and is specific to a certain transaction.[20]

Nontariff trade barriers   Governments have seemingly endless ways to restrict trade. Some of them are framed, with varying degrees of plausibility, in terms of health, safety, or environmental protection. They include:

- Embargoes, as noted, which can apply to imports, exports or both.

- Quotas, which, again as noted, limit rather than prohibit.
- Currency controls.
- The imposition of unique performance, environmental, health, or safety specifications that a foreign firm may not be prepared to meet. A commonly cited example is the EC's ban on American beef because U.S. ranchers use growth hormones.
- Preferential treatment given to the country's own suppliers when the government is procuring supplies for its own use. This is common in the major industrial nations. At least with regard to expensive items, there has been an effort through the Agreement on Government Procurement to limit such preferences.[21]
- Undue red tape in customs procedures.
- Various internal requirements, such as that the country's own system of measurement (e.g., the metric system) be used in any specifications or that a commodity be labeled in a certain way.
- Government subsidies or tax preferences to its own firms. Sometimes these provoke "countervailing duties" by other nations to level the playing field for their own suppliers.
- Constraints on "portfolio investment." Some nations totally bar a foreigner's purchase of securities in one of the country's firms, either in general or in certain industries. Others allow a temporary co-ownership, but with the provision that at some time the ownership must come to rest entirely with the country's own nationals.

Efforts to reduce trade barriers As previously noted, the consensus since World War II that the intense national protectionism that occurred during the Great Depression was a disaster has led to negotiations under the GATT, established in 1947, as a way to reduce not just tariffs but all trade barriers. By providing an

international forum, GATT makes it more possible for each government to resist its own producer interest-groups' pressures for protectionism. Since 1947, GATT negotiations, called "rounds," have lowered many barriers, although much remains to be done. The most recent round was the "eighth round," also called "the Uruguay round," which began in 1986, addressed, among other things, issues relating to intellectual property rights. The resulting agreement makes the World Trade Organization (WTO) the controlling agency over international trade, empowering the WTO to establish international panels to hear disputes about the decisions and laws of individual countries relating to trade. If a country does not comply with a decision after appeal, it is subject to trade sanctions or must pay compensation.

The central idea behind GATT is that member nations not discriminate in their conduct of trade. The most favored nation (MFN) rule calls for each country to give all other member nations the benefit of its lowest tariffs and least restrictive trade rules. Several exceptions have been developed, however, to allow preferential treatment for developing nations. A second rule, the national treatment rule, requires the country to treat foreign goods equally with domestically manufactured goods once they have entered the country.[22] Special rules have been worked out for free-trade areas in which tariffs are removed among two or more nations, and for customs unions, which go a step further by setting a common tariff for countries outside the group.

The United States fought back against trade barriers with the Omnibus Trade Act of 1988, which included the "Super 301" provision whereby a U.S. trade representative (USTR) could inform Congress if a country erected significant trade barriers against the United States or systematically discriminated against American business. Retaliation was then threatened against the country. Although successfully used against several adverse trade practices, the provision was opposed by other countries, and this experiment ended in 1991 when Sec. 301 was allowed to expire.

Retaliation against dumping   Most American states have laws against selling below cost with the intention of forcing a competitor out of business. Similar behavior, called *dumping, in* which imported goods are sold for "less than fair value" (LTFV), is frowned on in international trade. Fair value is determined by comparing the price with the cost of manufacture or with what the goods are being sold for at home.[23] In the United States, the International Trade Commission, part of the Department of Commerce, investigates whether dumping has occurred and whether it has adversely affected an entire American industry (not just individual firms). If these facts are found, a countervailing duty is placed on the goods. In recent years, the United States has experienced some friction with Japan over alleged dumping by Japan.

Expropriation, Confiscation, and Nationalization

The power of eminent domain involves a government's taking of what previously has been private property. The exercise of this power is called a *condemnation.* In the United States, Constitutional protections apply: A "taking" of private property must be for a "public purpose," and "just compensation" must be paid. In international affairs, the power was limited from the middle of the seventeenth to the nineteenth century by the doctrine enunciated in 1646 by Hugo Grotius that no government had a right to take the property of a foreigner, and that if it violated this principle it would owe the foreign owner full payment.[24]

The term *nationalization* refers to a state's assumption of ownership. Legal literature sometimes then distinguishes between *expropriation,* which involves meeting the tests of "a proper public purpose" and "just compensation," and *confiscation,* which in one or both ways does not.[25]

Competing doctrines   A modern traditional theory came into being early in the nineteenth century. It differs from Grotius in holding that a state may lawfully take the property of a foreigner; but it elaborates on and adds to the traditional requirements by calling for a proper public purpose, an absence of discrimination against the foreign owner, and "prompt, adequate and effective compensation." Developed countries typically treat this as established international law. The doctrine has also been gaining increasing acceptance worldwide, both among developing nations as they take on the attitudes of developed countries and among the formerly Communist countries as they adopt market economies.

An opposing doctrine has held sway for the past century, however, among many less developed nations, which have given private property less sanctity and have often seen themselves as exploited by outsiders. These countries have embraced the Calvo Doctrine, named after a Latin American professor, which insists strongly on the right of a government to take the property of a foreign investor and sees any intervention by the investor's home state as a violation of the sovereignty of the host government. Because they strongly assert the latter's sovereignty, these nations are known as sovereign rights states. Some remove the limits of public purpose and nondiscrimination entirely; others do not go quite so far, holding merely that there need be no showing of a public purpose as long as the foreigner is not discriminated against. In all these nations, the amount and terms of compensation tend to be far less generous than in developed countries. Before allowing foreign investment, many of these countries require the investor to agree to a "Calvo clause," which says that the investor gives up the right to seek assistance from its home state.

Creeping expropriation is a business risk that has its counterpart in the United States and that has grown with the increasing sophistication of governments in less developed countries. (The term uses *expropriation* as synonymous with *confiscation,* reflecting the overall lack of consistency in the use of such labels.) This consists of the host government's gradually imposing so many controls that the property's owners lose the incidents of ownership. Although the United States has sought to have it recognized, international law does not yet acknowledge the existence of creeping expropriation.[26]

Remedies   Because of all this, there is a high level of political risk for investors in less developed countries. The remedies are limited and often ineffectual. They include suing in the courts of the country that has made the seizure, suing in the home country, seeking the political support of the investor's home country, resorting to an international agency, or carrying insurance against the risk.

A lawsuit brought in the courts of a less developed country is often unrewarding, since the courts there are generally not independent and the attitudes included in the Calvo Doctrine will govern. The lawsuit may, however, be brought in the investor's home state, where the hope is to collect out of property that the seizing state may have there. But this route is almost entirely blocked by legal doctrines of long standing that reflect the reluctance of one nation to invite war or international friction by interfering with another. One of these is the *sovereign immunity doctrine.* In the United States, the Foreign Sovereign Immunities Act of 1976 bars a federal court from taking a case unless the other country's actions were a form of commercial activity. In addition, there is the *act of state doctrine,* which declines to declare the action of a foreign government invalid, and a propensity of courts in the United States to see the other country's law as controlling in deciding the case. In the context of these intergovernmental relations, remedies for the investor are often inadequate.[27]

Instead of relying exclusively on a lawsuit, the investor may solicit the political help of its home state. An American investor may ask assistance from the State Department, which has the final word on whether to grant it. Subject to some exceptions, the investor must first exhaust its remedies within the other country. A freezing of assets, such as occurred against Iran, is possible, although this does not result in immediate compensation to the investor whose property was taken; instead, the investor must prove its claim before the Foreign Settlement Claims Commission in order to share in anything the American government recovers.

Resort to an international tribunal is yet another possibility. The International Court of Justice (ICJ) is, however, empowered only to decide cases between governments or that are instigated by agencies of the United Nations. Individuals do not have standing to sue there. On the other hand, the International Center for the Settlement of Investment Disputes (ICSID), established at the World Bank's Washington Conference in 1965, is available to individuals and firms. About half the world's nations have ratified the convention that created the court, which handles disputes if several preconditions are met. The parties must look only to the ensuing arbitration, foregoing all court action or political assistance.[28]

The best protection would seem to be insurance, but it is often not available. The U.S. governmental agency OPIC serves this purpose. An important limitation is that the insurance is offered only for investments in countries that have entered into an executive agreement agreeing to arbitrate any claims (doing so with OPIC itself, which will have taken as assignment the investor's claim after paying the investor). OPIC's premium for the coverage varies with the risk. The coverage will sometimes include political violence such as terrorism, war, and revolution. OPIC is not required to insure an investment, and will turn down those that are too risky. Coverage can also apply to creeping expropriation if the entire investment has been af-

Philippines' Dispute with Westinghouse

During the Marcos era, Westinghouse Electric Corporation signed a contract to build a $2.3 billion nuclear power plant in the Philippines. While the construction was under way, a popular uprising toppled the Marcos government. The uprising and the subsequent free election brought to power Corazon Aquino, the widow of slain opposition leader, Bonito Aquino, as the new president of the Philippines. Shortly after the 620-megawatt plant was completed, the Aquino government mothballed the plant because of safety concerns. Then it filed suits against Westinghouse. In 1993, after it lost a bribery case against the electric company in federal court in New Jersey, the Philippines government reached an out-of-court settlement with Westinghouse.

The terms of the agreement called for Westinghouse to build two new 100-megawatt gas turbines at $49.5 million. In return, the Philippines government agreed to drop a breach-of-contract arbitration case pending against Westinghouse in Geneva.

Source: *The Wall Street Journal* (October 5, 1993), B13.

---

fected and if the investor agrees to abandon all rights to it. Beyond the United States, the World Bank set up the Multilateral Investment Guaranty Agency (MIGA) in 1987 to perform much the same functions as OPIC.

Privatization

The worldwide move toward a market economy in the 1970s and 1980s involved a trend that was the very opposite of nationalization. Deregulation and privatization (a government's passing of the ownership of property to individuals and firms) took hold in Europe, America, and many parts of the world. Then when Communism broke up in Eastern Europe and the former Soviet Union in the late 1980s and early 1990s, privatization became the byword for the transition of these areas to a market system.

Forms of privatization vary greatly. The state may issue script and auction the property, may grant concessions to private operators but with the property staying owned by the government, may pass ownership to those who had been employed at a certain facility or who were tenants, or may just sell a sometimes less-than-controlling interest. In the semi-chaos that prevailed in the former Soviet Union following the

fall of the Communist Party, much privatization occurred spontaneously without a controlling principle: People would simply take land to farm and the managers of industrial plants would simply declare them their own. Many of the powers of government were decentralized by a similar process as localities claimed autonomy.

Privatization does not necessarily imply an absence of governmental controls after ownership has passed into private hands. The whole range of governmental involvement, discussed earlier, remains possible.

International Legal Issues

Extraterritoriality

Although each nation's law normally extends only to matters that occur within its borders, the extraterritorial application of law to events taking place elsewhere has been growing rapidly. This has been evident in criminal law with the post–World War II Nuremberg trials, Israel's prosecutions of Adolph Eichmann and Jan Demjanjuk, and the United States' capture and prosecution of Manuel Noriega. The United States, applying the principles that have been developed internally by the U.S. Supreme Court relating to jurisdiction of state courts over non-residents, has been the principal proponent of extraterritoriality. The principle has several applications to business practices.

Bribery After scandals surfaced about American firms committing bribery overseas, Congress passed the Foreign Corrupt Practices Act of 1977, which outlaws the bribing of foreign political candidates and governmental officials if the particular office exercises judgmental powers relating to the subject matter of the bribe. The act applies even though the bribe occurs outside the United States and by an individual, working for an American company, who may not be an American citizen.

Securities regulation American courts have generally been willing to exercise jurisdiction over citizens of other countries, residing in those countries, to apply American securities regulation. The federal Securities Act of 1933 relates to new issues of securities, and the Securities Exchange Act of 1934 prohibits fraud in any securities transaction and has a number of rules that apply to large companies. Extraterritoriality is exercised to prevent a circumvention of those laws.

Labor law Historically, the U.S. Supreme Court has refused to apply American labor law to work done outside the United States, but in recent years the federal government has pressed hard to apply such law, especially antidiscrimination principles, to American businesses abroad.

Banking The war on drugs involves a massive struggle against the smuggling of illegal substances into the United States. The federal government, seeking to prevent foreign banks from playing a role in the laundering of profits from this and other illegal activity, has gone to court to get subpoenas to serve on the banks' branches in the United States requiring the branches to pass on information from their parent banks. This effort has not been wholly successful, since it often incurs opposition not just from other governments but from the American courts themselves.

Taxation The United States has a strong interest in preventing wealthy taxpayers from taking up residency in a country where taxes are lower, and has accordingly been the main exception to the rule, followed by most countries, that a nation will not tax its nonresident citizens.

Torts of subsidiaries In the 1984 tragedy at Bhopal, India, more than 2,000 people were killed and 200,000 injured by a toxic gas released by a plant operated by Union Carbide India Limited, a subsidiary of an American corporation, Union Carbide Corporation. Fifty-one percent of the Indian corporation was owned by the American company, the rest by the citizens or the government of India. The plant was built, operated, and managed entirely by Indians. The American company was sued on a newly fashioned theory known as the *single enterprise theory,* which argued that parent companies that have "a global purpose, organization, structure, and financial resources" should be liable for torts (civil wrongs) committed in any country by their subsidiaries.[29] The case was settled for $470 million. Automatic tort liability for actions of foreign affiliates, if it develops, will constitute a vast extension of extraterritoriality and will enormously increase the liability exposure of companies engaged in international business.

Antitrust Antitrust law in the United States contains a *per se* prohibition against some restraints on trade. An act that is illegal *per se* is illegal "in itself," without a court's looking at extenuating factors or overall effect. Other restraints are illegal only if they violate a rule of reason (reasonableness test) or have a reasonable probability of lessening competition. Civil and criminal penalties apply, including the possibility of treble damages (a tripling of the actual damages). The principal American antitrust statutes are the Sherman Act, which prohibits monopolies and restraints on trade; the Clayton Act, which bars certain acts if they have a reasonable probability of lessening competition; and the Robinson-Patman Act, which pertains to price discrimination.

Considerable friction has existed over the extraterritorial application of antitrust laws by the United States and the European Community. Largely because of the American treble damage remedy and an exemption granted to export associations, Britain has joined in the opposition voiced by many less developed countries. Some countries have adopted blocking legislation, and courts overseas have sometimes ordered one citizen of the country not to sue another citizen on an antitrust matter in American courts.

The Foreign Trade Antitrust Improvements Act of 1982 gave a statutory basis to earlier court decisions that extended American antitrust law to the behavior of foreign entities. For a court to apply American law, it must find several things: that the anticompetitive act had, or was intended to have, a substantial effect on either American exports or internal commerce; that the behavior was of the sort that would violate U.S. antitrust laws; and, after considering the need for international comity, that the American interest in regulation outweighs the interest of the other country in governing the activity.

Reexportation   As we saw in the earlier discussion of governmental restrictions on trade, it is illegal to export a good on the commodity control list to an embargoed country. This takes on an extraterritorial aspect in light of the responsibility that is placed on the American exporter to see to it that the recipient in one country does not send the goods on (reexport them) to someone at a prohibited destination.

Contract Enforcement

Those engaged in international business will want to do everything possible to arrive at enforceable contracts. This requires a knowledge of desirable contract provisions, the rules of law that apply, how payment is made, and the enforcement of judgments.

Contract provisions   It is wise to include certain provisions in an international contract. One is a *forum-selection clause* by which the parties agree on what nation's courts are to have

jurisdiction over a dispute if one arises. These should be crafted with competent legal advice, since the clause will not be enforced if it seems inequitable for any of several reasons. Another is a *choice-of-law clause* specifying which country's law should be applied by the court hearing the dispute. The 1986 Hague Convention on the Law Applicable to Contracts for the International Sale of Goods, known also as the Choice-of-Law Convention, lets the parties freely pick the law to be applied. Along similar lines, a *choice-of-language clause* is desirable, agreeing on the language in which the contract will be construed. A *force majeure clause* is also common. This provides for a party to be excused from performing if prevented from doing so by a force—such as war, expropriation, strikes, flood, embargo, and the like—that is beyond the party's control.

Law relating to sales   In the United States, the Uniform Commercial Code (UCC) was adopted in the early 1960s by all states except Louisiana, which derives its law from the Napoleonic Code. For international transactions, however, a source of law that is rapidly being adopted around the world is the United Nations' Convention on Contracts for the International Sale of Goods (CISG), which took effect in 1988.[30] It controls, preempting any given nation's law, if the parties' respective countries have adopted the convention (the United States is among those that have done so) or if a choice-of-law clause in the contract specifies that it, or the law of a member nation, is to apply. CISG relates to sales between merchants, not to consumers. It speaks to issues relating to the formation of the contract and the remedies, but doesn't deal with matters of competency, lawful purpose, product liability for harm caused by goods, or rights of third parties. These exclusions suggest that parties should continue to include a choice-of-law clause to cover those matters.

The CISG is partly based on the UCC and partly on the concepts that inhere in European civil law. Among its principles, which frequently differ significantly from the UCC, are rules that:

- Offerors will be required to hold offers open if the other party reasonably believes a commitment to do so was made.
- The offeree's response, to count as an acceptance, must fully match the offer rather than make any changes.
- Oral contracts are binding, since no contract has to be in writing.
- An acceptance is effective when it is received, not when it is dispatched.
- The *doctrine of consideration* (making a contract valid only if, for each promise, somebody gave something in return) is not used.
- A court can consider evidence from outside the contract itself, such as from the negotiations leading up to the contract. The *parol evidence rule,* which limits the court to considering what is in the contract itself, is not applied by the CISG unless the contract itself says that it should be.
- The provisions about implied warranties are similar to the UCC's, except that there is no limit placed on disclaimers of warranties.
- The concept of substantial performance is, in effect, included, since the CISG uses the concept of fundamental breach (similar to material breach in American law). This differs from the UCC, which embraces the *perfect tender doctrine,* which considers any breach, no matter how slight, a material breach.

Way of paying obligations Since the mid-1970s, rather than use the mail or telex, firms in a large number of countries have made payments of money owed to others under contracts through the Society for Worldwide Interbank Financial Telecommunication (SWIFT),

by which banks transfer funds rapidly from a buyer's bank to that of a seller.

Enforcement of judgments If one party sues the other in the courts of a certain country for the breach of a contract and obtains a judgment in that country's courts, collection of the judgment can possibly be obtained in another country through the entry of a corresponding judgment there. The courts of the second country, in doing this without requiring a new trial on the merits, extend "comity" to the judicial actions of the other nation.

This does not, however, work with perfect symmetry. While American courts will usually enforce foreign judgments in the absence of a strong public policy reason not to, many other countries attach conditions to enforcing U.S. judgments. Countries differ in the types of remedies they prefer. Specific performance, whereby a court orders a party to do what it promised under a contract, is more commonly used than money judgments in many countries.

Patents, Copyrights, Trademarks, and Trade Names

As noted previously, IPRs may constitute a valuable part of the assets of a firm doing business internationally.[31] It becomes important to protect the exclusivity of these rights by blocking unauthorized use. One of the more effective ways to protect an IPR, where the situation fits, is to maintain an unpatented right as a trade secret. Coca-Cola, for example, for more than a century has kept its formula secret. So long as careful steps are taken to maintain the secrecy, the law of individual countries, such as the law of a given state in the United States, relating to trade secrets provides remedies in case of theft.

The international registration of patents and trademark is governed by the 1883 Paris Convention for Protection of Industrial Property. Copyrights are governed either by the Berne Convention, promulgated in 1886 but revised in 1971, or the Universal Copyright Convention. Ninety-three countries belong to one, the other, or both. The conventions are administered by the World Intellectual Property Organization (WIPO), established in 1967.

Patents, trademarks and tradenames The Paris Convention does not provide a one-time, universally valid patent, trademark or trade name registration (although the Madrid Convention does set up such a system for trademarks and trade names among its participating nations, which do not include the United States). Instead, a separate registration is needed within each country where protection is desired, and the laws of different countries vary widely. Patent protection starts from the time an application is filed, and if an application is filed in another member country within one year of the initial filing, the protection in that second country dates back to the day on which the application was filed in the first country. This 12-month rule is called the *right of priority*. A similar dating-back applies to trademarks if the filing in the second country is done within six months. Some countries, including the United States, will judicially protect a trademark on the basis of its use even if it is not registered. Subject to some exceptions, United States patents are good for 17 years from the day the application is filed. In other countries, the period varies from as low as 5 to as long as 20 years.

The Paris Convention's *national treatment rule* requires that each member nation give foreign applicants the same protection it gives its own citizens, without discrimination. The *common rules principle* sets down certain principles for all member nations to follow, although much is then left to the nation's own laws.

Copyrights A one-time registration of copyright is available among the nations that have subscribed to the Berne Convention, so that the claimant need not register in each country. A major issue in recent years has been the protection of computer programs, since imitation can escape copyright protection if the programming is sufficiently rearranged. The trend in the technically advanced nations is to shift to

a patent rationale. A mixed system of patent and copyright has been established for computer chips. The Uruguay round of the GATT negotiations gave considerable attention to current issues relating to all forms of IPRs.

Transfer of IPRs The owner of an IPR may use it itself, convey it to another firm, or give a *license* (exclusive or nonexclusive) to one or more others. If the owner *franchises* the right, the owner gives a license and retains a large amount of control over its use. Many countries will grant a *compulsory license* to a potential user, without getting the owner's approval, if a certain period of time passes without the owner's using the IPR in the country's market.

Finally, since in effect IPRs are legally protected monopolies, given as an encouragement to invention, countries have developed a large body of law that concerns itself with the anticompetitive features and speaks to how the monopoly can be used. For example, most countries will treat it as illegal price fixing if the IPR owner and the licensee agree about what the licensee will charge its own customers.

Antitrust

In addition to the antitrust matters we have discussed in relation to extraterritoriality, it should be noted that it is illegal under the Export Administration Act of 1979 and the Internal Revenue Code for Americans either to take part in or to cooperate with an international boycott (concerted refusal to deal). Historically, the primary purpose of this provision was to prevent American participation in the Arab states' boycott against Israel. In fact, Americans are required to report to the IRS any request to take part in a boycott and any request to provide information about the religion or national origin of customers, employees, or suppliers. The U.S. government approves certain boycotts, however, such as the one that existed for several years against South Africa, and it is lawful to participate in those.

Many countries have merger legislation that in various ways limits acquisitions by foreign firms of part or all of a domestic company. Most particularly, developing nations want their own citizens to own at least part of each enterprise.

MNC Operational Disputes

MNCs face a number of potential operational disputes. In the following we discuss major operational disputes that can hamper international business.

Industrial Relations

The labor legislation that applies to international businesses is the law of the country in which employees are working, subject to any extraterritorial effect of the law of the employees' country of origin if the employees are not natives of the host country. The International Labor Organization (ILO), an agency of the United Nations, has proposed more than 150 conventions, and regional treaties also exist within such areas of the world as the European Community. A *convention* is an agreement, originated by an international organization, between two or more countries. Primarily, however, the law of specific nations controls, with there in general being no common body of law based on international agreement. It is essential that an international business get to know the labor laws and customs of the nations with which it deals, since they may differ greatly from those in the United States. Most employees, for example, are employed at will in the United States, but in such a nation as Japan there is an expectation of a long-term commitment.

The ILO seeks the adoption of standards by its member nations, proposes recommendations and conventions, and conducts conferences. Its administrative tribunal hears specific cases, but only involving employees of intergovernmental organizations (IGOs), such as the ILO itself.[32]

The situation regarding collective bargaining will vary depending on the strength of union organizations, labor militancy, and the extent to which union activities such as picketing and boycotts have been under legal constraint. Various aspects of labor relations were discussed in Chapter 10. Here we will only refer to pertinent legal issues.

Many countries put limits on the right to dismiss employees and to relocate or close plants. The United States has instituted a requirement of early notification for layoffs. In Germany, the company must work through the works council, which can insist on an arbitration. The discharge of an employee often requires consultation with the union, as in Britain, or with the works council, as in Germany. In the United States, union contracts invariably provide a grievance procedure, culminating in arbitration, in cases of employee discipline.

To be employed as a foreign worker in a country, a person must obtain the necessary visa and will be under the same laws as workers of that country. In addition, a myriad of regulations exist about pay, working conditions, percentage of foreign workers that can be employed, who will pay for their return to their home countries, etc. Prohibitions or restrictions are sometimes placed on the right of a worker to send his salary home.

Many countries have compensation systems for injury on the job. *Workers compensation,* a compulsory insurance system, is prevalent in the United States, where it was copied from the legislation in Bismarck's Germany. Countries generally provide for private insurance, a governmental fund, or a combination.

Environmental Laws

The developed nations have devoted increasing resources to protection of the environment, and most have extensive laws dealing with responsibility for and cleanup of pollution. This has not come nearly so far in the developing countries and the formerly Communist states, but businesses must be aware that lax standards, where they exist, may soon be tightened.

Internationally, the United Nations Environmental Programme (UNEP) is actively generating a series of agreements, supplemented by guidelines. More than a hundred countries, for example, have joined the Basal Convention on Transboundary Movements of Hazardous Wastes and their Disposal, which is mainly addressed to the problems that arise from one country's sending wastes to another (often a less developed country) for disposal.[33]

Transfer Pricing

Where a business has operations located in more than one taxing jurisdiction, such as in different states within the United States or in more than one country, and there are transactions among the company and its affiliates, taxes can be minimized for the enterprise as a whole by setting the charges made on the transactions so that the affiliate in the state or country with the lowest tax makes all or most of the profit. This is called *transfer pricing*.[34] Transfer pricing is the source of much dispute between host countries and MNCs. While flagrant cases of abuse are often detected, most subtle cases remain hidden. When, for example, MNCs use the same price for products sold both to subsidiaries and unrelated firms these transactions are different. Subsidiaries may receive different financing terms, warranties, advertising support, and after-sales services. Therefore, what may appear to be equal and fair prices offered to both parties in fact are not.[35] It appears that foreign-owned MNCs operating in the United States are reporting significantly less profit for their U.S. operations than their U.S. counterparts. In 1987, for example, U.S.-owned firms reported an average of 2.9 percent return on assets, nearly four times that of their foreign competitors.[36] Since 1980, sales by foreign firms in the U.S. have been steadily rising, reaching more than $540 billion in 1986. Their reported profit, however, barely changed during the same period. In 1986, only 43 percent of 36,800 foreign-owned companies reported any taxable income. They claimed deductions of $543 billion on only $500 billion of revenues.[37]

There are a couple of different ways that governments with the higher tax rates can defeat this. The most common one is to apply the *arm's length principle*. Here, the taxing authorities use a variety of standards to adjust the prices that one entity has charged another, seeking to make them comparable to what independent firms would have charged each other. Under this, the taxing agencies determine what profit each entity made.

Another approach is the *unitary business rule*. Here, the taxing authority starts with the total profit made everywhere by the international business and then decides what part of that profit should be attributed to the affiliate within its jurisdiction. Percentages are developed based on relative amounts of sales, property owned, and wages paid both worldwide and locally. American law adopts the arm's length principle for the federal government, but some states use the unitary business rule.

Research and Development

The Tokyo round of the GATT negotiations took place between 1973 and 1979. Among other things, it produced a Product Standards Code to set up a mechanism to create internationally recognized norms for product characteristics and product descriptions. Each member nation is required to have a central standards office, which for the United States is the National Center for Standards and Certification Information, which is maintained by the Department of Commerce's National Bureau of Standards.

Technology is often transferred in international trade, and provisions are sometimes put into contracts attempting to place constraints on the recipient. Those engaged in international business need to know that such constraints are often illegal.

Most countries outlaw a transferor's placing restrictions on further research and development by the transferee, either as to the improvement of the technology itself or as to a competing technology. The United States allows restrictions where there is a legitimate business interest to be served, such as shielding the transferor from legal responsibility or safeguarding the technology's reputation.

Grant-back provisions also have legal nuances that can make them illegal. Provisions of this sort require a party to convey knowledge that the party comes to have through the use of the technology. They can be reciprocal, where both parties must share information, or unilateral, where only one (ordinarily the licensee) must. Those that are unilateral are illegal in most countries, although the United States considers them so only if, given the market situation, they have an adverse effect on competition.

Conclusion

This chapter touches on a great many areas of law relating to international business, but it is important to be aware that there is much more. A single chapter leaves many topics untouched, and gives only the broad outline of the law on the topics that were selected. Even textbooks devoted entirely to the law of international business only scratch the surface on many things. Business firms find it necessary to go beyond a general knowledge and to master, with the aid of competent professional advice, the many specifics, often nation by nation.

Perhaps the primary purpose of a chapter such as this one is to create an awareness of legal issues so that a person or firm doing business internationally will seek competent legal advice.

Discussion Questions

1. Is the position of the dissenting justices in the Audi case (see the chapter vignette) similar to that of the Indian courts in the Bhopal case? Discuss.
2. What does each of the following acronyms stand for? IPRs, CISG, GATT, EEC, NAFTA, OPIC, COCOM, MFN.
3. What is a GATT round?
4. What basically did the Foreign Corrupt Practices Act of 1977 do?
5. How is the Mitsubishi Group organized?
6. What are four examples of the differences in attitude and policies between the developed and the less developed nations?
7. How does Subpart F of the Internal Revenue Code fight tax havens?
8. Describe the foreign exchange market.
9. What are the steps in the U.S. entry process for imports?
10. What is an embargo, and how can an exporter check to see whether it is lawful to export a certain item?
11. What are the two types of American export licenses?
12. Name six nontariff trade barriers.
13. What is the central idea behind GATT?
14. What is dumping, and how is it generally handled?
15. What distinction is sometimes made between expropriation and confiscation?
16. What doctrines and court practices make it difficult to win against a host state in a lawsuit brought in a home state?
17. When is OPIC insurance available to cover the risk of confiscation by a host state?
18. What factors must a court find present in order to apply American antitrust law to the behavior of foreign entities under the Foreign Trade Antitrust Improvements Act of 1982?
19. What is transfer pricing, and what steps are taken to defeat it?

Endnotes

1. For an extended discussion of the "legal families" that have formed world law, see R. August. *International Business Law: Text, Cases, and Readings* (Englewood Cliffs, NJ: Prentice-Hall, 1993), 44–52.

2. The concern over the anticompetitive impact of the

Foreign Corrupt Practices Act is expressed, for example, in August. *International Business Law,* 189.

3. For a discussion of how contract negotiations in Japan are affected by cultural influences, see R. Schaffer, B. Earle, and F. Agusti. *International Business Law and Its Environment* (Minneapolis/St. Paul: West Publishing Co., 1993), 121–3.

4. August. *International Business Law.* 159.

5. Schaffer. *International Business Law.* 47–8.

6. M. B. Metzger *et al., Business Law and the Regulatory Environment,* 8th ed. (Homewood, IL: Irwin, 1992), 1261.

7. Schaffer. *International Business Law.* 482.

8. Schaffer. *International Business Law.* 439.

9. Metzger. *Business Law.* 1276.

10. Metzger. *Business Law.* 1273.

11. P. J. Shedd and R. N. Corley. *Business Law* (Englewood Cliffs, NJ: Prentice-Hall, 1993), 157.

12. For a detailed discussion of the varied systems of taxation, see August. *International Business Law.* 688–97.

13. The methods of handling the problem of multiple taxation are discussed in August. *International Business Law.* 704–8.

14. August. *International Business Law.* 676.

15. August. *International Business Law.* 699–700.

16. For a more complete discussion of OPIC, see August. *International Business Law.* 83–8.

17. A discussion of the country-of-origin rules appears in Schaffer. *International Business Law.* 352–9.

18. The U.S. entry process is discussed at length in Schaffer. *International Business Law.* 332–40.

19. Shedd. *Business Law.* 160–1.

20. Shedd. *Business Law.* 160.

21. For a discussion of the Agreement on Government Procurement, see August. *International Business Law.* 347–8.

22. For further information about the most favored nation rule and the national treatment rule, see August. *International Business Law.* 315–8.

23. R. N. Corley *et al. The Legal Environment of Business,* 8th ed. (New York: McGraw-Hill, 1990), 664.

24. For a discussion of the history of international legal doctrines relative to a government taking of property, see Schaffer, *International Business Law,* pp. 453–460.

25. Corley. *Legal Environment.* 651.

26. As to creeping expropriation, see August. *International Business Law.* 83–4.

27. For a discussion of sovereign immunity and the act of state doctrine, see Corley. *Legal Environment.* 651–4.

28. August. *International Business Law.* 103–11, contains an extended discussion of arbitration through ICSID.

29. The case in which the U.S. Court of Appeals (Second Circuit) recounted the details of the Bhopal accident and held that the dispute should be heard in India, not the United States, is *In re Union Carbide Corporation Gas Plant Disaster at Bhopal,* 809 F.2d 195 (1987).

30. The CISG is dealt with extensively in the chapter on "Sales" in August. *International Business Law.* 422–74.

31. See the chapter on "Intellectual Property" in August. *International Business Law.* 586–664; and the chapter "Licensing and Other Transfers of Intellectual Property" in Schaffer. *International Business Law,* 425–52.

32. For a lengthy discussion of the ILO, see August. *International Business Law.* 259–68.

33. International environmental issues are examined in Schaffer. *International Business Law.* 517–27.

34. Transfer pricing is treated at length in August. *International Business Law.* 720-5.

35. H. Gleckman and T. Holden. "Can Uncle Sam Mend This Hole in His Pocket?" *Business Week* (September 10, 1990), 48–9.

36. Ibid.

37. L. Chambliss. "Holier Than Thou." *Financial World* (May 29, 1990), 20–1.

FOREMOST-MCKESSON, INC., AND PAK DAIRY: A NEW SOVEREIGNTY

MASOUD KAVOOSSI

Multinational enterprises (MNEs) face a multitude of problems in their efforts to succeed internationally. Not the least of these problems are the varying legal disputes and their effect on business transactions. Just as other uncontrollable factors, such as politics, affect international business activities, so do the legal aspects. Such legal questions as jurisdictional issues in disputes, are of primary concern to international business. Some of these disputes can be avoided through the judicious writing of clear contracts that provide for these potential pitfalls. Some conflicts will still occur between MNCs, between nations, or between nations and private parties.

Foremost-McKesson, Inc., a Maryland corporation with its principle place of business in California, assisted in establishing a dairy, the Sherkat Sahami Labaniat Pasturize Pak (Pak Dairy), in Iran, in 1959. From 1959 to the time of the Iranian revolution in 1979, Foremost provided the top management for the dairy and controlled its Board of Directors. During this period, Foremost held 31% of the equity interest in the dairy.

On January 22, 1982, Foremost and the Overseas Private Investment Corporation (OPIC) filed a complaint in a U.S. court against the Islamic Republic of Iran and several agencies and instrumentalities of Iran through which Foremost claims Iran acted. These agencies and instrumentalities include the financial organization for the expansion of ownership of productive units, the National Investment Company of Iran, Industrial and Mining Development Bank of Iran, the Foundation for the Oppressed, and Pak Dairy. Foremost alleges that Iran acting through agencies and instrumentalities, illegally divested Foremost of its investment in Pak Dairy. Foremost and OPIC sought compensation for the entire value of their jointly held 19.84% insured equity interest in Pak Dairy, estimated to value at no less than $7,040,000, plus interest; compensation for their share in any dividends declared; and various other damages, including attorneys' fees. On June 29, 1982, Iran responded to the suit stating that prosecution was barred by the Algiers Accord of January 19, 1981.[1] Pursuant to Iran's response Foremost and OPIC presented their claims against Iran to the United States-Iran Claims Tribunal (Claims Tribunal) in the Hague.[2]

The Foremost-McKesson, Inc., case was prepared for this book by Dr. Kavoosi, Howard University, and is printed with the author's permission.

[1] Under the Algiers Accord, Iran agreed to assume responsibility for compensating United States nationals for claims against Iran. Also for claims against any "political subdivision of Iran, and any agency, instrumentality, or entity controlled by the government of Iran, or any political subdivision thereof." See Declaration of the Government of the Democratic and Popular Republic of Algeria.

[2] Activity of the Tribunal can be found in the message by the President to the Congress of November 20, 1987, report on national emergency with respect to Iran, in *The Congressional Record*, Daily ed., November 20, 1987.

On April 10, 1986, Claims Tribunal concluded that interference with Foremost's right had not, by January 1981, amounted to an expropriation. However, the Claims Tribunal concluded that Pak Dairy had unlawfully withheld from Foremost cash dividends declared in 1979 and 1980, and it therefore awarded Foremost approximately $9000,000 plus interest against Iran. The Claims Tribunal also concluded that Pak Dairy unlawfully failed to deliver to Foremost stock certificates representing stock dividends declared in 1980 and that Pak Dairy had breached contractual obligations in failing to pay rental payments due and to return upon demand certain machines to Foremost. The Claims Tribunal awarded Foremost in excess of $500,000 in damages against Pak Dairy for the contract breaches. Iran paid the amounts awarded out of the security account established at the Hague pursuant to the provisions of the Algiers Accord.

On April 1, 1988, Foremost, still seeking damages for claimed losses, alleged that the dairy was expropriated, by bringing a lawsuit in a U.S. District Court. In response Iran moved to reject the complaint for lack of jurisdiction under the Foreign Sovereignty Immunity Act (FSIA).[3]

Before proceeding to consider the various questions raised in this case, one must first address Iran's attribution argument. In its suit, Foremost seeks to hold the foreign sovereignty of Iran responsible for the actions of Pak Dairy and/or entities holding the majority of Pak Dairy's shares. Iran claims that the courts cannot attribute to Iran the actions of the Board of Directors of Pak Dairy.

The Claims Tribunal held that "the two main indicators of government control of a corporation are the identity of its shareholders and the composition and behavior of its Board of Directors." Because it was found that government-controlled entities held the majority of shares in Pak Dairy and that these entities also held a majority of

seats on the Board of Directors, the Claims Tribunal held that Pak Dairy was a corporation controlled by the government of the Islamic Republic of Iran.

It seems clear that Foremost's complaint alleges actions that are both commercial and governmental in nature. However, there is no indication that Iran nationalized Pak Dairy by taking it over through a process of law. Indeed, Iran denies it controls Pak Dairy or that Pak Dairy is an agency or instrumentality of Iran. There has been no restriction or governmental decree or directive depriving persons outside Iran of the right to sell or transfer shares in an Iranian enterprise or of a government policy curtailing the payment of dividends. In the absence of such evidence one may conclude that the actions alleged were commercial in nature and subsequently should not involve Iran.

It appears that, business, law, and politics play with different rules and neither one fully understands each other's game in an international setting.

Discussion Questions

1. Is Iran immune from suit under FSIA? Is the defense of sovereign immunity applicable?
2. Another question is the issue of jurisdiction. Which country's courts have jurisdiction in such matters?
3. Is Iran right in its claim that the U.S. court erred in attributing to Iran the actions of Pak Dairy and its majority shareholders, which are allegedly agencies or instrumentalities of the Islamic Republic of Iran?
4. Did Iran waive its immunity by signing the Treaty of Amity?[4]

---

[3] FSIA applies to instrumentalities and agencies of the foreign sovereign as well as to the state itself.

[4] The Treaty of Amity provides that each contracting party should at all times accord fair and equitable treatment to nationals and companies of the other contracting party, and to their property and enterprises; shall refrain from applying unreasonable or discriminatory measures that would impair their legally acquired rights and interests.

Selected Bibliography

The Congressional Record, Daily ed., Nov. 20, 1987.

Brower, C., *et al.* "The Iran-United States Claims Tribunal After Seven Years: A Retrospective View from Inside." *Arbitration Journal,* 43 (December 1988), 16–30.

Baker, S. A., *et al.* "Arbitration Proceedings Under the UNCITRAL Rules—The Experience of the Iran-United States Claims Tribunal." *George Washington Journal of International Law and Economics (JIC),* 23 (1989), 267–347.

DRESSER AND THE SOVIET PIPELINE CONTROVERSY

CHARLES R. KENNEDY, JR.

On August 18, 1982, Rock Grundman, Government/Business Affairs Counsel for Dresser Industries, was awakened in the middle of the night by an urgent long-distance phone call from the company's French subsidiary.

Mr. Grundman's caller hurriedly related the latest chain of events and concluded by saying that a ship named the "Borodin" was en route to the French port of Le Havre to load three completed compressors for the Soviet pipeline. The situation was critical. Since June 18, 1982, when President Reagan had announced his expanded embargo, communications between the parent and its subsidiary had been consciously limited. A new embargo had extended the one of December 30, 1981, to include the foreign subsidiaries of U.S. firms who were producing equipment under U.S. licenses. The president's action in June meant that Dresser's French subsidiary could honor its Soviet pipeline contract only at the risk of U.S. government sanctions or

This case was prepared by Charles R. Kennedy, Jr., Associate Professor at the Darden Graduate School of Business Administration and Mary Buckle Williams, Darden MBA '86. Copyright © 1987 by the Darden Graduate Business School Foundation, Charlottesville, Virginia.

blacklisting. This action not only put Dresser in a difficult position, it put a strain on relations between the United States and its European trading partners, who would be beneficiaries of the Soviet pipeline. (See Exhibit 1 for a chronology of events.) The French government had requested that they be shipped on time. Arrival time of the ship was uncertain, but its likely departure date was late August.

Mr. Grundman saw Dresser as being "between a rock and hard place." If the company honored the U.S. president's directive, it would alienate the French government. If the company responded to the French government's request for shipment, the company could face repercussions from the U.S. government. Whichever direction the company took, the offended government could initiate civil or criminal action.

As he hung up the phone, Mr. Grundman pondered the significance of the ship's name, "Borodin." Aleksandr Borodin was a famous Russian composer in the mid-1800s. Were the Russians trying to get Dresser to dance to their music by sending the "Borodin" to France?

Over his first cup of coffee, Mr. Grundman notified officials of the U.S. State and Com-

Exhibit 1
Chronology of Events

June 1978	Contract for drill bit plant signed.
December 1979	Invasion of Afghanistan by Soviet troops.
January 1980	President Carter imposes sanctions and denies export licenses of technology transfer.
September 1981	Contract signed with Creusot-Loire, SA, and Machinoimport to manufacture and sell 21 compressors.
December 13, 1981	Martial law in Poland.
December 29, 1981	Last technical document to Dresser-France sent.
December 30, 1981	President Reagan imposes embargo.
June 18, 1982	President Reagan makes embargo retroactive, effective June 22, 1982.
June 20, 1982	Mr. Grundman flies to Maxwell Air Force Base for two-week reserve duty.
June 25, 1982	President Mitterrand makes public speech requesting completion and shipment of compressors.
July 3, 1982	Mr. Grundman returns from reserve duty.
July 25, 1982	President and chairman of Dresser puts Mr. Grundman in charge of situation.
August 10, 1982	President of Dresser-French receives letter from French Minister of Research and Industry stating that Soviet contract would be honored.
August 18, 1982	Mr. Grundman informed of "Borodin" destination.
August 23, 1982	French government issues legally enforceable requisition order to ship compressors.

merce Departments and the U.S. Trade Representative of the reported destination and name of the ship. These actions were followed by a call to France so that the French government would be fully informed as well. After these calls were completed, he wondered what the ultimate consequences of this dilemma to Dresser would be and what the company could do in response.

Dresser Industries

Dresser was founded in 1880 as a producer of new types of lead-free pipe couplings. The company grew during the 1960s through acquisitions and became a leading supplier of engineered products and technical services to energy and natural resources industries throughout the world.

In 1981 Dresser Industries was divided into five industry segments: petroleum operations, energy processing and conversion equipment, refractories and minerals operations, mining and construction equipment, and industrial specialty products. Total sales and service revenues

amounted to $4.6 billion in 1981, with earnings of $317 million. These levels reflected an increase over the previous year of 15 percent and 21 percent, respectively. Carefully developed functional policies, sophisticated planning and control, effective marketing programs, and a high level of capital and technical spending contributed to the achievement of this performance. Proprietary products and services in the energy-related markets were also important to maintaining Dresser's leading position in the world.

Headquartered in Dallas, Texas, Dresser employed over 57,000 people and operated in more than 100 countries. Dresser, in fact, had $1.5 billion in export sales in 1981. With this extensive network, the company and its subsidiaries had captured 20 percent to 30 percent of the world's market for compressors. Through advanced technology development, compressors continued to be one of the company's key strategic products, accounting for 86 percent of the energy-processing segment's sales, which totaled $900 million in 1981.

Dresser-France, one of the company's divisions within the Dresser Compressor Group, was owned by Dresser A. G. (Vaduz), a Liechtenstein corporation. Dresser Industries owned Dresser A. G. The French subsidiary contributed about $492 million in annual sales in 1981 and exported about 92 percent of its output. Gas compressors and other devices built in its plant were based on the technology developed by the Dresser-Clark Division in Olean, New York, and other U.S.-based divisions. Several of the company's other international manufacturing operations had similar licensing agreements to build identical compressors.

Dresser and the Soviet Connection

Dresser began exporting compressors to the USSR in the 1930s, and during the political cold war of 1949–1963, continued to conduct business with the Soviet Union without U.S. government intervention. As relations between the Soviet and U.S. governments thawed in the late 1960s, sales in general between the two countries accelerated. Western exports of manufactured goods flowed east, and eastern exports of mineral raw materials and labor-intensive goods flowed west. Transfer of western technology, in particular, grew dramatically. In fact, international sales of U.S. licenses increased three times faster than merchandise exports.

To encourage this favorable flow of trade, Congress passed the Export Administration Act of 1969 as a successor to the Export Control Act of 1949. The new act reduced restrictions of exports to communist countries of goods and technology for economic development. (Exports for military development were still prohibited.) The new legislation was further amended during the early 1970s (the Nixon *detente* years) so as to allow U.S. companies to compete for Soviet business on an equal basis with Western Eruopean counterparts.

The Soviets were anxious to purchase foreign equipment and technology to develop their oil and gas industry. In 1975 they initiated negotiations with Dresser for a $144 million contract to help them build a plant to manufacture drill bits. After careful reviews in the Department of Defense, the export license was finally issued in May 1978.

Support in Washington for liberalization of trade with the Soviets began to erode at about the same time. Incidents such as the trials of Soviet dissidents Shcharansky and Ginzberg, the Soviet support of insurrection in Africa, and the Soviet invasion of Afghanistan in 1979 ended the climate of *detente* between the two countries. With President Carter's ensuing export embargo, the Dresser drill-bit license was revoked. By this time, however, all the necessary goods had been shipped, and only the final phase of limited Soviet technical training remained. Similarly, General Electric's turbine technology had already been delivered to four European countries. That contract was the heart of the Soviet pipeline project.

The Soviet Pipeline

In the 1960s, the Soviet Union discovered a vast reserve of natural gas in the province of Urengoi in Siberia. A six-tube pipeline was initially planned to carry up to 65 billion cubic meters (bcm) per year to Western Europe, 3,700 miles away. (The length of this pipeline was four times longer than the Alaskan pipeline.) Contracted delivery of gas was later scaled down to 35 bcm/year, beginning with 10 bcm in 1984.

As the worldwide oil crisis had developed in the 1970s, consumers conserved energy and looked for alternative energy sources. Natural gas proved to be a cheaper alternative, with price differentials widening to 50 percent between 1974 and 1977. Gas consumption within the EEC countries grew sharply and was expected to reach 400 bcm by the end of the century. Because European production could not supply the total projected demand, other sources of natural gas supply were analyzed on the basis of cost, reliability, and potential impact on balance of payments. European leaders believed that the USSR was the only country that could reasonably satisfy their requirements. They were confident that the EEC would not become overly dependent on the Soviets because, despite the fact that the new Soviet pipeline would supply 20 percent of the EEC's total natural gas needs, only 5 percent of total energy supplies would be sourced from the Soviets. Furthermore, the Europeans were optimistic about the jobs that would be created to support the pipeline, since the countries were facing rising unemployment and inflation.

The pipeline project was the largest commercial transaction ever attempted between the East and the West. Originally, costs of construction were estimated to be $11 billion. Productive life of the pipeline was said to be 25 years, beginning in 1984.

Construction of the pipeline would require the cooperation of twelve nations, dozens of companies, and more than 120,000 Soviet workers. Financing of the project, including the imported equipment and pipe, would be negotiated through the Western European beneficiaries. The final costs were reestimated to be $25-$30 billion because of unforeseen problems and delays.

The French engineering firm Creusot-Loire was selected as the contractor for approximately eighty compressors valued at $1 billion. GE licensees in the EEC received the orders for the turbines to drive all 120 or so compressors in the pipeline project. On September 28, 1981, Dresser-France signed a contract with Creusot-Loire and the USSR for one group of twenty-two compressors to be powered by the GE turbines. The $20 million order required 20 percent of Dresser-France's total operations and represented a substantial portion of its annual workload in Le Havre. Deliveries were scheduled to begin in May 1982.

Previous energy projects with the USSR had been profitable for European businesses. Most of the ventures had been a type of countertrade known as compensation agreements: western exports were compensated with credits that the Soviets would repay, wholly or partly, in goods at some future time. Transfer of foreign exchange was minimal. In the new pipeline agreement, however, transfer of foreign exchange would flow in exchange for the natural gas.

U.S. Opposition to the Urengoi Pipeline

The U.S. government objected to the Soviet-EEC deal mainly from a political standpoint. The Reagan Administration believed that European dependency on Soviet oil threatened European security and increased Europe's vulnerability. Resistance to Soviet aggression might be weakened by actual or potential interruption of supplies. Such interruptions had been experienced before, but never during an international crisis, and supplies had always been restored.

Another argument addressed the sale of technologically advanced equipment that could strengthen the Soviet strategic position. Gas exports to Western Europe could earn the USSR $10-$15 billion in hard currency annually by the 1990s, which could be used to bolster its military forces.

The Reagan Administration argued that such a Soviet military buildup directly threatened U.S. national security. Therefore, building U.S. military forces and applying economic pressure against the Soviet Union became a top priority with some within the administration.

Export controls were believed to be effective only under certain conditions. An example of ineffective controls cited by some observers was the grain sales embargo imposed by President Carter in 1979. The desired effect was not achieved because other suppliers were readily available. On the other hand, when hard currency was used for grain purchases, that money was not available for arms purchases. This choice between guns and butter was believed to put effective pressure on Soviet action. "U.S. grain sales make the Russians dependent on us and force them to give up their hard currency every year," said one Reagan advisor. "The pipeline does just the opposite, it makes the Europeans dependent on the Russians." Such was the Reagan Administration's answer to European charges of hypocrisy when the U.S. president announced his pipeline sanctions policy while still allowing wheat sales to the Soviets.

The Sanctions

Precipitated by the Polish government's declaration of martial law on December 13, 1981, on December 30, President Reagan announced new economic sanctions against the Soviet Union. These sanctions expanded the 1978 restricted list of oil and gas equipment exports by domestic companies to include oil and gas transmission and related goods. It also restricted further issuance or renewal of validated licenses for export to the USSR of high-technology products, technical data, and oil and gas equipment and technology.

The proclamation had immediate implications for U.S.-based companies that had supply contracts for the Soviet pipeline. GE had a $175 million contract for the 125 turbine rotors; only twenty-three sets had been supplied so far. (Companies in France, the United Kingdom, and Italy were to build the turbines.) Caterpillar, which was already experiencing financial difficulties, had a $90 million contract for pipe-laying tractors. Other domestic companies also had outstanding contracts that might be denied licenses.

Prior to the December sanctions, Dresser Industries had conferred with the administration to verify the government's position on U.S.-Soviet business. Dresser had asked if the U.S. government had any strong objections to the compressor contract. The government gave a neutral reaction, neither a yes or no answer. Based on this response, Dresser signed the compressor contract in September 1981.

When the sanctions were announced three months later, all necessary technology and information had already been transferred to Dresser-France from Dresser-Clark. Mr. Grundman recounted those events this way:

> At that time, I was on vacation in Sante Fe, New Mexico. I was advised while in Santa Fe of what the president had done, and I discussed it with the operating units and lawyers involved and made sure that no data was transmitted to France subsequent to that date. In effect, we put a wall between the U.S. and Dresser-France from that day forward, but that was easier said than done, because we had just transmitted by mail another set of technical drawings, which was unnecessary to the completion of the contract. We actually required Dresser-France to return them unopened. I jokingly vowed never to go on vacation again.

Communications with the Reagan Administration were continuous at the same time. Dresser wanted to express its intentions clearly and to understand the interpretation of the government's regulations. Most importantly, Dresser did not want the U.S. government to act against its interests based on rumor or incorrect facts. Dresser thus took a proactive stance with the government. As Mr. Grundman described it:

> Immediately after New Year's weekend, I arranged a meeting with an assistant secretary of Commerce to give an interpretation of the regulation. I needed to be sure we could lawfully proceed with the contract or at least determine where we stood from a legal standpoint in order to make an informed business decision. The end result, however, was that the assistant secretary was noncommittal and gave no response to my inquiry as to whether the regulations applied retroactively or were intended to. Therefore, we had to rely on our legal judgment that they did not apply retroactively, and they knew that would be our interpretation.

On the international front, the EEC remained committed to participating in the natural gas pipeline despite the economic sanctions against the project. The countries contended that growth in trade with Eastern Europe and the USSR was necessary to maintain Western Europe's economy. West German industry officials indicated that more serious problems could arise if the Reagan Administration prohibited American companies from delivering parts and components to European manufacturers supplying equipment for the pipeline. A search for other suppliers was one option that was contemplated.

As far as Dresser was concerned, the spring of 1982 was business as usual. As Mr. Grundman recounted.

> Nothing happend except normal business. The commercial decision to proceed was made, with Dresser-France in the position to proceed without any further help from the United States. We understood that the regulations were not retroactive.

Reagan's "trade war" with the Soviets, however, was one of the top issues that consumed the Versailles summit meetings in June 1982, among the United States, United Kingdom, France, West Germany, Japan, Italy, and Canada. Their discussions were concluded with a loosely worded, hard-to-interpret agreement whereby the countries would proceed "prudently" in their economic approach to the Soviet Bloc. The European leaders left the summit believing that Reagan would ease his embargo policy in exchange for their agreement to review credit terms to Eastern Europe in the future.

A few days after the accord, France was the first to announce publicly its interpretation of the Versailles agreement. President Mitterrand expressed his intent to continue the current credit policy with the USSR. Therefore, in response to Europe's refusal to eradicate the policy of interest-rate subsidization for the pipeline, on June 18 President Reagan announced extensions to the sanctions effective as of June 22, 1982. The extensions covered foreign subsidiaries and licensees of U.S. companies.

The decision had been formulated in a National Security Council meeting. On Friday, June 18, Bo Denysyk, a Deputy Assistant Secretary of Commerce, called Rock Grundman to ask what the proposed sanctions would do to the Dresser-France contract. "Halt it" was the reply. Fifteen minutes later, the sanctions were announced.

Mr. Grundman was told that the sanctions would be retroactive, making it unlawful to transfer anything that was made with the assistance of U.S. technology. He immediately advised Dresser's president, Jim Brown, who sent a telex to Dresser-France on June 19 advising them to cease work on the contract and not to ship the three completed compressors to the Soviet Union.

Under the Export Administration Act of 1979 (see Exhibit 2), the President of the United States could initiate civil, criminal, and administrative penalties against violators of his trade sanctions, including placing the offending firm on a denial or "blacklist." U.S. export controls were implemented by the Commerce Department's International Trade Administration (see Exhibit 3). Any blacklisted company could be denied authority to export goods or technology, and other companies could be denied any transactions with that company. Such penalties could be targeted at either U.S. corporations as a whole, their overseas subsidiaries only, or foreign-owned companies. As Lionel H. Olmer, Under Secretary of Commerce for International Trade Administration, explained:

> We are putting our shoulder to the wheel to make these sanctions as effective as possible . . . denial list (companies) could be prohibited from receiving any export of any good or data from the United States, irrespective of whether it's related to oil or gas.

Olmer, moreover, predicted that President Reagan's actions would delay the pipeline project by at least two years and might even cause the project to collapse. He also estimated that

387.1 Sanctions

(a) Criminal

(1) Violations of Export Administration Act.

    1. *General.* . . . whoever knowingly violates the Export Administration Act ("the Act") or any regulation, order, or license issued under the Act is punishable for each violation by a fine of not more than five times the value of the exports involved or $50,000, whichever is greater, or by imprisonment for not more than five years, or both.

    2. *Willful violations.* Whoever willfully exports anything contrary to any provision of the Act or any regulation, order, or license issued under the Act, with the knowledge that such exports will be used for the benefit of any country to which exports are restricted for national security or foreign policy purposes except in the case of an individual, shall be fined not more than five times the value of the exports involved or $1,000,000, whichever is greater; and in the case of the individual, shall be fined not more than $250,000, or imprisoned not more than 10 years, or both. . . .

(b) Administrative

    1. Denial of export privileges. Whoever violates any law, regulation, order, or license relating to export controls or restrictive trade practices and boycotts is also subject to administrative action which may result in suspension, revocation, or denial of export privileges conferred under the Export Administration Act.

    2. Civil penalty. A civil penalty may be imposed for each violation of the Export Administration Act or any regulation, order, or license issued under the Act either in addition to, or instead of, any other liability or penalty which may be imposed. The civil penalty may not exceed $10,000 for each violation except that the civil penalty for each violation involving national security controls imposed under Section 5 of the Act may not exceed $100,000.

Source: Export Administration Regulations, January 25, 1983.

Exhibit 2   Export Administration Act Regulations, Excerpts

the sanctions would result in roughly $1.2 billion in lost sales for U.S. companies. When asked what the Commerce Department's reaction would be if France passed a law barring companies from complying with U.S. regulations, Olmer stated: "It would be a contentious matter. I hope it won't arise."[1]

A week after the sanctions were announced, President Mitterrand made a public statement requesting that all French-based companies honor their original contracts. Several weeks later, the French government sent a letter to Dresser-France asking the company to ship the three completed compressors on schedule and resume work on the remaining ones. On August 23rd, once the "Borodin" had arrived in Le Havre, the French government issued an "Order du Requisition" to Dresser-France requiring completion of the compressor contract with the USSR. Such orders by the French government

[1] *The New York Times,* June 24, 1982, p. 1.

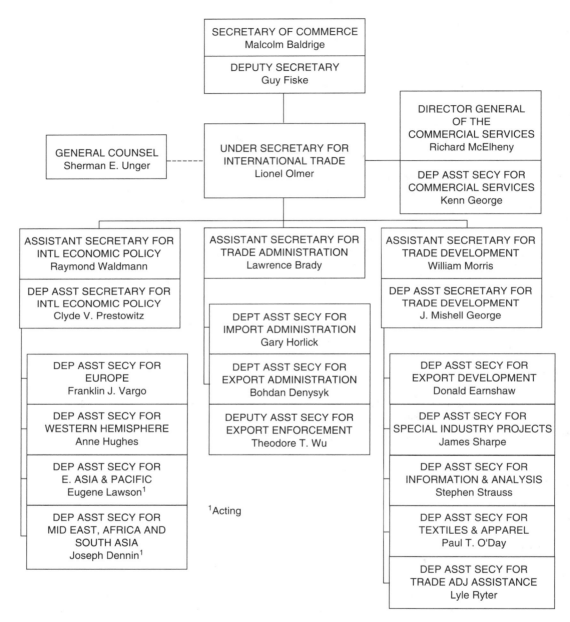

Exhibit 3   Commerce Department—International Trade Administration

could not be challenged in the French judicial system. Dresser now was caught squarely in between two governments. Noncompliance with the French order could cost the French affiliate and its managers $60,000 and up to twelve months in jail, in addition to a contractual penalty not to exceed 8 percent of the total contract price for failure to deliver.[2] Even nationalization of Dresser-France's facilities was considered a real possibility by managers in Dallas.

The reactions of other European governments were swift and angry as well. British Prime Minister Margaret Thatcher, who was considered a close friend and ally of President Reagan, was in fact the first European leader to condemn the June 18th sanctions. Like the government of France, she invoked a UK law, the Protection of Trading Interests Act, which compelled three British firms with compressor contracts to ignore American export controls. The governments of West Germany and Italy also urged their firms to honor pipeline contracts, thereby defying the U.S. embargo. The foreign ministers of the ten European Economic Community countries, moreover, issued a joint statement, which said: "The action, taken without consultation with the Community, implies an extraterritorial extension of U.S. jurisdiction, which in the circumstances is contrary to the principles of international law."

Mr. Grundman described the circumstances under which he managed this situation:

> Curiously enough, when the first shoe dropped, I was in Sante Fe. When the second shoe dropped, I was on my way to my last two-week duty in the Air Force reserve. Conducting business by express mail and pay telephone while at Maxwell Air Force Base during the last two weeks of June was interesting, but of course, the most important thing had been taken care of already—the telex to Dresser-France had been sent. Then, after I returned from reserve duty, President Jim Brown died. When

Chairman J. V. James resumed the role of the president, he called me into his office and said he wanted me to handle the Dresser-France situation. The immediate thing to do was to make sure that nothing was done precipitously by either the U.S. or French governments. The first decision was to keep them both informed completely, which we did.

Mr. Grundman told both governments about continued communications between Dresser-Headquarters and Dresser-France and with each respective government. Copies of formal correspondence were cross-issued to both governments. The U.S. government acknowledged the information but remained noncommittal in its response. Through informal discussions with many senior officers in the administration, Mr. Grundman argued that the sanction policy was harmful to the health of the companies involved as well as the countries. Some senior officials agreed with him privately, but not always publicly. The press reported:

> Some officials sympathized with Dresser's position noting that if the company is successful in stopping the shipment, its French executives face severe penalties. If, on the other hand, the shipment is delivered, the American parent company faces severe sanctions under the Export Administration Act.[3]

Unfortunately for Dresser, many administration officials were not sympathetic to the company's situation. In addition, the legal position of the Reagan Administration was strong. The law gave the president total discretion in implementing export controls for foreign policy reasons. Dresser's only viable legal argument was that in spite of any foreign policy rationale, Reagan's sanctions violated the intent of the Export Administration Act since sanctions were imposed retroactively and on companies outside U.S. jurisdiction. Nevertheless, as the "Borodin" approached Le Havre, it became

---

[2] *Oil and Gas Journal,* August 30, 1982, p. 74.

[3] *Washington Post,* August 23, 1982, p. A1.

clear that the Reagan Administration was going to react strongly if Dresser-France loaded those compressors. As reported in the press on August 23rd:

> Administration officials said yesterday that an interdepartmental working group of the National Security Council began last Friday to map out a strategy for legal and administrative actions against Dresser Industries, should the loading occur, as well as stern diplomatic messages to the French government. The group was chaired by Treasury Secretary Donald T. Regan. . . . Another administration official said yesterday that two specific options thus far studied by the working group are seeking a temporary restraining order in U.S. District Court against the Dresser subsidiary's shipment and taking administrative action against Dresser, perhaps going so far as to cut off its French subsidiary from future equipment supplies.[4]

Even the possibility of placing Dresser as a whole on a denial list was not out of the question.

Borodin Starts the Music

Since late July when the chairman and president of Dresser had given Mr. Grundman the lead role in managing the pipeline crisis, few other senior executives had been privy to the details of the situation. The General Counsel was not involved at this stage, because he was in Europe on other business. After Mr. Grundman received the phonecall from Dresser-France on August 18 informing him of the "Borodin" being en route to Le Havre, the days passed very quickly and the pressure mounted enormously. Unfortunately, Dresser was victimized by being the first test case of a foreign policy dispute between the U.S. and European governments. Other firms would face a similar dilemma in a few days, particularly a British firm, John Brown Engineering Ltd., whose compressors

were scheduled for shipment before the end of the month. Nevertheless, Dresser was first, and on August 23rd, the most pressing decision now rested on an accurate understanding of the company's possible options. Did the French subsidiary have any choice but to obey Mitterrand's order? If the French order was obeyed, the U.S. government had made it clear that a blacklisting of Dresser-French would probably follow. Given this threat, could headquarters close its eyes and let the French subsidiary make its own choice? Alternatively, should Dresser again order their subsidiary to ship or not to ship the compressors? Or should Mr. Grundman, keeping the Logan Act in mind,[5] request the U.S. government to allow headquarters to negotiate directly with the French government? Should Dresser take legal action against the U.S. government by challenging the President's authority in the Export Administration Act of 1979? Apparently challenging the French government's "Order du Requisition" was not an option. Since the ship was to be loaded with the compressors in a couple of days, Dresser would have to make its decisions quickly.

Certainly, the U.S. government had its preference. As reported in the press:

> "The hope is to go the diplomatic route," said one senior official, who emphasized that the president is adamant about not backing off from the sanctions. At the same time, this official said that no decision has been made on what course to take if the first loading occurs at Le Havre. He ruled out any American attempt to physically interfere with the loading. The official said that lawyers from the State, Defense, Commerce and Justice departments are still hopeful that Dresser officials can be persuaded to take additional steps to stop the shipment. Moreover, the official said, the administration is planning to tell the French gov-

---

[4] *Ibid.*

[5] Logan Act forbids U.S. private citizens from negotiating with a foreign government about U.S. foreign policy, unless prior approval by the government has been given.

ernment through the State Department that Reagan takes the export ban seriously and intends to enforce it.[6]

Another administration official, however, stated that:

Dresser officials already have done most of what a court order would require them to do to stop the shipment. This official said that Dresser's top management in Dallas has already ordered the French-based Dresser executives to stop the shipment. Those (French) executives, in turn, told the freight handling company in an August 11 letter that ". . . All shipment is forbidden until further instructions are given to you in writing . . ."[7]

---

[6] *Washington Post*, August 23, 1982.

[7] *Ibid.*

SIXTEEN

SOCIO-ETHICAL ISSUES AND INTERNATIONAL MANAGEMENT

Businesses are expected to be socially responsible and conduct themselves ethically. While there are some emerging agreements, at least in the United States, regarding the social responsibilities of domestic firms, the social responsibility and ethical aspects of international management are being hotly debated. Disagreements arise due to the nature of international business and different perspectives that nations hold regarding these issues. National priorities and cultural differences confound the problems further. This chapter examines these issues and highlights the differences.

The major topics covered in this chapter involve the problems of corruption and bribery and their effect on international management, ecological aspects of international business, special concerns of developing countries, problems of expanding free trade, and international conflict resolution. The chapter also discusses the role of supranational organizations, such as the United Nations, International Monetary Fund, and the World Bank in resolving international trade disputes and promoting global prosperity.

In 1974, in an attempt to increase the price of exported bananas, under the initiatives of the Panamanian dictator General Omar Torrijos and Costa Rica's president Jose Figueres, the seven banana-producing countries met in Panama. Participating countries were Colombia, Costa Rica, Ecuador, Guatemala, Honduras, Nicaragua, and Panama. They wanted to establish an organization of banana exporting countries (OBEC), a banana cartel modeled after the Organization of Petroleum Exporting Countries (OPEC).

At that time, banana production and export were controlled by the big three fruit firms of United Brands Company, Standard Fruit Company, and Del Monte Corporation, and prices had not been increased for nearly 20 years. The objective was to fix the price and curtail the production of exported bananas.

Their efforts failed due to the reluctance of Ecuador, the world's largest banana producer, to cooperate. Each country, however, began imposing its own export tax on bananas. For example, Honduras announced the imposition of a 50-cent tax on each 40-pound box of bananas; Costa Rica, 25 cents; and Panama, $1.00. These taxes, and increased labor costs, would add nearly $19 million to the United Brands' expenses annually. The company began negotiations with the banana exporting countries to reduce the banana taxes. Soon after, a deal was made with the Honduran government to reduce the banana tax to 25 cents a crate. This was a saving of $7.5 million to the firm. In exchange, a payment of $2.5 million was to be made to Honduran government officials. News reports indicated that in September, the funds from the United Brands' foreign subsidiaries were surreptitiously deposited in the Hondurans' Swiss bank accounts.

Shortly after, during the investigation of the Watergate scandal, the story of the bribes and the involvement of top executives of United Brands became public. It was disclosed that in addition to payments to banana exporting countries, United Brands had paid $750,000 to the Italians. Concerns over these bribes and similar corporate corruptions led to the passage of the

Foreign Corrupt Practice Act of 1977. A sad note on the misdeeds of United Brands: On February 3, 1975, the United Brands' CEO, Eli Black, distressed over the publicity surrounding the payoffs, jumped to his death from his forty-fourth floor office.

Sources: P. Kihss. "44-Story Plunge Kills Head of United Brands." *The New York Times* (February 4, 1975), 1, 10; K. H. Bacon, M. Bralove, and S. J. Sansweet. "United Brands Paid Bribe of $1.25 Million to Honduran Official." *The Wall Street Journal* (April 9, 1975), 1, 23; P. Nehemkis, "Business Payoffs Abroad: Rhetoric and Reality." *California Management Review,* 18, no. 2 (Winter 1975), 5–20.

Introduction

Corruption, bribery, and the demand for large illegal payoffs are not uncommon in the international marketplace. Although the case of the United Brands' misdeeds received wide publicity, many others go unnoticed. Besides grand briberies, there is widespread petty corruption perpetuated by the functionaries at the lower levels of many government institutions. With the rising volume of international trade and increased interdependencies among nations, corruption and bribery are but two of many socioethical issues with which international managers have to deal. In addition, international managers are faced with many ecological problems stemming from worldwide industrial activities that threaten life on earth.

No other issues are more challenging to international managers than socioethical and ecological problems. The complexity and interdependency involved in the multinational company (MNC) operations spill over into the area of social responsibility as well. While the impact, obligations, and responsibilities of a domestic business are limited to its home environment, those of the MNCs cross national boundaries and create a web of interdependent and often conflicting responsibilities that are not easily resolved.

Often what appears on the surface is far from the actual reality. Each subsidiary, for example, is governed by the laws, customs, norms, and business practices of the host country. As long as a subsidiary is able to operate independently of other subsidiaries, it can meet its minimal legal, ethical, and social responsibilities by observing the local standards. Of course, these standards govern the overt behavior, leaving covert behavior to the consciences of the managers. The dilemma that international managers experience stems from the interdependency of the MNC operations. Action and decisions by a subsidiary in one country may have repercussions for the rest of the MNC. Further complications arise from the differences in norms and standards of behavior in general, and managerial behavior in specific.

Not only are there no clear answers to most of the international ethical dilemmas, there are no commonly accepted bases for resolving many legal problems of the MNCs as well. This does not mean that there is no order in international business and that international management operates chaotically. It does, however, mean that for international management there is a wider area of potential misunderstanding, disagreement, and dispute. Recently, much progress has been made to establish standards and codes of conduct to govern the MNCs' operations globally. In the following sections we review the problem areas and discuss the efforts that could lead to their resolution.

Social Responsibilities of MNCs

The term *corporate social responsibility* refers to obligations of business organizations toward society. The society allows organizations to operate within certain parameters. These parameters are defined by the society, and therefore may vary across nations. The variations, however, are typically not in substance but in procedures. Business is expected to operate in a manner consistent with the society's interests. This is true for all nations and all businesses, MNCs are no exceptions. In the United States, while some believe that the social responsibility of business is limited to the economic sphere, the majority accept that business has noneconomic obligations as well. Although the domain of corporate social responsibility is not very well defined, there are certain areas of agreement. For instance, in addition to providing employment for people and goods and services to consumers, business is expected to help preserve the environment, to sell safe products, to treat its employees equitably, and to be truthful with its customers. In some cases business is also expected to train the hard-core unemployed, contribute to education and the arts, and help revitalize urban slum areas.[1]

Obviously, there is lack of agreement, even *within* a given society, about what an organization's social responsibilities should be, and even beyond the ambiguities in domestic corporate social responsibility, there are uncertainties regarding the social responsibility of MNCs. The uncertainties are due to the differences in norms and value systems with which the MNCs must deal when they conduct business in different countries, not to mention the variations in political and economic systems they face. The uncertainty is also partly due to the fact that for domestic businesses, certain implicit and explicit codes of conduct guide managerial decision making while there is much less guidance in the international arena. Although a few international organizations have issued guidelines for some aspects of MNC activities, other aspects are very much open to the discretion of individual firms. Additionally, unique MNC characteristics are a confounding factor. The operation of an international firm spans the globe and transcends the national boundaries. As De George puts it:

A global company internalizes the worldwide division of labor and stands ready to move its operations as necessary to take advantage of lower wages, attractive interest and tax rates,

and of available resources. Such companies loosen their national roots and identification, and assume a global stance. . . . they owe primary allegiance to no particular nation. American workers have no special claim on the jobs such companies make available; and their owners are as likely to be non-American as American. Although we can still speak of Ford, General Motors, IBM, Hewlett-Packard, and Johnson & Johnson as American corporations, the sense in which they are American is becoming more and more tenuous. . . . As the corporate ability to escape national constraints increases, the need for multinational and global restraints becomes more pressing.[2]

At present, due to the lack of global constraints and guidelines, the MNC executives are forced to rely more on personal judgment and corporate policies.

Although it is very difficult to make any definitive statement about precisely what is MNC social responsibility and how it should be determined, certain positions are emerging. These positions are discussed next.

The Stakeholder Perspective

One way of analyzing MNC social responsibility is the stakeholder approach. Similar to a domestic firm, an MNC has stakeholders, those whose prosperity and fortune are directly tied to the operation of the company. Actions taken by the company will have a direct impact on its stakeholders.

Major stakeholders of a typical firm are stockholders, customers, suppliers, creditors, employees, the community within which the firm exists and from which it draws its inputs, and the general public. The firm, whether domestic or international, is responsible to its stakeholders. Each stakeholder expects, and often demands, that the firm satisfy its claim in a responsible manner. Stockholders want higher returns on their investment in the firm. Customers want good quality products that are worth their money. Suppliers depend on the firm for their continued operation and are interested in a dependable business partner. Creditors want the firm to safeguard their capital with sound business practices. Employees want jobs that are economically and psychologically rewarding and secure. The local community expects the firm to act as a good neighbor and to be a responsible member of the community through its participation and contributions to various civic causes and activities. The general public is interested in the firm's continuous contributions to the society as a whole and the assumption of fair share of the burden of government and society. The general public also wants the firm to safeguard the ecosystem through environmentally safe business practices. Often these claims are in conflict with one another. Satisfying one claim has an impact on others. Reconciliation of these claims is a difficult task.

For those aspects of the business that could reasonably be confined to a single nation, the social responsibility of an MNC and a local firm are identical. There are, however, many facets of the MNC operation for which a single nation perspective is insufficient. The business activities of the MNCs are not limited to a single country. The impact of these activities spills over the national borders. In pursuit of profit, plants are relocated, suppliers are replaced, and resources are reallocated, all of which may benefit one country while causing problems for others. From this perspective, MNC social responsibility is a broader, more complex concept than that of a domestic business. The broader concept of MNC social responsibility embraces the MNC's world citizenship.

The world corporate citizen Kenichi Ohmae tells us that MNCs are operating in the borderless world. "Over the political map, the boundaries between countries are as clear as ever. But on a competitive map, a map showing the real flows of financial and industrial activity, those boundaries have largely disappeared."[3] While local variations in tastes abound, information flow has transformed the people of the world to global citizens: They demand the best, and they buy from whoever provides the best products, regardless of whether it is an American, a British, or a Japanese firm. Supplying goods and services to these global citizens is the task of the increasing numbers of MNCs. These MNCs are "the world corporate citizens." If they owe primary allegiance to no particular country, they owe it to the people of the world and to Mother Earth.

Assuring that the MNCs fulfill their social responsibility to the world community requires guidelines or a code of conduct, and it also requires some form of regulation and monitoring. Today, no comprehensive guidelines governing MNC behavior and no global institution for monitoring them exist. Given the complexity of issues involved, it is doubtful that either will be developed soon. The monitoring aspect represents a less pressing problem. At the present time national governments are dispensing such roles. However, while developed countries are well equipped to monitor and force compliance, developing countries do not have the infrastructure to do so. In the absence of comprehensive guidelines there are several institutions, both private and governmental, that have assumed a limited role in dealing with the conduct of the MNCs. Guidelines that have been established by these institutions cover many aspects of MNC conduct. These guidelines vary in their specificity and scope, and some essentially express "ideals" toward which a firm aspires. None contains exclusively or specifically ethical guidelines.[4] Often, compliance with these codes is voluntary or indirect.

Among the institutions that have assumed leadership in promoting ethical conduct and establishing codes and guidelines are the International Chamber of Commerce (ICC), the Organization for Economic Co-operation and Development (OECD), the International Labor Organization (ILO), and the United Nations Commission on Transnational Corporations. Most nations are members of these institutions. The membership of national governments in these institutions obligates the MNCs to comply with the codes. This is an indirect type of enforcement, since there are no direct measures for ensuring compliance. The codes themselves deal both with the MNCs' behavior and the national governments' activities. Major areas that these codes cover are the relationship between national governments, the public, and the MNCs; environmental protection; consumer protection; employment practices; and human rights. MNCs are morally bound to recognize these codes and consider them in their international activities. The incentive to do so is both moral and economic.[5] Some researchers, among them McGuire, Sundgren, and Schneeweis, for example, have found a positive correlation between socially responsible corporate behavior and profitability.[6]

While we do not have comprehensive guidelines for MNC conduct, some scholars have specified certain MNC behavior as appropriate for the conduct of business in developing countries.[7] De George has suggested that MNCs should act with integrity in their dealings with the people of the world. Acting with integrity necessitates taking six steps[8]:

1. The firm should act in accord with its own self-imposed values which cannot be less than an ethical minimum, but may well exceed this. For example, a firm may neither give nor accept bribes.
2. In addition to satisfying the basic moral norms applicable everywhere, the firm should uphold other equally obvious moral rules. For example, not only does one not kill a competitor, but one also does not maim or otherwise harm that person.
3. The firm should enter into business agreements by building on these rules. Business agreements should be fair and benefit both sides.
4. Because developing countries are poor in infrastructure, MNCs have special obligations toward them. We will deal with this aspect of MNC conduct in more detail later.

5. The firm should consider the ethical dimensions of its actions, projects, and plans before acting, not afterward. This means that the ethical dimensions should be an integral part of strategic planning.
6. Each person should be given his or her due. The firm should be open and receptive to complaints from those affected and address their claims with justice.

To deal with the special case of developing countries, De George suggests seven guidelines. These rules are not supposed to form an exhaustive list. Other rules could be added to them. The rules provide the basis for conducting business with developing countries that do not have the infrastructure institutions and resources matching those of the MNCs. When operating in, and doing business with, developing countries the MNCs should:

1. Do no intentional harm. This includes respect for the integrity of the ecosystem and consumer safety.
2. Produce more good than harm for the host country.
3. Contribute by their activity to the host country's development.
4. Respect the human rights of their employees.
5. To the extent that local culture does not violate ethical norms, MNCs should respect the local culture and work with and not against it.
6. Pay their fair share of taxes.
7. Cooperate with the local government in developing and enforcing just background (infrastructure) institutions (i.e., laws, governmental regulations, unions, consumer groups, which serve as a means of social control).

By following these rules the MNCs set a high moral standard and provide a sound basis for mutually beneficial business relationships. Ignoring them negatively impacts the MNC for many years. As an example, let us apply these rules to extractive industries in developing countries. Critics have accused the MNCs of past and some present exploitation of developing countries. The charges are that the MNCs extract minerals at low costs, pay very low prices, and ship them abroad where they are sold at handsome profits. Frequently, these raw materials are processed into products that are sold back to developing counties at inflated prices. In this way, these countries are exploited twice: once when their natural resources are bought for a pittance, and the second time when the products made from them are sold back to them at higher prices than those in developed countries where competition is greater. When applied to extractive industries in developing countries, for example, the first rule obligates the MNCs to use environmentally safe extractive methods that would preserve the natural habitats and would not harm the ecosystem. In negotiation for the exploration and mining rights, the MNCs should not take advantage of the developing countries' lack of administrative capability. A contract that does not give a developing country a fair market price for these rights is clearly in violation of rule 1 and rule 2 and possibly rule 3.

Following these rules not only is moral, it is practical. Consider the case of oil-producing countries before the formation of the Organization of Oil Exporting Countries (OPEC). These countries were asserting that they were being exploited by the MNCs. The assertion of exploitation was based on the fact that the international oil companies were paying about $2 for a barrel of crude oil. According to these countries, their oil was worth much more than the artificially low price of $2 a barrel. The large international oil companies in industrial countries, acting as a cartel, collectively were imposing low prices and conditions for sale of crude oil instead of negotiating equitable agreements or allowing the market forces to prevail. To these oil-exporting countries the choice was clear: fight fire with fire. They countered by forming a cartel of their own and hiking the prices consid-

erably. This sent a shock wave throughout the world and caused much financial difficulty for all. Eventually, however, the market forces brought the prices to a level lower than OPEC desired, but considerably higher than prior to the formation of the OPEC.

Problem Areas

The most pressing social responsibility and ethics issues arising from the operations of the MNCs are the ecological impact of industrial operations, along with bribery and corruption. These issues are concerns of all nations and their resolution requires worldwide cooperation by national governments. International cooperation is also needed for the resolution of other major problems. These include exploitation of global commons,* free trade, and the special concerns of developing countries.

Ecological Concerns

The most pressing and thorny international management problem is the ecological impact of industrialization around the globe. Modern industries all affect the environment to some degree. For generations, industrialization has taken place without much concern for its environmental consequences. Industrialization can be viewed as occurring in two waves. The first wave of industrialization concerned itself only with economic development. Developed countries of today, the first group of nations to industrialize, either were not completely aware of the negative impact of industrialization on the environment or they considered the impact so negligible that they were not much worried about the consequences. Either way the course of industrialization continued unabated with minimum concern for the environment. But after decades of industrialization and economic development, the resulting adverse environmental impact is very much evident.

Global commons refers to natural resources such as the oceans, outer space, and Antarctica.

It appears that at the beginning of the twentieth century, population growth and technology had a minimum impact on the planet earth. Today, the vastly increased population and expanded industrialization are threatening earth's fragile ecosystem. Major, unintended changes are occurring around us. Human activities are radically disturbing the symbiotic relationship between the atmosphere, soil, water, plants, and animals. Desertification, deforestation, pollution, and the poverty associated with environmental degradation are posing life-threatening problems to developing countries. The disappearance of rain forests in the tropics, the loss of plant and animal species, and changes in rainfall patterns are disasters for humanity and all life on earth. Increased toxic chemicals, toxic wastes, and acidification are creating the life-threatening challenges to industrial nations. Regardless of the level of economic development and geographic location, all nations suffer from carbon dioxides and gases that are released into the atmosphere by industrialized countries. These fumes react with the ozone layer and may produce irreversible damage to the ecosystem.[9]

Effects on the ecosystem   To protect the environment and people from the unintended consequences of industrialization, the developed countries, and particularly the United States, have established numerous regulations and enacted specific "environmental" legislation. Antipollution requirements, clean air and water standards, and hazardous waste disposal guidelines are but a few of these measures. Although, these measures are useful, they are not sufficient to halt the deterioration of the environment. In developing countries, the story of environmental protection is quite different. Developing countries neither have the administrative sophistication to establish similar protective measures, nor the resources to monitor compliance with those measures. Many people in developing countries are not well informed about the health and ecological consequences of modern industries. The ignorance of the general popula-

tion and the unpreparedness of their governments leave a large exploitation potential for the unscrupulous.

Today, because of the increased knowledge about the environmental impact of industrialization, there are worldwide pressures and demands to curb the damage to the environment. The second wave of industrialization, occurring now with the industrialization of developing countries, is faced with these demands. Developing countries that are beginning to industrialize are expected not to follow the practices of the past, which were employed by the present developed countries. They are expected to use the methods that are much more environmentally friendly. Of course, deployment of these methods has a price. Many of the methods that are ecologically oriented require more investment in technology and equipment than developing countries can afford. The more urgent needs of these nations are eradication of widespread disease and poverty, employment, education, and development of an infrastructure. Without economic development, at a cost which they can afford, ecological issues may not receive proper attention. Ecological matters are luxuries beyond the reach of these nations. The irony is that the less expensive and careless exploitation of natural resources may harm the environment and deplete natural resources in such a way that result in further impoverishment. This point has not been lost on the world leaders who, in 1992, convened the Rio Conference called Earth Summit. They called for a sustainable development in which the special needs of developing countries are considered. The conference acknowledged that these countries are environmentally vulnerable and therefore deserve special priority in terms of international assistance.

Before the Earth Summit was convened, the World Commission on Environment and Development set up by the United Nations to address major challenges of the world community on environmental issues asserted that:

Ecology and economy are becoming ever more interwoven—locally, regionally, nationally, and globally—into a seamless net of causes and effects. . . . Over the past few decades, life-threatening environmental concerns have surfaced in the developing world. Countrysides are coming under pressure from increasing numbers of farmers and the landless. Cities are filling with people, cars, and factories. . . . Dryland degradation sends environmental refugees in their millions across national borders. Deforestation in Latin America and Asia is causing more floods, and more destructive floods, in downhill, downstream nations. Acid precipitation and nuclear fallout have spread across the borders of Europe. Similar phenomena are emerging on a global scale, such as global warming and loss of ozone. . . .

The recent crisis in Africa best and most tragically illustrates the ways in which economics and ecology can interact destructively and trip into disaster. Triggered by drought, its real causes lie deeper. They are to be found in part in national policies that gave too little attention, too late, to the needs of smallholder agriculture and to the threats posed by rapidly rising populations. Their roots extend also to a global economic system that takes more out of a poor continent than it puts in. Debts that they cannot pay force African nations relying on commodity sales to overuse their fragile soils, thus turning good land to desert.[10]

No matter where they take place, environmental damages resulting from industrialization and the abuse of nature spread like cancer. We all live on the same planet, breathe the same air, and drink the same water. Poorly regulated imports, for example, can bring to developed countries contaminated agricultural products grown with harmful chemicals, which are sold in the developing countries by the firms who take advantage of their less stringent or nonexistent environmental regulations. Developed and developing countries' pollution become the world's problem.

Some MNCs have established manufacturing facilities in developing counties that have more lenient or even no environmental regulations. Since they are not required to abide by the stringent requirements that are common in many industrialized nations, most of these facilities are operating at lower costs. These practices may initially save some money, but considering the associated ecological and human costs, ultimately they are indeed quite expensive. A glaring example was the Bhopal factory, a subsidiary of Union Carbide in India, and the infamous accident that cost thousands of Indian lives. While Bhopal-type accidents are exceptional and isolated violations, when they happen the resultant tragedies underline the fragility of the ecosystem.

Compared to isolated grand incidents of the abuse by the unscrupulous MNCs, environmental damage resulting from poverty, overpopulation, and ignorance is widespread and their impact on the environment is very severe. According to the World Bank, less than 2 percent of the sewage in Latin America is treated. Two-thirds of the rivers near large cities in China are so polluted that fish cannot survive in them.[11] These countries can barely feed their people, let alone worry about protecting the environment. Their ecological problems, however, do not remain localized. We are all affected by them.

The inattention to the environment, over the long run, is a luxury that not only poor countries, but all of us cannot afford. Nevertheless, the fact remains that wealth and efficient use of natural resources go together. Below a certain level of earnings, people will only be concerned with short-term survival, and postpone the issues of their long-term welfare. Therefore, economic growth is needed to combat the poverty. "A world in which poverty is endemic will always be prone to ecological and other catastrophes."[12] But over the long run, unrestrained growth that harms the environment would be a self-defeating endeavor. What is needed is a "sustainable development" that preserves "natural capital." Air, water, and other ecological treasures are natural capital that we have to pre-serve for ourselves and the future generations. Sustainable development balances the human activity with nature's ability for renewal.

To practice sustainable development, devel-oping countries need assistance from the rich countries and the MNCs. Huge investments are needed to protect the ocean resources, promote sustainable agricultural practices, control toxic wastes, and reduce the adverse impact on the climate (the Greenhouse Effect and the loss of the ozone layer). It is estimated that developing countries need $125 billion annually to imple-ment the recommendations of Earth Summit.[13] These countries not only need capital for sus-tainable development, they also need informa-tion and technology transfer to achieve and manage such development. MNCs are in the best position and have a special responsibility to provide the assistance needed. "Multinational companies can play an important role in sus-tainable development, especially as developing countries come to rely more on foreign equity capital. But if these companies are to have a positive influence on development, the negotiat-ing capacity of developing countries vis-à-vis transnationals (MNCs) must be strengthened so they can secure terms that respect their environ-mental concerns."[14] Of course MNCs cannot be relied on to provide the needed negotiating ca-pacity to developing countries. This is where the United Nations and other supranational not-for-profit organizations can be—and traditionally have been—very helpful.

One area where MNCs can contribute is technology transfer. Through technology trans-fer, MNCs can provide developing countries with the knowledge and capability for environ-mentally sound production methods. If prac-ticed properly, such technology transfer could be mutually beneficial. Many case examples at-test to the practicality and profit potential of technology transfer that is environmentally friendly. In Poland, for example, mining opera-tions employ 700,000 people, and coal exports

constitute 10 percent of hard-currency revenues. Coal also provides 90 percent of domestic en-ergy consumption. The operation of its mines, however, is polluting the Polish rivers and caus-ing serious ecological harm. The Axel Johnson Group of Stockholm, Sweden, a worldwide trading, distribution, and retailing firm, supplied the Polish mines with antipollution technology. A total investment of $60 million provided a consortium of Polish companies with the needed technology including water purification and desalination equipment. The treatment of dirty, saltwater produces freshwater and salt, both of which are sold commercially. The tech-nology not only eliminates water pollution, it can generate nearly $9 million in additional rev-enues.[15]

Use of global commons   Developing coun-tries have long complained about their relation-ship with developed countries. They assert the relationship is more favorable to developed countries. They feel that rich nations are taking advantage of their lack of technological sophis-tication. Developing countries claim that not only their natural resources are exploited to the benefit of industrialized countries, the global commons are exploited disproportionately by the MNCs from rich nations. The global com-mons most in contention are the oceans, outer space, and Antarctica. At the present time, the ability to exploit these resources is limited to the MNCs from developed countries. As more na-tions industrialize and develop technological ca-pabilities, the rate of use will increase. The con-sequences of unrestricted exploitation of these resources can be disastrous.

The oceans.   "In the Earth's wheel of life, the oceans provide the balance. . . . they play a critical role in maintaining its life-support sys-tems, in moderating its climate, and in sustain-ing animals and plants. . . . The oceans also provide the ultimate sink for the by-products of human activities. Huge closed septic tanks, they receive wastes from cities, farms, and indus-tries. . . ."[16] We have to devise ways of pro-

tecting the oceans from excessive contamination and abuse. The rich fishing areas and the
large deposits of minerals under the seas are the
source of many grievances among nations.
Many of these minerals are far from the limits
of territorial waters. Without an international
ecosystem approach to protect the oceans from
excessive exploitation, contamination and abuse
may endanger life as we know it on earth.

Many nations claim three-mile coastal territorial waters, and do not allow outsiders within
that limit. Some have adopted a 200-mile
Exclusive Economic Zone (EEZ). The United
Nations Convention on Law of the Sea, has
given this expanded territorial zone its blessing.
Even when the 200-mile EEZ is accepted by all
nations, the oceans and much of the undersea
minerals fall outside this limit. Until there is an
international agreement for mining the seabed,
disputes and disagreement will rise. Who owns
this wealth? How should it be tapped? At what
rate should the ocean floor wealth be exploited?
The U.N. Convention on Law of the Sea has a
provision for creating an International Seabed
Authority. The authority would control all mining activities in the seabed beyond the 200-mile
EEZs. This is the most ambitious attempt ever
to provide an internationally agreed regime for
the management of the oceans, and to prevent
overexploitation. So far, 159 countries have
signed the convention, and 32 nations have ratified it. A small number of nations had indicated
that they are unlikely to ratify it. Without an international treaty, the danger of overexploitation
and life-threatening abuse of the oceans may
continue.[17]

At the present time capital requirements and
technological barriers limit the exploitation of
the oceans. Today, only a few nations have the
technology and resources to exploit deep sea
minerals. In 1994, for example, Shell Oil successfully drilled an oil well in the Auger field, at
a water depth of 2,860 feet, 137 miles south of
Louisiana shoreline. Not too many companies
can match the technological sophistication and

the capital needed for such an operation. Deep-
water drilling is not cheap. The Auger platform
cost some $780 million and required work by
740 American companies and 33 foreign contractors. The deck is the size of two football
fields and weighs about 23,000 tons. It houses
132 workers and supervisors in a five-story dor-
mitory.[18]

While today only a few companies and
fewer nations can accomplish what the Shell
company is doing, this exclusivity will not last
long. As more nations join the ranks of industrialized countries, they may participate in the exploitation of natural resources beyond their own
territories. At such time, the MNCs' operations
may not go uncontested. Without the international treaties covering exploration and exploitation of deep sea minerals and fishing,
simple problems could easily develop into full-
scale conflicts. A few years ago such a conflict
arose in the South Pacific.

Similar to the United States and some other
countries, the island nations of Solomons,
Kiribati, and Vanuatu have all claimed exclusive
economic zones of 200 miles around their
coasts. This is mainly to protect the tuna fish in
their coastal waters. Tuna fish is to them what
oil is to Saudi Arabia. It is a major natural resource. However, these countries do not have
navies to protect their coasts. This fact has not
gone unnoticed by the fishing vessels from other
countries, and they often fish around these islands with impunity. The country that these is-
landers are most bitter about is the United States.
Americans have long fished in the Pacific
coastal waters, and see no reason to stop. A few
years ago, an American fishing vessel was spot-
ted by a light aircraft flying around the
Solomon's exclusive zone. Unconcerned about
its violation, the vessel continued fishing, fully
aware that there is no force to stop it.
Coincidentally, a privately owned Australian pa-
trol boat was in the Solomons on a sales demonstration tour. Tally ho! The Solomons crew of
armed police on the Australian boat arrested the

astonished U.S. "pirate." The Solomons fined the owner and impounded the boat. In retaliation, the U.S. stopped importing Solomon fish, a major part of its export trade. The American sanction infuriated the Solomons. Eventually, a compromise was reached whereby the fishing vessel was sold back to its original owner for $700,000, and the U.S. trade sanction was lifted.[19]

Outer space. Telecommunication and the use of space are other areas of contention between the rich and the poor countries. As new technologies are developed, international management will have to deal with additional difficulties. Radio-frequencies and space are becoming crowded. Every day a new satellite is launched into space to orbit the earth. These satellites are used for various purposes, from weather forecasting to crop estimation to telecommunication. In particular, the use of a geostationary orbit 22,300 miles above the equator is a hotly contested property in space. Competition for the available positions and frequencies in space is resulting in resentment on earth. Most of the satellites belong to the Western world, Russia, and Japan. Except for a few nations, developing countries have no satellites, and many fear that the geostationary orbit will be crowded by the time they have the technology or the money to launch them. A satellite in the geostationary orbit travels at the earth's rotational speed, and therefore is a fixed target for radio signals. At a lower or higher orbit, satellites go faster or slower than the rotational speed of the earth. The physical position is not as important as the frequencies used by these satellites. Overlapping and garbling of radio beams carrying messages to and from the earth can happen in crowded locations. Every country is interested in positioning satellites in the geostationary orbit. The question is on what basis the orbital positions and frequencies should be allocated. Developed countries favor the first come, first served basis, while developing countries would like rationing the available frequencies and orbital positions.[20]

Antarctica. Antarctica is a desolate and inhospitable place. Extreme cold and heavy winds create a very hostile environment for life. The coldest continent, Antarctica's temperature can reach below -88 degrees Celsius (-126 degrees Fahrenheit). Winds of up to 200 miles per hour create extremely dangerous conditions. It has a very harsh environment where a person without protective gear can freeze to death in a few moments.

Except for a few bird species, especially the penguins, and a few scientific expeditions, no one would dare to venture into this frigid land. Yet, there are global ownership disputes over Antarctica. The seven nations of Argentina, Australia, Chile, France, Great Britain, Norway, and New Zealand have made territorial claims on Antarctica. These claims, however, are not recognized by other nations.

Because of the extreme cold and its isolation from the rest of the world, Antarctica's geological composition is not well known. It is believed, however, that it has large deposits of mineral resources. Coal and iron deposits are estimated to be large enough to be worth commercial exploitation. Antarctica's continental shelf may contain large deposits of oil and natural gas. The waters surrounding Antarctica support a rich marine life including krill, a tiny shrimp-like animal. Large numbers of whales around Antarctica feed on these creatures.

Scientific and commercial interest in Antarctica has prompted many debates. Since 1959, it has been managed under the Antarctic Treaty that was signed by representatives of 12 nations in Washington, D.C. The treaty dedicated the entire continent to scientific and peaceful purposes. It suspended all territorial claims. In 1991, a protocol to the treaty was approved by 24 nations prohibiting exploration for oil and other minerals for at least 50 years. The treaty is open to all nations who can demonstrate concrete interest in Antarctica by conducting substantial scientific research.

The present arrangement and the Treaty on Antarctica are considered unacceptable by many developing countries. Many developing countries lack the resources and technology to participate in the scientific exploration of Antarctica. While the treaty signatories claim to manage the continent in the interest of all people, developing countries assert that these interests should not be defined by self-appointed parties. It is, however, highly unlikely that we will see the commercialization of Antarctica any time soon. Legal ambiguities, and technological barriers, not to mention the enormous investment needed, make commercial endeavors close to impossible at the present time.

Bribery and Corruption

Often, in the course of doing business and carrying out normal daily transactions abroad, there is no escaping encounters dealing with bribery and corruption. Bribery and corruption are facts of doing business in many places. No geographic location or country has a monopoly on corruption. Business and political scandals in the United States, Europe, and Japan are testimony to this fact. The practice, however, is pervasive in some countries. Publicity around illicit payments by the U.S.-based MNCs in the mid-1970s, which culminated in the passage of the Foreign Corrupt Practice Act of 1977, and the Japanese political scandal of the early 1990s may give the impression that corruption is on the rise. In reality, business and government practices have never been so closely monitored by the people and the media. It follows, therefore, that corruption probably is on the wane. Certainly, a reading of the history of the world provides some encouraging notes that our time is not unique in the course of civilization. Polybius, the Greek historian living in the sec-

How to Deal with Petty Extortionists

Here is some advice from an international traveler who would gladly spend $100 to avoid paying a $20 bribe—if there is a chance of succeeding. In some situations there are no ways to avoid the illicit payments short of abandoning whatever you were trying to do. For example, if you want to leave the west central African country of Cameroon, the choice is to give the border guard the $20 he demands or else stay in Cameroon for God knows how long.

If you are going to pay the illicit money they demand of you, do it right. Never admit it is a bribe. Say you understand that your case requires additional efforts on the part of the official and you are willing to pay a fee for the extra work.

Do not be afraid to haggle and bargain. If you bargain, you often wind up paying less than what was initially demanded.

Never be rude and insult the functionaries, even though this may make you feel better. You may be arrested for that, and end up paying much more, not to mention the time lost in the process.

Under the right circumstances ask for a receipt. This may scare the extortionists and expedite your case. Otherwise, back home you could present the receipt to their consulate and demand a refund. Be ready to have a good laugh anyhow if your receipt turns out to be like the one the international traveler got from a Chinese policeman written in Chinese. Back in the United States it was translated to mean "stick it in your ear."

Adapted from Jim Rogers's advice to Stratford Sherman, which appeared in "Mr. Rogers Takes His Dream Trip." *Fortune* (February 24, 1992), 104–10.

ond century B.C., summarized Carthage's decline in a single sentence: "At Carthage nothing that results in profit is regarded as disgraceful." During the Renaissance, corruption was rampant, and business historian Jacob van Kalveren suggested that sixteenth- and seventeenth-century Europe should be characterized not as the age of mercantilism but as the age of corruption.[21]

Besides the harmful effect on the moral fabric of the society, corruption has economical costs. The bribes that bureaucrats receive to approve licenses inflate business costs. Tax officials who take bribes and allow income to go unreported deprive the national treasuries of significant revenues. Government officials who purchase expensive equipment with foreign aid money to receive a kickback from the seller divert resources from useful projects into useless ones. The real cost of corruption must also include the loss of confidence in the system and the stifling of entrepreneurial initiatives. The cost of bribes and illegal payments, for example, has been estimated to be 3 to 5 percent in China. Based on the 1993 foreign investment of $100 billion, this would be $3 to $5 billion. In Italy, it is estimated that corruption has inflated the total outstanding government debt by as much as 15 percent, or about $200 billion. A few years ago the Chinese government reported that state assets had fallen by more than $50 billion in value. They attributed this primarily to deliberate undervaluation by corrupt officials who were trading off big properties to private interests or to overseas investors for payoffs.[22]

There are two types of bribes, the whitemail bribe, and the lubrication bribe or "speed money." The lubrication bribe is to facilitate the process of normal bureaucratic functioning, such as the processing of a visa, clearing import papers, and issuing a driver's license. It does not involve any act that is not allowed by law. It is facilitation money without which the delay could disrupt normal business functions and therefore be costly. The lubrication bribe has al-

most been institutionalized in some developing countries. Everybody does it and everyone expects it. It is referred to in various parts of the world by various terms. In West Africa it is "dash," in Mexico "mordida" (the bite), in the Honduras "pajada" (a piece of the action), in Brazil "jeitinho (the fix), in some former British colonies in Asia "kumshaw" (thank you), and in the Middle East "bakhshesh" or "an-aam" (gift).

While lubrication money is paid to low-level bureaucrats, the whitemail bribe is elicited by high-level government officials. There are also other differences between the two types of bribes. The differences are in the method and the amount of payment, and the outcome. Lubrication money is relatively small and takes place directly between the client and the functionary for the purpose of starting the bureaucratic wheel rolling. Except for the payment, it involves no illegal act. The whitemail bribe involves large money and generally includes an elaborate system for concealing it. The recipients of whitemail are high-level government officials, and often it involves illegal transactions. Because of their illegality, the MNCs making these payments hide them with false accounting, fictitious bookkeeping entries, and bogus documentation. Sometimes payments are funneled through subsidiaries abroad, as consulting fees. In other cases, for example, in Italy and in South Korea, these payments take the form of contributions to political parties. Often, the whitemail bribe takes place with the assistance of a go-between who acts in other capacities too and helps to bridge the cultural gap. As Nehmkis suggested, if the Middle East's intermediaries didn't exist, they would have to be invented. For the Western business executives, the intermediaries are useful in many ways: they overcome the formidable language barriers and facilitate getting access into the power centers. Many Middle East rulers are still suspicious of, and uneasy with, financial and business transactions with foreigners. Moreover, in the Middle East, the network of powerful families is the repository of economic, financial, and political intelligence. The West does not have a equivalent system with which to compare them. Those with connections with these powerful families can provide a sense of confidence for the organizations that deal with foreigners.[23]

Evidence suggests that the MNCs are both the victim and the culprit of corruption. To combat bribery and corruption, the MNC executives should take certain steps. The first recommendation is to reject flatly the practice of bribery. Indulging in bribery has a corrosive effect on the business and the people. Respond to the suggestions and demands for illegal payments that you have a great respect for your counterpart, and you risk prosecution under the law if you pay. When a West African minister, for example, during a break in a negotiation session, poetically told a U.S. executive that the minister was "the first tree in the forest and needed water," the American replied in friendly but blunt terms, "If I pay you, I will go to jail." Considering the personal relationship they had developed during the negotiations, the official certainly would not want to see that happen.[24] If you are asked to do something that violates your moral beliefs, or your company's code of ethics, or is against the law, do not do it. There is an advantage in gaining a reputation as a person who will not make moral compromises.

Sometimes it is possible to please the government officials with worthy community projects instead of a bribe. Building a school, a road, a sport facility for the youths for which a bureaucrat can take the credit for its construction could go a long way in securing the government contract that otherwise would have been denied. Finally, keep in mind that in many cultures gifts and payments are an essential part of building relationships between persons and groups. To reject abruptly and moralistically any suggested request for a gift may be interpreted as a rejection of the relationship that the other side considers necessary to doing business with you.[25] As De George reminds us, ". . . ba-

sic morality does not vary from country to country, even though certain practices may be ethical in one country and not in another because of differing circumstances. Getting this subtle difference straight is the crux of the matter."[26]

While corruption is widespread internationally, it is more prevalent in developing countries. Why is corruption so rampant in many developing countries? One explanation, of course, is simple human greed, and the breakdown of moral values. Some argue that the low salaries of government workers are partly responsible for widespread bribery in most developing countries. While no two nations are similar, poor countries that pay subsistence level salaries to government bureaucrats are sowing the seed of corruption. Without sufficient income, when opportunities for generating additional money arise, not too many functionaries can resist the temptation. This is especially the case in many developing countries, where people make a distinction between morality and law. In their view, delaying paperwork for a wealthy foreign company to extract a fee may be illegal but is not an evil act. Another explanation takes into account cultural differences and value orientations. What one culture considers normal facilitation of business transaction another considers a bribe.

Many issues that make sense in one culture, when viewed through a different cultural perspective, would appear inappropriate and sometimes even wrong. The following anecdote vividly illustrates the cultural differences regarding ethical concerns.

> The cannibal was having a conversation with an educated and sophisticated man from the Western world. The Westerner asked him, "How exactly do you go about finding your food?" "When we run out of food," answered the cannibal, "we declare war on a neighboring tribe. We kill as many people as we want, bring them back and eat them. How about you? I heard that there was a huge war in your part of the world a few years ago. How many did you

Corporate Taxes: The Italian-Style

A leading American bank opened a subsidiary in a major Italian city. At the end of the first year of operation, the firm's local lawyers and tax accountants advised the bank to file its tax return "Italian-style," meaning to understate its actual profit significantly. The American general manager of the bank, who was in his first assignment abroad, refused to do so because he considered it dishonest and unacceptable. A few months after filing its "American-style" tax return, the bank was invited to discuss its taxes with Italian tax authorities. They suggested that the bank's taxes were at least three times higher. It is a customary practice that Italian corporations understate their profits by anywhere between 30 to 70 percent. Italian tax authorities aware of this practice usually assess taxes owned by the corporations based on what they assume the actual earning should be. Of course, this amount is open to negotiation, which opens up room for the work of tax negotiation agents called *commercialista*. The *commercialista's* fee, a lump sum, is included in the payment to the government, the *bustarella*. Corporations never learn how much of the money paid was *bustarella* and how much was the fee. The total amount, however, is a deductible expense on the firm's tax return for the next year.

Source: Adapted from A. L. Kelly. "Case Study—Italian Tax Mores." In Thomas Donaldson, ed. *Case Studies in Business Ethics* (Englewood Cliffs, NJ: Prentice Hall, 1984), 14–7.

kill?" Visibly embarrassed, the Westerner said, "Millions." "Wow!" the cannibal could not hide his surprise. "And did you eat them all?" "Certainly not! We do not eat people," answered the shocked companion. It was the cannibal's turn to look surprised and confused, even a little disgusted. With a puzzled voice he inquired "What a waste, why did you kill them in the first place then?"[27]

If bribery were the rule that everyone followed, it would cease to be bribery, and instead become a cost of doing a certain kind of business. Tipping in the United States is an example. It is widely and openly practiced. While tipping is customary in the United States, it is considered demeaning and insulting in other countries. Similarly, in some countries civil servants are known to earn a part of their salaries from the small payments made by the clients. These payments ensure better and more timely service. Since Americans do not tip civil servants this does not mean the practice is wrong everywhere. The distinction may involve prevalence

of the practice and the openness with which it is followed. Unless, the payment is truly a common and open practice, it is ethically questionable.[28]

Lobbying is another example of an action that is sanctioned in one country but frowned on in others. Lobbying legislators and government agencies is an accepted legal practice in the United States. Some other nations consider it influence peddling and mislabeling of buying votes and favors. Table 16.1 provides a list of foreign governments and the amount of money they spent on lobbying in 1992. Japan is on the top of the list of the countries that spend the most money on lobbying in the United States. Why do the Japanese spend so much money? Some say that Japanese want to tie up the country's talented trade lawyers, making them unavailable for cases that are brought against them. Others say that Japanese take a long view of their relationship with Washington and are well aware that today's lawyer may be tomorrow's senior official. Formerly representing

Table 16.1
The Money Foreigners Spent Lobbying America, 1992

Country	Million $
Japan	60.434
Canada	22.710
Germany	13.140
France	12.857
Mexico	11.046
Hong Kong	10.046
Kuwait	9.522
Taiwan	8.309
Australia	8.308
Ireland	7.829
Indonesia	7.398
United Arab Emirates	6.890
Britain	6.775
Netherlands	3.945
Israel	3.771
Austria	3.654
Turkey	3.337
Sweden	3.109
Brazil	3.090
Venezuela	2.999
Saudi Arabia	2.709
South Korea	2.708
Scotland	2.363
Angola	2.326
Singapore	2.316
Italy	2.107
Colombia	1.600
Bermuda	1.541
U.S.S.R./Russia	1.541
Poland	1.323

Source: *The New York Times* (November 2, 1993), A1. The original data is from the Justice Department.

Japan, these officials might be more sympathetic toward the Japanese views and more inclined to support their interests. "When you represent the Japanese, and your source of income is Japanese, your perceptions change," a former Japanese lobbyist noted.[29]

There are other reasons for rampant corruption in developing countries too. Kolde,[30] for example, has traced the cultural and historical roots of bureaucratic corruption and bribery in some developing countries to the clashes of cultures and colonial legacy.

Many developing countries were colonies of the West. Kolde asserts that confused loyalties, weak identification with nationhood, and a lack of internal cohesion are common to most ex-colonies. In these countries, under the rule of Western powers, tribes were not integrated into nations. They were kept in tribal minisovereignties. To prevent the formation of anticolonial coalitions among tribes, intertribe conflicts and rivalries were fomented and cultivated. When these ex-colonies gained their independence, they lacked the substance of nationhood. The problem was confounded by the fact that the Western powers did rule indirectly through native chieftains and community elders. These native leaders were, therefore, viewed by the general population as the agents of the colonizing authority. Their traditional authority and legitimacy was weakened in the eyes of the local people. Upon independence the traditional sources of social order were not in place.

Moreover, Western legal systems that were superimposed on the tribal structures resulted in the breakdown of the discipline of indigenous society. In these societies, legal technicalities and multitudes of regulations replaced simple honesty and personal accountability, which in most preindustrial societies serve as the main instrument of order and control. Many of these regulations were a matter of relabeling and redefinition of the old practices. If previously witchcraft was sanctioned by the indigenous system as legitimate, for example, the newly imported law declared it a crime. Gift giving to chiefs and elders was not only considered right and proper by the natives, but purifying and sanctifying. But these were declared to be bribes by the imported Western law. Moreover, to deal with the natives, the foreign rulers relied on the go-betweens. The go-betweens, while themselves natives, had learned the way of the rulers, and often were the lawyer-translator-opportunist who exploited the ignorance of both the rulers and the ruled.

The Colonial Legacy

They are tall and narrow featured, and during the colonial era in central Africa, the Tutsi were among Africa's most remarkable elites. While they numbered only a small minority among the majority Hutu, the Tutsi not only administered Rwanda and neighboring Burundi, but the Germans and, later, the Belgians celebrated them with a kind of Wagnerian romanticism, assuring them the best kind of jobs and favored treatment. . . .

[A]fter the Belgians left Africa and Rwanda began to grapple with the uncertainty and turbulence of majority rule, the Tutsi sinecure unraveled. Tribal uprising among the Hutu singled out the Tutsi for reprisal; hundreds of thousands fled, tens of thousands were massacred. . . . Beyond central Africa, . . . much of the developing world has been struggling for nearly half a century to come to terms with grinding ethnic and tribal rivalries that remain, in a way, one of the most enduring legacies of their colonial past. . . .

For the French or the British or the Germans, the tendency to settle and show favoritism on one group among many underscored, at heart, a practical and economic necessity: to administer their far-flung holdings, the European powers needed locals to rule in their place. . . . In superimposing what in some cases was a new hierarchy atop an existing social system, colonialism gave a new shape and tension to relationships between different ethnic groups, even if it did not reorder them entirely. . . . In some ways, the very tribalism or contemporary ethnic politics in northern India or parts of Africa were, at root, European inventions. . . .

Excerpted from W. E. Schmidt. "One Chosen, Tribal Elites Now Suffer Consequences." *The New York Times* (April 17, 1994), E3. Copyright © 1994 by the New York Times Company. Reprinted by permission.

When the independence came, the colonial legacy was often a lawyer-ridden bureaucratic system deluged with favoritism and corruption. Highly repugnant to the native population, this colonial inheritance greatly increased the difficulty of building confidence between the new national government and the people. . . . National authorities have had but modest success in restructuring this colonial legacy and in changing public perceptions of government.[31]

The Issue of Free Trade

The premise of expanding international trade is that all participants will benefit from it. To increase international trade, we have to remove barriers to free trade. To begin to remove trade barriers, bilateral and multilateral trade agreements have been established. The most important multilateral trade agreements take place under the auspices of the General Agreement on Tariffs and Trade (GATT). These agreements are aimed at reducing tariff and nontariff trade barriers.

Free trade and open markets have consequences for domestic industries. Foreign competition forces inefficient domestic businesses out of the market and out of being. This creates displacement of jobs in the host country. Over the long run, most analysts believe that the resultant efficiency creates more jobs, but in the short run there will be pockets of unemployment in declining industries. The short-run consequences put pressure on the host country's government to protect inefficient industries. Based on trade agreements, government cannot protect inefficient domestic firms against effi-

Transparency International

There is a high cost to bribery and corruption. Under-the-table payments increase the cost of doing business and lower the morale without adding any value to the outcome. Often, the outcome is lower quality products and services at higher costs. Development banks have known this for a long time. The beneficiaries of the bribery are corrupt government officials and foreign firms who acquiesce to it. It is estimated that some African leaders, for example, have accumulated more than $20 billion in Swiss bank accounts by setting up useless or phony projects with the help of unscrupulous MNC executives. The sole purpose of these projects is to siphon out money borrowed from foreign sources.

Having observed such practices for long, Peter Eigen, a former official of the World Bank, has started a new, nonprofit organization called Transparency International (TI). TI held its inaugural meeting in Berlin, on May 1993. It is dedicated to combating "grand" corruption that usually takes place at the highest level of government in some countries with the MNCs involvement.

TI is modeled after Amnesty International. As the name stands, TI wants business transactions to take place in a more "transparent" and, therefore, honest fashion. The members pledge to fight bribe-assisted business transactions. Among TI members are government officials and the MNCs who are interested in fighting corruption. American MNCs such as General Electric and Boeing are among the early members and supporters of TI. Since passage of the Foreign Corrupt Practice Act in 1977, American companies have been at a competitive disadvantage with other MNCs. While the act forbids the U.S. firms to participate in illegal payments, it cannot prevent corrupt actions by other MNCs, which may be getting business contracts through illicit means. The officials of TI are convinced that the membership will expand because everyone sees the destructive impact of corruption on the business, and the benefit of stamping it out by joining TI.

Sources: K. Pennar. "A New Globo-Cop for Crooks in High Places." *Business Week* (December 6, 1993), 136; and "Clean, Not Laundered." *The Economist* (May 8, 1993), 78.

cient foreign competition by tariffs. Some governments, however, use less obvious measures such as subsidies to domestic firms and regulations and tariffs on foreign companies. These measures make it very difficult for foreign firms to establish footholds in the country. There are other problems too. Environmental protection measures are not uniform around the world. In countries with more stringent regulations, industries are forced to invest in capital equipment for ecologically cleaner production. Such an investment adds to the production costs, and puts these businesses at a competitive disadvantage against firms from other countries with less

demanding regulations or no regulations at all. GATT, which was initially established to solve tariff and nontariff barriers, now has to deal with these problems as well.

General Agreement on Tariffs and Trade
The GATT is a multilateral agreement setting out rules for the conduct of international trade. It was founded in 1948 on a provisional basis to make rules for the conduct of trade among its members. A parallel organization, the International Trade Organization (ITO), was set up to enforce those rules. However, the charter for the ITO was never ratified, leaving the GATT as an interim agreement. The goals of the agreement

Invisible Trade Barriers

For many years American and European companies have complained that the Japanese market is closed to foreigners. While there are not many visible barriers for trading with Japan, invisible obstacles are many. Often foreign businesses, and particularly Americans, are blamed for not trying hard enough and giving up easily when they face difficulties in Japan. While this might be true, experience is a very powerful teacher. The American construction firms, for example, after many attempts and apparent success at the beginning, learned that the clubby environment of the industry in Japan cannot be penetrated. By a gentleman's agreement foreigners are excluded from the construction industry. Then, why try at all? In retailing the story is totally different. A tightly controlled Byzantine distribution system keeps foreign competition out of many consumer products and inflates prices to consumers. The laws that are designed to protect thousands of small shops prevent the establishment of discount stores and supermarkets. A foreign competitor faces a very difficult task cracking the system. Because of long-standing exclusive agreements between the wholesalers and retailers it is almost impossible to find a distributor. There are many layers to this distribution system, and products change many hands before they get to the final consumer. Each layer adds more to the price of the product without adding any value to it. For example, one pint of ice cream that costs less than $3 in New York is more than $8 in Tokyo, or an AM/FM cassette player that is less than $40 in New York costs more than $200 in Tokyo. A women's scarf purchased by an import agent for $30 is sold to a wholesaler for $60. The wholesaler then sells it to a department store for $90, which charges the consumer $160 for it. How could an exporter build a customer base with a $160 scarf?

Sources: J. Sterngold. "Making Japan Cheaper for the Japanese." *The New York Times* (August 29, 1993), E6; D. E. Sanger. "Discounting Finally Makes It to Japan." *The New York Times* (October 11, 1993), D1, D2; L. W. Tuller. *Going Global: New Opportunities for Growing Companies to Compete in World Markets* (Homewood, IL: Richard D. Irwin, 1991); J. M. Schlesinger. "U.S. Contractors Find They Rarely Get Work on Projects in Japan." *The Wall Street Journal* (June 10, 1991), A1, A9.

---

are to create a more predictable environment for international trade and to liberalize trade so that investment, job creation, and trade can flourish.

As an interim arrangement, GATT has been very successful. The objective of GATT was the elimination of trade tariffs. Under its auspices governments cut the average tariff on manufactured goods from 40 percent in 1947 to an average of approximately 5 percent in 1991. GATT operates on the basis of three guiding principles[32]:

1. *Reciprocity:* If one country lowers its barriers to another country it can expect the other country to lower its barriers in return.

2. *Nondiscrimination:* Countries should not grant one GATT member or group of members preferential trade treatment over the others. This is also known as the most favored nation rule.

3. *Transparency:* GATT urges countries to replace nontariff barriers with tariffs, and then to bind these tariffs by promising not to raise them in the future. This is to replace hidden barriers, which are difficult to measure, with those that are transparent to all and easy to estimate their costs. While foreign firms could defeat tariff barriers through efficiency, they could not overcome nontariff obstacles through improved productivity.

Operating together, the combination of these principles forms a powerful combination. Theoretically, if one country lowers its barriers to another in order to gain access to that country's markets (reciprocity) it must then lower its barriers to all such imports regardless of which GATT country they come from (nondiscrimination). This leads to further reductions in tariffs as additional countries are obliged to reciprocate. GATT "insures that any initial spark of liberal intentions is fanned into a healthy flame."[33]

So far there have been seven agreements under the GATT, each called a *round*. The eighth round, the Uruguay round, was concluded in December 1993. When ratified it will become the eighth agreement.

The Uruguay round. It took seven years to conclude the Uruguay round of GATT, the most ambitious of the eight rounds to date. It began in 1986 at Punta del Este, Uruguay, and ended in a signing ceremony attended by 120 government delegations in January 1994 in Marakesh (Morocco). Its aim was to reduce all remaining tariffs by 30%, to tighten up the rules, and to extend them into areas not previously covered. These areas included services, trade-related intellectual property rights (TRIPs), trade-related investments and mergers (TRIMs), and agriculture. The general strategy of the talks was that the rich countries would liberalize trade restrictions and tariffs on agriculture and textiles, and thus developing countries would be the principal beneficiaries. The developing countries, in return, would open their markets to rich country providers of services and capital and furnish better protection of intellectual property rights.[34] Other subjects negotiated were subsidies, antidumping safeguards, dispute settlement, and nontariff measures.

GATT will become the World Trade Organization (WTO) when it is ratified by the members. WTO is intended to be more powerful than GATT. It incorporates trade in goods, services, and ideas and has more binding authority. GATT was never more than a provisional set of

rules with a small office in Geneva. The WTO will be the umbrella organization covering the old GATT and all the new agreements reached in the Uruguay round. A key part of the new organization will be its dispute settlement procedures, which was supposed to be the original role of ITO. Unlike GATT, which had no effective way to impose sanctions on the violators and suffered from continual delays and blockages, the WTO will have a dispute settlement panel and an appeals body. If the reports of the panel are challenged, the appeals body makes a final and binding judgment. The judgments of the appeals body will have to be implemented within a reasonable period. Sanctions can be imposed against the recalcitrant country.

Criticisms of GATT. Critics of GATT cite several shortcomings. They charge that GATT's 1940s era assumptions have become largely irrelevant to the world economy of today. There is a growing school of pragmatic thought which holds that the real world does not act like a computer-generated economic model. As economist Pat Choate notes, "In world trade, you're dealing with a messy political, as well as economic, system at both ends of the transaction. It's naive and unrealistic to conduct real world policy based on theory of economic advantage that says one free trade shoe fits every country."[35]

According to Prestowitz, Tonelson, and Jerome,[36] there are three problems concerning GATT. First, the global preeminence of the United States has significantly eroded. They argue that it was the U.S. strength and its ability to impose its views on its trading partners that gave the system its early vitality. In the 1950s and 1960s the overwhelming U.S. economic strength in virtually all key industries combined with the geopolitical motive of containing Communism combined to create momentum for a stable and prosperous free world. This also allowed the United States to absorb the costs of world economic leadership and unequal trade liberalization in the name of GATT progress.

Second, the shift of GATT's focus from its early tariff cutting to eliminating nontariff barriers caused members to retreat into intractable conflicts over their sovereign rights. Each nation insisted on setting its own economic and social priorities. Third, the basic underlying principles such as "national treatment" and "most favored nation" are inherently disadvantageous to the most liberal and open societies. Under "national treatment" a government agrees to treat foreign businesses exactly as it treats domestic companies. In exchange other GATT countries agree to do the same. The problem is that the treatment afforded firms—whether domestic or foreign— varies widely among nations. For example, there are major differences in the treatment of antitrust regulations, bureaucratic intervention, and industrial targeting policies between the governments of the United States and Korea.

There are similar problems with most favored nation status. According to GATT rules of nondiscrimination, any liberal concessions negotiated between two countries must be extended to all other member countries. This means that the latter countries can pick up the benefits from the liberalization of the first two countries while keeping their concessions at a minimum. The results of these problems are that companies from restrictive countries will penetrate the more liberal countries' markets over a period of time.[37]

Other charges against the GATT system are more specific in nature. Critics charge that the GATT system is based on the economic concept of comparative advantage. The traditional paradigm based a country's advantage on relatively static factors such as natural resources, labor, and capital inputs. Today, the ability to innovate and adapt, diffuse, and implement technologies is the key to competitiveness. Comparative advantage is now governed largely by microelectronics, information, and technology, and is much more dynamic.[38]

Another charge against the GATT system is that it has been unable to eliminate the increased use of nontariff measures for creating barriers to foreign competition. Tariff barriers are transparent, and few argue GATT's effectiveness against these protectionist policies. However, the most popular instruments of modern protectionist policy take a variety of other forms. These policies include the various forms of research and development subsidies. R&D support for domestic producers gives them advantages in the global market and can distort trade as much as protectionist barriers. Other methods include so-called "gray area measures." These can take the form of voluntary export measures (VERs), orderly marketing arrangements (OMAs), voluntary import expansion (VIEs), or antidumping rules. Critics charge that the GATT system is largely ineffective against these types of protectionist policies.

Another problem with the system of institutionalized trade talks is that the system encourages countries to keep barriers as bargaining chips. GATT is even being attacked on environmental grounds. Ralph Nader recently told Congress that GATT was a "radical deregulation of consumer and environmental standards around the world." Friends of the Earth, Greenpeace, and Public Citizen have even sued to force the U.S. trade representative to conduct an environmental impact statement before proceeding with the GATT talks.[39]

Pro-GATT arguments. The pro-GATT side charges that the world's extraordinary economic progress since World War II owes much to international trade, and that, in turn, owes nearly everything to GATT. The pro-GATT forces charge that the increase in bilateral and unilateral negotiations will undermine, if not ruin, all that GATT has accomplished, and lead the world into another protectionist era similar to that of the 1930s. Proponents of GATT point out that national attempts to control trade through nontariff mechanisms, especially subsidies, cannot prevail in the long run. They are undesirable because they tend to make domestic producers less competitive internationally.[40]

The pro-GATT camp charges that GATT has always been a good tool, and now that the developing countries are coming around to free trade, it can work better than ever. Supporters of GATT argue that if governments are genuinely interested in free trade, they can use the existing GATT to promote it. Moreover, in that case, regional free-trade deals, such as NAFTA, need not pose a threat to liberalization across a broader front. If, on the other hand, governments doubt the case for free trade, they will use whatever trading arrangements are at hand in a search for strategic advantage, or to satisfy special interests. At the end of this road lies mismanaged trade—with or without GATT, with or without regional trading blocks.[41]

Proponents of GATT argue that free trade enriches everyone, and that prosperity is the best defense against resurgent totalitarianism or authoritarianism. Peace and prosperity go hand in hand, and peace is better than war. The Canadian ambassador to the GATT spoke for many when he commented that: "The GATT is a system and an institution that exists, that functions, and that remains the only safeguard against the law of the jungle in trade. For the moment the GATT is all we have. We have to look after it."[42]

Concerns of Developing Countries

There is a division in the world economy. The world is divided into two camps of "haves" and "have-nots," or North and South. Not only do these two groups live under different socio-economic conditions, they have different approaches and orientation to the world problems. The "have-nots," many of them old colonies of industrialized countries, based on their past experience believe that the North is attempting to hold them down and exploit them. At the Earth Summit, for example, the North was trying to build a consensus, and probably an agreement, limiting destruction of rain forests, reduction of pollution, and safeguarding of nature. The South saw the meeting as an opportunity to get the North to commit resources for protection of

nature. In their opinion, the North, by its unrestrained industrialization had endangered the planet and would have to pay for its cleanup. If the South was going to forego cheap and dirty technology, and stabilized population, the North would have to assist and pay at least part of the bill. To Brazil, China, India, Malaysia, and Mexico, for example, the unfettered ability to industrialize was essential, and pollution, in their opinion, was an unavoidable consequence.

The tendency of developing countries to follow easy and less expensive economic development strategies and the reluctance of developed countries to assist in the use of more expensive but environmentally safer methods will have grave consequences for the world. Consider the scenario of increased car ownership by the people of developing countries. The United Nations demographers estimated that the world population was 5.7 billion in 1994, and that it will double to more than 10 billion by 2050. If we extrapolate the rate of car ownership by the people of developed countries to the rest of the world, the increased pollution from additional cars certainly will have adverse effect on the planet. Safeguarding the ecosystem calls for population control and environmentally friendly means of transportation; these, in turn, require investment in education, family planning, and a coherent approach to economic development globally. At the present time the United Nations is supporting programs and attempts that are aimed at stabilizing the earth's population at 7.8 billion by that year.[43]

Many years ago Perlmutter stated that increased international trade is the best hope for world peace: bombing customers, suppliers, and employees is in nobody's interest.[44] We should add that the worst enemy of peace is poverty. No international trade is possible with destitute people, and poverty cannot be eradicated without equitable world trade. Many developing countries' intellectuals believe that the MNCs are partly to blame for the plight of poor nations. They cite examples of past flagrant exploitation, and point out the statistics that indicate these countries not only did not benefit from the relationship with the MNCs, but instead actually suffered. Between 1960 and 1968, for example, profit remittance to the MNCs by Latin American countries exceeded 6.7 billion.[45] The belief that developing countries are heavily dependent on developed countries and draw decreasing benefit from the relationship is called "dependencia." The Dependencia school of thought paints an exploitive picture of the world, where the MNCs are moving away wealth and benefits from poor developing countries to rich developed countries. The process of wealth transfer is assisted by an "unequal exchange," in which commodities incorporating high value labor are purchased by consumers whose labor has been sold at a low value. In this way, global inequalities are built into the prices we pay on the open market.[46] Consider, for example, the New Guinea villagers who produce coffee for the world market. After coffee beans leave the village, they are transported overseas, change many hands, go through several processes, and finally end up in the form of processed coffee in jars and cans available to the world market. The villagers receive just enough cash to support a local store which sells, among other things, cans of *Nescafe* coffee. The difference between the price paid to the villagers for their coffee, and the price they have to pay for the cans of Nescafe, is 48 times.[47] In this way, dependencia is increasing the gap between the rich and the poor. Between 1948 and 1988, per capita income in Latin America declined relative to Western Europe and North America by 26 percent.[48] In 1990, a majority of developing countries had lower per capita income than a decade before.[49]

Frequently, in order to expand to developing countries, the MNCs build close relationships with the governments and the elites of these countries. Unfortunately, often these governments are not representative of the people and are not acting in their best interests. Particularly, international bankers have had their share of acquiescing to the schemes of governments and elites who were lining their own pockets at the expense of the people. Many attribute much of the developing countries' economic problems and huge external debts to these relationships. Some have suggested a circular relationship between capital flight, political instability, and economic hardship in these countries.[50] There are some indications that international bankers and financiers have had an active role in and contributed to capital flight from developing countries.[51] Thus, international bankers, through their participation in capital flight may have contributed to the plight of these countries. De George describes this peculiar relationship:

> [International] Banks in less developed countries face a dilemma: the best prospect for large loans are the government and the country's elite. But the government and the elite do not always use their loans for the good of the country; indeed, they tend to use them for themselves and their own narrowly conceived interests. . . . Banks do not only lend money; they also receive money. Offering customers secret unnumbered accounts and evincing a willingness to accept deposits without question make banks accomplices to exploitation, crime, and the flight of investment capital from less developed countries.[52]

Such relationships perpetuate the dependency of developing countries on technology and capital from developed countries. The dependency phenomenon has been the subject of much debate. Many have argued that if this pattern continues, developing countries may never attain a level of economic development comparable to the United States and the more prosperous European nations.[53] The experiences of a few Asian countries, such as Korea, Taiwan, Singapore, and Malaysia, however, indicate otherwise. While these countries are not comparable to the United States now, the continuation of the present rate of growth and industrialization could bring them to that level. Nevertheless, the abject poverty of many developing countries leaves ample room for worry and concern.

While acknowledging the unscrupulous past practices of some MNCs, and the potential for abuse, no one denies that the MNCs can play a very constructive role in assisting developing countries. The nature of their involvement and assistance, however, remains an open question. Probably, what we all need is an understanding that the problems of poor nations cannot be solved with the approaches that have worked for the rich. Insistence by the World Bank and the International Monetary Fund on fiscal restraint and export push by these countries, while all that is available for exports are raw materials, falls into this category. We need new ideas and practical solutions. Recent efforts at alleviating the developing countries' debt burden and preserving rain forests are good examples. In this case, environmental groups have initiated a drive to retire developing countries' external debt in exchange for saving forests, the wildlife's natural habitat. This exchange works as follows: A private conservation organization purchases the commercial debt of a developing country at a steep discount from a bank or in the secondary market and agrees to cancel the debt in exchange for setting aside a nature area for conservation. Based on similar ideas, the World Bank now incorporates environmental concerns into its loan programs. An example is a 20-year environmental action plan for Madagascar. The plan is jointly developed by the World Bank and the World Wide Fund for Nature. It is aimed at increasing public awareness of environmental issues, establishing and managing protected areas, and encouraging "sustainable development."[54]

International Conflict Resolution and Supranational Organizations

Civilization has come a long way in conflict resolution. While pockets of regional animosities remain, we are beginning to accept that wars are not the best method of resolving our disputes. We are beginning to see that all members of the "global village" are better off when mutually beneficial solutions are applied to common problems. The harmony and prosperity of a village is directly related to its ability to resolve the differences and disputes among its members in an orderly and peaceful fashion. The chief, the elders, or the village council are usually the arbitrators of disputes among the villagers. Although our "global village" does not have a chief, there are certain supranational organizations that resemble the village council. While their mandate may be the same as that of the village council, the power and authority of these institutions is not the same. For problems that lie within the national borders, these institutions do not have any power at all. The most prominent of these institutions are the United Nations (U.N.), the World Bank, and the International Monetary Fund (IMF).

All intranation business problems are handled by the national governments and domestic legal systems. There is no dispute regarding the power and sovereignty of national governments in domestic conflict resolution. Not all business problems and disputes, however, are purely of a domestic nature. Most MNC operations cross national borders and involve multiple jurisdictions. Certain questions arise for the MNC operations that are not confined to one country. For instance, in the case of disputes between firms from two different countries, whose legal system should apply? In some cases there are no clear jurisdictional demarcations to show where the sovereignty of one country ends and that of the other one begins. Moreover, certain issues do not fall within the jurisdiction of any nation. One such example is the use of global commons. As the MNCs expand their operations and as more countries industrialize, the need for and the importance of supranational institutions for resolving international problems will increase.

The United Nations[55]

In the midst of euphoria and optimism of the end of the World War II, the United Nations was established in 1945. The mission of the U.N. is to ensure peace on earth and to serve as arbitrator of international conflicts. It was patterned after the League of Nations, but unlike the League of Nations, all major world military and economic powers were included as its charter members. All nations were invited to join the U.N. by accepting its mission and abiding by its charter. The U.N. charter comprises 111 articles. Articles 1 and 2 deal with the purposes of the U.N., which is basically promoting and maintaining world peace.

Charter of the United Nations. Chapter 1. Purpose and Principles

Article 1. The purposes of the United Nations are:

1. To maintain international peace and security, and to that end: to take effective collective measures for the prevention and removal of threats to the peace, and for the suppression of acts of aggression or other breaches of the peace and to bring about by peaceful means, and in conformity with the principle of justice and international law, adjustment or settlement of international disputes or situations which might lead to a breach of peace.
2. To develop friendly relations among nations based on respect for the principle of equal rights and self-determination of peoples, and to take other appropriate measures to strengthen universal peace;
3. To achieve international co-operation in solving international problems of an economic, social, cultural, or humanitarian character, and in promoting and encouraging respect for human rights and for fundamental freedoms for all without distinction as to race, language, or religion; and
4. To be a centre for harmonizing the actions of nations in the attainment of these common ends.

Article 2. The Organization and its Members, in pursuit of the Purposes stated in Article 1 shall act in accordance with the following Principles.

1. The Organization is based on the principle of the sovereign equality of all its Members.
2. All Members, in order to ensure to all of them the rights and benefits resulting from membership, shall fulfill in good faith the obligations assumed by them in accordance with the present Charter.
3. All Members shall settle their international disputes by peaceful means in such a manner that international peace and security, and justice, are not endangered.
4. All Members shall refrain in their international relations from the threat or use of force against the territorial integrity or political independence of any state, or in any other manner inconsistent with the Purposes of the United Nations.
5. All Members shall give the United Nations every assistance in any action it takes in accordance with the present Charter, and shall refrain from giving assistance to any state against which the United Nations is taking preventive or enforcement action.
6. The Organization shall ensure that states which are not Members of the United Nations act in accordance with these Principles so far as may be necessary for the maintenance of international peace and security.
7. Nothing contained in the present Charter shall authorize the United Nations to intervene in matters which are essentially within the domestic jurisdiction of any state or shall require the Members to submit such matters to settlement under the present Charter; but this principle shall not prejudice the application of enforcement measures under Chapter VII.

To carry out its mission, the U.N. charter provided for creation of six primary organs: the General Assembly, the Security Council, the Economic and Social Council, the Trusteeship Council, the International Court of Justice, and the Secretariat.

The General Assembly is the organ that reflects the total membership of the U.N. It is one of the most influential organs of the U.N. All members have equal voting power in the assembly, and because of this it has been referred to as the "town-hall meeting" of the world. The primary functions of the General Assembly include discussion and recommendation of issues presented before it, control of finances, election and admission of new members, and initiation of proposals for charter review and amendment.

The Security Council is responsible for making specific and binding decisions where the issue of peace and security are concerned. Membership in this council includes five permanent members: the United States, Russia, the United Kingdom, France, and China. These five countries were given permanent membership in the council assuming they would be responsible for enforcing any binding decisions the council makes. There are also 10 (originally 6) other countries that are elected by the General Assembly. The nonpermanent members are chosen on the following geographical basis: three Africans, two Asians, one Eastern European, two Latin Americans, and two from Western Europe and other states. Resolutions of the council require nine favorable votes, including those of the permanent members, on all nonprocedural matters. In effect, the permanent members have veto power in the council. Over the years, this feature has greatly restricted the effectiveness of the council.

The Secretariat comprises the permanent administrative staff of the U.N. and is directed by the chief administrative officer, the Secretary-General. The Security Council recommends a nominee for the secretary general to the General Assembly for approval. Although the charter has not specified the term of the office, the secretary general usually serves for five years. Members of the Secretariat staff are appointed by the secretary general on as wide a geographical basis as possible. They take an oath to serve as international civil servants. However, many of these administrators later will go back to their countries, and may resume employment with their governments upon return. Therefore, while with the U.N., they may not be able to divorce themselves totally from influence attempts by their governments.

The International Court of Justice, which is composed of 15 judges, is elected by the General Assembly and the Security Council voting concurrently. The court has two functions. It serves as the tribunal for the final settlement of disputes submitted to it by the parties. It also acts in an advisory capacity to all other organs of the U.N. in regards to questions of legal nature.

A cluster of some 20 intergovernmental agencies operate around the U.N. to promote the general welfare in the world through economic, social, and cultural programs. Six of these agencies, along with the U.N. itself, are headquartered in Geneva, Switzerland. They include International Telecommunication Union (ITU), World Health Organization (WHO), International Labor Organization (ILO), World Meteorological Organization (WMO), World Intellectual Property Organization (WIPO), and the General Agreement on Tariffs and Trade (GATT). Two agencies, the World Bank and IMF are located in Washington, D.C. The rest of the agencies are scattered among various cities, primarily in Europe and North America. The Food and Agricultural Organization (FAO) is in Rome. The U.N. Educational, Scientific and Cultural Organization (UNESCO) is in Paris. The International Civil Aviation Organization (ICAO) is located in Montreal. Berne is the headquarters of the Universal Postal Union (UPU). London is the location for the Intergovernmental Maritime Organization (IMO). The headquarters of the International Atomic Energy

Agency (IAEA) is in Vienna, and the U.N. Environmental Protection Agency (UNEP) is in Nairobi.

The World Bank and the International Monetary Fund[56]

Like the GATT, the World Bank and the IMF were created during the Bretton Woods (New Hampshire) meetings on July 1, 1944. Because of the total dependence of the Allied countries on the United States, the role and influence of the United States on the conference and its outcome was decisive. As a result, both the World Bank and the IMF are strongly influenced by the United States in philosophy and direction.

The World Bank   The original function of the Bank was to provide funds for the reconstruction of Europe. After Europe recovered, the bank shifted its focus and became exclusively a development advisor and financial intermediary between state-sponsored projects and private investors. It borrows on commercial terms, by selling bonds, then it lends the proceeds to finance development projects around the world.

The World Bank is comprised of a group of institutions that specialize in various aspects of economic development. The group consists of three internationally oriented institutions and four regionally oriented banks. The three are the International Bank for Reconstruction and Development (IBRD), the International Development Association (IDA), and the International Finance Association (IFS). Through its triple-A credit rating, the IBRD has been able to borrow in excess of $10 billion a year in private capital markets, and thus is able to fund a substantial portion of the money the World Bank lends. Its primary focus is financing the medium- and long-term projects. IDA lends only to the poorest countries on concessional (below-market) terms. Some of their typical projects include primary school classrooms and technical assistance and loans to poor farmers. When a country pays its loans back, it will become a donor and adds to the funds available for loan to oth-

ers. The four regionally oriented banks are the Inter-American Development Bank (IDB), the Asian Development Bank (ADB), the African Development Bank (AFDB), and the Caribbean Development Bank (CarDB).

Membership in the IMF is a condition for admission to membership in the World Bank. Therefore, the bank's member governments are also members of the IMF. Voting privileges are in proportion to the capital stock owned by the members in the bank. Slightly more than 20 percent of votes belongs to the United States. As the largest shareholder, the U.S. chooses the bank's president. For this reason, and for the fact that it is located in Washington, D.C., and its origin goes back to Bretton Woods, some have called it "America's institution."[57] Other large shareholders are the United Kingdom, Germany, France, and Japan. All matters before the bank are decided by the majority vote.

The International Monetary Fund   The IMF is not a bank, but a club. Member countries pay a subscription and agree to abide by a mutually advantageous code of conduct. The IMF's original objective was to promote trade by creating a reliable exchange rate system. The IMF functioned by providing a pool of money from which members could borrow short term, in order to adjust their balance of payments with other members.

Over the years, both the World Bank and the IMF have changed. The Marshall Plan eclipsed the bank's role in European reconstruction in the late 1940s. Likewise, when Richard Nixon took the United States off the gold standard in 1971 and switched to floating exchange rates, the IMF's original function disappeared. These developments resulted in a change in priorities for both. The bank and the IMF focused their attention on world poverty, and shifted their operations from serving the rich countries to serving the middle income and poor nations. Today, the Bank's main goal is to promote long-term economic growth that reduces poverty in developing countries. To do this the bank has become a development advisor and financial intermediary between state-sponsored projects and private investors, corporations, and commercial banks. The bank sponsors primarily specific infrastructure projects, such as roads or dams. It also makes loans for "policy adjustments," which enhance a country's economic, financial, or political environment for private investment.

The IMF started on a new path in 1982 when it came to the aid of Mexico, when it had nearly defaulted on its loans from commercial banks. The action seemed consistent with the agency's goal of overseeing the international monetary system and helping member countries overcome short-term financial problems. Since then, the IMF has been operating in a three-way arrangement with heavily indebted countries and commercial banks. Because of their new roles, with the bank making policy adjustments and the IMF involved in long-term structural loans, the duties of the two institutions overlap.

Criticisms against IMF and the World Bank
Critics charge that despite their goals, neither organization has been successful in promoting real market-oriented policy reform. The result of their approach to lending, they argue, is massive impoverishment and indebtedness around the globe. They point out that despite the bank's and the IMF's efforts and large amount of lendings, there are more people living in absolute poverty than ever before.

Critics cite several problems with IMF and bank lending. They charge that the IMF's short-term adjustment lending can do more harm than good when applied to the structural problems of the Third World. According to these critics, the fund focuses on narrow accounting data, ignoring the broad policies that have slowed development. For instance, because the fund typically demands that a borrowing nation reduce its current account deficit, the country restricts imports, or by insisting that a country cut its budget deficit, it causes the government to raise taxes, thereby, slowing growth. One of the main criticisms leveled at the World Bank and the

IMF stems from the concept that funds are "fungible" (negotiable in kind or substitutable, exchangeable). Because of this, critics charge that no matter how conscientiously the bank examines a project or how it is economically justified, the project that is actually financed becomes an altogether different one, and probably much less sensible. They argue that the truly good projects would have gone ahead anyway, paid for out of the country's own resources, and that the bank ends up financing the marginal project, one that would not have proceeded without the additional funds.

The concept of fungibility extends to the IMF also. Because the IMF makes loans to governments, not specific projects, these funds can be redirected. Critics charge that the IMF underwrites any country, no matter how venal or brutal, and that these funds are frequently redirected toward economically nonproductive ends.

Another criticism is that the IMF and the World Bank do little to enforce the conditions of their loans. If a country violates its agreement, the organizations will simply suspend the loan, negotiate a new agreement, and funds will flow again. When the country violates the new conditions the process starts anew. Members are required to consult with the IMF annually on their economic and financial policies. These consultations should provide IMF with an opportunity to review and influence the members' policies. Since IMF has no formal sanctions against noncompliance, it is not clear how effective the consultation process is. As Paul Volcker, the U.S. Undersecretary of the Treasury for monetary affairs, has stated ". . . when disagreement arose between the IMF and member countries on the need for policy changes, if the country was small, it fell into line; if it was large, the IMF fell into line; if several large countries were involved, the IMF disappeared."[58]

There are a host of other complaints and criticisms. Debtor countries charge that because of the IMF's insistence that to renegotiate a loan the country must have in hand an agreement with its bankers, and that there be not interest in arrears, the IMF is simply a collector for the commercial banks. Conservationists charge that the World Bank and IMF collude in their dealings with developing countries, and that they support programs that do not work. There are accusations that the World Bank and IMF apply identical remedies, irrespective of a country's circumstances, and that they have a market-oriented, free-enterprise philosophy, which they apply in a doctrinaire way.

Pro-IMF and World Bank arguments The World Bank counters the fungibility charge with the argument that in many of the countries its operations account for a big share of the total investment program. In sub-Saharan Africa, for example, gross investment accounts for 15 percent of national income. Therefore, it is implausible that without the World Bank's aid most of the projects would have gone ahead anyway. The bank also points out that it does not merely select projects from a list offered by its borrowers, leaving the country free to move down the list once it has obtained the funds. In fact, most of the affected countries do not have the skills to frame an investment program and design projects within it. In these countries the bank may devise projects almost from scratch. The bank maintains that without its involvement those projects could not have gone forward. Finally, the bank points to its debt repayment record and its AAA rating.

In countering the criticisms, IMF points out South Korea as an example of its accomplishments. The IMF maintains that it assisted that country's recovery from the devastation of the Korean War, provided crucial foreign capital, and acted as a catalyst in facilitating foreign investment. The Fund also points out that it is the only international institution concerned with its borrowers' economic policies, and that its role of "surveillance" is more important than ever. Both the bank and the IMF point out that they provide a great deal of technical assistance, such

as feasibility studies, engineering services for project design and construction, and human resources development and training to the developing world. Both agencies claim that they are still the cheapest way for taxpayers of the richest countries to come to the aid of the poor.

What Is Next?

We are witnessing a transition period in the world. While we are not quite sure exactly where the transition will take us, it is our hope that nations in a leadership role are keeping their focus on the ideal destination and are selecting their present paths accordingly. We hope that the present path will take us all to prosperity and peace.

Like any transition period, this one is governed by the forces of change. Technological advancement in telecommunications, computers, and the convenience of traveling are reducing physical distances and bringing the countries of the world ever closer to a "global village." Political changes are pushing the world into two different directions. The fall of international Communism is changing military-political rivalries to economic-political rivalries and consequently creating ever-increasing market competition. At the same time, ethnocultural differences that were suppressed by the rivalry between capitalist democracies and Communism are coming to the limelight. Increased understanding of the ecosystem and the impact of people on the environment, coupled with the disastrous consequences of a few blatant cases of industrial negligence, such as the Bhopal disaster and the Chernobyl accident, are galvanizing the forces of environmentalism in demanding better safeguards for the ecosystem.

New players are emerging on a scene dominated by economic and political rivalry, and even new aspects of competition are appearing. No longer can the United States be assured of undisputed world leadership. Such new developments create advantages as well as drawbacks. The period from the end of the second world war until the fall of global Communism was characterized by U.S. political and economic leadership. Many attribute the success of GATT and the growth of world trade during this period to the dominant power of the United States and the willingness of the United States to support the emergence of an economically strong Europe and Japan to combat the expansion of international Communism. The dominant position of the United States gave it the power to set the rules that all participants followed. With a large market and dominant position, the U.S. was able to and did absorb some of the costs. At present, however, the threat of international Communism is vanishing and the United States is opting out of its leadership position to look after its own interests.

During this transition period, who is going to set the rules? No matter who sets them and what form their contents take, why should anybody follow these rules? Since there is no undisputed front-runner, and no dominant power to handle disputes, how do we resolve trade conflicts and who will be the arbitrator? Of course, one immediate need is to strengthen supra-national organizations such as the U.N., but doing this is, in itself, a slow, arduous task.

There are certain signs of additional emerging answers to the questions of leadership and role-setting. To answer these questions, we should take into consideration the intertwining of international management and international relations and note four observable trends.[59] First, there is a growing diffusion and ambiguity of power. The U.S. hegemony is on the decline and other superpowers are faced with increasing internal and external problems. Europe is moving closer to an economic and, possibly, political unity, and ministates are emerging that are at times capable of frustrating the will of major powers. Second, international alignments are becoming more fluid. The fall of international Communism is bridging the ideological gap between Eastern and Western Europe. The growing number of newly industrializing countries is blurring the line between the "haves" and "have-nots," and there is an increasing localization of politics related to ethnicity and other issues that exist beneath the global level. Third, the pattern of interdependencies is becoming more intricate. This is due to an expanding agenda of concerns that merges the economics, ecology, and politics, leading to a broader concept of national security beyond traditional military considerations. Fourth, the role of nonstate actors is on the rise, and links between the activities of local, national, international, and intergovernmental levels are increasing. There are signs of emerging nonterritorial organizations through growing networks of nongovernmental organizations (NGOs, e.g., Amnesty International), and alliances among MNCs. While we may not ever see a world map defined by the MNC logos, their influence may match those of most national governments.

The increased complexity of international management, propelled by these four trends, gives market power and size a new prominence. Some[60] argue that those who control the world's largest markets will be informally writing the rules of international business. If this assertion is true, the Europeans may be writing the *de facto* rules of international trade in the next century. While the specifics of those rules are not predictable, their directions are discernible from certain observable trends. In the world trade, to be considered fair, the rules must apply to all participants. We must have "a level playing field." There must be broadly similar taxes, regulations, and private modes of operation. Much of the benefits that are now local may become global or vanish. German firms, for example, may not be able to continue giving three years' leave to new mothers if the rest of the world is not willing to match its generosity. If in one country, such as Japan, commercial laws provide opportunities to businesses to work out common strategies of conquest in home or foreign markets, others will be forced to respond. Similarly, in an open world economy the high minimum wages of Western countries are threatened by the low minimum wages of Asians. Given short vacations in Japan, long European vacations are not viable. No nation alone can compel businesses to honor ecological standards. MNCs simply move production to those parts of the world with no fringe benefits and no environmental regulations. In effect, hidden benefits and covert costs will become overt in wages and prices. Likewise, extreme variations on return on investment cannot last long. Previously localized issues will become global. "The capitalist who is willing to work for the lowest rate of return in the world sets the maximum rate of return for everyone else. If the Japanese capitalist will accept a 3 percent return, Americans cannot have 15 percent."[61]

Conclusion

Similar to their domestic counterparts, MNCs have social responsibilities. Because of cultural and market diversity, however, the MNCs face a much more difficult challenge in fulfilling their social responsibilities. The MNCs not only have an obligation to abide by the local laws of the host countries, but also to preserve the ecological well-being of the planet, respect the host culture, and follow overall ethical standards. Although basic morality does not vary among nations, due to differing circumstances, certain practices are locally determined. The MNCs' executives need to understand those variations and consider them in their day-to-day business.

While compliance with national laws and ethical norms is of local concern, other issues such as ecological problems, harvesting the riches of the oceans, exploration of Antarctica, and exploitation of outer space are global matters. There are wide areas of disagreement regarding these issues. With the changing emphasis from a military-political rivalry to an economic-political rivalry among nations, the handling of these issues is gaining added urgency. Supranational organizations such as the U.N., the GATT, the World Bank, and the IMF are well positioned to take leadership in global conflict resolution in all of these issues. The nature of these organizations, and the method of resolving global differences they adopt, will be debated for many years to come. What is clear at this point is that our transformation toward a "global village" is well under way.

Discussion Questions

1. It is suggested that for many social responsibility issues the MNCs have a special obligation toward developing countries. Explain the reason for such a special obligation.

2. The newly independent country of Neverland is interested in selling exploration rights to its minerals. Since this is the Neverland's first international venture, you can probably negotiate a very lucrative deal for your company. You may be able to negotiate a below-market price for its minerals. In all likelihood, your agreement will become the industry pattern for other MNC negotiations. What will you do? Support your decision on practical and moral grounds.

3. Why are global ecological problems difficult to solve?

4. Do you agree with the claim that we need to develop global standards to protect the ecosystem? Support your opinion.

5. Why should the rule of "first come, first served" not be applied to the use of outer space?

6. In the case of lubrication money, why shouldn't an executive simply follow what everybody else is doing.

7. What are the benefits of GATT?

8. What are the criticisms of GATT?

9. Elaborate on the changing mission and strategies of the World Bank and the IMF.

10. Do you agree that the U.N. should be strengthened?

11. Do you think that the United States can maintain its global leadership role? If the answer is yes, explain your reasons. If the answer is no, what type of leadership will emerge?

Endnotes

1. P. Wright, C. D. Pringle, M. Kroll, and J. A. Parnell. *Strategic Management* (Boston, MA: Allyn and Bacon, 1994), 64.

2. R. T. De George. *Competing with Integrity in International Business* (New York: Oxford University Press, 1993), 3–4.

3. K. Ohmae. *The Borderless World* (New York: Harper Collins Publishers, 1991), 8.

4. De George. *Competing with Integrity.* 44.

5. K. A. Getz. "International Codes of Conduct: An Analysis of Ethical Reasoning." *Journal of Business Ethics,* 9 (July 1990), 567–77.

6. J. B. McGuire, A. Gundgren, and T. Schneeweis. "Corporate Social Responsibility and Firm Financial Performance." *Academy of Management Journal,* 31, no. 4 (1988), 854–72.

7. G. R. Bassir. "Multinational Corporations in Less Developed Countries: An Alternative Strategy." *Human Systems Management,* 10 (1991), 61–9.

8. De George. *Competing with Integrity.* 23–58.

9. World Commission on Environment and Development, *Our Common Future* (Oxford, England: Oxford University Press, 1990), 22.

10. World Commission on Environment. *Our Common Future.* 5.

11. J. A. Baden. "Business, Science and Environmental Politics." *Columbia Journal of World Business,* 27, no. 3–4 (Winter 1992), 27–35.

12. World Commission on Environment. *Our Common Future.* 8.

13. "Earth Summit Approves Agenda 21, Rio Declaration." *UN Chronicle* (September 1992), 59–65.

14. World Commission on Environment. *Our Common Future.* 18.

15. A. A. Johnson. "Traders." *Stanford Business School Magazine,* 61, no. 2 (December 1992), 16.

16. World Commission on Environment. *Our Common Future.* 262.

17. World Commission on Environment. *Our Common Future.* 273–4.

18. A. Salpukas. "2,860 Feet Under the Sea, A Record-Breaking Well," *The New York Times* (April 24, 1994), F9.

19. "Fishy Business in the Pacific." *The Economist* (November 16, 1985), 37–8.

20. T. W. Nether. "Third World Seeks Its Place in Space." *The New York Times* (September 15, 1985), E7.

21. H. Schollhammer. "Ethics in an International Business Context." *MSU Business Topics* (Spring 1977), 56.

22. K. Pennar, P. Galuszka, D. Lindorff, and R. Jesurum. "The Destructive Costs of Greasing Palms." *Business Week* (December 6, 1993), 133–8.

23. P. Nehemkis. "Business Payoffs Abroad: Rhetoric and Reality." *California Management Review,* 18, no. 2 (Winter 1975), 5–20.

24. J. W. Salacuse. *Making Global Deals* (Boston, MA: Houghton Mifflin Co., 1991), 101–2.

25. Salacuse. *Making Global Deals.* 101.

26. De George. *Competing with Integrity.* 11.

27. Told in 1994, by Parvathy Menon, a graduate student at Barton School of Business, Wichita State University, who had heard the joke in Russia.

28. De George. *Competing with Integrity.* 13.

29. S. Engelberg and M. Tolchin. "Foreigners Find New Ally Is U.S. Industry." *The New York Times* (November 2, 1993), A1, B8.

30. E.-J. Kolde. *Environment of International Business* (Boston, MA: PWS-Kent Publishing Co., 1985), 152–3.

31. Kolde. *Environment of International Business.* 152.

32. J. Hegarty. "Why We Can't Let GATT Die."*Journal of Accountancy* (April 1991), 74–7.

33. G. L. Crovitz. "GATT's Last Gasp?" *Barrons* (January 20, 1992), 44–7.

34. "Once and Future GATT." *The Economist* (June 1, 1991), 65.

35. L. Reynolds. "Getting the GATT Talks Back on Track." *Management Review,* 80, no. 7 (July 1991), 31–2.

36. C. V. Prestowitz, A. Tonelson, and T. W. Jerome. "The Last Gasp of GATTism." *Harvard Business Review* (March–April 1991), 130–8.

37. Ibid.

38. C. Stevens. "Technoglobalism vs. Technonationalism: The Corporate Dilemma." *Columbia Journal of World Business,* 25, no. 3 (Fall 1990), 42–9.

39. D. Bandow. "The IMF: Forever in Debt." *Business and Society Review,* no. 73 (Spring 1990), 4–7; Crovitz. "GATT's Last Gasp?" 44–7.

40. J. Hegarty. "Why We Can't Let GATT Die." *Journal of Accountancy* (April 1991), 44–7.

41. "Once and Future GATT." 65.

42. S. Ostry. "The Implications of Developing Trends in Trade Policy." *Business Economics,* 25, no. 1 (January 1990), 23–7.

43. S. Chira. "Women Campaign for New Plan to Curb the World's Population." *The New York Times* (April 13, 1994), A1, A12.

44. H. V. Perlmutter. "The Tortuous Evolution of the Multinational Corporation." *Columbia Journal of World Business* (January–February 1969), 9–18.

45. A. Pinto and J. Knalkel. "The Centre-Periphery System 20 Years Later." *Social and Economic Studies,* 22 (1973), 34–89.

46. P. J. Taylor. "Understanding Global Inequalities:

A World-System Approach." *Geography,* 77 (January 1992), 17.

47. T. P. Bayliss-Smith. *The Ecology of Agricultural Systems* (Cambridge, MA: University Press, 1981), 35.

48. G. Arrighi. "World Income Inequalities and the Future of Socialism." *Conference Paper* (Binghamton, NY: Fernand Braudel Center, SUNY, 1991), reported in Taylor. "Understanding Global Inequalities." 10–21.

49. World Commission on Environment. *Our Common Future,* 6.

50. K. Fatehi. "Capital Flight from Latin America as a Barometer of Political Instability." *Journal of Business Research,* 30, no. 2 (1994), 187–95.

51. R. T. Naylor. *Hot Money and the Politics of Debt* (New York: The Linden Press/Simon and Schuster, 1987); W. Ingo. *Secret Money: The World of International Financial Secrecy* (Lexington, MA: Lexington Books, 1985); M. R. Sesil, K. Witcher, and D. Hertzberg. "Flight Capital's Destination Often Is U.S.: Political Security Attracts Billions of Dollars." *The Wall Street Journal* (May 27, 1986), 2.

52. De George. *Competing with Integrity.* 71.

53. K. Paul and R. Barbato. "The Multinational Corporation in the Less Developed Country: The Economic Development Model Versus the North-South Model." *Academy of Management Review,* 10, no. 1 (1985), 8–14.

54. M. J. Moline. "Debt-for-Nature Exchanges: Attempting to Deal Simultaneously with Two Global Problems." *Law and Policy in International Business,* 22 (1991), 133–57.

55. This section is based on information gleaned from several sources including P. R. Baehr and L. Gordenker. *The United Nations* (New York: Praeger Publishers, 1984); L. M. Goodrich. *The United Nations in a Changing World* (New York: Columbia University Press, 1977); J. M. Rochester. *Waiting for Millennium* (Columbia, SC: University of South Carolina Press, 1993).

56. Information in this section was culled from a variety of sources including *The World Bank, IFC and IDA: Policies and Operations* (Washington, DC: International Bank for Reconstruction and Development, 1962); A. L. Acheson, J. F. Grant, and M. F. J. Prachowny. *Berton Woods Revisited* (Toronto: University of Toronto Press, 1972); E. Coady. "Global Change and the World Bank." *Bankers' Magazine,* no. 3 (1992), 25; P. Mistry. "World or Wonderland Bank?" *Banker,* no. 788 (1991), 40; B. Orr. "Are the IMF and the World Bank on the right track?" *ABA Banking Journal* (March 1990), 74–82; and D. Bandow. "The IMF: Forever in Its Debt." *Business and Society Review* (Spring 1990), 4–7.

57. D. Bandow. "The IMF: Forever in Its Debt." 4–7.

58. R. Solomon. *The International Monetary System, 1945–76* (New York: Harper and Row, 1977), 250.

59. Rochester. *Waiting for the Millennium.* 237.

60. L. Thurow. "New Rules for Playing the Game." *National Forum* (Fall 1992), 10–13.

61. Thurow, "New Rules for Playing the Game." 13.

MARKETING HOT MILK

ROLF HACKMANN

Background

The nuclear accident at Chernobyl in the Soviet Union on May 26, 1986, had far-reaching effects—not only from a geographical but also political and economic point-of-view. Within thirty-six hours, the radioactive cloud generated by the blast drifted over Poland, then Scandinavia—where it was first discovered—and other parts of Western Europe. Spring precipitation caused vast amounts of cesium 134 and 137, with half-lives[1] of two and thirty years, respectively, plus iodine 131, with

[1] Half-life is the time period required for half of the atoms of a radioactive substance present at the beginning to become disintegrated.

a half-life of 120 days, to be deposited on the newly emerging vegetation, water supplies, animals and humans alike.

Discovered in Sweden three days before the official Soviets announcement, the accident jolted Europe into a new reality which left neither time for preparation nor the possibility for any defence measures. Rapidly accumulating in all kinds of fresh produce like vegetables, lettuce, mushrooms, nuts and fruits, the radiation posed an immediate threat to human health. By traveling up the food chain through animal uptake of contaminated vegetation or other organic matter and water, the fallout was increasingly found in fish, milk and meats for human or animal consumption. Untold economic damage resulted from field crops that had to be plowed under or were declared unfit for human consumption.

The Swedish government had to reimburse the Lapps for condemned reindeer meat. German and Italian authorities averted economic hardships for their vegetable and fruit growers in the same manner. Demand for venison that could be sold on the open market fell almost to zero as high contamination levels were reported. Many people changed their dietary habits from fresh to frozen foods in the face of real or imagined health hazards.

In order to avoid a panic, public officials did everything to play down the implications of the accident, but it became painfully evident how little they themselves were prepared for an emergency of such proportions. There was enough equipment and trained man-power to monitor radiation levels, but the problem was that no universally accepted standards had been set for Europe to divide the innocuous from the dangerous.

Since many of the foodstuffs produced on the continent were crossing national boundaries, even those of Eastern Europe, the often wide differences in officially accepted radiation standards among countries led to protective measures at the borders and in some cases outright

suspicion of the sellers' ethics. All imports of live sheep and goats, freshwater fish, milk, vegetables and fruits were temporarily banned from Eastern European nations in May. When the ban was lifted on May 31, 1986, imports were restricted to goods from areas outside a 650-mile radius around Chernobyl.

In forcing the adoption of a unified system of radiation standards for the European Community (EC) and non-member nations, the Chernobyl accident may actually have been a blessing in disguise. However, these standards arrived in December, 1987—too late to be of immediate benefit, and in a revised form in June of 1988.

Because of lack of clear-cut guidelines, another area of confusion was the question of disposal of contaminated materials and merchandise. Did the responsibility for this fall into the competence of private business, municipal, state or even federal authorities? What were proper disposal methods that prevented, or decreased, further dangers for the public health? Should the materials be contained, treated, diluted, sold, burned, stored underground, or could the problem be solved in some other manner? As there was no precedent to spawn such guidelines, nor had any ever been formulated in anticipation of just such an emergency, there is no doubt that the problem was often addressed in the wrong, yet most expeditious, manner.

Many countries found a patent solution in exporting the burdensome material to unsuspecting customers. The "Austrian Solution" was simply dumping any unwanted goods into the Danube and letting the river carry them downstream. Where possible, radiating materials might have been diluted or mixed with untainted inventories to reduce the hazards to acceptable levels. This practical, even though unorthodox, manner of self-help is suggested by reports that Brazil and the Philippines took highly contaminated milk powder off their retail shelves. The milk had come from England, the Netherlands, and Denmark. Singapore had returned 240 ships carrying contaminated European foodstuffs by October. Malaysia, in a similarly defensive action, returned butter ghee from Holland, cream from England, and Italian vegetables. Sri Lanka prohibited the sale of Polish preserves and Bulgarian plums. In January 1987, the Egyptian navy escorted a Dutch ship out of the harbor of Alexandria with 61 tons of radioactive Austrian milk powder on board. The incident led to the Foreign Ministry of Egypt warning all harbor and airport officials to keep a watchful eye on possible attempts to import contaminated dried milk from Germany.

The atmosphere of near panic, confusion, official bungling and a general lack of preparedness for such nuclear emergency is demonstrated by the following sequence of events overwhelming a major German food processor.

Meggle Milchindustrie GMBH

Meggle is one of the largest dairy companies in all of Germany and certainly the leading one in the southern part of Bavaria where 70% of all German cheese is produced.

When the full extent of the radioactive contamination of milk in that region had became known, officials at the Bavarian department of agriculture advised all dairies to switch their production of milk and yogurt to cheese. The reason for this measure was that up to seventy-five percent of radio nucleids are eliminated from milk solids by the cheese making process, to be concentrated in the whey, the watery component of milk that separates from curdled milk.

At the same time, the authorities urged Meggle to acquire most of the contaminated whey from other dairies and dry it in their modern processing plant. At Meggle's insistence, they apparently committed themselves to whatever assistance necessary to dispose of the material which would result from this action. All in all, Meggle accumulated 5,046 metric tons of such dried whey during the spring and summer of 1986. Under normal circumstances this commodity is used in the production of human foods and animal feeds because it is rich in sugars, minerals and lactalbumin. Meggle's product, however, was far from being a normal commercial item as it showed highly elevated levels of radioactivity, in the vicinity of 8,000 becquerel (Bq) per kilogram of powder or several times the official norm of 1,850 Bq/Kg established for trade merchandise after Chernobyl.

The Federal Department of Agriculture of Germany had declared this level safe in July 1986, three months after the incident. The reasoning behind the rather late decree was arbitrary; therefore, somewhat questionable as it rested on the assumption that whey powder used in the manufacture of human alimentary products, such as baby foods or candy, does not exceed twenty percent by volume. The norm for radioactivity in dried milk products had previously been set at 370 Bq/Kg by the EC (European Community) authorities. Multiplying this level by a factor of five resulted in the 1,850 Bq/Kg for the whey powder. This kind of arithmetic obviously leaves little or no room for any radioactivity occurring naturally or otherwise in other components of the end product.

The same ministry also decreed that all whey powder with excessive contamination levels be taken off the market, and the owner would be reimbursed by a special Chernobyl fund set up by the federal government. Meggle claimed DM 4.6 million but received only DM 3.8 million in damages, which was equivalent to the full market price of normal dried whey. Another DM 700,000 in storage expenses for railroad cars was denied. Why railroad cars? Because the federal railway system was the only place that would accept the contaminated food in storage.

By establishing the maximum level of contamination for trade merchandise, the ministry turned the Meggle whey into a product without commercial value with a stroke of the official pen. But they left the final responsibility for the disposal of this unwanted material unclear. If it had been declared normal waste its removal would become public responsibility, and even more so if it had been labeled radioactive waste. Officials refused to take either step simply because they did not know how to handle this mountainous problem. Instead, they offered all kinds of advice and assistance to Meggle in disposing of the hot item but steadfastly refused to acquire ownership of the problem.

That strange position is explained by the fact that they saw no practical way of disposing of the material and were unprepared to shoulder the expense. Alternatives were underground storage, incineration, or as the most costly solution decontamination.

Underground storage was impossible because the material could not be compacted and solidified, and thus might leach into the underground water supply. Incineration was equally unacceptable. Burning the material on land in one of several incinerators available would spread the contaminated ashes over inhabited areas, because radioactivity cannot be neutralized by incineration. Burning at sea was not feasible because this was not approved by the Federal Ministry for the Environment. Decontamination also had to be ruled out for lack of a proven process at that time.

Attempts to put the problem into the hands of the newly created German "Federal Ministry for Environmental Protection and Reactor Safety" proved futile as this organization quickly pointed out that this matter was the responsibility of the concerned states. The disputes over legal competence went on for months without resolution.

By the end of November, a ray of hope brightened the dismal atmosphere. Two different parties appeared on the scene and offered to sell the goods to Africa. Exports had never been ruled out and the ban on domestic sales apparently did not affect its disposal in foreign markets. How could it with the jurisdiction of a federal ministry extending only up to the country's borders, but not beyond? Delighted to have found a viable solution to the intractable prob-

lem, questions about ethics were not raised by any of the key actors in this drama. It seemed to be such a wonderful alternative: if we cannot handle the problem here, why not export it?

There had been other interested parties throughout the summer and fall who wanted to buy at favorable prices and then sell abroad. One businessman from Nigeria was willing to acquire the goods but could not get the import license and the necessary foreign exchange allocation approved by his government. It is not clear whether this was a result of concerns about the material or a consequence of the very tight finances of the deeply indebted country. There were others, among them a Swiss businessman and government representatives from Poland, Bulgaria, and the People's Republic of Mongolia. Some came to offer disposal and others with all intentions to "process" the shipment. But none of these deals ever materialized for one reason or another. Bulgaria was concerned with the publicity surrounding such a deal and its effect on its very lucrative western tourist business. Poland did not want to believe the guarantees that pork raised with the contaminated feed supplement would not be exported to western markets, etc.

Two gentlemen planned to export the whey to third-world countries. One was a mystery man, referred to only as Mr. K., and the other was an engineer, Mr. Sprang, who exported fish farms to Africa and South America. The only thing both had in common as competitors was their plan to export the whey to Third World countries.

Meggle and the Bavarian authorities approved their export plan in principle provided: a. the ultimate buyers had full knowledge of the contamination problem, b. the material would not be used in agricultural products for export, and c. any danger to the local population was effectively eliminated.

A very sophisticated package, indeed, designed to relieve all parties from further responsibility. The fact that this very same material had been officially declared completely unfit for human consumption in any form only a few short months earlier was suddenly of no concern anymore. Actually, it now served as the official rationalization for the whole plan. The contamination level of 1,850 Bq of cesium per kilogram of material had been established with foodstuffs for humans, but not animal feeds. This was correct. Whey powder is used as a growth product for pigs and calves after some sugars have been partially removed, and Meggle sells such a product under the trade name "Anilac."

This seemed to be a perfect solution, especially since feeding experiments with the contaminated powder in September yielded only fractional residues in the animal tissues. But, if that would have been an innocuous solution to the problem, why didn't Meggle use the hot whey in its own product after they had spent so much money on it, one might ask.

Anyhow, despite the fact that Mr. K. nor Mr. Sprang were unable to provide the required official import approvals of the merchandise, Mr. Sprang placed an order with Meggle for 4,826,050 kilograms on December 3, 1986. Terms of the sale provided for the merchandise to be shipped by oceanfreight via Trieste, and for the total tonnage to be shipped by the end of January 1987, with a declared final destination of Egypt and Nigeria. Meggle accepted and confirmed the order that very same day and ministerial approval came five days later, even though the agreed purchase price was way below the current price of DM 800/ton of whey powder. On December 17, another ministerial approval was issued. This time for the export of only one ton of the powder "for feeding experiments in third countries." No mention was made of the previously required declaration of consent and approval by informed buyers.

Even though all parties were reticent about this latest step, it was established that the one ton went to Egypt where it was shipped by Mr. K. In an unfriendly commentary, Mr. Sprang alleged that his competitor "must have falsified the tariff code of the goods. The required analysis of the imported material may be purchased for a few hundred dollars in Egypt and after you have imported one ton of an officially approved tariff position, you may later import as much as you like."

By this time the German press had gotten wind of the secretive activities. One paper asked its readers whether the radioactive material would be used to produce baby foods. Such publicity caused the Bavarian ministry to distance itself from Mr. K., much to the delight of Mr. Sprang who was now rid of the only competitor for the powder.

Left as the only prospective buyer for the goods, Mr. Sprang disclosed his plan to mix the contaminated material with other feeds until contamination levels of the end product fell below the 600 Bq/Kg limit established by the EC. Again Meggle and the ministry in Munich approved this plan with the provision that the contamination levels be monitored by an official authority.

Taking advantage of the untoward publicity created by the latest incident, Mr. Sprang renegotiated the original purchase contract entered into in December and signed a new contract on January 23. New terms: uptake of 3,000 tons at DM 50/ton, payment 30 days net and an option on the rest of 2,000 tons. Once more, Meggle promptly agreed and even offered to advance the transportation charges.

Sprang planned to have the KoFu company—a giant feed mill in Cologne—do the mixing at a 10 : 1 ratio into animal feed products for fish, chicken and cattle. Such an order would bury the whey powder in a veritable mountain of 50,000 tons of animal feeds destined for Egypt, the Sudan, and Nigeria.

With all contracts and approvals in hand, Mr. Sprang let the hot merchandise roll on January 28, when 150 of the 260 freight cars used for storage of the material started their journey to Cologne and Bremerhaven, and ultimately Africa as planned. This date was only three days after the general federal election. Everything probably would have proceeded according to schedule had not the German public intervened once more.

Civil vigilantes monitored every station of the train's route and even tried to block the train on several occasions. Their actions, focused public attention on the potential dangers of the cargo that, after all, carried 15 billion Bq of cesium through densely populated regions without special permits or precautions. A spokesman of the federal ministry for environmental protection played down the hazards to the public by declaring that the "specific activity" of the whey powder would have to reach 74,000 Bq/Kg before official approvals would become mandatory.

Such argument did little to calm the concerns of the general public nor those of the authorities in Cologne and Bremerhaven who forced the return of the trains under threat of stiff penalties. Even the Federal Minister of Health, Mrs. Suessmuth, found it scandalous and "irreconcilable with ethical principles to make a distinction between health protection measures for people in Europe and developing nations."

Suddenly, a high level of public awareness was created that spilled over into other countries. In Germany, the suspicion grew that producers, merchants, and even officials used the Third World as a "dumping ground" for Chernobyl waste. Egypt's semiofficial newspaper *Al Ahram,* published praise to Allah for "waking up the German authorities" and demanded disclosure of identity of all local importers "who want to make exorbitant profits at the expense of the public's health." More fundamentalist news media even accused the West of inundating Egypt with poisoned foods to make the population infertile.

The international uproar reached such proportions that it finally called for long overdue decisive and definitive action by the German authorities. It came on February 5, 1987, when the Minister for Environmental Affairs, Mr. Walter

Wallmann, invited Mssrs. Meggle and Sprang into his office for an "informative discussion," at the end of which both gentlemen relinquished their ownership rights to 4,826 tons of whey powder to the federal government, as of midnight February 6, 1987. The legality of this operation was questioned only by the infuriated Mr. Sprang, while Mr. Meggle and the State of Bavaria heaved a big sigh of relief.

This decision, unfortunately, was not the end of the episode because no one had officially declared the powder to be either a waste product or a commercial good—the central problem of the whole affair. Despite this legal flaw, Mr. Wallmann placed the merchandise into the hands of the German armed forces a few days after its expropriation. The 150 railroad cars in Cologne and Bremerhaven were transferred to isolated army proving grounds in northern Germany and the remaining 92 cars were stationed in southern Germany. A decision on the final disposal of the material was promised to be forthcoming within twelve weeks.

When everything appeared to be heading for a satisfactory finale, bad news hit the press once more. By mid-February 1987, another 2,000 tons of contaminated powder was discovered in a Meggle warehouse. This time the radioactivity reached only 2,000 Bq/Kg as a result of feeding summer hay to the dairy herds. The discovery led to a very interesting calculation by the Green Party (environmentalists) who established that another 8,000 tons of contaminated whey powder should actually have surfaced. There was no trace of it. The embarrassed authorities admitted that dairies either disposed of it in the environment or, more likely, had simply sold it to the market.

Rather than report their contaminated milk and filing for indemnification from the federal government, the other dairies opted to avoid the bureaucratic hassle Meggle was finding itself in. They decided to either not check the milk or, if it was found to be contaminated, use it anyway. Taking a loss by discarding the material seemed unlikely in view of the government's reimbursement policy. The simplest solution seemed to be to unload it on the consumer and forget about the consequences.

The Ministry for Environmental Affairs solicited expert testimony on how to best dispose of the nuisance. The Radiation Protection Commission advised them to feed it to animals or use it as fertilizer. Feeding it would pose no problem as long as the animals are taken off the feed long enough before being shipped to market. The only problem this time was that the radiant material would have to be mixed to bring the contamination down to acceptable levels. In view of the quantities involved this process would take years, but whey powder may be stored for only two years before it degrades.

Spreading the 5,000 tons as fertilizer over an area of 100 square kilometers would result in a normal radiation level, comparable to that of the widely used phosphate fertilizers! In theory this proposal was correct, but not very reassuring in view of the elevated radiation levels in the ground after the accident. In short, it was no practical solution.

Mr. Wallmann preferred decontamination by the ion-exchange method, proposed by another expert, which could be handled economically with regular dairy equipment. At the end stage there would be whey powder with very low radioactivity and a residual but highly radioactive cesium salt. Amounting to only two to five percent of the total volume, it could be easily stored underground as radioactive waste. The ministry opted for this proposal as the most reasonable solution to the problem and began the search for a processing site.

In May of 1988, the Lingen city council, in northern Germany, voted unanimously to accept the material for decontamination by a plant, yet to be built for the proposed process. The vote caused a public uproar in this small town which had launched an initiative against such a project the previous fall. The political argument of new

workplaces and the influx of DM 20 million of federal funds could not overcome the deep concern for the safety of its citizenry. 11,442 people signed a petition to abandon the project but were rejected. The city council stood firm and counting on the backing of the ruling party, the Christian Democrats, proceeded with its plans.

Two years after Chernobyl, the episode was finally brought to conclusion. But the problem of radioactive contamination is still vexing Europe and will continue to do so for decades to come. While the accident led to the discovery of practical countermeasures on a limited scale, it has solidified a broad political movement against the further use of atomic energy.

Bibliography

Der Spiegel
Giftmuell—Her mit dem Zeug, November 24, 1986, pp. 47/8.
Molke—In toto, February 16, 1987, pp. 116/7.
Molke—Saure Briketts, March 3, 1987, pp. 99/101.
Die Zeit
Lieber strahlen als zahlen, No. 30, July 25, 1986, pp. 10/1.
Unternehmen Molkepulver, No. 15, April 10, 1987, pp. 15/7.
Die Molke rollt, No. 22, June 3, 1988, pp. 11/2.
Official Journal of the European Communities
No. C 232/41, August 31, 1987, pp. 41/54, Report of the subcommittee on Chernobyl.
No. L 371/11, December 30, 1987, pp. 11/9, Council Regulation (EURATOM) No 3954/87 of December 22, 1987, laying down maximum permitted levels of radioactive contamination of foodstuffs and feedingstuffs following a nuclear accident or any other case of radiological emergency.
European Communities Commission
Background Report, ISEC/B21/86, October 16, 1986, The European Community and Chernobyl, pp. 1/3.
Commission of the European Communities
Background Report, ISEC/B1/88, January 14, 1988, Radiation Protection Programmes After Chernobyl, pp. 1/3.
Com(88) 293 final, Brussels, June 7, 1988, Commission Communication on completion of Annex to Council Regulation (EURATOM) No. 3954/87 of 22 December, 1987, laying down maximum permitted levels of radioactive contamination of foodstuffs and of feedingstuffs following a nuclear accident or any other case of radiological emergency.

UNION CARBIDE, BHOPAL: TECHNOLOGICAL HAZARDS

SITA C. AMBA-RAO

The Accident

Union Carbide (India), Limited (UCIL) is a subsidiary of Union Carbide, U.S.A., located at Bhopal in the central part of India. On the night of December 2, 1984, operators at the UCIL plant noticed a rise in the pressure in the tank containing methyl isocyanate (MIC), a deadly potent and highly volatile gas used to make pesticides. The pressure and a small leak were misinterpreted as harmless, common occurrences. The situation reached a crisis. Because the safety backup systems were not in order, the employees were unable to control the leak, and fled from the scene. The gas escaped in the atmosphere before the tank was sealed. The plant had a single manual alarm system, which was sounded once, but few people heard or could understand its significance.

The cloud of gas quickly spread across the city resulting in death and injury of thousands of people. By the end of the week an estimated 2,500 people were dead and about 200,000 injured, many of them incapacitated to the point of inability to earn a living. Other long-term ef-

This case is based on the following source: S. C. Amba-Rao. "Whither Bhopal: Technological Hazards and Social Responsiveness in the Third World." *Social Development Issues,* 12, no. 2 (1989), 11–22. Sources for the update included issues of *The Wall Street Journal, Business Week,* and *The New York Times,* except where otherwise indicated. The Union Carbide Bhopal case was especially prepared for this book by Professor Sita C. Amba-Rao, Indiana University, Kokomo.

fects on health were uncertain. Thousands of cattle and other animals also fell victim and the environment was polluted. The accident was the worst industrial disaster. The plant was closed and the license to operate it was canceled.

Union Carbide Corporation (UC)

At the time of the accident UC had over 99,000 employees worldwide. The company was the third largest chemical company in the U.S. and seventh largest in the world; it was the 31st largest of the world's multinational companies. Its subsidiary, UCIL was 25th in total sales in India. The company's products included a number of consumer and industrial items. The sales in 1983 were nine billion dollars, down from a high of $10.17 billion in 1981. The company's net income fell from $310 million in 1982 to $79 million in 1983. In December 1983, its assets exceeded $10 billion with a book value per share of $69.95. However, the company's receipts on pesticides were $14 million in 1983 comprising only eight percent of the corporation's total sales of $175 million. And, the Bhopal plant was operating at less than one third of its capacity.[1]

Union Carbide had a reputation for environmental concerns and was rated first by the U.S. National Council of Economic Priorities among the country's eight largest chemical companies in complying with the Occupational Safety and Health Administration's standards, between 1972 and 1979.

Union Carbide (India), Limited (UCIL)

Union Carbide's manufacturing operations in India go back to 1934 with its first battery plant. It was one of the few foreign firms in India that could hold majority equity interest, with 50.9 percent ownership of UCIL, because of its sophisticated technology, and its role in agricultural growth and exports. Otherwise, the equity limit for foreign investment in India was 40 percent under the Indian Foreign Exchange Regulations Act (1973). The Bhopal plant was built in 1969 under a technology transfer agreement, against recommendations by experts because of its hazardous nature. Manufacturing of MIC began in 1979. At the time of construction, the plant was outside the city of Bhopal, with a population of 672,000. In later years many poor people settled near the plant, attracted by its water lines and roads. In 1975 the municipal corporation official had asked the plant to be moved away from the city because of the hazards. In response the official was terminated from office. Later, in 1984 the Indian Department of Environment announced banning location of plants with hazardous substances near populous areas.

Throughout the period the Bhopal plant had been having operating problems because of reduced demand, increased competition, and the consequent cost-cutting measures. Further, this plant made an insignificant contribution to the company's profits. Consequently, UC decided in 1984 to sell the plant. Throughout the period, however, the relations between UC, the city, and the government had been good because of the company's contribution to the jobs and population growth in the area.

The Chemical Industry and Safety

Despite the high level of potentially dangerous activities in the chemical industry, the safety record of the industry is one of the best and better than manufacturing. In 1983 the chemical industry had 5.2 occupational injuries per 100 workers versus 7.5 for all manufacturing. The chemical companies contend that they apply the same standards of safety in foreign operations as at home. However, implementation and enforcement problems made it difficult to maintain the standards and avert the possibility of disaster. While the environmental agencies in developing countries have risen considerably (11 in 1972 to 110 in 1984), these are understaffed and underfinanced by the governments. In India, the Department of Environment had a staff of 150, while the U.S. Environmental Protection Agency had a headquarters staff of 4,400. Further, the inspectors in the developing countries were found to have low status, poor pay, and large areas to cover, setting the stage for disasters as in Mexico City where gas tanks exploded in storage in November 1984. Yet such workplaces were adopting complex industrial processes similar to those in the U.S., without the requisite controls.[2]

Antecedents of the Accident

In addition to the external developments described above, prior to the accident the Bhopal plant had operational difficulties, employee problems, and technological shortcomings. In 1982 there was an internal audit of the plant's design and operations whereby, human, technological, and organizational factors needing attention were identified. The company had an action plan to rectify the problems. In 1984, the company reported correcting several deficiencies, except two on which work was in progress: malfunction of a safety valve and potential overfilling of the MIC storage tank erroneously.

Employee issues reported in the audit included low morale, lack of staff, inadequate training, and managerial experience. High turnover of plant managers affected attention to plant maintenance and contingency plans for dealing with such major accidents.

Technological problems needing attention, according to the report, included flaws ranging from design to operation of the plant, equipment, materials, and operating procedures. A postaccident investigation had confirmed various system failures in the MIC production process and neglect of safety and maintenance.

Company Response

Following the accident Union Carbide immediately mobilized its resources and took several actions worldwide. It was a strategy of damage control and reaction. However, as in any such major event, the company responded in three stages: immediate, short-term, and long-term efforts. The corporate actions, both symbolic and concrete, included the following.

Immediate: The company stopped production and shipment of MIC worldwide. Union Carbide's Chairman Warren Anderson visited India to provide relief to the victims. A technical investigating team was sent to Bhopal. Money and essential items were contributed. Employees worldwide were informed on the events, assuring functioning of the safety processes in all plants. The company's overall excellent safety record was publicized. So were the procedures and equipment at the plants in West Virginia. Employees around the world expressed their concern by observing silence. Stockholders were assured of the financial soundness of the company.

Intermediate: Five million dollars worth of safety improvements were installed at West Virginia, the only other place where MIC was produced. Further, aid was given to the victims in various forms, although it was rejected by the Indian government. The long-term plans included the rehabilitation of the surviving victims and families. The company proposed major projects such as building training and rehabilitation facilities, and a $10 million hospital.

These steps should be viewed in perspective. Chairman Anderson expressed the company's moral responsibility, but not legal liability. While not accepting blame, on behalf of UC, he desired out-of-court settlement of compensation. Further, the worldwide reaction from various quarters—the media, international agencies, interest groups, and the chemical industry—had their influence in the company's post-Bhopal response. Many, including senior executives of chemical firms were critical of UC's inattention to the developing crisis despite internal warnings. They expressed that under such highly hazardous operations, the company had hierarchial responsibility for safety as the parent corporation and could not rely on a foreign infrastructure to enforce legal compliance.

Role of the Indian Government

In order to gain a proper perspective, the role of the government with regard to UC, both historically and surrounding the accident, may also be noted. The government represents the country's interest while collaborating with domestic and global businesses. The Indian government acted in the interest of the nation's economic growth and industrialization. However, it failed to provide the appropriate structure and environment. Initially the government insisted on introducing the complex operations against expert advice, without the necessary infrastructure and later permitted manufacturing in a densely populated area, influenced by its historically good relations with UC. Further, it legalized the occupation of squatters around the plant despite the company's reminder about the risk.

Yet, in response to the crisis, the government avoided acknowledging its share of responsibility in creating the accident, distanced itself from UC, rejected relief efforts by UC and controlled information in order to maintain its political legitimacy. Nevertheless, following the Bhopal accident, the government acted swiftly providing money, food and medical care, spending $40 million. Legal action was also taken, arresting plant officials for negligence.

As explained above, manufacturing with complex technology and plants has to be supported by appropriate levels of infrastructure.

The latter refers to both physical and social aspects. In the Bhopal case, the required level of infrastructure was absent. This was evident in various forms: The slums around the company prevented speedy evacuation of people in an emergency. The need for training, rather than drilling, employees in the understanding of safe operating procedures and the reason behind them was not recognized. The constant alertness and discipline required in working under hazardous conditions needed to be internalized. Similarly, the plant and government officials involved in environment, health, and safety had to be sensitized and trained at the point of importing technology as well as in its later use. For example, the mayor of Bhopal had no idea of the potential dangers involved in the MIC plant.[3] Further, as already mentioned, the Indian Department of Environment was understaffed; and the state government had 15 inspectors to cover over 8,000 plants located in the state.[4] Such gaps existed despite greater efforts toward safety enforcement in India than in most Third World countries.[5]

The tragic events of Bhopal did appear to have an impact on government complacency because, since the accident, environmental legislation and legal actions have been initiated.[6] For example, an Indian petroleum plant was ordered by a state government to relocate for safety, and in another case, the Supreme Court ruled that the parent company has the absolute responsibility for the safety of its plant operations.[7]

Legal Issues

Besides relief activities, the Indian government took legal action, arresting plant officials for negligence. Also arrested were top executives and Warren Anderson immediately on his arrival in India. Later Anderson was ordered to leave the country. Meanwhile thousands of lawsuits were filed in the U.S. and India on behalf of the victims, amounting to over $15 billion. The allegation against UC was that the company was negligent in designing the plant and had not warned the residents about the potential danger of the chemical; and that it lacked the warning system similar to its counterpart in West Virginia in the U.S., which had an automatic, computerized system.[8]

In March 1985 the company and the government began negotiations. The government rejected UC's offer and filed a suit against UC. The suit held UC accountable for "the design, development and dissemination of information and technology worldwide."[9] Further, the suit contended that UC was negligent in the design, maintenance, and safety of the plant, particularly misrepresenting to the government about safety, and storing "dangerously large quantities" of MIC without warning systems. Later, as lawyers for the victims were negotiating, the government intervened and preempted action on behalf of the victims.

A major legal question was whether the case should be tried in the U.S. because UC, the U.S. corporation, was the majority owner of UCIL, or in India where the accident had occurred. The plaintiffs' lawyers and the Indian government preferred the U.S. because of faster resolution and larger awards. The company desired India for the lesser awards, besides being the site of action and evidence. The award based on the value of lost earnings due to death or disability in India would be far less than the amount set in the U.S.[10] The company was also concerned about possible punitive damages, which are not covered by insurance.

The lawsuits in the U.S. were referred to the U.S. Federal District Court in New York under Judge John F. Keenan. After unsuccessful efforts to settle the case, Keenan ruled in May 1986 that the case should be tried in India.[11] He viewed the trial in the U.S. as tantamount to imposing the U.S. standards and values on a developing country; and stated that the Indian courts are capable of awarding fair and equitable justice. Thus the case was adjudicated to the Indian Supreme Court.

On February 14, 1989, the parties reached a settlement when the Indian Supreme Court awarded $470 million to the government on behalf of the victims. All criminal charges and civil suits against the company were dropped.[12] The settlement evoked arguments from both proponents and opponents. Proponents believed that this sends a message of multinational parent responsibility for subsidiary liability. Opponents, including activists and victims' lawyers, challenged the constitutionality of the settlement as being very low considering the number of victims and the level of suffering, and filed petitions on their behalf. The Supreme Court heard their arguments, and in October 1991 the Court upheld the settlement paid by UC but removed immunity from prosecution granted earlier, leaving the company open for criminal charges.[13] In April 1992 UC's assets were seized by the court as the company had not responded to criminal charges[14]; and trial was ordered for UCIL officials in May 1993.[15] As for victim compensation, reports indicate a very slow pace for the compensation process for survivors. Meanwhile, people are dying every day due to the aftereffects.

Social Concerns and Corporate Actions

In order to enable assessment of the corporation's social responsibility, this section includes relevant corporate behaviors at various times, to observe the consistency between the company's espoused commitment and its implementation.

Following the Bhopal accident the company undertook several affirmative steps to respond to the tragic consequences. To an extent these actions were undoubtedly on UC's initiative. But external pressure, particularly from the statements of other chemical company executives about parent company responsibility, was inevitable. Chairman Anderson proclaimed that the company is morally responsible for the events at Bhopal and asserted his company's commitment to stay in India and work at the

problem until it is resolved. Similarly, historically the company had developed positive relationships with the government providing economic opportunities to the community. Thus, the company had attempted to establish the image of a good corporate citizen.

Considering the historical and post-Bhopal events, however, there were incongruencies in what the company projected and what occurred in effect. These became evident particularly in UC's relationship with the subsidiary and certain steps taken relative to the two MIC producing plants in Bhopal and West Virginia. Some of these events, which occurred at different times are briefly presented as illustrations.

1. As was explained earlier, the corporation commissioned the MIC production plant against the advice of technical experts; and later continued to operate in the populous area without adequate infrastructure.
2. The Bhopal community, as a stakeholder, had no influence on what was happening as antecedents to the crisis were developing in and around the plant. The community was neither aware of the deteriorating conditions in the plant, the increasing risk, or the emergency procedures, nor could they prevent the slum settlement. They perceived only the beneficial purpose of the product (pesticide). Moreover, the problem posed by lack of transportation and communication facilities to evacuate quickly such a mass of people under an emergency was overwhelming.[16]
3. As the postaccident events unraveled in 1985, UC attributed the cause of the accident to local mismanagement and distanced itself from the Bhopal subsidiary. Yet over the years UC failed to provide support to UCIL, despite corporate control of UCIL's governance. This was apparently due to the corporation's decision to sell the pesticide plant because of its strategic insignificance to UC (low proportion of total profits and high competition).[17] A related event was that, following the accident, UCIL management was

caught in the legal battle between the parent company and the Indian government. The plant management was constrained in its movement, actions, and communication with outsiders, although it maintained contact with employees and suppliers.

The following three events illustrate the extent of the company's commissions and omissions in the 1980s that led to major and smaller accidents both at Bhopal and at its West Virginia plant: (1) Not following up on the safety audit of UCIL in 1982, which revealed chronic operational deficiencies that finally led to the accident; (2) not sharing its findings at the West Virginia plant in 1984 with UCIL about the possibility, and the dire consequences, of a MIC "runaway reaction" prior to the Bhopal accident (which may have reduced the seriousness of the accident); and (3) installing expensive safety features in the West Virginia plant after the Bhopal crisis without appropriate operational training and neglect of operational procedures, resulting in a toxic gas leak and crises affecting 135 people in 1985.

The response of UC to the accident itself was called a "strategy of containment."[18] The intention of the company was to protect its assets at any cost and "downplay the seriousness of the situation, to minimize the adverse impacts, especially to health, and seek to implicate others. . . . It also appears to be a typical, if not standard, industry response. . . ."[19]

Post-Bhopal Consequences on the Corporation and Elsewhere

As the information on the accident spread, there was a wide reaction. The corporation faced resistance to its business operations elsewhere in the world. There were bomb explosions and public demonstrations against the company in Germany. An MIC shipment to France was stopped by its Environment Ministry, and negotiations were stalled on plant construction proposals elsewhere. Other repercussions included

bitterness of UC employees with the news that allegedly a few Indian workers were responsible for the accident; the employees felt that this blemished the company's and its employees' reputation.[20] The negligent attitude of UC was generalized to the chemical industry and all U.S. multinationals, as well, by critics. Questions were raised on risks and benefits to companies and countries in such hazardous operations, on the need for increasing safety measures, and on informing residents about hazards. The minor accidents after the Bhopal incident increased fear about safety among residents living near chemical plants in the U.S. This resulted in passage of right-to-know laws in several states. And the U.S. Occupational Safety and Health Administration passed a regulation requiring companies to inform all concerned about the nature of substances used and any precautions required.[21]

More specifically, immediate repercussions were felt on the corporations's financial and market status. The company's share value fell to $35 from $49; the company went through restructuring, and sold many of its businesses including profitable ones, closed plants and laid off 4,000 employees. In addition, the GAF Corporation attempted a takeover of UC. UC had to incur heavy debt to prevent the takeover.

On the whole, the Bhopal tragedy acted as a catalyst for chemical companies and the U.S. Chemical Manufacturers Association to review and revise their practices in handling, storing, transporting, and utilizing dangerous substances.

Discussion Questions

1. Evaluate the social strategy of Union Carbide and the Indian government considering the antecedents and consequences of the Bhopal accident, before and after the occurrence.
2. To what extent should developing countries consider individual rights or social welfare in

the use of hazardous technology? Analyze the ethical aspects of the case.

3. What corporate actions or policies could have prevented the Bhopal disaster?

4. Should global firms have a universal policy regarding their business operations? Should this include use of sophisticated technology in developing countries?

5. "Use of hazardous technology in developing countries requires pluralistic involvement by the parties concerned, namely, the corporations, governments, and communities. The three parties are mutually dependent for resources, finances, and information." Explain the statement indicating the role of the three parties involved.

6. Can developing countries that are striving to raise the general standard of living of their population pay attention to the environment to the same extent as developed countries? Should they? Would this issue be any different with the new privatization and globalization efforts by India and other developing countries?

Endnotes

1. "A Calamity for Union Carbide." *Time* (December 17, 1984), 38.

2. W. C. Frederick, K. Davis, and J. E. Post. *Business and Society,* 6th ed. (New York: McGraw-Hill Co., 1988).

3. J. R. Long and D. J. Hanson. "Bhopal Triggers Massive Response from Congress, The Administration." *Chemical and Engineering News,* 63, no. 6 (February 11, 1985), 60.

4. L. R. Ember. "Technology in India: An Uneasy Balance of Progress and Tradition," *Chemical and Engineering News,* 63, no. 6 (February 11, 1985), 62.

5. C. Trost. "Danger Zone: Chemical Plant Safety Is Still Just Developing in Developing Nations." *The Wall Street Journal* (December 13, 1984), 1.

6. F. Bordewich. "The Lessons of Bhopal." *Atlantic* (March 1987), 30–3.

7. *The Wall Street Journal* (March 11, 1987).

8. "Union Carbide Fights for Its Life." *Business Week* (December 24, 1984), 53–6.

9. R. Friedman and M. Miller. "Union Carbide Is Sued by India in U.S. Court." *The Wall Street Journal* (April 9, 1985), 14.

10. "Union Carbide Fights for Its Life." 55.

11. "Nobody Wins in the Carbide Ruling." *Business Week* (May 26, 1986), 41–2.

12. S. Hazarika. "Bhopal Payments by Union Carbide Set at $470 Million." *The New York Times* (February 15, 1989), 1.

13. S. McMurray. "India's High Court Upholds Settlement Paid by Carbide in Bhopal Gas Leak." *The Wall Street Journal* (October 4, 1991), B3.

14. S. Hazarika. "Court in India ito Seize Union Carbide Assets." *The New York Times* (May 1, 1992), C7, D7.

15. S. Kumar. "Union Carbide Officials Face Prosecution." *New Scientist,* 38, no. 187, (May 1, 1993), 8(1).

16. Trost. "Danger Zone." 1.

17. Frederick *et al. Business and Society.* 585.

18. H. Deresky. *International Management* (New York: Harper Collins, 1994), 557.

19. W. Morehouse and M. A. Subramaniam. *The Bhopal Tragedy: What Really Happened and What It Means for American Workers and Communities at Risk—A Preliminary Report for the Citizens' Commission on Bhopal* (New York: The Council on International and Public Affairs, 1986), 40–1.

20. *Business Week* (November 25, 1985), 45.

21. *Chemical Hazard Communication* (Washington, DC: U.S. Department of Labor, OSHA #3084, 1988).

INDEX